Trade Secret Protection

Trade Secret Protection

Asia at a Crossroads

Edited by

Kung-Chung Liu

Reto Hilty

Wolters Kluwer

Published by:
Kluwer Law International B.V.
PO Box 316
2400 AH Alphen aan den Rijn
The Netherlands
E-mail: international-sales@wolterskluwer.com
Website: lrus.wolterskluwer.com

Sold and distributed by:
Wolters Kluwer Legal & Regulatory U.S.
7201 McKinney Circle
Frederick, MD 21704
United States of America
E-mail: customer.service@wolterskluwer.com

ISBN 978-94-035-3053-6

e-Book: ISBN 978-94-035-3104-5
web-PDF: ISBN 978-94-035-3105-2

Editors

Professor Kung-Chung Liu, Singapore Management University/Renmin University of China/NCCU, Taiwan
kcliu@smu.edu.sg

Professor Reto Hilty, Director, Max Planck Institute for Innovation and Competition

Contributors

Professor Byungil Kim (project lead), Hanyang University, Korea
kimbyungil66@yahoo.com
Overview and Summary
Chapter 2 (Topics 1, 2 and 4)

Farizah Mohamed Isa, Faculty of Law, Universiti Tecnologi Mara, Malaysia
farizahisa@gmail.com
Chapter 8 (Topics 1, 4)

Associate Professor Hao-Yun Chen, National Taipei University, Taiwan
hychen@mail.ntpu.edu.tw
Chapter 4 (Topic 2)

Associate Professor Hsiao-Fen Hsu (project lead), National Cheng-Kung University, Taiwan
hfhsu@ncku.edu.tw
Overview and Summary
Chapter 4 (Topic 3)

Jingwen Liu, Ph.D. student, the Chinese University of Hong Kong
jingwenliu@link.cuhk.edu.hk

Professor Jyh-An Lee (project lead), the Chinese University of Hong Kong
jalee@cuhk.edu.hk

Professor Kung-Chung Liu, Singapore
Management University/Renmin University of China/NCCU, Taiwan
kcliu@smu.edu.sg
Chapter 3 (Topics 3 and 6) Chapter 4 (Topics 3, 4, 5 and 6)

Adjunct Professor Kyoung-Shin Park, Ewha Womans University, Korea
vengerov21@gmail.com
Chapter 2 (Topic 3)

Prof Dr. Lim Heng Gee (project lead), Faculty of Law, Universiti Teknologi MARA, Malaysia
henggeelim@yahoo.com
Overview and Summary
Chapter 8 (Topics 2, 4)

Professor Ng-Loy Wee Loon, National University of Singapore
loy.weeloon@nus.edu.sg

Dr. Luc Desaunettes-Barbero, UClouvain
luc.desaunettes@uclouvain.be

Associate Professor Luo Li, Renmin University of China
luoliq@gmail.com
Chapter 3 (Topic 4)

Makoto Hattori, Attorney-at-Law, Abe, Ikubo & Katayama
makoto.hattori@aiklaw.co.jp
Chapter 1 (Topic 4)

Associate Professor Man Zhang, Law School, Northwest University, China
xdfxyzm@126.com
Chapter 3 (Topic 2)

Professor Masabumi Suzuki (project lead), Nagoya University Graduate School of Law
msuzuki@law.nagoya-u.ac.jp
Overview and Summary
Chapter 1 (Topics 4 and 5)

Prashant Reddy T. Lawyer, India
preddy85@gmail.com

Senior Lecturer Sik Cheng Peng, Faculty of Law, Universiti Malaya
sikcp@um.edu.my
Chapter 8 (Topics 3, 5)

Dr. Siping Zeng, Xiamen University of Technology
2015000023@xmut.edu.cn
Chapter 3 (Topic 5)

Associate Professor Su-Hua Lee, National Taiwan University, College of Law
leesh@ntu.edu.tw
Chapter 4 (Topic 1)

Judge Sutatip Yuthayotin (project lead), Panel Head at Udonthani Provincial Court, Thailand
sutatippp@yahoo.com

Professor Takakuni Yamane, Doshisha University
tyamane@mail.doshisha.ac.jp
Chapter 1 (Topic 6)

Professor Takeshi Maeda, Kobe University
tmaeda@harbor.kobe-u.ac.jp
Chapter 1 (Topic 1)

Professor Tatsuhiro Ueno, Waseda University
uenot@waseda.jp
Chapter 1 (Topic 2)

Professor Tieguang Liu, Kenneth Wang School of law of Soochow University
tieguangl@126.com
Chapter 3 (Topic 1)

Research Judge Tosaporn Leepuengtham, the Supreme Court of Thailand
juffy67@gmail.com

Professor Won Bok Lee, Ewha Womans University
wonbok.lee@ewha.ac.kr
Chapter 2 (Topic 3)

Associate Professor Xiaojun Wang, School of Law of Guizhou Normal University
junexj@vip.126.com
Chapter 3 (Topic 3)

Professor Xiuqin Lin (project lead), Xiamen University
xqlin@xmu.edu.cn
Chapter 3 (Overview and Summary)

Xuan Wang, Ph.D. student, Xiamen University
32520200156814@stu.xmu.edu.cn
Chapter 3 (Topics 5 and 6)

Professor Yasuto Komada, Sophia University
komada-y@sophia.ac.jp
Chapter 1 (Topic 3)

Summary of Contents

Editors v

Contributors vii

Introduction 1

PART I
Asian Civil Law Jurisdictions with No Sui Generis Law 5

CHAPTER 1
Japan 7

CHAPTER 2
Trade Secret Law in Korea (Country Report) 71

CHAPTER 3
China 115

PART II
Asian Civil Law Jurisdictions with Sui Generis Law 169

CHAPTER 4
Taiwan 171

CHAPTER 5
Thailand 225

PART III
Asian Common Law Jurisdictions 269

CHAPTER 6
Singapore 271

CHAPTER 7
Hong Kong 287

CHAPTER 8
Malaysia 331

CHAPTER 9
India 395

PART IV
Some References from the Occident 431

CHAPTER 10
Trade Secrets Protection in the European Union 433

Index 451

Table of Contents

Editors v

Contributors vii

Introduction
Kung-Chung Liu & Reto Hilty 1

Part I
Asian Civil Law Jurisdictions with No Sui Generis Law 5

Chapter 1
Japan 7
Overview and Summary
Masabumi Suzuki 7

1. Related Legal System 7
2. Definitions and Requirements of Trade Secrets 8
   2.1. Definition 8
   2.2. Requirement (1): Usefulness 8
   2.3. Requirement (2): Being Kept Secret 9
   2.4. Requirement (3): Being Not Publicly Known 10
3. Types of Acts of Unfair Competition Related to Trade Secrets 10
   3.1. Overview 10
   3.2. Wrongful Acquisition of Trade Secrets and Subsequent Unauthorized Use or Disclosure 10
      3.2.1. Wrongful Acquisition and Subsequent Use or Disclosure (Article 2(1), Item (iv)) 10
      3.2.2. Acquisition and Use or Disclosure of Wrongfully Acquired Trade Secrets (Article 2(1), Items (v) and (vi)) 11
   3.3. Unauthorized Use of Legitimately Acquired Trade Secrets 11

3.3.1. Unauthorized Use or Disclosure (Article 2(1), Item (vii)) 11
3.3.2. Acquisition and Use or Disclosure of Wrongfully Disclosed Trade Secrets (Article 2(1)(viii) and (ix)) 12
3.4. Distribution of Things Created by Unauthorized Use of Technical Secrets (Article 2(1)(x)) 12
3.5. Exclusion from Application 13
4. Civil Remedies 13
4.1. Injunction 13
4.2. Damages 14
5. Criminal Penalties 15
6. Special Measures for Judicial Proceedings Involving Trade Secrets 15
7. International Jurisdiction and Choice of Law 16

Topic 1 The Requirements for Trade Secrets in Japan
Takeshi Maeda 17
1. Legal Issues 17
2. The Statutory Law 17
3. The Case Law 17
4. The Leading Case 19
4.1. Case Information 19
4.2. Summary 19
4.3. Facts 19
4.4. The Reasoning of the Court 19
4.4.1. Secrecy Management 19
4.4.1.1. The Customer Information Was Managed as a Secret 19
4.4.1.2. Secrecy Management Does Not Have to Be Perfect 20
4.4.2. Usefulness and Non-public Domain 21
4.5. Legal Analysis 21
4.5.1. Secrecy Management 21
4.5.1.1. Recognizability Is the Most Important Requirement 21
4.5.1.2. How to Determine the Recognizability 22
4.5.1.3. Evaluation of the Present Decision 23
4.5.2. Usefulness 24
4.5.3. Non-public Domain 24
4.6. Commercial or Industrial Significance 25

Topic 2 The Validity and Scope of Confidentiality and Noncompetition Clauses
Tatsuhiro Ueno 26
1. Legal Issues 26
2. The Statutory Law 26
2.1. Obligation of Confidentiality under Labor Law and Contract Law 26
2.2. Noncompetition Obligation under Labor Law and Contract Law 26

2.3. Trade Secret Protection under the UCPA 27
3. The Case Law 28
3.1. Contractual Obligation of Confidentiality and Trade Secret Protection 28
3.2. Contractual Noncompetition Obligation and Trade Secret Protection 29
4. The Leading Case 30
4.1. Case Information 30
4.2. Summary 30
4.3. Facts 30
4.4. The Reasoning of the IP High Court 31
4.4.1. General Principle 31
4.4.2. The Invalidity of Employment Regulations and the Pledge 32
4.4.3. The Validity of the Noncompetition Agreement at the Time of Joining the Company 32
4.4.4. The Defendant Did Not Violate the Confidentiality Agreement by Asking the Customer Medical Records to Be Sent? 33
4.5. Legal Analysis 33
4.6. Commercial or Industrial Significance 33
Topic 3 International Jurisdictions and the Applicable Law on Trade Secret Infringement Litigation
Yasuto Komada 34
1. Legal Issues 34
2. The Statutory Law 34
2.1. International Jurisdiction 34
2.2. Applicable Law 34
3. The Case Law 35
3.1. International Jurisdiction 35
3.2. Applicable Law 37
4. The Leading Case 38
4.1. Case Information 38
4.2. Summary 38
4.3. Facts 38
4.4. The Reasoning of the Court 39
4.4.1. Regarding the Applicable Law 39
4.4.2. Regarding the Existence of Y's Unfair Competition Act 39
4.5. Legal Analysis 39
4.5.1. International Jurisdiction 39
4.5.2. Applicable Law 40
4.5.2.1. Academic Theories 40
4.5.2.2. Our View 41

Topic 4 Protective Order System
Masabumi Suzuki & Makoto Hattori 43
1. Legal Issues 43
2. The Statutory Law 43
3. The Case Law 45
4. The Leading Case 45
4.1. Case Information 45
4.2. Summary 45
4.3. Facts 46
4.4. The Reasoning of the Court 46
4.5. Legal Analysis 47
4.5.1. Significance of This Judgment 47
4.5.1.1. Provisional Dispositions for Injunction Frequently Used in Practice 47
4.5.1.2. Purpose of the Protective Order System 48
4.5.1.3. Protective Order and Provisional Disposition Procedure 48
4.5.2. Actual Operation of the Protective Order System 49
4.5.2.1. Who Can Make a Motion? 49
4.5.2.2. Kinds of "Litigation" in Which a Motion Can Be Made 49
4.5.2.3. Trade Secrets Subject to Protective Orders 49
4.5.2.4. The Addressee of Protective Orders 50
4.5.2.5. Necessity 50
4.6. Commercial or Industrial Significance 50
Topic 5 Damages
Masabumi Suzuki 52
1. Legal Issues 52
2. The Statutory Law 52
3. The Case Law 54
3.1. Cases That Applied Article 5(1) 54
3.2. Cases That Applied Article 5(2) 55
3.3. Cases That Applied Article 5(3), Item (iii) 55
3.4. Others 56
4. The Leading Cases 56
4.1.1. Case Information 56
4.1.2. Summary 56
4.1.3. Facts 57
4.1.4. The Reasoning of the Court 57
4.1.5. Legal Analysis 58
4.1.6. Commercial or Industrial Significance 59
4.2.1. Case Information 59
4.2.2. Summary 59
4.2.3. Facts 59
4.2.4. The Reasoning of the Court 59

4.2.5. Legal Analysis 60
4.2.6. Commercial or Industrial Significance 61
Topic 6 The Criminal Punishment for Trade Secret Infringement and the Element of "Purpose of Wrongful Gain" in Japan
Takakuni Yamane 62
1. Legal Issues 62
2. The Statutory Law 62
3. The Case Law 63
4. The Leading Case 65
4.1. Case Information 66
4.2. Summary 66
4.3. Facts 66
4.4. The Reasoning of the Court 67
4.5. Legal Analysis 68
4.5.1. Significance of the Supreme Court's Judgement 68
4.5.2. How to Determine the "Purpose of Wrongful Gain" under Article 21(1)(iii) 69
4.6. Commercial or Industrial Significance 69

CHAPTER 2
Trade Secret Law in Korea (Country Report) 71
Overview and Summary
Byungil Kim 71
1. Historical Development 71
2. Definition of Trade Secrets 72
3. Infringing Acts 72
3.1. General Aspects 72
3.2. Acquisition of Trade Secret by Unfair or Unlawful Means 73
3.3. Breach of Confidentiality 74
4. Protection of Trade Secrets Within a Trial 74
5. Remedies 76
5.1. Injunctive Relief 76
5.2. Damages 77
6. Criminal Sanctions 79
6.1. The 2019 Amended UCPA Expanded the Scope of Punishable Acts 79
6.2. Exceptions for Innocent Acquisition 80
Topic 1 The Requirements of Secrecy Management: From "Reasonable Efforts" to "Managed as a Secret"
Byungil Kim 81
1. Legal Issues 81
2. The Statutory Law 81
3. The Case Law 81
3.1. Positive Examples from the Supreme Court 82
3.2. Negative Examples from the Supreme Court 82

4. The Leading Case 84
4.1. Case Information 84
4.2. Summary 84
4.3. Facts 84
4.4. Reasoning of the Court 85
4.5. Legal Analysis 87
4.5.1. Definition of Trade Secrets 87
4.5.2. Lowered Maintenance Requirement for Trade Secrets 88
4.6. Commercial or Industrial Significance 88
Topic 2 The Validity and Scope of Confidentiality and/or Noncompetition Clauses
Byungil Kim 89
1. Legal Issues 89
2. The Statutory Law 89
3. The Case Law 90
4. The Leading Case 90
4.1. Case Information 90
4.2. Summary 90
4.3. Facts 91
4.4. Reasoning of the Court 92
4.5. Legal Analysis 93
4.5.1. Breach of Confidentiality Obligation 93
4.5.2. The Duty of Noncompetition 93
4.5.3. Article 10(1) of the UCPA as Legal Basis for Noncompete Obligation 95
4.5.4. Employee's General Skills and Knowledge and the Particular Knowledge of Employer's Trade Secrets 95
4.6. Commercial or Industrial Significance 96
Topic 5 Length of Permanent Injunctive Relief for Trade Secret Infringement
Won Bok Lee & Kyoung-Shin Park 97
1. Legal Issues 97
2. Statutory Law 97
3. Case Law 97
4. Leading Case 98
4.1. Case Information 98
4.2. Summary 98
4.3. Facts 98
4.4. Reasoning of the Court 99
4.5. Legal Analysis 100
4.5.1. The "Trade Secret Protection Period" Coined by the Korean Supreme Court 100
4.5.2. A Trifurcated Approach Based on Whether the "Trade Secret Protection Period" Is Over, Not Over, or Indeterminable 101

4.5.3. Whether a Bifurcated Approach Based on Whether the "Trade Secret Protection Period" Is Determinable or Not 101
4.5.4. Misplaced Critique on Korean Supreme Court's Holding 102
4.5.5. Unresolved Issues 103
4.6. Commercial or Industrial Significance 104
Topic 5 The Damages
Byungil Kim 106
1. Legal Issues 106
2. The Statutory Law 106
3. The Case Law 108
4. The Leading Case 108
4.1. Case Information 108
4.2. Summary 109
4.3. Facts 109
4.4. Reasoning of the Court 110
4.5. Legal Analysis 111
4.5.1. Civil Remedies 111
4.5.2. Damages Determination 111
4.5.3. Apportionment (Contributory Percentage) of Damages 112
4.6. Commercial or Industrial Significance 113

Chapter 3
China 115
Overview and Summary
Xiuqin Lin 115
1. Legislative Efforts 115
1.1. Summary of Civil Protection of Trade Secrets 115
1.2. Summary of Criminal Protection of Trade Secrets 117
1.3. Summary of Administrative Protection of Trade Secrets 118
2. Judicial Practice on Trade Secrets 118
Topic 1 The Requirements of Trade Secret
Tieguang Liu 120
1. Legal Issues 120
2. The Statutory Law 120
3. The Case Law 121
3.1. Not Generally Known 121
3.2. Of Economic Value 122
3.3. Corresponding Measures 122
4. The Leading Case 123
4.1. Case Information 123
4.2. Summary 123
4.3. Facts 123
4. Reasoning of the Courts 124
4.1. The First Instance 124

4.2. The Second Instance 125
4.2.1. The Technology of the Mold Design Was Already Known to the Public 125
4.2.2. The Tray Design Has No Commercial Value 126
4.5. Legal Analysis 126
4.5.1. The Secrecy Requirement 126
4.5.2. Economic Value 127
4.6. Commercial or Industrial Significance 127

Topic 2 The Validity and Scope of Confidentiality and/or Noncompetition Clauses
Man Zhang 129
1. Legal Issues 129
2. The Statutory Law 129
3. The Case Law 131
4. The Leading Case 132
4.1. Case Information 132
4.2. Summary 132
4.3. Facts 133
4.4. The Reasoning of Courts 133
4.4.1. Whether the Customer List Met the Requirements of Commercial Secrets 133
4.4.2. Whether an Infringement of Commercial Secrets Took Place 134
4.4.3. The Balance Between the Protection of Trade Secrets and the Employee's Freedom to Work and Use His Expertise Obtained During Previous Employment 134
4.5. Legal Analysis 135
4.5.1. Confidentiality and Noncompetition Agreement in General 135
4.5.2. Striking the Right Balance? 135
4.6. Commercial or Industrial Significance 136

Topic 3 The Shifting of Burden of Proof for Trade Secret Infringement
Kung-Chung Liu & Xiaojun Wang 137
1. Legal Issues 137
2. The Statutory Law 137
3. The Case Law 139
4. The Leading Case 140
4.1. Case Information 140
4.2. Summary 140
4.3. Facts 140
4.4. Reasoning of the Courts 141
4.4.1. On the Issue of Secrecy (Not Generally Known to the Public) 141
4.4.2. On the Issue of Protective Measures Taken 142
4.5. Legal Analysis 143

4.5.1. Tilting the Scale Too Much in Favor of the Right Holder? 143
4.5.2. How to Apply Article 32 of the AUCL in a Balanced Way 144
4.6. Commercial or Industrial Significance 144
Topic 4 Preliminary Injunction
Luo Li 145
1. Legal Issues 145
2. The Statutory Law 146
3. The Case Law 147
4. Leading Case 148
4.1. Case Information 148
4.2. Summary 149
4.3. Facts 149
4.4. The Court's Reasoning 150
4.4.1. The Information at Issue Constitutes Trade Secrets 150
4.4.2. The Defendant's Conduct Constituted Trade Secret Infringement 150
4.4.3. It Is Necessary to Take Behavior Preservation Measures 150
4.5. Legal Analysis 151
4.5.1. "Likelihood of Judgment in Favor of the Applicant" as Factor to Consider When Determining Application for Behavior Preservation 151
4.5.2. The Present Decision Was Heavily Influenced by eBay 151
4.6. Commercial/Industrial Significance 152
Topic 5 Damages
Siping Zeng & Xuan Wang 153
1. Legal Issues 153
2. The Statutory Law 153
2.1. Three Statutory Methods for Calculating Compensatory Damages 153
2.1.1. The Actual Losses Method 153
2.1.2. The Benefits Method 154
2.1.3. The Statutory Damages Method 154
2.2. Punitive Damages 154
2.3. Reasonable Expenses 155
2.4. Commercial Value and Competitive Advantages 155
3. The Case Law 155
3.1. Cases That Applied the Actual Loss Method 155
3.2. Cases That Applied the Benefits Method 156
3.3. Cases That Applied the Statutory Damages Method 156
3.4. Cases That Awarded Punitive Damages 156
3.5. Cases That Granted Commercial Value of Trade Secrets 157
4. The Leading Case 157
4.1. Case Information 157
4.2. Summary 157

4.3. Facts 157
4.4. Reasoning of Courts 158
4.4.1. Factors Affecting Profits of Real Estate Projects 158
4.4.2. The Plaintiffs' Loss Was Limited to the Value of a Consulting Service 158
4.4.3. Expected Benefits from Obtaining the Right to Develop the Real Estate Project Are Not the Loss the Plaintiffs Suffered 159
4.4.4. The Investigation and Research Costs (I&R Costs) Can Be the Basis for Evaluating the Loss of the Trade Secret Infringement 159
4.5. Legal Analysis 159
4.6. Commercial/Industrial Significance 160

Topic 6 Criminal Punishment for Trade Secret Infringement
Kung-Chung Liu & Xuan Wang 161
1. Legal Issues 161
2. The Statutory Law 161
3. The Case Law 163
4. The Leading Case 164
4.1. Case Information 164
4.2. Summary 164
4.3. Facts 164
4.4. Reasoning of the Courts 165
4.4.1. The First Instance Court 165
4.4.1.1. Commercial Value of the Trade Secret as Losses Caused to Its Holder 165
4.4.1.2. Synthesis Fees for Structural Formulas Are the R&D Costs 165
4.4.1.3. Factors Affecting the Sentencing of Criminal Punishment 166
4.4.2. The Second Instance Court 166
4.5. Legal Analysis 167
4.5.1. Setting Fixed Monetary Thresholds for Trade Secret Crimes Is Problematic 167
4.5.2. Asking Criminal Court to Determine the Losses the Trade Secret Holder Suffered Is Also Problematic 167
4.6. Commercial/Industrial Significance 168

PART II
Asian Civil Law Jurisdictions with Sui Generis Law 169

CHAPTER 4
Taiwan 171
Overview and Summary
Hsiao-Fen Hsu 171

1. Development and Practice of Trade Secrets Act 171
2. Confidentiality Preservation Order and Investigation Confidentiality Protective Order 172
3. Definitions and Requirements of Trade Secrets 173
4. The Validity and Scope of Confidentiality and/or Noncompetition Clauses 173
5. Five Types of Trade Secret Infringement 173
6. The Burden of Proof 174
   6.1. The Principle of Burden of Proof and the Specific Defense Requirement 174
   6.2. Preliminary Showing of Infringement or Possible Infringement by the Plaintiff 174
7. Civil Remedies 174
   7.1 Injunction 174
   7.2. Damages 175
8. Criminal Penalties 176
9. Special Measures for Judicial Proceedings Involving Trade Secrets 176

Topic 1 The Requirements of Trade Secret Protection
Su-Hua Lee 178
1. Legal Issues 178
2. The Statutory Law 178
3. The Case Law 178
   3.1. Requirement of Secrecy 179
   3.2. Requirement of Economic Value 179
   3.3. Requirement of Reasonable Measures to Maintain Secrecy 180
4. The Leading Case 181
   4.1. Case Information 181
   4.2. Summary 181
   4.3. Facts 181
   4.4. Reasoning of the Courts 182
      4.4.1. The Taiwan IP and Commercial Court 182
      4.4.2. Supreme Court 183
   4.5. Legal Analysis 184
      4.5.1. Information Protected by the TSA Shall Be Closely Related to the Industry 184
      4.5.2. The Secrecy Requirement Assessed "As a Whole" 184
      4.5.3. Improperly High Requirement of Reasonable Measures to Maintain Secrecy 185
   4.6. Economic or Commercial Significance 185

Topic 2 The Validity and Scope of Confidentiality and Noncompete Clauses
Hao-Yun Chen 186
1. Legal Issues 186
2. The Statutory Law 186
3. The Case Law 187
4. The Leading Case 189

4.1. Case Information 189
4.2. Summary 189
4.3. Facts 189
4.4. Reasoning of the Court 191
4.5. Legal Analysis 191
4.5.1. A Differentiated Approach to Noncompete Clause Should Be Favored 191
4.5.2. Applying the TSA in a Way to Hollow Out Labor Standards Act? 192
4.5.3. Explicit Criteria for Determining the Necessity and Reasonableness of Noncompete Injunction under the TSA Are Needed 193
4.6. Commercial or Industrial Significance 193
Topic 3 A Ping-Pong Between Burden of Proving Trade Secret Infringement and Specific Defense Requirement
Hsiao-Fen Hsu & Kung-Chung Liu 194
1. Legal Issues 194
2. The Statutory Law 194
3. The Case Law 194
4. The Leading Case 195
4.1. Case Information 195
4.2. Summary 195
4.3. Facts 195
4.4. Reasoning of the Courts 196
4.4.1. Lower Courts: The Plaintiff Bears the Burden of Proof When the Defendant Denies Wrongdoing 196
4.4.2. The Supreme Court 197
4.4.3. The Retrial Court 198
4.4.3.1. The Defendants Had Violated Himax's Confidentiality Rules 198
4.4.3.2. The Defendants Could Not Use "Business Needs" as a Defense 198
4.5. Legal Analysis 199
4.5.1. Legislative Background of Article 10-1 of the IPCAA 199
4.5.2. Lower Courts Failed to Apply Article 10-1 of the IPCAA 199
4.5.3. Preliminary Showing of Infringement or Possible Infringement by the Plaintiff 200
4.5.4. Obligation of Specific Defense Does Not Transfer Burden of Proof 201
4.6. Commercial or Industrial Significance 201
Topic 4 Orders by Courts or Prosecutors to Protect Trade Secrets
Kung-Chung Liu 202
1. Legal Issues 202
2. The Statutory Law 202
2.1. Court Orders 202

2.1.1. The Closed-Door Trial Order 202
2.1.2. The Partial Publication Order 202
2.1.3. The Confidentiality Preservation Order 203
2.2. The Investigation Confidentiality Protective Order by Prosecutors 204
2.2.1. When and to Whom Can the Order Be Issued? 204
2.2.2. Forms and Taking Effects of the Order 204
2.2.3. Cancelation or Amendment of the Order 204
2.2.3.1. By Prosecutors 204
2.2.3.2. By Courts 205
2.2.4. Criminal Punishment for Violating an Investigation Confidentiality Protective Order 205
3. The Judicial Practice 205
4. The Notorious Case 206
5. Critique of the Investigation Confidentiality Protective Order by Prosecutors 206
5.1. It Expands the Power of Prosecutors and Poses a Threat to the Rule of Law Principle 206
5.2. It Is Not Necessary 207
5.3. Trade Secret Cases Should Be Reserved for Judges 207
5.4. Prosecutors Lack the Technical Capability 207
6. Can Confidentiality Preservation Orders and Investigation Confidentiality Protective Orders Be Applied to General Civil and Commercial Cases? 208
Topic 5 A New Direction for Calculating Damages for Trade Secret Infringement?
Kung-Chung Liu 209
1. Legal Issues 209
2. The Statutory Law 209
3. The Case Law 210
4. The Leading Case 210
4.1. Case Information 210
4.2. Summary 210
4.3. Facts 211
4.4. Reasoning of the court 212
4.4.1. Resorting to Discretionary Power Recognized by the CCP 212
4.4.2. The Plaintiff Was Unable to or under Difficulty to Prove the Damages Amount 212
4.4.3. Using the R&D Costs as Proxy for Damages 212
4.4.4. Punitive Damages 213
4.5. Legal Analysis 214
4.5.1. Two Peculiarities of the Present Case 214
4.5.2. Using R&D Costs as a Proxy for Damages Is Acceptable, but … 214
4.5.3. The Estimated R&D Costs Seem Unreasonably High 215
4.6. Commercial or Industrial Significance 216

Topic 6 The Criminal Punishment of Trade Secret Theft and Economic Espionage in Taiwan
Kung-Chung Liu 217
1. Legal Issues 217
2. The Statutory Law 217
3. The Case Law 218
4. The Leading Case 219
4.1. Case Information 219
4.2. Summary 219
4.3. Facts 220
4.4. Reasoning of the Court 221
4.4.1. The Executives of UMC, Mr. Rong and Mr. Chen, Had Not Done Their Utmost to Prevent the Theft 221
4.4.2. Committing Trade Secret Theft with the Intention of Using it in Mainland China (Economic Espionage) 221
4.4.3. Mr. Rong Is the Most Reprehensible Among the Three Defendants 221
4.4.4. UMC's Fine 222
4.4.5. Confiscation of Salary as Illicit Gains 222
4.5. Legal Analysis 222
4.5.1. Did USDOJ's Settlement with UMC Pre-empt Taiwanese Courts' Finding of Economic Espionage? 222
4.5.2. Preventing Economic Espionage or Hindering Employees' Mobility? 223
4.5.3. Economic Espionage Requires Trade Secrets Held by Taiwanese 224
4.6. Commercial or Industrial Significance 224

Chapter 5
Thailand 225
Overview and Summary
Sutatip Yuthayotin & Tosaporn Leepuengtham 225
1. Brief History 225
2. The Scope of Protection 226
3. Trade Secret Owners and Their Rights 227
4. Infringement of Trade Secret 227
5. Prescription Period 228
6. Criminal Penalty 228
7. Injunctive Relief 230
8. Presumption for the Benefit of a Trade Secret Controller 230
9. Compensation and Punitive Damages 231
10. Practice 231
Topic 1 The Requirements of Trade Secret
Sutatip Yuthayotin 232
1. Legal Issues 232

2. The Statutory Law 232
3. The Case Law 232
4. The Leading Cases 233
4.1. Supreme Court Decision 15697/2557 233
4.1.1. Case Information 233
4.1.2. Summary 233
4.1.3. Facts 233
4.1.4. The Reasoning of the Court 234
4.1.4.1. The List of Customer Names and Other Information in Question Were Not Trade Secrets 234
4.1.4.2. Personal Expertise or Skill Acquired Through the Course of Employment 235
4.1.5. Legal Analysis 236
4.1.5.1. It Must Be Commercial Information 236
4.1.5.2. The Information Is Unknown to the Public and Not Accessible by Unconnected Persons 236
4.1.5.3. The Information Has Commercial Value Derived from Its Secrecy 236
4.1.5.4. The Trade Secret Controller Has Implemented Appropriate Measures to Keep the Information Confidential 236
4.1.6. Commercial and Industrial Significance 238
4.2. The Appeal Court for Specialized Cases, IP&IT Division Decision 165/2562
Tosaporn Leepuengtham 238
4.2.1. Case Information 238
4.2.2. Summary 238
4.2.3. Facts 239
4.2.4. Reasoning of the Court 239
4.2.4.1. Kitchen Design and Layout Were Not Secret 239
4.2.4.2. No Sufficient Steps Were Taken with Regards to Wood-Fired Pizza Oven 239
4.2.4.3. The Pizza Dough Recipe Is a Trade Secret 240
4.2.4.4. The Second Defendant Misappropriated the Confidential Information 241
4.2.4.5. Dissenting Opinion 242
4.2.5. Legal Analysis 243
4.2.5.1. A Recipe *Is* an Eligible Subject Matter for Trade Secret Protection 243
4.2.5.2. The Recipe Must Be Sufficiently Different from Similar Recipes Which Are Freely Available 244

4.2.5.3. Reasonable Steps to Preserve the Secrecy 244
4.2.5.4. The Recipe Would Seem to Be of Sufficient Economic Value 244
4.2.6. Commercial or Industrial Significance 245

Topic 2 The Validity and Scope of Confidentiality and Non-competition Clauses
Sutatip Yuthayotin 246
1. Legal Issues 246
2. The Statutory Law 246
3. The Case Law 247
4. The Leading Cases 247
4.1. Supreme Court Decision 1275/2543 (Decided on March 20, 2005) 247
4.1.1. Summary 247
4.1.2. Facts 248
4.1.3. Reasoning of the Court 248
4.2. Supreme Court Decision 6075/2549 249
4.2.1. Case Information 249
4.2.2. Summary 249
4.2.3. Facts 250
4.2.4. Reasoning of the Court 250
4.2.5. Legal Analysis 250
4.2.5.1. Form of Confidentiality and/or Non-competition Clauses 250
4.2.5.2. Legal Requirements 251
4.2.5.3. Criteria under the Supreme Court Precedents 251
4.2.6. Commercial and Industrial Significance 252

Topic 5 Civil Remedies: Injunctive Relief and Damages 254
1. Injunctive Relief
Sutatip Yuthayotin 254
1.1. Legal Issues 254
1.2. The Statutory Law 254
1.3. The Case Law 256
1.4. The Leading Cases 256
1.4.1. CIPIT Court Decision Tor. Por. 31/2549 256
1.4.1.1. Case Information 256
1.4.1.2. Summary 257
1.4.1.3. Facts 257
1.4.1.4. The Reasoning of the Court 257
1.4.2. CIPIT Court Decision Tor. Por. 98/2552 258
1.4.2.1. Case Information 258
1.4.2.2. Summary 258
1.4.2.3. Facts 258
1.4.2.4. The Reasoning of the Court 259
1.4.2.5. Legal Analysis 260

1.4.2.5.1. Thai Courts Are Very Careful in Granting Provisional Injunction 260
1.4.2.5.2. Legal Requirements for Granting Provisional Injunction 260
1.4.2.6. Commercial and Industrial Significance 261

2. Damages
Tosaporn Leepuengtham 262
2.1. Legal Issues 262
2.2. The Statutory Law 262
2.3. The Case Law 262
2.4. The Leading Cases 263
2.4.1. Supreme Court Decision 7769/ 2557 263
2.4.1.1. Case Information 263
2.4.1.2. Summary 263
2.4.1.3. Facts 263
2.4.1.4. Reasoning of the Court 264
2.4.2. The Appeal Court for Specialized Cases Decision 185/2562 A.D. 2019 264
2.4.2.1. Case Information 264
2.4.2.2. Summary 264
2.4.2.3. Facts 264
2.4.2.4. Reasoning of the Court 265
2.4.3. Supreme Court Decision 9072/2547 A.D. 2004 265
2.4.3.1. Case Information 265
2.4.3.2. Summary 265
2.4.3.3. Facts 265
2.4.3.4. Reasoning of the Court 266
2.4.3.5. Legal Analysis 266
2.4.3.5.1. Under Section 438 of the Civil and Commercial Code 266
2.4.3.5.2. Punitive Damages 267
2.4.3.6. Commercial or Industrial Significance 268

PART III
Asian Common Law Jurisdictions 269

CHAPTER 6
Singapore
Ng-Loy Wee Loon 271
Overview and Summary 271
Topic 1 The Legal Criteria in an Action for Breach of Confidence 272
1. First Element: The Plaintiff's Information Must Qualify as Confidential Information 272

1.1. The Requirement for *Relative* Secrecy 272
1.2. The Requirement to Assess the Information *as a Whole* 274
2. Second Element: The Defendant Must Owe an Obligation of Confidentiality to the Plaintiff (To Keep the Information Confidential) 275
2.1. Contractual Obligations of Confidentiality 276
2.2. Equitable Obligations of Confidentiality 277
3. The Third Element: The Defendant Must Have Breached the Obligation of Confidentiality by Using or Disclosing the Information Without the Authorization of the Plaintiff 280
4. Defense of Public Interest 281
Topic 2 The Enforceability of Confidentiality and/or Non-compete Clauses 283
Topic 3 The Burden of Proof 284
Topic 5 Monetary Awards 285
Topic 6 Criminal Sanctions 286

CHAPTER 7
Hong Kong
Jyh-An Lee & Jingwen Liu 287
Overview and Summary 287
1. The Equitable Action for Breach of Confidence 288
1.1. The Necessary Quality of Confidence 288
1.2. Circumstances Importing an Obligation of Confidence 288
1.3. Unauthorized Use to the Detriment of the Plaintiff 289
2. Civil Remedies 290
2.1. Injunctions 290
2.2. Damages 291
3. Efforts Towards Criminalization 292
Topic 1 The Requirements of Trade Secret in Hong Kong
Jyh-An Lee & Jingwen Liu 294
1. Legal Issues 294
2. The Statutory Law 294
3. The Case Law 294
4. The Leading Case(s) 294
4.1. Case Information 294
4.2. Summary 295
4.3. Facts 295
4.4. Reasoning of the Court 296
4.4.1. The General Principle Applicable to the Grant of Interlocutory Injunctions 296
4.4.2. Five-Step Test for Determining Whether There Is a Serious Question to Be Tried 297
4.5. Legal Analysis 298
4.5.1. Trade Secrets Enjoy Stronger Protection than Confidential Information 298
4.5.2. PCI's Breach of Confidence 299

4.6. Commercial or Industrial Significance 300
Topic 2 The Validity and Scope of Confidentiality and/or Non-competition Terms
Jyh-An Lee & Jingwen Liu 302
1. Legal Issues 302
2. The Statutory Law 302
3. The Case Law 302
4. The Leading Case(s) 303
4.1. Case Information 303
4.2. Summary 303
4.3. Facts 303
4.4. Reasoning of the Court 305
4.4.1. The Validity and Enforceability of the Restrictive Covenant 305
4.4.2. Misappropriation of Trade Secrets and Confidential Information 306
4.5. Legal Analysis 307
4.6. Commercial or Industrial Significance 308
Topic 3 The Burden of Proof and Its Reversal
Jingwen Liu & Jyh-An Lee 310
1. Legal Issues 310
2. The Statutory Law 310
3. The Case Law 310
4. The Leading Case(s) 311
4.1. Case Information 311
4.2. Summary 311
4.3. Facts 311
4.4. Reasoning of the Court 313
4.4.1. Whether the Customer Database and the Price List Were Trade Secrets of the Plaintiff 313
4.4.2. Whether the Defendants Had Breached Their Duties of Confidence 314
4.5. Legal Analysis 315
4.5.1. Confidentiality and Relevance of the Information 315
4.5.2. An Express or Implied Duty of Confidence 316
4.5.3. The Misuse of the Information to the Detriment of the Plaintiff 316
4.5.4. The Validity of a Covenant in Restraint of Trade 317
4.5.5. The Damage Caused to the Plaintiff 317
4.6. Commercial or Industrial Significance 318
Topic 5 The Damages
Jingwen Liu & Jyh-An Lee 319
1. Legal Issues 319
2. The Statutory Law 319
3. The Case Law 319

4. The Leading Case(s) 320
4.1. Case Information 320
4.2. Summary 320
4.3. Facts 321
4.4. Reasoning of the Court 322
4.4.1. The First-Instance Decision 322
4.4.2. The Court of Appeal Decision 323
4.4.2.1. The Applicability of Exemplary Damages in General 323
4.4.2.2. The Applicability of Exemplary Damages Against Equitable Wrongs 324
4.2.2.3. The Assessment of Exemplary Damages 324
4.5. Legal Analysis 325
4.5.1. The Availability of Damages in Breach of Confidence Cases 325
4.5.2. Different Types of Damages 326
4.5.2.1. Compensatory Damages 327
4.5.2.2. Nominal Damages 327
4.5.2.3. Aggravated Damages 328
4.5.2.4. Exemplary Damages 328
4.6. Commercial or Industrial Significance 329

CHAPTER 8
Malaysia 331
Overview and Summary
Lim Heng Gee 331
1. Introduction 331
2. The Elements Essential to a Cause of Action for Breach of Confidence 332
3. The Validity and Scope of Confidentiality and/or Non-competition Clauses 333
3.1. The Distinction Between Confidential Information and the Employee's General Stock of Knowledge 333
3.2. Section 28 of the Contracts Act and Restraint of Trade 333
4. The Burden of Proof for Trade Secret and Infringement and Its Reversal 334
4.1. The Legal Burden of Proof for Establishing the Cause of Action 334
4.2. The Legal Burden of Proof for the Remedies Sought 335
4.3. Interlocutory Applications 335
5. The Order for Protecting the Secrecy of Trade Secret During Prosecution and Trial 336
5.1. Anton Piller Order 336
5.2. Mareva Injunction 337
5.3. Interim Injunction and Interlocutory Injunction 337
6. The Damages 338

Topic 1 The Requirements of Trade Secret
Farizah Mohamed Isa 340
1. Legal Issues 340
2. The Statutory Law 340
3. The Case Law 340
4. The Leading Case 341
4.1. Case Information 341
4.2. Summary 341
4.3. Facts 341
4.4. The Reasoning of the Court 342
4.4.1. Duty of Fidelity 342
4.4.2. Requirements of an Action for Breach of Confidence 344
4.4.3. The Confidential Nature of the Information 344
4.4.4. That the Information in Question Was Communicated in Circumstances Importing an Obligation of Confidence 345
4.4.5. Unauthorized Use of That Information to the Detriment of the Party Communicating It 345
4.5. Legal Analysis 346
4.5.1 A Trade Secret Extends to Information Which Would Prejudice Its Owner When Used Without His Consent or Knowledge 346
4.5.2. Duty of Fidelity after the Employee Leaves His/Her Employment 347
4.5.3. Unauthorized Use 347
4.5.4. Restraint of Trade? 347
4.6. Commercial or Industrial Significance 348
Topic 2 The Validity and Scope of Confidentiality and/or Non-competition Clauses
Lim Heng Gee 349
1. Legal Issues 349
2. The Statutory Law 349
3. The Case Law 349
4. The Leading Case 349
4.1. Case Information 349
4.2. Summary 349
4.3. Facts 350
4.4. The Reasoning of the Court 351
4.4.1. The Customer List, Customer Preferences and Business Know-How Are Considered to Be Confidential Information 351
4.4.2. The Contractual Prohibitions Do Not Contravene Section 28 of the Contracts Act 1950 352
4.4.3. The Restriction in Perpetuity Was Reasonable and Thus Valid 353

4.4.4. Defendant's Livelihood and Access to Customers Would Not Be Affected 354
4.5. Legal Analysis 354
4.5.1. The Validity and Scope of Confidentiality and/or Non-competition Clauses 354
4.5.2. Section 28 Is Indeed Inconsistent with the Common Law Doctrine of Restraint of Trade 356
4.6. Commercial or Industrial Significance 357

Topic 3 The Burden of Proof for Trade Secret and Infringement and Its Reversal
Sik Cheng Peng 359
1. Legal Issues 359
2. Statutory Law 359
3. Case Law 359
4. The Leading Case 360
4.1. Case Information 360
4.2. Summary 361
4.3. Facts 361
4.4. The Reasoning of the Court 362
4.4.1. Lack of Sufficient Particularity in the Claim 362
4.4.2. Enforcement of Contractual Covenants on Confidentiality 364
4.4.3. Lack of Evidence on the Alleged Breach 364
4.5. Legal Analysis 365
4.5.1. Careful Pleading 365
4.5.2. The Rationale of Detailed Specifications 366
4.6. Commercial or Industrial Significance 367

Topic 4 The Order for Protecting the Secrecy of Trade Secret During Prosecution and Trial: Interlocutory Injunction
Farizah Mohamed Isa 369
1. Legal Issues 369
2. The Statutory Law 369
3. The Case Law 369
4. The Leading Case 369
4.1. Case Information 370
4.2. Summary 370
4.3. Facts 370
4.4. The Reasoning of the Court 372
4.4.1. Principles Applicable to Interim Injunctions 372
4.4.2. The Springboard Doctrine/Injunction 374
4.5. Legal Analysis 376
4.5.1 No Bona Fide Serious Matter to Be Tried 376
4.5.2. The Restraint of Trade Provision 377
4.6. Commercial or Industrial Significance 377

Topic 4 The Order for Protecting the Secrecy of Trade Secret During Prosecution and Trial: Anton Piller Order
Lim Heng Gee 378
1. Legal Issues 378
2. The Statutory Law 378
3. Case Law 378
4. The Leading Case 378
4.1. Case Information 379
4.2. Summary 379
4.3. Facts 379
4.4. The Reasoning of the Court 380
4.4.1. The Plaintiff Failed to Make a Full and Frank Disclosure When Applying for the Order 380
4.4.2. The Anton Piller Order Was Too Wide, Imprecise, Vague and Oppressive 382
4.5. Legal Analysis 382
4.5.1. Three Essential Preconditions for the Making of Anton Piller Order 382
4.5.2. Identification of the Specific Confidential Information Sought to Be Seized Is Important 384
4.6. Commercial or Industrial Significance 385
Topic 5 Damages
Sik Cheng Peng 386
1. Legal Issues 386
2. The Statutory Law 386
3. The Case Law 386
4. The Leading Case 387
4.1. Case Information 387
4.2. Summary 387
4.3. Facts 387
4.4. The Reasoning of the Court 388
4.4.1. Method of Assessment 388
4.4.2. The Duty to Prove Loss 388
4.4.3. Insufficient Evidence of Loss 389
4.4.4. Remoteness 390
4.5. Legal Analysis 391
4.5.1. The Objective of Damages 391
4.5.2. The Burden of Proof 392
4.5.3. Proof of Loss 393
4.6. Commercial or Industrial Significance 394

CHAPTER 9
India
Prashant Reddy T. 395
Overview and Summary 395

Topic 1 The Requirements of Trade Secrets 400
1. Legal Issues 400
2. The Statutory Law 401
3. The Case Law 401
4. The Leading Cases 401
4.1. Case I 401
4.1.1. Case Information 401
4.1.2. Summary 401
4.1.3. Facts 401
4.1.4. Reasoning of the Court 402
4.1.5. Legal Analysis 403
4.1.6. Commercial or Industrial Significance 404
4.2. Case II 404
4.2.1. Case Information 404
4.2.2. Summary 404
4.2.3. Facts 405
4.2.4. Reasoning of the Court 405
4.2.5. Analysis 406
4.2.6. Commercial/Industrial Significance 407
Topic 2 The Validity and Scope of Confidentiality and/or Non-competition Clauses 408
1. Legal Issues 408
2. The Statutory Law 408
3. The Case Law 409
4. The Leading Cases 409
4.1. Case I 409
4.1.1. Case Information 409
4.1.2. Summary 409
4.1.3. Facts 409
4.1.4. Reasoning of the Court 410
4.1.5. Legal Analysis 411
4.1.5.1. The Disclosure of Trade Secrets Is Not Inevitable 411
4.1.5.2. Section 27 Contracts Act Represented a Clean Break from English Law 412
4.1.6. Commercial or Industrial Significance 412
4.2. Case II 412
4.2.1. Case Information 413
4.2.2. Summary 413
4.2.3. Facts 413
4.2.5. Legal Analysis 415
4.2.5.1. No Point Granting an Injunction Whose Compliance Could Not Be Monitored 415
4.2.5.2. Golikari Needs Not Be Complied with in a Rigid Manner 415

4.2.6. Commercial or Industrial Significance 415

Topic 4 'Confidentiality Club' to Protect the Secrecy of Trade Secrets During Trials 417

1. Legal Issues 417

2. The Statutory Law 417

3. The Case Law 419

4. The Leading Cases 420

4.1. Case I 420

4.1.1. Case Information 420

4.1.2. Summary 420

4.1.3. Facts 420

4.1.4. Reasoning of the Court 421

4.1.5. Legal Analysis 422

4.1.6. Commercial or Industrial Significance 423

4.2. Case II 423

4.2.1. Case Information 423

4.2.2. Summary 423

4.2.3. Facts 423

4.2.4. Reasoning of the Court 424

4.2.5. Legal Analysis 425

4.2.6. Commercial or Industrial Significance 425

Topic 6 The Criminal Punishment for Trade Secret Infringement 426

1. Legal Issues 426

2. The Statutory Law 426

3. The Case Law 427

4. The Leading Case(s) 427

4.1. Case Information 427

4.2. Summary 427

4.3. Facts 428

4.4. Reasoning of the Court 428

4.5. Legal Analysis 429

4.6. Commercial or Industrial Significance 429

PART IV
Some References from the Occident 431

CHAPTER 10
Trade Secrets Protection in the European Union
Luc Desaunettes-Barbero 433

1. Overview 433

1.1. Historical and Institutional Background 433

1.2. Structure, Influence and Overall Balance 435

1.3. A Broad and Fuzzy Definition 436

1.4. A Strong Legal Protection 436

1.5. Exceptions for Journalists and Whistle-Blowers 437

1.6. Enforcement: The Requirement of an In-Depth Proportionality Analysis 437
2. The Requirements of Trade Secrets 438
2.1. A Questionable Alignment with Article 39(2) TRIPS 439
2.2. Analysis of the Requirements 439
3. The Validity and Scope of Confidentiality and/or Non-competition Clauses 441
4. The Burden of Proof for Trade Secrets and Infringement and Its Reversal 443
5. The Order for Protecting the Secrecy of Trade Secrets During Trial 444
5.1. Preservation of Confidentiality of Trade Secrets in the Course of Legal Proceedings 444
5.2. Provisional and Precautionary Measures 445
6. The Damages 446
6.1. Need for Demonstration of the Violator's Accountability 446
6.2. Calculation Method 447
7. The Criminal Punishment for Trade Secret Infringement 447
8. Conclusion 448

Index 451

Introduction

Kung-Chung Liu & Reto Hilty

Trade secret protection law has been an important complement to patent law and gained increasing importance over the last three decades, especially in Asia, due to the staggering commercial value of trade secrets, fierce cross-border competition, and 'large-scale global labour mobility'.[1] Thus far, no systematic study of trade secret protection law of major Asian jurisdictions has been made, except a recent publication that deals with China, Japan, and Korea[2], and one volume that deals with Korea and China[3]. More importantly, Asian economies are now at a crossroads, with the following changes:

(1) Various countries are following the US approach in criminalizing trade secret infringement, with imprisonment of up to 10 years in Japan, China, and Korea, up to 5 in Taiwan, and up to 1 in Thailand. However, these economies are of a civil law tradition which generally lacks an effective civil discovery process. This will lead to more criminal cases than civil cases to prosecute trade secret infringement. In addition, criminal cases have greater smearing effects on defendants in Asia and could place defendants in a less favourable situation.

(2) Four of the above countries are also following the US approach in penalizing cross-border trade secret infringement, or the so-called economic espionage, including Japan (up to 10 years), Korea (up to 15 years), Taiwan (up to 10

1. Anselm Sanders, The 'Actio Servi Corrupti' from the Roman Empire to the Globalised Economy, in Christopher Heath & Anselm Sanders (eds.), 'Employees, Trade Secrets and Restrictive Covenants' (Wolters Kluwer 2017), 3.
2. Christopher Heath & Anselm Sanders (eds), 'Employees, Trade Secrets and Restrictive Covenants' (Wolters Kluwer 2017), Part III Employees, Trade Secrets and Restrictive Covenants in Asia.
3. Meng Yanbei & Lee Hwang (eds), 'China-Korea IP & Competition Law Annual Report 2018' (Volumes I & II, Beijing 2019).

years), and China (up to 15 years).[4] It happens that there is underlying historical and geopolitical tension among these four Asian economies, which might provide the hotbed for nationalist and populist responses and twists to this type of cases. This can only reinforce the existing tension against the background of ever-intensifying competition.

(3) Japan and Korea rely on unfair competition prevention law to protect trade secrets, leaving it as a reflective interest, rather than a full-blown legal right. China, although also relying on unfair competition prevention law to protect trade secrets, specifically recognizes trade secrets as one of the objects of intellectual property rights in Article 123(2) of the Civil Code. However, Taiwan and Thailand follow the US approach in enacting sui generis trade secret protection law. A sui generis trade secret protection law has the propensity of propertizing trade secrets, rather than being purely behavioural or relational regulation. For example, according to section 5 of the Thai Trade Secrets Act, trade secrets owners are exclusively entitled to disclose or use, or license someone else to disclose or use, trade secrets and to stipulate any terms and conditions for the maintenance of the secrecy. Trade secret owners can also transfer their trade secrets by juristic act or by inheritance.

(4) Punitive damages are foreseen for intentional or wilful trade secret infringement by Korea (up to treble damages), Taiwan (up to three times the amount of compensatory damages), Thailand (up to two times the amount of compensation) and China (one to five times the actual loss suffered or benefits obtained by the infringer). This is noteworthy, as the compensation principle for torts in these economies is compensatory in nature, and courts are generally reluctant to award punitive damages.

These trends raise the questions of their compatibility with Asian commercial realities of being net importers of technology and vibrant economies for start-ups premised on employee mobility. If un-reflected, these trends might have ramifications for other Asian jurisdictions, not the least those of common law heritage. In addition, given that China, Japan, Korea, Malaysia, Singapore, and Thailand (six of the fifteen members) are key drivers of the Regional Comprehensive Economic Partnership (RCEP), and their regimes on trade secret protection might shape the future direction of the RCEP.

The present book provides a detailed analysis of the statutory and case law of nine major Asian economies, namely Japan, Korea, China (civil law traditions with no sui generis trade secret protection law), Taiwan and Thailand (civil law traditions with sui generis trade secret protection law), and Singapore, Hong Kong, Malaysia, and India (common law traditions). In addition, a chapter on EU trade secret protection law, which looks critically at EU's modelling on the US law, is included to serve as a reference for Asian economies, as it addresses many of the overlooked public interests,

4. By the end of 2020, there has not been even one convicted economic espionage case in Japan. As of June 2021, there has been three final convictions of economic espionage in Taiwan, but all with probation.

such as the freedom of expression and information, including freedom of the media, mobility of workers or employees, and exemption of certain whistle-blowing practices.

This book strives to give a clear overview of national laws and practices by examining the six topics that purportedly best reflect the Asian features: topic 1 the requirements of trade secrets, topic 2 the validity and scope of confidentiality and/or non-competition clauses, topic 3 the burden of proof and its shifting or reversal, topic 4 the order for protecting the secrecy of a trade secret during prosecution and trial, topic 5 civil remedies (injunctive relief and damages), and topic 6 criminal punishment for trade secret infringement. However, each chapter might have a slightly different format, number of leading cases, and even choice of topics, as the actual situations of each jurisdiction may differ from one another. For example, in Japan, the burden of proof is not particularly an issue, as there are detailed statutes for trade secret protection and there is no case law on this topic. On the other hand, there are hot debates on international jurisdiction and choice of law concerning trade secret infringement cases with foreign aspects. Therefore, in Chapter 1, the topic of international jurisdiction and choice of law replaces the topic of the burden of proof and its shifting or reversal. In Thailand, there is no case law on topics 3-5, and case law on topic 6 does not really establish any guidance beyond what is already stated in the Trade Secrets Act. As a result, Chapter 5 does not have case reports on those topics. Singapore, Hong Kong, and Malaysia do not have any specific law to penalize trade secret infringement, and there will be no case report on topic 6 in the respective chapter. However, topic 6 will still be addressed in Chapter 9 although there is no specific law in India that criminalizes the unauthorized use of trade secrets, as there is no shortage of cases wherein employers have attempted to use conventional criminal law to prosecute former employees for alleged trade secret infringement. The EU does not have any case law.

Worth mentioning is the large number of contributors to this book, 31 in total. This is because we would like Asian IP laws to be an area of common interest among as many IP scholars, judges, and practitioners as possible. We would like to sincerely thank them for their contribution. Mr Wang Xuan is also thanked for his help in preparing the index.

This book was preceded by an International Conference on Trade Secret Protection: Asia at a Crossroads, held on 7 December 2020 at College of Law, National Taiwan University jointly by the IP Initiative (previously the Applied Research Center for Intellectual Assets and the Law in Asia (ARCIALA)) of the Center for Artificial Intelligence and Data Governance (Yong Pung How School of Law, Singapore Management University), Max Planck Institute for Innovation and Competition, Center for Law, Technology and Ethics (College of Law National Taiwan University), and Taiwan Intellectual Property Law Association. We would also like to thank them for providing a venue for contributors to discuss their preliminary findings and exchange views.

PART I Asian Civil Law Jurisdictions with No Sui Generis Law

CHAPTER 1
Japan

OVERVIEW AND SUMMARY
Masabumi Suzuki

1. RELATED LEGAL SYSTEM

The protection of trade secrets in Japan is primarily based on the Unfair Competition Prevention Act (UCPA). The Act provides for the definition of trade secrets, acts of unfair competition related to trade secrets, civil remedies, and criminal penalties. The first provisions related to trade secrets were introduced into the UCPA by its revision in 1990 and came into force in 1991. That amendment was made in response to the GATT (General Agreement on Tariffs and Trade) Uruguay Round negotiations, which eventually led to the establishment of the World Trade Organization (WTO) and the conclusion of the Agreement on Trade-Related Aspects of Intellectual Property Rights (the TRIPS Agreement)[1]. This chapter will mainly focus on the protection of trade secrets by the UCPA.

The provisions related to trade secrets in the UCPA have since been amended many times to expand the types of targeted acts and to strengthen remedies. There have been also many court decisions accumulated with regard to the interpretation of the provisions. One of the main reasons for the stronger protection of trade secrets is changes in Japanese society, especially its labor markets, i.e., increase in mobility of employees, shares of non-regular employment, and numbers of foreign workers.

Besides the UCPA, the Civil Code and labor laws are also relevant in disputes concerning trade secrets, particularly with regard to contractual obligations to protect

1. During the Uruguay Round negotiations, the Japanese government recognized that a resulting agreement on intellectual property would contain an obligation to protect undisclosed information, and therefore submitted a bill to introduce trade secret protection to the Diet, aspiring to have an influential position in the negotiations.

confidential information and to avoid competition between employers and employees[2]. The general tort law (Article 709 of the Civil Code) can also be applicable to disputes involving fraudulent acts related to trade secrets. However, after the trade-secret-related provisions were introduced in the UCPA, claims for the protection of confidential information based on the general tort law have rarely been successful. This is because the provisions of the UCPA are considered to supersede the general tort law for the protection of confidential information, and if claims based on the UCPA fail, courts do not usually affirm the presence of tortious conduct[3].

2. DEFINITIONS AND REQUIREMENTS OF TRADE SECRETS

2.1. Definition

Article 2(6) of the UCPA defines trade secrets as follows:

> The term "trade secret" as used in this Act means technical or business information useful for business activities, such as manufacturing or marketing methods, that are kept secret and that are not publicly known[4].

The definition provides three requirements for any information to be deemed as trade secrets, i.e., (1) usefulness, (2) being kept secret, and (3) being not publicly known. They correspond to the three requirements set forth in Article 39.2 of the TRIPS Agreement. However, in comparison with Article 39.2, the definition in the UCPA is more detailed as to the requirement of usefulness ("commercial value" in Article 39.2 (b)) but much simpler as to the other requirements. In particular, the requirement of "being kept secret" is so simply defined that there have been controversies over the interpretation of its meaning. Each requirement is briefly explained below. In addition, *Topic 1* introduces a leading case in which these requirements were discussed.

2.2. Requirement (1): Usefulness

A trade secret is, first of all, "technical or business information useful for business activities, such as manufacturing or marketing methods." This requirement is also called the utility requirement. "Useful" means that the information is useful for business activities such as research and development and the production and sale of goods or services. The purpose of the requirement is to limit the subject of protection to kinds of information that have a certain social significance and necessity to be protected[5].

2. *Topic 2* in this Chapter deals with the issues of the validity of contractual obligation of confidentiality as well as noncompetition obligation, and the relationship between such contractual obligations and the protection of trade secrets under the UCPA.
3. The case discussed in *Topic 1* involves the issue of applicability of the general tort law to acts not covered by the UCPA.
4. An English translation of the UCPA provided by the Japanese government is available on WIPO Lex, https://wipolex.wipo.int/en/legislation/members/profile/JP. This chapter does not necessarily follow that translation.
5. Tokyo District Court, Heisei 12 (Wa) 9499 (decided on February 14, 2002, public works unit price list case).

Specifically, product design drawings, manufacturing methods, customer lists, sales manuals, and supplier lists are examples of "technical or business information useful for business activities." To meet the utility requirement, it is not necessary that the information be presently and actually used in business activities. However, the information should be effective in, for example, cost savings and improvement of operational efficiency[6]. It is also said that information that meets the two requirements of "being kept secret" and "being not publicly known" is usually found to be useful[7].

In contrast, information that is offensive to public order and morals, such as information that teaches methods of crimes or tax evasion, or shows how to manufacture and obtain prohibited items such as narcotics and stimulants, is not worthy of legal protection and does not meet the utility requirement[8]. In addition, information on antisocial behavior such as the release of harmful substances into the environment is not useful for business activities and does not fall under the definition of trade secrets[9].

2.3. Requirement (2): Being Kept Secret

This requirement is also called the "confidentiality management" requirement in the sense that managerial measures need to be taken by the lawful holder of the information to satisfy this requirement. Therefore, this requirement is essentially the same as the requirement of "reasonable steps ... to keep it secret" provided in Article 39.2(c) of the TRIPS Agreement.

In the past, the pervasive view interpreted this requirement as demanding (1) that a limit be imposed on those who have been given access to specific information (restricted access), and (2) that measures be taken to make it possible for those who access the information to recognize its confidentiality (recognizability)[10]. There have been many court decisions taking this interpretation. However, this interpretation has been criticized as too strict in recent years, and currently, the dominant view is that the second factor (2) (recognizability) should be decisive[11].

6. IP Policy Office, Ministry of Economy, Trade and Industry, *Commentaries on the Unfair Competition Prevention Act* (2nd ed., 2019) ("METI, *Commentaries*") 43. There are court decisions that denied the utility requirements in cases where courts could not discern any effects of the technical information at issue. *See*, e.g., Tokyo District Court, Heisei 13 (Wa) 7445 (decided on October 1, 2002, crepe mix liquid). There is no objection, however, to the interpretation that the utility requirement does not mean a high level of unpredigctability as the requirement of inventive step (nonobviousness) for patents.
7. Ministry of Economy, Trade and Industry, *Management Guidelines for Trade Secrets* ("METI, Guidelines") 19, https://www.meti.go.jp/english/policy/economy/chizai/chiteki/pdf/0813mgtc.pdf. The Guidelines were first published in 2003 and have been revised in 2005, 2010, 2011, 2013, 2015, and 2019 to reflect trends in court decisions.
8. Tokyo District Court, *supra* note 5.
9. METI, *Commentaries*, *supra* note 6, at 43.
10. *See*, e.g., METI, *Guidelines*, *supra* note 7, at 6 (n. 6).
11. *See*, e.g., Tokyo High Court, Heisei 28 (U) 974 (decided on March 21, 2017, customers' information) (Because this is a criminal case, it is subject to the jurisdiction of the Tokyo High Court (not the IP High Court).); Osaka District Court, Heisei 27 (Wa) 4169 (decided on October 19, 2017, alumina textile). METI issued its *Guidelines* (*see supra* note 7) for the first time in 2003, and has revised them several times. The *Guidelines* introduce court decisions related to the three requirements for trade secrets, with a focus on the requirement for confidentiality management,

2.4. Requirement (3): Being Not Publicly Known

This requirement is understood to mean that the information is generally unknown or not readily available to the public[12]. In essence, it is the same as Article 39.2(a) of the TRIPS Agreement.

This requirement can become an issue, for example, where information available from reverse engineering was alleged to be publicly unknown. For example, in one case where the plaintiff sought to protect information (such as drawings of parts) regarding the manufacture of its products (aluminum shutters) as trade secrets, the Intellectual Property High Court (IP High Court) concluded that "information easily obtainable from products in circulation in the market cannot be deemed to be information 'that is not publicly known' as provided in Article 2(6) of the UCPA," and the parts presented in the drawings claimed as trade secrets by the plaintiff could not be regarded as "publicly unknown" because they could "be easily reproduced from the plaintiff's products themselves by using general technical means."[13]

3. TYPES OF ACTS OF UNFAIR COMPETITION RELATED TO TRADE SECRETS

3.1. Overview

In Article 2(1), items (iv) through (x) of the UCPA, the types of acts related to trade secrets that are regarded as acts of unfair competition are stipulated. They can be roughly divided into the following three types:

(1) Wrongful acquisition of trade secrets and subsequent unauthorized use.
(2) Unauthorized use of legitimately acquired trade secrets.
(3) Distribution of things resulting from unauthorized use of technical secrets.

3.2. Wrongful Acquisition of Trade Secrets and Subsequent Unauthorized Use or Disclosure

3.2.1. Wrongful Acquisition and Subsequent Use or Disclosure (Article 2(1), Item (iv))

"Wrongful acquisition" is defined as "acts of acquiring trade secrets by theft, fraud, duress, or other wrongful means." Use or disclosure of trade secrets by the person who

---

and indicate the minimum level of measures for business entities to receive the protection of trade secrets. The *Guidelines* used to take the formerly prevailing interpretation of the requirement for confidentiality management. In the 2015 revision, however, the *Guidelines* changed the interpretation, and began to explain the requirement as ultimately demanding recognizability of confidentiality, while the access restriction should be taken as just one of the possible means to ensure recognizability and not always indispensable.

12. METI, *Guidelines*, *supra* note 7, at 19. Incidentally, METI's English translation of the *Guidelines* uses the term "non-public domain" for this requirement. This is not an appropriate translation, because Article 2(6) of the UCPA states "that are not publicly known" and its meaning is different from the concept of the information's not being in the public domain (e.g., patented inventions can be publicly known, but not in the public domain).
13. IP High Court, Heisei 23 (Ne) 10023 (decided on July 21, 2011, aluminum shutter).

wrongfully acquired them is also an act of unfair competition. For example, an employee stealing a confidential document kept by an employer and delivering it to another company would belong to this type.

3.2.2. Acquisition and Use or Disclosure of Wrongfully Acquired Trade Secrets (Article 2(1), Items (v) and (vi))

Item (v) designates acts to acquire trade secrets that were originally acquired wrongfully by a third party (a person whose wrongful acquisition belongs to the type provided in item (iv)), and to use or disclose such trade secrets, knowing or not knowing due to gross negligence the fact of wrongful acquisition by the third party as acts of unfair competition. For example, an employee who buys confidential documents of another company from a thief of the documents with the knowledge of the theft, and discloses the documents to his employer would be regarded as committing this type of act.

If the above actor did not know without gross negligence, at the time of his acquisition of the trade secrets, about the wrongful acquisition of the trade secrets by the third party, his conduct does not fall under item (v). However, if he learns, or has gross negligence in not learning, the fact of the wrongful acquisition by the third party, and then uses or discloses the trade secrets, such acts would constitute acts of unfair competition under item (vi). For example, if an employee buys documents from a person nonnegligently, and then, he shows the documents to his employer after having come to know that the seller stole the documents illegally, his act of disclosure constitutes an act of unfair competition.

3.3. Unauthorized Use of Legitimately Acquired Trade Secrets

3.3.1. Unauthorized Use or Disclosure (Article 2(1), Item (vii))

Item (vii) prescribes acts of using or disclosing trade secrets for the purpose of wrongful gain or damaging the trade secret holder by a person who has been shown them by the business entity holding the trade secrets. Here, the "business entity holding the trade secrets" includes not only business operators who hold the trade secrets from the beginning (e.g., a business operator who holds technical information developed in-house) but also business operators who have taken over from the person who developed the information or have obtained the right to use the information.

There is controversy about the meaning of "shown" by the holder. Specifically, when an employee of a company creates a trade secret on the job (e.g., when an in-house researcher creates an invention as a job), has the employee been "shown" the trade secret? Opinions are divided on this question. The first view is that the trade secret created as a job belongs to the company that is the employer of the creator, and the employee, even though having created the trade secret, is a person who has been "shown" it[14]. The second view criticizes the first view, arguing that it is often not possible to clearly determine the attribution of trade secrets, and the employee who

14. *See*, e.g., Tsuneyuki Yamamoto, *Outline of the Unfair Competition Prevention Act* (4th ed., Hatsumei Kyokai, 2006) (in Japanese) p. 162.

created the trade secret should not be deemed a person who has been "shown" it[15]. According to the second view, unauthorized use and disclosure by the employee who creates trade secrets should be treated as a breach of contractual obligation. No precedent has yet been reached by the court on this issue.

With regard to this type of conduct, there is a court decision which held that disclosing the prices in the wholesale contract between the parties would not be disclosing trade secrets shown by the holder, as they are formed through negotiation between the parties and initially acquired by both parties[16].

3.3.2. Acquisition and Use or Disclosure of Wrongfully Disclosed Trade Secrets (Article 2(1)(viii) and (ix))

Item (viii) designates acts to acquire trade secrets that were wrongfully disclosed by a third person (a person whose wrongful disclosure would either fall under item (vii) or constitute a breach of legal obligation for confidentiality), and to use or disclose such trade secrets, knowing or not knowing due to gross negligence the fact of wrongful disclosure, as acts of unfair competition. For example, suppose an employee of a robot manufacturer participates in the establishment of a different company that operates the same type of business, and discloses to the new company the confidential information on robot manufacturing technology that was shown to him by the original company, and taken out without permission at the time of his retirement. His disclosure to the new company would be an act of unfair competition under Article 2(1), item (vii). Then, if the new company uses the information for manufacturing robots, knowing that the employee leaked the information in violation of a confidentiality obligation with the original employer, the use by the new company would fall under Article 2(1), item (viii).

If the above actor of acts under item (viii) did not know without gross negligence, at the time of his acquisition of the trade secrets, about the wrongful disclosure by a preceding holder, his conduct does not fall under item (viii). However, if he learns, or has gross negligence in not learning, the fact of the wrongful disclosure by a preceding holder, and then uses or discloses the trade secrets, such acts would constitute acts of unfair competition under item (ix).

3.4. Distribution of Things Created by Unauthorized Use of Technical Secrets (Article 2(1)(x))

This type covers transferring, delivering, exporting, importing, and other acts for distribution of things created by the unauthorized use (which would fall under one of

15. *See.* e.g., Yoshiyuki Tamura, *Unfair Competition Law* (2nd ed., Yuhikaku, 2003) (in Japanese) p. 343.
16. Tokyo District Court, Heisei 13 (Wa) 10472 (decided on February 5, 2002, Daikoku). The case was between a major pharmaceutical company (the plaintiff) and a drug store (the defendant). The plaintiff alleged that the drug store committed acts of unfair competition (Article 2 (1)(vii) of the UCPA) by disclosing the prices in the wholesale contract between the parties. The Tokyo District Court dismissed the claim, stating that the prices were not trade secrets shown by the plaintiff to the drug store.

items (iv) through (ix)) of technical secrets. For example, selling a car that has been manufactured using illegally stolen secrets of assembly technology would belong to this type. If the distributor is unaware with no gross negligence of the fact that the things were created by unauthorized use, the act of distribution is exempted from the scope of acts of unfair competition.

This type was introduced by the 2015 revision of the UCPA. While the acts in the formerly existing provisions were directly related to the misappropriation of trade secrets, the new type is only indirectly related to trade secrets[17]. It also differs from the other types in that it only covers acts related to technical secrets rather than trade secrets generally.

This type of conduct has the following problems[18]. First, the scope of the subject matter, i.e., things "created by" the use of trade secrets, is unclear, and there is room for a very broad interpretation[19], thus lacking predictability and legal stability. Second, while it is necessary that the information be a trade secret (technical secret) at the time of its use for creating things, it is not required that the information used for the creation of the things remain a trade secret at the time of the act of distribution of things (i.e., the act specified by item (x)). For example, distribution of things after the information used for their creation became known to the public may still be an act of unfair competition. It is questionable whether it is really necessary to regulate without limit the distribution of things using information that is no longer a trade secret.

3.5. Exclusion from Application

Article 19 of the UCPA designates certain acts that are within the scope of acts of unfair competition but subject to neither civil remedies nor criminal penalties under the Act. With respect to acts related to trade secrets, if a person acquires trade secrets by transaction, not knowing without gross negligence of the wrongful acquisition or unauthorized disclosure of the information by a preceding holder, the person can use the trade secrets within the scope of title acquired through the transaction (Article 19(6)). The purpose of this exclusion is to ensure the safety and security of business transactions.

4. CIVIL REMEDIES

4.1. Injunction

A person whose business interests are infringed or likely to be infringed by acts of unfair competition may claim injunctive relief (Article 3(1) of the UCPA), destruction

17. The type of acts provided by Article 2(1)(x) is similar to that provided by Article 4.5 of the EU Trade Secret Directive (2016/943) which relates to acts concerning "infringing goods".
18. Masabumi Suzuki, *Reflections on International Aspects of the Protection of Trade Secrets (in Japanese)*, 49(6) Patents & Licensing 8 (2020), https://papers.ssrn.com/sol3/papers.cfm?abstract_id=3812080.
19. For example, things created by a production process using confidential information of measuring methods would fall under the scope of the subject of this type. In contrast, if that information is a patented invention, the patent right would not extend to distribution of products manufactured by use of the invention (*see* Article 2(3)(iii) of the Japanese Patent Act).

of things that constitute the act of infringement, and other measures necessary to make injunction relief effective (Article 3(2)).

For example, in a case where the plaintiff, who held a customer list as a trade secret, claimed suspension of the use of the list by the defendant, the court issued the following orders[20]:

(1) The defendant shall not request a meeting, give a call nor send mail to persons on the plaintiff's customer list, to conclude a contract for making or sale of men's wigs, to solicit such a contract, or to engage in business activities associated with such a contract.
(2) The defendant shall not conclude a contract for making or sale of men's wigs, solicit such a contract, nor engage in business activities associated with such a contract with persons listed on the plaintiff's customer list who visit the defendant or make a telephone contact to the defendant in order to conclude such a contract or to receive services associated with such a contract.
(3) The defendant shall discard the copy of the plaintiff's customer list.

The right to claim injunctive relief against acts explained in 3.2 and 3.3 above is extinguished by prescription if the actor continues the acts and the infringed person does not exercise the right within three years after the person comes to know about the fact of infringement and the identity of the actor. The right to injunction also expires when twenty years have elapsed from the beginning of the acts (Article 15).

4.2. Damages

A person whose business interests have been infringed due to intentional or negligent acts of unfair competition may seek damages from the actor (Article 4). However, no compensation for damages will be granted for the act of using trade secrets after the right to claim an injunction against the act has expired (Article 4 proviso).

The UCPA has provisions to make it easier for an infringed person to prove the amount of damages by presenting presumptions for the amount. Specifically, (1) the infringed person's profit per unit of things the person could have sold but for infringement, multiplied by the quantity of things transferred by the actor of the act of unfair competition (this assumption is available only for the damages caused by unfair use of technical secrets), (2) the amount of profits received by the actor due to the act of unfair competition, or (3) the amount that the infringed person would have been able to charge the actor for the use of the trade secret may be presumed as the amount of damages suffered by the infringed person (Article 5(1) through (3))[21]. *Topic 5* discusses court decisions that applied these provisions.

20. Osaka District Court, Heisei 6 (Wa) 4404 (decided on April 16, 1996, customer list of men's wig store).
21. Similar provisions for the presumption of the amount of damages exist in many Japanese IP laws such as the Patent Act, Trademark Act, Utility Models Act, Industrial Design Act and Copyright Act.

5. CRIMINAL PENALTIES

No criminal penalties were set when trade secret provisions were introduced in the UCPA for the first time in 1990. That was because there was concern that the criminal punishment would adversely affect the public interest by giving chilling effects on, for example, the freedom of the press and the freedom of choosing occupation. However, as the need for the protection of trade secrets increased, criminal penalties were introduced in 2003. Afterward, several amendments to the UCPA have been made to expand and strengthen penalties. In particular, there is an increasing number of cases in which trade secrets of Japanese companies are alleged to have been illegally acquired by foreigners or illegally used in foreign countries. Therefore, the UCPA has introduced provisions regarding foreign offenses.

Under the current provisions, the maximum penalties for acts of unfair competition related to trade secrets are, in principle, a maximum of 10 years in prison and/or a fine of JPY 20 million (about USD 190,000). The amount of fines can be increased up to JPY 30 million (about USD 290,000) for crimes aimed at the use of trade secrets in foreign countries. In addition, if the actor of the crime is an employee, the employer may be subject to joint liability with the employee for a fine of up to JPY 1 billion (for crimes aimed at use in foreign countries) or JPY 500 million (for other crimes). These penalties are heavier than general theft (the maximum penalty for theft is either imprisonment of 10 years or a fine of JPY 500,000 (about USD 4,800 under Article 235 of the Penal Code).

Topic 6 introduces a decision by the Supreme Court that provides an interpretation of a provision of criminal penalties for illegal acquisition of trade secrets (Article 21(1)(iii) of the UCPA). Specifically, the issue was whether or not there was a "purpose of gaining fraudulent benefits" required by the penalty provision, and the Supreme Court affirmed that the accused had that purpose at the time of committing the crime.

6. SPECIAL MEASURES FOR JUDICIAL PROCEEDINGS INVOLVING TRADE SECRETS

In recent years, with the increased concern about misappropriation of trade secrets, provisions to protect trade secrets in court proceedings have been expanded. First, there are general provisions to protect confidential information in the Code of Civil Procedure (CCP), for example, provisions for restrictions on viewing litigation materials (Article 92 of the CCP), right to refuse testimony (Article 197 of the CCP), and right to refuse the submission of documentary evidence (Article 220 of the CCP). In addition, IP laws provide special procedures for judicial proceedings regarding infringement of IP (including trade secrets). Relevant special procedures include the protective order system (Article 105-4 of the Patent Act, Article 30 of the Utility Model Act, Article 41 of the Industrial Design Act, Article 39 of the Trademark Act, Article 10 of the UCPA, etc.), in-camera procedure for examining the reason for rejection of submission of documents (Article 105 of the Patent Act, Article 30 of the Utility Model Act, Article 41 of the Industrial Design Act, Article 39 of the Trademark Act, etc.), suspension of open trials (Article 105-7 of the Patent Act, Article 30 of the Utility Model Act, and Article 13 of the

UCPA), and court decisions on keeping the confidentiality of trade secrets in criminal proceedings (Article 23 of the UCPA). *Topic 4* introduces court cases and actual practices related to the protective order system.

7. INTERNATIONAL JURISDICTION AND CHOICE OF LAW

In Japan, international jurisdiction and choice of law are being discussed with respect to civil cases related to trade secrets that involve international aspects. *Topic 3* deals with a civil lawsuit between Japanese companies in which the defendant was accused of having acquired a trade secret illegally, but counterargued that it obtained the trade secret from a Chinese company or a Taiwanese company in good faith. In that case, the IP High Court stated that the legal nature of claims for civil remedies in such disputes is tortious, and the governing law should be the law of the place where the result of the infringing act occurred, determining that the law of Japan should be applied to that specific case.

TOPIC 1 THE REQUIREMENTS FOR TRADE SECRETS IN JAPAN

Takeshi Maeda

1. Legal Issues

The requirements for trade secrets are (1) secrecy management (controlled as a secret), (2) non-public domain (not publicly known), and (3) usefulness (useful technical or operational information). Being a trade secret is a requirement for receiving protection under the UCPA. In Japan, the most contentious issue in determining whether or not specific information satisfies the definition of a trade secret is the requirement of secrecy management.

2. The Statutory Law

Article 2(6) of the UCPA provides that the term "trade secret" as used in this Act shall mean a production method, sales method, or any other technical or operational information useful for business activities that is controlled as a secret and is not publicly known.

Article 2(1)(vii) of the UCPA provides that acts of using or disclosing a trade secret, which has been disclosed by the holder of such trade secret, for the purpose of unfair business competition or otherwise acquiring an illicit gain, or causing injury to such holder constitute "unfair competition."

Article 2(1)(viii) of the UCPA provides that acts of acquiring a trade secret with the knowledge or, without the knowledge due to gross negligence, that there has been an improper disclosure of such trade secret or that such trade secret has been acquired through improper disclosure, or acts of using or disclosing a trade secret so acquired constitute "unfair competition."

The importance of "trade secrets" such as technical or business know-how has increased significantly. In response, the 1990 amendments to the UCPA created protection for trade secrets. With the 1993 amendments to the UCPA, the definition clause of trade secrets moved to Article 2(6). Still, the definition of trade secrets itself has remained unchanged through the amendments.

The METI Guidelines summarizes the definition of trade secrets[22]. The Guidelines are legally not binding but embody one way of thinking based on innovation, overseas trends, and domestic and international court cases. However, it is a handy resource for learning about trends in Japanese practice. It is believed that many companies follow this guideline for trade secrets management.

3. The Case Law

From the establishment of the IP High Court in 2005 to the writing of this case report (November 12, 2020), there have been more than 200 cases involving trade secrets in the district courts, and 52 cases in which trade secrets have been at issue in the IP High

22. *See supra* note 7.

Court[23]. However, there is no Supreme Court precedent on the trade secret requirement. Almost half of the trade secret decisions by the IP High Court were issued after 2016, which indicates that the importance of trade secrets has increased sharply in recent years.

Regarding the criteria for judging the secrecy management requirement, Professor Tamura has classified court cases into three periods based on whether information could be recognized as secret by those who had access to it: First, the mitigation period before 2003, the strict period of 2003-2008, and the shaky period of 2007 to present[24]. In the mitigation period, for example, in the Tokyo District Court case of December 26, 2002, Heisei 12 (Wa) 22457, the court found that the information hold by the temporary staffing business company was kept in an unlocked cabinet and there was no specific "do not take out" notice. However, the employees have to make written pledges to maintain the secrecy of the clients' information and not to compete for two years after leaving the company. In conclusion, the court affirmed the secrecy management, focusing on the fact that the employees could recognize such information as a secret.

In the strict period, according to Professor Tamura, some court cases require systematic control for information and found that it is not enough to satisfy secrecy management if those who have access to the information can recognize it as a secret. For example, in the Tokyo District Court case Heisei 15 (Wa) 10721 (decided on April 13, 2004), the secrecy management of information such as customer lists was at issue. The court denied the secrecy management based on the fact that there was no access restriction on the file and that there was no secrecy management agreement in the work rules or the written oath.

From around 2007, court cases that reverted to the mitigation period began to reappear and became mainstream again. At present, many court cases judge secrecy management based on whether the information is kept secret to the extent that a person with access to the information would know that the information is being maintained as a secret. Examples are the IP High Court cases Heisei 24 (Ne) 10084 (decided on July 4, 2012), which I will later introduce as the leading case, and Heisei 26 (Ne) 10028 (decided on August 6, 2014), and Osaka District Court case Heisei 27 (Wa) 4169 (decided on October 19, 2017). The METI Guidelines also state that "for secrecy management requirements to legally satisfy the definition, it is necessary that the intent to maintain confidentiality within of a specific company regarding a specific, legally owned trade secret, has been clarified to its employees by using appropriate confidentiality measures, thereby allowing the employees and other workers to recognize the said intention of confidentiality."[25]

---

23. This is the results of the search at https://www.courts.go.jp/app/hanrei_jp/search7?reload = 1.
24. Yoshiyuki Tamura, *Changes in Judicial Decisions on the Requirements for Confidentiality Management of Trade Secrets and Their Relevance (Part 1) (in Japanese)*, 64(5) Intellectual Property Management 621 (2014).
25. METI *Guidelines*, *supra* note 7, at 4.

4. The Leading Case

The decision on secrecy management represents the current trend in court decisions that focus on the recognizability of trade secrets to employees. It is one of the most symbolic rulings of the shaky period after 2007.

4.1. *Case Information*

The IP High Court, Heisei 23 (Ne) No. 10084 (decided on July 4, 2012), and Heisei 24 (Ne) No. 10025 (supplemental appellate case).

Presiding Judge Yoshinori Tomita, Judge Yoshiki Tanaka, and Judge Sumiko Maseki.

4.2. *Summary*

The present case involved former employees being sued for infringing their previous employers' trade secrets. The district court found unfair competition related to Article 2(1)(vii) and (viii) of the UCPA and partially allowed the claims[26]. The defendants appealed, and the plaintiffs filed a supplemental appeal. The IP High Court dismissed the appeal, finding that the customer information constituted a trade secret

4.3. *Facts*

Plaintiff Next is a corporation engaged in selling and purchasing real estate, primarily investment condominiums. Plaintiff Community is a wholly owned subsidiary of plaintiff Next and is engaged in managing real estate sold by plaintiff Next. Defendants A and B were employees of Plaintiff Next and were involved in the sales of Plaintiff Next's investment condominiums. Defendant A resigned from Plaintiff Next and established a corporation, Defendant Rentrex, and employed Defendant B. Defendant Rentrex was engaged in the rental and management of the real estate, primarily investment condominiums, and competed with Plaintiff Community.

The plaintiffs sued the defendants for unfair competition, namely obtaining the plaintiffs' customer information, which is a trade secret, and contacting the plaintiffs' customers to solicit them to change their rental management contractor from the plaintiff Community to the defendant Rentrex. The plaintiffs sought damages among others.

4.4. *The Reasoning of the Court*

4.4.1. *Secrecy Management*

4.4.1.1. The Customer Information Was Managed as a Secret

Plaintiff Next is a company listed on the second section of the Tokyo Stock Exchange with a capital of over JPY 1.8 billion, and Plaintiff Community is also a joint-stock

26. Tokyo District Court, 2009 (Wa) No. 24860.

company with a capital of JPY 50 million. Since the plaintiffs jointly own the customer information in question, they should be required to have an appropriate information management system together.

The customer information in question is centrally managed by the sales division, which supervises the sales department of Plaintiff Next, as electronic data stored in customer files and customer management systems. The customer files and the customer management systems were all stored in a locked room with restricted access. The former was available only to employees belonging to the sales division or employees of the division who had gone through the prescribed application process and login procedure.

Although the sales division employees kept the customer information as a copy of the contract details report, this was based on the business need to respond quickly to customer inquiries and to narrow down the number of prospective customers for additional sales. The plaintiffs defined the confidentiality obligations in the work rules, which are always available in each department, asked employees to submit confidentiality agreements, implemented various information security measures, including obtaining ISMS and ISO/IEC27001 certifications, conducting the annual assessment, distributing the "ISO27001 Handbook" to employees, and holding seminars and examinations based on this handbook. Therefore, the decision found that the plaintiffs have made it easy for their employees to recognize that the customer information is confidential.

Taking all of the above into account, the decision concluded that the plaintiffs restricted access to the customer information so that a person with access to the customer information recognizes it as a secret, and therefore, the customer information was managed as a secret by the plaintiffs.

4.4.1.2. Secrecy Management Does Not Have to Be Perfect

(a) The defendants argued that the customer information lacked secrecy management because the plaintiffs managed it sloppily. However, the decision conceded that even if the employees distributed the related documents to their superiors, took them home, kept them in notebooks, and did not destroy them even after the sales contract was concluded, this was based on business necessity. Besides, there was no circumstance indicating that a person other than the employees in the plaintiffs' sales-related departments would have had access to the related documents and notebooks. As stated above, the plaintiffs ensured that their employees could easily recognize the customer information as confidential. There was no evidence to prove that the documents related to the customer information were left on the plaintiffs' desks.

Therefore, the defendants' argument that the customer information in question lacked secrecy management could not be accepted.

(b) In addition, the defendants argued that although the Plaintiffs must mark each piece of the customer information of Plaintiff Next as a trade secret, they failed to do so; therefore, pieces of the customer information lacked secrecy management.

However, because Plaintiff Next had strict control over the customer information and made it easy for its employees to recognize the customer information as confidential, the decision concluded that individual pieces of information included in the customer information also satisfied the secrecy management requirement even if they were not marked as secret themselves.

4.4.2. Usefulness and Non-public Domain

Because the plaintiffs' customers often buy investment condominiums sold by the Plaintiff Next and consign their rental management to the Plaintiff Community, the customer information enables the plaintiffs to efficiently get a sales contract or a rental management contract of investment condominiums. The customer information is about 7,000 people who purchased investment condominiums for sale and is not generally known. Therefore, the customer information is useful information for the plaintiffs' business activities and is not publicly known.

The defendants argued that the customer information is neither useful nor non-public information because one can easily obtain the names, addresses, telephone numbers, and the names and addresses of their workplaces from the registration summaries, NTT's (Nippon Telegraph and Telephone Corporation) directory, list agencies, and the Internet.

However, the decision determined that "the customer information is not just the names and other information of a few individuals, but the names and other information of approximately 7,000 individuals who purchased investment condominiums sold by Plaintiff Next. It is clear that such information is not readily available in the registration summaries, NTT's directory, list agencies, or on the Internet."

4.5. Legal Analysis

4.5.1. Secrecy Management

4.5.1.1. Recognizability Is the Most Important Requirement

In this case, whether customer information constitutes a trade secret or not was disputed. The court ruled affirmatively, finding that the secrecy management requirement was satisfied. The court followed the trend of recent cases and judged the secrecy management based on whether "a person with access to the information recognizes it as a secret." The decision is significant, as it presents the criteria for judging secrecy management.

The purpose of the secrecy management requirement is to provide predictability to employees by specifying which items within a specific corporation are to be kept confidential by employees (the scope of information)[27]. The METI Guidelines before the 2015 revision stated that secrecy management requires that (1) access to the information be restricted, and (2) the information be recognizable as a trade secret by those who have access to it. The two requirements must be satisfied at the same time.

27. METI, *Guidelines*, *supra* note 7, at 4.

Therefore even if the information is recognizable as a secret, if there is an objectively low restriction of access, the secrecy management will still be denied.

However, the current METI Guidelines understand that "restricted access" is only one means of ensuring "recognizability."[28] Thus, even if a company's secrecy management measures are inadequate and access restrictions are not sufficiently structured, as long as a person with access to the information can recognize it as a trade secret, the secrecy management requirement will be satisfied.

Such an interpretation is justified because the purpose of the secrecy management requirement is to ensure the foreseeability for employees and others who have access to the information, so recognizability is the most important requirement. As Professor Tamura has pointed out, the law does not have to protect information for which a company does not have secrecy management measures because it does not care about divulging it and needs no incentive to develop it. From this perspective, a certain level of secrecy management measures may be necessary, but a high degree of such measures would rigidly constrain corporate activities. After all, it is sufficient for a company to make clear its intention to manage the information as a secret, so if the management measures are sufficient to ensure the employees' recognition of it as a secret, it is sufficient[29].

4.5.1.2. How to Determine the Recognizability

The METI Guidelines state that "for secrecy management requirements to legally satisfy the definition, it is necessary that the intent to maintain confidentiality within a specific company regarding a specific, legally owned trade secret has been clarified to its employees by using appropriate confidentiality measures, thereby allowing the employees and other workers to recognize the said intention of confidentiality."[30] The intention of confidentiality is the company's intention to treat the information as confidential. The Guidelines state that the ultimate criterion for secrecy management is whether the intention of confidentiality is recognizable. The Guidelines state that the company should show it in the objective form of "secret management measures."

According to the METI Guidelines, the extent of the secrecy management measures required depends on the size, type of business, the employees' duties, the nature of the information, and other company circumstances[31]. In this decision, as discussed below, the size of the company, the duties of the employees, and the nature of the information are taken into account in determining whether the secrecy management requirement is satisfied. These circumstances affect whether or not an employee can recognize the information as secret. Many court cases have considered such circumstances as well[32].

---

28. METI, *Guidelines*, *supra* note 7, at 6.
29. Tamura, *supra* note 24.
30. METI, *Guidelines*, *supra* note 7, at 6.
31. *Ibid.*
32. The Osaka District Court case Heisei 13 (Wa) 10308 (decided on February 27, 2003), and the IP High Court case Heisei 22 (Ne) 10039 (decided on September 27, 2011) acknowledged the recognizability of the rare technical information.

According to the METI Guidelines, secrecy management measures consist of two different factors[33]. One is a measure that reveals whether a company reasonably separates trade secrets from general information (Reasonable Classification). The other is a measure which clarifies the information is a trade secret[34]. Reasonable Classification means that a company reasonably separates trade secrets from general information according to the nature of the information, the selected medium, secrecy management, and the amount of information, intending to indicate to employees the subject of secrecy management. This reasonable classification does not require labeling each piece of paper or each electronic file as either a trade secret or general information for a medium containing the information. Instead, it is enough for such classification to allow the employees to determine whether a specific piece of information contains trade secret information (which may also contain general information), or consists only of general information, according to an ordinary management method suited to a specific scale, business style, or other relevant facets of the corporation in question[35]. It should be noted that the degree of Reasonable Classification is only an indicator for judging recognizability, and even if the degree of Reasonable Classification is lenient, the secrecy management requirement may be satisfied in some cases in light of other circumstances.

4.5.1.3. Evaluation of the Present Decision

The decision first states that the plaintiffs should prepare a commensurate secret management system because they are listed companies on the Tokyo Stock Exchange. The larger the company, the more extensive the restrictions on access to sensitive information should be. In this judgment, the court found that the customer information was managed centrally as customer files or electronic data stored in the customer management system, which were kept in a locked room with restricted access, and their use was limited to employees of the sales division who had gone through specific procedures. In the present case, the plaintiffs had taken Reasonable Classification and further clarified the secrecy management of the information. This level of measures is sufficient to meet the requirements of a listed company.

On the other hand, the court also found that there were inadequate restrictions on access. First, employees in the sales division sometimes kept customer information on hand. However, this was unavoidable due to business necessity, and the court finally affirmed the secrecy management after finding that the company made its employees aware that customer information was a trade secret. Second, individual pieces of information included in the customer information should have been marked as a trade secret, but no explicit indication was made. However, the court found that even without such a clear indication, so long as employees fully understood that the unauthorized misappropriation of customer information, even a piece of it, would constitute unauthorized misappropriation of a trade secret, this does not matter. This

33. METI, *Guidelines*, *supra* note 7, at 7.
34. *Ibid.*
35. *Ibid.*

ruling means that even inadequate restriction of access may satisfy the secrecy management requirement if a person with access to the information recognizes it as a secret, after all.

4.5.2. *Usefulness*

To be useful, the information must be objectively useful for business activities. It can be either technical or operational information. However, information about the company's antisocial activities, for example, will not be considered useful[36]. Any information with commercial value in a broad sense is eligible for trade secret protection, while information having no legitimate interest to be legally protected as a secret is denied the utility requirement and excluded from trade secret protection.

It does not have to be presently used in a business activity to meet the usefulness requirement, and this includes potentially valuable cases[37]. It also includes so-called negative information, such as data from previous failed studies[38]. Some court cases have denied the usefulness of the composition information of a beverage on the grounds that the benefit of the composition was not known[39]. However, the information seems to have been considered not a trade secret primarily because it was almost identical to publicly known information, rather than because it lacks usefulness[40].

According to the above, the usefulness requirement is denied only in exceptional cases, such as information that is only a slight modification of publicly known information, or information for which there is no legal justification to be protected as a secret[41]. The customer information in this case is the information of approximately 7,000 people who purchased investment condominiums sold by plaintiff Next, and it seems clear that it would be beneficial to the plaintiffs' business activities.

4.5.3. *Non-public Domain*

The non-public domain requirement is satisfied when the information is not generally known or readily available to the public[42]. Specifically, it means that the information is not generally available to the public outside of the holder's control.

Even if the information was previously made public in a foreign country, for example, the non-public domain requirement will still be satisfied if the acquisition of the information requires substantial time and financial costs[43]. In a court case, it was decided that even when it is possible to obtain secret technical information by reverse engineering, the non-public domain requirement has been met because presumably, it

36. METI *Guidelines, supra* note 7, at 16.
37. *Ibid.*
38. *Ibid.*
39. The Tokyo District Court case Heisei 13 (Wa) 7445 (decided on October 1, 2002).
40. Hirasawa Takuto, Usefulness (in Japanese), Jurist 248, p. 213.
41. METI *Guidelines, supra* note 7, at 17 says that information that satisfies secrecy management and the non-public domain requirement is usually recognized as useful.
42. METI *Guidelines, supra* note 7, at 17; *see also* TRIPS Agreement, Article 39(2)(a).
43. METI *Guidelines, supra* note 7, at 17.

would be necessary for experts to analyze the information over a long period at great expense[44].

Also, a trade secret is usually a combination of various pieces of knowledge. However, the fact that a fragment of information is published in various publications and that collecting those fragments could lead to a reconstruction of information similar to the information that constitutes the relevant trade secret does not immediately mean that the information is in the public domain[45].

The customer information in this case includes the names, addresses, and telephone numbers of the individual customers, which may be public knowledge by themselves. However, it would involve a large cost to link these pieces of information with the information on the customers who purchased the condominiums and to accumulate 7,000 items. The customer information as such is no longer the same as its components, namely the names and addresses of the individual customers. The court found the customer information met the non-public domain requirement for this reason, which is a sound judgment.

4.6. *Commercial or Industrial Significance*

Recently, as represented by this decision, whether "a person with access to the information recognizes it as a secret" has become the standard for judging secrecy management. The METI Guidelines also summarize that access restrictions are just one factor to be considered in determining the recognizability of the information as a secret. Under this criterion, a company does not necessarily need to impose strict access restrictions for it to be protected as a trade secret. It is sufficient to limit access to the information to the extent that employees are made aware of its secrecy management, depending on the actual circumstances.

44. The Osaka District Court case Heisei 13 (Wa) 10308 (decided on February 27, 2003).
45. METI *Guidelines, supra* note 7, at 20.

TOPIC 2 THE VALIDITY AND SCOPE OF CONFIDENTIALITY AND NONCOMPETITION CLAUSES

Tatsuhiro Ueno

1. Legal Issues

Employees are often obliged not to divulge confidential information acquired in the course of their work (obligation of confidentiality) and to refrain from competitive activities that are significantly contrary to the interests of the employers (noncompetition obligation), not only during their employment but also after the termination of the employment contract. However, questions arise as to the validity of contractual obligation of confidentiality as well as noncompetition, and the relationship between such contractual obligations and the protection of trade secrets against the disclosure and use by resigned employees under the UCPA.

2. The Statutory Law

2.1. Obligation of Confidentiality under Labor Law and Contract Law

Article 3(4) of the Japanese Labor Contracts Act[46] stipulates, "[a] Worker and an Employer must comply with the labor contract, and must exercise their rights and perform their obligations in good faith." As a matter of good faith under Article 3(4) of the Labor Contract Act or as a concomitant obligation derived from the labor contract, workers are obliged not to divulge confidential information acquired in the course of their work during their employment[47].

Even after the termination of the labor contract, an obligation of confidentiality would be regarded valid, if there is at least a clear and concrete basis for the obligation, such as a confidentiality management regulation or individual agreement, and if the obligation is considered reasonable in light of various circumstances (e.g., the reasonableness of the former employer's interests, the former employee's position and duties, and the specificity and scope of the confidentiality) and does not excessively restrict the worker's freedom of conduct, according to the dominant theories[48] and case law[49].

2.2. Noncompetition Obligation under Labor Law and Contract Law

As a matter of good faith under Article 3(4) of the Labor Contract Act or as a concomitant obligation derived from the labor contract, workers are also obliged to

---

46. Act No. 128 of 2007. A translation is available <http://www.japaneselawtranslation.go.jp/law/detail/?id=2578&vm=04&re=01&new=1>.
47. *See* Hisashi Araki, *Rôdôhô [Labor Law]* (3rd ed., Yûhikaku, 2016) p. 279 (in Japanese); Kazuo Sugeno, *Rôdôhô [Labor Law]* (11th ed., Kôbundô, 2017) p. 151 (in Japanese); Michio Tsuchida, *Rôdôkeiyakuhô [Labor Contract Law]* (2nd ed., Yûhikaku, 2016) p. 123 (in Japanese).
48. *See* Tsuchida, *supra* note 47, at 708 et seq.
49. Tokyo District Court decisions 838 Rôdô-Hanrei 32 [Daiohs Case] (decided on August 30, 2002), 2040 Hanrei-Jihô 126 [Dance Music Record Case] (decided on November 26, 2008);, 2246 Rôdôkeizai-Hanrei-Sokuhô 3 [Legacy Case] (decided on March 27, 2015), and Case No. 7143(Wa) of 2016 [Eishin-Foods Case] (decided on October 25, 2017).

refrain from competitive activities that are significantly contrary to the interests of the employers (noncompetition obligation)[50].

Even after the termination of the labor contract, a noncompetition obligation would be regarded valid, if there is at least a clear and concrete basis for the obligation, such as a noncompetition obligation regulation or individual agreement, and if the obligation is considered reasonable in light of various circumstances (e.g., the former employee's position and duties, the legitimacy of the former employer's interests, the restricted acts, period and area, and the existence and content of compensatory measures), and sufficient compensatory measures are provided for the resigned employee, according to the major theories[51] and case law[52].

In one recent court case, the IP High Court held that "even if the employer and the employee individually reach an agreement on a non-competition obligation after the resignation to prevent the employee from working for a company that competes with the employer or from opening his/her own business, the validity of such agreement should be examined in light of the interests of the employer, the previous position of the resigned employee, the scope of the restriction, and the existence and content of compensatory measure, because it restricts the retiree's freedom of business and choice in employment." It denied the validity of the agreement on noncompetition obligation in the case at issue, on the grounds that it prevents the employee from working for a company that competes with the employer for three years without locational restrictions, the scope and period of the restriction being excessive, that the interests of the employer for the noncompetition obligation were not legitimate, and that the compensatory measure for the resigned worker was not sufficient[53].

2.3. *Trade Secret Protection under the UCPA*

Trade secrets are defined by the UCPA as "technical or business information useful for business activities, such as manufacturing or marketing methods, that are kept secret and that are not publicly known" (Article 2(6)). Article 2(1)(iv) to (x) of the UCPA provides for certain acts of unfair competition with respect to trade secrets which include "the act of using or disclosing trade secrets disclosed by the company that owns them (hereinafter referred to as the 'trade secret owner') for the purpose of wrongful gain, or causing damage to the trade secret owner" (Article 2(1)(vii)).

---

50. *See* Araki, *supra* note 47, at 281; Tsuchida, *supra* note 47, at 125.
51. *Ibid.*
52. Nara District Court, 624 Hanrei-Jihô 78 [Foseco Japan Ltd. Case] (decided on October 23, 1971); Tokyo District Court, 1556 Hanrei-Jihô 83 [Tokyo Legal Mind Case] (decided on October 16, 1995), 838 Rôdô-Hanrei 32 [Daiohs Case] (decided on August 30, 2002), 2144 Rôdôkeizai-Hanrei-Sokuhô 23 [Kantôkôgyô Case] (decided on March 13, 2012), 2265 Hanrei-Jihô 59 [Apartment Management Case] (decided on February 12, 2015); Osaka District Court case No. 7562(Wa) of 2012 [Matsui Case] (decided on September 27, 2013); IP High Court decided on August 7, 2019, 1579 Kinyûshôji-Hanrei 40 [Eyelash Extension Case]; 10037(Ne) of 2019 [Opening Tool Case] (decided on October 9, 2019).
53. *See supra* note 52, IP High Court, 10037(Ne) of 2019 [Opening Tool Case] (decided on October 9, 2019).

3. The Case Law

3.1. Contractual Obligation of Confidentiality and Trade Secret Protection

With respect to the question of whether a resigned employee's conduct after the termination of the labor contract may constitute a breach of the contractual obligation of confidentiality, even if it does not constitute a wrongful disclosure of trade secrets as an act of unfair competition under Article 2(1)(vii) of the UCPA, there are largely two different opinions in Japan.

One opinion admits or emphasizes the differences between the contractual obligations of confidentiality and the protection of trade secrets against the wrongful disclosure by resigned employees under the UCPA[54]. Therefore, their answer to the abovementioned question is yes. The reasons for this opinion include (a) information that fails to be kept secret and information that lacks usefulness (e.g., scandalous information) are not considered trade secrets under the UCPA; (b) an act of disclosure that is not aimed at wrongful gain or causing damage to the trade secret owner is not considered unfair competition under the UCPA; (c) information developed by the employee him/herself does not constitute "trade secrets disclosed by the company that owns them" under Article 2(1)(vii) of the UCPA[55]; and (d) the remedies under the UCPA include not only civil remedies such as claims for injunction (Article 3) and compensation for damages (Article 4) but also criminal penalties under certain circumstances (Article 21(1)).

Another opinion admits or emphasizes the similarities between the contractual obligations of confidentiality and the protection of trade secrets against the wrongful disclosure by resigned employees under the UCPA. Therefore, their answer to the abovementioned question is no. The reasons for this opinion include (a) both of them share the same purpose of striking a proper balance between the interests of employers and employees; (b) recently, there has been a tendency with respect to the secrecy management requirement under the UCPA to emphasize the importance of providing predictability to employees[56]; and (c) the employee's freedom of business and choice in employment (Article 22(1) of the Constitution) should be ensured and the chilling effect should be reduced to promote employment mobility. In fact, some court cases

---

54. *See* Araki, *supra* note 47, at 282 et seq.; Tsuchida, *supra* note 47, at 124 and 708. *See also* Tokyo District Court, 938 Rôdô-Hanrei 14 [Nissan Century Security Case] (decided on March 9, 2007).
55. Regarding this issue, *see* Takakuni Yamane, *Fuseikyôsôbôshihô 2 jo 1 ko 4 go / 7 go no kiritsu niokeru jikanjiku to kôisha no ninshiki no kôzô [The Structure of the Timeline and the Recognition of the Doer under Article 2(1)(iv) and (vii) of the Unfair Competition Prevention Act]*, 57 Tokkyokenkyû 43 (2014) (in Japanese); Mio Ishii, *Jûgyôshakaihatsu, sôsaku no eigyôhimitsu to fuseikyôsôbôshihô 2 jo 1 ko 7 go no "shimesareta" yôken [Trade Secret Developed or Created by an Employee and the Requirement of "Disclosed" under Article 2(1)(vii) of the Unfair Competition Prevention Act]*, in Naoki Koizumi & Yoshiyuki Tamura (eds), *Habataki*, Kôbundô, 2015 (in Japanese), p. 892.
56. *See* METI *Guidelines*, *supra* note 7, at 4 (stating "[t]he spirit of the secrecy management requirements is to provide predictability to employees by specifying for which items within a specific corporation employees are to maintain confidentiality (the scope of information), thereby ensuring stability in business practices"). *See also* Tokyo High Court, 70(1) Kôtôsaibansho-Keiji-Hanreishû 10 [Benesse Case] (decided on March 21, 2017).

determined the scope or object of a contractual noncompetition obligation by complying with the definition of trade secret under Article 2(6) of the UCPA[57].

3.2. *Contractual Noncompetition Obligation and Trade Secret Protection*

With respect to the question of whether a resigned employee's conduct after the termination of the labor contract may constitute a breach of the contractual noncompetition obligation, even if it does not constitute a wrongful use of trade secrets as an act of unfair competition under Article 2(1)(vii) of the UCPA, there are also largely two different opinions in Japan.

One opinion admits or emphasizes the differences between the contractual noncompetition obligation and the protection of trade secrets against the wrongful use by resigned employees under the UCPA[58]. Therefore, their answer to the abovementioned question is yes. The reasons for this opinion include (a) the protection against the wrongful use of trade secrets under the UCPA is limited in terms of its object and purpose; (b) the remedies under the UCPA include not only civil remedies such as claims for injunction (Article 3) and compensation for damages (Article 4) but also criminal penalties under certain circumstances (Article 21(1)); and (c) even very broad noncompetition obligation can be regarded as valid if there is a clear individual agreement and sufficient compensatory measures are provided for the resigned employee.

Another opinion admits or emphasizes the similarities between the contractual noncompetition obligations and the protection of trade secrets against the wrongful use by resigned employees under the Japanese UCPA. Therefore, their answer to the abovementioned question is no. The reasons for this opinion include (a) both of them share the same purpose of striking a proper balance between the interests of employers and employees; and (b) the employee's freedom of business and choice in employment (Article 22(1) of the Constitution) should be ensured and free competition should be promoted. In fact, one court case seems to have denied the validity of a part of the noncompetition contractual agreement, which imposes unlimited restriction on the resigned employee by preventing the employee from engaging in any competitive business activities for three years after leaving the employer with or without the use of confidential information obtained during the employment. It concluded that the part went beyond the level of protection against the wrongful use of trade secrets under the UCPA[59].

57. *See supra* note 52, Tokyo District Court, [Kantôkôgyô Case]; *supra* note 49, [Legacy Case]; *supra* note 49, and [Eishin-Foods Case] (decided on October 25, 2017).
58. *See* Araki, *supra* note 47, at 282 et seq.; Tsuchida, *supra* note 47, at 719.
59. Fukuoka District Court (Kokura Branch), 1360 Rôdôhôritsu-Shunpô 48 [Seibushôji Case] (decided on April 19, 1994,). *See also supra* note 52, IP High Court, [Opening Tool Case]; [Eyelash Extension Case].

4. The Leading Case

The leading court case concerning the validity of contractual noncompetition obligation and the relationship between the obligation and trade secret protection under the Japanese UCPA is the one by the IP High Court in 2019, which was the first and most detailed judgment and was affirmed by the Supreme Court on January 31, 2020, as it refused to receive the appeal, without providing any detailed reason.

4.1. Case Information[60]

IP High Court, First Division, 1579 Kinyushojihanrei 40, Case No. 10016(Ne) of 2019 [Eyelash Extension Case] (decided on 7 August 2019).

4.2. Summary

Contractual noncompetition obligation for resigned employees would be valid if there is an individual agreement or a provision in the employment regulations and the restriction is considered reasonable in light of the content and degree of the employer's interest to be protected by the restriction, the position of the resigned employee during the time of employment, the scope of the restriction on competition, and the existence and content of compensatory measures for the resigned employee. In this case at issue, the agreement on noncompetition obligation concluded at the time of the employee's joining the company is not invalid, because the restriction is limited to the period of two years, the location of Kokubunji City, and the use of confidential information which is considered trade secrets under the Japanese UCPA.

4.3. Facts

The plaintiff operates an eyelash extension shop in Kokubunji City, Tokyo. The defendant had been employed by the plaintiff from October 3, 2016 to September 18, 2017, as a so-called eyelist (eyelash stylist).

On October 3, 2016, when joining the company, the defendant signed the "Pledge at the time of joining the company," which stated that the defendant pledged "not to engage in any competitive business activities in Kokubunji City for two years after leaving the plaintiff using confidential information obtained during the employment" (Article 13) and "confidential information means important information (information relating to management, sales, technology or customers) which is kept secret by the company" (Article 10).

The plaintiff's employment regulations stipulate that "employees shall observe the non-competition obligation even after the resignation and shall not work for a company in a competitive relationship" (Article 28(1)), that "employees shall not, after the resignation or dismissal, work for or become an officer of another company in the same industry, or otherwise engage in the business of another company in the same

60. The judgment in Japanese is available at <https://www.courts.go.jp/app/files/hanrei_jp/887/088887_hanrei.pdf>.

industry, regardless of the form, or engage in a competing business" (Article 28(2)), and that "the company shall conclude with employees a 'written pledge and confirmation' stipulating the period of restriction, restricted areas, etc." (Article 28(3)).

In September 2017, after the defendant decided to resign, the plaintiff requested that the defendant submit a "written pledge and confirmation" which contains the statement, "I promise not to work for or become an employee of a competing business in Kokubunji City for two years after my resignation, nor to establish a competing business by myself." However, the defendant handwrote, "I cannot promise anything about not working for a competing business in Kokubunji City for two years after my resignation because, as I have already told you, I am going to work in a place decided by the other company" beneath the statement, signed and sealed the document, and submitted it to the plaintiff.

The defendant is engaged in eyelash extension work at another eyelash extension salon in Kokubunji City, after resigning from the plaintiff.

On December 9, 2017, the defendant asked an employee of the plaintiff to send records which describe the medical history, care, and treatment history (hereinafter referred to as "customer medical records") of two customers whom the defendant had treated during the employment, and the employee took a photograph of the customer medical records by using a smartphone and sent it to the defendant.

The plaintiff sought an injunction against the defendant's engagement in eyelash extension work at an eyelash extension salon in Kokubunji City for two years, primarily based on the agreement and preliminarily based on the UCPA.

After the Tokyo District Court (Tachikawa Division) dismissed the plaintiff's claim on January 18, 2019[61], the IP High Court dismissed the plaintiff's appeal on August 7, 2019. The plaintiff appealed to the Supreme Court, which refused to receive the appeal on January 31, 2020[62].

4.4. *The Reasoning of the IP High Court*[63]

4.4.1. *General Principle*

Contractual noncompetition obligation for resigned employees would be valid if there is an individual agreement or a provision in the employment regulations and the restriction is considered reasonable in light of the content and degree of the employer's interest in being protected by the restriction, the position of the resigned employee during the time of employment, the scope of the restriction on competition, and the existence and content of compensatory measures for the resigned employee.

61. Tokyo District Court (Tachikawa Division), Case No. 609 (Wa) of 2018 (decided on January 18, 2019).
62. Supreme Court, Second Division, Case No. 1525(O) of 2019 (decided on January 31, 2020).
63. The judgment contains no paragraph number.

4.4.2. *The Invalidity of Employment Regulations and the Pledge*

The plaintiff's employment regulations, which contain the following provisions: (a) employees shall observe the noncompetition obligation even after the resignation and shall not work for a company in a competitive relationship; and (b) employees shall not, after the resignation or dismissal, work for or become an officer of another company in the same industry, engage in the business of another company in the same industry in any other form, or engage in a competing business themselves, are considered invalid, on the ground that these provisions cannot be regarded as reasonable, as they impose unlimited restriction on the resigned employee regardless of his/her status.

The "written pledge and confirmation" submitted by the defendant at the time of the resignation contained, as mentioned above, the reservation that the defendant could not promise anything about not working for a competing business in Kokubunji City for two years after the resignation, and therefore no valid agreement on the restriction of competition was concluded between the plaintiff and the defendant.

4.4.3. *The Validity of the Noncompetition Agreement at the Time of Joining the Company*

With regard to the agreement at the time of joining the company, the "pledge at the time of joining the company" stated that the defendant pledged "not to engage in any competitive business activities in Kokubunji City for two years after leaving the plaintiff using confidential information obtained during the employment." However, according to the text of Article 10 of the pledge, the term "confidential information" in this agreement means information that "is kept secret by the company." Considering the content of the "pledge at the time of joining the company," the provisions relating to confidential information in this pledge should be understood to have the same purpose of protecting trade secrets as the UCPA. As there is no definition of the term "kept secret" in this agreement, the meaning of the term should be understood as the same as the term "kept secret" under the UCPA.

The term "competitive business activities" in this agreement should be understood as managing other eyelash extension salons and engaging in so-called eyelist work at other eyelash extension salons, according to the nature of the services provided by the defendant during the employment. Hence, the agreement at the time of joining the company is regarded as an agreement that the defendant will not manage any other eyelash extension salons in Kokubunji City or engage in so-called eyelist work at any other eyelash extension salons for two years after leaving the company using the "confidential information" that the defendant learned during the employment, and the "confidential information" means information that "is kept secret by the company" in this agreement. The agreement at the time of joining the company is not invalid, as the restriction is limited to a period of two years, the location of Kokubunji City, and the act of competition using confidential information, therefore it does not unreasonably restrict the defendant's freedom of business and choice in employment.

4.4.4. *The Defendant Did Not Violate the Confidentiality Agreement by Asking the Customer Medical Records to Be Sent?*

The defendant asked an employee of the plaintiff to send the customer medical records of two customers.

However, the customer medical records could be viewed by any employee in the plaintiff's salons, and no measures such as locking were taken where the files containing the customer medical records were kept, and there was no other evidence to prove the existence of a measure for keeping the customer medical records secret. Therefore, the customer medical records were not "kept secret" and cannot be considered "confidential information" under the agreement at the time of joining the company. Hence, the defendant did not violate the agreement at the time of joining the company.

4.5. *Legal Analysis*

Immediately after the present decision, the IP High Court rendered another decision on October 9, 2019[64], which followed the same direction as the present decision. It seems that the IP High Court tends to admit the similarities between the contractual noncompetition obligations and the protection of trade secrets against the wrongful use by resigned employees under the UCPA, on the ground that both of them share the same purpose of striking a proper balance between the interests of employers and employees.

As mentioned before, the Japanese Supreme Court refused to receive the appeal, and thus officially affirmed by the judgment of the IP High Court, although with no detailed reason. Therefore, it is highly likely that the abovementioned understanding of the IP High Court regarding the similarity between the contractual noncompetition obligations and the protection of trade secrets under the UCPA will continue to be accepted in future case law in Japan.

4.6. *Commercial or Industrial Significance*

According to recent court cases in Japan, a contractual noncompetition obligation would be valid if there is an individual agreement or a provision in the employment regulations and the restriction is considered reasonable in light of the content and degree of the employer's interest in being protected by the restriction, the position of the resigned employee during the time of employment, the scope of the restriction on competition, and the existence and content of compensatory measures.

In particular, if the restriction of a contractual noncompetition obligation is limited to a period of two years and the location of a particular city, and restricts only the act of competition by using confidential information, then it would be considered reasonable and valid because it does not unreasonably restrict the employee's freedom of business and choice in employment.

64. *See supra* note 52, IP High Court, [Opening Tool Case] and *supra* text accompanying note 53.

TOPIC 3 INTERNATIONAL JURISDICTIONS AND THE APPLICABLE LAW ON TRADE SECRET INFRINGEMENT LITIGATION[65]

Yasuto Komada

1. Legal Issues

How are the international jurisdiction and the applicable law to be determined in trade secret infringement cases?

2. The Statutory Law

2.1. International Jurisdiction

In general, when determining the international jurisdiction in a trade secret infringement case, both the defendant's domicile (Article 3-2 of CCP) and the place of the infringement (the place where the tort occurred, Article 3-3 item 8 of the CCP)[66] are to be considered. It is also widely accepted that the place where the tort occurred includes two elements: the place where "the wrongful act" was committed and the place where "its result" occurred.

2.2. Applicable Law

In 2006, *Hôrei* (General Rules for Application of Laws), the old Japanese private international law (PIL), was totally revised and superseded by *Tsûsokuhô* (Act on General Rules for Application of Laws). The relevant provisions of *Tsûsokuhô* are as follows:

> Article 17
>
> The formation and effect of a claim arising from a tort shall be governed by the law of the place where the result of the wrongful act occurred only if the occurrence of the result at said place was ordinarily unforeseeable.
>
> Article 19
>
> Notwithstanding the provisions of Article 17, the formation and effect of a claim arising from a tort of defamation of others shall be governed by the law of the victim's habitual residence (in cases where the victim is a juridical person or any other association or foundation, the law of its principal place of business).

65. Because there are detailed statutes for trade secret protection in Japan, the burden of proof is not particularly an issue, and there are no cases with regard to this topic. On the other hand, there are hot debates on international jurisdiction and choice of law concerning trade secret infringement cases involving foreign aspects. Therefore, we chose this topic.
66. Article 3-3 item 8 of the CCP provides: "An action set forth in one of the following items may be filed with the Japanese courts in the case specified in said item: (viii) an action for a tort: if the place where the tort was committed is within Japan (excluding instances where the results of a wrongful act that was committed in a foreign country have arisen within Japan and it would not ordinarily have been possible to foresee those consequences arising within Japan)."

Article 20

Notwithstanding the preceding three Articles, the formation and effect of a claim arising from a tort shall be governed by the law of the place with which the tort is obviously more closely connected than the place indicated in the preceding three Articles. In determining the place with which a tort is closely connected, the court shall consider whether the parties had their habitual residence in the places governed by the same law at the time of the occurrence of the tort and whether the tort was committed in breach of an obligation under a contract between the parties. The court shall also take into account any other circumstances concerned.

Article 21

Parties to a tort may, after the tort occurs, change the law applicable to the formation and effect of a claim arising from the tort. However, if that change prejudices the rights of a third party, it will not be asserted against the third party.

Article 22

(1) In a case where a tort is governed by a foreign law, if the facts to which the foreign law should be applied do not constitute a tort under Japanese law, no claim under the foreign law may be made for damages or any other remedies.
(2) In a case where a tort is governed by a foreign law, even if the facts to which the foreign law should be applied constitute a tort under both the foreign law and Japanese law, the victim can claim damages or any other remedies only as permitted under Japanese law.

Both *Hôrei* and *Tsûsokuhô* follow the principle of *lex loci delicti commissi*. However, *Tsûsokuhô* goes a step further to specifically point to "the place where the result of the wrongful act occurred" (Article 17) instead of just pointing to "the place where the event causing the claims occurred" (Article 11(1) of *Hôrei*). Notably, *Tsûsokuhô* also contains some exceptions. As far as a defamation claim is concerned, the applicable law shall be the law of the victim's habitual residence or if it is a juridical person, its principal place of business (Article 19). From these provisions, clearly, two factors should be considered: the law of the place where the parties had their habitual residence at the time of the occurrence of the tort and the law applicable to the contract when the tort was committed in breach of the obligation thereunder. However, if there is a law that is obviously more closely connected to the tort in question than the law indicated in Articles 17 and 19, such a law shall be applicable (Article 20). *Tsûsokuhô* also recognizes the parties' autonomy clause, which allows the parties to choose laws that are different from the ones indicated in Articles 17, 19, and 20. However, if such a law prejudices the rights of a third party, it may not be asserted against him or her.

3. The Case Law

3.1. International Jurisdiction

The "result" mentioned in Article 3-3 item 8 of the CCP is generally considered to be the one arising directly from "the wrongful act," i.e., the infringement of the alleged legitimate interest[67], to curb any unnecessary expansions of the jurisdiction. For example, if the plaintiff brings an action on the grounds that the defendant seized the plaintiff's ship in a foreign country and such seizure constitutes a tort, the fact that the sailing of the ship became impossible should be considered the "result," while the fact that the plaintiff had to cancel the charter and lost the charter fee in Tokyo should be considered a secondary or a derivative result that cannot afford a Japanese court the international jurisdiction of tort over the action[68].

It is also worth noting that the international jurisdiction of the Japanese court cannot be affirmed under Article 3-3 item 8 of the CCP if it was not ordinarily foreseeable that "its result" would arise in Japan when "the wrongful act" was committed. For example, if a certain machine is not usable in Japan but is usable in a certain foreign country due to technical reasons and a Japanese customer bought it in that foreign country, it can safely be said that the customer cannot bring an action against the manufacturer before a Japanese court on the grounds that his use of the machine in Japan occasioned some accident and made him suffer damages[69]. In such a case, it was not ordinarily foreseeable that the accident would occur in Japan when the manufacturer sold the machine.

In the context of a trade secret infringement, "the wrongful act" can be a disclosure, a transfer, or an exploitation of a trade secret. The place of the act can be identified rather easily, while the place of "its result" (the infringement of the alleged legitimate interest) might not be clear, making it difficult to identify[70]. Case law is not helpful on this point, because in Japan there seem to be only a few cases in which the international jurisdiction of tort over an action arising out of a trade secret infringement has been disputed[71].

---

67. *See*, Yasunori Homma et al., *Kokusaiminjisoshôhô* [International Civil Procedure Law], (2nd ed., Yuhikaku, 2012) p. 61; Shoichi Kidana (ed.), *Kokusaishihô* [Private International Law (PIL)], (Seibundo, 2016) p. 372 (Shunichiro Nakano); Jun Yokoyama, *Kokusaishihô*, (Sanseido, 2012), p. 338.
68. Cf. Tokyo District Court, *Hanreijihô* (*Hanji*), no. 1135, p. 70 (decided on February 15, 1984).
69. This example is shown in Tatsubumi Sato & Yasuhiko Kobayashi, *Ichimon-itto*: *Heisei* 23 *Nen Minjisoshôhôtôkaisei* (Questions and Answers: Revision of Civil Procedure Law etc. in 2011), Shojihomu, 2012, p. 71.
70. Supreme Court already clarified that for a Japanese court to affirm its international jurisdiction, it is in principle sufficient for the plaintiff to establish the objective factual relationship between the act made by the defendant in Japan and the damage occasioned to the plaintiff's legitimate interest by the act. Cf. Supreme Court, June 8, 2001, *Saikôsaibanshominjihanreishû* (Supreme Court Civil Case Reports, *Minshû*), vol. 55, no. 4, p. 727. This ruling was made before the introduction of the provisions on international jurisdiction into the CCP, but it is thought to be still effective for the interpretation of Article 3-3 item 8 of the present code. For analysis *see*, Yasuto Komada, *International Jurisdiction of Tort, Property Location, and Annexation over Copyright Claims*, in Kung-Chung Liu (ed.), *Annotated Leading Copyright Cases in Major Asian Jurisdictions*, City University of Hong-Kong Press, 2019, pp. 453 et seq.
71. There is at least one case related to unfair competition in which the international jurisdiction was disputed. In the case, the court denied its international jurisdiction on the grounds that the plaintiff could not succeed in establishing the fact that the defendant, an ex-employee of the plaintiff's subsidiary, unduly disclosed the trade secret and caused damages to the plaintiff in Japan or made an unfaithful business trip to Japan and caused the plaintiff to bear the cost. *See*, Osaka District Court, *Heisei* 13 (*Wa*) no. 8485 (decided on February 5, 2004).

3.2. *Applicable Law*

In Japan, there are at least 13 judicial decisions related to unfair competition that clearly detail the facts considered in the choice of law process[72]. In all these cases, Japanese law is chosen, except in one case in which the court applied the law of the State of New Jersey to one of the plaintiff's claims[73]. Indeed, it is safe to say in general that once it is established that the court has international jurisdiction based on a certain link between Japan and the case in question, Japanese law is likely to apply.

A trade secret infringement is considered by most decisions to be an unfair competition act and tort matters under PIL. However, some cases rely on *ratio legis* to choose the applicable law for an injunction claim and a claim of publication of an apology[74]. Others (including the leading case discussed below) consider an injunction claim as a tort matter and try to ensure that it conforms to the law chosen under the provisions of PIL[75].

As already seen, the connecting factors provided for under Article 17 of *Tsû-sokuhô* and Article 11(1) of *Hôrei* are "the place where the result of the wrongful act occurred" and "the place where the event causing the claims occurred." Generally, courts have been considering various allegedly illegal acts as facts that may come under these connecting factors.

When looking at trade secret infringement cases, for example, the leading case discussed below and a more recent case[76], the alleged illegal disclosure, and exploitation of the relevant information are considered facts that come under the notion of "the result" in *Tsûsokuhô*. However, in earlier cases where the alleged illegal acts occurred in plural countries[77], the act held by the courts to be the primary or most important act was considered "the events causing the claims" in *Hôrei*.

To sum up, courts consider the alleged illegal acts and the relevant facts to be those coming under the notions of the connecting factors provided for in PIL. These

72. *Trade secret infringement cases*: [Gould Inc.] Tokyo District Court, *Hanji*, no. 1429, p. 80 (decided on September 24, 1991); [LG Display] Tokyo District Court, *Heisei* 24 (*Wa*) no. 10567 (decided on June 30, 2016); IP High Court, *Heisei* 28 (*Ne*) no. 10089 (decided on March 8, 2017); [High-performance multi-nuclide removal equipment] IP High Court, *Heisei* 30 (*Ne*) no. 10049 (decided on September 20, 2019). *Product design imitation cases*: [Petit holder] Tokyo District Court, July 4, 2008, *Heisei* 19 (*Wa*) no. 19275; [Saxophone strap] IP High Court, January 24, 2019, *Hanji*, no. 2425, p. 88. *Tarnishment cases*; [Coral sand] Tokyo District Court, *Hanji*, no. 1874, p. 23 (decided on October 16, 2003); [Soft blaster] IP High Court, *Heisei* 17 (*Ra*) no. 10006 (decided on December 27, 2005), [Ultraman], *Heisei* 21 (*Ra*) no. 10006 (decided on December 15, 2009), and [*Kozureôkami*] *Heisei* 25 (*Ne*) no. 10094 (decided on March 27, 2014); [Blu-ray disc] Tokyo District Court, *Hanji*, no. 2257, p. 87 (decided on February 18, 2015); [D'Angelico] IP High Court, *Heisei* 25 (*Ne*) no. 10104 (decided on, March 25, 2015). It is important to note that some decisions in Japan do not provide any reasoning as to why the Japanese UCPA is applied despite the fact that the backgrounds of those cases contain foreign elements.
73. Cf. D'Angelico case, *ibid*.
74. Cf. Petit holder case and Soft blaster case, *supra* note 72.
75. Cf. Gould Inc. case; High-performance multi-nuclide removal equipment case; Coral sand case; Ultraman case; *Kozureôkami* case; Blu-ray disc case, *supra* note 72.
76. Cf. High-performance multi-nuclide removal equipment case, *supra* note 72.
77. Cf. Gould Inc. case and LG Display cases, *supra* note 72.

interpretations[78] make it easier for courts to apply the forum law because they are able to choose the acts that were committed in Japan, just saying (with no clear reason) that those acts are the most relevant to the case in question.

4. The Leading Case

4.1. *Case Information*

IP High Court, Division 4, *Hanrei Taimuzu*, No. 1452, p. 80 (decided on January 15, 2018).

It is the first IP High Court decision which characterizes the claims for both injunction and damages as results of a trade secret infringement as tort matters under *Tsûsokuhô*.

4.2. *Summary*

X alleged that Y disclosed and exploited X's trade secret in Japan, which constitutes unfair competition acts under Japanese law. The court of the first instance rejected X's claims under the Japanese UCPA without providing the reasons behind the choice of that law as the applicable law[79]. According to the court, it could not be established that Y had acquired the documents without the knowledge of the existence of any previous wrongful disclosures due to its gross negligence (Article 2(1) item 8 of UCPA). X appealed to the IP High Court, which was rejected. Both parties are Japanese companies and, therefore, neither the international jurisdiction of the court nor the applicable law is disputed.

4.3. *Facts*

X is a Japanese company that was manufacturing polarized light irradiation devices for photo-alignment ("X devices"). X made some documents for a sales promotion of X devices in China and sent them via e-mail to its agency in Taiwan (P). P then shared these documents via e-mail with certain Chinese companies (Q and R). All these companies (P, Q, and R) had signed confidentiality agreements with X before the documents were disclosed to them.

Y, a Japanese company, brought actions for an interim injunction against X, alleging that by manufacturing X devices, X was infringing the Japanese patent right possessed by Y. Y submitted to the court the abovementioned documents to help ascertain the structure of X devices. X brought an action against Y alleging that such an

78. This way of interpretation (under *Hôrei*) is highly recommended by Noboru Kashiwagi, who insists that, even if the same type of unfair competition is concerned, the type of fact coming under the notion of connecting factor can be different, and it should be determined on a case by case basis. *See* his case note in *Shôgaihanreihyakusen* (100 PIL Cases), 3rd ed., 1995, p. 96 et seq., spec., p. 97. We, however, believe that such an approach is too distant from the wording of the provisions of *Hôrei*, and under *Tsûsokuhô*, "the result" of unfair competition acts should be identified to avoid arbitrary interpretation.
79. Tokyo District Court, *Heisei* 28 (*Wa*) No. 35978 (decided on July 12, 2017).

act constituted a wrongful disclosure of X's trade secrets, and X sought an injunctive relief to stop Y from disclosing and exploiting the relevant information.

4.4. *The Reasoning of the Court*

4.4.1. *Regarding the Applicable Law*

X, a Japanese company, demands that Y, a Japanese company too, stop using and disclosing information on its (X's) trade secrets, dispose of the documents or other media on which the information is recorded, and publish an apology. X alleges that Y acquired the documents from either the Taiwanese company, P, or the Chinese companies, Q and R, without knowing that such disclosures were wrongful.

Since X's claims for injunctive relief, etc., are based on the premise that Y's act is unlawful and any of the claims of injunction, disposal, and publication of an apology made by the person whose right or interest has been infringed by any unlawful act is nothing but the civil remedy for the act, the legal relationship around these claims should be characterized as a tort, and the applicable law to the claims should be chosen under Article 17 of *Tsûsokuhô*. Therefore, the claims, which are concerned with "the formation and effect of a claim arising from a tort" provided for in the provision, shall be governed by "the law of the place where the result of the wrongful act occurred."

"X alleges that Y used and disclosed the information on its trade secrets in Japan and these acts are unlawful. In addition, it is undisputed between the parties that X is a Japanese company having its headquarters in Japan and Y used and disclosed the information there. Based on these facts, the place where the result of the wrongful act occurred should be regarded as Japan because it is the place where the use and the disclosure of the information was made and the infringement of X's legal interests (a result) occurred."

"Consequently, the Japanese unfair competition law shall apply in the present case."

4.4.2. *Regarding the Existence of Y's Unfair Competition Act*

"X does not insist that Y acquired the documents with the knowledge that a wrongful disclosure had occurred before.

However, in the present case, a question arises as to whether Y acquired the documents without the knowledge that there were wrongful disclosures due to its gross negligence. Regarding this question, we, as the judges who sit in this court, wish to agree with the opinion of the court of the first instance."

4.5. *Legal Analysis*

4.5.1. *International Jurisdiction*

In the present case, Y is a Japanese company and has its principal office in Japan, and therefore the Japanese court clearly has international jurisdiction over the case, as provided for under Article 3-2 of the CCP. This explains why it was not disputed in the present case. As already seen, Article 17 of *Tsûsokuhô* also espouses the notions "the wrongful act" and "the result" as the connecting factors. Theoretically speaking, judges have no legal obligation to take an identical interpretation of these notions between the CCP and *Tsûsokuhô* in individual cases. However, interpreting them in a different way seems to be unnecessarily complex. In our opinion, "the result" in the CCP should in principle have the same meaning as in *Tsûsokuhô* to guarantee consistent and uniform results for all parties.

4.5.2. *Applicable Law*

4.5.2.1. Academic Theories

In Japan, the question of the applicable law for trade secret infringement acts is often discussed as a part of the question of the applicable law for unfair competition acts. There are two important theories in this field. The first one is the "classification theory," which classifies various unfair competition acts into two types: acts exclusively related to a certain operator's business (two-faced type; headhunting of another company's employee, trade secret infringement, tarnishment of another company's business, etc.) and acts related to not only a certain operator's business but also the collective interests in the market (three-faced type; deceptive advertising, etc.). The supporters of this theory argue that the tort provisions of PIL should cover both types, but the connecting factors within a case ("the place where the events causing the claims occurred" in Article 11(1) of *Hôrei* / "the place where the result of the wrongful act occurred" in Article 17 of *Tsûsokuhô*) be interpreted differently depending on the type of unfair competition act committed[80]. They come up with the conclusion that the law applicable to the two-faced type should be the law of the country in which the victim has its principal place of business, and the law applicable to the three-faced type should be the law of the country in which the competitive relations or the collective interests of consumers are affected by the relevant act (the law of the marketplace)[81].

The second theory is the "unification theory," which treats all unfair competition acts as a unit. The supporters of this theory argue that the law applicable to unfair competition acts should be determined under *ratio legis* and it should be the law of the marketplace. Therefore, according to this theory, not only the three-faced but also the two-faced type shall be governed by this law, and there is no chance to derogate from or distort this principle under Article 20, 21 or 22 of *Tsûsokuhô*[82]. In Japanese academia, the classification theory is considered stronger than the unification theory.

80. Ryoichi Yamada & Yoshiro Hayata, *Enshû Kokusaishihô Shimpan* (Practice on PIL, A New Edition), Yuhikaku, 1992, p. 138 (Yoshiharu Aizawa); Naoe Fujisawa, case note in *Jurisuto*, no. 1287 (2005), pp. 143 et seq., spec., p. 146; Yoshiharu Aizawa, *Kokusaifuseikyôgyôhô no Kenkyû* (Study on International Unfair Competition Law), Daigakukyoikushuppan, 2016, pp. 505-506.
81. Zempachi Okamoto, case note in *Tokkyo Kanri* (Patent Administration), vol. 44, no. 2 (1944), pp. 159 et seq., spec., p. 161; Yamada & Hayata, *ibid.* (Yoshiharu Aizawa); Fujisawa, *ibid.*
82. Koji Deguchi, *Kokusaifuseikyôsô no Junkyohô* (Law Applicable to Unfair Competition), Nihonkokusaikeizaihôgakkainempô (Yearbook of Japan's Association of International Economic Law), vol. 23 (2014), pp. 106 et seq, spec. pp. 112-117. Akinobu Tanso et al. (ed.), *Kokusaikeizaihô Shimpan* (International Economic Law, A New Edition), Seirinshobo, 1993, p. 360. Shoichi

4.5.2.2. Our View

The place of "the result" provided for in Article 17 of *Tsûsokuhô* is generally interpreted as the place where the victim's legitimate interest is infringed. Therefore, when choosing the law applicable for unfair competition acts, it is important to identify such a place. In unfair competition cases, the marketplace should generally be considered to be the place where the legitimate interest is infringed. This conclusion is backed by the development of unfair competition law in most industrialized countries. This law started as civil law and then developed into a law regulating the collision of interests among enterprises. Finally, unfair competition law developed into an economic law that focuses on the preservation of market order, so that market players can enjoy fair and free competition and consumers can enjoy the fruits of such competition. These interests have a strong link with the market, thereby corroborating our interpretation.

As already seen, the unification theory takes the view that the law of the marketplace should apply exclusively in all types of unfair competition acts. It posits that all unfair competition acts should be treated as a unit and that their center of gravity can never be found in any place other than in the market. We think that these arguments are reasonable. However, we cannot accept this theory claiming that an unfair competition act should be characterized as a non-tort or a special tort in order to prevent the forum law from interfering with Article 22 of *Tsûsokuhô*, whose purpose is to maintain public order or, more precisely, to exempt Japanese industries from any tort responsibility that is heavier than that arising out of the forum law. Unfair competition matters can touch upon public order more frequently than common torts. It is quite strange that in the case of a common tort, the forum law may interfere, while in the case of an unfair competition act, the law may not. Although Article 22 should be abolished someday because it is too introverted, we believe that invalidating its provisions in unfair competition cases through interpretation is not a good idea[83].

In addition, it is not reasonable to classify unfair competition acts into two types, because acts that fall under the two-faced type can also affect third-party operators and influence market order. For example, tarnishment can make the distributors exclude the victims from their trading partners list because they would not want to associate themselves with the negative acts of the tarnisher. Similarly, a trade secret infringement can alter the conditions of competition among all operators because the infringer can take advantage of other operators and benefit by saving on the cost of obtaining the relevant information in a fair manner.

For the above reasons, the law of the marketplace should apply to all types of unfair competition acts under Article 17 of *Tsûsokuhô*. The same goes for

Kidana is often cited as having the same opinion, but the author simply mentions the possibility of such an interpretation and even proposes another interpretation, which is closely related to the classification theory.

83. The provisions of Article 21 should also apply in cases of unfair competition, which means the parties can choose the law after the relevant act was committed. Of course, such an application of the law other than the law of the marketplace may somewhat distort the conditions of the competition therein. However, permitting party autonomy in the choice of law may not be a big problem, as party autonomy in the disposition of the litigation, including a settlement, is normally allowed under the substantive law in this field.

tarnishment—we believe that Article 19 only covers disputes between parties who are not in competition (e.g., defamation or slander by media). As already seen, some cases rely on *ratio legis* to choose the applicable law, especially in injunction claims (or the claim of publication of an apology). This trend can be attributed to the Supreme Court's[84] ruling that a damage claim arising out of a patent infringement should be governed by the law applicable to tort matters while an injunction claim should be governed by the law applicable to the effect of the patent right[85]. This ruling has been vehemently criticized by several authors who think that such a division can break the delicate balance between these two remedies[86]. Arguably, this division cannot be justified, because any matter of illegality can be qualified as a tort under PIL.

In our view, unfair competition acts should be covered by the tort provisions of *Tsûsokuhô*. Therefore, it is theoretically possible for any law, other than that of the marketplace, to apply under Article 20. However, this depends on each individual case. As already explained, the legitimate interest that unfair competition law aims to secure is usually found in the market; that is why, in most cases, the center of gravity is in the market. We can hardly think of a case where any law other than that of the marketplace is "obviously more closely connected" to any unfair competition act. Even in cases where a trade secret infringement is made in breach of a confidentiality agreement, a closer connection is presumed for the law of the country in which the products or services for which the secret is applied are provided to the consumers (the law of the marketplace) than for any other law applicable to the agreement.

There might be cases where only acquisition or disclosure of a trade secret has been made and the infringer's target market might still not be clear at the time of bringing an action. Such cases are rare and the victim is usually able to demonstrate the market targeted by the infringer even before the secret is unduly exploited. However, if such a case happens, the law of the place in which the victim has its principal place of business should apply, because at this point the case only concerns the relationship between the infringer and the victim.

84. Supreme Court, *Minshû*, vol. 65, no. 7, p. 1551 (decided on September 26, 2002). For analysis, *see* Yasuto Komada, *Applicable Law When an Act Implemented in Japan Allegedly Infringed a US Patent Right*, in Kung-Chung Liu (ed.), *Annotated Leading Patent Cases in Major Asian Jurisdictions*, City University of Hong-Kong Press, 2017, pp. 392 et seq.
85. Mari Nagata also points out its influence. *See* her case note in JCA Journal, 65(1) (2018), pp. 39 et seq., spec., p. 41.
86. They say that different laws should not apply to these two remedies because each country tends to strike a balance by adopting the system in which it is difficult to get injunction relief but easy to get a large amount of compensation, or the system in which it is easy to get injunction relief, but difficult to get a large amount of compensation. Shoichi Kidana, case note in *Hatsumei* (Invention), 100(6) (2003), pp. 93 et seq., spec., p. 100, p. 105 note 4; Nobuhide Ohtomo, case note, *Jurisuto*, no. 1171, p. 109.

TOPIC 4 PROTECTIVE ORDER SYSTEM

Masabumi Suzuki & Makoto Hattori

1. Legal Issues

In judicial proceedings, the parties may be forced to show their confidential information[87] when presenting arguments or proof. For example, in litigation concerning unauthorized use of trade secrets or patent infringement, the defendant may need to present evidence about the actual process of manufacturing its products that contains the defendant's confidential information, in order to show that the defendant is not using the plaintiff's secrets or inventions.

In Japan, in the past, there were few measures to protect confidential information in judicial proceedings except for general restriction on third parties' access to case records (Article 92 of the CCP and Article 53(2) of the Code of Criminal Procedure), and parties' activities might be restricted due to concerns about the leakage of confidential information. In response, in 2004, relevant laws were amended to incorporate new measures to protect confidential information in court proceedings, namely: (i) the protective order system, (ii) (expansion of) in-camera trial procedures, and (iii) a system for suspending the disclosure of cross-examinations in proceedings in which trade secrets are an issue. The laws amended for this purpose were the Patent Act, the Industrial Design Act, the Trademark Act, the UCPA, and the Copyright Act[88]. The protective order system has been in effect since April 1, 2005.

Under the relevant statutory provisions, it is possible for parties to request protective orders in "litigation" concerning the infringement of IP rights, or infringement of commercial interests by unfair competition conduct. There were different views as to whether a protective order may be requested in a provisional disposition case.

2. The Statutory Law

Article 105-4 (Protective order) of the Patent Act typifies provisions concerning protective orders and provides as follows:

> (1) In litigation concerning the infringement of a patent right or exclusive license, where there is prima facie evidence of the fact that trade secrets (referring to trade secrets as provided in Article 2 (6) of the UCPA (Act No. 47 of 1993), the same shall apply hereinafter) possessed by a party satisfy all of the following paragraphs, the court may, upon a motion of the party, order by a ruling that

87. In this section, the term "confidential information" means information that is valuable for its holder and kept secret irrespective of whether or not it satisfies the requirements to be regarded as a "trade secret" as provided in Article 2(6) of the UCPA. The term "trade secret" is used as defined by the UCPA. For the text and interpretation of Article 2(6) of the UCPA, *see* the "Summary" of this chapter.

88. Similar provisions concerning protective orders were also introduced to the Plant Variety Protection and Seed Act in 2007, which entered into effect in December 2007.

the parties, etc., attorneys or assistants shall neither use the trade secrets for any purpose other than those for the proceedings of the litigation nor disclose the trade secrets to any person other than those who receive the order regarding the trade secrets under this provision; provided, however, that this shall not apply where the parties, etc., attorneys or assistants have, prior to the filing of the motion, already obtained or been in the possession of the trade secrets by a method other than by reading of the briefs under item (i) or through the examination or disclosure of evidence under the said item:

(i) where the trade secrets possessed by the party were or are contained in the briefs already submitted or to be submitted or such trade secrets were or are contained in the evidence already examined or to be examined (including documents disclosed under Article 105 (3) and under Article 105-7 (4)); and

(ii) where it is necessary to restrict the use or the disclosure of the trade secrets under the preceding paragraph to prevent any possible interference with the party's business activities based on the trade secrets that might arise if the trade secrets are used for any purpose other than those for the proceedings of the litigation or if the said trade secrets are disclosed.

(2) A motion requesting the order under the preceding paragraph (hereinafter referred to as a "protective order") shall be made in writing specifying the following matters:

(i) the person(s) to whom the protective order is to be issued;

(ii) the facts that clearly identify the trade secrets to be protected by the protective order; and

(iii) the facts corresponding to the reasons each of the items in the preceding paragraph is applicable.

(3) Where the protective order is issued, a written ruling thereof shall be served to the person(s) to whom the protective order is issued.

(4) The protective order shall take effect as of the date the written ruling is served to the person(s) to whom the protective order is issued.

(5) The decision dismissing a motion requesting the protective order shall be subject to immediate appeal.

If an addressee does not abide by a protective order, he will be subject to criminal penalties. For example, Article 200-2(1) of the Patent Act provides for penalties of imprisonment with labor for five years or less, and/or a fine of JPY five million. It is an offense subject to prosecution only upon complaint (paragraph (2) of the same article). Foreign offenders are also punished (paragraph (3) of the same article).

In addition, a person who violates a protective order may be regarded as having acted illegally against the holders of the trade secrets that are the subject of the order. The persons whose business interests have been adversely affected by the conduct of the violator may claim civil remedies (such as injunctions and damages) based on the general tort law (Article 709 of the Civil Code) or the UCPA.

Similar provisions are contained in the Industrial Design Act, the Trademark Act, the UCPA, the Copyright Act, and the Plant Variety Protection and Seed Act[89].

The Intellectual Property Benches of the Tokyo District Court published a document entitled "On a Motion for Protective Orders"[90] in December 2008. The document provides guidelines on such issues as prior consultation (consultation among both parties and the court), a method of making a motion, methods for hearing and deciding on the motion, and a method for filing a request for revocation of a protective order.

3. The Case Law

According to one survey, there were 4 to 8 applications for protective orders at the Tokyo District Court per year between 2008 and 2012. The total number of applications in that period was 26. About half (14) were granted, while 8 were withdrawn and 2 were rejected[91]. Another survey informs that there were 3 to 5 applications at the Tokyo District Court per year from 2013 to 2015 (5 in 2013, 3 in 2014, and 3 in 2015)[92].

4. The Leading Case

4.1. Case Information

Japanese Supreme Court, Third Petty Bench, Heisei 20 (Kyo) 36, Minshu Vol. 63, No. 1, p. 271 (decided on January 27, 2009).

4.2. Summary

This ruling has significance not only for resolving the specific issue of the availability of protective orders but also for the implementation of the protective order system in general.

In this case, the Japanese Supreme Court confirmed that a provisional disposition case to seek an injunction against infringement of a patent right or exclusive license falls within the category of "litigation concerning the infringement of a patent right or exclusive license" prescribed in the main clause of Article 105-4(1) of the Patent Act, and it is allowable to file a motion for a protective order under the said paragraph in such a provisional disposition case. In discussing the issue related to the scope of "litigation," the Supreme Court elaborated on the purpose of the protective order system.

---

89. English translations of these acts are available from WIPO Lex, https://wipolex.wipo.int/en/members/profile/JP.
90. The original document (in Japanese) is available at https://www.courts.go.jp/tokyo/saiban/sinri/sinri_himitsu/index.html.
91. Shinji Oda, *Actual Status of Implementation of Protective Orders*, 59 Law & Technology (in Japanese) 3, at 6 (2013).
92. *Report of the 2015FY Discussion between the Courts and the JFBA Committee on Intellectual Property Rights*, 2 Law & Technology (Special Edition) (in Japanese) 1, at 27 (2016).

4.3. *Facts*

Party A filed a petition for an order of provisional disposition to seek an injunction against the importation and sale of LCD television sets and LCD monitors and other acts conducted by party X, alleging that such acts infringe A's patent right (the case pertaining to this motion shall hereinafter be referred to as the "Provisional Disposition Case"). In the Provisional Disposition Case, a hearing was held on the date on which X was able to attend.

X filed a motion (hereinafter the "Motion") for a protective order under Article 105-4(1) of the Patent Act against Y1, Y2, and Y3, who were A's attorneys or assistants in court, in order to protect X's trade secrets, alleging that these trade secrets were stated in the brief and other documents that X planned to submit in the Provisional Disposition Case.

Both the courts of first instance (the Tokyo District Court) and second instance (the IP High Court) dismissed the Motion without prejudice. X petitioned the IP High Court for permission to appeal to the Supreme Court, which was granted by the IP High Court. The Supreme Court quashed the decision of the IP High Court, revoked the decision by the Tokyo District Court, and remanded the case to the Tokyo District Court[93].

4.4. *The Reasoning of the Court*[94]

"The point at issue is whether or not it is allowable to file a motion for a protective order under Article 105-4(1) of the Patent Act in a case pertaining to a petition for an order of provisional disposition to seek an injunction against the infringement of a patent right, etc.

The court of prior instance dismissed the Motion without prejudice, holding that since 'litigation concerning the infringement of a patent right or exclusive license' prescribed in the main clause of the principal part of Article 105-4(1) of the Patent Act does not include a provisional disposition case to seek an injunction against the infringement of a patent right, it is unallowable to file a motion for a protective order in the Provisional Disposition Case.

However, we cannot affirm the determination of the court of prior instance mentioned above, on the following grounds.

In litigation concerning the infringement of a patent right or exclusive license, if any trade secrets are included in the brief or documentary evidence to be submitted to the court, it could happen that the party who holds these trade secrets, out of fear that the trade secrets will be used by the other party for purposes other than the purpose of conducting the suit or be disclosed to a third party, which would cause hindrance to the

93. The quashing of the decision of the IP High Court was based on Article 325(5) of the CCP, and the revocation of the decision of the Tokyo District Court and the remand of the case to that court were based on Articles 331 and 307 of the CCP.
94. This part is a quotation of the ruling based on an English translation provided by the Japanese Supreme Court, https://www.courts.go.jp/app/hanrei_en/detail?id=983. Some changes were made in order to keep consistency with the other parts of this section, and for grammatical reasons.

party's business activities involving the trade secrets, refrains from showing those trade secrets at court and ends in failing to make sufficient allegations and proof. It can be construed that in order to avoid such a situation, the Patent Act provides for the protective order system (Articles 105-4 to 105-6, 200-2, and 201) and prohibits, by a protective order with criminal punishment, such trade secrets from being used for purposes other than the purpose of conducting the suit or disclosed to a party other than the one who has received the protective order.

A provisional disposition case that seeks an injunction against the infringement of a patent right or exclusive license addresses a specific issue, i.e., whether or not an order of provisional disposition is necessary, which is not disputed in a case on the merits. However, other issues that are addressed in a provisional disposition case are also disputed in a case on the merits, and therefore there is no difference between these cases in that the party who holds the trade secrets is likely to face the abovementioned situation, which the protective order system cannot be deemed to accept. Even if we construe that a motion for a protective order may be filed in provisional disposition cases, this construction cannot be said to be contrary to the features of provisional disposition cases, such as the requirement that the case should be handled promptly.

Under the Patent Act, the term 'litigation' is not only used to refer to a case on the merits but also includes a civil preservation case in some provisions (Articles 54(2) and 168(2)). In light of the purpose of the protective order system described above, it is appropriate to construe that a provisional disposition case to seek an injunction against the infringement of a patent right or exclusive license falls within the category of 'litigation concerning the infringement of a patent right or exclusive license' prescribed in the main clause of Article 105-4(1) of the Patent Act, and it is allowable to file a motion for a protective order in provisional disposition cases.

The determination of the court of prior instance goes against this reasoning, violates laws and regulations and apparently affects its decision. The appeal counsels' arguments are well grounded, and the decision in prior instance should inevitably be quashed. We have decided to revoke the decision of the first instance and remand the case to the court of first instance for further examination."

4.5. *Legal Analysis*

4.5.1. *Significance of This Judgment*

4.5.1.1. Provisional Dispositions for Injunction Frequently Used in Practice

A provisional disposition requesting the suspension of infringement of IP rights in Japan (hereinafter referred to as a "provisional disposition for injunction") is a provisional disposition that temporarily establishes a provisional status that will bring about the ultimate realization of rights (Article 23(2), the Civil Provisional Remedies Act[95]). Therefore, the content of the decision to approve the petition for the disposition is almost the same as that of the decision affirming claims in proceedings on the merits.

95. Article 23(2) of the Civil Provisional Remedies Act states "An order of provisional disposition that determines a provisional status may be issued when such status is necessary in order to

The decision approving a provisional disposition can be immediately enforced by notification. In addition, making a petition for a provisional disposition is cheaper than filing a lawsuit on the merits, and can be withdrawn based on the petitioner's unilateral intention. For these reasons, provisional dispositions for injunction are frequently used in practice as a means of prompt dispute resolution.

4.5.1.2. Purpose of the Protective Order System

As quoted above, this judgment states that the purpose of the protective order system is to avoid a situation where "the party who holds these trade secrets, out of fear that the trade secrets will be used by the other party for purposes other than the purpose of conducting the suit or be disclosed to a third party, which would cause hindrance to the party's business activities involving the trade secrets, refrains from showing those trade secrets at court and ends in failing to make sufficient allegations and proof." This understanding is based on discussions in the legislative process for the introduction of the protective order system. This judgment also determined that the issuance of a protective order would be permitted even in the provisional disposition case, because in the provisional disposition procedure, the above situation may occur for the party who holds trade secrets, which is no different from the case of the proceedings on the merits, and the protective order system cannot be deemed to accept such detrimental results.

4.5.1.3. Protective Order and Provisional Disposition Procedure

Typical situations in which the protective order system is used are: (i) when the other party or its attorney is involved in the in-camera procedure in determining the necessity of an order for a document submission, and (ii) when one of the parties submits its trade secrets to the proceeding in order to prove its own arguments (e.g., in a patent infringement case, when the defendant tries to clarify the specific mode of the alleged infringing act, or in a case concerning trade secret infringement, when the defendant claims to have developed the trade secret independently).

Evidence that can be submitted in the provisional disposition procedure in Japan is limited to "evidence that can be examined immediately" (Article 13(2), the Civil Provisional Remedies Act; Article 188, the CCP), and thus orders to submit documents (Article 223, the CCP) cannot be used. Therefore, the situation (i) mentioned above does not occur in provisional disposition procedures.

On the other hand, the situation (ii) above can occur in provisional disposition procedures as well as in proceedings on the merits. In addition, the former proceedings are not significantly different from the proceedings on the merits with regard to the period of time necessary for examinations, and it is therefore acceptable even if it takes several weeks to deal with a protective order in provisional disposition procedures.

---

avoid any substantial detriment or imminent danger that would occur to the obligee with regard to the relationship of rights in dispute".

Based on these considerations, the decision by the Supreme Court is generally supported by practitioners in Japan.

4.5.2. *Actual Operation of the Protective Order System*

4.5.2.1. Who Can Make a Motion?

The parties to the proceedings who hold trade secrets can propose a motion for a protective order. Interveners in lawsuits can also make a motion[96].

Parties or interveners who are not holders of trade secrets cannot make a motion for a protective order. In this context, those who "hold" trade secrets need to be broadly understood. Specifically, it is understood that not only the person who created the trade secret by himself/herself but also the person who has been shown the trade secret by another person and has the obligation to keep it secret is understood as the "holder."

4.5.2.2. Kinds of "Litigation" in Which a Motion Can Be Made

It is provided that protective orders may be issued in "litigation concerning the infringement" of a patent right or other relevant IP rights, or business interests in cases concerning unfair competition. Since the related articles (for instance, Article 105-4 of the Patent Act) can be the basis for criminal punishment (according to, for example, Article 200-3 of the Patent Act), they should be strictly understood, and interpretation by analogy is not allowed. Therefore, protective orders cannot be issued in, for example, proceedings regarding remuneration for employee inventions, suits against appeal or trial decisions made by the Japan Patent Office, or proceedings concerning license agreements. However, as already discussed with respect to the present decision, it is possible to issue protective orders in provisional disposition cases.

4.5.2.3. Trade Secrets Subject to Protective Orders

The subject of protective orders is a trade secret as defined in Article 2(6) of the UCPA; i.e., "a production method, sales method, or any other technical or operational information useful for business activities that is controlled as a secret and is not publicly known." In a patent infringement lawsuit against generic drugs, the defendant proposed a motion for a protective order for the materials to be examined by the authority that was attached to the application for import approval of generic drugs, and the court granted the motion, affirming the information contained in the materials was a trade secret[97].

As is clear from the related provisions (e.g., Article 105-4(1), item (i) of the Patent Act), only those trade secrets described in case briefs or included in the evidence can be the subject of protective orders. In addition, if the addressee of the protective order has already acquired or held the trade secrets independently of the proceedings before

96. Osaka District Court, 2008 (Mo) 363 (decided on April 18, 2008, accepting a petition by an intervener in a patent infringement case).
97. Tokyo District Court, 2006 (Mo) 9933 (decided on September 15, 2006).

the motion for the order for the same secrets is made, the motion will be rejected (Article 105-4(1), proviso)[98].

4.5.2.4. The Addressee of Protective Orders

Protective orders may be addressed to the party of the case (including its agents or employees) and its attorneys or assistants. In practice, who will actually be addressed will be coordinated and determined in prior consultation among the parties and the court. It is understood that at least one attorney representing the opposite party should be included in the addressees in order to facilitate subsequent proceedings. Furthermore, there is an opinion that a patent attorney representing (or assisting the representing attorneys for) the opposite party, and a representative (or an employee entrusted with the proceedings by the board of directors) of the opposite party should also be included in the addressees in principle[99]. However, in reality, it seems that there are many cases in which the opposite party (including its agents or employees) is not included in the addressees. In particular, when the parties are direct competitors in the market, the party requesting a protective order tends to have a strong wish to exclude agents or employees of the opposite party from the addressees. It also seems that US companies tend to only agree on disclosing their trade secrets to attorneys, probably because they are accustomed to "Attorney's Eyes Only" practices in the discovery procedure.

4.5.2.5. Necessity

Relevant provisions (e.g., Article 105-4(1), item (ii) of the Patent Act) require that the need for the issuance of a protective order is recognized by the court to grant a motion for the order; i.e., the need to "restrict the use or the disclosure of the trade secrets ... to prevent any possible interference with the party's business activities based on the trade secrets, that might arise if the trade secrets are used for any purpose other than those for the proceedings of the litigation or if the said trade secrets are disclosed."[100] Here, according to the pervasive view, the possibility of "interference" does not need to be concrete; an abstract likelihood is enough.

4.6. *Commercial or Industrial Significance*

The protective order system in Japan has been implemented in a strict way by the court, partly because it is coupled with criminal punishment. As a result, the number of orders actually issued is not large. From the perspective of the parties, there is an opinion among practitioners which alleges that a nondisclosure agreement concluded

98. Osaka District Court, 2008 (Mo) 799 (decided on December 25, 2008, rescinding a once-issued protective order based on provisions including Article 105-4 (1), proviso).
99. *See* Motoji Nakajima, *Practical Issues Concerning the Implementation of the Protective Order System*, in Tetsuya Obuchi et al. (eds) *Patent Litigation (in Japanese)* 1217, at 1224 (2012).
100. For an example of court decisions that discussed the need for a protective order, *see* Tokyo District Court, *supra* note 97.

between the parties is preferable because it may enable a more flexible implementation than a protective order. However, as a matter of course, reaching an agreement on handling trade secrets between litigating parties can be difficult, and criminal penalties are expected to guarantee the effectiveness of the protective order system. Therefore, holders of trade secrets who happen to be parties to lawsuits over infringement of IP should seriously consider the use of the protective order system.

TOPIC 5 DAMAGES

Masabumi Suzuki

1. Legal Issues

What kinds of acts concerning trade secrets can be grounds for claims for damages? Who can claim damages for such acts, and how will the amounts of damages be calculated? The answers to these questions are as follows with regard to the practice in Japan: (i) damages can be claimed against the person who conducted intentionally or negligently any of the trade-secret-related acts that are listed in the UCPA (UCPA), (ii) any person whose business interests have been infringed can claim damages caused by the act, (iii) the amount of damages is calculated under the compensatory principle, namely in order to compensate the loss suffered from the infringement. In view of the difficulty in proving damages in actual litigation, the UCPA has provisions for presumption of the amount of damages. Therefore, the interpretation of these provisions for the presumption of the amount of damages often becomes a problem in litigation over acts of unfair competition related to trade secrets.

2. The Statutory Law

In Article 2(1), items (iv) to (x), the UCPA stipulates the types of acts of unfair competition related to trade secrets. For an explanation of the types of acts, *see Overview and Summary* of this chapter.

Article 4 of the UCPA stipulates the right to claim damages as follows:

> A person that intentionally or negligently infringes on the business interests of another person through unfair competition is held liable to compensate for damages which result, provided, however, that this Article does not apply to damages resulting from the act of using trade secrets ... after the rights prescribed in Article 15 have extinguished pursuant to the same Article.

Claim for damages can be made only by a person whose business interests have been infringed, and only against a person who committed acts of unfair competition intentionally or negligently. The proviso states that damages cannot be claimed for an act of using trade secrets after the time when the right to seek an injunction against the use of the trade secrets has expired. The right to seek injunction is extinguished specifically in two cases. First, when the person conducting the act does so continuously and the trade secret owner whose business interests have been infringed or are likely to be infringed on by the act does not exercise the right within three years from the time when the person comes to know of the fact and the identity of the person conducting the act. Second, when twenty years have elapsed from the time the act began.

Article 5 of the UCPA provides a presumption of the amount of damages in order to make it easier for a person who has his or her business interests infringed to prove the amount of damages:

(1) When a person whose business interests have been infringed due to the unfair competition set forth in Article 2(1), items (i) through (xvi) or (xxii) (with regard to the unfair competition set forth in items (iv) through (ix) of the same paragraph, limited to unfair competition that involves a technical secret) (hereinafter referred to as the "infringed party" in this paragraph) makes a claim for compensation for damages suffered due to the infringement, from a person that has intentionally or negligently infringed on the business interests, if the infringer has transferred things that constituted the act of infringement, the quantity of the things transferred (hereinafter referred to as the "transferred quantity" in this paragraph) multiplied by the amount of profit per unit of the things that the infringed party could have sold in the absence of the act of infringement may be fixed as the amount of damages suffered by the infringed party, within the limits of an amount proportionate to the infringed party's ability to sell or conduct other acts concerning the things; provided, however, that if there are circumstances that would have prevented the infringed party from selling a number of things equivalent to all or part of the transferred quantity, an amount proportionate to the number of things corresponding to the circumstances is deducted.

(2) When a person whose business interests have been infringed on due to unfair competition makes a claim for compensation for damages suffered by him from a person that intentionally or negligently infringed on the business interests, if the person has made a profit through the act of infringement, the amount of profit is presumed to be the amount of damages that the person whose business interests were infringed on has suffered.

(3) A person whose business interests have been infringed on due to the unfair competition set forth in Article 2(1), items (i) through (ix), ... may make a claim for compensation for damages against a person that has intentionally or negligently infringed on the business interests, in an amount equivalent to the amount of money that the infringed party should have been entitled to receive for the act prescribed in the relevant item of the following ones for the classification of unfair competition set forth therein, as the amount of damages suffered by the infringed party:
   (i) unfair competition set forth in Article 2(1), items (i) or (ii) —use of an indication of goods or business pertaining to the infringement;
   (ii) unfair competition set forth in Article 2(1), item (iii) —use of a configuration of goods pertaining to the infringement;
   (iii) unfair competition set forth in Article 2(1), items (iv) through (ix)—use of trade secrets pertaining to the infringement;
   (iv) unfair competition set forth in Article 2(1), items (xi) through (xvi) —use of "shared data with limited access" pertaining to the infringement;
   (v) unfair competition set forth in Article 2(1), item (xix) —use of a domain name pertaining to the infringement; and
   (vi) unfair competition set forth in Article 2(1), item (xxii) —use of a trademark pertaining to the infringement.

(4) The provisions of the preceding paragraph do not preclude a claim for compensation of damages exceeding the amount prescribed in that paragraph. In such a case, if the person that infringed on the business interests did not do so intentionally or through gross negligence, the court may take this into consideration in determining the amount of damages to be compensated.

Simply put, the ways of calculation provided by these provisions are: (i) the infringed person's profit per unit of things the person could have sold but for infringement, multiplied by the quantity of things transferred by the actor of unfair competition (this assumption is available only for the damages caused by unfair use of technical secrets), (ii) the amount of profits received by the actor due to the act of unfair competition, and (iii) the amount that the infringed person would have been able to charge the actor for the use of the trade secrets. These are merely presumptions of the amount of damages, and it is not necessary for the plaintiff to request the application of either of them when making a claim for damages. In addition, even when requesting the application of these provisions, such damages as those on reputation and attorney's fees do not fit into these provisions, so the amount can be separately asserted and proved.

Besides the application of the UCPA, a person who has been damaged by an act related to trade secrets may be able to claim damages based on Article 709[101] of the Civil Code, which is a general tort law. However, the pervasive view is that any acts that are similar to but not included in those acts of unfair competition listed in the UCPA are basically not recognized as torts under Article 709 of the Civil Code.

3. The Case Law

In the 10 years from 2006 to 2015, there were 94 trade-secret-related civil cases and 118 judgments in these cases in Japan, of which 87% (82 out of 94) involved claims for damages while 55% (52 out of 94) involved claims for injunctions. The rate at which claims for damages were approved was 17% (14 out of 82), while it was 13% for injunctions (7 out of 52)[102].

Regarding the provisions of the UCPA that were applied, according to a survey[103] of 31 court decisions (the total number of the decisions that became final) in which damages were granted between 1991 and 2019, two decisions applied Article 5(1), 13 decisions applied Article 5(2), four decisions applied Article 5(3)(iii), and ten decisions calculated the damages without applying Article 5 (there were other decisions that awarded damages based on the arguments and proof by the plaintiff with regard to lost profits, damages on its reputation, and extra costs caused by unfair competition acts). The largest amount of damages awarded was JPY 1,023 million (equivalent to about USD 9 million. *See* "the leading cases" below), although there were other cases where much larger amounts were claimed, the parties reached settlements before the courts gave decisions.

3.1. *Cases That Applied Article 5(1)*

Article 5(1) is a relatively new provision introduced by the 2003 amendment of the UCPA. The purpose of the provision is to presume the amount of lost profits due to a decrease in sales of products caused by unfair competition acts related to trade secrets.

101. Article 709 of the Civil Code provides that "[a] person that has intentionally or negligently infringed the rights or legally protected interests of another person is liable to compensate for resulting damage in consequence."
102. Takakuni Yamane, *Damages for Trade Secret Infringement*, 70 Patent Studies 51 (2020) (in Japanese), https://www.inpit.go.jp/content/100871116.pdf.
103. *Ibid.*, at 67.

The decisions that applied this provision are IP High Court, Heisei 29 (Ne) 10007 (decided on March 26, 2018), and Tokyo District Court, Heisei 27 (Wa) 16423 (decided on November 29, 2018). The former will be introduced later as a leading case.

3.2. *Cases That Applied Article 5(2)*

Article 5(2) is the most commonly used provision in Article 5. The reasons for the active use are probably, first, that the applicable cases are not limited to those involving technical secrets as in Article 5(1), second, that the plaintiff (a trade secret holder) does not need to disclose its accounting (profits, etc.) in applying the provision, and third, that larger amounts of damages can often be presumed than under Article 5(3), item (iii).

A decision by the IP High Court explained the purpose of Article 5(2) as follows: "the paragraph presumes the lost profit, based on the rule of thumb that when the infringer has benefited from the infringing act, the infringed party could have obtained the same amount of profit." The same decision also clarified that the paragraph cannot be applied if the holder of the trade secret was not carrying out business activities using the secret (IP High Court, decided on February 19, 2015, Heisei 25 (Ne) 10095). Other decisions that applied Article 5(2) include Osaka District Court, Heisei 13 (Wa) 10308 (decided on February 27, 2003); Nagoya District Court, Heisei 17 (Wa) 3846 (decided on March 13, 2008); and Tokyo District Court, Heisei 21 (Wa) 32104 (decided on February 13, 2013), and Heisei 24 (Wa) 35742 (decided on April 17, 2014).

3.3. *Cases That Applied Article 5(3), Item (iii)*

Article 5(3), item (iii) deems the amount equivalent to reasonable royalty to be the amount of damages. IP High Court, decided on February 19, 2015, Heisei 25 (Ne) 10095 stressed that the amount presumed by the provision is not "the amount equivalent to the value of the trade secret," but "equivalent to the amount of money that the infringed party should have been entitled to receive for the use of the trade secret pertaining to the infringement," and stated that the amount "should be calculated by comprehensively considering factors including the significance of the trade secret, the modes of the acts of unfair competition, the profits gained by the infringer through the act of unfair competition, the business relationship between the infringed and the infringer, and the business policy of the infringed." The IP High Court determined that 3% of the sales earned through the sales activities based on the customer information which was the trade secret of the plaintiff was the presumed amount of damages in that specific case. Other court decisions that awarded damages calculated by Article 5(3), item (iii) include Osaka District Court, Heisei 18 (Wa) 5172 (decided on June 12, 2008); IP High Court, Heisei 22 (Ne) 10039 (decided on September 27, 2011), and Reiwa 1 (Ne) 10044 (decided on January 31, 2020). The last one will be discussed later as a leading case.

3.4. *Others*

There are cases where the court awarded damages without applying Article 5 but based on the arguments and proof by the plaintiff. Such decisions include Osaka District Court, Heisei 5 (Wa) 8314 (decided on December 22, 1998); Fukuoka District Court, Heisei 11 (Wa) 1102 (decided on December 24, 2002); IP High Court, Heisei 25 (Ne) 10084 (decided on July 4, 2014); Osaka District Court, Heisei 27 (Ne) 12149 (decided on June 23, 2018).

4. The Leading Cases

This part analyzes two cases. The first one interprets Article 5(1) of the UCPA in detail, presenting guidelines for the future application of that provision. The second one is an example of cases applying Article 5(3), item (iii) as well as a significant case where the courts directed the plaintiff's former employee to pay a huge amount of damages, in fact, the largest amount of damages in disputes on trade secrets so far in Japan.

4.1.1. *Case Information*

IP High Court, Heisei 29 (Ne) 10007 (decided on March 26, 2018).

4.1.2. *Summary*

This decision has precedential significance, as it explains how to apply Article 5(1) in detail and in a general way. To summarize the decision:

(i) the purpose of the provision is to present the method of calculating the amount of damages in cases where the plaintiff is seeking compensation for lost profits due to a decrease in sales volume;

(ii) the "things that the infringed party could have sold in the absence of the act of infringement" is the product of the infringed which has a competitive relationship with the infringing product in the market;

(iii) the "amount of profit per unit" is the amount obtained by deducting the manufacturing cost and variable costs that increase according to the sales of the infringed party's product from the selling price of that product (the amount of marginal profit), and the burden of proof for the amount lies with the infringed party; and

(iv) the "circumstances that would have prevented the infringed party from selling" in the proviso of Article 5(1) mean the circumstances that inhibit a reasonable causal relationship between the infringing conduct and the decline in sales of products of the infringed party, and include, for example, the existence of competing products in the market, the sales efforts of the infringer (brand power and advertising), the performance of the infringing product (function, design, etc.), and the nonidentity of the markets (price and sales form).

4.1.3. *Facts*

The plaintiff and the defendant were both companies manufacturing and selling cable-television-related equipment. The defendant was established by A, a former employee of the plaintiff. The plaintiff alleged that the defendant obtained trade secrets of the plaintiff (technical information on software for equipment related to digital wave reception, etc.) which were illegitimately disclosed by former employees of the plaintiff who were now employed by the defendant, and the defendant used the secrets for manufacturing products. Based on the allegation, the plaintiff requested injunction against the defendant's manufacturing and selling of the products, disposal of the manufactured product, and the payment of JPY 11.83 million as compensation for damages. The court at first instance granted the plaintiff's injunction and disposal claims and ordered the defendant to pay JPY 4,498,700 as damages[104]. The defendant appealed.

4.1.4. *The Reasoning of the Court*

The IP High Court upheld the first instance decision but decreased the amount of damages. Specifically, the IP High Court found that the defendant's act was an unauthorized use of the plaintiff's trade secrets (technical secrets) as prescribed in Article 2(1), item (viii) of the UCPA, and an infringement of the plaintiff's business interest. Then, the Court applied Article 5(1) of the UCPA for the calculation of damages. In that context, the Court presented its interpretation of that provision in a general way as follows:

> Article 5(1) of the UCPA stipulates the method of calculating the amount of damages when compensation for lost profits due to a decrease in sales volume is sought based on Article 709 of the Civil Code[105]. ... [The provision] reverses the burden of proof for the reduced sales quantity which has a reasonable causal relationship with the infringing act, and thus aims to provide more flexible determination of the decrease in sales volume, which used to be determined in a rigid all-or-nothing way.
>
> In light of the wording and the purpose of Article 5(1), the "things that the infringed party could have sold in the absence of the act of infringement" should be understood as the products of the infringed party whose sales volume is affected by the act of infringement, namely the infringed party's products that have a competitive relationship with the infringing products in the market ... The "amount of profit per unit of the things" is the amount obtained by deducting the manufacturing cost and the variable cost that increases according to the sales quantity of the product from the selling price of the infringed party's product (the amount of marginal profit). The burden of proving the amount, as well as the sales ability, should be understood to be on the side of the infringed party.
>
> Furthermore, the infringer bears the burden of proof for the "circumstances that would have prevented the infringed party from selling a number of things

104. Tokyo District Court, Tachikawa Branch, Heisei 26 (Wa) 1519. However, the decision was not published, so its details are not available.
105. The Court should have cited Article 4 of the UCPA here, rather than Article 709 of the Civil Code.

equivalent to all or part of the transferred quantity" in the proviso of Article 5(1). When the circumstances are proved, the quantity corresponding to the circumstances is deducted. The "circumstances that would have prevented the infringed party from selling" mean the circumstances that inhibit a reasonable causal relationship between the infringing conduct and the decline in sales of products of the infringed party, and include, for example, the existence of competing products in the market, the sales efforts of the infringer (brand power and advertising), the performance of the infringing product (function, design, etc.), and the nonidentity of the markets (price and sales form).

The IP High Court then applied the interpretation of the provision to this case. In the calculation of damages, the Court found the ratio of the contribution of the trade secrets to the sales of the plaintiff's products to be 20%, took that ratio into account in determining the "amount of profit per unit," and calculated the amount of damages caused by the sales of the infringer's products as JPY 1,499,476, and the attorneys' fees as JPY 200,000, awarding the plaintiff a total of JPY 1,699,467.

4.1.5. *Legal Analysis*

Article 5(1) of the UCPA was introduced after the model of Article 102(1) of the Patent Act. On February 28, 2020, the IP High Court gave an *en banc* decision interpreting Article 102(1), and that interpretation was essentially the same as the interpretation of Article 5(1) of the UCPA by the above decision[106]. Therefore, this decision's interpretation of Article 5(1) of the UCPA was, in essence, supported by the *en banc* decision of the IP High Court, and thus has a considerably high precedential significance.

While the interpretation of this decision is basically a sound one, there is a problem as to the way of taking into account the ratio of the contribution of the trade secrets to the sales of the products (either the infringer's or the infringed party's). The IP High Court considered that ratio in the determination of the "amount of profit per unit of the things," but not in the recognition of the "circumstances that would have prevented the infringed party from selling." However, it is not reasonable to examine the ratio of the contribution independently, separate from the examination of the "circumstances that would have prevented the infringed party from selling," because factors affecting the sales of products are interrelated. The ratio of trade secrets contributing to (or not contributing to) product sales is just one of the circumstances that hinder a causal relationship between the infringement and the decrease in sales of the infringed party's product. It is not persuasive to distinguish the ratio of the contribution of the trade secrets from other factors and to do so, there is a risk of double evaluation of the same factor. Therefore, it is more appropriate to evaluate the ratio of trade secrets contribution to product sales in the analysis of the "circumstances that would have prevented the infringed party from selling."[107]

106. The presiding judge in charge of the two decisions was Judge Makiko Takabe, then Chief Judge of the IP High Court.
107. For a detailed discussion on this point, *see* Masabumi Suzuki, *Recent Trends Concerning Article 102 of the Japanese Patent Act—Court Judgements and Law Amendments Relating to Calculation of Damages for Patent Infringement*—291 Patents and Licensing, 8 (2021), https://ssrn.com/abstract=3812036.

4.1.6. *Commercial or Industrial Significance*

As explained above, Article 5(1) is the newest provision of Article 5 of the UCPA. The number of cases where the provision was invoked is not large yet. However, it is expected that the provision will be used more often in accordance with the clarification brought by courts' interpretation, and the above decision will be one of the leading cases in the application of Article 5(1).

4.2.1. *Case Information*

Tokyo District Court, Heisei 29 (Wa) 29604 (decided on April 24, 2019) and IP High Court, Reiwa 1 (Ne) 10044 (decided on January 31, 2020).

4.2.2. *Summary*

The Tokyo District Court affirmed the plaintiff's claim for damages due to unauthorized disclosure of trade secrets, applying Article 5(3), item (iii) of the UCPA. The IP High Court dismissed the appeal by the defendant. The amount of damages awarded by the courts in this case is the largest that has been awarded in trade-secret-related cases so far in Japan.

4.2.3. *Facts*

This case is related to a dispute between Nippon Steel (NS) and POSCO, the two big steel companies in Japan and South Korea respectively. NS alleged that POSCO used NS's trade secrets that were disclosed by the defendant of this case for manufacturing and sales of advanced types of steel products. NS claimed damages of JPY 98.6 billion against POSCO in a lawsuit in Japan. The dispute between NS and POSCO was resolved in 2015 by a settlement under which POSCO paid NS JPY 30 billion. However, the plaintiff, NS, sued the defendant in 2017, an individual who used to be an employee of NS, for illegal disclosure of NS's trade secrets (technical information on electrical steel sheets) to POSCO, and claimed damages of JPY 1,023 million. The case continued and was decided by the courts. The Tokyo District Court affirmed NS's claim for damages of JPY 1,023 million in full, and the IP High Court upheld the decision.

4.2.4. *The Reasoning of the Court*

The plaintiff claimed damages of JPY 1,023 million, arguing that the "amount equivalent to the amount of money that the infringed party should have been entitled to receive for the act" of unauthorized disclosure of the technical information at issue in this case, calculated under Article 5(3), item (iii) was equivalent to the license fee of the technical information, amounting to at least JPY 930 million, and the attorney's fees, which was at least 10% of the above damages. In response, the Tokyo District Court granted the claim in full, stating:

The average royalty rate in the industrial field of steel and nonferrous metals is 3.5% with initial payments and 3.3% without initial payments. In addition, as for the number of cases, the one with the royalty rate of 3 % is the largest. ... Then, in the 10 years from 2007 to 2016, the amount equivalent to the license fee for technical information is at least JPY 4,104 million [applying the royalty rate of 2 %].

Based on the above, it is recognized that the defendant has to pay the plaintiff, based on Article 4 of the UCPA, at least JPY 930 million in damages and JPY 93 million in attorney's fees, totaling JPY 1,023 million, together with interest arising between April 30, 2012, and the payment date.

As a rebuttal, the defendant argued that POSCO and the defendant had inauthentic joint liability[108] for the damages toward the plaintiff, and because POSCO had already paid JPY 30 billion to the plaintiff as a result of the settlement, the defendant's liability for the damages had disappeared. Neither the Tokyo District Court nor the IP High Court accepted this argument. Specifically, the IP High Court stated:

> However, since the debt owed by POSCO and the defendant is an inauthentic joint debt, even if some agreement is reached between POSCO and the plaintiff regarding the amount of debt owed by POSCO, the effect of the agreement does not extend to the defendant. In addition, the litigation between POSCO and the plaintiff was an action seeking damages of JPY 98.6 billion due to acts of trade secret infringement by POSCO and others, and there is not enough evidence to determine how much of, and for what purpose, the JPY 30 billion resulting from the settlement was used. ... Therefore, the defendant's rebuttal about the payment is rejected.

4.2.5. *Legal Analysis*

The significance of these decisions is, first, that the case is an example of how disputes would be resolved where the person who made the unauthorized disclosure of trade secrets and the entity who misused them are both sued, and secondly, that the case attracted social attention because of the magnitude of the economic effects of the illegal conducts concerning trade secrets. However, the decisions do not present an in-depth interpretation of Article 5(3), item (iii) of the UCPA.

In this case, the plaintiff (NS) sued a former employee who committed unauthorized disclosure of the trade secret (technical information). The plaintiff also filed a lawsuit against the company (POSCO) that used the trade secret in its business following the unauthorized disclosure, in which the plaintiff claimed damages of JPY 98.6 billion. The latter proceeding ended with a settlement. In the settlement, the parties agreed that POSCO would pay JPY 30 billion to NS. It is not clear whether NS was satisfied with the amount of the payment under the settlement. Nevertheless, the fact that NS received the payment may have affected how much NS would claim in the present case. Specifically, the amount of damages the plaintiff claimed was JPY 1,023 million, while the Tokyo District Court found that the actual damages would have been as much as JPY 4.1 billion or more. The court also applied a rather low royalty rate (2 %) in the calculation of damages under Article 5(3), item (iii), although the average

108. The "inauthentic joint liability" or "inauthentic joint liability" is a concept (without a specific statutory basis) for a kind of joint liability where the mutual relationship between the joint debtors is comparatively weak.

royalty rates were found to be more than 3%. In this way, the settlement of the dispute between the plaintiff and POSCO might have affected the plaintiff's policy for litigation and the courts' decisions of lowering the amount of damages.

On the other hand, as a matter of law, the courts clarified that the payment by POSCO to NS as a result of the settlement did not excuse the defendant from the liability for damages. Because the defendant was an individual and JPY 1,023 million was a huge amount of money for an individual to owe, this case gave a warning to the Japanese society that illegal acts related to trade secrets can have serious consequences.

The dispute between the two companies attracted such attention in Japan that, as a result, the UCPA was amended in 2015 to introduce heavier criminal sanctions than the usual sanctions for the act of illegal acquisition and disclosure of trade secrets for the purpose of using them abroad[109].

4.2.6. *Commercial or Industrial Significance*

In recent years, various discussions have been held in Japan regarding the damage system for infringement of IP rights. Specifically, the interpretation of provisions for presumptions of the amount of damages (e.g., the IP High Court has recently issued several important *en banc* decisions on such provisions of the Patent Law), and whether Japan should introduce an enhanced damage system are being hotly debated. At present, the majority view is that the compensatory principle should be maintained, and under that principle, courts should interpret the related provisions in a flexible way so that the right holders can get sufficient compensation for their damages.

Under such circumstances, there are growing expectations that the damage system will be an effective remedy for illegal acts related to trade secrets. It seems that the courts are also taking a positive stance in finding relatively large amounts of damages.

109. *See* Article 21(3) of the UCPA.

TOPIC 6 THE CRIMINAL PUNISHMENT FOR TRADE SECRET INFRINGEMENT AND THE ELEMENT OF "PURPOSE OF WRONGFUL GAIN" IN JAPAN

Takakuni Yamane

1. Legal Issues

Criminal punishment for trade secret infringement in Japan was introduced by the 2003 amendment of the UCPA[110]. One of the difficult issues in applying criminal punishment is the determination of whether the accused has acted with the "purpose of wrongful gain." This case report deals with this legal issue.

2. The Statutory Law

Multiple amendments of the UCPA have taken place, including expansion of the coverage of criminal offenses and the introduction of measures to protect confidentiality of trade secrets in criminal courts.

Article 21(1)(i)-(viii) of the UCPA provides that a person who acquires, uses, or discloses trade secrets through an act of fraud, etc, or through the usurpation of management for the purpose of wrongful gain or causing damage to the owner of the trade secrets, or a person who obtains trade secrets in breach of the legal duties regarding the management of the trade secrets, will be punished by imprisonment with work for not more than 10 years or a fine of not more than JPY 20 million, or both.

Of these, the offense prescribed in Article 21(1)(iii) applies most frequently. This offense was introduced in the 2009 amendments of the UCPA. One of the characteristics of this offense is that it is possible to penalize the act of reproducing and obtaining a trade secret in breach of the duty regarding the management of the trade secret before it is used or disclosed[111]. Article 21(1)(iii) prescribes that:

> (1) A person who falls under any of the following items will be punished by imprisonment with work for not more than 10 years or a fine of not more than 20 million yen, or both:
>
> (iii) a person to whom the owner of a trade secret has revealed the trade secret, and who, for the purpose of wrongful gain or causing damage to such owner, obtains the trade secret by any of the following means, in breach of the duty regarding the management of the trade secret:
>
> (a) embezzling a medium containing a trade secret, etc. (meaning a document, a drawing, or a data storage medium in which a trade secret is described or recorded; the same shall apply hereinafter in this item) or a property that represents a trade secret;
>
> (b) reproducing a description or a record from a medium containing a trade secret, etc., or a property that represents a trade secret;
>
> (c) not deleting a description or a record that should be deleted from a medium containing a trade secret, etc., and disguising this act as if the

110. METI, *Commentaries*, *supra* note 6, at 89.
111. *See* Article 21(1)(iii)(b) of the UCPA.

description or record in the medium containing the trade secret, etc. had been deleted.

Article 21(1)(ix) provides that a person who—for the purpose of obtaining a wrongful gain or causing damage to the owner of trade secrets—assigns, delivers, displays for the purpose of transfer or delivery, exports, imports or provides through a telecommunications line things created through trade secret infringement (excluding a person who has received the things by transfer without knowing that the things were created by an act of illegal use) will also be punished by imprisonment with work for not more than 10 years or a fine of not more than JPY 20 million, or both.

Article 22(1)(ii) provides that the corporation to which the person who conducted such trade secret misappropriation belongs will be punished by a fine of not more than JPY 500 million. Such a fine will be levied in addition to the fine imposed on the individual.

If those actions are conducted for the purpose of using trade secrets outside Japan, the criminal fines will be higher:

- for an individual, a fine of not more than JPY 30 million (Article 21(3));
- for a corporation, a fine of not more than JPY 1 billion (Article 22(1)(i)).

Article 21(4) provides that an ultimately unsuccessful attempt of trade secret infringement (excluding Article 21(1)(iii)) will also be punished.

Article 21(6) provides that the offenses prescribed in Article 21(1)(i)-(viii), 21(3), and 21(4) also apply to a person that commits the offenses outside Japan in connection with trade secrets of the trade secret owner conducting business within Japan. This provision was introduced in the 2015 amendments of the UCPA. Prior to that, wrongful acquisition of a trade secret outside Japan would not have resulted in criminal liability in Japan under the principle of territoriality.

3. The Case Law

Criminal penalties for trade secret misappropriation were not actively used for the first five years since 2003. However, criminal investigations are now being used more frequently. Table 1.1 shows that the numbers of consultations received by the police and arrests for trade secret infringement cases in Japan have been increasing in recent years[112]. It is said that many of the recent civil cases have been under concurrent or prior criminal investigation. It is becoming a typical approach for a victim to consult with the police to start a criminal investigation and obtain necessary evidence from the files of the criminal case to be used as the plaintiff's evidence in a civil case[113].

112. National Police Agency, *Sgtatus of Arrests for Lifestyle and Economic Offenses in 2019 (in Japanese)* (March 2020), at 22. https://www.npa.go.jp/publications/statistics/safetylife/seikeikan/R01_seikatsukeizaijihan.pdf.

113. Madoka Shimada, Toshihiko Hamano & Nobuhiro Tanaka, *Japan Law & Practice*, in *Chambers Global Practice Guides—Trade Secrets 2020*, Chambers and Partners, 2020, at p. 10.

Table 1.1 Trends in the Number of Consultations Received and Arrests for Trade Secret Infringement Cases

Year	*2013*	*2014*	*2015*	*2016*	*2017*	*2018*	*2019*
The number of consultations received by the police	12	29	26	35	72	47	49
The number of arrests	5	11	12	18	18	18	21

According to my research[114], from 2003, when criminal penalties for trade secret infringement were introduced, to December 2020, there were at least 30 criminal court cases involving trade secret infringement[115]. Table 1.2 summarizes the distribution of these 30 cases by year of judgment. This table shows that the number of criminal trade secret cases has increased rapidly since 2012. Of these cases, 23 were judged by district courts, 5 by high courts, and 2 by the Supreme Court[116].

Table 1.2 Changes in the Number of Criminal Trade Secret Cases

2003-2008	*2009*	*2010*	*2011*	*2012*	*2013*	*2014*	*2015*	*2016*	*2017*	*2018*	*2019*	*2020*
0	1	0	0	5	0	2	5	6	3	4	1	3

The following four points can be summarized as the characteristics of these criminal trade secret cases.

The first is the conviction rate. All 30 cases have resulted in convictions[117].

The second is the types of trade secrets. Cases involving business information account for 63% of the total (19 of 30 cases), which is higher than the percentage of cases involving technical information (50% (15 of 30 cases))[118]. In the cases of business information, the largest percentage of cases involves customer information (58% (11 of 19 cases)).

The third is the relationship between the owner of trade secrets and the accused. Of the 30 cases, 28 were committed by those who had been granted access to trade secrets by the owners of the trade secrets. In other words, the vast majority of criminal

114. In searching cases, I used three commercial databases: Westlaw Japan, LEX/DB, and D-1 law.
115. All of these 30 criminal cases are based on public trial procedures. However, it is said that court orders are often issued without going through trial procedures, and such summary court orders are not listed in the database. It is important to note that the actual number of criminal court cases for trade secret infringement is higher than 30.
116. However, one of the two Supreme Court cases was formally dismissed without showing any substantive reasoning. *See* Supreme Court judgment, Heisei 27 (A) 1351 (decided on October 31, 2016).
117. In one case, the accused violated his duty of confidentiality and took two pieces of information: product planning data for a new car and an instructional text on parts distribution. The court found the product planning data to be a trade secret and convicted him of trade secret infringement. On the other hand, with regard to the instructional text, the court denied the requirement of reasonable measures to maintain secrecy and acquitted him of trade secret infringement. Yokohama district court judgment of October 31, 2016, Heisei 26 (wa) 1529.
118. In 4 of the 30 cases, both business information and technical information were involved.

trade secret cases involve those who owe a confidentiality duty to the trade secret holder, for example, employees. Cases involving unknown persons who used improper means to acquire information are far rarer—only 7% of the total (two of 30 cases).

The fourth is that Article 21(1)(iii)(b) was applied in 77% of the cases (23 of 30 cases). In 43% of these cases (10 of 23 cases), the accused was charged not only with the act of reproducing and obtaining a trade secret in breach of the duty regarding the management of the trade secret under Article 21(1)(iii)(b) but also with the subsequent acts of use and disclosure under Article 21(1)(iv)[119]. In the remaining 57% of the cases (13 of 23 cases), however, the accused was charged only with the act of reproducing and obtaining a trade secret in breach of the duty regarding the management of the trade secret under Article 21(1)(iii)(b). This has been considered the result of the 2009 amendment of the UCPA, which was intended to arrest the accused before the use or disclosure of the trade secret is made[120].

The fifth is that, so far, there have been no cases in which Article 21(3), which relates to the actions conducted for the purpose of using trade secrets outside Japan, has been applied. According to news reports, there has been one case of arrests in December 2018 applying Article 21(3), but no decision has been issued yet.

4. The Leading Case

The leading case on Article 21(1)(iii)(b) is the one and only Supreme Court judgment that was decided with substantive reasoning. The ruling is of practical significance as a precedent, in that it shows how to determine the "purpose of wrongful gain" in cases where an employee makes copies of the trade secrets of the company where he/she works immediately before leaving said company and making a career move to another company in the same business[121].

119. Article 21(1)(iv) provides that a person who falls under any of the following items will be punished: "(iv) a person to whom the owner of trade secrets has revealed the trade secret and who, for the purpose of wrongful gain or causing damage to such owner, uses or discloses trade secrets obtained through the means set forth in (a) to (c) of the preceding item, in breach of the duty regarding the management of the trade secret."
120. For example, Professor Mitsue Kimura, a criminal law scholar, pointed out the following: "In recent years, the number of cleared cases for trade secret infringement has been increasing. The ability to arrest those who obtained trade secrets in breach of the duty regarding the management of the trade secrets is effective in cases in which it is difficult to prove the use or disclosure of trade secrets. It can be said that the 2009 amendment of the UCPA is having an effect." Mitsue Kimura, *The Crime of Violating Trade Secrets and Criminal Protection of Information (in Japanese)*, 59(1) Tokyo Metropolitan University Journal of Law and Politics, 55 (2018).
121. As a commentary on this case by the judicial research official of the Supreme Court, *see* Hirokazu Kure, *A Commentary on the Supreme Court Judgement of Dec. 3. 2018 (in Japanese)*, 72(10) Hoso jiho 184-186 (2020). *See also*, Takakuni Yamane, *Duplication of Trade Secret Data by Employees upon Resignation and the Offense of Trade Secret Infringement (in Japanese)*, 85 Law & Technology 3, 11-12 (2019).

4.1. *Case Information*

Supreme Court, the Second Petty Bench, judgment, Heisei (A) 582 (of December 3, 2018), Keishu Vol. 72, No. 6. Page 569.

4.2. *Summary*

An employee can be considered to have had the "purpose of wrongful gain" under Article 21(1)(iii) of the UCPA if he had been authorized to access data files that were trade secrets and stored in the server computer of the company where he had worked, made copies of said data files to his own hard disk immediately before leaving the said company and making a career move to another company in the same business, said copies were not made for the purpose of performing duties for the first company, and there were no circumstances hinting any other justifiable purpose. The first instance court found that the accused had the purpose of unlawful gain in making copies of the data files, such as utilizing the relevant information as a direct or indirect reference at another company to which the accused was to make a career move, and found the facts of the crime mentioned above. In the appeal, the appellate court upheld this finding of facts. The Supreme Court upheld the judgment in prior instance and dismissed the appeal.

4.3. *Facts*

(1) The accused is a person who worked at Company A, an automobile company. The accused engaged mainly in product planning operations of Company A. The accused later found a job at Company B, another automobile company, and was to leave Company A on July 31, 2013. At Company B, the accused was supposed to engage in duties, such as the development, planning, etc., of automobiles.

(2) Company A had provided the accused an identification code and a password to access the information stored in Company A's server computer concerning Company A's automobile product planning, etc., which Company A kept secret and was not publicly known.

(3) The accused was given a personal computer ("company's PC") by Company A and was authorized to bring out the company's PC and use it to access the corporate network from outside the company. On the other hand, at Company A, the accused was prohibited from using his own recording media for performing duties for the company or for accessing the corporate network, and also from storing the company's information on his PC or external recording media.

(4) On July 16, 2013, the accused made at home copies of folders that contained eight data files, including the information concerning the automobile product planning, which were stored in the company's PC, to the accused's own hard disk. Furthermore, on July 18, 2013, the accused made at home copies of said

folders from his own hard disk to his PC ("accused's own PC"). After that until July 26, which was set as the last working day at Company A, the accused did not conduct any routine work or remaining work, etc. for Company A by using the eight data files.

(5) On July 26, 2013, the accused requested to come to the office on the next day (July 27) for "stowing the accused's personal belongings, etc." and obtained permission to do so. On the said day, at Company A's technical center, the accused connected his own hard disk to the company's PC and attempted to make copies of four folders, which contained 5,074 data files in total (about 12.8 GB), including the data files concerning the automobile product planning. The accused was able to make copies of only 3,253 data files in the end due to the volume limit of the hard disk, which contained operational information covering the whole process relating to Company A's automobile development from the initial stage of planning operations to the stage immediately before release.

(6) The counsel of the accused argued that the making of copies mentioned in (4) above was carried out for the purpose of organizing operation-related data, and the making of copies mentioned in (5) above was carried out for the purpose of collecting commemorative photographs, and thus the accused did not have the purpose of utilizing the relevant information as a direct or indirect reference at another company to which the accused was to make a career move when making these copies. The counsel argued further that in order to find the accused guilty of having acting with the "purpose of wrongful gain" under Article 21(1)(iii) of the UCPA, a highly punishable purpose must be found in addition to the absence of a justifiable purpose and reason, and an ambiguous purpose of utilizing the information as a direct or indirect reference at another company to which one was to make a career move, etc. did not constitute the purpose of wrongful gain.

4.4. *The Reasoning of the Court*

"The counsel argues that the making of copies mentioned in (4) above was carried out for the purpose of organizing operation-related data. However, there is no fact that shows the accused performed duties for Company A by using the copies of the data files, and moreover, it is not necessary or reasonable for the accused, who was authorized to use the company's PC outside the company, etc. and actually brought the company's PC home on July 16, 2013, to make copies of the data files mentioned in (4) above from the company's PC to the accused's own hard disk and PC in order to perform duties for Company A. Taking these facts into consideration, it is found that the making of copies mentioned in (4) above was carried out for a purpose other than performing duties for Company A."[122]

"In addition, the making of copies mentioned in (5) above is found to have been carried out for a purpose other than performing duties for Company A because it is clear that the accused did not need to perform duties for Company A

122. Supreme Court, Heisei (A) 582, Keishu Vol. 72, No. 6., at 573.

on the day following the last working day at the company. Incidentally, although the four folders contained image data that can be commemorative photographs as argued by the counsel, such as photographs in the 'photographs of corporate gatherings' folder, the number of such image data accounts for a small portion of the whole, and the number of data files of automobile product planning, etc. makes up a significant majority. Moreover, the accused intended to make copies of the full contents of all four folders, which is shown by the fact, for example, that the accused had attempted to make copies of the same four folders two days before (July 25), and did not try to sort out the relevant image data that can be commemorative photographs. In light of these facts, the making of copies mentioned in (5) above cannot be considered to have been carried out only for the purpose of collecting commemorative photographs."[123]

"As mentioned above, the accused made copies of the data files mentioned in (4) and (5) above, which were trade secrets of the company where the accused worked, to the accused's own hard disk, immediately before leaving said company and making a career move to another company in the same business. Said making of copies was not carried out for the purpose of performing duties for the company where the accused worked and there are no circumstances suggesting the existence of any other justifiable purpose. Based on these facts of the case, it can be reasonably inferred that said copies were made for the purpose of using them for the benefit of the accused, the company to which the accused was to make a career move or any other third party other than the company where the accused worked, after leaving said company. Therefore, the accused can be considered to have had acted with the 'purpose of wrongful gain' under Article 21(1)(iii) of the UCPA. The determination of the court of prior instance that upheld the judgment in the first instance to the same effect as above is justifiable."[124]

4.5. *Legal Analysis*

4.5.1. *Significance of the Supreme Court's Judgement*

In order for Article 21(1)(iii)(b) to be applied, the prosecutor must prove the following: the accused to whom the owner of a trade secret has revealed the trade secret (α), for the purpose of wrongful gain or causing damage to such owner (β), obtained the trade secret by means of reproducing a record from a medium containing the trade secret (γ), in breach of the duty regarding the management of the trade secret (σ).

In this case, there was no dispute that the accused had been granted access from Company A to the server containing the data file of trade secrets (α), had made copies of the data files on the accused's personal hard disk, etc. (γ), in violation of internal regulations prohibiting the storage of the Company's information on his/her PC or external recording media (σ). Therefore, the only issue was whether or not the accused had acted with the "purpose of wrongful gain."(β)

If the trade secret was later used or disclosed after it was obtained, it is possible to determine the purpose of the act of obtaining from the manner of use or disclosure. However, in the present case, the accused was arrested immediately after the making of copies of the data files on July 27, 2013, so it is difficult to determine the purpose of

123. *Ibid.*
124. *Ibid.*, at 573-574.

the accused's obtaining them. The Supreme Court's judgment is significant in that it clarified specifically how to determine the "purpose of wrongful gain."[125]

4.5.2. How to Determine the "Purpose of Wrongful Gain" under Article 21(1)(iii)

The Supreme Court has inferred the "purpose of wrongful gain" first from the timing and manner of the accused's obtaining of the trade secrets. Specifically, the Supreme Court emphasized the fact that the accused made copies of a large amount of the data files containing the trade secrets of Company A to the accused's own hard disk, immediately before leaving Company A and making a career move to another company in the same business.

The Supreme Court then examined whether such making of copies was carried out for justifiable purposes, such as performing duties for Company A. With respect to the making of copies at home, the Supreme Court emphasized that there was no fact that showed the accused performed duties for Company A by using the copies of the data files, and moreover, it is not necessary or reasonable for the accused to have bothered to make copies of the data files from the company's PC to the accused's own hard disk and PC in order to perform duties for Company A. With respect to the making of copies on July 27, 2013, the Supreme Court also emphasized that it is clear that the accused did not need to perform duties for Company A on the day following the last working day at the company.

Based on the above facts, the Supreme Court concluded that it could be reasonably inferred that the copies by the accused were made for the purpose of using them after leaving Company A for his own benefit or for the benefit of the company to which the accused was to make a career move, etc., and therefore the accused can be considered to have had acted with the "purpose of wrongful gain" under Article 21(1)(iii).

4.6. Commercial or Industrial Significance

The ruling has drawn attention from industries. First, the ruling shows that criminal measures can be effective in preventing the spread of damage to companies that have suffered trade secret infringement. As soon as it is discovered that an employee breached the confidentiality obligation and took out a trade secret at the time of retirement, the company can immediately collect logs, room entry/exit records, or other evidence showing the fact of unauthorized reproduction and consult with the investigative authorities, thereby preventing the trade secret from spreading or being leaked overseas. A wide range of companies, including automakers, electrical equipment manufacturers, paint manufacturers, cutting tool manufacturers, telecommunications carriers, banks, electronics retail stores, and distance learning providers, are increasingly resorting to criminal measures against trade secret infringement regardless of their size.

---

125. Kure, *supra* note 121, at 165; Yamane, *supra* note 121, at 9-10.

Second, the ruling indicates that companies that accept job changers need to pay more attention to the risk that the job changers will bring trade secrets from their previous jobs to their company. Companies that hire job changers need to take measures to prevent them from bringing in and disclosing trade secrets of other companies to their own companies. In some cases, investigative authorities have even investigated the companies to which the employees were transferred. With the increasing mobility of human resources, more attention is needed.

CHAPTER 2
Trade Secret Law in Korea (Country Report)

OVERVIEW AND SUMMARY

Byungil Kim

1. HISTORICAL DEVELOPMENT

Until the early 1990s, there was no direct legal protection of trade secrets in Korea. Now and then, the infringement of trade secrets was qualified as theft or misappropriation of property under criminal law. Occasionally, civil law protection of trade secrets was granted within the framework of contracts, e.g., licensing, distribution, and employment agreements. In some cases, legal protection could be obtained under tort law[1]. But hardly any case law developed under these provisions, since establishing intent or negligence appeared difficult. In addition, under a civil law action based on torts, only damages rather than injunctive relief could be obtained.

In order to comply with international obligations, acquiesce to the requests of the relevant domestic circles and encourage investment in research and development in Korea, the Korean legislature amended the Unfair Competition Prevention Act (UCPA)[2] on December 31, 1991. By virtue of this amendment, technical or operational information could be protected as a trade secret as of December 15, 1992. The amendment

1. For details, *see* Byung-Il Kim, The Protection of Trade Secrets in Korea, *IIC* Vol. 30 (1999) 403.
2. *Bujeong Gyeongjaeng Bangjibeob* Act. No. 911, December 30, 1961, wholly amended by Act No. 3897, on 31 December 1986. The title of the Act was changed from "The Unfair Competition Prevention Act" to "The Unfair Competition Prevention and Trade Secret Protection Act" in 1998 by Act No. 5621, last amended by Act No. 17727, of December 22, 2020. *See* Byung-Il Kim, Protection Against Unfair Competition, in Byung-Il Kim & Christopher Heath (eds), Intellectual Property Law in Korea, Wolters Kluwer, 2015, 147-173. An English translation of all major IP laws can be found at the website of the Legislative Center of Korea, Legislation Research Institute, http://elaw.klri.re.kr/eng_service/main.do.

aimed at protecting trade secrets from misappropriation or unauthorized use, which was to encourage innovation and to promote technology transfer from foreign countries[3].

Korea amended the UCPA in 1999 to broaden the scope of trade secret protection. This amendment was an attempt to prevent corporate spying in Korea by imposing criminal penalties on former employees for divulging trade secrets. In 2004, the government further strengthened the scope of protection for trade secrets by extending the scope of punishable offenses and increasing the penalty for the employer of infringers, etc. In 2006, the Industrial Technology Leak Prevention and Protection Support Act (ITPA) was enacted to increase the protection of domestic industrial technology by seeking to prevent certain key technologies from flowing outside of Korea, thereby promoting technological development and national security. Since 2009, the UCPA has been amended to include: (i) relaxation of trade secret requirements (Article 2(2)); (ii) certification of the original document of trade secrets (Article 9*bis*); (iii) "punitive damages" for intentional or willful trade secret Infringement; and (iv) strengthening penalties for trade secret infringements (Article 18).

2. DEFINITION OF TRADE SECRETS

A definition of a "trade secret" can be found in Article 2(2) of the UCPA. According to this provision, a trade secret is any technical or business information deemed useful for production, sale methods, and other business activities, which is not known to the public, is of independent economic value and is managed as a secret[4]. *Topic 1* introduces a leading case in which these requirements were discussed. Trade secrets can be classified into two categories: "technical" and "business or administrative." Technical trade secrets related to technical information such as design methods, blueprints, get-ups, devices, patterns or manufacturing processes[5], experimental data, know-how[6], raw material ratios, or formulae for measuring strength. Protectable "business" information includes such diverse aspects as customer lists, production and selling programs for new products, selling systems, bookkeeping rules, and office management rules.

3. INFRINGING ACTS

3.1. General Aspects

In Korea, the UCPA provides a number of provisions for various types of trade secret infringement. The provisions may overlap with the contractual protection of trade secrets, which is not limited to contractual relationships.

3. Byung-Il Kim, *supra*, note 1, at 404.
4. Seoul High Court decision 95La193 (June 29, 1996). The UCPA requires the owner to make some efforts to maintain secrecy. The necessary effort was broadly described as "considerable," or "reasonable." However, Article 2(2) of the 2019 revised UCPA relaxes the criterion for trade secrets from "maintained as a secret by reasonable effort" to "managed as a secret."
5. Supreme Court decision 96Da16605 (December 23, 1996).
6. Supreme Court decision 7Da8229 (June 13, 1997).

Infringement of trade secrets is divided into six categories but basically falls into two types: unfair acquisition (Article 2(3)(a)), and the breach of an obligation to maintain the confidentiality of trade secrets (Article 2(3)(d)). The four other types of infringement can be described as ex post facto behavior. The following six acts enumerated in the UCPA are considered an infringement of trade secrets:

- obtaining a trade secret by theft, fraud, coercion or other unfair means, or use of the trade secret, or disclosure to the public (or a specific person) (Article 2(3)(a));
- obtaining, using or disclosing a trade secret knowing that it was unfairly obtained, or without knowledge of the fact owing to gross negligence (Article 2(3)(b));
- use or disclosure to the public of any trade secret with knowledge after the fact that it was obtained unfairly, or without knowledge of the fact owing to gross negligence (Article 2(3)(c));
- using or publicly disclosing a trade secret contrary to contractual secrecy, with the intention of obtaining an unfair benefit or inflicting loss on the owner of the trade secret (Article 2(3)(d));
- obtaining, using or disclosing a trade secret knowing that it was disclosed to the public under the conditions stated in subsection (d), or without knowledge of the fact owing to gross negligence (Article 2(3)(e)); and
- using or disclosing a trade secret to the public with subsequent knowledge that it was disclosed to the public under the conditions of subsection (d), or without knowledge of the fact owing to gross negligence (Article 2(3)(f)).

3.2. Acquisition of Trade Secret by Unfair or Unlawful Means

Article 2(3)(a) UCPA covers all cases where trade secrets are acquired by unlawful means and is applicable particularly to cases where persons obtain knowledge of another's trade secrets by means that contravene criminal law or ethical standards[7]. "Unfair or unlawful means" include the use of physical force, break-ins, and theft, as well as obtaining disclosure through misrepresentation or other forms of industrial espionage[8]. On the other hand, Article 2(3)(a) cannot be applied to cases of discovery by independent research or by reverse engineering, by starting with the known product and working backward to find the method by which it was developed[9].

In addition, and according to Article 2(3)(b) UCPA, it is considered a misappropriation to obtain a trade secret knowing that it has been obtained by an act of improper acquisition, or even without knowing, should this be due to gross negligence. This provision applies to cases where third parties are involved in the subsequent misappropriation of improperly acquired trade secrets. Therefore, any user of a trade secret

7. Supreme Court decision96 Da 16605 (December 23, 1996).
8. Kook-Hyun Kim, *Yeongeob Bimil Boho e Kwanhan Peob Silmu* (Trade Secret Law) (Seoul, 2010), at 63.
9. Supreme Court decision 96Da16605 (December 23, 1996); Jun-Seok Park, in Sang-Jo Jong (ed.), *Bujeong Gyeongjaeng Bangjibeob Juhai* [Commentary on the Unfair Competition Prevention Act], Seoul, 2020, at 343.

who subsequently receives notice that the trade secret has been misappropriated will have to cease using it. In addition, Article 2(3)(c) is applicable to acts of use or disclosure even if at the time of acquisition the subsequent user had no knowledge of the fact that the trade secret was obtained by unfair means, or had no reasonable grounds to suspect this.

3.3. Breach of Confidentiality

Article 2(3)(d) UCPA concerns the misappropriation of trade secrets lawfully acquired from the rightful owner. Article 2(3)(d) UCPA is applicable to the use or public disclosure of a trade secret contrary to a contractual obligation to secrecy with the intention of obtaining an unfair benefit or of inflicting loss on the owner of the trade secret. Trade secrets are usually disclosed to third parties in various business relationships, such as licensing, engineering, or employment agreements[10]. In these cases, the obligation to confidentiality arises from the circumstances in which the information was imparted. In its most common form, such an obligation is established by means of a contract with express terms dealing with confidentiality, or in the absence thereof, by implied terms depending on the nature of the contract[11]. The obligation of confidentiality may extend beyond the termination of such an agreement. However, the same applies when a trade secret has already been disclosed before a contractual agreement can be reached, even if negotiations should subsequently fail. In addition, the obligation can arise from statutory law[12] or fiduciary relationships[13]. Therefore, any breach of confidentiality constitutes not only a breach of contract (with contractual remedies to the injured party)[14] but also a misappropriation of trade secrets under the UCPA[15]. Topic 2 deals with the validity and scope of confidentiality and/or noncompetition clauses.

Furthermore, according to Article 2(3)(e) UCPA, it is a misappropriation of trade secrets to obtain, use or disclose a trade secret knowing that it was disclosed to the public under the conditions stated in clause (d), or without knowing such fact owing to gross negligence. Where the subsequent owner or user should have known that the trade secret was disclosed contrary to a secrecy obligation or had reasonable grounds to suspect such a fact, such conduct constitutes a misappropriation of trade secrets.

This applies even if the disclosure contrary to an obligation of secrecy was unknown at the time of acquisition (Article 2(3)(f) UCPA).

4. PROTECTION OF TRADE SECRETS WITHIN A TRIAL

The practical aspects of maintaining secrecy in court proceedings are difficult to handle. In order to seek a legal remedy for trade secret infringement, the owner of the

10. *See* Kook-Hyun Kim, *supra*, note 8, at 67-68.
11. Byung-Il Kim, *supra*, note 1, at 40; Kook-Hyun Kim, *supra*, note 8, at 68-69.
12. Article 60 of the Public Officials Act, Article 52 of the Local Officials Act, Article 26 of the Attorney's Act, and Article 23 of the Patent Attorney's Act.
13. Seoul High Court decision 94Na37303 (May 25, 1995).
14. For example, *see* Article 350 of the Civil Code (Breach of Contract).
15. Supreme Court decision 96Da16605 (December 23, 1996).

trade secret has to specify the alleged trade secret and prove the misappropriation[16]. This may make the owner fear that the status of the trade secret will be lost in the proceedings unless measures are taken to protect it within a trial. Since the Korean Constitution requires court trials to be open to the public[17], there is still the possibility that trade secrets may be leaked or disclosed to the other party or a third party during the trial process. So, the owner of a trade secret needs in camera proceedings[18] where the public is excluded and only the opposing parties and their attorneys may participate[19].

The principle of open trial, which gives the right to be heard priority over the interest in protecting trade secrets, may result in a party having to decide between disclosing trade secrets or losing the action due to lack of evidence[20]. At the same time, it must be taken into account that property is protected under Article 23 of the Constitution. This is why the Code of Civil Procedure (CPA) must try to balance both interests, i.e., an enterprise's concern in relation to property and the public's interest in an open trial.

Under the 2011 amended UCPA, in trade secret infringement lawsuits related to the infringement of business interests, the court, at a party's request, may order the other party, its legal counsel, or any other entity that has acquired the trade secret due to such lawsuit not to use such trade secrets for purposes other than for continuing the lawsuit nor to disclose these trade secrets to others, provided that the applicant shows or vindicates that the evidence contains or would contain trade secrets and there is a risk of business disruption without such confidentiality order (Article 14-4). Furthermore, if a party can prove that the case files contain its trade secrets, a court, at the party's request, may prohibit nonparties from accessing or copying the case files (Article 163 of CPA). Although trade secrets are protected de jure by the UCPA, de facto there is no effective protection. Article 163 of CPA allows exclusion of third parties from the inspection of court records, but this is no help for the other party to the suit. For the effective protection of trade secrets, one would essentially have to reform the CPA to

16. The extent of specificity of a trade secret should be determined by considering various factors, including the content and nature of the individual information alleged as a trade secret; content of information known in the relevant field; specific aspects of trade secret misappropriation and content of claim for injunction; and relationship between the trade secret owner and the other party. If the trade secret is not specific enough, the court will dismiss the plaintiff's claim (*see* Supreme Court decision 2011Ma1624 (August 22, 2013).
17. According to Article 109 Korean Constitution, trials and decisions of the courts shall be open to the public. However, trials may be closed to the public by court decision, when there is a danger that such trials may undermine the national security or disturb public safety and order, or be harmful to public morals.
18. In the USA, this was acknowledged in the following decisions: *John T Lloyd Laboratories, Inc. v Lloyd Broat Pharmacist, Inc.*, 131 F.2d 703, 707 (6th Cir. 1942); *E.L. Bruce Co. v Bradley Lumber Co.*, 79 F. Supp. 176 (W.D. Ark. 1948).
19. Rudolf Callmann, *The Law of Unfair Competition, Trademarks and Monopolies*, Vol. 2 (4th ed, Wilmette, Ill. 1982) § 14.41.
20. Kab-Ju Jung, "*Know-how ui Boho*" (The Protection of Know-How), in Beobweon Haengjeongcheo (ed.), "Chitcheok Soyukkweon e daehan Jemunje (Ha)" (Problems in Intellectual Property Law (Vol. II), Jaepan Jaryo, Vol. 57, 1992, at 254.

include provisions for in camera proceedings, sealing court records, and prohibiting any disclosure of the trade secret without the court's permission[21].

Recently, Korean Intellectual Property Office (KIPO) has initiated steps to introduce a discovery system adapted to the judicial regime of Korea. The KIPO is contemplating improving the effectiveness of current evidence-gathering procedures, plans to complete the revisions to the Patent Act and the UCPA by the end of 2021, and implement the new discovery system by 2022.

5. REMEDIES

The UCPA provides for the right to claim injunctive relief and damages as civil remedies for the infringement of a trade secret[22]. In addition, a claim to restore one's business reputation is also provided (Articles 10-12).

5.1. Injunctive Relief

According to Article 10(1) UCPA, any person whose business interest is likely to be damaged as a result of another person infringing a trade secret may file a restraint action with the court. A claim for injunctive relief can be granted not only against acts which have already occurred but also against those that are imminent. Article 10(2) UCPA allows for a preventive claim for an injunction if there are objective circumstances whereby infringement is likely to be committed by a potential infringer. In addition, the UCPA provides that any person whose business interests have been or are likely to be damaged as a result of the infringement may not only request cessation of the unlawful act, but also the implementation of measures to prevent future infringement, e.g., destruction and removal of the medium on which the trade secret is recorded, or any measures necessary to prohibit or prevent any further infringement. The person causing the infringement must take proper measures to eliminate concrete disturbances and to prevent recurrences[23].

A claim for injunctive relief ensues from an objective act of infringement so that in principle a perpetrator's good or bad faith does not matter, and neither does intention or negligence, which is different from general tort law. Hence, proof of the offense as such, for example, the unlawful acquisition of a trade secret[24], is sufficient for a claim for injunctive relief.

A claim for a no-fault injunction may be brought before a civil court only by a person whose business interests have been or are likely to be damaged as a result of an

21. *See* Kyung-Jik Kwak, "*Yeongeob Bimil eui Chimhae wa Guje & Sosongsang eui Jemunje*" (Infringement of a Trade Secret and Its Remedies), *Human Rights and Justice*, Vol. 250 (1997), at 59 et seq.
22. In the case of contractual protection, a breach of contract gives the injured party a right to an action for damages (Article 390 of the Civil Code) or specific performance (Article 389 of the Civil Code). Unlike under the German Civil Code, injunctive relief may not be claimed in a case of breach of contract.
23. Supreme Court decision 7Daka90 (April 12, 1988).
24. *See* Byung-Il Kim, *supra*, note 1, at 413.

infringement[25]. Injunctive relief would thus be available to owners of trade secrets, but not to trade associations or consumers, because they cannot produce any proof of direct injury to their business interests[26]. The concept of "business interests" must always be broadly interpreted[27]. Business interests do not refer to commercial transactions in a strict sense—simple activities of an economic nature are sufficient[28].

Korean courts normally do not grant permanent injunctions in trade secret cases, but rather for a period of only two to three years[29]. Proceedings for provisional injunctions are available according to Article 300 of the Civil Enforcement Act[30]. Courts generally require a security to be furnished before issuing an interlocutory injunction[31]. Exactly what type of claims can be allowed for such an injunction is not completely clear.

The right to injunctive relief is time-barred for three years after obtaining knowledge of the facts that would give rise to such claim, or after ten years have elapsed from the date of the wrongful act (Article 14). In addition to injunctive relief, the plaintiff may request the destruction of articles that constituted the trade secret misappropriation, removal of the equipment used for the misappropriation, or other measures for suspension or prevention of the misappropriation[32]. *Topic 5* introduces a Supreme Court case related to the length of permanent injunctive relief for trade secret misappropriation.

5.2. Damages

According to Article 11 UCPA, any person whose business interests have been damaged as a result of a trade secret infringement may bring a claim for damages before a civil court if the infringer has acted intentionally or negligently. Unlike injunctive relief, an action for damages requires proof of damages as a result of unfair competitive activities and a causal link between the infringement and the damages. Article 11 UCPA is *lex specialis* to the general tort clause under Article 750 Korean Civil Code.

However, an infringer is presumed to have acted at least negligently according to Article 112 Trade Mark Act, Article 130 Patent Act, Article 30 Utility Model Act, and Article 116 Design Act, unless proven otherwise. Yet the UCPA does not contain a

25. Supreme Court decision 80Da829 (December 9, 1980).
26. Sang-Jo Jong, "Uncertainties Relating to Computer Program Protection in Japan and Korea" *Korean Journal of Comparative Law*, Vol. 20 (1992), at 62.
27. *See* Ui-Chang Hwang and Kwang-Yeon Hwang, *Bujeong Kyungjaeng Bangji Yeongeob Bimil Boho e Kwanhan Peob* [Unfair Competition and Trade Secret Law] (Seoul, 2011), at 245-246.
28. Supreme Court decision 73Da1238 (February 24, 1976).
29. Supreme Court decisions 96Da16605 (December 23, 1996) and 97Da24528 (February 13, 1998).
30. Supreme Court decisions 97Da24528 (February 13, 1998).
31. Seoul District Court decision 94Gahab12987 (March 27, 1995).
32. *See* Supreme Court decision 96Da16605 (December 23, 1996) (ordering a defendant to return to a plaintiff a note on which the defendant had written down the plaintiff's trade secret).

comparable provision with such a legal presumption. Therefore, the plaintiff bears the burden of proving intention or negligence on the part of the defendant[33].

The amount of damages is determined by the general principles of tort law[34]. According to Article 394 Civil Code, the method of recovery is by a monetary award. In the event of a trade secret infringement, it is very difficult to prove: (1) that damages have been sustained, and (2) the extent of such damages. Under the UCPA, there are generally three methods for calculating damages for infringement of a trade secret infringement: lost profit (Article 14*bis* (1)), infringer's profit (Article 14*bis* (2)), and reasonable royalty (Article 14*bis* (3)). The UCPA included a special provision allowing the amount of damages to be presumed to be equivalent to the sales of the infringing product multiplied by the claimant's profit per product (Article 14*bis* (1)). This calculation method, however, is subject to the limitation that if the infringer's sales exceed the patentee's own production capacity, damages under this method cannot be awarded for such excess sales. The 2021 Amendment increases the scope of damages available to a trade secret's owner under this provision, by allowing the patentee to claim some damages for the infringer's sales beyond the owner's own production capacity. The trade secret's owner will now be allowed to claim (i) damages for infringing products up to the owner's own production capacity based on a "lost profits" calculation where the sales of infringing products are multiplied by the owner's profit per product, and (ii) damages for infringing products exceeding the owner's production capacity in an amount calculated by multiplying the sales of such excess infringing products by a reasonable royalty rate profit (Article 14*bis* (1)). The profit that the infringer has gained is presumed to be the damages that the trade secret's owner sustained profit (Article 14*bis* (2)). The infringer's profit can include the infringer's increased revenues, decreased production cost, avoided development costs, etc. As a minimum amount of damages, the owner is entitled to a reasonable royalty, which would normally be charged for a license for the same kind of technology (Article 14*bis* (3)). In addition, Article 14*bis* (4) provides for damages compensation exceeding reasonable royalty and reduction of damages considering minor negligence. *Topic 5 also* discusses court decisions on damages calculation.

If proving damages by any of the above methods is not possible due to the facts of a particular case, the court has the discretion to determine a reasonable amount of damages based on an examination of all of the evidence and the parties' arguments (Article 14*bis* (5)). In case the trade secret infringement is found wilful, the court may award up to treble damages (Article 14*bis* (6)). In addition, the court may order the defendant to produce documents which prove the turnover of the infringing goods (Article 14*ter*).

---

33. *See* Young-Jun Yang, "Yeongeob Bimil eui Boho" [Protection of Trade Secrets], in Sang-Jo Jong (ed.), *Chitcheok Chaesankkweon Peopgangeui* [Explanation of Intellectual Property Law], Seoul, 1997, at 594.
34. *Ibid.*, at 595.

6. CRIMINAL SANCTIONS

Trade secret infringement may be criminally prosecuted as larceny (Article 329) or breach of trust (Article 355) under the Korean Penal Code, in addition to the UCPA and the ITPA.

6.1. The 2019 Amended UCPA Expanded the Scope of Punishable Acts

The UCPA criminalizes trade secrets infringement only in the following circumstances: acquisition of a trade secret, in order to gain improper profits or to inflict harm on the owner of such trade secret; unauthorized use of a trade secret; and unauthorized disclosure of a trade secret. However, the 2019 amended UCPA expanded the scope of infringement and now includes the following forms of trade secret infringement: (i) taking information outside of a designated area without authorization; (ii) refusing to comply with the owner's request to return or destroy information; (iii) acquisition by improper means; and (iv) re-acquisition and use of misappropriated trade secrets with knowledge of (i), (ii), or (iii). The UCPA clarifies that while employees have an obligation to either destroy or return the employers' trade secrets before resigning, employers have an obligation to (i) clearly designate areas and boundaries where information can be taken and (ii) expressly require employees to either return or destroy trade secrets. Although employers would have a burden of setting up and maintaining compliance programs for their trade secrets, e.g., designated areas and assigning compliance personnel, employers equipped with such compliance programs can now effectively claim trade secret theft even against a mere data leak, and thus will be entitled to strong protection under the UCPA[35]. In addition, the UCPA strengthens statutory punishment for trade secret infringement as follows[36]:

Type of Act	*Classification*	*Previous → Amendment*
Domestic trade secret Infringement (Article 18(2))	Imprisonment	Up to 5 years → up to 10 years
	Penalty	Up to KRW 50 million → up to KRW 500 million (If ten times of the proprietary benefit exceeds KRW 500 million, the penalty shall be two to ten times the proprietary benefit)
Foreign trade secret Infringement (Article 18(1))	Imprisonment	Up to 10 years → up to 15 years
	Penalty	Up to KRW 100 million → up to KRW 1.5 billion (If ten times the proprietary benefit exceeds KRW 1.5 billion, the penalty shall be at least two to ten times the proprietary benefit and up to ten times the proprietary benefit)

35. *Yulchon LLC*, Korea Strengthens Protections of Patents and Trade Secrets—Treble Damages, Changes in Burdens of Proof, and More, https://www.lexology.com/library/detail.aspx?g=264c775e-e702-4009-8979-190a962731cf (last visit March 23, 2021.)
36. *Ibid.*

According to Supreme Court's Sentencing Guidelines (May 15, 2017), sentencing periods related to trade secret infringements follow as:

Classification	*Mitigated Sentencing Range*	*Standard Sentencing Range*	*Aggravated Sentencing Range*
Infringement within the Country	~ 10 month	8 month ~ 2 yrs	1 yr ~ 4 yrs
Infringement outside of the Country	10 month ~ 1 yr 6 months	1 yr ~ 3yrs 6 months	2 yrs ~ 6 yrs

Unlike the Sentencing Guideline, the maximum sentence for foreign infringement is 12 months between 2017 and 2019, which is similar to or even lower than domestic infringement[37].

It must be noted that the UCPA punishes attempts, preparation, and conspiracy (Articles 18*bis* and 18*ter)* and that actions described in Article 18(1) and (2) can be pursued by prosecutors without a request by the infringed party. Further, if an employee commits the violation, the employee's employer is vicariously liable for the violation unless the employer can prove that it was not negligent in preventing such violations (Article 19). However, it is very difficult to prove the duty of supervisory attention to employee violations, although the Supreme Court holds that the issue of whether a corporation neglected its duty of considerable attention or supervision shall be determined by comprehensively taking into account all the circumstances related to the violation in question[38]. Therefore, an employer has to set up and maintain a compliance program for trade secret protection and provide education to its employees about their obligations under the UCPA.

6.2. Exceptions for Innocent Acquisition

The provisions of Articles 10-12 do not apply to the use or disclosure of a trade secret lawfully acquired by a transaction permissible under Article 13 UCPA. "A person who has lawfully acquired a trade secret through a legitimate transaction" is one who has acquired the trade secret in a manner described in Article 2(2)(c) or (f), without knowing or being grossly negligent in failing to know at the time of acquisition that the trade secret had been improperly disclosed or acquired. In this way, the UCPA tries to minimize unforeseeable risks for an inadvertent buyer. Therefore, a person who acquires a trade secret in good faith through a business transaction is exempt from liability so long as the trade secret is used or disclosed within the authorized scope.

37. KIPO, 2017-2019 UCPA cases analysis study (in Korean), 2020, at 142-143.
38. Supreme Court decision 2009Do5824 (February 25, 2010).

TOPIC 1 THE REQUIREMENTS OF SECRECY MANAGEMENT: FROM "REASONABLE EFFORTS" TO "MANAGED AS A SECRET"

Byungil Kim

1. Legal Issues

The major issues in the present case are the meaning of "reasonable efforts to maintain secrecy" of the requirements of trade secrets under UCPA.

2. The Statutory Law

Under Article 2(2) of the UCPA amended by Act No. 8767, December 21, 2007, trade secrets were defined as any technical or business information that is useful for the production, sales method, and other business activities, not known to the public, of independent economic value, and kept secret through considerable effort. In other words, requirements for trade secret protection were: not known to the public, considerable efforts taken to maintain secrecy and independent economic value.

There had been criticism that the requirements for secrecy management were too strict, making it difficult for small- and medium-sized enterprises (SMEs) to protect a business or technical secrets. Therefore, the term "considerable effort" was replaced by "reasonable effort" on January 28, 2015[39].

However, the misappropriation claims were often dismissed due to lack of "considerable or reasonable effort" to protect trade secrets, so the newly revised Article 2(2) of the UCPA (amended by Act No. 16204, January 8, 2019), replaces the requirement to show "reasonable effort" with "maintained as a secret"[40] and now reads "The term 'trade secret' means information, including a production method, sales method, useful technical or business information for business activities, that is not publicly known, is maintained as a secret, and has an independent economic value."

3. The Case Law

Since the 2015 amendment to the UCPA, which replaced "considerable effort" with "reasonable effort," there has been no Supreme Court precedent applying the "reasonable effort" standard. The Supreme Court has not provided a criterion for distinguishing the "reasonable effort" standard from the "considerable effort" standard. Rather, Korean courts seem to take a similar approach regarding the requirements of "reasonable effort" and "considerable effort."

---

39. The meaning "considerable" seems to have the same meaning as "reasonable" under the Uniform Trade Secret Act (published by the Uniform Law Commission (ULC) in 1979 and amended in 1985, promulgated for adoption by states in the United States). *See* Hyun-Soo Kim, "Trade Secret Law, Intellectual Property and Innovation: Theoretical, Empirical, and Asian Perspectives" (Ph.D. dissertation, University of Illinois at Urbana-Champaign 2010), at 126-127.
40. Kim & Chang, Amended Patent Act and Trade Secret Act to Provide Stringer Protection of Right Holders, Newsletter (2019, 8, 6).

3.1. *Positive Examples from the Supreme Court*

Decision 2012Do7874 (October 25, 2012)

The court acknowledged a reasonable degree of effort to maintain secrecy when the company (holder of the trade secret) had required a confidentiality agreement that prohibited disclosure of trade secrets and incorporated a noncompetition clause. In addition, the company restricted access to the natural source compounding room and the powder sauce compounding room when making the fish soup, and installed and managed closed-circuit monitors around the entrances.

Decision 2006Do7916 (July 9, 2009)

The court acknowledged a reasonable degree of effort to maintain secrecy when a company took internal measures to restrict access to a computer aided design (CAD) file and technical data at issue. The company also imposed confidentiality obligations on the Korea Railroad Corporation when entering into a resource purchase contract, and explicit and implied confidential obligations on the company (pertaining to the files above) that commissioned the creation of an electronic manual for the CAD file at issue.

Decision 2007Do11409 (July 24, 2008)

The court acknowledged a reasonable degree of effort to maintain secrecy when IP addresses, ID's and passwords were necessary to access the server of the company (the holder of the source files constituting the program on the internet).

Decision 2004Do6576 (September 15, 2005)

The court acknowledged a reasonable degree of effort to maintain secrecy when the plaintiffs received confidentiality pledges from the defendants and enforced a transfer security system and industrial security management regulations on them.

Decision 96Da16605 (December 23, 1996)

The court acknowledged a reasonable degree of effort to maintain secrecy when the plaintiff company set up a separate laboratory in the factory so that no unauthorized personnel could enter, imposed a confidentiality obligation on all the employees, and strictly controlled the technical information under the management of the director of research.

3.2. *Negative Examples from the Supreme Court*

Decision 2008Do3436 (September 10, 2009)

The court did not acknowledge a reasonable degree of effort to maintain secrecy when the defendant entered a confidentiality agreement with the company the day before his retirement, the computer where the material of this case was kept had no password and separate lock, anyone could easily access, read and copy the material through any computer in the company, and the drawer which contained the backup CD for the material was always open.

Decision 2006Do8498 (January 30, 2009)

The court did not acknowledge a reasonable degree of effort to maintain secrecy when the company did not provide separate security education or classify the experiment results of this case as secure data. On top of that, the computer in which the experiment results were stored was placed on the desk where the defendant was working without any security devices, the office where the defendant worked was not separated from other people, and there was no one to stop the defendant when he took the computer out. Thus, although the defendant executed a general security agreement when he joined the company, secrecy management was denied.

Decision 2008Do3435 (July 10, 2008)

Although some of the defendants had executed a general trade secret confidentiality agreement when joining the company, there was no security manager assigned for the files created at work, and no security devices or security controls. There was no classification according to importance or any special marks to indicate that the material was confidential or secret files. Information stored on the file server could be accessed, read, and copied freely by even production staff and from individual computers on the internal network. A reasonable degree of effort was not acknowledged.

To summarize, "considerable effort" required taking into account the following: intention to maintain confidentiality, storing the trade secret in a place with limited access (e.g., at a physical location or in a server or folder in the case of electronic information), limiting access to such storage, specifying the method of storing or destroying the confidential data, assigning specific staff to handle the secret, or imposing confidentiality obligations. Courts found it difficult to acknowledge secrecy management when any employee could access the information without special restrictions, or when the information was of a type that a long-time employee would know of it[41]. Therefore, if the owner simply executes a general business confidentiality agreement, and does not specify the business secret or takes no separate action, it would be difficult to recognize "considerable effort." However, it may be possible to manage the secrecy by appropriate methods that are commensurate with the size of the company or the value of the secrets to avoid excessive costs from incurring to maintain secrecy[42].

41. Supreme Court decisions 2008Do3435 (July 10, 2008), 2011Do139 (August 25, 2011), and 2012Do12828 (August 20, 2014).
42. The 2019 UCPA amendment has been expected to make it substantially easier to pursue legitimate claims against parties who misappropriate trade secrets. However, a certain level of effort is required to meet the secrecy requirement. Reasonable effort standards will continue to be considered in evaluating the owner's efforts to protect secrecy. However, Korean courts will respect the purpose of the UCPA amendment and relax the level of "effort" in interpreting the

4. The Leading Case

The present decision is the leading case because it was a representative precedent which provides comprehensive criteria for considerable effort. The case also clarifies that in evaluating the owner's efforts to protect secrecy, courts usually consider several factors and circumstances, in order to balance the costs of keeping the information secret with the benefits of the alleged trade secrets that vary from case to case.

4.1. Case Information

Supreme Court Decision 2017Do13791 (October 31, 2019).

4.2. Summary

The Supreme Court reversed the appellate court's ruling for evaluating the trade secret owner's efforts to protect secrecy, based on the following factors: details of the preventive measures of the owner; business needs to grant access to the corresponding information; confidential relationship between the owner and the invader of the trade secrets and its extent; economic value of the trade secrets; and business scale and economic capacity of the owner of the trade secrets.

4.3. Facts

The defendant company granted wholesale stores a specific liquor license of a one-year exclusive right to sell liquor in a certain area, and the wholesale stores handled only the product of the defendant company in return.

The wholesale store managers in this case ("the instant managers") are independent merchants who have registered and do business independently. The instant managers respectively managed and utilized their own information about transactions and customers through personal computers (PC) or account books. In 2002, the defendant company established the wholesale store computer system at its own expense to efficiently manage and utilize the information about customers with whom the wholesale stores traded. In 2006, the defendant company provided personal digital assistants (PDA) to wholesale stores and had the wholesale stores enter the transaction information into the PDA. The wholesale stores entered the information on sales partners, sales information, and transaction terms, etc. of liquor products ("the instant information") through the PDA or a PC.

The instant information entered by the instant managers were stored on the server owned and managed by the defendant company. The defendant company also used the instant information for business operations when necessary for the establishment of a business plan, setting sales targets for each retail shop within wholesale stores, inventory management, etc. The instant managers knew of the fact that the defendant company was using the instant information, and did not raise any objection

current law. Jun-Seok Park, in Sang-Jo Jong (ed.), *Bujeong Gyeongjaeng Bangjibeob Juhai* [Commentary on the Unfair Competition Prevention Act], Seoul, 2020, at 315-316.

for six to seven years prior to the occurrence of this case. The instant managers and the defendant company did not conclude any confidentiality agreement for the instant information.

Within the defendant company, employees in charge of the management of wholesale stores could only access the instant information entered by the instant managers within the scope of their work. However, employees at the business headquarters of the defendant company, who maintained and managed the wholesale store computer system, could see the instant information, and no security procedures were established. The instant managers set a password in the wholesale store computer system according to their ID, but also informed the sales staff of the defendant company managing their wholesale store of the password and requested that they place orders for business convenience.

The instant managers obtained the instant information in the course of conducting business with the exclusive right to sell liquor in a certain area granted by company B. The instant managers and the defendant company jointly used the instant information for the duration of the business relationship. However, the instant managers whose business relationship with the defendant company had ended could no longer use the information. Around May 2010, the defendant company added that it "provides the portal system to the wholesale store free of charge, and the ownership of various data generated by the wholesale store using the portal system shall be shared by it and the wholesale store during the contract period, and the ownership shall be owned by it after the contract period" to Article 14(2) of the newly amended wholesale store contract.

The defendant company, without the permission of the instant managers, supported the company in competition with the instant managers by using the instant information. The instant managers sued the defendant company on the ground that from March 2009 to March 2010 the defendant company infringed on their trade secrets, and the prosecutor indicted company B for infringing trade secrets.

The first instance court held that the instant information stored in the wholesale store computer system was not known publicly, had independent economic value, was maintained by considerable effort, and therefore constituted "trade secret" under Article 2(2) of the UCPA, and the defendant had infringed upon it[43]. The appellate court affirmed the first instance judgment[44]. However, the decision was reversed by the Supreme Court upon appeal.

4.4. Reasoning of the Court

The Korean Supreme Court reiterated the holding from its previous decisions: "The term 'trade secret' as referred to in Article 2(2) of the UCPA means information, including the production method, sales method and useful technical or business information for business activities, that is not known publicly, is the subject of

43. Seoul Central District Court decision 2014Godan9055 (October 25, 2016).
44. Seoul Central District Court decision 2016No4411 (August 18, 2019).

considerable effort to maintain its secrecy, and has independent economic value."[45] The meaning of "being the subject of considerable effort to maintain its secrecy" is a condition by which it can be objectively shown that the information is kept and managed securely by using marks or notices that enable the public to recognize that the information includes secrets, limiting access to the said information in terms of either persons or means, or imposing confidentiality duty upon those having access to the information[46].

The Korean Supreme Court ruled further that whether the effort for such maintenance and management is considerable ought to be determined by comprehensively taking into account the following: details of the preventive measures of the owner of the trade secrets; business needs to grant access to the corresponding information; the confidential relationship between the owner and the invader of the trade secrets and its degree; the economic value of the trade secrets; and the business scale and economic capacity of the owner of the trade secrets. The Supreme Court then pointed out that:

- The instant managers recognized that the defendant company had managed the instant information through the wholesale store computer system, but did not raise any objection. Therefore, it was difficult to say that they were willing to keep and manage the instant information confidentially.
- The instant managers seemed to have actually delegated the management of the wholesale store computer system to the defendant company.
- It could not be seen that the instant managers had taken measures such as preventing the defendant company and its employees from accessing the instant information, and it seemed difficult for its employees to recognize that "the instant information was maintained and managed as confidential by the instant managers."
- The instant managers needed to enter an ID and password to access the wholesale store computer system. However, this was only a basic identity verification procedure set by the defendant company to access the wholesale store computer system, so it was difficult to view it as a preventive measure for the instant information. Even if the person in charge of the defendant company's business had a duty not to disclose the instant information to an organization in a competitive relationship under the principle of good faith, it was difficult to pursue the confidentiality of the information by itself.

Therefore, it could not be said that the instant managers, who were trade secret holders, managed the instant information as confidential in relation to the defendant company.

45. Supreme Court decision 98Do4704 (March 12, 1999).
46. Supreme Court decision 2008Do3435 (July 10, 2008).

4.5. Legal Analysis

4.5.1. Definition of Trade Secrets

Under Article 2(2) of the UCPA, the three requirements for trade secret protection under the UCPA are:

- the information must not be known to the public;
- it must have independent economic value; and
- reasonable efforts must have been made to keep it secret.

The first requirement is that the information must not be known to the public at large. Secrecy may still exist where there is not sufficient access to the elements necessary for its economic application, even though certain other elements are known[47]. Information can qualify as secret even if it can be readily accessed by persons other than one's competitors. Information readily obtainable does not fall within the definition of a trade secret. The Supreme Court has affirmed the principle that the owner of a trade secret will not lose the trade secret if the information is revealed to another party in confidence and under the implied obligation not to use or disclose it[48]. As distinct from protection under patent law, the information need not be novel or inventive[49]. This applies to trade secrets as a whole, but also components thereof. The information may already be widely known, but still be protected if its composition is applicable in a different way, with different results, or in a different context unknown to third parties[50]. It is important to note that information is regarded as secret if accessible only under great expenditure of time and money, for example, reverse engineering of products[51]. Furthermore, any protectable information has to have an independent economic value. The trade secret is valuable insofar as it gives a competitive advantage to the owner vis-à-vis its competitors[52]. In one case, the Supreme Court found that a competitor could not duplicate the information without investing a significant amount of time, effort, and expense and that the level of secrecy was sufficient for the owner to derive significant economic value therefrom[53]. Thus, a

47. Ho-Yeol Chung, *Bujeong Kyungjaeng Bangji Peob* [Unfair Competition Law] (Seoul 1993) 247-248; Kook-Hyun Kim, *supra*, note 8, at 18-26.
48. *See* Supreme Court decision 96Da16605 (December 23, 1996).
49. *Ibid.*; Kook-Hyun Kim, *supra*, note 8, at 27-28; Sang-Jeong Lee, "Yeongeob Bimil eui Boho" [Protection of a Trade Secret], *Human Rights and Justice* Vol. 3 (1994), 97.
50. *See* Supreme Court decision 98Da45751 (decided on November 10, 1998) (If the fundamental operating principle or composition of the machinery of this case was already known to the public, it cannot be said that it is a trade secret in itself. However, if the specifications, materials, processing methods, design drawings, etc., of each part of the machinery of this case are not publicly known and have independent economic value, and the production method of or information thereon is kept confidential by considerable efforts, it constitutes trade secret as prescribed by Article 2(2) of the UCPA.).
51. *See* Seoul District Court decision 95Gahab3954 (December 27, 1995); Seoul High Court decisions 95La211 (decided at May 27, 1996) and 95La193 (June 29, 1996); Supreme Court decision 96Da16605 (December 23, 1996).
52. Seoul High Court decision 95La193 (June 29, 1996).
53. Supreme Court decision 96Da31574 (decided on January 26, 1996).

competitor's lack of knowledge can constitute and contain protectable information[54]. Independent value means that the owner of the information has a competitive advantage over his competitor due to the information, which requires substantial costs or effort to obtain or develop[55].

The third and most essential requirement for the protection of trade secrets is the management measures to keep the information secret. The UCPA does not require extreme and unduly expensive measures[56]. The trade secret owner must take reasonable steps to maintain the secrecy of the information in question to qualify for trade secret protection in a way that can be objectively acknowledged as a trade secret, including limiting access to those with a need to know and instructing employees as to what information is secret and how it should be handled[57].

4.5.2. *Lowered Maintenance Requirement for Trade Secrets*

The requirement "reasonable effort" often resulted in the dismissal of misappropriation claims. Therefore, Article 2(2) of the newly revised UCPA relaxes the criterion for trade secrets from "maintained as a secret by reasonable effort" to "managed as a secret." The amendment broadens the scope of information which can be protected as a trade secret and is expected to make it substantially easier to pursue legitimate claims against parties who misappropriate trade secrets in Korea[58]. Information could now be recognized as a trade secret as long as it is managed as a secret even if there was no reasonable effort taken.

4.6. Commercial or Industrial Significance

Legislative relaxation of standards for trade secrets and therefore for trade secret infringement is expected to contribute to the maintenance of a healthy trade order in the Korean industry.

54. *See* Ui-Chang Hwang and Kwang-Yeon Hwang, *Bujeong Kyungjaeng Bangji Yeongeob Bimil Boho e Kwanhan Peob* [Unfair Competition and Trade Secret Law] (Seoul, 2011), at 46-47, 197-198.
55. Supreme Court decision 2005Do6223 (decided on February 16, 2008).
56. *See* Ho-Yeol Chung, *supra*, note47, at 251-252; Sang-Jo Jong, "Protection of Trade Secrets in the Context of Employment" (in Korean), *Beobhag*, Vol. 30, No. 1 (1995) at 164, 172, and 179.
57. Ho-Yeol Chung, *supra*, note 47, at 250-251; Kook-Hyun Kim, *supra*, note 8, at 40-46.
58. Sun R. Kim, Protection of Trade Secrets Through IP and Unfair Competition Law, AIPPI Report Q215, Korea (2010), at 2; Kim & Chang, *supra* note 40.

TOPIC 2 THE VALIDITY AND SCOPE OF CONFIDENTIALITY AND/OR NONCOMPETITION CLAUSES

Byungil Kim

1. Legal Issues

The major issues in the present case are the validity and scope of confidentiality and/or noncompetition clauses under UCPA.

2. The Statutory Law

Under Article 2(Definitions) the terms used in the UCPA shall be defined as follows:

(3) The term "infringement of trade secrets" means any of the following:
  (a) Acquiring trade secrets by theft, deception, coercion or other improper means ("act of improper acquisition"), or subsequently using or disclosing the trade secret improperly (including informing any specific person of the trade secret while under a duty to maintain secrecy; hereinafter the same shall apply).
  (b) Acquiring trade secrets or using or disclosing them with the knowledge that an act of improper acquisition of the trade secrets has occurred or when the lack of such knowledge was caused by gross negligence.
  (c) After trade secrets have been acquired, using or disclosing them with knowledge that an act of improper acquisition of the trade secrets has occurred or when the lack of such knowledge was caused by gross negligence.
  (d) Using or disclosing trade secrets to obtain improper benefits or to damage the owner of the trade secrets while under a contractual or other duty to maintain secrecy of the trade secrets.
  (e) Acquiring trade secrets, or using or disclosing them with the knowledge that the trade secrets have been disclosed in a manner provided in item (d) or when gross negligence was the cause of the disclosure or the lack of such knowledge.
  (f) After acquiring trade secrets, using or disclosing them with the knowledge that they have been disclosed in a manner provided in item (d), or when gross negligence was the cause of the disclosure or the lack of such knowledge.

Article 10 (Injunction against Infringement of Trade Secrets, etc.):

(1) A person who possesses trade secrets may seek a court injunction or preventive order against a person who infringes or is likely to infringe such trade secrets if the business interest of the person who possesses the trade secrets has been or is likely to be damaged by the infringement.
(2) If a person who possesses trade secrets files a claim under paragraph (1) of this section, the person may request the destruction of goods used in the infringement, the removal of facilities used in the infringement, or any other measures necessary to prohibit or prevent the infringement.

Any breach of duty to maintain secrecy constitutes not only a breach of contract under Article 350 of the Civil Code (Breach of Contract) with contractual remedies to the injured party but also a misappropriation of trade secrets under the UCPA. Therefore, Article 2(3)(d) UCPA may overlap with the contractual protection of trade secrets, and both may concurrently apply. If a director of a company is responsible for a breach of confidentiality obligation, the act can be considered a breach of trust under Article 382-4 of the Commercial Code[59] and Article 681[60] of the Civil Code[61].

3. The Case Law

The Korean Supreme Court has found that the "duty of confidentiality" can arise not only from express consent (nondisclosure agreements, confidential agreements, or restrictive covenants) but also from a trust relationship in which the recipient has implicitly consented to the duty of confidence[62]. The Korean Supreme Court further recognized the duty of confidence that arises during the employment relationship or even after termination of the employment relationship[63].

4. The Leading Case

This is a leading case because the Supreme Court for the first time recognized the duty of confidence that arises during the employment relationship or even after termination of the employment relationship and Articles 2(3)(d) and 10(2) of the UCPA as a legal basis for an injunction to prohibit an employee from engaging in specific work in a competing firm in violation of a duty of confidence.

4.1. Case Information

Supreme Court Decision 96Da16605 (December 23, 1996).

4.2. Summary

A former employee took trade secrets concerning an ink formula to a competing company directly after termination of employment, and a preliminary injunction was granted in favor of the proprietor of the trade secret. The Korean Supreme Court agreed

59. Article 382-4 (Directors' Duty of Confidentiality) provides "No director shall divulge any trade secret of the company which has come to his or her knowledge in the course of performing his or her duty, not only while in the office but also after retirement."
60. Article 681 (Mandatary's Duty of Care and Due Diligence) provides "A mandatary shall manage the affairs entrusted to him with the care of a good manager in accordance with the tenor of the mandate."
61. *See* Kab-Ju Jung, "Know-how ui Boho" [The Protection of Know-How], in Beobweon Haengjeongcheo (ed.), *Chitcheok Soyukkweon e daehan Jemunje (Ha)* [Problems in Intellectual Property Law (Vol. II)], *Jaepan Jaryo*, 1997, Vol. 57, 244.
62. Supreme Court decisions 96Da31574 (November 26, 1996), 96Da16605 (December 23, 1996), and 2002Ma4380 (July 16, 2003).
63. Supreme Court decisions 97Da8229 (June 13, 1997), 97Da24528 (February 13, 1998), and 2002Ma4380 (July 16, 2003).

with the appellate court's decision that injunctive relief was available to the plaintiff, based on the principle that the duty of confidentiality can arise from not only an express contract but also an implied duty derived from the facts and circumstances surrounding a particular relationship.

4.3. *Facts*

The technical information relates to the formation ratio and method of ten chemicals, products, and colors, which are the raw materials for ink manufacturing. Information is one of the most important management factors for a writing instrument manufacturer. Company A researched and developed the information by investing 2 to 32 years of time and a lot of human and physical facilities. The information has an independent economic value as technology information which is a key element of Company A's business, and its contents are not generally known. This information is confidential because it is difficult even for employees of company A's research institutes to understand its contents

Company A, since its establishment, has had a separate department in charge of ink R&D and production. Only one copy of the "Manufacturing Data Notes" on 400 kinds of ink manufacturing methods was made and was kept secret by a secrecy marking on the cover. In addition, company A prevented researchers from leaking "research notes" and related data and demanded strict adherence to confidentiality. Company A allowed only relevant personnel to enter the laboratory and imposed an obligation on all employees to maintain confidentiality.

C, as the head of the research department of company A, had been responsible for the research, development, and manufacturing of oil-based ink, and of water-based ink. During his tenure at company A, C wrote down various technical information in his own notebook for reference in developing new ink in the future.

Company A and company B were competing companies that produced and sold writing instruments, such as ballpoint pens. C retired from company A on January 8, 1993, and joined company B on January 1, 1993, and was in charge of R&D and production of ink. When C joined company B, company B had only two employees in charge of development work, and the equipment required for research and development of ink was also inferior to that of company A. C agreed to take charge of the ink manufacturing business at company B, receiving a higher level and salary than that at company A.

C joined company B and worked in the ink production department after leaving company A with his own notebook and used it for business. Company B scouted C to use the ink manufacturing method acquired by C while working for A. After recruiting C, company B produced highlighters that seemed to be the same as or similar to company A's products, without any research.

Consequently, company A filed a lawsuit against company B and C to prohibit infringement of trade secrets by using A's technical information, disclosing it to a third party, or disposing of the notes recorded in C's notebook. The first instance court issued an injunction against the use and disclosure of the trade secrets and held that "The technical information on the manufacturing method of ink, etc. in this case was a trade secret under the UCPA. Defendant C is obligated to maintain confidentiality regarding the technical information for a considerable period of time even after resigning from the plaintiff (company A) based on contractual relations and good faith. The act of acquiring the trade secret and writing it in the notebook owned by C was not a trade secret infringement. However, the act of disclosing the trade secret to company B by manufacturing ink using the technical information written in the notebook while working for company B was a trade secret infringement."[64]

The defendants appealed with the Seoul High Court, which upheld the decision of the first instance court[65]. As to the duty of confidentiality, the appellate court determined that "'Duty to maintain trade secrets as confidential by contract relationship, etc.' under Article 2(3)(d) of the UCPA exists not only where there is contract that explicitly agreed to bear the confidentiality duty, but also where it is deemed to agree or implicitly agree in light of the characteristics of personal trust relationship to assume such duty according to the good faith principle." The Seoul High Court also held that the notebook containing the trade secrets should be considered corresponding to the "goods used in the infringement" in Article 10(2) of the UCPA, so there was a reason for the destruction of this notebook if there was a concern that the infringement of trade secrets would continue. The Supreme Court affirmed the appeal court's decision on this issue.

4.4. *Reasoning of the Court*

The Korean Supreme Court reiterated the holding from its previous decisions.

"Duty to maintain trade secrets as confidential by contract relationship, etc." under Article 2(3)(d) of the UCPA includes not only the case where the contracting party has explicitly agreed to bear the duty to maintain confidentiality but also the case where it is deemed that the contracting party has agreed to assume such duty according to the good faith principle implied in light of the characteristics of a personal trust relationship.

The Korean Supreme Court noted that "Considering various circumstances such as the nondisclosure agreement between company A and C, company A's rules of employment to maintain secrecy, the nature and economic value of the technical information, and the comparison of profits between company A and C, C is obligated to maintain confidentiality of the technical information for a reasonable period after resignation from company A in accordance with the principle of good faith under contractual relationship." Considering "(i) C has benefited from company B, such as receiving a high salary and a higher position and disclosed the technical information to company B in order for company B to use the technical information to profit in terms of reduced time and economic costs in manufacturing ink, (ii) company B itself used the technical information to produce or tried to produce ink," the Korean Supreme Court held that "C's act is committed for the purpose of obtaining unjust profits against

64. Seoul Southern District Court decision94Gahap3033 (February 22, 1994).
65. Seoul High Court decision 95Na14420 (February 22, 1996).

good morals and other social order in light of the principle of fair competition, and constitutes an infringement of trade secrets under Article 2(3)(d) of the UCPA."

Furthermore, the Supreme Court held that inducing a breach of duty to maintain secrecy is "improper means" under Article 2(3)(a) of the UCPA, and pointed out that "Company B did not hire C just to use the general knowledge, skills, and experience that C had acquired during years of working at company A, but to induce violation of a confidential agreement by hiring former employee of company A."

4.5. *Legal Analysis*

4.5.1. *Breach of Confidentiality Obligation*

Article 2(3)(d) UCPA concerns breach of confidentiality obligation. A typical case would involve an employee disclosing a trade secret, lawfully obtained during his employment, to a competing enterprise. The obligation of confidentiality is established by means of a contract with express terms dealing with confidentiality, or in the absence thereof, by implied terms depending on the nature of the contract or by fiduciary relationships[66]. Apart from the explicit consent to maintain secrecy, there may be cases where such duty is recognized based on implicit consent or under a principle of trust[67]. The obligation of confidentiality may extend beyond the termination of such an agreement[68]. However, the same applies when a trade secret has already been disclosed before a contractual agreement can be reached, even if negotiations should subsequently fail.

4.5.2. *The Duty of Noncompetition*

An employee owes a general obligation of secrecy to his employer. This duty may be stated in the employment contract and may include obligations not to use a trade secret or not to compete with the employer[69]. Furthermore, in the absence of any express terms, there are implied terms imposing a duty of good faith or trust on the employee towards his employer (Article 2 of Civil Code)[70]. This duty of trust is based on the close relationship resulting from the employment. The duty of noncompetition is broader and more comprehensive than the one to maintain the confidentiality of trade secrets, and likewise independent of any contractual agreement[71]. The extent of these obligations depends on the position of the employee[72]. Judicial precedents define noncompete clauses as "an agreement that the employee will not engage in competitive behaviour such as being hired by the employer's competitors or establishing and

66. Seoul High Court decision 94Na37303 (May 25, 1995).
67. Supreme Court decision 96Da16605 (decided on December 23, 1996).
68. Byung-Il Kim, *supra*, note 1, at 408; Kook-Hyun Kim, *supra*, note 8, at 68-69.
69. Byung-Il Kim, *supra*, note 1, at 409.
70. *Ibid.*
71. *Ibid.* Restrictive terms are often expressly used to prevent an employee from working for a competitor or setting up a competing business within a given geographical area and for a given period of time.
72. Seoul High Court decision 94 Na 37303 (May 25, 1995).

managing a competing company."[73] It is also impermissible to engage in preparations for setting up a competing enterprise while still in employment. However, there is no general obligation not to prepare post-contractual activities in advance. Such agreements are impermissible if no specific trade secret is involved[74].

The noncompete clause between the employer and the employee is in principle enforceable under the freedom of contract principle. However, such restrictive covenants are enforceable only to the extent they are reasonable and necessary in terms of time, activity, and territory to protect the employer's interests[75]. The covenant will be enforced only if the interests of both parties have been fairly balanced and do not contravene the public interest by depriving the employee of his means of livelihood, restrict the employee's freedom of choice of occupation, or lead to an unjust monopoly[76].

To examine the validity and enforceability of the covenant, courts in Korea have principally considered three aspects: the rights of the freedom to choose an occupation and to engage in work[77], the interests of employers in protecting valuable information[78], and public policy (good morals and other social order, or restraint of free competition)[79]. The reasonableness of a post-employment covenant has been examined based on several factors: the existence of protectable interests of the employer, the former employee's position in the company, duration and geographical scope of the restraint, the field of work, the existence of compensation offered to an employee, reasons for termination of the employment relationship, public interests, and so on[80].

The "protectable interests of the employer" include not only the employer's trade secrets but also exclusive knowledge and information of the employer that the employee agrees to keep as a secret[81]. As for "the former employee's position in the company," covenants not to compete are more likely to be deemed valid if, for example, the employee was a high-ranking executive officer responsible for handing confidential business information or handled such confidential business information for a long period of time. As for "the scope of the restriction," covenants not to compete are likely to be deemed invalid if the scope of the covenants is excessively wide because the employee's freedom to choose an occupation becomes too limited[82]. "The existence

73. Supreme Court decision 2009Da82244 (March 11, 2013).
74. *See* Ho-Yeol Chung, *supra*, note 47, at 279.
75. Seoul District Court decision 96Da16605 (November 7, 1997); Seoul High Court, 94Na36386 (September 13, 1995).
76. Courts have found that it was legal and effective to impose an obligation on a former employee not to engage in any competing business for a limited period of time for the purpose of protecting an employer's trade secret acquired by the employee. *See*, Seoul District Court decision 94Gahab12987 (March 27, 1995).
77. Supreme Court decision 2006Ma1303 (March 29, 2007).
78. Suwon District Court decision 2002Gahab95 (June 7, 2000).
79. Seoul Central District Court decision 2007Gahab3903 (March 19, 2008).
80. Supreme Court decisions 2007Ma1303 (March 29, 2007) and 2009Da82244 (March 11, 2013).
81. They also include the employer's relationship with its customers and maintenance of the employer's credibility. Supreme Court decision 2009Da82244 (March 11, 2013).
82. The Court also found that in the absence of a territorial limitation, such an obligation might be invalid due to the employee's right to freedom of profession as guaranteed under Article 37(2) of the Constitution. Seoul Central District Court decision 2007Gahab3903 (March 19, 2008).

of compensation offered to an employee" has recently been considered an important factor in determining the validity of covenants not to compete. There are precedent cases, however, where covenants not to compete were deemed to be valid in light of other factors despite an absence of compensation[83]. Therefore, compensation is not absolutely necessary. Benefits provided in nonmonetary forms such as promotion, or opportunities to study abroad, can constitute consideration in connection with covenants not to compete.

Without a valid covenant not to compete, a former employee does not owe a duty of noncompetition derived from the employment contract because, unlike a nondisclosure agreement, covenants not to compete may directly restrict the constitutional right of the employee to choose occupation freely and engage in work (Article 15 of the Korean Constitution)[84]. However, explicit contractual clauses with excessive restrictions could be invalidated on the grounds that they are contrary either to the freedom of occupation under the Constitution or to the public order and good morals under Article 90 of the Civil Code[85].

4.5.3. *Article 10(1) of the UCPA as Legal Basis for Noncompete Obligation*

However, the law of post-employment restraints, which was only based on the ancillary duties derived from the employment contract, changed after the UCPA was adopted in 1991 because it provided a new statutory legal basis for regulating this field[86].

In 2003, the Supreme Court reaffirmed that even without a valid covenant not to compete, a former employer could seek an injunction to prevent a former employee from working in a specific position in which a trade secret would be used in or disclosed to a competing firm, holding that:

> when it would be impossible to protect the trade secret of the plaintiff unless the former employee was prohibited from engaging in the trade-secret-related work in the new firm, it may be possible to prohibit the former employee from engaging in the trade-secret-related work in the new firm as a necessary measure to prohibit or prevent a misappropriation of the trade secret on the basis of Article 10(1) of the UCPA[87].

4.5.4. *Employee's General Skills and Knowledge and the Particular Knowledge of Employer's Trade Secrets*

The former employer and former employee sometimes dispute whether or not certain information qualifies as "confidential information" or "company property" and whether such information or property is subject to the confidentiality obligation. It has

83. Incheon District Court decision 2011Gahab340 (May 20, 2011).
84. Seoul District Court decision 94Gahab12987 (March 27, 1995); *See* Hyun-Soo Kim, *supra*, note 39, at. 140.
85. Sang-Jo Jong, "Protection of Trade Secrets in the Context of Employment," *Beobhag*, Vol. 36 No. 1 (1995), at 164, 179.
86. Hyun-Soo Kim, *supra*, note 39, at 140.
87. Supreme Court decision 2002Ma4380 (July 16, 2003).

to be observed in this respect that courts distinguish between an employee's general skills and knowledge, and the particular knowledge of an employer's trade secrets[88]. It has been recognized that the general skills and knowledge obtained in the course of employment are not the property of the employer and cannot be legally protected as trade secrets[89]. Therefore, restrictions concerning a former employee's use of his general skills and knowledge are void, as they are contrary to the freedom of occupation under the Constitution and to good morals under the Civil Code. Nevertheless, the line between unprotectable general skills and information and protectable trade secrets belonging exclusively to the employer's sphere is often difficult to draw. In addition, proof that trade secrets have been disclosed contrary to post-contractual secrecy obligations can be extremely difficult.

4.6. *Commercial or Industrial Significance*

In the present decision, the Supreme Court for the first time recognized that Articles 2(3)(d) and 10 of the UCPA can be a legal basis for an injunction to prohibit an employee from engaging in specific work in a competing firm in which the trade secret of the former employer would be used or disclosed. This means that businesses in Korea have one more avenue to stop their employees from competing. However, courts have tried to strike a particular balance between the employer's interests in maintaining trade secrets and the employee's freedom of profession and freedom of choosing one's work.

88. Supreme Court decision 96Da16605 (December 23, 1996); Sang-Jo Jong, *supra*, note 85, at 169-170.
89. Supreme Court decision 97Da8229 (June 13, 1997).

TOPIC 5 LENGTH OF PERMANENT INJUNCTIVE RELIEF FOR TRADE SECRET INFRINGEMENT

Won Bok Lee & Kyoung-Shin Park

1. Legal Issues

The major issues in the present case are the appropriate length for an injunction and its adjustment under Korea's Unfair Competition Prevention and Trade Secret Protection Act.

2. Statutory Law

Under Korea's Unfair Competition Prevention and Trade Secret Protection Act, the statutory ground for injunction against the misappropriator of a trade secret is as follows: "Article 10 (Right to Request Prohibition of Infringement of Trade Secrets)

(1) A person who possesses trade secrets may file a request with the court for prohibition or prevention of infringement against any person who infringes or is likely to infringe trade secrets, if business interests of the person who possesses the trade secrets are damaged or are likely to be damaged by such infringement.
(2) If a person who possesses trade secrets files a request under paragraph (1), the person may request the destruction of goods constituting the infringement, the removal of facilities used in the infringement, or any other measures necessary to prohibit or prevent the infringement."

3. Case Law

The Korean Supreme Court has fixed the length of a permanent injunction in the following cases: Decision 96Da16605 (December 23, 1996)[90], Decision 97Da24528 (February 13, 1998)[91], Decision 2002Ma4380 (July 16, 2003)[92], and Decision 2016Ma1630 (April 13, 2017)[93]. However, in the following cases, the Korean Supreme Court set an indefinite length for the permanent injunction: Decision 2008Ma1087 (March 16, 2009), Decision 2001Da17557 (March 4, 2014), and Decision 2018Ma7100 (March 14, 2019).

90. The Supreme Court agreed with the trial court's decision that granted an injunction for a three-year period starting from the conclusion of the litigation.
91. The Supreme Court agreed with the trial court's decision that granted an injunction for a three-year period starting from the date the defendant resigned from the plaintiff.
92. The Supreme Court agreed with the trial court's decision that granted the trade secret protection period of one year, which started when the defendant resigned from the plaintiff and had already lapsed by the time of the litigation.
93. The Supreme Court agreed with the trial court's decision that granted the trade secret protection period of two years at most, which started from the date the defendant resigned from the plaintiff and had already lapsed by the time of the litigation.

As will be explained below, the Korean Supreme Court grants an injunction of an indefinite length when there is insufficient evidence to prove that either the defendant or the trade would be able to develop the same technology as protected by trade secret in a finite number of years.

4. Leading Case

This case is a leading case because the Supreme Court solidified the "lead time" theory as the principle for determining the length of an injunctive relief against the misappropriator of a trade secret. The case also makes it clear that a permanent injunction has a limited length unless the defendant fails to prove that either the defendant or the industry would have developed the same technology through legitimate means.

4.1. *Case Information*

Supreme Court Decision 2017Da34981 (September 10, 2019)

4.2. *Summary*

The Korean Supreme Court agreed with the appellate court's calculation for the duration of possible injunctive relief available to the plaintiff, based on the principle that the objective of an injunctive relief on grounds of a trade secret is to prevent the infringer from gaining an undue advantage over other competitors and to place the trade secret owner in the situation that he would have been in but for the trade secret infringement.

4.3. *Facts*

In 2008, the plaintiff, a navigation system manufacturer, developed an automobile navigation system called ASIA Navigation, built specifically for automobiles made by a global automaker Z, which were sold in Korea and Japan. Defendant X, the owner of another navigation system manufacturer, which was also a co-defendant in this case ("Defendant Company"), solicited defendant Y, then an employee at the plaintiff, to transfer the plaintiff's technical data, which happened between March 2009 and March 2010. The Defendant Company successfully produced its own lines of navigation systems called NAVIGATION SYSTEM A and NAVIGATION SYSTEM B, respectively. NAVIGATION SYSTEM A units were sold in China while NAVIGATION SYSTEM B units installed in automobiles sold in Korea received clearance from car companies for installation.

The plaintiff filed a lawsuit and sought damages and injunction against the defendants, enjoining them from using or disclosing the plaintiff's trade secrets for car navigation, as well as manufacturing, selling, or exporting products in which the plaintiff's trade secret was used. The first instance court decided that KRW 6.7 billion should be the compensation for damages caused by infringement of trade secrets that occurred until March 2012, but dismissed the request for injunction. The court explained that "the purpose of prohibiting infringement of trade secrets is to prevent a party from unfairly taking advantage of another party who is engaged in fair competition, from a superior position and to allow the non-infringing party (i.e., trade secret holder) to return to its original position as if there had not been such infringement. Moreover, the period for the prohibition of infringing trade secrets should be equal to a considerable time necessary for the infringer or other fair competitor to acquire the trade secret through legal means, such as independent development or reverse engineering." The court interpreted "the end of the period of protection of trade secrets to be around March 2012, about one year and six months from the start of the defendant's development efforts, and as of the last day of the hearing in this case, the plaintiff's right to prohibit infringement of trade secrets and to prevent infringement was deemed to have lapsed, therefore the injunction request was dismissed."[94]

Both the plaintiff and the defendants appealed with the Seoul High Court, which upheld the decision of the first instance court[95]. As to the duration of injunctive relief, the appellate court determined that the Defendant Company would have been able to develop its own navigation system without relying on the plaintiff's trade secrets in eighteen months. Based on that calculation, the appellate court determined that injunctive relief for the plaintiff would no longer be available past March 2012, or 18 months after the defendant started developing navigation systems and denied the plaintiff's petition for injunction long after March 2012.

The decision was appealed, and the Korean Supreme Court affirmed the appeal court's decision on all issues.

4.4. *Reasoning of the Court*[96]

The Korean Supreme Court reiterated the holding from its previous decision:

> "The purpose of injunctive relief for trade secret misappropriation is to prevent the perpetrator from unjustly benefiting from a head start or lead time advantage that is attributable to the misappropriation and to put the holder of a trade secret in a position he would have been in in the absence of such misappropriation. In order to achieve that purpose, an injunction against an infringer of a trade secret will have its force during the *trade secret protection period*. The *trade secret protection period* will be determined in light of the nature and complexity of the technological information kept as trade secret, whether the infringer or the industry may have been able to decipher the trade secret through legal means such as reverse engineering, how long it took the trade secret owner to develop the technology, the speed at which related technologies are advancing, the human and non-human resources of the infringer, and the former employee's freedom to profession and freedom to conduct business." (emphasis added)[97]

94. Korean Presidential Council on Intellectual Property, 2019 Annual Report on Intellectual Property Protection and Enforcement in Korea, 163-164. Available at: https://www.ipkorea.go.kr/Eng/2019.pdf.
95. Seoul High Court Decision 2015Na9945 (July 6, 2017).
96. The citation of the present decision is without a specific page, paragraph or line number, because Korean court decisions are published without such numbers.
97. Cited from Supreme Court Decision 97Da24528 (February 13, 1998).

4.5. *Legal Analysis*

4.5.1. *The "Trade Secret Protection Period" Coined by the Korean Supreme Court*

The length of a permanent injunction enjoining the infringer of a trade secret from using or disclosing the misappropriated information is not a straightforward issue to decide. At the heart of the controversy is the somewhat complicated nature of trade secret protection. In contrast to a patent with a limited 20-year life, the life of a trade secret can be "perpetual" in the sense that it will not lose secrecy unless and until it is made public. Also, in contrast to a patent, which prevents anyone other than the patent holder from using the patented technology, a trade secret only prevents misappropriation of the trade secret. Reverse engineering a trade secret is not prohibited. Thus, it becomes a logically challenging issue to decide whether to perpetually enjoin the infringer of a trade secret from using the trade secret even if the infringer would have reverse engineered the trade secret on his own at some point.

Notwithstanding its common law origin, the conflicting case law in the United States demonstrates the difficulty of setting the length of a permanent injunction in a trade secret infringement case and could therefore provide a good reference for Korean law. Three rules exist as to the length of the permanent injunction against a trade secret misappropriator. The Shellmar rule holds that a perpetual injunction can be issued against the misappropriator of a trade secret regardless of whether the trade secret becomes public[98]. The Conmar rule sits at the opposite end of the spectrum, by denying injunction once the trade secret has become public through no fault of the misappropriator[99]. Finally, the Winston Research rule takes the middle ground[100]. Also referred to as the "lead-time rule," it calculates the length of a permanent injunction by determining a theoretical point in time at which the infringer of a trade secret would have independently discovered the secret through reverse engineering or other legitimate means, and enjoining the misappropriator from using the trade secret until such time. If it so happens that such time has already passed at the time of litigation, the court will simply deny permanent injunction.

One commentator describes this split as a "balancing of three conflicting interests the entrepreneur's proprietary claim to knowledge achieved by research and initiative, the employee's interest in using his knowledge for his own benefit, and the general public's interest in the benefits of free competition in the relevant technology."[101]

As can be seen from the statutory provision, Korean law does not specify how long a permanent injunctive relief should be or how it should be calculated. Thus, it is left for the judiciary to decide.

---

98. *Shellmar Products Co. v Allen-Qualley Co.*, 87 F.2d 104, 32 U.S.P.Q. 24 (C.C.A. 7th Cir. 1936).
99. *Conmar Products Corp. v Universal Slide Fastener Co.*, 172 F.2d 150, 80 U.S.P.Q. 108 (2d Cir. 1949).
100. *Winston Research Corp. v Minnesota Min. & Mfg. Co.*, 350 F.2d 134, 146 U.S.P.Q. 422 (9th Cir. 1965).
101. Remedies—Duration of injunctive relief (federal preemption again), 3 Callmann on Unfair Comp., Tr. & Mono. § 14:40 (4th Ed.)

Thus, it is clear that the Korean Supreme Court has adopted the "head start" or "lead time" theory, along the same lines as the Winston Research rule of the U.S. More interestingly, as can be seen from the above holding, the Korean Supreme Court is of the view that trade secret protection is, by default, not perpetual. The Korean Supreme Court even coins the term "trade secret protection period," which implies that trade secret is protected for a limited duration. The term "trade secret protection period" is not found anywhere in UCPA.

4.5.2. *A Trifurcated Approach Based on Whether the "Trade Secret Protection Period" Is Over, Not Over, or Indeterminable*

The Korean Supreme Court, in one of its previous decisions, also provided more concrete guidance on the length of injunctive relief:

> At the end of a trial, if the trade secret protection period is not over, the misappropriator will be enjoined from using the trade secret for the remainder of the trade protection period. If the trade secret protection is over, permanent injunction should not be granted. If the expiration of the trade secret protection period cannot be determined with certainty due to, for example, lack of evidence that the infringer or the trade can decipher the trade secret, then a permanent injunction can be granted with an *indefinite length* (emphasis added). Even when an indefinite injunction is issued, it does not remain *perpetual* (emphasis added, as the defendant may later prove the expiry of the trade secret protection period in a subsequent suit[102].

In other words, the Korean Supreme Court preaches a trifurcated approach based on whether the "trade secret protection period" is over, not over, or indeterminable at the end of trial. The trade secret owner enjoys any duration of injunctive relief only if the trade secret protection period remains or is at least indeterminable. In the latter case still, the trade secret owner will not be entitled to a perpetual injunction; the injunction will be indefinite, with room for the defendant to terminate the injunction.

4.5.3. *Whether a Bifurcated Approach Based on Whether the "Trade Secret Protection Period" Is Determinable or Not*

Alternatively, the Korean Supreme Court's approach can be described as a bifurcated one, too: cases where the trade secret protection period is determinable versus cases where the trade secret protection period is indeterminable. In the former cases, the injunctive relief will last until the end of the trade secret period, unless it is already over at the time of trial; in the latter cases, the injunctive relief will not have an initial expiration date but is subject to termination nonetheless if the defendant can prove the expiration of the period later. It naturally follows that the defendant bears the burden

102. Korean Supreme Court Decision 2018Ma7100 (March 14, 2019).

of providing evidence that the trade secret protection period has a determinable end[103]. Otherwise, the defendant will be faced with an injunction n of indefinite length.

In the present case, the Korean Supreme Court also held that the duration of the "trade secret protection period," as well as the starting point of an injunction, are matters of fact and, thus, under the discretion of the trial court. However, since the Korean Supreme Court espoused the "head start" theory as the rationale behind enjoining a trade secret infringer, trial courts will be bound by the principle and will not be allowed to adopt a Shellmar-like rule or Conmar-like rule. Instead, the discretion of the trial court will be limited to determining the end of the "trade secret protection period."

4.5.4. *Misplaced Critique on Korean Supreme Court's Holding*

Not all scholars support the Korean Supreme Court's holding that is based on the "lead time" theory. For example, one article written by a prominent scholar argues that a non-public trade secret deserves perpetual injunctive relief against the misappropriator[104]. One exception is when there is a compelling reason to believe that the trade secret will be made public in the near future at the time of trial, in which case the injunctive relief will have a time limit rather than being perpetual. The same article also argues that the "lead time" theory comes in if, and only if, the trade secret at issue has been disclosed to the public before the end of the trial. In such a case, according to the article, the owner is still entitled to a limited-time injunction based on the Winston Research rule.

However, that is not a correct understanding of U.S. case law. As discussed earlier, the U.S. case law on the length of permanent injunction on trade secret infringement differs from one state to another. There is no single "U.S. law" on the length of a permanent injunctive relief in trade secret infringement cases. In addition, it is unambiguously clear that the Winston Research rule also does apply even when the trade secret is still non-public[105]. While the Winston Research rule itself dealt with

103. Under U.S. law, many courts also put the burden on the defendant. F.g., *Hyde Corp. v Huffines*, 158 Tex. 566, 314 S.W.2d 763, 776, 117 U.S.P.Q. 44 (1958) ("[W]hen a plaintiff makes out a case for injunctive relief, the duty devolves upon the opposing party to show by competent evidence that an order of less duration than a permanent order will afford the injured party adequate protection."); *Halliburton Energy Services, Inc. v Axis Technologies*, LLC, 444 S.W.3d 251, 2014 I.E.R. Cas. (BNA) 166626, 112 U.S.P.Q.2d 1599 (Tex. App. Dallas 2014), reh'g overruled, (October 7, 2014) and rule 53.7(f) motion granted, (January 22, 2015) ("[T]he burden is on the defendant to show at trial that an injunction for a period of time less than perpetual will be adequate to protect the rights of the injured plaintiff.")

104. Chaho JUNG & Guanghong ZHANG, "Period-Limited or Perpetual Injunction of a Trade Secret Infringement: Seoul High Court 2014Na2011824 Decision", *The Journal of Intellectual Property*, Vol. 14, No. 2 (2019).

105. This is the conclusion the authors have reached after perusing authoritative U.S. trade secret law commentaries, such as Melvin F. Jager, *Trade Secrets Law* (C. Boardman, 1985). Also, according to this commentary, "There is a trend in the law to withdraw from the extreme positions of Shellmar and Conmar, and to fashion injunctions which relate to the duration needed for a competitor to independently develop the trade secret material by fair means." (Permanent injunctions—Limited injunctions, 2 Trade Secrets Law § 7:14). Another commentary states "[I]njunctive relief should ordinarily continue only until the defendant could have

a situation where the trade secret at issue had become public, there are plenty of other cases that followed the Winston Research rule while the trade secret at issue was not public at the time of trial. In one U.S. case, the trade secret at issue was customer information, not a technological one. Unlike a technology, which may be developed eventually by the trade, confidential customer information is not amenable to independent development in the same manner, unless the owner of the customer information voluntarily discloses it. Yet, the court limited the duration of the permanent injunction against the infringer of the customer information to such time as would require a diligent salesperson to develop comparable customer information[106].

The authors believe the misunderstanding was probably caused by the state-level protection of trade secrets in the U.S. Unlike the federal patent law in the U.S., which necessarily results in a single, uniform interpretation of the law, trade secret law in the U.S. is an assembly of 50 different state laws[107]. Unless one consults a case law commentary that comprehensively reviews the case laws from all 50 states, one may fall into the mistaken view that one rule prevails over another. This pitfall should be an alarm for comparative legal scholarship not just in the context of the length of permanent injunction against the infringer of a trade secret, but for many other important legal issues involving trade secrets in general.

4.5.5. *Unresolved Issues*

The present case, in combination with other precedent cases that dealt with the length of injunctive relief in trade secret infringement cases, still leaves some issues unresolved.

For one, it is not clear how the willfulness of the infringer is factored into the length of an injunctive relief. At least the Korean Supreme Court did not specifically list the "willfulness of the infringer" as an element in determining the "trade secret protection period."[108] In contrast, under the Winston Research rule, the court took the bad faith of the infringer into consideration in issuing a two-year injunction. This is an interesting issue, because, through a 2019 amendment, the Korean trade secret law now allows enhanced damages against a willful infringer, while the injunctive relief

acquired the information by proper means. Injunctions extending beyond this period are justified only when necessary to deprive the defendant of a head start or other unjust advantage that is attributable to the appropriation." Restatement (Third) of Unfair Competition § 44 (1995).

106. *Surgidev Corp. v Eye Technology, Inc.*, 828 F.2d 452, 4 U.S.P.Q.2d (BNA) 1090 (8th Cir. 1987). Another case in which the trade secret at issue had not become public at the time of the trial is, e.g., *K-2 Ski Co. v Head Ski Co.*, 506 F.2d 471, 473, 183 U.S.P.Q. 724 (9th Cir. 1974).

107. Although the U.S. promulgated the Defend Trade Secrets Act in 2016, it does not preempt state trade secret laws.

108. As described above, the Korean Supreme Court lists "the nature and complexity of the technological information kept as trade secret, whether the infringer or the trade may have been able to decipher the trade secret through legal means such as reverse engineering, how long it took the trade secret owner to develop the technology, the speed at which related technologies are advancing, the human and non-human resources of the infringer, and the former employee's freedom to profession and freedom to conduct business" as the factors to be considered in determining the trade secret protection period.

clause remains the same. Of course, there is the possibility that the lower courts, with the full discretion to determine the duration of the "trade secret protection period," can fashion a longer injunction against a bad-faith infringer without mentioning the reason, even before the Supreme Court specifically allows elongated injunction against a bad-faith infringer.

Another unresolved issue is the implication of the disclosure of the trade secret to the public before the end of trial. As mentioned above, the disclosure of the trade secret to the public does not foreclose injunctive relief under the Shellmar rule or even under the Winston Research rule under certain circumstances[109]. However, the holding of the Korean Supreme Court would make it very awkward to grant injunctive relief for a trade secret already disclosed to the public. The Korean Supreme Court's logic is centered around the concept of trade secret protection period," which would lapse if the trade secret has been disclosed to the public. Only an alternative theory, such as the necessity for punitive punishment against a bad-faith infringer, along the lines of the Winston Research rule, would be able to overcome the "trade secret protection period" architecture. Time will tell.

Lastly, the Korean Supreme Court has yet to hear a case where the misappropriated trade secret is not a technology but business information, such as customer list. It is not immediately conceivable that diligent competitors can aggregate a similar list, although some U.S. courts still limited the duration of a permanent injunction based on such a possibility[110]. The factors mentioned by the Korean Supreme Court in calculating the "trade secret protection period" are geared towards technology, not business information, either. Still, that does not necessarily mean that business information will be entitled to perpetual injunctive relief. Again, it will take another Supreme Court case to have the answer.

4.6. *Commercial or Industrial Significance*

The present case reaffirmed the Korean Supreme Court's previous reasoning on the purpose of an injunctive relief in a trade secret infringement case, as well as the proper length of an injunctive relief. The burden of proof falls on the defendant to prove that the "trade secret protection period" is finite, rather than indeterminable, to avoid an indefinite permanent injunction. The defendant will have to prove that the technology protected by trade secret was not impermeable to reverse engineering and would have been deciphered. Alternatively, the defendant must prove that either the defendant or the trade had the knowledge and experience to eventually develop the same technology in the foreseeable future.

As the length of an injunctive relief only reflects the "lead time" that the infringer enjoyed from misappropriating a trade secret, according to the opinion, without any consideration for possible bad-faith behavior of the infringer, the injunctive relief may sound insufficient to deter misappropriation. The criminal provision as well as the

109. Some courts, however, deny permanent injunction if the trade secret has been disclosed to the public. Restatement (Third) of Unfair Competition § 44 (1995).
110. *Surgidev Corp. v Eye Technology, Inc.*, 828 F.2d 452, 4 U.S.P.Q.2d (BNA) 1090 (8th Cir. 1987).

enhanced damages provision under the Korean trade secret law will probably have a bigger role as a deterrent mechanism against trade secret misappropriation.

TOPIC 5 THE DAMAGES

Byungil Kim

1. Legal Issues

The major legal issues are damages determination under the UCPA.

2. The Statutory Law

Article 11 (Liability for Damages for Infringement of Trade Secrets)

A person who damages the business interests of a person who possesses trade secrets through an intentional or negligent infringement of trade secrets shall be liable for compensation of such damages.

Article 14bis (Presumption, etc., on the Amount of Damages)

(1) Where a person whose business interests have been infringed by an act of unfair competition, a violation as referred to in Article *3bis* (1) or (2) or an infringement of trade secrets, claims compensation for damages under Article 5 or 11, and where the person who has infringed the business interests transfers the goods causing the act of unfair competition, violation as referred to in Article 3*bis* (1) or (2) or infringement of trade secrets, the amount obtained by multiplying the transferred amount in subparagraph 1 by the presumed profit per unit in subparagraph 2, may be determined as damages for the person whose business interests have been infringed. In such cases, the compensation may not exceed an amount calculated by multiplying the estimated profit per unit by the number of articles that the person whose business interest has been infringed could have produced subtracted by the number of units actually sold: Provided, that where a person whose business interest has been infringed was unable to sell the product for reasons other than the act of unfair competition, violation referred to in Article 3*bis* (1) or (2), or infringement of trade secrets, a sum calculated according to the number of articles subject to the following shall be deducted:
   (1) The amount of goods transferred.
   (2) Profit per unit of the goods which a person whose business interests have been infringed would have been able to sell if there had been no such act of unfair competition, violation as referred to in Article 3*bis* (1) or (2)) or infringement of trade secrets.

(2) Where a person whose business interests have been infringed by an act of unfair competition, violation as referred to in Article 3*bis* (1) or (2) or infringement of trade secrets claims compensation for damages under Article 5 or 11, the profits gained by the infringer through the infringement, if any, are presumed to be the amount of damages suffered by the person whose business interests have been infringed.

(3) Where a person whose business interests have been infringed by an act of unfair competition, violation as referred to in Article 3*bis* (1) or (2) or infringement of trade secrets claims compensation for damages under Article 5 or 11, he/she may claim as damages the amount of money that the person would normally be entitled to receive for using a mark applied to goods if the mark was the object of an act of unfair competition or a violation referred to in Article 3*bis* (1) or (2), or for using trade secrets that were the object of the infringement.

(4) Where the amount of actual damages caused by an act of unfair competition, violation as referred to in Article 3*bis* (1) or (2) or infringement of trade secrets exceeds the amount under paragraph (3), the excess amount may also be claimed as compensation for damages. In such cases, when awarding damages, the court may consider whether the person who has infringed the business interest was willful or grossly negligent.

(5) Where the court recognizes the difficulty of proving the amount of damage that has occurred in litigation related to an act of unfair competition, violation referred to in Article 3*bis* (1) or (2) or infringement of trade secrets owing to the nature of the case, the court may determine a reasonable amount after examining the evidence and reviewing all the arguments related to the calculation of damages on the basis of the entire contents of the oral proceedings and the result of evidence investigations, notwithstanding paragraphs (1) through (4).

(6) *Notwithstanding Article 5 or 11, the court may award damages up to three times the amount of damages determined pursuant to paragraphs 1 to 5, if* violation as referred to in Article 2(1)(i) or infringement of trade secrets *is found to be willful.*

(7) The court shall consider each of the following factors in considering the damages pursuant to paragraph 6:
   (i) whether the infringer has a dominant position;
   (ii) whether the infringer knew the act of infringement would cause harm to the infringed party;
   (iii) the significance of any such damages;
   (iv) the economic benefits to the infringer from the infringement;
   (v) how frequently and how long the infringing activity was committed;
   (vi) the criminal penalty for the infringing activity;
   (vii) the infringer's financial status; and
   (viii) what efforts the infringer has made to reduce the harm to the infringed party.

The 2019 amendment to the UCPA provides *punitive damages* for intentional or willful trade secret infringement, up to treble damages (Article 14*bis* (6) and (7)[111]. The introduction of treble damages for willful infringement is expected to redress certain distortions in the technology market, encourage licensing between companies and help victims of trade secret misappropriation by enabling them to sufficiently recover their damages through litigation.

3. The Case Law

Between 2015 and 2019, there were a total of 48 cases in which damages for trade secret infringement were recognized and the amount of damages was calculated based on Article 14*bis* UCPA. Out of the 48 cases, 5 cases were based on Article 14*bis* (1), 5 cases were based on Article 14*bis* (2), 1 case was based on Article 14*bis* (3) and (4), and 37 cases were based on Article 14 *bis* (5) (*see* Table 2.1).

Table 2.1 Number of Cases on Each Different Damages Calculation Method and Damages Amount Rate Thereof[112]

	Lost Profit (Paragraphs 1)	*Infringer's Profit (Paragraph 2)*	*Reasonable Royalty (Paragraphs 3 & 4)*	*Loss under Court's Discretion (Paragraph 5)*
Number of cases (2015-2019)	5	5	1	37
Damages determined/revenue of infringing products (%)	10.4	10.4	0.02	79.0

4. The Leading Case

This is a leading case because the Supreme Court for the first time ruled on damages apportionment for an infringing trade secret.

4.1. *Case Information*

Supreme Court Decision 2012Da77761 (decided on December 24, 2014).

111. Myunghoon Kim, Changes in Law Allow South Korean Courts to Impose Treble Damages, https://www.ibanet.org/Article/NewDetail.aspx?ArticleUid=758472AD-2804-4B7A-895A-36531CEA464A (last visit March 23, 2021).
112. KIPO, 2017-2019 UCPA cases analysis study (in Korean), 2020, at 130.

4.2. *Summary*

The Supreme Court recognized that the amount calculated by deducting the necessary fluctuating expenses for product sales from the infringing products' profit (infringer's profit) shall be the amount of damages in trade secret misappropriation. The Supreme Court further reviewed the question of whether the amount of damages can be reduced considering the contribution rate of trade secrets. Defendant argued that damages award should be curtailed by limiting the damages base upon the contribution rate. However, the court did not admit the damages apportionment jurisprudence in this case.

4.3. *Facts*

Company A (plaintiff), a confectionery manufacturer, registered an invention patent[113] on "rice cake[114] coated with chocolate and its manufacturing methods" and then developed and launched a product called "Choco Chaltteok Pie." Thereafter, Company A, in addition to the existing patented invention, adjusted the raw materials and mixing ratio of the product, which extended the preservation period of the cake to 5 months. Company A received a pledge from all its employees that they shall not divulge the plaintiff's trade secrets while maintaining and managing the above manufacturing information as confidential.

B was in charge of the development work at Company A and separately stored and kept files such as the composition and blending ratio table of the rice cake in a personal notebook. B later left Company A and joined Company C. B submitted file contents to Company C, which Company C adopted to manufacture and sell a product called "Chaltteok Cookie," with raw materials and mixing ratio similar to the manufacturing information of Company A.

Company A filed a lawsuit against Company C and B and claimed that its technical information corresponded to the trade secret definition set forth in Article 2(2) of the UCPA, seeking compensation for damages caused by the infringement of the trade secret. With respect to the calculation of damages, Company A argued that the amount of profit that Company C has incurred as a result of the infringement of trade secrets should be presumed to be the damages of Company A. Company C argued that the manufacturing method of the rice cake does not constitute a trade secret, and by the time Company C started producing and selling the product, the trade secret was already extinguished, and A's damage did not occur.

The first instance court held that the technical information constituted "trade secret" under Article 2(2) of the UCPA and the defendant infringed upon it, pointing out that "The plaintiff has invested more than KRW 3 billion in human and physical facilities over a five-year period to research and develop the product. It was a key technology of A's flagship product, Choco Challtteok Pie. The plaintiff prevented

113. Coated Rice Cake and Producing Method Thereof, Application No. 1019970011345 (March 29, 1997) and No: 1002138580000 (May 17, 1999).
114. ***Chaltteok*** (찰 떡 , *[tɕʰal.t͈ʌkɕ* also called ***Chapssal-tteok*** (찹 쌀 떡 ; *[tɕʰap̚ɕ͈al.t͈ʌk̚]*)), is a *tteok*, or Korean rice cake, made of *glutinous rice*.

leakage by marking and classifying the technical information as confidential. Only a few employees had access to the confidential information. The plaintiff demanded a written pledge from its employees of not only general confidentiality obligations but also a specific promise not to divulge any trade secrets about the Choco Challtteok. B was the only employee of Company A who was able to manage information on product development and manufacturing process as the head of the R&D department of A."[115] Furthermore, the court ruled that "According to Article 14*bis* (2), the profits gained through the infringement shall be presumed to be the amount of damages suffered by an infringed party. The profit is the amount calculated by deducting necessary *fluctuating* expenses from the amount of sales."

The defendants appealed with the Seoul High Court, arguing that "The trade secrets, the infringement of which is recognized, are the manufacturing technology of rice cake, and the component ratio of rice cake in rice cake cookies is 38%, and considering that the infringed trade secrets are not important technologies, the contribution ratio of the infringed trade secrets should be 10%-20%. The amount of damages should be calculated by multiplying the infringer's profit by this contribution rate." However, the Seoul High Court upheld the decision of the first instance court[116]. As to the apportionment in damages of trade secret infringement, the appellate court further determined that "Even if the infringing part is a part of the product, if it is the main cause of attraction or the purchase motive for the product's customers, or if it plays a key function in the development, production, and sales of the product the benefits of the product as a whole should be calculated and the contribution rate should not be considered by drawing mechanical figures based on the quantitative ratio, price ratio, etc. of the product." The Supreme Court affirmed the appeal court's decision on this issue.

4.4. *Reasoning of the Court*

Article 14*bis* (2) of the UCPA prescribes a legal presumption: the infringer's profit is presumed as trade secret holder's damages. If the infringer proves that the trade secret holder's actual loss is less than the infringer's profit, such presumption is rebutted and the actual loss is set as the maximum of damages compensation. In addition, the infringer's profit may be derived from other factors, such as the infringer's capital power, sales network, promotional efforts, brand power, unique design, etc. The infringer's profit is calculated by deducting relevant costs from the infringing product revenue.

The Korean Supreme Court noted that the amount of damages was determined by deducting the expenses incurred for the sale of the product from the sales proceeds generated from the act of infringement. Furthermore, the Korean Supreme Court reiterated the holding from its previous decisions: The infringed trade secret is the manufacturing technology of sticky rice cake (*chaltteok)* among the sticky rice cakes cookies (*chaltteok cookies)*, but based on the *chaltteok cookies*, the total amount of

115. Uijeonbu District Court decision 2009Gahap7325 (September 8, 2011).
116. Seoul High Court decision 2011Na78967 (August 3, 2012).

material costs, labor costs, and expenses for the entire *Pocheon-plant* are calculated based on the ratio of the sales amount of the *chaltteok cookies*, and after deducting the necessary and variable expenses. In addition, the marginal profit calculated by deducting necessary variable expenses from the sales of the cookie product should be regarded as the amount of compensation for the trade secret holder's damages. Also, there is no reason for the defendant's claim that the amount of damages should be reduced in consideration of the "contribution rate" of the trade secrets related to sticky rice cake because the *chaltteok cookies* is a product in which sticky rice cake is added to ordinary cookies, but it is recognized and sold as discriminatory characteristics that distinguish from other products due to the ingredients of *chaltteok*.

4.5. *Legal Analysis*

4.5.1. Civil Remedies

The UCPA provides for the right to claim injunctive relief (Article 10)[117], damages (Article 11), and. measures to restore one's business reputation as civil remedies for trade secret infringement(Article 12).

Claiming damages is a typical remedy for tort actions in Korea and is governed by the basic principles enumerated in the Civil Code. However, Article 11 UCPA is *leges speciales* to the general tort clause under Article 750 of Civil Code. In general, there are four requirements for damage claims: intention or negligence, existence of an act of infringement, damage and causality between damage and the acts of infringement.

However, intention shall be presumed according to Article 68 Trade Mark Act, and negligence shall be presumed according to Articles 130 Patent Act, Article 46 Utility Model Act, and Article 116 Design Act, thereby shifting the burden of proof to the defendant. In contrast thereto, the UCPA does not provide provisions concerning such legal presumption. Therefore, the plaintiff bears the burden of proving the defendant's intention or negligence[118].

4.5.2. Damages Determination

The UCPA of 2001 went further by providing various methods for the calculation of damages: actual damages, lost profit (Article 14*bis* (1)), infringer's profit (Article 14*bis* (2)), and reasonable royalty (Article 14*bis* (3)), from which the plaintiff may freely choose any one method[119]. In addition, the plaintiff may suggest evidence for two or three methods and choose the best one at the end of the proceeding. Where the infringing party's infringing act is the sale of goods, the unit price of such goods

117. Moreover, injunctions may be made in the normal course of litigation, and in the form of provisional dispositions (or preliminary injunctions) under the Korean Civil Execution Act. Among these remedies, interestingly enough, the most frequently used relief is the provisional injunction (Article 300 of Civil Execution Act).
118. In practice, once the existence of acts of unfair competition or trade secret misappropriation has been proven, negligence on the part of the alleged infringer can be presumed.
119. *See* details, Chaho Jung, Patent Damages Determination in Korea, *IIC* 49(7) (2018), 267, 271-291.

multiplied by the number of goods which the infringed party could have sold in the absence of the infringement may be estimated as the amount of damage suffered by the infringed party within a limit of not exceeding an amount attainable under the working capacity of the infringed party (Article 14*bis* (1)). According to Article 14*bis* (2), the profits gained through the infringement shall be presumed to be the amount of damages suffered by an infringed party. An infringed party may seek the larger amount between "the profits gained by the infringer from the use of the trade secret" and "an ordinary royalty generally accepted for the use of the trade secrets" as damages, in addition to legal expenses (Article 14*bis* (3)). If the amount of damages exceeds the prescribed amount, the claim for damages may be made in this amount. In this case, the court shall consider the intent or gross negligence on the side of the infringer when determining the amount of the damages (Article 14*bis* (4)). Furthermore, the court may recognize a corresponding amount of damages based on arguments and the result of evidence examination as a whole, in a case where it is extremely difficult to prove facts necessary to prove the amount of damages owing to the character of the facts, notwithstanding Article 14*bis* (1) to (4) (Article 14*bis* (5)).

However, the "lost profits" calculation method is subject to the limitation that damages will not be awarded beyond the infringed party's own production capacity. As a result, the damages available to the trade secret holder under this calculation method have tended to be quite low, even where the infringer is a much larger company with a greater ability to produce and market the relevant products or services. This situation has been criticized as insufficient to deter trade secret infringement, particularly infringement by large companies. To solve this problem, through the 2020 amendment, the UCPA provides that if the "sales amount of an infringer" exceeds the infringed party's own production capacity, the infringed party will be entitled to receive reasonably expected royalties for such excess sales (Article 14*bis* (1) (ii)). By increasing the potential liability for damages through explicit provisions in the UCPA, the amendment is expected to strengthen trade secret protection in Korea.

4.5.3. *Apportionment (Contributory Percentage) of Damages*

In the case of manufacturing infringing products using the trade secrets of others, the trade secrets in question are often related to only a part of the product. In such a case, the calculation of the trade secret contribution rate from the total profit can be considered in calculating the amount of damages. In the 2002Da18244 decision, the Supreme Court set forth general jurisprudence that can be applied to the calculation of damages and infringement of other intellectual property rights, such as patent infringement. The Supreme Court held that "In the case where only a part of a product is related to infringement of intellectual property, the entire profit that an infringer gains by manufacturing and selling the product cannot be regarded as profit of the infringement." The Supreme Court also stated that "a contributory rate (contribution) of the part related to infringement of the intellectual property to the total profit obtained by the infringer through manufacture and sales of the product shall be calculated, and according thereto an amount of profit by the infringement shall be calculated. Such a contribution rate can be only comprehensively assessed by taking into consideration the indispensability, importance, price ratio, quantitative ratio, etc., of the part related to the infringement of the intellectual property with respect to the total profit obtained by the infringer."[120] In the present decision, the Supreme Court did not admit the damages apportionment jurisprudence but made clear that the application of the contribution rate depends on the importance of the parts that made up the entire product. In one recent trade secret case, the Supreme Court holds that the determination of the facts or contribution rate of trade secrets shall fall within the exclusive authority of the fact-finding court unless it is deemed considerably unreasonable in light of the principle of equity. Based on the facts acknowledged by the lower court, the lower court's determination that the contribution ratio was 3% is not considerably unreasonable under the principle of equity."[121]

4.6. *Commercial or Industrial Significance*

Under the UCPA, calculating the amount of damages in trade secret infringement cases is rarely easy. The calculation of damages is based on Article 14*bis* (5) in most cases. The courts have not yet developed a clear and consistent standard applicable to trade secret damages.

120. Supreme Court decision 2002Da18244 (June 11, 2004). *See* details, Boohan Kim, "Presumption on Damages Based on Infringer's Profit", *IP Law Journal*, Vol. 3, Patent Court of Korea (2016), at 135-139.
121. Supreme Court decisions 2017Da34981 (September 10, 2019) and 2017Da24113 (November 29, 2017).

CHAPTER 3
China

OVERVIEW AND SUMMARY
Xiuqin Lin

The protection of trade secrets in China has been substantially improved in recent years, as demonstrated by two rounds of legislative revision, newly adopted judicial interpretation by the Supreme People's Court (SPC) in 2020, enhanced judicial practice, and announced policy on the protection of trade secrets. Three major achievements can be summarized. First, the scope of undisclosed information protected as trade secrets is expanded, and algorithms and data are recognized as new types of technical information, etc. Second, the enforcement of trade secret protection has been strengthened. Furthermore, the newly revised *Anti-Unfair-Competition Law* (AUCL) imposes punitive damages on malicious infringement of trade secrets and lowers the threshold for establishing trade secret crimes. The number of trade secret cases handled by Chinese courts in the past five years exceeds that of the previous fifteen years. It is reasonable to expect that in China trade-secret-related cases will continue to rise and the protection will be strengthened.

1. LEGISLATIVE EFFORTS

Since China's economic reform and opening-up in the 1980s, its legislation on trade secrets has gone from scratch to a basically systematic framework. At present, China has a set of rules on protecting trade secrets, which include civil norms as well as administrative and criminal norms. A separate trade secret law is lacking.

1.1. Summary of Civil Protection of Trade Secrets

The "*General Principles of Civil Law,*" implemented in 1986, did not explicitly provide for trade secret protection. At that stage, the protection of trade secrets could only seek remedy in the provisions for the protection of "other scientific and technological achievements[1]." Later, in the 1987 "*Technology Contract Law,*" the civil protection for "trade secrets" emerged.[2] As a legal term, "trade secrets" first appeared in the Civil Procedure Law (CPL) enacted in 1991. The CPL stipulates that any evidence involving trade secrets should be kept confidential, and that cases involving trade secrets, if the parties apply for nonpublic hearings, may be heard in camera, rather than in public.[3] In 1992, the *SPC's Court's Opinions on Several Issues Concerning the Application of the Civil Procedure Law* explained that the scope of trade secrets mainly includes technical secrets, business intelligence, information such as production technology, formulas, trade contacts, purchase and sales channels, and other business secrets that the parties do not want to disclose.[4]

The substantive law concerning the protection of trade secrets first appeared in the AUCL promulgated in 1993, which defined trade secrets as the technical information and business information that are not known to the public, can bring economic benefits to its holder, and are practical and subject to corresponding confidentiality measures taken by right holders.[5] In addition, there are other laws and regulations in China that cover the protection of trade secrets. For instance, Company Law stipulates the confidentiality obligations of directors and senior managers of the company; whereas the Labor Law, Labor Contract Law, and relevant judicial interpretations provide for the protection of trade secrets in the context of the employer-employee relationship.

In 2007, the SPC promulgated the "*Interpretation on Several Issues Concerning the Application of Law in the Trial of Civil Cases of Unfair Competition* " to set out detailed rules on the constitutive elements of trade secrets, reverse engineering, and burden of proof[6]. In 2017, the revised AUCL made a few amendments to the protection of trade secrets. First, it refines the definition of trade secrets by deleting the requirement of "practicality[7]" Second, it explicitly imposes sanctions on employees and former employees of trade secret holders for infringement of trade secrets[8]. Third, it imposes a duty of confidentiality on the supervision and inspection authority for business trade secrets that came to their knowledge during their investigation[9]. In addition, the amendment also introduces statutory damages for the infringement of trade secrets of up to RMB 3 million[10].

In 2019, due to external pressure during United States (US)-China trade negotiations and strong calls from the domestic market for strengthening the protection of

1. Article 118, *General Principles of Civil Law of the People's Republic of China* (1986).
2. Articles 7 and 39, *Technology Contract Law of the People's Republic of China* (1987). The Technology Contract Law was later abolished in 1999 due to the introduction of the Contract Law, which was absorbed by the new Civil Code in 2021.
3. Articles 66 and 112, CPL (1991).
4. Article 154, *SPC's Opinions on Several Issues Concerning the Application of the Civil Procedure Law* (1992).
5. Article 10, AUCL (1993).
6. Articles 9-17, SPC, Interpretation on Several Issues Concerning the Application of Law in the Trial of Civil Cases on Unfair Competition (2007), Fa Shi [2007] No. 2.
7. Article 9(3), AUCL (2017).
8. Article 9(2), AUCL (2017).
9. Article 15, AUCL (2017).
10. Article 17(4), AUCL (2017).

trade secrets, China revised the AUCL again. Among others, the amended law raises the maximum statutory damages for infringement from CNY 3 million to RMB 5 million and introduces punitive damages for malicious infringement with the aim of effectively deterring trade secret infringement. The amount of punitive damage shall be one to five times the actual loss suffered by the infringement or benefits obtained by the infringer due to the infringement[11]. Moreover, the amendment explicitly extends the infringing acts to cover electronic intrusion as a means of illegally obtaining trade secrets,[12] and acts that instigate, induce, and help others to infringe trade secrets[13]. Furthermore, potential infringers of trade secrets are extended to include "other natural persons, legal persons and unincorporated organizations other than business operators." Meanwhile, the definition of trade secrets is further expanded to cover "commercial information such as technology information and business information[14]." In addition, the rules on burden of proof in civil procedures involving trade secrets are radically improved to favor trade secret holders[15].

In 2020, the SPC issued the *Provisions on Several Issues concerning the Application of Law in the Trial of Civil Cases involving Infringement of Trade Secrets* (*Provisions on the Trial of Infringement of Trade Secrets*), which stipulates detailed rules for the trial of civil cases involving the infringement of trade secrets[16].

Notably, in 2017 China enacted the *General Provisions of Civil Law* as the first step toward the enactment of a grand Civil Code to replace the 1986 "General Principles of Civil Law," which cannot cope with social development. Article 123(2)6 of the *General Provisions of Civil Law* clearly lists trade secrets as a type of intellectual property, which is incorporated into the *Civil Code* enacted in 2020[17]. The explicit recognition of trade secrets as intellectual property reflects the increased significance of trade secrets, highlights a new stage of trade secret protection in China, and hopefully will settle the long-standing controversy over whether trade secrets are intellectual property[18].

1.2. Summary of Criminal Protection of Trade Secrets

In terms of trade secret protection in criminal law, Article 219 of *Criminal Law*, revised in 2020 (effective March 1, 2021), increases the imprisonment punishment for serious crime on trade secrets from three to seven years to three to ten years, among other revisions. The amendment also introduced Article 219-1, which follows the US model and adopts enhanced imprisonment punishment for economic espionage (from up to five years to a minimum of five years and up to fifteen years for serious offenses).

11. Article 17(3), AUCL (2019).
12. Article 9(1), AUCL (2019).
13. Article 9(1)(4), AUCL (2019).
14. Article 9(2), AUCL (2019).
15. Song Jian, Impacts of Article 32 of the AUCL 2019 on Trial Rationale for Trade Secret Infringement Cases, in China Patents and Trademarks, No. 4, 2020, 22-31.
16. SPC, Fa-Shi [2020] No. 7.
17. Article 123(2)6, Civil Code.
18. Xiuqin Lin, Jurisprudential Foundation for Treating Trade Secret as Intellectual Property (in Chinese), GanSu Social Science, 2, 2020, 11-20.

Basically, the definition of trade secrets and the criminal acts listed in the *Criminal Law* are the same as those in the AUCL.

In 2004, the SPC and the Supreme People's Procuratorate (SPP) jointly issued the "*Interpretation on Several Issues Concerning the Specific Application of Law in Handling Criminal Cases of Infringement of Intellectual Property Rights,*" which clearly stated that cases in which holders of trade secrets suffer a loss of RMB 500,000 and above shall be deemed a case of " substantial loss." In 2020, the SPC and the SPP jointly revised the "Interpretation on Several Issues Concerning the Specific Application of Law in Handling Criminal Cases of Infringement of Intellectual Property Rights," partially as a response to the request of China's trading partners. This revision lowers the monetary threshold for "substantial loss" from RMB 500,000 to RMB 300,000 and covers two more situations: (1) the infringement directly causes the trade secret holder to go bankrupt or go out of business due to major business difficulties; (2) the infringement causes other major losses to the owner of the trade secret[19].

These new rules reflect China's readiness to enhance the protection of trade secrets and to create a better business environment with integrity and fair competition.

1.3. Summary of Administrative Protection of Trade Secrets

The AUCL of 1993 stipulates administrative liability for the infringement of trade secrets. In order to enhance the protection of trade secrets, the State Administration for Industry and Commerce of China (SAIC) formulated a regulation on the prohibition of infringing trade secrets in 1995. This regulation enumerated in detail the constitutive requirements of trade secrets, protection measures, and infringing acts of trade secrets. In 1998, the SAIC revised relevant regulations, among others, to impose on some professionals and public servants the obligation to maintain trade secrets obtained in the course of their work, violation of which will bear corresponding legal liabilities. These provisions are scattered in Accounting Law, Lawyers Law, Banking Law, Statistics Law, Judge Law, Prosecutor's Law, and Administrative Punishment Law of Public Servants. In 2020, the State Administration for Market Regulation (SAMR)[20] issued the *Draft Provisions on the Protection of Trade Secrets for Comment*, which further strengthens the administrative protection of trade secrets[21].

2. JUDICIAL PRACTICE ON TRADE SECRETS

As of October 11, 2020, at least some 2,309 civil decisions and some 262 criminal decisions on infringement of trade secrets, including the first and second instance, were retrieved through China's official portal for courts' decisions[22].

19. SPC and SPP, Fa-Shi [2020] No. 10, Article 4.
20. SAMR is the governmental authority for regulating areas, such as market competition, monopolies, intellectual property, and drug safety. Created in the 2018 Chinese overhaul of government administration, SAMR consolidates in one ministry the market regulation functions previously shared by three separate ministries, the General Administration of Quality Supervision, Inspection and Quarantine (AQSIQ), the China Food and Drug Administration (CFDA), and the SAIC.
21. http://www.moj.gov.cn/news/content/2020-09/04/zlk_3255343.html.
22. https://wenshu.court.gov.cn/.

In terms of geographical distribution, these cases are mainly handled in Guangdong (15.75%), Shanghai (15.72%), Zhejiang (11.56%), Beijing (10.47%), Jiangsu (7.89%), Shandong (6.8%), etc. The number of cases heard in the last five years (2016-2020) is 1,663 in total, which is more than the total number of 1,622 cases in the previous fifteen years (2001-2015). The sharp increase in cases reflects the rising awareness among trade secret holders of the need to protect their business advantage through trade secrets.

The proliferation of trade secret cases has brought many challenges to the judicial organs. According to the statistics of the Wolters Kluwer database, as of October 11, 2020, 34.05% of trade secret cases were tried by the district people's courts, and 44.81% were tried by the intermediate people's courts. Among others, three specialized intellectual property courts in Beijing, Shanghai, and Guangzhou have tried 111 cases in total. Several courts have handled more than 60 cases, including Shanghai Second Intermediate People's Court (102), SPC (90), Shenzhen Intermediate People's Court of Guangdong Province (87), Hangzhou Intermediate People's Court of Zhejiang Province (75), Shanghai First Intermediate People's Court (64), Shanghai Higher People's Court (63), Chaoyang District People's Court of Beijing (62), and Pudong People's Court Shanghai New District (61)[23].

In terms of compensation for infringement, as of October 11, 2020, the highest amount of compensation awarded in a trade secret civil dispute by Chinese courts was rMB 35 million,[24] and the biggest fine imposed in a criminal case of trade secret infringement was RMB 37 million[25].

In a nutshell, China's judicial practice on the protection of trade secrets suffers from a few frequently alleged difficulties, including the identification of trade secrets, identification criteria of trade secrets, evidence, and determination of damages. Some of these problems are endogenous to the trade secret protection system, while some are caused by legislative shortcomings, such as ambiguity in relevant laws. Nevertheless, the recent revision of Chinese laws on trade secret protection and the establishment of *the Intellectual Property Court of the SPC* could alleviate these difficulties.

23. https://law.wkinfo.com.cn/judgment-documents/list?q=%E5%95%86%E4%B8%9A%E7%A7%98%E5%AF%86%C7%81titleExtend:((%22%E5%95%86%E4%B8%9A%E7%A7%98%E5%AF%86%22))&tip=%E5%95%86%E4%B8%9A%E7%A7%98%E5%AF%86.
24. Zhejiang Higher People's Court (2017) Ming Zhong No. 123.
25. Zhuhai Intermediate People's Court Guangdong Province (2013) Xing No. 87.

TOPIC 1 THE REQUIREMENTS OF TRADE SECRET

Tieguang Liu

1. Legal Issues

According to Article 9(4) of China's AUCL, information must meet three requirements in order to qualify as a trade secret: (1) it must be unknown to the public (secrecy requirement); (2) it must derive economic value (value requirement); and (3) it must be the subject of corresponding measures taken by the right holder to maintain its secrecy (corresponding measures requirement). However, the meaning of the three requirements of trade secrets, especially the first and the third ones, is not very clear, and its interpretation by courts on a case-by-case basis is not always consistent.

2. The Statutory Law

In China, trade secret protection was explicitly introduced in the legislation in 1993, when the AUCL was first adopted (amended in 2017 and 2019 respectively). Article 9(4) of the AUCL now reads as follows: "the term 'trade secrets' as mentioned in this Article refers to the 'know-how' and business information that are not known to the public and can bring economic value to the right holder, and for which the right holder has taken confidentiality measures."

To sum up, there are three requirements of trade secret: "secrecy requirement," "value requirement," and "corresponding measures requirement." In order to guide courts to apply the requirements in a unified way, the SPC issued its *Interpretation on Several Issues Concerning the Application of Law in the Trial of Civil Cases on Unfair Competition* in 2007 (2007 Judicial Interpretation), providing detailed guidance on the interpretation of the three requirements[26].

In 2020, the SPC further issued its *Provisions on the Trial of Infringement of Trade Secrets*[27]. It interprets the first requirement of secrecy or being unknown to the public as "not generally known and not easily accessible by relevant persons in the relevant field when an alleged infringement occurs" (Article 3). According to Article 4(1) of the 2020 Judicial Interpretation, the concept of "being generally known to the public" includes five situations: (1) The information falls within common sense or industrial practices in the relevant field. (2) The information only involves such contents as the product size, structure, materials, and simple combination of components, which may be directly obtained by relevant persons in the relevant field through observation of products on the market. (3) The information has been disclosed to the public in open publication or publicized in any media. (4) The information has been disclosed to the public through public meetings, exhibitions, and other methods. (5) The information may be obtained by relevant persons in the relevant field through other public channels. Further, if new information derived from sorting out, improving, and

26. SPC, Fa-Shi [2007] No. 2, Articles 9, 10 and 11.
27. SPC, Fa-Shi [2020] No. 7.

processing the information known to the public meets the abovementioned requirements, it shall be deemed not known to the public (Article 4(2)).

The second requirement of trade secret, namely, "of economic value," is interpreted *as* "realistic or potential economic value due to the fact that it is not known to the public[28]."

As for the third requirement of trade secret, namely the "corresponding measures requirement," Article 5 of the 2020 Judicial Interpretation states that if a right holder has taken reasonable protection measures, prior to the occurrence of any alleged infringement, to prevent the disclosure of a trade secret, the court should rule that the requirement of corresponding measures is met. When the court determines whether a right holder has taken corresponding protection measures, it shall take into consideration the following factors: the nature of the trade secret and its carrier, the economic value of the trade secret, the degree of identifiability of protection measures, the degree of correlation between protection measures and the trade secret, and the right holder's willingness to keep the trade secret confidential. Furthermore, Article 6 of the 2020 Judicial Interpretation provides that "if one of the following circumstances is sufficient to prevent the disclosure of trade secrets under normal circumstances, the people's court shall determine that the right holder has taken corresponding confidentiality measures." The seven listed circumstances include: (1) a confidentiality agreement has been signed or confidentiality obligations have been agreed upon in a contract; (2) setting confidentiality requirements for employees, former employees, suppliers, clients, visitors, etc., who are able to access and obtain trade secrets through bylaws, training, rules and regulations, and written notification; (3) restricting visitors or conducting differentiated management on sensitive factories, workshops, and other production and business places; (4) differentiating and managing trade secrets and their carriers by means of marking, classification, isolation, encryption, sealing, and limiting the scope of persons who can access or obtain the trade secrets; (5) taking measures such as prohibiting or restricting the use, access, storage, copying, etc., of computer equipment, electronic equipment, network equipment, storage equipment, software, etc., that can access and obtain trade secrets; (6) requiring employees who are leaving the employment to register, return, clear, and destroy the trade secrets and their carriers accessed or obtained by them, and to continue to assume the confidentiality obligation; and (7) taking other reasonable confidentiality measures.

3. The Case Law

Several cases may shed some light on how Chinese courts interpret the three requirements in practice.

3.1. Not Generally Known

In *Beijing Rongqiniu Information Technology Co., Ltd v Zhao Yuanjiao*, the defendant, who was a former employee of the plaintiff, which was a financial service platform,

28. Article 7, 2020 Judicial Interpretation.

was sued for disclosing the plaintiff's trade secret, including information about its online marketing service suppliers and terms of transaction, to a competitor. The plaintiff argued that it made substantial investment in obtaining the information about creditable marketing service suppliers, and had kept it confidential through reasonable measures. The Beijing Intellectual Property Court held that the information disclosed was the plaintiff's "internal business data," which includes the combined record of its different marketing service suppliers and the description of their marketing results, not merely the names of isolated and scattered companies. Such information does not fall within "the business information which is generally known or is readily available," and thus meets the secrecy requirement[29].

In *Fujian Jinjiang Bocan Shoes Co., LTD v Spenco Medical Corporation, Yageshi (Xiamen) Plastic Products Co., Ltd*, the Fujian Provincial Higher People's Court held the information had been disclosed in several publications so that it does not meet the requirement of "unknown to the public[30]."

3.2. *Of Economic Value*

The requirement of economic value is commonly interpreted by courts to mean that the information can bring competitive advantage to the right holder. For example, in *Beijing Rongqiniu Information Technology Co., Ltd v Zhao Yuanjiao*, the Beijing IP Court held that information about good marketing service suppliers can bring competitive advantage to business operators in the same field by reducing their transaction costs and is thus of economic value[31].

In *Youya Wujin Company v Hua Li, Jiajia You, Jia'en, Lao Shenzhen Xinuo Metal Products Co., Ltd.*, the court was asked to decide whether a customer list is of economic value. The Shenzhen Intermediate People's Court held that information about the plaintiff's customers and suppliers, obtained through continuous business transactions, would enable the plaintiff to control the initiative of trading with its customers and suppliers, and to better conclude transactions, and thus meets the "economic value" requirement[32].

3.3. *Corresponding Measures*

As for the requirement of corresponding measures, the SPC held that a right holder should make reasonable efforts which are sufficient to maintain the secrecy of relevant information under normal circumstances. In *Zhang Peiyao, Hui Deyao, Jiangsu Funing County Dust Removal Equipment Factory v Suzhou Nanxin Cement Co. Ltd.*, the SPC held that reasonable measures should at least enable the counterparty or the third party to know that the right holder has the intention to keep the relevant information confidential or at least enable ordinary business operators who have paid normal

29. *See* Beijing IP Court (2020) Jing-73-Min-Zhong-Zi, No. 2581.
30. *See* Fujian Provincial Higher People's Court (2009), Min-Min-Zhong-Zi, No. 344 civil decision.
31. *See* Beijing IP Court (2020) Jing-73-Min-Zhong-Zi, No. 2581.
32. *See* Shenzhen Intermediate People's Court, Guangdong Province (2019) Yue-San-Min-Zhong, No. 4816.

attention to draw similar conclusions. When the product which embodied the trade secret is legally possessed and used by others, a declaration or confirmation of the ownership of the product is not sufficient to qualify as a reasonable confidentiality measure for the relevant technical information[33].

4. The Leading Case

Fujian Jinjiang Bocan Shoes Co., LTD (Bocan) v Spenco Medical Corporation (Spenco), Yageshi (Xiamen) Plastic Products Co., Ltd (Yageshi) is chosen as the leading case because it highlights the typical difficulties of determining the requirements of trade secrets and is very detailed in its fact-finding and reasoning.

4.1. Case Information

Fujian Provincial Higher People's Court, (2009) Min-Min-Zhong Zi, No. 344 (decided on August 31, 2011).

4.2. Summary

The key issue of the present case is whether the technical information meets the requirements of secrecy and economic value required of trade secrets. The first instance court relied on a technical evaluation which confirmed the trade secret nature of the technical achievement involved. However, the court of the second instance came to a completely opposite conclusion and overturned the decision of the first instance.

4.3. Facts

The plaintiff, Bocan Company, was established in 1995 and is mainly engaged in the export business of its own products and technologies. The defendant, Spenco Corporation, was a buyer and seller of medical products, registered and established in the US in 1967. Founded in April 2006, the defendant Yageshi (Xiamen) Plastic Products Co., Ltd. was a foreign-owned enterprise engaged in the production and processing of various footwear materials and other products.

Bocan had a long business relationship with Spenco by providing Spenco GEL insoles and other products. Spenco had certain access to Bocan's trade secrets, as its employees were sent to Bocan's factory to verify Bocan's eligibility as a supplier and to oversee Bocan's production to ensure the quality. Therefore, on October 31, 2003, Spenco and Bocan signed an *"Agreement on the Conditions of Disclosure of Trade Secrets,"* according to which Spenco agrees not to use or disclose the trade secrets of Bocan in any form except for the transactions with Bocan, the termination of the confidentiality agreement does not end Spenco's obligation to protect Bocan's trade secrets, and all documents in writing, printing or in any other form and information disclosed to Spenco, including all backups and copies of the documents, shall be the

33. *See* SPC (2000) Zhi-Zhong-Zi No. 3.

assets of Bocan, and should be returned to Bocan upon Bocan's request or upon termination of the purchase agreement.

Bocan also signed a confidentiality agreement with its employees, which does not end employees' obligation to protect Bocan's trade secrets with the termination of employment. In addition, Bocan signed a confidentiality agreement with its business partners such as the mold factories for insoles.

Huang Liyang was a shareholder and an employee of Bocan and worked in the departments of sales, procurement, and quality inspection. Huang was subject to confidentiality obligations under the Equity Transfer Agreement. Huang later left Bocan and is the brother-in-law of the legal representative of Yageshi. Zhang Yinfeng and Yu Sanlong, former employees of Bocan, also signed a confidentiality agreement with Bocan. Both Zhang and Yu left Bocan and became employees of Yageshi. Ever since Yageshi was established, it was a supplier to Spenco.

Bocan filed a lawsuit against Spenco and Yageshi on the grounds that the two defendants had infringed its trade secrets by breaking the confidentiality agreement as well as disclosing and using the plaintiff's know-how. The claimed trade secrets include mainly two parts, the design of a double-flow channel and double-gate GEL insole mold with color inserts (the mold design) and a tray made of high-temperature foam material and the tray scaffolding of 20 stories (the tray design).

4. Reasoning of the Courts

4.1. The First Instance[34]

The first instance court commissioned Beijing Zitu Intellectual Property Judicial Authentication Center to assess two questions, whether Bocan's technical information was not known to the public and whether Yageshi had used Bocan's technical information. Beijing Zitu issued an Appraisal Report (Beijing Zitu [2008] no. 26) and concluded that the two pieces of technical information, namely, the "mold design" and the "tray design" were not known to the public and met the requirements of a "trade secret," and that Yageshi had used the two pieces of technical information owned by Bocan.

As for the first technical secret, the Appraisal Report's conclusion was based on two grounds. First, the mold design had not been disclosed by the published technical documents provided by the court; secondly, the mold design was new and reflective of the creative work of the designer.

As for the second technical secret, the Appraisal Report concluded that such design of choosing materials of low conductivity and soft quality solved the problems of cooling and saving space for placing products, and is "a technical measure that breaks convention and overcomes prejudice," as it deviates from the conventional way of applying materials that are smooth in surface and have good thermal conductivity.

34. Quanzhou Intermediate People's Court, Fujian Province (2007) Quan-Min-Chu-Zi No. 18 civil decision.

Mainly based on the Appraisal Report, Quanzhou Intermediate People's Court held that the two pieces of technical information used by the plaintiff Bocan fall within the definition of "know-how," as it is unknown to the public and of practical economic value and can bring a competitive advantage to Bocan. Moreover, Bocan had taken strict measures to protect it. The defendant Spenco violated the confidentiality agreement with the plaintiff by disclosing the abovementioned trade secrets to the defendant Yageshi for use. The defendant Yageshi used the trade secrets, knowing that Spenco had breached its confidentiality agreement with Bocan. The two defendants have jointly infringed the plaintiff's trade secrets and should bear the corresponding civil liability.

The court granted Bocan's application for a permanent injunction to stop infringement, and awarded RMB 3 million damages and reasonable expenses incurred for stopping the infringement. Both Spenco and Yageshi appealed the decision.

4.2. *The Second Instance*

Fujian Provincial Higher People's Court revoked the decision of the first instance.

It interpreted the requirements of trade secret by citing the 2007 Judicial Interpretation Article 9 of the 2007 Judicial Interpretation, which provides that the following information shall not be considered "unknown to the public": (1) information that falls under common sense or industrial practices in the relevant field; (2) information that only involves such contents as the product size, structure, materials, and simple combination of components, which may be directly obtained by relevant persons in the relevant field through the observation of products on the market; (3) information that has been disclosed to the public in any open publication or publicized in any other media; (4) information that has been disclosed to the public through public report meetings, exhibitions, and other methods; and (5) information that may be obtained by relevant persons in the relevant field. Article 10 further defines that relevant information that has realistic or potential economic value and can bring competitive advantages to the right holder shall be deemed "can bring economic benefits to the right holder[35]."

Then Fujian Provincial Higher People's Court rejected the view of the Appraisal Report, holding that the claimed know-how does not meet the requirement of a trade secret for the following two reasons.

4.2.1. *The Technology of the Mold Design Was Already Known to the Public*

The mold design had been disclosed in earlier relevant public publications, including teaching materials at the College of Light Industry for professionals, such as *"Plastic Moulding Mold"* (first edition) published in June 1982, *"Injection Mold Design and Production Application"* (first edition) published in March 2005, and *"Plastic Molding Technology and Mold Design"* (first edition) published in January 2006. Some of these

35. Articles 9 and 10 of the 2007 Judicial Interpretation are similar to Articles 3 and 4 of the 2020 Judicial Interpretation.

teaching materials explain the design principles and requirements of double (or more) runner, double (or more) gate for double (or more) cavity molds, while others directly disclose the technical solution of such a design. Moreover, Xiamen Mold Industry Association and its technical committee concluded that a "double-flow channel and double-gate design" falls within the common selection of the design profession. Therefore, the claimed know-how of "double-flow channel and double-gate design of GEL insole mold with color inserts," claimed by Bocan to be a technical secret, does not meet the legal requirements of unknown to the public and does not constitute a technical secret.

4.2.2. *The Tray Design Has No Commercial Value*

As for the second know-how, the court disqualified the tray design as a trade secret from the perspective of its lack of commercial value. It held that the fact that in Yageshi's workshops some trays are equipped with high-temperature resistant foam material while some are made with other materials, shows that for newly produced shoes just off the mold, which are 50-60°C, the cooling-off does not necessarily have to use foam material and using other materials will not have substantial impact on shoes' quality. In other words, foam materials are not an indispensable cooling material and mainly serve the function of containing products. As such, the foam material has no real or potential economic value, and cannot bring competitive advantage for manufacturers. Moreover, the number of layers in the tray scaffolding should not be considered a technical secret at all.

To sum up, the court of second instance held that the claimed know-how owned by the plaintiff, Bocan, does not meet the requirements of a trade secret, and thus rejected the plaintiff's claims.

4.5. *Legal Analysis*

4.5.1. *The Secrecy Requirement*

The most critical issue in a case of trade secret infringement is whether the claimed know-how meets the requirements of trade secret. According to the current legislation, the requirements of trade secrets should be secrecy, value, and corresponding protection measures. The present decision demonstrates the difficulties in China to meet the requirements of a trade secret, as courts seem to have taken a cautious, strict approach to establishing a trade secret.

However, unlike patent, a trade secret does not require novelty. As long as the know-how involved is not freely and legally available to the public, it would meet the requirement of secrecy. According to Article 9(4) of the *AUCL* and Article 3 of the 2020 Judicial Interpretation, if the information is not generally known to the public, it would meet the requirement of secrecy.

However, it is always a difficult task to prove that something does not exist, such as "unknown to the public." As Cui Guobin rightly pointed out, the secrecy of trade secrets is a typical negative fact and is difficult to prove[36]. In contrast, it is easier to prove a positive fact, such as that the information already exists in the public domain and does not meet the requirement of secrecy. Fujian Provincial Higher People's Court in the present decision took this approach, finding that the claimed confidential information was already in the previous professional publications, and thus known to the public.

For this reason, some scholars advocate that once the plaintiff has provided prima facie evidence on the confidentiality measures he has taken, the burden of proof of secrecy should be reverted to the defendant, who should bear the burden to prove that there is no secrecy. This viewpoint is reflected in the newly added Article 32 of 2019 amendment to *the AUCL,* which provides that in civil trial proceedings for infringement of a trade secret, if the right holder of the trade secret provides prima facie evidence to prove that it has taken confidentiality measures for the claimed trade secret and reasonably indicates that the trade secret has been infringed upon, the alleged tortfeasor shall prove that the trade secret claimed by the right holder is not a trade secret.

4.5.2. Economic Value

It is often said that it is relatively easy to meet the requirement of economic value of a trade secret. However, this is not always the case, and the determination of economic value can be rather subjective. In the present decision, the first instance court recognized the commercial value of the tray design due to two factors, one is the cooling-off and the other is holding and containing products. The second instance denied the first factor, rather convincingly. However, it did not touch upon the second factor, namely, the issue of whether saving space can be of commercial value.

Again, trade secret is not like a patent and does not require an inventive step. It is advisable to caution against the misuse of the commercial value factor in the trade secret context so that at the end of the day inventive step will not be required of trade secrets.

4.6. Commercial or Industrial Significance

It is important for trade secret holders to take reasonable measures to protect their trade secrets, such as signing confidentiality agreements with business partners and employees. Bocan has shown good business acumen in signing confidentiality agreements with its supplier, Spenco, and its employees. Businesses also need to be prepared to meet the rigorous requirements of a trade secret by putting in place sound protective measures and education to raise awareness among employees about the importance of trade secret protection.

Moreover, when litigating over trade secret infringement cases, businesses should be aware of the possibility of commissioning a professional third party to do a

36. Cui Guobin, Distribution of Burden of Proof in Trade Secret Infringement Litigation (in Chinese), SJTU Law Review, 4, 2020, 10.

technical assessment about whether the trade secret at dispute is already known to the public. Notably, in the present case, the first instance court relied entirely on the finding of an authentication center, while the opinion of the technical committee of Xiamen Mould Industry Association affected the second instance court's denial of the claimed trade secrets.

TOPIC 2 THE VALIDITY AND SCOPE OF CONFIDENTIALITY AND/OR NONCOMPETITION CLAUSES

Man Zhang

1. Legal Issues

Signing a confidentiality agreement or noncompetition agreement has been considered an effective means to protect trade secrets[37]. In light of the principle of autonomy of private law, such agreements can be established by the parties of their free will, but they may affect the employee's labor rights; thus some scholars argue that the noncompetition agreement may affect the employees' right to subsistence[38]. Therefore, it is necessary to pay special attention to balancing the interests of both employers and employees when determining the validity of such agreements and resolving resultant disputes. Generally speaking, the legal disputes involving such agreements focus on the following issues: the scope of confidentiality and noncompetition, the relationship between the performance of confidentiality or noncompetition obligations and the payment of compensation, and the calculation of compensation and liquidated damages. Particularly, there are a few difficult questions to be answered: first, whether there is a difference between the legal consequence of leaking secrets to third parties and that of using the secret for the obligor's own business; second, whether noncompetition only refers to inter-business prohibition; third, whether the employer's failure to pay or inadequate compensation would affect the effectiveness of the confidentiality agreement or noncompetition agreement.

2. The Statutory Law

There is no statutory law on the scope and validity of confidentiality obligations in China. To fill the lacuna, the SPC has issued *Provisions on the Trial of Infringement of Trade Secrets* (2020)[39]. Article 2(2) provides that if a customer conducts transactions with an employer due to his trust in a particular employee, and the employee can prove that the customer voluntarily conducts a transaction with the employee or the employee's new employer after the employee leaves, it shall be held that the employee has not obtained trade secrets by improper means. Article 10(1) clearly qualifies any confidentiality obligation as the confidentiality obligation referred to in Article 9(1) of the AUCL[40], and Article 10(2) expands on the grounds from which confidentiality obligations arise[41]. Article 11 stipulates that the management personnel and other

37. Li Yongming, Some Issues Concerning Non-Competition Clauses (in Chinese), Journal of Legal Studies, 5, 2002, 84-97.
38. Li Zaijun, Competition-Constraining Contracts and Confidentiality Contracts (in Chinese), [. Journal of the Central Academy of Political Science and Law, 1, 2000, 50-52.
39. SPC, Fa-Shi [2020] No. 7.
40. Article 10(1) of Provisions on the Trial of Infringement of Trade Secrets provides: The confidentiality obligation assumed by the law or contract shall be recognized by the court as the confidentiality obligation referred to in Article 9(1) of the AUCL.
41. Article 10(2) of Provisions on the Trial of Infringement of Trade Secrets provides: The confidentiality obligation is not stipulated in the contract, but in accordance with the principle

personnel, if having employment relations with legal persons or unincorporated organizations, can be identified as employee and former employee. Article 12 provides that when the court determines whether employees and former employees have channels or opportunities to obtain the holder's trade secrets, it should take into account the following factors:

(1) their position, responsibilities, and authority;
(2) their duties or tasks assigned by the employer;
(3) the specific circumstances of participating in production and operation activities related to trade secrets;
(4) whether they get to keep, use, store, copy, control, or through other means contact or obtain trade secrets and their carriers;
(5) other factors that should be considered.

Notably, in order to balance the protection of trade secrets and the autonomy of employees, Article 13(2) of SPC, *Several Issues Concerning the Applicable Laws in the Trial of Unfair Competition Civil Cases Interpretation*(2007)[42] provides that where a client conducts market transactions with an organization out of confidence in an individual employee of that organization, after such employee leaves the organization, if it can be proved that the client, of its own accord, chooses to conduct market transactions with such employee or his/her new employer, it shall be deemed that no improper means have been used, unless otherwise agreed between the employee and the original employer. Furthermore, Article 22 of China's Labor Law (1995) and Article 23(1) of the Labor Contract Law (2008, 2012) recognize the freedom of employers and employees to conclude a confidentiality clause in the labor contract. Article 22 of the Labor Law provides "The parties to the labor contract may agree on matters related to the protection of the employer's business secrets in the labor contract." Article 23(1) of Labor Contract Law stipulates a similar but slightly detailed provision, which reads, "The employer and the employee may agree in the labor contract a confidentiality clause regarding the employer's business secrets and intellectual property rights." Furthermore, under Articles 23(2) and 24 of the Labor Contract Law, when an employer enters into a noncompetition agreement with its former executives, senior technicians, and other employees with a confidentiality obligation, the time period of noncompetition shall not exceed two years upon the dissolution or termination of the labor relationship; and the employer should pay monthly economic compensation to the employees involved. If the employee violates the agreement, he shall be liable for

---

of good faith, the nature and purpose of the contract, the contracting process, and trading habits, the accused infringer knows or should know that the information obtained is business secrets, then the accused infringer shall assume the obligation of confidentiality.

42. SPC, Fa-Shi [2007] No. 2. Article 13(1) of this interpretation defines the concept of "client list" as specific client information such as "clients' names, addresses and contact details, and the usual practice, intention and details of transactions, which comprise specific client information that is different from the relevant information in the public domain. Such information includes a directory of numerous clients, and specific clients with long-term and stable business relationships."

payment of the agreed damages. However, the above provisions are silent on the scope of confidentiality and the geographical region of restrictions.

In 2009, the SPC issued the "Guiding Opinions on the Proper Trial of Labor Dispute Cases under Current Situations," to remind the courts to maintain public interests and public order, while balancing the interests of employers and employees when handling competition restriction disputes[43]. Moreover, in 2013, the SPC issued the *Interpretation of the SPC on Several Issues Concerning the Application of Law in the Trial of Labor Dispute Cases (IV)* (Judicial Interpretation IV)[44], which provides further regulations to deal with the situations where the noncompetition agreement is not clearly stipulated: the employee who has fulfilled the noncompetition obligations may claim 30% of his average salary in the 12 months before the dissolution or termination of the labor contract as the monthly compensation, which may not be lower than the local minimum wage. The termination of the labor contract does not affect the validity of the noncompetition clause with economic compensation; and if the employer fails to pay compensation for more than three months, the employee can request the cancellation of the noncompetition agreement. The employer may terminate the agreement during the noncompetition period, at which time the employee has the right to claim an additional three months' compensation. Even if the employee has paid liquidated damages for violating a noncompetition clause, his former employer can continue to ask him to uphold the obligation of noncompetition (Articles 6-10, Judicial Interpretation IV).

3. The Case Law

As of September 13, 2020, some 70,898 judgment documents with the keywords "Validity and Scope of Confidentiality Agreement (clauses)" and 2,308 judgment documents with the keywords of "Validity and Scope of Non-competition (clauses)" can be retrieved from China Judgments Online Network[45] and Openlaw[46]. This section limits our search to the so-called classic cases and bulletin cases[47] of the SPC and of courts from China's major commercial regions, including Beijing, Shanghai, Guangdong, Jiangsu, and Fujian. This section selects seven cases for detailed analysis. Currently, when courts handle civil cases on the validity and scope of confidentiality agreements or clauses and noncompetition agreements or clauses, they usually need to discuss the following three points: the validity of noncompetition agreements or clauses, liquidated damages, and economic compensation.

To sum up, the people's courts at all levels seem to have shown the same or similar opinions on the following issues. First, the confidentiality and the noncompetition agreements or clauses, as the expression of the parties' true intention, do not

43. SPC, Fa-Fa [2009] No. 41.
44. SPC, Fa-Shi [2013] No. 4
45. https://wenshu.court.gov.cn/website/wenshu/181029CR4M5A62CH/index.html.
46. http://openlaw.cn.
47. The SPC has a practice of selecting and publicizing courts decisions from all level of courts as examples for courts to follow. The cases published in the Gazette of the SPC are called bulletin cases, while others are called classic cases.

violate the mandatory provisions of laws and administrative regulations, and thus should be recognized as legally binding and effective[48]. Second, when dealing with the noncompetition obligation, courts seem to be less tolerant toward the employee's violation by establishing his own competing business than toward his working for other competitors[49]. Third, the employee cannot defend his violations of confidentiality and noncompetition obligations by citing the employer's failure to pay compensation, wages, dividends, and social insurance premiums[50]. Fourth, if an employee or employer violates the confidentiality or noncompetition agreements or clauses, the court may adjust the amount of agreed damages by comprehensively weighing multiple factors[51].

4. The Leading Case

This section selects the SPC (2019) Min Zai No. 268 case to conduct a comprehensive discussion, based on three reasons: First, in this case, the SPC overturned the judgment of the first and second instance courts, and the final decision has guiding significance for courts in handling similar cases. Second, it conducted a detailed analysis on whether the customer list composed of customer information meets the elements of trade secrets, and it clarifies that customer information protected by trade secrets is special information different from that which is publicly known. Third, the SPC elaborated at great length on the proper balance between the protection of trade secrets and that of employees' freedom to work and move.

4.1. Case Information

SPC (2019) Min Zai No. 268 (decided on December 16, 2019), retrial case of trade secret infringement dispute between Midacre (Tianjin) Technology Co., Ltd. (Midacre) and Huayang Xinxing Technology (Tianjin) Group Co., Ltd (Huayang).

4.2. Summary

The plaintiff Huayang filed a suit, claiming that the four defendants' use of the plaintiff's customer list to facilitate their own business at Midacre constituted infringement of trade secret and should be stopped immediately, and the defendants should jointly compensate Huayang for its economic losses, RMB 3,157,062.9 in total. The case was first tried by the Tianjin First Intermediate People's Court, and then tried by the Tianjin High People's Court and retried by the SPC.

The Court of First Instance ruled in Huayang's favor: (1) the defendants should stop infringing on the trade secrets of Huayang, the client list, during the period in

48. For example, Beijing Haidian District People's Court (2005) Hai Min Chu Zi No. 5106.
49. For example, Shenzhen Intermediate People's Court (2014) Shen Zhong Fa Zhi Min Zhong Zi No. 30.
50. For example, Fuzhou Intermediate People's Court (2014) Rong Min Zhong Zi No. 722; Beijing Higher People's Court (2016) Min Zhong No. 127.
51. Fuzhou Intermediate People's Court (2014) Rong Min Zhong Zi No. 722.

which the claimed trade secrets were not known to the public; (2) Midacre should compensate Huayang RMB 600,000, for which the other defendants shall be jointly and severally liable[52]. Huayang appealed to Tianjin Higher People's Court, which rejected the appeal and upheld the original judgment[53]. Upon the appeal of Midacre, the SPC retried the case and held that the first and second instance courts erred, as a matter of facts and the application of the law, in their finding that Midacre had used Huayang's list of 43 customers and infringed on Huayang's business secrets. The SPC revoked the decisions and dismissed the claims of Huayang.

4.3. *Facts*

The plaintiff Huayang is an enterprise engaged in research and development, production, and sales of industrial cleaning and maintenance products. Its products are mainly industrial chemicals such as cleaning agents, lubricants, and sealants. The first defendant, Midacre, established on October 30, 2015 by Wang Chenggang, mainly engaged in the production and sales of cleaning agents. The registered legal representative at that time was Zhang Shujuan, who was later replaced by Wang.

The second defendant, Wang, joined Huayang in 1996 and served in a series of posts, such as a director, deputy general manager, general manager, vice president, and the legal representative of Huayang (from 2012 to 2016). Two other defendants, Zhang Hongxing and Liu Fang were both former department managers of the plaintiff and later joined the defendant company. Huayang had signed confidentiality agreements with Zhang and Liu, but not with Wang. There were no noncompetition agreements between Huayang and Wang, Zhang, or Liu.

4.4. *The Reasoning of Courts*

4.4.1. *Whether the Customer List Met the Requirements of Commercial Secrets*

The lower courts in this case held that the customer list, composed of customers' information (including 43 customers' names, phone numbers, addresses and transaction contents, prices, and quantities), was information not generally known and easily accessible to relevant persons in the field, and Huayang had also adopted reasonable protection measures commensurate with its commercial value (a user name and password were required to enter the EPR system[54]) so that the customer list qualified as a trade secret.

The SPC dismissed the above decisions. It started by citing Article 13 of the "Interpretation of the SPC on Several Issues Concerning the Application of Law in the Trial of Unfair Competition Civil Cases." The SPC held that the list of customers protected by trade secrets should be specific information that is different from those publicly known, and the customer list at dispute did not qualify as specific information for the following reasons.

52. Tianjin First Intermediate People's Court (2017) Jin 01 Min Chu No. 50.
53. Tianjin Higher People's Court (2018) Jin Min Zhong No. 143.
54. EPR system is a special measure to protect trade secrets made by Huayang.

In the internet environment, it is easy to obtain the relevant demand-side information and relevant industry practitioners can easily know the information given their work skills; the information in the customer list regarding the order dates, order numbers, product names, product specifications, sales order quantity, unit price is general information and does not reflect a customer's trading habits, intentions, and other contents. Without in-depth information covering the specific transaction habits and intentions of relevant customers, it is difficult to determine that the demand-side information is a trade secret protected by the AUCL.

4.4.2. *Whether an Infringement of Commercial Secrets Took Place*

The lower courts found an infringement of the plaintiff's business secrets and violation of the statutory and contractual obligations with the plaintiff on the following grounds: First, several defendants had access to the claimed trade secrets. Second, the defendants had a statutory or contractual obligation of confidentiality. The defendant, Wang, should bear statutory confidentiality obligation because he had been the director and legal representative of the plaintiff company, and he broke the obligation by establishing the defendant company Midacre and serving as its legal representative. The remaining defendants joined the defendant company and held important positions shortly after leaving the plaintiff's company. The defendant company was competing with the plaintiff, as it produced and sold the same products as those of the plaintiff. Within a short period of time after the establishment, the defendant's clients overlapped with those of the plaintiff. Finally, the defendant company failed to prove how it cultivated the 43 customers in a short period of time.

However, the SPC found no infringement of trade secrets on the following grounds: First, Huayang did not sign a noncompetition agreement with Wang and the others, nor did the defendant Midacre have a noncompetition obligation. Second, the specific content of the two parties' client information was largely different. The contact persons for 40 of the 43 clients, accounting for 93%, were different, and the contact persons and contact numbers for 37 of the 43 clients, or 86%, were different.

4.4.3. *The Balance Between the Protection of Trade Secrets and the Employee's Freedom to Work and Use His Expertise Obtained During Previous Employment*

The SPC elaborated that when there exist no obligations of noncompetition or of protecting trade secrets, an employee may use the knowledge, experience, and skills, either learned in previous employment or through other channels in the market, to carry out market development or compete with his previous employers. When there is no statutory prohibition or contractual obligation, employees are not prohibited from engaging in business in the same industry. If an employee were prohibited from competing with his previous employer merely due to the reason that the employer had multiple previous transactions or stable transactions with a particular client, it is essentially restricting the client's opportunity to choose transaction entities. This would result in restriction on market competition, and also not be conducive to safeguarding the legitimate rights and interests of workers in their legitimate employment and entrepreneurship. Such a potential result would run counter to the legislative purposes of the AUCL to safeguard the healthy development of the socialist market economy, to encourage and protect fair competition, to stop unfair competition, and to protect the legitimate rights and interests of business operators and consumers. In addition, the knowledge, experiences, and skills that employees have acquired and accumulated through their work, except for those belonging to trade secrets, constitute a part of their personality, and the basis of their survival ability and work ability, and employees should have the freedom to make use of them independently after leaving the employer.

4.5. *Legal Analysis*

4.5.1. *Confidentiality and Noncompetition Agreement in General*

In theory, the term confidentiality agreement refers to an agreement between an employer and an employee that the employee shall not use, disclose or permit a third party to use the employer's technical information or business information without permission. A noncompetition agreement means an employer and an employee agree that the employee must not engage in industrial competition, so as to prevent the employee from causing competitive disadvantage to the employer's business. Confidentiality and noncompetition agreements also have many similarities. From the perspective of their legal nature, they are both an agreement between employers and employees and fall within the scope of contract law. In terms of form, they may appear as separate agreements or related clauses in the employment contracts. In terms of subject, it is generally believed that statutory duty of loyalty includes confidentiality and noncompetition of directors, supervisors, and other high-ranking management personnel. Therefore, confidentiality and noncompetition agreement are common, explicitly or implicitly, between employers and current and former employees who hold a management role or have access to business secrets.

4.5.2. *Striking the Right Balance?*

Viewed in light of China's recent trend of strengthening the protection for trade secrets, it might seem that the balance shown in this case is rather odd and should be readjusted.

However, as the present decision rightly points out, in trade secret protection and noncompetition cases, consideration must be given to workers' freedom to choose jobs, reasonable flow of talents, preservation of the legitimate interests of workers in rightful employment and starting new businesses, and the enhancement of a reasonable flow of the workforce and workers' independent choice of jobs. Noteworthy is that the present decision even emphasizes the personality character of expertise that employees have acquired and accumulated in the course of work, and the freedom they must enjoy to use it after leaving employment, so long as it does not belong to trade secrets of the former employer.

The above decision that advocates a balanced consideration of multiple factors was decided on December 16, 2019, and was not reflected in the *Provisions on the Trial of Infringement of Trade Secrets* that the SPC promulgated almost one year later (September 10, 2020). Whether it was an intentional rejection or negligent omission remains to be resolved by future case law.

4.6. *Commercial or Industrial Significance*

It is undeniable that intangible assets such as intellectual property rights and trade secrets have increasingly become essential tools for boosting or maintaining the competitiveness of enterprises. Enterprises can mitigate the risk of infringement of these assets in two major ways. For one thing, companies should actively protect and deploy intellectual property rights and trade secrets to create a safe and reliable internal environment for innovation. For another, enterprises should sign confidentiality agreements with employees in general and sign noncompetition agreements with senior managers, and senior technical personnel engaged in research and development, manufacturing, and management specifically. It is necessary to clarify the object, scope, region, term, and compensation of noncompetition agreements. Enterprises can better enforce noncompetition agreements if they agree to pay the leaving employees corresponding compensation.

TOPIC 3 THE SHIFTING OF BURDEN OF PROOF FOR TRADE SECRET INFRINGEMENT

Kung-Chung Liu & Xiaojun Wang

1. Legal Issues

The traditional evidence rule of "whoever asserts he provides evidence" has been applied to trade secret infringement cases in China since 2007, which led to difficulties faced by trade secret holders to prove their cases. In addition, the issue of economic espionage has become a concern for Chinese businesses. In 2019, Article 32 of the AUCL was added to provide solutions to the above problems. How to correctly understand and apply the new provision is one big legal issue.

2. The Statutory Law

In China, the *AUCL,* ever since its inception in 1993, protects trade secret holders from misappropriation. However, there is no express provision on the distribution of burden of proof in trade secret infringement cases. In the early days since the enactment of the *AUCL,* the SPC had accepted presumption and even the reversal of burden of proof to some extent[55]. However, in 2007 the SPC changed its view when it issued its *Interpretation of the SPC on Some Issues Concerning the Application of Law in the Trial of Civil Cases Involving Unfair Competition (*2007 Interpretation*)*[56] to provide the basis for determining the burden of proof.

Article 14 of 2007 Interpretation clearly increased the burden of proof for the holders of trade secrets. A plaintiff needs to prove that: (1) the trade secrets claimed meet the legal requirements, (2) the defendant's information is identical or substantially identical to the plaintiff's trade secrets, and (3) the defendant has obtained the plaintiff's trade secrets by improper means or disclosed them in violation of contractual agreement. These three things must be established at the same time to prove that the defendant infringed the plaintiff's trade secrets. As long as any of these three points is not proven, the plaintiff's case of trade secret infringement will fail. In a 2011 document, the SPC tried to reduce the plaintiff's burden of proof by allowing the establishment of secrecy through "reasonable explanations."[57] However, courts have paid little heed to it[58].

To mitigate the plaintiff's plight, some provincial courts have lowered the standard of proof. For example, Jiangsu Provincial Higher People's Court has in its "Guidelines on the Adjudication of Trade Secret Infringement Cases" (2010) adopted the "preponderant evidence principle": "Given that the element (*of not generally*

55. *See* Cui Guobin, The Distribution of Burden of Proof in Trade Secret Infringement Litigation (in Chinese), SJTU Law Review, 4, 2020, 12.
56. SPC, Fa-Shi [2007] No. 2 (effective February 1, 2007).
57. SPC, Article 25 of Opinions on Several Issues on Sufficient Exercise of Intellectual Property Judicial Function to Promote Socialist Cultural Development and Prosperity and to Stimulate Economic Autonomous and Harmonious Development, 16 December 2011. Fa-Fa [2011] No. 18.
58. Song Jian, Impact of Article 32 of the AUCL 2019 on Trial Rationale for Trade Secret Infringement Cases, China Patents and Trademarks, 4, 2020, 26-27.

known to the public) is a negative fact and the plaintiff faces a greater burden of proof, courts may lower the standard of proof when appropriate, such as following the preponderant evidence principle. In practice, courts may lower the plaintiff's burden of proof by inviting judicial assessment or asking the defendant to prove that the information at dispute is already generally known to the public (2.8.2.)[59]."

In April 2019, China modified the AUCL and introduced the "shifting of burden of proof" against the background of negotiations to defuse the trade war between China and the US. Article 32 of *the AUCL provides:*

> In the civil trial procedure for infringement of a trade secret, if the right holder of the trade secret provides preliminary evidence proving that he has taken protection measures for the claimed trade secret and reasonably explained that the trade secret has been infringed, the alleged infringer shall *prove* (emphasis added) that the trade secret claimed by the right holder is not a trade secret as described in this Law.
>
> If the right holder of a trade secret provides preliminary evidence and reasonable explanations that the trade secret has been infringed, and provides any of the following evidence, the alleged tortfeasor shall *prove* (emphasis added) the absence of such infringement:
>
> (1) Evidence that the alleged infringer has a channel or an opportunity to access the trade secret and that the information he uses is substantially the same as the trade secret.
> (2) Evidence that the trade secret has been disclosed or used, or is at risk of disclosure or use, by the alleged infringer.
> (3) Evidence that the trade secret is otherwise infringed upon by the alleged infringer.

Some eight months later, the US and China signed on January 15, 2020 the Economic and Trade Agreement. Article 1.5(2) of the Agreement (Burden-Shifting in a Civil Proceeding) provides a verbatim translation of Article 32 of *the AUCL, but lessening the tortfeasor's burden from "prove" to "show"*:

> China shall provide that: (a) the burden of proof or burden of production of evidence, as appropriate, shifts to the accused party to *show* (emphasis added) that it did not misappropriate a trade secret once a holder of a trade secret produces: (i) evidence that the accused party had access or opportunity to obtain a trade secret and the information used by the accused party is materially the same as that trade secret; (ii) evidence that a trade secret has been or risks being disclosed or used by the accused party; or (iii) other evidence that its trade secret(s) were misappropriated by the accused party; and (b) under the circumstance that the right holder provides preliminary evidence that measures were taken to keep the claimed trade secret confidential, the burden of proof or burden of production of evidence, as appropriate, shifts to the accused party to *show* "[emphasis added]" that a trade secret identified by a holder is generally known among persons within the circles that normally deal with the kind of information in question or is readily accessible, and therefore is not a trade secret.

59. *See* Cui Guobin, The Distribution of Burden of Proof in Trade Secret Infringement Litigation (in Chinese), SJTU Law Review, 4, 2020, 13; Song Jian, Impact of Article 32 of the AUCL 2019 on Trial Rationale for Trade Secret Infringement Cases, China Patents and Trademarks, 4, 2020, 17.

3. The Case Law

"Burden of proof," "reversal of burden of proof," and "trade secret infringement" were used as keywords to search for relevant trade secret infringement cases. The result shows that there are rarely cases that deviated from the traditional rule of burden of proof before the 2019 amendment of *the AUCL*. According to one study, in China from 2013 to 2017, plaintiffs in trade secret infringement cases have a losing rate of 63.19%, a winning rate of 9.27%, and a partial winning rate of 25.74%[60]. On the whole, the winning rate for plaintiffs in trade secret infringement cases is clearly lower than that of patent, trademark, and copyright infringement cases[61]. The commonly held opinion attributes this to the plaintiff's inability to prove to the court's satisfaction that information at dispute was a trade secret[62].

In the following, two cases (one from the SPC and the other from Shanghai) are introduced to show that the plaintiff bears a relatively heavy burden of proof.

In *(2012) Min-Shen-Zi No. 1403*[63], the SPC held that under Article 14 of the 2007 Interpretation, the plaintiff needed to prove three points to establish a trade secret infringement, namely that the claimed information meets the requirements of trade secrets, the defendant's information is identical or substantially identical to the plaintiff's trade secrets, and the defendant has misappropriated the trade secrets by improper means. In the current case, the plaintiff failed to prove that the technical information used by the defendant was essentially identical to his trade secrets and that the defendant had disclosed his trade secrets in violation of the agreement. Therefore, the plaintiff's claim was dismissed.

In (2012) Hu-Gao-Min-San-Zhong Zi No. 43[64], the Shanghai Higher People's Court followed Article 14 of the 2007 Interpretation and held that when the appellants claimed that the appellees had infringed their trade secrets, they should have provided evidence to prove that the appellees had obtained the trade secrets through unfair means and disclosed or used them. Since the appellants failed to provide evidence to prove the facts as required, their claims of trade secret infringement could not be established.

---

60. *See* Tao Guandong, Reflection on Burden of Proof in Trade Secret Infringement Dispute—Written on the Occasion of the Addition of Article 32 of the AUCL, China Patents and Trademarks, 3, 2019, 68.
61. Song Jian, Impact of Article 32 of the AUCL 2019 on Trial Rationale for Trade Secret Infringement Cases, China Patents and Trademarks, 4, 2020, 27.
62. Cui Guobin, The Distribution of Burden of Proof in Trade Secret Infringement Litigation (in Chinese), SJTU Law Review, 4, 2020, 18.
63. The SPC (2012) Min-Shen-Zi No. 1403 (decided on December 25, 2012). This case was chosen by the SPC as a bulletin case (The SPC has a practice of selecting and publicizing court decisions from all levels of courts as examples for courts to follow. The cases published in the Gazette of the SPC are called bulletin cases, while others are called classic cases).
64. Shanghai Higher People's Court, Hu-Gao-Min San (Zhi) Zhong Zi No. 43, *Tianxiang Investment Consulting Co., Ltd., Beijing Tianxiangtonghe Information Technology Co., Ltd. v Shanghai Wande Information Technology Co., Ltd. and Shanghai Wande Investment Management Co., Ltd.* (decided on September 14, 2012).

4. The Leading Case

This section selects the decision in which the plaintiff was awarded RMB 35,000,000 for economic losses and RMB 220,000 for reasonable expenses, which was the highest amount of compensation in trade secret infringement cases as of the writing of this report[65]. The decision was chosen by Zhejiang Higher People's Court as one of the ten IP cases in 2018 in Zhejiang Province.

4.1. *Case Information*

Zhejiang Shaoxing Intermediate People's Court (2014) Zhe-Shao-Zhi-Chu-Zi No. 500 civil decision (not published).

Zhejiang Higher People's Court (2017) Zhe-Min-Zhong No. 123, *Fujian Fukang Pharmaceutical Co., Ltd., Fujian Haixin Pharmaceutical Co., Ltd., and Yu Ke v Zhejiang Xinhecheng Co., Ltd.* (decided on May 21, 2018).

This case is currently pending retrial before the SPC.

4.2. *Summary*

Xinhecheng Company sued Fukang Company, Haixin Company, and Yu Ke on the grounds that they jointly infringed its technical secrets, and requested that the court order the defendants to immediately stop the infringement and to compensate the economic losses of RMB 50 million and reasonable expenses of RMB 1 million.

Zhejiang Shaoxing Intermediate People's Court ruled that the defendants should immediately stop infringing the trade secrets of Xinhecheng Company, and Haixin Company should compensate Xinhecheng Company for economic losses of RMB 35,000,000 in addition to reasonable expenses of RMB 220,000, while Fukang Company and Yu Ke bear joint and several liability for the compensation. Fukang Company, Haixin Company, and Yu Ke appealed to Zhejiang Higher People's Court, which rejected the appeal.

4.3. *Facts*

In 2008, Fukang Company contacted Yu Ke, an employee of Xinhecheng Company through an intermediary, and purchased technical information for manufacturing vitamin E from Yu Ke for RMB 800,000. Yu Ke then handed over to Fukang Company the technical information, such as a manufacturing flowchart for vitamin E intermediates and engineering specifications that he came into contact with during his work for Xinhecheng Company, however removing signs indicating Xinhecheng Company. In 2010, Yu Ke joined Fukang under a fake name as the deputy general manager. In 2011, some shareholders of Fukang set up Haixin Company, to which the vitamin E project team of Fukang was transferred. Yu Ke also worked as the deputy general manager of Haixin. While working for Fukang and Haixin, Yu actively referenced and used

65. Noteworthy is that, on February 26, 2021, the SPC has in (2020) Zhi-Min-Zhong-Zi 1669 decision awarded damages of RMB159 million in a trade secret infringement case.

technical information data he illegally copied from Xinhecheng's No. 606 workshop and technical data he stole from the director of Xinhecheng's No. 603 workshop.

Xinchang police department started to investigate Yu Ke, Fukang, and Haixin in 2013. In 2015, Xinchang People's Court found them guilty of the crime of trade secret infringement. It imposed a RMB 14 million fine on Fukang and a RMB 17 million fine on Haixin and sentenced Yu Ke to six years' imprisonment with a fine of RMB 200,000. Xinhecheng brought a civil suit against the three defendants and sought a cease and desist order, destruction of equipment for manufacturing and testing vitamin E and its intermediates, destruction of drawings and files containing the trade secrets at dispute, and damages of RMB 50 million.

4.4. *Reasoning of the Courts*[66]

The first instance court follows the "preponderant evidence principle" adopted by Jiangsu Provincial Higher People's Courts in its "Guidelines on the Adjudication of Trade Secret Infringement Cases" (2010), which is confirmed by the second instance court. The first instance court started by reciting Article 9 of the Interpretation on Several Issues Concerning the Application of Law in the Trial of Civil Cases on Unfair Competition issued by the SPC in 2007 (2007 Judicial Interpretation): "(1) If the relevant information is not generally known and not easily accessible by relevant persons in the relevant field, it should be considered not generally known to the public. (2) In any of the following situations the relevant information may be considered generally known to the public: (i) The information falls within common sense or industrial practices in the relevant field. (ii) The information only involves such contents as the product size, structure, materials, and simple combination of components, which may be directly obtained by relevant persons in the relevant field through observation of products on the market. (iii) The information has been disclosed to the public in open publication or publicized in any media. (iv) The information has been disclosed to the public through public meetings, exhibitions, and other methods. (v) The information may be obtained through other public channels. (vi.) The information can be easily obtained without paying certain prices."

4.4.1. *On the Issue of Secrecy (Not Generally Known to the Public)*

The first instance court further decided that vitamin E and its intermediates are not new products, and its manufacturing methods are often documented in public literature. However, the trade secrets in the present case involve the manufacturing skills and dedicated equipment for the intermediates of vitamin E, which are company-specific depending on its scale, existent equipment, technical capacity, and working experience. The exploration of manufacturing skills and dedicated equipment requires huge efforts and wisdom. As a result, there are only a few companies in China that manufacture the intermediates of vitamin E, with each earning different profit margins.

66. The following discussion focuses exclusively on the court's finding of trade secrets based on the evidence provided by the parties.

Given the potential value of manufacturing skills and dedicated equipment, vitamin E manufacturers generally adopt a certain level of protective measures, making them not generally known to relevant persons in the relevant field and difficult to acquire.

The court went on to discuss the six scenarios where "not generally known to the public" may be negated, in other words, the information at dispute is not generally known to the public or lacks secrecy: (1) The fact that only a few technicians such as Yu Ke knew the manufacturing process and dedicated equipment for the intermediates, and Fukang was unable to completely control the know-how with the technology brought from Yu Ke shows that the information in question could not be common sense or industrial practices in the relevant field. (2) The relevant public or even professionals could not directly obtain the trade secrets, namely the drawings of the manufacturing process and dedicated equipment, at dispute by observing the products of manufactured intermediates and vitamin E products. (3) Following the novelty check for patents, if the information at dispute possesses novelty, it can show that it is not domestically or internationally known to the public prior to the date of the novelty check. The novelty check by the patent search center of China National Intellectual Property Administration did not find the same or substantially the same technical solution as the one in question. It is therefore not disclosed in open publication or publicized in any media, or disclosed to the public through public meetings, exhibitions, or obtainable through public channels. (4) The sale of the trade secret shows that it cannot be obtained without paying huge prices. The defendants could have found proof to disprove that the information at dispute is not generally known to the public, which is much easier than Xinhecheng's burden of proof, as he would need to disprove only one of the six scenarios. However, the defendants did not sufficiently disprove them, and only disputed the adoption of a novelty check for patents, without factual or legal basis.

4.4.2. On the Issue of Protective Measures Taken

The first instance court holds that Xinhecheng adopted "reasonable protective measures" for the secrets involved. It recites Article 11 of the 2007 Judicial Interpretation: The reasonable protective measures adopted by the right holder to prevent information leakage which correspond to the specific circumstances of the case, such as its commercial value, shall be regarded as a "protective measure." The court shall determine whether the right holder has taken reasonable protective measures based on factors such as the characteristics of the medium that carries the information involved, the right holder's willingness to keep secrets, the identifiability of the protective measures, and the difficulty for others to obtain [the secrets] through legitimate means. Xinhecheng has set up a confidentiality system which specifies the scope of confidentiality, protective measures, and consequences for breaching a confidentiality system.

Yu Ke had signed the 1999 confidentiality agreement. Although the defendant disputed this, asserting without valid evidence that the stamp was later added, that does not change the fact that Yu Ke knew of the confidentiality agreement and was willing to fulfill his confidentiality obligation. The defendant further disputed that he had signed the 2008 confidentiality agreement. However, the criminal decision has confirmed that Yu Ke did write his ID number and address on the 2008 confidentiality agreement. This, in the absence of valid evidence to disprove the facts by the defendant, at least proves that Yu Ke knew of the content of the agreement. The fact that the information in question has up to now not been disclosed shows that the protective measures adopted by Xinhecheng were reasonable and valid. Therefore, it can be concluded that Xinhecheng had adopted reasonable protective measures that correspond to the commercial value of the trade secrets.

4.5. *Legal Analysis*

The present decision reasonably allocates the burden of proof and remedies the rigidity of the burden of proof rule prior to the revision of *the AUCL*. The following discussion will be focusing not on the present decision, but rather on the future application.

4.5.1. Tilting the Scale Too Much in Favor of the Right Holder?

Plaintiffs in Taiwan have also been troubled by the difficulty of proving the existence and infringement of trade secrets. Taiwan's Intellectual Property Case Adjudication Act was introduced in 2014. Its Article 10-1 plays a different ping-pong game with regards to burden of proof in trade secret infringement cases. It provides that in trade secret infringement cases, if a party has made a preliminary showing that his/her trade secret has been or is likely to be infringed, and the other party denies such allegation, the court shall order the other party to raise a specific defense as to the reasons for the denial.

The court may, subject to the circumstances, find the preliminary showing of the infringed party true if the other party mentioned in the preceding paragraph fails without good cause to raise a defense within the prescribed time limit or to raise a specific defense[67]. This provision does not involve the reversal or shifting of burden of proof. Rather it only urges the defendant to conduct good-faith defense.

In stark contrast, Article 32 of the AUCL clearly tilts the scale in the holder's favor and perhaps a bit too much. It only requires the right holder to provide preliminary evidence for taking protective measures for the claimed trade secret and reasonable explanations that the trade secret has been infringed. However, it then demands that the alleged infringer *"prove"* that the trade secret claimed by the right holder is not a trade secret or to *"prove"* the absence of such infringement. While it is in principle not difficult for the right holder to provide preliminary evidence and reasonable explanations, it can be cumbersome or even an unsurmountable hurdle for the defendant to prove. Therefore, Cui Goubin criticizes Article 32 as "unreasonably burdening the load of disadvantaged defendants, hampering free movement of talents, increasing

67. For discussion of Taiwan's law on burden of proof, please refer to Hsiao-Fen Hsu and Kung-Chung Liu, A Ping-Pong between Burden of Proving Trade Secret Infringement and Specific Defense in the present book.

management costs for businesses, breaking the balance of interests between right holders and the public, and harming the long-term industrial interests of China[68]."

Looking forward, to reduce the defendants' burden to also providing preliminary evidence and reasonable explanations after the plaintiff did his part, as the word "to show" in Article 1.5(2) of the US and China Economic and Trade Agreement suggests, may be a preferred future law (lex ferenda) so that a balanced ping-pong game can go on.

4.5.2. How to Apply Article 32 of the AUCL in a Balanced Way

Song Jian suggests, first, distinguishing between infringement through theft, bribery, fraud, coercion, electronic intrusion, or any other illicit means, and infringement through breach of contract, and, second, clearly lowering the plaintiff's burden of providing preliminary evidence and reasonable explanations in the former case[69]. However, that would further tilt the scale to the holder's favor. In contrast, Cui Guobin suggests requiring that the plaintiff's burden of providing preliminary evidence and reasonable explanations cover the secrecy element of the trade secret and the misconduct of the defendant[70]. We agree with Cui's suggestion and additionally propose to apply the preponderant evidence principle to the defendant who committed infringement through breach of contract, which is less culpable than infringement through theft, bribery, fraud, coercion, electronic intrusion, or any other illicit means.

4.6. Commercial or Industrial Significance

It is expected that Article 32 of the AUCL coupled with the revised Article 219 and added Article 210-1 of the Criminal Law will lead to more success for the holders of trade secrets and thus more trade secret infringement cases[71]. It is advisable for trade secret holders to actively formulate a trade secret management system and take corresponding protective measures, such as signing confidentiality agreements. This would easily enable them to provide preliminary evidence for taking protective measures for the claimed trade secret and reasonable explanations that the trade secret has been infringed and to trigger the shifting of the burden of proof to the defendant.

As for the defendants, especially those leaving their previous employers to join new ones, they should realize that their burden of proof can be quite onerous and difficult to satisfy. Therefore, arranging an amicable work transition between different employers is imperative.

68. Cui Guobin, The Distribution of Burden of Proof in Trade Secret Infringement Litigation (in Chinese), SJTU Law Review, 4, 2020, 33.
69. Song Jian, Impact of Article 32 of the AUCL 2019 on Trial Rationale for Trade Secret Infringement Cases, China Patents and Trademarks, 4, 2020, 29.
70. Cui Guobin, The Distribution of Burden of Proof in Trade Secret Infringement Litigation (in Chinese), SJTU Law Review, 4, 2020, 32.
71. For more, *see* Topic 6 of the present chapter.

TOPIC 4 PRELIMINARY INJUNCTION

Luo Li

1. Legal Issues

Chinese law recognizes preservative measures which are equivalent to preliminary injunctions in common law countries. There are three types of preservative measures: evidence preservation, property preservation and "behavior preservation[72]." While there was no doubt that the former two preservative measures can be applied to trade-secret-related legal disputes, whether behavior preservation was applicable to trade secrets legal disputes was highly controversial because it would prohibit respondents from using the information in dispute, which could seriously affect their business. Owners of trade secrets, however, called for behavior preservation because of the fear that their trade secrets would be leaked during litigation, which was the main reason that discouraged many owners from taking legal action.

Arguments opposing the application of behavior preservation in trade secret disputes include the following[73]. First, it is very difficult for the judge to know whether there exists a legally recognized trade secret before the completion of the whole process, let alone to evaluate the possibility of the plaintiff winning the case, which are the conditions for applying behavior preservation. Second, the considerably lower winning rate of plaintiffs in trade secret disputes, as opposed to other intellectual property cases, speaks against the application of behavior preservation. Third, behavior preservation, as a very powerful instrument that could greatly affect the normal business operation of the respondent, could be used by applicants to compete unfairly.

Arguments supporting the application of behavior preservation in trade secret disputes are as follows[74]: It can prevent the unnecessary disclosure of trade secrets during the litigation and better protect owners who are afraid of a second leak of trade secrets during the litigation. Second, Article 50 of TRIPS prescribes provisional measures which could include behavior preservation. Third, other countries, especially the US, have had many successful experiences in applying preliminary injunctions in trade-secret-related disputes.

In summary, the main issue regarding the application of preliminary injunction in trade-secret-related disputes is the applicability of behavior preservation and how to balance the interests of right owners to prevent their trade secrets from unnecessary disclosure and the interests of respondents in keeping their normal business operation.

---

72. An injunction to do or not do certain behaviors.
73. *See*, e.g., Kong Xiangjun (ed.), Practice of Judicial Protection of Trade Secrets (in Chinese), China Legal Publishing House, 2012, 192-193.
74. *See*, e.g., Huang Wushuang, The Inevitable Disclosure Rule of the U.S. Trade Secret Law and Its Inspiration (in Chinese), Legal Science, 8, 2007; Peng Xuelong, Injunctive Relief in U.S. Trade Secret Law (in Chinese), Intellectual Property, 4, 2004, P58.

2. The Statutory Law

Preservative measures were first codified into Chinese law by the Chinese Civil Procedural Law (CPL) of 1991, which prescribes evidence preservation (Article 74) and the requirements and enforcement of property preservation (Articles 92-99). Although Chinese Patent Law[75], Trademark Law[76], and Copyright law[77] all introduced behavior preservation before China's accession to World Trade Organization (WTO) in 2001, behavior preservation was not available to trade secret owners until 2012, after the 3rd amendment of the CPL: a People's court may order the respondent to do or not to do certain behaviors based on the application of another party or ex officio (Article 100).

In 2018, the SPC promulgated Regulations on Several Issues Concerning Application of Behavior Preservation in Intellectual Property Disputes[78] (Regulations on Behavior Preservation) and provided in Articles 100 and 101 of CPL classification as an "urgent situation" when the applicant's trade secrets will be illegally disclosed if no immediate behavior preservation measures are taken (Article 6(1)). This eventually cleared the way for applying behavior preservation to trade secret disputes.

In order to balance the interests of the trade secret owners on the one side and the respondents and the public on the other side, the court must consider the following factors when determining whether to grant the behavior preservation measure:

(1) whether the applicant's request has a factual basis and legal ground, including whether the validity of the intellectual property for which protection was requested is stable;
(2) whether failure to take behavior preservation measures will cause irreparable damage to the applicant's lawful rights and interests or cause difficulty in enforcing the decision of the case;
(3) whether the damage to the applicant caused by failure to take preservation measures exceeds the damage caused to the respondent by taking the preservation measures;
(4) whether the adoption of behavior preservation measures harms the public interests of society;
(5) other factors that should be considered (Article 7 of Regulations on Behavior Preservation).

The applicant must provide a guarantee that is sufficient to compensate the loss that the respondent might suffer as a result of the behavior preservation measure (Article 11 of Regulations on Behavior Preservation). If the court decides to take behavior preservation measures, it shall reasonably determine the time limit of the

75. Article 61 of Chinese Patent Law of 2000, which is revised to only include evidence preservation in 2008 and remains so in Article 67 of Chinese Patent Law of 2020.
76. Article 57 of Chinese Trademark Law of 2001, which is renumbered to Article 65 in 2019, yet its content remains unchanged.
77. Article 49 of Chinese Copyright Law of 2001, which is renumbered to Article 56 in 2020, yet its content remains unchanged.
78. SPC, Fa-Shi [2018] No. 21

preservation measures based on the applicant's request or the specific circumstances of the case (Article 13 of Regulations on Behavior Preservation).

3. The Case Law

The SPC has taken a very cautious approach in applying provisional measures, especially behavior preservation, and asked Chinese courts to carefully examine actual circumstances and strictly apply the rules on provisional measures[79]. There have only been a handful of trade secret cases in which the application of behavior preservation has been granted in trade secret litigation before 2019, which are briefly reported in the following.

In Shanghai First Intermediate People's Court, (2014) Hu Yi Zhong Min Bao No. 1 (decided on January 8, 2014), the defendant, a former employee of Novartis China, made copies of many confidential documents before leaving the plaintiff, without its consent. The plaintiff sent the defendant a warning letter demanding that the latter delete or destroy all the confidential documents. Having not received any response from the defendant, the plaintiff brought this issue before the court and filed an application for behavior preservation, which was granted.

In Shanghai Huangpu District Court, (2014) Huang Pu Min San (Zhi) Chu Zi No. 204 (decided on January 9, 2015), the plaintiff claimed that its former employee, Mr. Kang, downloaded a huge number of documents from the plaintiff's database without authorization. The plaintiff requested behavior preservation measures to prohibit Mr. Kang from using the documents in question. The court ruled in favor of the plaintiff.

In the Haitian Food Company case[80], the defendant was the plaintiff's former employee in charge of the technical team, and had downloaded confidential information to his personal computer, then reported the loss of his office computer on the day he quit his job unexpectedly. Considering the defendant's wife was suing the plaintiff's associated company, the plaintiff filed a lawsuit against the defendant for stealing trade secrets and requested behavior preservation under a RMB 1 million guarantee, which was granted by Foshan Intermediate People's Court.

In Zhejiang Higher People's Court (2017) Zhe Min Zhong No. 123 (decided on May 21, 2018), appellant one (defendant in the first instance), an employee of the respondent (a pharmaceutical company, plaintiff in the first instance), sold technical information which he collected from the respondent to appellant two (also a defendant in the first instance) to enable the manufacture of vitamin E. Later appellant one left the respondent and worked for appellant two as deputy general manager, bringing with him a great deal of technical data he copied secretly from the respondent. After some shareholders of appellant two formed another company, namely appellant three (also a defendant in the first instance), appellant one and the vitamin E production line were

79. The SPC's Opinions on Several Issues Regarding Intellectual Property Trials Serving the Overall Situation under the Current Economic Situation, Fa-Fa [2009] No. 23.
80. Press release of Foshan Intermediate People's Court on May 28, 2014: To prevent key personnel from leaking secrets, Haitian applied for behavior preservation, available at: http://www.fszjfy.gov.cn/pub/court_7/gongzuodongtai/fayuanyaowen/meitijujiao/201405/t20140528_19634.htm? clicktime = 1582815292&enterid = 1582815292.

both transferred to appellant three. The respondent sued for trade secret infringement and applied for behavior preservation. The court of first Instance decided in favor of the respondent and granted behavior preservation against appellant three, ordering appellant three to stop manufacturing and selling vitamin E using the trade secrets in dispute immediately, which was upheld by the court of second instance.

In Tianjin Binhai New District People's Court (2019) Jin 0116 Min Chu No. 2091 (decided on March 18, 2019), both the applicants and the respondent are social media platforms. The respondent asked its new users, who have already been users of the applicants, to allow it to access their account information on the applicants' platform, including nicknames, profile photos, etc., without the applicants' permission. The respondent not only kept this information for its own use, for example, to simplify the registration process but also sold it to another social platform. The court agreed with the applicants that the users' account information can qualify as trade secrets and belongs to the applicants, therefore the applicants' request for behavior preservation has legal and factual ground. The court held that the applicants should be protected against continuous harm by the act of the respondent during what was expected to be a lengthy trial, given the complexity of the case. The necessity of taking behavior preservation measures is justified by the following facts: (1) The respondent's act may greatly impair the applicants' competitive advantage in the relevant market given the rapid development and frequent updates of products and services on the internet. (2) The respondent's act would do irreparable harm to users of the applicants due to the fast and boundless nature of internet transfer. (3) The respondent's act endangers the personal information of the applicants' users and thus harms the applicants' goodwill.

In all the abovementioned cases, the behavior preservation measures are adopted upon the application of the plaintiffs. No behavior preservation order was made ex officio. There are no cases in which ex-employees are banned from working for competitors before the final judgments are made. In all cases where ex-employees are banned from working for competitors, the ban was granted by the final decision, and not behavior preservation measure, and was based on noncompete contracts.

It is, however, to be anticipated that there will be an increase in both the application and granting of behavior preservation measures after the Regulations of Behavior Preservation took effect in 2019[81].

4. Leading Case

4.1. Case Information

Shanghai First Intermediate People's Court (2013) Hu Yi Zhong Min Wu (Zhi) Chu Zi No. 119 (2013), Eli Lilly and Company, Eli Lilly (China) Research and Development

81. There are no official statistics regarding cases that applied Regulations of Behavior Preservation yet. The author only found on China Judgment Online (中国裁判文书网) one case in which behavior preservation is discussed after 2019. However, this does not suggest that the Regulation of Behavior Preservation doesn't have an encouraging effect on trade secret owners in applying for behavior preservation measures. Presumably, the reason for the small number of cases lies in two facts: (1) not all the relevant decisions have been made publicly accessible yet when trade secrets are involved; (2) the COVID-19 pandemic dissuaded people from bringing lawsuits.

Corporation v Huang Mengwei, decided on December 25, 2013. This is the first case in which behavior preservation measures were adopted in a trade secret dispute.

4.2. *Summary*

Plaintiff two (Eli Lilly (China) Research and Development Corporation) is owned by plaintiff one (Eli Lilly and Company). In 2012, the defendant started working for plaintiff two, signed a confidentiality agreement and received training on trade secret protection. In 2013, the defendant downloaded 48 documents from the server of plaintiff two and saved them on his private devices, 21 of which contained core trade secrets of the plaintiffs. After plaintiff two confronted him, the defendant promised to delete these documents in dispute but failed to do so. Plaintiff two then fired the defendant and together with plaintiff one filed a lawsuit against him, asking the court to order the defendant not to disclose, use or allow others to use the trade secrets stolen from them. The court ruled in favor of the plaintiffs.

4.3. *Facts*

The information and documents at issue are owned by the plaintiffs. The contents of the 21 documents mainly relate to the pathological principles and paths of diabetes treatment, as well as the compounds of related drug candidates developed for certain pathologies, the drug response of the compounds, the roadmap of clinical research and development, and the internal compounds. The information and documents at issue involve the most confidential content of pharmaceutical companies. It has never been made public in any form and cannot be easily obtained by those skilled in the art. The plaintiffs spent heavy human, material, and financial resources and obtained the abovementioned information through countless experiments. As interim research results of new drug research and development, they have foreseeable commercial value. Also, the plaintiffs took a variety of confidentiality measures to protect the information, including limiting the scope of the personnel who have access, adopting encryption measures on the documents, marking confidentiality signs, monitoring the accessing and downloading of the documents, signing confidentiality agreements with employees, and conducting confidentiality training. The defendant did not deny the content of the disputed information file but argued that the basic compound involved was publicly known information, and the experimental data were a simple combination that could be easily obtained by those skilled in the art. However, the defendant failed to provide robust evidence to confirm the argument.

The defendant obtained the documents at issue without the plaintiff's consent and breached the confidentiality agreement. The plaintiff's regulations stipulate that employees shall not download or store company information on electronic devices or media other than the ones belonging to the plaintiffs. Although the defendant had the authorization to access the information at the workplace, he violated the obligation of confidentiality by downloading the information and storing it on his personal devices without either the permission of the plaintiff or notifying the plaintiff.

The defendant did not delete or destroy the information in dispute as he had promised and as was required by the plaintiffs. The defendant had promised in written form that he would allow the company to check his personal devices to ensure that the information at issue was not leaked or used, and also to delete the information. However, the defendant later refused the plaintiff's access to his personal devices.

4.4. *The Court's Reasoning*

4.4.1. *The Information at Issue Constitutes Trade Secrets*[82]

According to Article 10 of the AUCL of 1993, the information constitutes trade secrets when it is unknown to the public, able to bring economic benefits to the right holder, is practical, and is under protective measures. The court held that although the information at issue included the basic compound, which is publicly known information, it does not mean that the method of combining the known compounds is also known to the public. The fact that the plaintiffs adopted various effective measures to protect the information suggests that the information at issue was not easy to obtain. Regarding the issue of the practical value of the disputed information, the court reasoned that although the information at issue could not bring any economic benefit at this stage, it was still valuable because it could help speed up the experiment and production process, establishing the plaintiffs' competitive advantage in research and development. The court also recognized the plaintiffs' various efforts in adopting protective measures, such as limiting personnel's access to the disputed information, encrypting the files with the information at issue, marking confidentiality signs, monitoring of accessing and downloading of the files, signing confidentiality agreements, and providing trade secret protection training to their employees. Therefore, the court concluded that the information of the 21 files in dispute constituted trade secrets protected by the AUCL.

4.4.2. *The Defendant's Conduct Constituted Trade Secret Infringement*

The defendant's act of downloading the disputed information and saving it on his personal devices violated the company's rules and was improper, and could be classified as "obtaining rightholder's trade secrets by other improper means" under Article 10 of the AUCL, and thus constituted trade secret infringement.

4.4.3. *It Is Necessary to Take Behavior Preservation Measures*

The court believed it was not necessary to adopt behavior preservation measures if there was only a general possibility of unauthorized disclosure or use of the information at issue. The court took into account the substantial possibility of the applicant winning the case; whether the applicant would suffer a substantial threat of irreparable loss if no behavior preservation was taken; whether the applicant would suffer more

82. The decision available to the public does not contain page, paragraph or line numbers.

damage than any potential damage to the respondent; and whether behavior preservation measures would violate public interest and other factors. In conclusion, the court held that it was obvious that the respondent obtained the applicants' trade secrets by improper means, that once trade secrets were disclosed there would no longer be any way to protect them, as they would be lost forever, and that to prohibit the defendant as an individual from disclosing, using or authorizing others to use the documents in dispute would do less harm to the defendant than the harm done to the plaintiffs through the leak of trade secrets.

Based on the above reasoning and evaluation, the court ruled that it was necessary to adopt behavior preservation measures during the trial.

4.5. *Legal Analysis*

4.5.1. *"Likelihood of Judgment in Favor of the Applicant" as Factor to Consider When Determining Application for Behavior Preservation*

The court in the Eli Lilly case listed some factors to be considered when determining the applicability of the behavior preservation rule, namely how likely it was that the applicant would win the case; whether the applicant would suffer a substantial threat of irreparable loss if no behavior preservation were taken; whether the applicant would suffer more damage than any potential damage to the respondent; and whether behavior preservation measures would violate the public interest.

However, one of the major differences between the consideration of behavior preservation and permanent injunction is of course that the court has to decide whether to grant a behavior preservation application before it knows which party wins the case, whereas the court only has to decide whether a permanent injunction is the proper remedy for the plaintiff after he won the case. In the Eli Lilly case, the court cautiously avoided the potential conflict between the behavior preservation ruling and the final judgment by using the expression "the respondent is prohibited from disclosing, using or allowing others to use the 21 *documents claimed by the applicant as trade secret.*"

Furthermore, both the CPL and the Regulations on Behavior Preservation require the applicant to provide a guarantee for behavior preservation measures, which could compensate the respondent in case the behavior preservation measures were later revoked and harm to the respondent occurred as a result. Therefore, it is correct that the Regulations on Behavior Preservation require the applicant to demonstrate that its request of behavior preservation measures has a factual and legal ground, rather than to demonstrate the substantial possibility of winning the case.

4.5.2. *The Present Decision Was Heavily Influenced by eBay*[83]

In the eBay case, the U.S. Supreme Court required that a plaintiff who requested a permanent injunction against a defendant demonstrate: (1) that it had suffered an

83. *Ebay Inc. et al. v MercExchange,* L.L.C. 547 U.S. 388 (2006).

irreparable injury; (2) that remedies available at law were inadequate to compensate for that injury; (3) that considering the balance of hardships between the plaintiff and defendant, a remedy in equity was warranted; and (4) that the public interest would not have been disserved by a permanent injunction.

The court in the Eli Lilly decision was heavily influenced by the eBay case and clarified that "other damages to parties" stipulated in Article 100 of the CPL requires that the applicant suffer "a substantial threat of irreparable loss" and that the damage to the applicant caused by the failure to take behavior preservation measures exceed the damage caused to the respondent by the behavior preservation measures. This understanding is clearly picked up by Article 7(2) and (3) of Regulations on Behavior Preservation.

4.6. Commercial/Industrial Significance

With the development of digital technology and the free movement of people, trade secrets are more vulnerable to infringement than ever. The Eli Lilly case and the behavior preservation rules under Chinese law suggest that, in order to better protect their trade secrets, avoid disputes and reduce damage, companies should:

(1) Establish detailed rules on trade secrets protection, including the scope of trade secrets and what employees should and shouldn't do. In the Eli Lilly case, the defendant argued that Eli Lilly China's rules didn't forbid employees from downloading confidential information from the company's server and storing it on personal devices. While it is true with Eli Lilly China's own policy, Eli Lilly China's parent company, Eli Lilly and Company, has a global policy regarding the use of the company's electronic resources which clearly prohibits its employees from downloading or storing any communication or information related to the company on any non-company devices. This Global Policy is also applicable to Eli Lilly China's employees including the defendant because Eli Lilly China not only made the employees aware of it but also required them to sign an acknowledgment of this. Otherwise, Eli Lilly China could have lost the case.

(2) Take effective protective measures, such as signing confidentiality agreements with their employees, providing training on trade secret protection, encrypting trade secrets where necessary, limiting personnel that can access trade secrets, and prohibiting employees from bringing confidential documents out of the company through the internet, as hard copies or on electronic devices.

(3) File a lawsuit and apply for provisional measures, especially behavior preservation measures, as soon as possible. Behavior preservation is probably more important for trade secret owners than for any other right holders because once the information is improperly disclosed, the trade secret is lost forever. In this sense, behavior preservation is often a more powerful means to protect trade secret owners than compensation, and application for it should almost be a routine for trade secret owners during litigation.

TOPIC 5 DAMAGES

Siping Zeng & Xuan Wang

1. Legal Issues

In a trade secret infringement case, the determination of damages can lead to a series of legal issues, such as what are the methods for calculating damages, how to define the causation between infringers' profits and infringement acts, how to calculate the loss of competitive advantages, whether R&D costs could be calculated in the "actual loss of the business," and whether there are statutory and/or punitive damages.

2. The Statutory Law

2.1. Three Statutory Methods for Calculating Compensatory Damages

As a civil law jurisdiction, China follows the principle of compensatory damages to restore the infringed to the situation he would have been in but for the infringement[84]. AUCL lists three methods for determining the amount of the compensatory damage in the following sequence, which are further explained by the SPC.

2.1.1. The Actual Losses Method

Primarily, the method for calculating damages is per the actual losses of the business incurred as a result of the infringement according to Article 17(3) of the AUCL. As for the application of this method, the SPC states, "where a right holder requests the determination of the actual loss with reference to the license fee of the trade secret, a court may determine the damages according to the nature, content, actual performance of the existing license and the nature, circumstances and consequences of the infringement[85]." The actual loss may also be calculated by analogously applying methods for determining actual loss in the patent cases[86], namely by multiplying the total amount of the patentee's reduced sales of the products using trade secret due to the infringement by the reasonable profit of each product. Where it is difficult to determine the total amount of the patentee's reduced sales of the products, the actual

84. This principle is embodied in Articles 1182 and 1184 of the Civil Code. Article 1182 provides: "Where any harm caused by a tort to a personal right or interest of another person gives rise to any loss to the property of the victim of the tort, the tortfeasor shall make compensation as per the loss sustained by the victim as the result of the tort or as per any benefit obtained by the tortfeasor from the tort." Article 1184 provides: "Where a tort causes any harm to the property of another person, the amount of loss to the property shall be calculated as per the market price at the time of occurrence of the loss or by any other reasonable means."
85. Article 20 of the "Provisions of the SPC on Several Issues Concerning the Application of Law in the Trial of Civil Cases Involving infringement of Trade Secrets." SPC, Fa-Shi [2020] No. 7.
86. Article 17(1) of the "Interpretation of the SPC on Some Issues Concerning the Application of Law in the Trial of Civil Cases Involving Unfair Competition (Fa-Shi [2007] No. 2)" provides that "the determination of damages for the acts infringing trade secrets may be governed by the methods of determining damages for patent infringements by analogy."

loss could be calculated by multiplying the total amount of the infringing products sold on the market by the reasonable profit of the right holder[87].

2.1.2. *The Benefits Method*

If it is difficult to calculate the actual loss, the benefits acquired by the tortfeasor from the infringement can be used to calculate damages. Such benefits may be calculated by multiplying the total amount of the infringing product sold on the market by the reasonable profit of each infringing product. Generally, the benefits obtained by the infringer from the infringement are calculated according to the "operating profits" of the infringer; as for the infringer whose entire business is the infringement, the loss may be calculated according to the "sales profits[88]." The amount of "sales profits" is generally higher than the "business profits," as the latter must deduct reasonable overheads and expenses[89].

2.1.3. *The Statutory Damages Method*

Where it is difficult to determine the actual loss suffered by the right holder due to the infringement or the benefits acquired by the tortfeasor from the infringement, the people's court may, based on the circumstances of the infringement, award compensation in the amount of not more than RMB 5 million to the right holder. Article 17(4) of the 2019 AUCL increases the statutory damages introduced in 2017 from RMB 3 million to RMB 5 million. Where a court applies the "statutory damages method" to determine the amount of compensation, it may consider the nature of the trade secret, the commercial values, the R&D costs, the degree of innovation, the competitive advantage that can be brought about, as well as the subjective fault of the infringer, the nature, the circumstances, and the consequences of the infringement[90].

2.2. *Punitive Damages*

Article 17(3) of the AUCL introduced punitive damages in 2019, which has been generally applied to all intellectual property by the Civil Code in 2020. Article 1185 of the Civil Code states, "Where intentional intellectual property infringement has resulted in serious consequences, the infringed person has the right to request corresponding punitive damages." As for the amount of punitive damage, Article 17(3) of the AUCL states, if an operator maliciously commits an act of infringing on trade secrets and the circumstances are serious, the amount of compensation may be

87. Article 20 of the "Several Provisions of the SPC on Issues concerning the Application of Law in the Trial of Cases on Patent Disputes (Fa-Shi [2015] No. 4)."
88. *Ibid.*
89. Article 106 of the "Accounting System for Business Enterprises" (December 29, 2000 No. 25 [2000] of the Ministry of Finance).
90. Article 20(2) of the Provisions of the SPC on Certain Issues Concerning the Application of Law in the Trial of Civil Cases Involving infringement of Trade Secrets (Fa-Shi [2020] No. 7).

determined at not less than one time and not more than five times the amount determined by the "actual loss method" or "benefits method."

2.3. *Reasonable Expenses*

Under Article 17(3) of the AUCL, the amount of damages shall also include reasonable expenses made by the right holders to stop the infringement, in addition to the compensation amount determined by the above methods based on right holders' actual loss, benefits of infringers and punitive damages.

2.4. *Commercial Value and Competitive Advantages*

Compared with the trade secret infringement that benefits exclusively or predominantly the infringer, infringement that leads any trade secret to be known to the general public would cause much bigger harm to the owner of the trade secret, as the trade secret is lost for good. The SPC foresees the need for courts to reflect the commercial value of the trade secret in the amount of compensatory damages[91]. The commercial value shall be determined by factoring in the R&D costs, the proceeds from implementing the trade secret, possible benefits, the lead time for maintaining competitive advantage, etc[92].

3. The Case Law

The amount of damages determined by courts varies substantially depending on the specific facts of the case and evidence introduced by the parties. Three methods for calculating the compensatory damages are all widely applied by courts, among which the statutory damages method has the highest frequency of application because in many cases, it is difficult for parties to prove the actual loss or the profit caused by the infringement. Therefore, courts tend to determine the amount of damages by flexibly applying the statutory damages method while taking into account the comprehensive situations of infringement.

3.1. *Cases That Applied the Actual Loss Method*

In Second Branch of *Shanghai People's Procuratorate v Zhou Delong, Chen Weiming, Tao Guoqiang*[93], Shanghai Second Intermediate People's Court calculated the actual loss by multiplying the sales volume of infringing products by the average sales profit of the right holder before the infringement.

91. SPC (2007) Min-San-Zhong-Zi No. 1.
92. Article 19 of the Regulations of the SPC on Several Issues Concerning the Application of Law in the Trial of Civil Cases Involving Infringement of Trade Secrets (Fa-Shi [2020] No. 7).
93. Shanghai Second Intermediate People's Court (2003) Hu-Er-Zhong -Xing-Chu-Zi No. 150.

3.2. Cases That Applied the Benefits Method

In *Xi'an People's Procuratorate v Pei Guoliang* (2006)[94], the defendant used stolen technical secrets in signing technical contracts with others. Shanxi Provincial Higher Court applied the benefits method to calculate the damages by multiplying the total amount of contracts (equivalent to sales revenue) by 12 % (the average profit margin of the industry).

In *Ningxia Zhengyang Products Import and Export Co., Ltd. v Ningxia Fumin Vegetable Dehydration Group Co., Ltd.*[95], the court of first instance took the defendant's sales profit plus half of the plaintiff's R&D costs as the total damages. However, the SPC overturned this approach for two reasons. First, the R&D costs shall not be included because the benefits method and the R&D cost method cannot be applied simultaneously. Second, the defendant is not a company engaged entirely in infringement, therefore the operating profit of the company, instead of the sales profit, shall be taken as the basis.

3.3. Cases That Applied the Statutory Damages Method

In *Hebi City Reflective Materials Co., Ltd. v Song Junchao, Li Jianfa, Hebi Rui Mingte Technology Co., Ltd*[96], Henan Provincial Higher People's Court eventually determined the compensation amount by referring to factors such as the nature, subjective fault, trading time, and quantity of the defendants' infringement, the transaction price of similar products in the past and the efforts made by the plaintiff to obtain the trade secret, as it is difficult to determine the plaintiff's loss and the defendants' profit.

3.4. Cases That Awarded Punitive Damages

Zhejiang NHU Company v Fujian Fukang Pharmaceutical Company, Fujian Haixin Pharmaceutical Company, and Yuke[97] is the first trade secret infringement case that awarded punitive damages. This judgment was made on May 21, 2018 when the then-current AUCL (2017) did not provide for punitive damages. However, the court analogously applied the punitive damages rules for malicious infringement in the Trademark Law (2013). The Zhejiang Higher People's Court ordered punitive damages based on the following factors: the defendant's deliberate infringement, the large scale of the manufacture and sale, the wide scope of the sale, the long duration of the sale, the special importance of the technology involved to the plaintiff, and the defendant's delay action and dishonesty during the litigation. The court calculated that the defendant's operating profit due to the infringement was approximately RMB 15.47 million. In the end, the court determined punitive damages in the amount of RMB 35 million. It also supported the claim of compensation for reasonable expenses incurred

94. Shanxi Higher People's Court (2006), Gazette of the SPC, 2006.12.
95. SPC (2007) Min-San-Zhong-Zi No. 1.
96. Henan Provincial Higher People's Court (2016) Yu-Min-Zhong No. 347.
97. Zhejiang Higher People's Court (2017) Zhe-Min-Zhong No. 123.

by the plaintiff to stop the infringement. This decision is listed as one of the "Ten Annual IP Cases of Zhejiang Province in 2018."

3.5. *Cases That Granted Commercial Value of Trade Secrets*

In *Xinli Media Group Co., Ltd. v Beijing Paihua Culture Media Co., Ltd.*[98], Chaoyang District People's Court of Beijing focused on the commercial value of the trade secret involved in determining the amount of compensation, as the trade secret has been made known to the public. The court also fully supported the plaintiff's claim for reasonable expenses to stop the infringement.

4. The Leading Case

This section selects *Cheng Jizhong (Cheng) and Shandong Greentown Real Estate Marketing Planning Co., Ltd., (Greentown Company) v Hongya Real Estate Development (Group) Co., Ltd., (Hongya Company)* as the leading case, as it was heard by the SPC and selected as one of the "Top 10 Cases on Judicial Protection of Intellectual Property Rights by Jiangsu Provincial Courts in 2015."

4.1. *Case Information*

The first instance: Jiangsu Provincial Higher People's Court, 2010 Su-Zhi-Zi No. 1 (decided on May 14, 2013).

The second instance: the SPC, 2013 Ming-San-Zhong-Zi No. 6 (decided on April 29, 2015).

4.2. *Summary*

The Jiangsu Provincial Higher People's Court and the SPC both held that the claimed information contained in the two project profit analysis reports constituted a trade secret, and Hongya Company committed an infringement of the involved trade secret. The court of first Instance ordered Hongya Company to compensate Cheng and Greentown Company for losses of RMB 1 million but dismissed other claims of the plaintiffs. The plaintiffs and the defendant appealed to the SPC respectively, which was rejected.

4.3. *Facts*

During 2006, Cheng and Greentown's employees went to Inner Mongolia to conduct research and a survey on the real estate market there and obtained benchmark land price lists, real estate sales advertisements, brochures of local construction companies, and various newspapers from some cities. They completed two analysis tables and

98. Chaoyang District People's Court, Beijing (2017) Jing 0105 Min-Chu No. 68514.

reports on the sales prices, construction costs, and progress of some real estate development projects in Wuyuan County.

On October 31, 2006, Cheng and the Government of Wuyuan County signed a "Project Development Agreement" for the development of roads and commercial and residential construction projects on both sides of Longxingchang Street, Wuyuan County. On November 12, 2006, the two parties signed another "Supplementary Agreement" in order to start the project as soon as possible. Then Cheng and Greentown Company published an advertisement in the local newspapers between November 2006 and January 2007 to invite "Project Cooperation Investment Partners." Wu Zuliang contacted Cheng by telephone on January 19, 2007, and two project profit analysis reports and related documents were faxed to Wu, while the specific place names of the projects were concealed. Then the two parties signed a letter of intent for cooperation, which stipulated that the trade secrets in the project profit analysis reports provided by Cheng should be kept confidential and that the content of the letter of intent for cooperation is also a business secret and should not be disclosed to any third party.

However, on February 3, 2007, Cheng discovered that Wu and Hongya Company had signed a project development contract with the Wuyuan County government without Cheng's participation. Hongya then obtained the necessary governmental approval and completed the real estate development project in the location specified in the abovementioned confidential information, with substantial profit (approximately RMB 800 million) by August 2012.

4.4. Reasoning of Courts

4.4.1. Factors Affecting Profits of Real Estate Projects

When it was controversial whether the profit of the real estate projects should be accounted as the "losses of the trade secret infringement," the SPC reasoned that the profits of real estate projects are affected by at least the following factors: whether the company's research report on the real estate market can help the company make correct development and investment decisions; whether the real estate development enterprise itself has sufficient market competitiveness, and has actually obtained the development and construction approval; whether the real estate development enterprise can actually invest manpower, material, and financial resources according to the needs of the project in the development and construction process, and properly operate and manage the project; and various market risks that may appear and have actually occurred in the end.

4.4.2. The Plaintiffs' Loss Was Limited to the Value of a Consulting Service

The SPC held that the trade secret claimed by Cheng and Greentown Company was embodied in the two project profit analysis reports about a real estate development project in a specific place. The commercial value of this trade secret lay only in providing market information that helped Hongya Company locate a real estate project among many real estate investment options. For Cheng and Greentown Company, the loss of profit due to the infringement of the trade secrets should be equivalent to the loss of value of "providing a consulting service about real estate information" to Hongya Company. The value of such a hypothetical consulting service should be the benchmark for the "benefits obtained by Hongya Company due to its infringement of the trade secret in this case."

4.4.3. *Expected Benefits from Obtaining the Right to Develop the Real Estate Project Are Not the Loss the Plaintiffs Suffered*

The SPC also held that the expected benefit claimed by Cheng and Greentown Company was not the losses suffered by them due to the infringement of their trade secrets. Cheng and Greentown Company argued that they would have obtained the profit if they had executed the real estate project, which was dismissed by the SPC on the ground that such benefit and profit could not be achieved by merely controlling and using the claimed trade secret.

4.4.4. *The Investigation and Research Costs (I&R Costs) Can Be the Basis for Evaluating the Loss of the Trade Secret Infringement*

Although the trade secret in dispute did not leak to the public, the plaintiffs demanded the compensation of their I&R costs for developing the two profit analysis reports which contained confidential information. The courts held that the I&R costs incurred in developing the trade secret can be compensated as the loss of the infringement. But the I&R costs must meet two qualifications: first, the costs must have been incurred before the formation of the carrier of the trade secret—the two "Project Profit Analysis Reports"; second, the costs must be related to the development of the trade secret.

4.5. *Legal Analysis*

In China, the methods of calculating compensation in trade secret infringement cases include the actual losses method, the benefits method, and statutory damages. Furthermore, for malicious and serious infringement, the amount of compensation may be one to five times the amount determined by the aforesaid methods (punitive damages).

In most cases, it is difficult for the plaintiff to prove its actual losses because it often suffered no actual losses except the loss of expected profit. In the field of intellectual property, the loss of expected profit is particularly difficult to prove, as the profit in a market economy is affected by various factors, including the emergence of alternative technologies, changes in consumer preferences, and so on.

As for the calculation of the infringer's profit, it is very difficult for plaintiffs to obtain the defendants' financial account books. In addition, the contribution rate of trade secrets to the profit of infringing products is difficult to calculate. Thus, courts tend to adopt the statutory damages method, which could reduce the burden of proof on the part of the plaintiff and the pressure of the court on fact discovery. Indeed, the statutory damages method gives judges wide discretion to determine the amount of compensation within the maximum limitation by taking into account the relevant circumstances of a particular case. However, it has been argued that the excessive application of the statutory damages method leads to low amount of compensation.

In this case, the court of the first instance held that it was difficult to calculate the loss of the victim and the profit of the infringer since the value of the involved trade secret was only to provide information for decision makers to make quick decisions, and the commercial value of this trade secret could not be accurately determined. Therefore, the first instance court determined the amount of compensation by comprehensively considering factors such as the specific content of the trade secrets involved, the difficulty of obtaining relevant information, and the nature and circumstances of the infringement. The plaintiffs appealed, arguing that the amount of compensation should be based on "the profit of the infringer." The SPC dismissed this argument and upheld the decision of first instance. The SPC further held that the defendant Hongya had used the confidential information and obtained the economic value, which should be attributed to the plaintiffs who made the efforts and spent the costs to complete the two project profit analysis reports. The SPC rightly determined the amount of the compensation by considering the real value of the business information, instead of the profit of the real estate projects. However, it was regrettable that the courts failed to take into account the fact that the defendant abandoned the plaintiff just one week after obtaining the relevant trade secrets and using them without authorization when deciding the amount of damages.

4.6. *Commercial/Industrial Significance*

The present case demonstrates the difficulties involved in determining the amount of compensation for the infringement of a trade secret, especially when the infringed trade secret is only one of many contributory elements to the business success of the infringer. It can be expected that courts would follow the approach and in-depth analysis of costs of developing the involved trade secret and the contributory factors to the profit of the alleged infringer used by the SPC in the present case.

It is also worth noting that the recently added punitive damages in Article 17 of the AUCL will be more frequently applied in the future when the infringements are malicious and have serious consequences. In order to correctly implement the punitive damages system for intellectual property rights, the SPC issued "Interpretation of Supreme People's Court on the Application of Punitive Damages in Hearing Civil Cases of Infringement upon Intellectual Property Right" on March 2, 2021 and published typical cases of applying punitive damages in the field of trade secrets. These actions show China's commitment to comprehensively strengthening the protection of intellectual property rights.

TOPIC 6 CRIMINAL PUNISHMENT FOR TRADE SECRET INFRINGEMENT

Kung-Chung Liu & Xuan Wang

1. Legal Issues

It remains difficult to enforce criminal punishment in China due to the following factors: (1) it is difficult to determine the content of trade secrets; and (2) the threshold for initiating a criminal investigation over alleged trade secrets is not uniform throughout China. Recently, China has lowered the threshold of conviction for trade secret crimes and strengthened criminal liability. How are the new provisions to be understood and applied?

2. The Statutory Law

The first Criminal Law of the People's Republic of China, introduced in 1979, provided no explicit clauses on protecting intellectual property, let alone trade secrets. When the Criminal Law was revised in 1997[99], the crime of trade secret infringement was added by incorporating the trade secret provisions of the 1993 AUCL. It was not until 2020 that China revised its provisions on trade secret crimes to bring them in line with the revision of the AUCL[100].

The eleventh Criminal Law Amendment (XI), passed by the National People's Congress (NPC) on December 26, 2020 (effective March 1, 2021), included the revision of the crime of trade secret infringement. The NPC did not provide any reasons for this amendment. However, clearly, it was partially driven by the Economic and Trade Agreement between the USA and China signed on January 15, 2020[101], and partially driven by the domestic need to deal with the rising issue of cross-border economic espionage[102].

---

99. Zhigang Zhang, Review of Chinese Criminal Law Legislation in the 40 Years since the Reform and Opening-up (in Chinese), Academic Exploration (in Chinese) No. 10, 2018, 53-58.
100. Guangquan Zhou, Criminal Legislation Progress and Judicial Outlook: General Comment on "Criminal Law Amendment (XI)" (in Chinese), Law Science (in Chinese), 470(1), 2021, 1. For the revised content of the AUCL, please refer to the Overview and Summary of this chapter (Summary of civil protection of trade secrets).
101. Articles 1.3 and 1.4 of the Agreement require China to define "operators" in trade secret misappropriation to include all natural persons, groups of persons, and legal persons, and to enumerate additional acts constituting trade secret misappropriation, especially: (a) electronic intrusions; (b) breach or inducement of a breach of duty not to disclose information that is secret or intended to be kept secret; and (c) unauthorized disclosure or use that occurs after the acquisition of a trade secret under circumstances giving rise to a duty to protect the trade secret from disclosure or to limit the use of the trade secret.
102. In a famous case involving economic espionage between China and Australia, Stern Hu (Hu Shitai; born 1963 in Tianjin, graduated from Peking University before obtaining Australian citizenship in 1994), formerly an executive of Rio Tinto mining group in Shanghai, and three Chinese colleagues were detained by the Chinese government on July 5, 2009, during contentious iron-ore contract talks between top mining companies and the steel industry in China. On March 29, 2010, Hu was sentenced to 10 years' jail after pleading guilty to stealing commercial secrets and receiving bribes (5 years for trade secret theft and 7 years for taking bribes as a non-state official. A total of 10 years was the combined term). *See* (2010) Hu-Yi-Zhong-Xing-Chu-Zi No. 34 criminal decision by Shanghai First Intermediate People's

The amendment modifies some of the constituent elements of the crime for infringing trade secrets, notably, replacing the requirements of "heavy losses" for the average trade secret crime with "serious circumstances" and "especially serious consequences" for heightened trade secret crime with "especially serious circumstances" respectively. This means that courts will pay attention to not only the amount of damages the right holder has suffered but also the severity of the infringement. Second, it raises the maximum sentence for crime of trade secret infringement from seven years to ten years. Third, it punishes the crime of economic espionage.

Article 219 stipulates: "Whoever commits any of the following conduct to infringe upon a trade secret shall, if the circumstances are serious, be sentenced to imprisonment of not more than three years and a fine or be sentenced to a fine only; or if the circumstances are especially serious, be sentenced to imprisonment of not less than three years nor more ten years and a fine:

(1) Obtaining a right holder's trade secret by theft, bribery, fraud, coercion, electronic intrusion, or any other illicit means.
(2) Revealing, using, or licensing any other person to use a trade secret obtained from a right holder by any means mentioned in the preceding paragraph.
(3) Revealing, using, or licensing any other person to use a trade secret under his control in violation of confidentiality obligations or the right holder's requirements for keeping the trade secret confidential.

Whoever knows of any conduct set forth in the preceding paragraph but still acquires, reveals, uses, or licenses any other person to use a trade secret shall be punished for infringing the trade secret.

For the purposes of this article, 'right holder' means the owner of a trade secret and any person permitted by the owner to use the trade secret."

The SPC and the SPP have jointly issued the Interpretation of the SPC and the SPP on Several Issues Concerning the Specific Application of Law in Handling of Criminal Cases of Intellectual Property Infringement in 2004 (2004 Interpretation)[103]. It set up monetary thresholds for "heavy losses" and "especially serious consequences": RMB 500,000 and RMB 2.5 million (Article 7). In 2020, the SPC and the SPP updated the Interpretation (Interpretation 3)[104], reduced the monetary threshold of "heavy losses" to RMB 300,000, and added two other forms of "heavy losses," which still has important reference value for clarifying what might constitute "serious circumstances."

Article 4 of Interpretation 3 provides that "Committing the acts prescribed in Article 219 of the Criminal Law with any of the following circumstances shall be deemed 'causing heavy losses to the right holder of a trade secret': (1) the amount of

Court, and also https://en.wikipedia.org/wiki/Stern_Hu. In 2018, Stern Hu was released from jail after nine years in detention in China; *see* https://www.abc.net.au/news/2018-07-04/stern-hu-explainer-why-china-jailed-the-former-mining-executive/9936578.

103. SPC, Fa-Shi [2004] No. 19.
104. SPC, Fa-Shi [2020] No. 10 (effective September 14, 2020).

losses caused to the right holder of a trade secret or the amount of illegal proceeds obtained from infringement upon a trade secret is no less than RMB 300,000; (2) directly leading to the bankruptcy or closedown of the right holder of a trade secret due to major operating difficulties; or (3) causing other serious losses to the right holder of a trade secret.

Where an act causes the right holder of a trade secret to suffer losses or where the amount of illegal proceeds derived from infringement on a trade secret is RMB 2.5 million yuan or more, the act shall be deemed causing especially serious consequences stipulated in Article 219 of the Criminal Law."

Article 219-1 punishes economic espionage. It provides that "Whoever steals, pries into, buys, or illegally provides any trade secret for any overseas institution, organization, or individual shall be sentenced to imprisonment of not more than five years and a fine or be sentenced to a fine only; or if the circumstances are serious, be sentenced to imprisonment of not less than five years and a fine." According to Article 45 of China's Criminal Law, the maximum term of any fixed-term imprisonment can be up to fifteen years. Therefore, serious economic espionage can be sentenced from five years to fifteen years.

3. The Case Law

According to the search result from the official case database (https://wenshu.court.gov.cn/), there are some 259 cases concerning the crime of infringing trade secrets between 2002 and October 2020 and some 2,283 trade secret civil cases.

A study on a total of 62 trade secret criminal cases in Beijing, Shanghai, Guangdong, and other places shows that the defendants in all the cases were convicted, and 97% of them were due to conviction of infringement of trade secrets[105]. The high conviction rate is perhaps due to the strong prosecution power in collecting evidence and arguing cases before the court.

Worth mentioning is the case which imposed the highest fine. Jiangxi Yibo Electronic Technology Co., Ltd. and others committed trade secret crimes[106].

It is one of the "Eight Classical IP Cases in 2013" selected by the SPC and the highest penalty criminal cases so far. The total fine imposed by the court amounted to RMB 36 million. The defendants, Yu Zhihong, Luo Shihe, Li Yinghong, Xiao Wenjuan, former employees of Zhuhai Saina Printing Technology Co., Ltd.(SPTC), resigned in March 2011 and went to work for Jiangxi Yibo Electronic Technology Co., Ltd. and Zhongshan Ward Co., Ltd. The four defendants brought the former employer's undisclosed information such as the price system, customer list they obtained during the process of their work to use in their new employment. Such behaviors violated the confidentiality agreement signed with their former employer. Further, the two companies, the new employers, used the customer information of SPTC to snatch its

105. Global Law Office, Case Retrieval Report of Crime of Violating Trade Secrets (Criminal Section) (in Chinese), available at: https://www.lexology.com/library/detail.aspx?g=7421413d-e2ad-4584-b38e-802e68f97b1a.
106. Zhuhai Intermediate People's Court Guangdong Province (2013) Zhu Zhongfa Xing Zhong Zi No. 87.

customers. As of April 2012, they had caused SPTC a loss of RMB 23,200,264.31 in total. The four individual defendants and the two companies were found guilty. However, the second instance reduced the fine on five defendants and sentenced Jiangxi Yibo Electronic Technology Co., Ltd. to a fine of RMB 21.4 million, Zhongshan Ward Printer Equipment Co., Ltd. a fine of RMB 14.2 million, Luo Shihe three years' imprisonment, and a fine of RMB 200,000, Li Yinghong two years' imprisonment with three years' probation and a fine of RMB 100,000, and Xiao Wenjuan to two years' imprisonment with three-year probation and a fine of RMB 100,000.

4. The Leading Case

The decision that this section selects as the leading case was introduced on the website of the SPP as a representative case, as it involved the biggest outsourced R&D company for drug-manufacturing, biotech, and medical equipment in Shanghai, and Pfizer, the world's biggest biopharmaceutical company. It was the first case in Shanghai that dealt with infringement of trade secrets on structural formulas for chemical compounds[107].

4.1. *Case Information*

The first instance: Shanghai Pudong New Area People's Court (2012) Pu-Xing (Zhi) Chu Zi No. 42 (decided on October 22, 2013).

The second instance: Shanghai First Intermediate People's Court (2013) Hu-Yi-Zhong-Xing (Zhi) Zhong-Zi No. 10 (decided on July 24, 2014).

4.2. *Summary*

Wu Guang, as a researcher of Shanghai Yoa Ming Kang De (YMKD), had signed a confidentiality agreement with the company, but repeatedly stole data from the computers of other researchers and disclosed secret information, including 89 undisclosed formulas of compounds, on the Internet. Wu was accused of the crime of infringing trade secrets. The first instance court held that Wu had infringed the commercial secrets involved and caused "especially serious consequences," and gave Wu a three-and-a-half-year prison sentence and a fine of RMB 100,000. The defendant appealed, which was dismissed by the second instance court.

4.3. *Facts*

YMKD signed an agreement with Pfizer to provide chemical-synthetizing services on Pfizer's orders. Under this agreement, the intellectual property of the synthesis research shall belong to Pfizer, and YMKD is obliged to keep the undisclosed information about the Pfizer project confidential. During the execution of the agreement, Pfizer placed an order and provided some suggestions on a structural synthesis path to

107. Available at: https://www.spp.gov.cn/ztk/2016/gyssgztj_3204/dxal/201607/t20160715_145980.shtml.

YMKD, which conducted specific synthesis experiments, partially on the basis of Pfizer's path suggestions and partially on its self-designed synthesis paths. YMKD delivered an experimental report, marked with the sign "confidential," and the corresponding compounds to Pfizer. The content of the experiment report included order information, the synthesized target compounds, the specific synthesis methods, and processes, etc.

The defendant Wu worked for YMKD since March 18, 2008 as a researcher of the Pfizer project, and signed a confidentiality agreement with the company, according to which Wu was obliged to keep confidential all materials related to the company's research materials and other confidential information during and after their employment. YMKD had taken the following protection measures: equipping the laboratory with an access control system, allowing the employees to only use their own account and password to log onto their working computers, and setting up series of prohibitive regulations for the use of computers. Thus, employees were not allowed to take company data out of the company, to connect to the company's network from outside, or to download internal company information.

Between September and October 2010, Wu stole relevant research data from the computers of other researchers of the company by secretly dismantling and changing computer hard disks to transfer data and information. The stolen information includes the structure and synthesis process information of 89 compound formulas protected as trade secrets. On the evening of October 16, 2010, Wu was caught on-site by the company's security guards while stealing the research materials in the abovementioned manner. Wu resigned on October 20, 2010 and confirmed in writing that he would not disclose any business secrets of the company or its clients to anyone after resignation. However, on March 2 and 11, 2011, in order to demonstrate the R&D capabilities of the company that he later on set up and to attract potential customers, Wu publicly disclosed the stolen structure formulas of the compounds on websites of SciFinder and ACDFIND as well as his company.

4.4. *Reasoning of the Courts*

4.4.1. *The First Instance Court*

4.4.1.1. Commercial Value of the Trade Secret as Losses Caused to Its Holder

The first instance court found the accused had stolen and published 80 structural formulas, which made those formulas known to the public. Therefore, the losses caused to the holder can be based on the commercial value of those formulas. The commercial value of structural formulas can be determined based on factors such as the R&D costs, profits derived from the implementation of the trade secrets in question, expected profits, and the lead time for maintaining competitive advantages.

4.4.1.2. Synthesis Fees for Structural Formulas Are the R&D Costs

The prosecutor used the synthesis fees for structural formulas as the R&D costs. Before agreeing with the prosecutor, the first instance court took a hard look at the R&D

procedure of structural formulas and associated costs, which included three stages: (1) the stage of designing the formulas, and the design costs; (2) the stage of verifying whether the formulas can synthesize the targeted compounds, and the verification costs; (3) the stage of repeating the synthesis process to improve or prepare for further research and the repetition costs. The defendant argued that some R&D costs incurred in the second and third stages were not necessary for developing the involved formulas and should be deducted.

However, the first instance court rejected such arguments and held that costs Pfizer spent during these three stages are all R&D costs, as "according to the rule of scientific experiments, no single experiment can lead to success; rather multiple synthesis complies with the rule of experiment and is part of the R&D process for structural formulas."

The court concluded that Pfizer had already suffered a loss of RMB 2.6 million in terms of R&D costs at the stage of synthesizing the structural formulas, causing significant losses, and therefore the defendant's acts constituted a crime of trade secret infringement.

4.4.1.3. Factors Affecting the Sentencing of Criminal Punishment

According to the first instance court, factors that worked in the defendant's favor should be considered, such as that he conceded to his criminal acts, that only structural formulas and not the entire technical information were revealed, and thus the R&D costs Pfizer spent were not lost completely, as they still could be used for further R&D. On the other hand, the court also took into account factors that worked against the defendant. For instance, the defendant used stealth as a means to acquire trade secrets at issue, which was an especially serious offense; additionally, its acts had directly hurt YMKD's reputation as an outsourcing contractor for pharmaceutical R&D, and in the international community negatively affected China's pharmaceutical R&D service industry. The court's determination of the fine of RMB 100,000 was based on the consideration that the defendant had not used the trade secrets to manufacture and sell products, had no other illegal gains, nor other loss caused to the holder nor harm to society.

4.4.2. The Second Instance Court

The second instance court basically agreed entirely with the first instance court's rulings on the above three points. In addition, it also emphasized that what Wu had done not only harmed the reputation of YMKD but also damaged the international image of the Chinese pharmaceutical R&D industry.

4.5. *Legal Analysis*

4.5.1. *Setting Fixed Monetary Thresholds for Trade Secret Crimes Is Problematic*

Obviously, the SPC and the SPP have tried to provide legal certainty and uniformity to crimes on intellectual property rights by fixing various exact and detailed monetary thresholds since 2004 when they first issued joint interpretation. However, such an effort is bound to be futile, given the differences in technologies, commercial value, industries, companies, geographic locations of infringement involved, and the rapidly changing economic situation. Therefore, Interpretation 3 has correctly given up monetary thresholds previously set up for crimes for infringing trademarks, copyright, and patents (e.g., Articles 1-6 of the 2004 Interpretation).

More importantly, from the perspective of legal policy, the crime with "especially serious circumstances" is a felony punished with a minimum of three years' imprisonment. For a felony, it should be a crime of moral turpitude or *mala in se* crime. However, the numerical threshold and the calculation hassle would only render the crime as *malum prohibitum* (wrong [because] prohibited).

In the present decisions, both parties and two courts went into great detail and length to argue and counterargue which R&D costs for which specific technical items should be recognized as damages and which not, hoping either to reach or escape the monetary threshold. This is highly subjective, contentious, and not an ideal task for criminal judges to handle. Comparatively speaking, rarely is similar practice being adopted by other jurisdictions.

4.5.2. *Asking Criminal Court to Determine the Losses the Trade Secret Holder Suffered Is Also Problematic*

Bundled with the problem of setting fixed monetary thresholds for trade secret crimes are the problems of asking a criminal court to determine the losses the trade secret holder suffered from trade secret crime, as these losses are difficult to prove with certainty (or at least beyond reasonable doubt). Article 5 of Interpretation 3 provides detailed ways for determining losses caused to the holder or illegal proceeds stipulated by Article 219 of the Criminal Law, which are the thresholds for crime with "serious circumstances" and crime with "especially serious circumstances":

(1) the reasonable royalty for using the trade secret at issue if the trade secret was acquired through improper means but not yet revealed, used or licensed to others for use;
(2) the reduced sales profits of the holder as the result of infringement if the trade secret was revealed, used or licensed to others for use after it was acquired through improper means, or reasonable royalty for using the trade secret if the reduced sales profits were lower than the reasonable royalty;
(3) the reduced sales profits of the holder as the result of infringement if the trade secret was revealed, used or licensed to others for use after it was acquired by breach of contract or confidentiality requirement demanded by the holder of the trade secret;

(4) the reduced sales profits of the holder as the result of infringement if the trade secret was revealed, used or licensed to others for use after knowing that it was acquired through improper means, or revealed, used or licensed for use by breach of contract or confidentiality requirement demanded by the holder of the trade secret;
(5) the commercial value of the trade secret if its secrecy has become known to the public or lost as the result of infringement, which can be determined comprehensively based on the R&D costs and the profits of implementing the trade secret;
(6) goods or proprietary interests derived from the revealing of or licensing of others to use the trade secret (which should be deemed illegal proceeds)

The reduced sales profits of the holder as the result of infringement as stipulated in (2)-(4) of the preceding paragraph may be calculated by multiplying the holder's unit reasonable profit with the holder's reduced amount of sales caused by the infringement, by multiplying the holder's unit reasonable profit with the sold volume of the infringing goods (if the holder's reduced amount of sales caused by the infringement could not be ascertained), by multiplying the unit reasonable profit of infringing goods with the sales volume of the infringing goods (if the holder's reduced amount of sales caused by the infringement and the holder's unit reasonable profit could not be ascertained), or the reduced sales profits of the holder as the result of infringement if the trade secret was used for service or other related business activities.

Damages to the holder of the trade secret include the holder's expenditures on mitigating losses to business operation or plans, or on reinitiating information security system of computers or other security systems.

As pointed out above, these calculations are extremely complicated for criminal judges and cases and can lead to the unpredictable application of Article 219 and even of Article 219-1 of the Criminal Law if the SPC and the SPP were to follow the inertia of using a monetary threshold for determining economic espionage when they later update Interpretation 3.

4.6. *Commercial/Industrial Significance*

It can be expected that the number of criminal cases over trade secret infringements will increase after the recent revision of the statutory laws, which expands the scope of trade secret infringement, lowers the monetary threshold, and introduces punishment for economic espionage. Criminal prosecution looks tempting in China, as prosecutors enjoy great investigative power. However, parties embroiled in such criminal cases should be mindful of the strict monetary thresholds for crime with "serious circumstances" and crime with "especially serious circumstances" and be ready to argue and calculate the reasonable royalty, the reduced sales profits of the holder, the commercial value of the lost trade secret, etc.

Part II Asian Civil Law Jurisdictions with Sui Generis Law

CHAPTER 4
Taiwan

OVERVIEW AND SUMMARY
Hsiao-Fen Hsu

1. DEVELOPMENT AND PRACTICE OF TRADE SECRETS ACT

Trade secrets in Taiwan were protected through relevant provisions of the Civil Code and Criminal Code before 1991. While the Fair Trade Act was implemented in 1991, the protection of trade secrets was expanded to the fight against unfair competition. The "inefficiency of the current Civil Code, Criminal Code, and the Fair Trade Act, namely incomprehensive coverage, limited addressees, and indirect consequences" combined with Taiwan's promise under United States (US) pressure to enact the Trade Secrets Act (TSA), led to the passage of the TSA (16 articles) in 1996. The Fair Trade Act's continued protection against misappropriation of others' manufacturing and sales secrets, information on transacting counterparties, or other technological secrets in parallel with the TSA ceased on February 4, 2015 when it was rescinded.

It must be noted that the Taiwan Intellectual Property Court (IP Court) was set up in 2008, and according to Articles 1 and 4 of the Intellectual Property Court Organization Act and Article 7 of the Intellectual Property Case Adjudication Act (IPCAA), the Taiwan IP and Commercial Court has jurisdiction over the first and second instances of civil cases involving intellectual property rights, including trade secrets. However, district courts have jurisdiction over first-instance cases as well if the parties choose to allow it. In terms of criminal suits, the Taiwan IP and Commercial Court serves only as the second instance court, the first-instance trial remains at the district court.

The 2013 amendment to the TSA introduced criminal liability of imprisonment of up to five years in addition to a fine of up to TWD 10 million (approximately USD 360,000). Moreover, following the Korean and Japanese trend to deter cross-border infringement of trade secrets, Article 13-2(1) and (2) of the TSA double the criminal punishment and provide that any person committing a crime of infringing a trade secret for the purpose of using it in foreign jurisdictions, Mainland China, Hong Kong, or Macau shall be sentenced to imprisonment between one and ten years, with a fine between TWD 3 million and TWD 50 million. An attempt to commit such a crime is punishable. Article 13-2(3) raises the fine to an unprecedented level of "two to ten times the illicit gain" by the violator if his gain exceeds the maximum fine. The latest amendment to TSA on January 15, 2020 allows an unrecognized foreign juridical person to file a complaint, initiate a private prosecution, or institute a civil suit in respect of matters governed by this Act (Article 13-5).

According to the Statistics Report on Trade Secrets Cases ("Statistics Report") published by the Statistics Office of the Taiwan IP and Commercial Court[1], from July 2008 to June 2019, there were 80 cases related to trade secret misappropriation brought to the first instance of the Taiwan IP and Commercial Court, and 37 civil cases were brought to the Taiwan IP and Commercial Court in its capacity as the second instance. The winning rate for the plaintiff of trade secrets cases heard by the Taiwan IP and Commercial Court is approximately 31.03 %, with 9 cases (partial and total win) out of the total 29 cases decided on the merits.

The average days required to close a civil case on trade secret infringement is 179 days for district courts and 304 days for the Taiwan IP and Commercial Court. For those closed with court decisions, the appeals upheld 90.91 % and 91.23 % of decisions by district courts and the Taiwan IP and Commercial Court respectively. The average days required for the Taiwan IP and Commercial Court to close appeal civil cases is 301 days, and 66.67 % of its decisions have been upheld by the Supreme Court.

District courts closed 49 first-instance criminal cases under the TSA from 2013 to June 2019[2]. The conviction rate is 30.30% among 99 defendants. However, after breaking down to cases under Article 13-1 of the TSA (on trade secret crime) and Article 13-2 (on economic espionage), the conviction rates are 27.14% and 70% respectively. Between 2016 and June 2019, a total of 17 criminal cases were appealed to and closed by the Taiwan IP and Commercial Court, ten of which were rejected, and seven revoked and remanded. The conviction rate is 31.03 %[3].

2. CONFIDENTIALITY PRESERVATION ORDER AND INVESTIGATION CONFIDENTIALITY PROTECTIVE ORDER

To keep the confidentiality of evidence and information about the trade secret in question submitted by the parties, Articles 11-15 of the IPCAA foresee issuance of a confidentiality preservation order by courts during court proceedings. Any violation of the order is subject to imprisonment of up to three years and/or a fine of TWD 100,000 (Article 35 of the IPCAA).

For the second-instance civil cases, 65 applications for a confidentiality preservation order were filed, and 64 of them were closed. Among the cases closed, 43 cases

1. Statistics Office of the Taiwan IP and Commercial Court, Statistics Report on Trade Secrets Cases 2019, 2020, available at https://ipc.judicial.gov.tw/tw/dl-1922-fb68aed4416c47be8b7e3cc7f440e35a.html
2. The Statistics Report includes only the statistics for criminal cases after the 2013 amendment to the TSA, which introduced criminal liability.
3. The Statistics Report, I, II.

were entirely approved (approximately 67%), 9 cases were dismissed, 6 cases were partly approved and 6 cases were withdrawn respectively[4].

Since 2020, Article 14-1 to 14-4 of the TSA additionally provide for the investigation confidentiality protective order to be issued by prosecutors during the criminal investigation stage. Anyone who violates a confidentiality order shall be liable to imprisonment for a period not exceeding three years, and/or a fine not exceeding TWD 1 million. For discussion of the two orders and whether they can be extended to cover general civil and commercial cases please *see* Topic 4.

3. DEFINITIONS AND REQUIREMENTS OF TRADE SECRETS

The definition and requirement of trade secrets by Article 2 of the TSA follow the international standards. However, in practice, the Taiwan IP and Commercial Court set too high a standard on the requirement of reasonable measures to maintain secrecy, among others. Questioning the Taiwan IP and Commercial Court's stance, the Supreme Court has revoked the former's decision twice. For more details, *see* Topic 1.

4. THE VALIDITY AND SCOPE OF CONFIDENTIALITY AND/OR NONCOMPETITION CLAUSES

In Taiwan, the validity and enforceability of noncompete clauses are enshrined in Article 9-1 of the Labor Standards Act and its enforcement rules. In *TSMC v Liang*, the Supreme Court accepted a noncompete claim based on the TSA, rather than contractual agreement, subject to the condition that the restriction beyond the agreement-based noncompete period is "necessary" and "reasonable" for excluding or preventing trade secret misappropriation. Notably, the Supreme Court did not specify the criteria for reviewing the necessity of injunction in this type of case under the TSA. Nor did the Court specifically identify any factors in assessing the reasonableness of restriction under the TSA. For more discussion, *see* Topic 2.

5. FIVE TYPES OF TRADE SECRET INFRINGEMENT

After defining the scope of trade secrets protection and its use, Article 10(1) of the TSA lists five types of acts that infringe trade secrets: (1) Misappropriating trade secrets by improper means. (2) Acquiring, using, or disclosing a trade secret as defined in the preceding item knowingly or unknowingly due to gross negligence. (3) Using or disclosing an acquired trade secret knowing, or not knowing due to gross negligence, that it is a trade secret as defined in item one. (4) Using or disclosing by improper means a legally acquired trade secret. (5) Using or disclosing without due cause a trade secret for which the law imposes a duty to maintain secrecy.

4. The Statistics Report, IV.

6. THE BURDEN OF PROOF

6.1. The Principle of Burden of Proof and the Specific Defense Requirement

According to Article 277 of the Code of Civil Procedure (CCP), a party bears the burden of proof with regard to the facts which she alleges in her favor unless the law provides otherwise or the circumstances render it manifestly unfair. However, to duly reduce the plaintiff's burden of proof, which is exacerbated by the uncertainty of the contents of trade secrets, the IPCAA introduced in 2014 Article 10-1 a specific defense requirement on the defendant which provides that:

> (1) In trade secret infringement cases, if a party has made a preliminary showing that his/her trade secret has been or is likely to be infringed, and the other party denies such allegation, the court shall order the other party to raise a specific defense as to the reasons for the denial. (2) The court may, subject to the circumstances, find the preliminary showing of the infringed party true if the other party mentioned in the preceding paragraph fails without good cause to raise a defense within the prescribed time limit or to raise a specific defense. (3) The parties shall be accorded an opportunity to present their arguments before the judgment is rendered, under the circumstances mentioned in the preceding paragraph.

6.2. Preliminary Showing of Infringement or Possible Infringement by the Plaintiff

According to Article 284 of the CCP, to make a preliminary showing of a factual allegation, all kinds of evidence may be used to establish the truthfulness of such allegation to the belief of the court, except for the kind of evidence which cannot be submitted immediately. The evidence provided by the party does not need to convince the court thoroughly, but needs to allow the court to form a weak conviction, believing that the claim may be the approximate truth; the party should then be deemed to have fulfilled the obligation of preliminary showing. With regards to the specific defense requirement, the defense must be substantiated by facts and plausible explanations. Simple denial does not suffice. The more a defendant has acted in culpable ways, the more a specific defense will be expected of him, and he cannot use the subjective and unilateral excuse of "business needs" as a specific defense. For more discussion, please *see* Topic 3.

7. CIVIL REMEDIES

7.1 Injunction

Article 11 of the TSA allows an injured party to demand infringers stop or prevent such infringement through an injunction. Trade secret owners are entitled to apply for an injunction and request removal of such misappropriation, or prevention if a likelihood of misappropriation exists. The injured party may request the destruction or other necessary disposition of products generated from the misappropriation or items used exclusively in the misappropriation[5]. According to a 2001 Supreme Court decision, if there exists a trade secret misappropriation, it is necessary for the trade secret owners to specify the content and scope of the trade secret in dispute. However, if a likelihood of misappropriation exists, the requirement of specifying the content and scope of the trade secret in dispute can be lower, needing only a preliminary showing of the likelihood of misappropriation to allow the court to form a weak conviction[6].

In addition to Article 11 of the TSA, Article 538 of the CCP, and Article 22 of the IPCAA also provide that, where necessary for purposes of preventing material harm or imminent danger or other similar circumstances, an application may be made for an injunction maintaining a temporary status quo with regard to the legal relation in dispute. To obtain a preliminary injunction order, a rights holder will have to prove (1) the preliminary injunction application is necessary to prevent material harm; or (2) there is imminent danger or other similar circumstances.

The Supreme Court in its ruling in 108 (2019) Tai-Kan-Zi No. 213 clarified the factors which need to be considered in a preliminary injunction petition for a trade secret case[7]:

(1) whether there is legal relation between the parties and there is a need to maintain the temporary status quo;
(2) whether there is the likelihood of success for the petitioner (the rights holder); or
(3) whether the granting or rejection of the petition will cause irreparable harm to the petitioner or opposing party, balance on the degree of damage to both parties, and impact on public interest.

7.2. Damages

TSA provides two civil remedies for trade secret owners whose secrets were misappropriated, namely monetary damages for restoration of the *status quo ante* and punitive damages that would have some deterrent effects on preventing future infringement. Article 13(1) of TSA provides three possible ways to calculate damages:

(1) Actual damages (actual loss).
(2) Unjust enrichment damages.
(3) Punitive damages (not to exceed three times the amount of compensatory damages).

In addition to the abovementioned ways to calculate damages, the Court can also apply Article 222(1) of the CCP, which allows the courts to exercise discretionary power: "Where a party has proved injury but is unable to or is under great difficulty to

5. Supreme Court civil decisions104 (2015) Tai-Shang-Zi No. 1589 and 95 (2006) Tai-Shang-Zi No. 1043.
6. Supreme Court 100 (2001) Tai-Kan-Zi civil ruling No. 63; Taiwan IP and Commercial Court 108 (2019) Min-Zan-Kan civil ruling No. 3 and 107 (2018) Min-Yin-Su-Zi civil decision No. 4.
7. *See also* Taiwan IP and Commercial Court 104 (2015) Min-Zan-Kan civil ruling No. 7.

prove the exact amount, the court shall, taking into consideration all circumstances, determine the amount by its conviction."

In the Taiwan IP and Commercial Court's 102 (2013) Min Yin Su Zi No. 6 civil decision since the plaintiff was unable to or under difficulty to prove the damages amount, the Taiwan IP and Commercial Court applied Article 222(1) of the CCP to determine an amount of damages according to its discretion and applied the maximum punitive damages of three times for intentional infringement by the defendant. For more details, please refer to Topic 5.

8. CRIMINAL PENALTIES

Since the criminal punishment was introduced in 2013, only five decisions were found in which the defendant was guilty as charged. However, of these five, one was based on fraud, one was overruled, and only three were based on trade secret theft. In contrast, there were seven acquittals during this period. However, as reported in Topic 6, in an economic espionage case involving high-tech companies from Taiwan, China, and the US, Taichung District Court imposed the harshest criminal sentence on all three defendants (4.5 years, 5.5 years, and 6.5 years of imprisonment respectively) without probation. It is also the first case where a corporate defendant was also fined. It remains to be seen whether this represents a watershed for Taiwanese courts to take a very strict stance on the issue of economic espionage in the confrontation between the US and China and even between China and Taiwan, or whether the Taichung District Court is simply mimicking the Eastern District Court of Texas by taking an approach extremely in favor of trade secret holders.

9. SPECIAL MEASURES FOR JUDICIAL PROCEEDINGS INVOLVING TRADE SECRETS

Protection for trade secrets of the parties or third parties during litigation is provided for in the IPCAA. When a party's means of attack or defense involves its own trade secrets or those of a third party, the trial may be held in private upon motion of the party and approval of the court; the same applies where both parties have agreed to have a private trial. Where litigation materials involve trade secrets, the court may refuse or otherwise allow limited reviews, transcription, or videotaping of such litigation materials upon motion or on its own initiative (Article 9). Where preservation of evidence may violate the trade secrets of an opposing party or a third party, the court may, upon a motion by the movant or the opposing party or third party, set limits on or prohibit the presence of the persons on the premises of the preservation of evidence, and may preserve the evidence separately, or set limits on or prohibit the review of the evidence (Article18(5)).

In addition, according to Article 14 of TSA, at the request of parties, the court may, as it deems appropriate, close the trial to the public and/or restrict access to the files of the litigation. According to the Statistics Report, the Taiwan IP and Commercial Court has closed 40 civil cases at the first instance, 20 civil cases at the second instance, and 12 criminal cases at the second instance, each exceeding 50% of the received cases[8]. The Statistics Report did not reveal the percentage of closed trials of district courts. However, in Taiwan Taichung District Court 2017 Zhi-Su-Zi 11 criminal decision (decided on June 12, 2020), all 13 trial sessions were held behind closed doors.

8. The Report, III. According to the Report, since the content of closed trials will not be revealed to the public, the Statistics Office of the IP Court searched decisions with the keyword "Closed" in the decision database to obtain the number of closed civil cases. As for criminal cases, the Statistics Office verified the cases one by one to obtain the number of closed penal cases.

TOPIC 1 THE REQUIREMENTS OF TRADE SECRET PROTECTION

Su-Hua Lee

1. Legal Issues

The prerequisite for the owner of a trade secret to assert civil or criminal liability against the infringer is that the asserted trade secret shall satisfy the relevant legal requirements. The definition and requirements of trade secret protection stipulated in Taiwan's TSA are in line with the Agreement on Trade-Related Aspects of Intellectual Property Rights (TRIPs) of the World Trade Organization (WTO)[9]. However, the case law sets a relatively high standard when applying the law to facts.

2. The Statutory Law

The TSA was introduced in 1996. Before that, trade secrets were protected by the Fair Trade Act, Articles 317 and 318 of the Criminal Code, and contract and torts law under the Civil Code. When the TSA was drafted, the legislators relied on TRIPs as guidance. In addition, the US Uniform Trade Secrets Act (UTSA) by the Uniform Law Commission (ULC) in 1979 served as a reference.

Article 2 of the TSA defines trade secrets and the requirements for protection, by referring to Article 1 of the UTSA[10]. It stipulates that "'trade secret' as used in this Act shall mean any method, technique, process, formula, program, design, or other information that may be used in the course of production, sales, or operations, and that also meets the following requirements: (1) it is not known to persons generally involved in the information of this type; (2) it has economic value, actual or potential, due to its secretive nature; and (3) its owner has taken reasonable measures to maintain its secrecy."

3. The Case Law

As mentioned, the case law sets a relatively high standard when applying the law to facts.

9. Article 39 (1) and (2) of TRIPS provides that natural and legal persons shall have the possibility of preventing information lawfully within their control from being disclosed to, acquired by, or used by others without their consent in a manner contrary to honest commercial practices so long as such information (a) is secret in the sense that it is not, as a body or in the precise configuration and assembly of its components, generally known among or readily accessible to persons within the circles that normally deal with the kind of information in question; (b) has commercial value because it is secret; and (c) has been subject to reasonable steps under the circumstances, by the person lawfully in control of the information, to keep it secret.
10. Article 1(4) of UTSA provides that "trade secret means information, including a formula, pattern, compilation, program, device, method, technique, or process ... ."

3.1. *Requirement of Secrecy*

Information protected by the TSA needs to satisfy the requirement of secrecy. This is a characteristic that a trade secret should have. Any information already published, publicly used, or accessed in Taiwan or other countries, or information generally known among or readily accessible to persons within the circles that normally deal with the information in question, shall belong to the public domain and cannot be protected by the TSA. The requirement of secrecy doesn't mean "absolute" secrecy. Instead, limiting access to information to a few people could fulfill the secrecy requirement, as long as it is shared under confidentiality agreements[11]. In this context, "industry standard" can be an important reference.

Information that is not freely available in the public domain could fulfill the requirement of secrecy, regardless of whether access to this information is difficult. Disputes commonly seen in practice have involved information such as customer lists and sales prices. Some decisions[12] have confirmed the secrecy of such information. However, some courts found a lack of secrecy, if the individual components of the information are already in the public domain. To take 105 (2016) Min-Ying-Shang-Yi-Zi No. 1 civil decision as an example, the Taiwan IP and Commercial Court ruled that the client information could satisfy the requirement of secrecy and economic value if it is obtained by investing manpower or capital, collecting, filtering, and sorting raw data, not from the public domain. By contrast, information should not be protected if it is only a client list with names, addresses, and contact information, which can be acquired easily such as from yellow pages or business directories, and it is not sorted or analyzed according to the client's preference, special needs, relevant background or internal communication data[13]. Remarkably, decisions like Taipei District Court 88 (1999) Su-Zi No. 2826 civil decision (臺北地方法院88年度訴字第2826號民事判決) deny the fulfillment of the secrecy requirement simply because the obtainment of such information doesn't need investment of lots of time or money.

3.2. *Requirement of Economic Value*

The requirement of economic value means the information should have actual or potential commercial value due to its secrecy. That is to say, if the non-public information does not possess any significance in terms of competition or competitiveness, it is not protectable. Whether the information has a transaction value is irrelevant. As long as the information helps its owner to save money, make money, or

11. KAI-NA CHANG ET AL., INTRODUCTION TO INTELLECTUAL PROPERTY LAW (IN CHINESE), 326 (13th ed. 2020).
12. Taiwan High Court 100 (2011) Lao-Shang-Yi-Zi No. 122 civil decision, Taiwan IP and Commercial Court 105 (2016) Min-Ying-Shang-Geng-(I)-Zi No. 1 civil decision, and Taiwan High Court Taichung Branch 102 (2013) Shang-Yi-Zi No. 1077 criminal decision.
13. For case laws taking a similar view that customer lists and sales price data are publicly accessible information and fail to satisfy the secrecy requirement, *see* Supreme Court 99 (2010) Tai-Shang-Zi No. 2425 civil decision, 102 (2013) Tai-Shang-Zi No. 235 civil decision, 104(2015) Tai-Shang-Zi No. 1654 civil decision, Taiwan IP and Commercial Court 105(2016) Xing-Zhi-Shang-Su-Zi No. 11 criminal decision, Taiwan High Court 100(2011) Lao-Shang-Yi-Zi No. 52 civil decision.

improve efficiency in product sales, or operation management, the requirement of economic value is fulfilled[14]. The owner of a trade secret can prove that competitors would be advantaged in competition if they obtain such information. The requirement of economic value is fulfilled if the publication of the information would cause a negative competitive impact on the owner of a trade secret. However, illegal information such as tax fraud or insider information, or information on a cocaine refining process, does not meet the requirement of economic value.

Furthermore, it is irrelevant whether the secret owner can actually make a profit due to the information or not. Even information on the reasons for failure could enjoy actual or potential economic value. For instance, information on the cause of a clinical trial failure is valuable, since competitors can avoid the same failure and shorten their development time[15]. Therefore, the concept of economic value under the TSA is absolutely different from the requirement of nonobviousness or inventive step in the Patent Act[16].

Generally, customer lists, information on transaction prices[17], testing methods, and procedures for using equipment could be considered valuable by courts[18].

3.3. *Requirement of Reasonable Measures to Maintain Secrecy*

In addition to secrecy and economic value, for a trade secret to be protectable the owner must satisfy the requirement of reasonable measures to maintain secrecy. That is, the owner of such information should take reasonable steps of protection. It also resonates with the secrecy requirement, since the information that is not protected by reasonable measures is usually not secret.

In some court decisions[19], the fulfillment of the requirement of reasonable measures is determined on the basis of two facts: (1) whether the trade secret owner takes reasonable steps, such as labeling documents explicitly as "confidential," to express the owner's intention of protecting trade secrets (subjective intention); and (2) whether the protection measures are of such a nature that interested parties could know the protection intention (objective protection measure). Objective protection measures include storing confidential information at different management and protection levels, locking or setting passwords for such information, and signing nondisclosure agreements with employees. Only "reasonable" steps of protection are needed, but they need not be unbeatable[20]. For instance, it should be regarded as reasonable

---

14. Kai-Na Chang et al., Introduction to Intellectual Property Law (in Chinese), 326 (13th ed. 2020).
15. Taiwan IP and Commercial Court 105 (2016) Min-Ying-Shang-Geng-(I)-Zi No. 1 civil decision.
16. Ming-Yan Shieh, Intellectual Property Law (in Chinese), 161 (10th ed. 2020).
17. Supreme Court 106 (2017) Tai-Shang-Zi No. 441 civil decision.
18. Taiwan High Court 96 (2007) Shang-Zi No. 198 civil decision.
19. Taiwan IP and Commercial Court civil decisions102 (2013) Min-Ying-Shang-Zi No. 4, 103 (2014) Min-Ying-Shang-Zi No. 5, and criminal decisions107 (2018) Xing-Zhi-Shang-Su-Zi No. 19, and 107 (2018) Xing-Zhi-Shang-Su-Zi No. 24.
20. Taiwan IP and Commercial Court civil decision 101 (2012) Min-Ying-Su-Zi No. 2, criminal decisions105 (2016) Xing-Zhi-Shang-Su-Zi No. 11, 107 (2018) Xing-Zhi-Shang-Su-Zi No. 19, and 107 (2018) Xing-Zhi-Shang-Su-Zi No. 24.

steps if no one can easily access such information with proper means. In determining whether the measures are reasonable, the nature of the trade secret, the actual operation of the enterprise, and common sense shall be taken into consideration[21].

4. The Leading Case

The importance of this case is that the Supreme Court disagreed with the Taiwan IP and Commercial Court's determination on the fulfillment of requirements, vacated the decision, and remanded the case back to the Taiwan IP and Commercial Court twice.

4.1. Case Information

Supreme Court civil decisions106 (2017) Tai-Shang-Zi No. 350 (decided on June 3, 2017) and 108 (2019) Tai-Shang-Zi No. 36 civil (decided on June 10, 2019).

4.2. Summary

The plaintiff owned the formula of a health supplemental, "Resveratrol," and signed an original equipment manufacture (OEM) agreement with the defendant. The plaintiff asserted that the defendant violated the nondisclosure agreement and improperly used the information protected by the TSA. The defendant argued that the claimed trade secret does not satisfy the protection requirements. The second instance of the Taiwan IP and Commercial Court affirmed the first instance's judgment in favor of the defendant. However, the Supreme Court vacated it and remanded the case back to the Taiwan IP and Commercial Court twice.

4.3. Facts

The plaintiff asserted that it owned the formula of a health supplemental, "Resveratrol," and that its production method was protected by the TSA. The plaintiff signed an OEM agreement with the defendant, which manufactured the "Resveratrol" product in capsule dose form. When the plaintiff provided the "Resveratrol" information to the defendant, such documents were labeled "business confidentiality" or "confidential." To avoid disclosing the "Resveratrol" information, the plaintiff differentiated the "confidential ingredients" and "actual manufacturing ingredients" from the "labeling ingredients," which were listed on the products to comply with the Commodity Labeling Act and the Health Food Control Act. The plaintiff accused the defendant of using the "Resveratrol" information to manufacture products in powder form without authorization and applying for an invention patent for the formula in Taiwan. The plaintiff asserted trade secret infringement and claimed damages. The plaintiff also requested that the court prohibit the defendant and its affiliates from using the said formula to manufacture products and to order recall and destruction of the infringing products.

21. Supreme Court 102 (2013) Tai-Shang-Zi No. 235 civil decision.

The defendant argued that the formula of "Resveratrol" was accessible to the public since the plaintiff's legal representative had already published a book entitled "Resveratrol—the End of Disease and Aging," which had disclosed the ingredients of this formula. Further, according to Article 13(1) of the Health Food Control Act and Article 9 of the Commodity Labeling Act, the manufacturer is obligated to fully disclose the ingredients and additives. Thus, the "Resveratrol" products were labeled with names, product names, and merchandise content, including main ingredients, materials, net weight, volume, quantity, measurement, etc. The defendant also claimed said formula did not enjoy economic value since the ingredients and materials were used in the healthcare industry and the formula merely combined the freely accessible ingredients. After such a combination, it did not have any unexpected positive effect. The defendant also asserted that "Resveratrol" products in powder form were developed by the defendant's R&D teams and irrelevant to the information provided by the plaintiff.

4.4. *Reasoning of the Courts*

4.4.1. *The Taiwan IP and Commercial Court*[22]

The second instance of the Taiwan IP and Commercial Court affirmed the adjudication of the first instance court, which was not published[23], and ruled that the formula of "Resveratrol" products was not confidential and the requirement of reasonable protection measures was not met either.

The court held that the legal representative of the plaintiff had disclosed the main ingredients of "Resveratrol" products in publications, apart from the ingredient label on products. Even though the plaintiff differentiated the "confidential ingredients" and "actual manufacturing ingredients" from the "labeling ingredients," the court believed it was not difficult for competitors like the defendant to obtain the information of "confidential ingredients" and "actual manufacturing ingredients." The court emphasized that said formula is merely a combination of common food and medicine, and the confidential ingredients claimed by the plaintiff, such as grape seeds, fleece flower root, and bonito, are of which all common Chinese herbs and supplements. Thus, any professionals in the healthcare industry could easily figure out the information of "Resveratrol" products and reproduce them via routine and limited experimentation. The court also ruled the plaintiff failed to submit evidence to prove that such ingredients were sorted, analyzed, and collected by himself. Thus, the requirement of secrecy was not satisfied.

Regarding the requirement of reasonable protection measures, the court held that the plaintiff did not adopt proper safeguard measures, as the claimed confidential information was delivered by fax. Although the recipient's names and "business

---

22. Taiwan IP and Commercial Court civil decisions102 (2013) Min-Ying-Shang-Zi No. 4, and 106 (2017) Min-Ying-Shang-Geng-(I)-Zi No. 2.
23. Taiwan IP and Commercial Court 101 (2012) Min-Ying-Su-Zi No. 3 civil decision. On the online database of the Judicial Yuan, it is indicated that this is a not-to-be-published decision based on automated assessment by programs.

confidentiality" were noted on the document, anyone on the receiver site could learn about or obtain the information, and the plaintiff did not sign a nondisclosure agreement with the recipients of the faxed documents. Also, the court emphasized the secret information claimed by the plaintiff was not entrusted to specific persons' keeping and no measures were taken to restrict access.

4.4.2. *Supreme Court*[24]

The Supreme Court revoked the Taiwan IP and Commercial Court's decision and pointed out the mistakes it made while applying the law. The court held that the requirement of secrecy is satisfied, as long as the information is not known by persons within the circles at stake and cannot be obtained easily through proper means. The concept of secrecy is totally different from the requirements of novelty (not part of the prior art) and inventive step (not easily made by the person skilled in the art based on the prior art) under the Patent Act. In addition, the nature of trade secrets, the actual operation of the enterprise, and common sense shall be taken into consideration on a case-by-case basis when determining whether the protection measures adopted by the trade secret owner are reasonable or not. If persons that normally deal with the kind of information in question cannot easily learn about the information, such measures are reasonable and satisfy the protection requirements[25].

The Supreme Court pointed out that the plaintiff delivered the formula to the defendant several times since 2008, and each formula had a different delivery date, ingredients, and quantity. Health products produced by those formulas were different, and therefore, the Taiwan IP and Commercial Court should review the facts separately for whether the formula delivered by the plaintiff each time satisfied the protection requirements and whether it was infringed[26].

The Supreme Court also questioned the Taiwan IP and Commercial Court's lack of an explanation as to how professionals in the healthcare industry could easily learn about the formula on the basis of the published book and product labeling, as the product packaging only indicated "30mg of garlic extracts," and the confidential ingredients claimed by the plaintiff were not disclosed. The publication only mentioned certain ingredients that are commonly seen in Chinese herbal medicine, but the amount and weight of each ingredient and the detailed compounding of the "Resveratrol" products were not disclosed. The court pointed out that the effect and function of healthcare products depend on the ingredients, amount, manufacturing process, and product stability, which might change due to the interaction among the product's physical and chemical characteristics, form (e.g., powder or liquid), and its ingredients with healthcare effect. Three types of "Resveratrol" products were involved in this litigation, which were produced with 19 to 29 ingredients in different amounts and forms. The Taiwan IP and Commercial Court failed to explain how a person skilled in the art could learn about such

24. Supreme Court civil decisions106 (2017) Tai-Shang-Zi No. 350 and 108 (2019) Tai-Shang-Zi No. 36.
25. Supreme Court 108 (2019) Tai-Shang-Zi No. 36 civil decision, pp. 4-5.
26. Supreme Court 108 (2019) Tai-Shang-Zi No. 36 civil decision, p. 5.

information and reproduce the "Resveratrol" products through regular, routine, and limited experimentation[27].

4.5. *Legal Analysis*

The author agrees with the Supreme Court's viewpoint and found the Taiwan IP and Commercial Court's interpretation of the protection requirements of trade secrets improper.

4.5.1. *Information Protected by the TSA Shall Be Closely Related to the Industry*

The definition of trade secrets protected by the TSA is broad. The nature of whether it is technological or non-technological business information is irrelevant. For instance, information on marketing strategy, investment plans, marketing investigation, pricing, cost estimates, or employee salaries is a protectable secret. However, information protected by the TSA must be closely related to the industry. It must be used in production, sales, or operations in a commercial course. By contrast, national security secrets, information on military sites, military operations, or campaigning tactics for a presidential election are not protected secrets defined in the TSA[28].

4.5.2. *The Secrecy Requirement Assessed "As a Whole"*

The trade secret involved in this case is the formula and manufacturing method for a healthcare food, "Resveratrol" products. The Taiwan IP and Commercial Court held that the main ingredients were disclosed by the published book and product label, so the competitors could easily figure out the information and reproduce the same product. Also, the Taiwan IP and Commercial Court denied the trade-secret protection since such information was not sorted, analyzed, and accumulated by the plaintiff. With regard to information like formulas for food and healthcare products, chemical compounds, and customer lists, the author is of the opinion that the determination of the secrecy requirement should be assessed "as a whole." Thus, even when the individual components of the information are already in the public domain, it could still be protected by the TSA, as long as the information as a combined package is not freely available in the public domain.

The author therefore questioned the Taiwan IP and Commercial Court's opinion. Whether a piece of information is difficult to obtain or takes money or time to obtain and whether the individual components of the information are already in the public domain are irrelevant. Regarding the formulas of food and healthcare products, the requirement of secrecy could be fulfilled even if all of the ingredients are known to the public. There is a substantial body of case law on this in the U.S., such as *Coca-Cola Bottling Co. of Shreveport, Inc. v Coca-Cola Co.* (Coca-Cola case)[29], *Peggy Lawton Kitchens, Inc v Hogan*

27. Supreme Court 108 (2019) Tai-Shang-Zi No. 36 civil decision, pp. 5-6.
28. Ming-Yan Shieh, Intellectual Property Law (in Chinese), 159 (10th ed. 2020).
29. 563 F. Supp. 1122 (D. Del. 1983).

(chocolate cookie case)[30], *Huntington-McGill v Old Mother Hubbard Dog Food Co., Inc.* (dog food case)[31] and *Interbake Foods, LLC v Tomasiello*[32] (ice cream and pancake formula case). Taking the formula of Coca-Cola as an example, sugar, corn syrup, and other ingredients are all information known to the public. However, such a formula still satisfies the requirement of secrecy since it should be assessed "as a whole," instead of as the individual components of the information.

4.5.3. Improperly High Requirement of Reasonable Measures to Maintain Secrecy

The Taiwan IP and Commercial Court held that the protection requirement of reasonable measures was not satisfied, as the plaintiff delivered the formula by fax, anyone on the receiver site could learn about the information, and the plaintiff did not sign a nondisclosure agreement with the recipients of the fax.

The author disagreed with the Taiwan IP and Commercial Court's opinion. As mentioned, the protection measures are only required to be "reasonable," not unbeatable. The nature of trade secrets, actual business operation, and common sense shall be taken into account on a case-by-case basis. The plaintiff already indicated "business confidentiality" on the faxed documents as well as the recipient's names. Under this circumstance, certain measures to maintain secrecy have been taken. Considering the industry practice and the small- and medium-sized enterprises status of the plaintiff and defendant, it can be argued that such measures were reasonable.

4.6. Economic or Commercial Significance

This dispute over trade secret infringement has been appealed to the Supreme Court twice. The Taiwan IP and Commercial Court's adjudications have been vacated by the Supreme Court twice, as well. The Supreme Court questioned the Taiwan IP and Commercial Court for setting too high standard on the requirement of reasonable measures to maintain secrecy, among others. However, the Taiwan IP and Commercial Court adhered to the high standard on protection requirements in the retrial.

It must be stressed that a high standard on requirements of secrecy and protection measures means that trade secrets holders will face more difficulties in protecting their trade secrets. After being vacated and remanded by the Supreme Court for the second time, the second instance of the Taiwan IP and Commercial Court is currently retrying the case the third time. Beyond any doubt, the court's decision will have substantial effects on companies' strategies for protecting trade secrets and assertion of trade secret infringement in the future.

30. 18 Mass. App. Ct. 937 (1984).
31. 22 Mass. App. Ct. 966 (1986).
32. 461 F. Supp. 2d 943 (2006).

TOPIC 2 THE VALIDITY AND SCOPE OF CONFIDENTIALITY AND NONCOMPETE CLAUSES

Hao-Yun Chen

1. Legal Issues

Companies often require their employees to sign employment contracts with confidentiality and noncompete clauses as a condition of employment. The confidentiality clause typically stipulates that an employee shall not use or disclose to third parties confidential information that they learn from the company. Such clauses are intended to keep certain information confidential. On the other hand, the noncompete clause is normally structured to prevent an employee from entering into competition with the company for a specific period of time after their employment ends, because they might take advantage of confidential information they learned during the employment to gain a competitive edge over the company. The noncompete clause, together with the confidentiality clause, may limit the employee's right to work and bring about adverse effects on the mobility of the employee. It is thus a common understanding that these clauses are valid and enforceable provided that the scope of noncompete and its duration specified therein are reasonable and not excessive or broader than necessary to achieve the abovementioned purposes. However, a recent Supreme Court case in Taiwan raised an intriguing question about whether an employee is still obliged not to use the confidential information or join the company's competitor after the expiration of the noncompete period, and if so, whether such obligation arises from the original employment contract or under the TSA.

2. The Statutory Law

In Taiwan, confidentiality and noncompete clauses generally impose contractual obligations on employees. A violation of either of the clauses may constitute a breach of contract and result in liability for damages. As to the scope and validity of the confidentiality and noncompete clauses, there are currently no specific provisions regarding this matter in the TSA, as issues surrounding confidentiality and especially noncompete clauses are not confined to trade secret protection, but instead associated with a broader context of conflict between freedom of contract and labor's rights. It is for this very reason that Taiwanese labor law has placed restrictions on the noncompete clause after termination of employment. Article 9-1 of the Labor Standards Act provides that:

> (1) An employer shall not make an after-resignation business strife limitation agreement with an employee unless the following requirements have been met:
>
> (i) The employer has proper business interests that require being protected.
>
> (ii) The position or job of the employee entitles him or her to have access to or be able to use the employer's trade secrets.
>
> (iii) The period, area, scope of occupational activities and prospective employers with respect to the business strife limitation shall not exceed a reasonable range.

(iv) The employer shall reasonably compensate the employee concerned who does not engage in business strife activities for the losses incurred by him or her.

(2) The reasonable compensation referred to in Subparagraph 4 of the preceding paragraph shall not include the remuneration received by the employee during employment.

(3) Any agreement in violation of any of the provisions of Paragraph 1 shall be null and void.

(4) The period of business strife limitation shall not exceed a maximum of two years. If such a period is more than two years, then it shall be shortened to two years.

Article 7-2 of the Enforcement Rules of the Labor Standards Act issued by the Ministry of Labor sets out the substantive requirements of "a reasonable range" stipulated in Article 9-1(1)(iii) of the Act[33]. Article 7-3 of the Enforcement Rules provides for factors to be taken into consideration in determining "reasonable compensation" stipulated in Article 9-1(1)(iv) of the Labor Standards Act[34]. In addition, the procedural requirements of the noncompete agreements are defined in Article 7-1 of the Enforcement Rules[35].

3. The Case Law

With respect to the number of cases involving injunctive relief based on the TSA, the author has searched the judicial database[36] of Taiwan for court decisions within the period of January 1, 2001 to November 30, 2020, using the keywords "confidential," "noncompete," "trade secret" and "Article 11 of the TSA" which provides injunctive relief as a remedy. After filtering out irrelevant decisions that are not related to the

33. Article 7-2 of Enforcement Rules of the Labor Standards Act provides that the "not exceeding a reasonable range" referred to in Article 9-1(1)(iii) of the Act shall be subject to the following requirements: (i) The period of business strife limitation shall not exceed the trade secrets or the lifecycle of technological information protected by the employer, but with a maximum up to two years. (ii) The area of business strife limitation shall be limited to the area of the employer's actual business activities. (iii) The scope of occupational activities of business strife limitation shall be concretely specified and shall be identical or similar to the scope of the employee's current occupational activities. (iv) The prospective employer of business strife limitation shall be concretely specified and have business activities that are identical or similar to and competitive with those of the employer.
34. The four factors include: (i) the amount of compensation per month shall be no less than 50% of one month's average wage of the employee upon resignation; (ii) the amount of compensation shall be sufficient to support the resigned employee during the period of business strife limitation; (iii) the amount of compensation shall be equivalent to the loss incurred by the employee in compliance with the period, area, scope of occupational activities and prospective employer of the business strife limitation; (iv) other matters relevant to the consideration of reasonable compensation criteria.
35. Article 7-1 of Enforcement Rules of the Labor Standards Act provides that "the after-resignation business strife limitation agreement shall be made in writing, and shall also specify in detail the contents of the provisions referred to in Article 9-1(1)(iii) and (iv) of the Act. The employer and the employee shall respectively keep a copy of the agreement with their signatures or seals on it."
36. Judicial Yuan, https://law.judicial.gov.tw/default.aspx.

confidentiality and/or noncompete clauses, there are 34 decisions touching on substantive issues of the validity and scope of confidentiality and/or noncompete clauses in the past two decades. After further classifying these decisions according to court instances, the author found only one decision by the Supreme Court[37], 2 decisions by Taiwan High Court (including Tainan Branch Court), 20 decisions by Taiwan IP and Commercial Court, and 11 decisions by district courts. As to the content of these decisions, in 6 decisions the court awarded damages or penalties for the departing employee's breaching the confidentiality and/or noncompete agreements; in 12 decisions (6 of which are preliminary injunctions) the court ordered the employee not to use or disclose secrets; in seven decisions the court prohibited employees from joining their employer's competitors (5 of which are preliminary injunctions, and the remaining 2 are judgments of the second and final instances of the same case).

Prior to the introduction of Article 9-1 of the Labor Standards Act in 2015, Taiwanese courts had been tackling the issue of the validity and enforceability of noncompete agreements mainly by applying the general principles of public order and good morals in the Civil Code. For example, in its decision of 1986 Tai-Shang-Zi No. 2446 (November 27, 1986), the Supreme Court held that a noncompete agreement did not violate the right to work under the Constitution and is thus valid and enforceable. The grounds for this decision are that the agreement had a definite two-year duration and a specific limitation on the type of work in which the employee should not engage during the noncompete period and that the agreement itself did not violate any imperative law or public order. Additionally, courts have ruled that a noncompete agreement concluded before the enactment of Article 9-1 of the Labor Standards Act could still be examined by courts regarding whether it should be held void for its manifest unfairness under Article 247-1(1) of the Civil Code[38]. In such circumstances, the rationales of Article 9-1 of the Labor Standards Act and Article 7-3 of the Enforcement Rules of the Labor Standards Act were taken into account as the jurisprudence prescribed in Article 1 of the Civil Code, which provides that a civil case shall be decided according to the jurisprudence in the absence of applicable law or custom.

As to the factors for determining the validity of a noncompete agreement, in 2010 Tai-Shang-Zi No. 599 (April 8, 2010), the Supreme Court held that in light of the principle of freedom of contract, such clauses are legal and valid provided that the scope of restriction defined in the noncompete clause is specific, reasonable and necessary, and that the employee has been reasonably compensated for any losses or damages resulting therefrom.

The focus then turns to how to evaluate the necessity and reasonableness of restriction.

---

37. Supreme Court *TSMC v Liang*, 2015 Tai-Shang-Zi No. 1589 (decided on August 21, 2015).
38. Article 247-1(1) of the Civil Code provides that if a contract has been constituted according to the provisions which were prepared by one of the parties for contracts of the same kind, the agreements which include the agreements stipulated in the following paragraph and obviously unfair under that circumstance are void.

4. The Leading Case

As mentioned, there was only one Supreme Court decision in the past two decades that addressed the issue of noncompete claims based on the TSA. How the issue was deliberated and decided by the apex court has implications for whether Taiwanese courts are ready to embrace the case law doctrine of inevitable disclosure established in the US which permits a court to enjoin a company's former employee from working for the company's competitor despite the absence of noncompete agreements.

4.1. *Case Information*

Taiwan Supreme Court 2015 Tai-Shang-Zi No. 1589 (decided on August 21, 2015).

4.2. *Summary*

The key point at issue in this case was whether the court should allow the plaintiff's claim to enjoin the defendant, a former employee having knowledge of the plaintiff's trade secrets, from working for the plaintiff's competitor under the TSA when the noncompete agreement has expired.

The Supreme Court upheld the Taiwan IP and Commercial Court's decision to grant the plaintiff's injunction against the defendant, holding that a trade secret can be protected for an unlimited period of time under the TSA insofar as the secret is kept confidential. The subject matters, requirements, and purposes of trade secret protection under the TSA differ from those of a noncompete agreement. In order to protect its trade secrets, a company may put restrictions on the departing employee's right to choose work by virtue of a noncompete agreement. This, however, does not affect the company's right prescribed in the TSA. If a reasonable restriction on the departing employee's right to choose work is necessary for excluding or preventing misappropriation, such restriction is permitted under Article 11(1) of the TSA[39] irrespective of whether the noncompete period set forth in the agreement has expired.

4.3. *Facts*

Liang Mong-Song had worked for 17 years (1992-2009) in Taiwan Semiconductor Manufacturing Co., Ltd (TSMC), the biggest OEM foundry manufacturer in the world. Liang was a senior director of the R&D department when he departed from TSMC in 2009. According to TSMC's "Confidential Information Protection Policy," every employee is obliged to keep TSMC's confidential information confidential.

On February 13, 2009, in connection with his departure, Liang entered into a separate agreement with TSMC. The agreement contained a two-year noncompete clause and a confidentiality clause stating that the obligation to maintain the confidentiality of TSMC's confidential information would not terminate even after Liang's

39. Article 11(1) of the TSA provides that if a trade secret is misappropriated, the injured party may request the removal of such misappropriation. If there is a likelihood of misappropriation, a prevention may be requested.

departure. After his resignation on February 21, 2009, Liang had become a faculty member at Sungkyunkwan University in Korea on August 1, 2009, which lasted until April 30, 2011. Sungkyunkwan University is a university closely connected with Samsung, a well-known top competitor of TSMC. In May 2011, Liang commenced employment at Samsung in Korea.

TSMC filed a lawsuit against Liang seeking the following legal remedies: (i) enjoining Liang from using or disclosing TSMC's confidential information or trade secrets which he knew during his employment, and from acquiring any of TSMC's trade secrets from third parties (e.g., TSMC's employees, suppliers or clients) by improper means, (ii) imposing a Samsung-specific noncompete ban on Liang (prohibiting Liang from working for Samsung) until December 31, 2015, and (iii) enjoining Liang from providing Samsung with personal information of TSMC's engineers for the purpose of assisting Samsung in poaching them.

In the first instance, the Taiwan IP and Commercial Court allowed TSMC's first and third claim[40], but refuted the second, although it admitted that Liang could infringe TSMC's trade secrets if allowed to work at Samsung. The reason is that the plaintiff's claim under the TSA to further prohibit Liang from joining Samsung after the expiration of the agreement-based noncompete period should be deemed an attempt to extend the noncompete period in a disguised manner, and is thus subject to court review under the principle of proportionality[41]. After taking into account the social interests and the balance of the interests of both parties, the court ruled that the extension (an additional four years) would be too long to be a necessary and reasonable measure[42].

In the second instance, the Taiwan IP and Commercial Court reversed the first-instance decision and granted TSMC's all three claims[43]. Liang argued that since technology in the semiconductor field evolves speedily, and he had departed from TSMC years earlier and had already worked at Samsung for three years, it was not possible for him to misappropriate TSMC's trade secrets anymore. Thus, he refuted TSMC's second claim, contending that the prohibition from employment at Samsung until 2015 would not only unlawfully extend the noncompete period but also unduly limit his freedom of choosing jobs. The Taiwan IP and Commercial Court was not persuaded by Liang's argument, and, after taking the following factors into consideration, held that there is a strong possibility that Liang may misappropriate TSMC's trade secrets during his employment at Samsung: (1) The TSA prescribes no limitation on the duration of a trade secret insofar as the secrecy is maintained. (2) Liang's position at TSMC was unique and highly irreplaceable. (3) TSMC and Samsung are both R&D-intensive companies, and they compete in the field of semiconductors, which is one of the core industries that the TSA focuses on. (4) Liang had a close relationship with Samsung immediately after his departure from TSMC. The Court accordingly ruled that a prohibition on working for Samsung would be the only effective measure for preventing TSMC's trade secrets from being misappropriated. Based on this finding, the Taiwan IP and Commercial Court held that the

40. Taiwan IP and Commercial Court 101 (2012) Min-Ying-Su-Zi No. 2 civil decision (decided on June 21, 2013).
41. *Ibid.*, line 1693-99.
42. *Ibid.*, line 1779-85.
43. Taiwan IP and Commercial Court 2013 Min-Ying-Shang-Zi No. 3 civil decision (decided on May 1, 2014).

TSMC's claim under the TSA should not be deemed an extension of the noncompete period. The Taiwan IP and Commercial Court distinguished the noncompete period specified in the separate agreement from that claimed by TSMC under the TSA. The latter, in the Court's view, is on the grounds that Liang is liable for misappropriation of TSMC's trade secrets or that there is a strong possibility of misappropriation. The claim under the TSA thus should not be deemed an extension of the agreement-based noncompete period. In addition, while TSMC argued that the so-called "inevitable disclosure doctrine" should be introduced and applied, the Taiwan IP and Commercial Court disagreed with the argument, noting that a comprehensive application of the doctrine to noncompete cases involving trade secrets would unduly limit the employee's right to work.

4.4. *Reasoning of the Court*

The Supreme Court affirmed the appellate court's decision, holding that, "trade secret protection is a part of intellectual property … . No limitation is prescribed on the duration of trade secrets under the TSA. If a trade secret is misappropriated, or if there is a likelihood of misappropriation, the injured party may apply for an injunction under Article 11(1) of the TSA, insofar as the secrecy of the trade secret is still maintained. This application for an injunction is eligible pursuant to the TSA, absent an agreement between the parties. As to the non-compete clause … the parties are bound by the noncompete clause provided that the clause is necessary and that the scope of its restriction does not exceed a reasonable level and is thus not improper. The subject matters, requirements and purposes of the TSA and the noncompete clause are different from each other. Accordingly, for the purpose of protecting its trade secrets, a company may restrict the departing employee's right to choose work by virtue of noncompete agreement. This does not mean that the company's right prescribed in Article 11(1) of the TSA is affected. The plaintiff is entitled to seek an injunction restricting the defendant's right to choose work thereunder irrespective of whether the noncompete period specified in the agreement has expired, provided that its trade secret is misappropriated or there is a likelihood of misappropriation, and that a reasonable restriction on the departing employee's right to choose work is deemed a necessary measure for excluding or preventing the misappropriation."

4.5. *Legal Analysis*

4.5.1. *A Differentiated Approach to Noncompete Clause Should Be Favored*

This case highlights the difficulty in balancing employers' legitimate economic interests (trade secret), employees' rights (right to choose work), and social interests. It is normal that employers take preventive measures against misappropriation of confidential information or trade secrets. One of the measures is to conclude confidentiality and noncompete agreements with employees. Another measure is to bring a lawsuit against employees, under either the TSA or the so-called inevitable disclosure doctrine[44]. These measures, however, impose restrictions on post-employment competition and thus raise concerns. On the one hand, from the perspective of promoting innovation, some scholars dispute whether noncompete clauses should be deemed valid and enforceable, as information spillovers play a critical role in spurring innovation in high-tech industries[45], which favor more mobility in the labor market[46]. On the other hand, some scholars take the opposite view, namely trade secret protection is a legitimate interest which justifies noncompete clauses[47]. Rather than prohibiting all types of restrictions on post-employment competition, a differentiated examination on the necessity and reasonableness of each type of restriction may better address potential concerns while balancing employers' business interests and employees' right to choose work[48].

4.5.2. *Applying the TSA in a Way to Hollow Out Labor Standards Act?*

As mentioned above, in Taiwan, the validity and enforceability of noncompete clauses are enshrined in Article 9-1 of the Labor Standards Act and its enforcement rules. A noncompete agreement is valid and enforceable if the legal requirements are satisfied. However, in terms of trade secret protection, scholars have no consensus on whether the inevitable disclosure doctrine should be introduced into the application of the TSA. This is exactly the case with *TSMC v Liang*, where the Supreme Court accepted TSMC's noncompete claim based on the TSA subject to the condition that the restriction beyond the agreement-based noncompete period is "necessary" and "reasonable" for excluding or preventing trade secret misappropriation. Notably, in contrast to the clear requirements for a noncompete agreement stipulated in the Labor Standards Act, the

44. *See* Sharon K. Sandeen & Elizabeth A. Rowe, *Debating Employee Non-compete and Trade Secrets*, 33 Santa Clara High Tech L.J. 438, 456-457 (2017) (suggesting inevitable disclosure is a way for an employer to impose the restraints of a noncompete agreement in the absence of one).
45. Robert W. Gomulkiewicz, *Leaky Covenants-Not-to-Compete as the Legal Infrastructure for Innovation*, 49(1) U.C.D. L. Rev. 251, 254 (2015). For example, Ronald J. Gilson, *The Legal Infrastructure of High Technology Industrial Districts: Silicon Valley, Route 128, and Covenants Not to Compete*, 74 N.Y.U. L. Rev. 575, 629 (1999) concluded that California's ban on noncompetes led to the rise of California's Silicon Valley; Andrea Contigiani, David H. Hsu & Iwan Barankay, *Trade Secrets and Innovation: Evidence from the "Inevitable Disclosure" Doctrine*, 39 Strategic Mgmt. J. 2921, 2923 (2018) (suggesting that "the average effect of IDD [the inevitable disclosure doctrine] on innovation quality ... is negative.").
46. *See*, e.g., Viva R. Moffat, *Making Non-competes Unenforceable*, 54 Ariz L. Rev. 939, 979 (2012)(arguing that a rule of unenforceability is more preferable for both employees and employers because "the labor market is more mobile and there is more innovation where non-competes are not enforceable"); Office of Economic Policy, U.S. Department of the Treasury, Non-compete Contracts: Economic Effects and Policy Implications 18-23 (2016), https://home.treasury.gov/system/files/226/Non_Compete_Contracts_Econimic_Effects_and_Policy_Implications_MAR2016.pdf (analyzing potential effects of noncompete enforcement on mobility, wages, and the economy as a whole.)
47. Sandeen & Rowe, *supra* note 43, 455-456 ("when trade secrets are genuinely at risk, NCAs [non-competing agreements] provide an additional level of protection that is often better suited to the circumstances than nondisclosure agreements.")
48. Sandeen & Rowe, *supra* note 43, 461-464 (discussing how legislation and the courts can address concerns about noncompete agreements without banning them completely.)

Court did not specify the criteria for reviewing the necessity of injunction in this type of case *under the TSA*. Nor did the Court specifically identify any factors in assessing the reasonableness of restriction *under the TSA*. This way of applying the TSA might hollow out the substance of the relevant provisions of the Labor Standards Act in the long run.

4.5.3. *Explicit Criteria for Determining the Necessity and Reasonableness of Noncompete Injunction under the TSA Are Needed*

To avoid such risk and increase the predictability of TSA enforcement, explicit criteria for determining the necessity of noncompete injunction *under the TSA* need to be established[49]. Also, judges should identify relevant factors in assessing the reasonableness of restriction, because reasonableness rests on the nature and state of the employer's legitimate interests (the content of trade secrets) and may vary depending on the employee's position, the length of noncompete duration, and the industry involved. Especially with respect to the necessity of noncompete injunction, it seems that the Supreme Court took a pro-trade-secret approach that noncompete injunction is basically deemed necessary under the TSA insofar as the secrecy is maintained[50]. How to strike a balance between trade secret owners' (employers') interests and employees' rights was, however, not mentioned. In view of the purposes of the TSA, i.e., to protect trade secrets, maintain industrial ethics and order in competition, and balance societal and public interests, judges should consider more aspects, such as employees' rights and post-employment competition, when deciding the necessity of a noncompete injunction.

4.6. *Commercial or Industrial Significance*

TSMC v Liang is a high-profile case, symbolizing the intense cross-border competition in the semiconductor industry. Many high-tech companies that heavily invested in R&D are facing the threat of their employees being poached by domestic and foreign competitors. The Supreme Court's decision made it clear that working for a former employer's competitor in the absence of noncompete agreements may still be enjoined under the TSA. The decision might be long-awaited good news from an employer's perspective but has far-reaching implications for trade secret protection cases involving high-level employees' movement. Due to its vaguely defined requirements on TSA enforcement, the decision has increased risk and uncertainty in the post-employment movement of employees among rival companies.

---

49. For example, the South Korean Supreme Court has explicitly identified major factors for determining the length of noncompete injunction for trade secret infringement. For a thorough analysis under Korean law, *see* Chapter 2 of this volume.
50. In contrast, the Supreme People's Court in China took the view that if the length of injunction for trade secret infringement is obviously unreasonable, the Court may only grant injunction within a definite period. (*See*, e.g., Article 16(2) of the Interpretation of the Supreme People's Court on Some Issues Concerning the Application of Law in the Trial of Civil Cases Involving Unfair Competition.)

TOPIC 3 A PING-PONG BETWEEN BURDEN OF PROVING TRADE SECRET INFRINGEMENT AND SPECIFIC DEFENSE REQUIREMENT

Hsiao-Fen Hsu & Kung-Chung Liu

1. Legal Issues

How is the requirement of "preliminary showing of infringement or possible infringement" interpreted by courts? How is "a specific defense" required of the defendant who denies the infringement?

2. The Statutory Law

To duly reduce the plaintiff's burden of proof in order to avoid the dilemma of "where the burden of proof lies, lies the loss of the case" exacerbated by the uncertainty of the contents of trade secrets, The Intellectual Property Case Adjudication Act (IPCAA) introduced in 2014 Article 10-1:

> (1) In trade secret infringement cases, if a party has made a preliminary showing that his/her trade secret has been or is likely to be infringed, and the other party denies such allegation, the court shall order the other party to raise a specific defense as to the reasons for the denial.
> (2) The court may, subject to the circumstances, find the preliminary showing of the infringed party true if the other party mentioned in the preceding paragraph fails without good cause to raise a defense within the prescribed time limit or to raise a specific defense.
> (3) The parties shall be accorded an opportunity to present their arguments before the judgment is rendered, under the circumstances mentioned in the preceding paragraph.

3. The Case Law

A search on the database operated by the Judicial Yuan by entering "Article 10-1 of the IPCAA " as the keyword for relevant judgments yields one Supreme Court decision[51], one High Court decision[52], and five Taiwan IP and Commercial Court decisions and rulings[53]. Among which, only the Supreme Court decision considered Article 10-1 of the IPCAA as a major issue. The High Court did not consider the allegation of the appellee fulfill the preliminary showing requirement and did not order the appellant to raise a specific defense. The two other rulings rendered by the Taiwan IP and Commercial Court concerned the confidentiality preservation order and did not take Article 10-1 of the IPCAA as a major issue.

---

51. Supreme Court, 106 (2017) Tai-Shang-Zi No. 55 civil decision.
52. Taiwan High Court, 104 (2015) Zhong-Lao-Shang-Zi No. 54 civil decision.
53. Taiwan IP and Commercial Court civil decisions 103 (2014) Min-Ying-Su-Zi No. 1, 103 (2014) Min-Ying-Su- Zi No. 3, 106 (2017), Min-Ying-Shang-Gen (1)-Zi No. 1; and civil rulings 108 (2019) Min-Mi-Sheng-Shang-Zi No. 9, and 108 (2019) Min-Mi-Sheng-Shang-Zi No. 16.

4. The Leading Case

It was the first time that the Supreme Court has provided a clear explanation about the defendant's obligation to provide a specific defense in a trade secret infringement case.

4.1. Case Information

Supreme Court 106 (2017) Tai-Shang-Zi No. No. 55 civil decision (decided on January 4, 2017).

Taiwan IP and Commercial Court, 106 (2017) Ming-Ying-Shang-Geng-(I)-Zi No. 1 civil decision (decided on February 27, 2018).

4.2. Summary

The plaintiff (appellant) Himax Technologies Inc. ("Himax") discovered after the departure of the defendants (appellees), i.e., its former employees Tsai and Hsiao, that these two employees sent the company's secret files to their personal email addresses in an encrypted or scrambled manner during the period between their resignation applications and departure. Thus, in accordance with the provisions of the Employee Confidentiality and Intellectual Property Transfer Agreements (the "Agreements") signed with the two employees, the plaintiff brought suit against the defendants and claimed the default penalty and damages. The first instance court Tainan District Court[54] and the second instance court Taiwan IP and Commercial Court[55] ruled against Himax for failing to fulfill the burden of proof in proving the specific contents of trade secrets. Upon Himax's appeal, the Supreme Court found that the Taiwan IP and Commercial Court had failed to order that the defendants (appellees) fulfill their duty of providing a specific defense, among other things, and revoked the Taiwan IP and Commercial Court's decision and remanded the case back to the Taiwan IP and Commercial Court for retrial.

Subsequently, the Taiwan IP and Commercial Court at retrial sustained Himax's claim and ordered that TWD 900,000 (approximately USD 30,000) and TWD 400,000 (approximately USD 13,000) damages be paid by Tsai and Hsiao respectively. It also allowed the request for removal and prevention by ordering Tsai and Hsiao to delete and destroy files containing Himax's trade secrets in their possession, and not to keep, use or disclose, advise or deliver the files to third parties or otherwise allow third parties to learn about or use such trade secrets.

4.3. Facts

Himax sued its former employees Tsai and Hsiao for sending sensitive files to their personal mailboxes during their employment period without the company's consent. The attachments to the mails were either encrypted or scrambled so that the company could not know what had been sent in the attachments. Based on its information

54. Tainan District Court, 102 (2013) Zhi-Zi No. 4 civil decision (decided on June 23, 2014).
55. Taiwan IP and Commercial Court, 103 (2014) Ming-Ying-Shang-Zi No. 3 civil decision (decided on April 30, 2015).

system records, Himax was able to successfully decode and reverse part of the mails sent and determined that there had been misappropriation of its trade secrets. Thus, in accordance with the Agreements signed with Tsai and Hsiao, the plaintiff sought default penalty, removal of misappropriation, and damages from the defendants.

Defendants Tsai and Hsiao argued that, even though the mails had been sent, it was required by overtime work, constituting the exception "required for business activities" under Article 1(1) of the Agreements, and that they had never disclosed or given such files to any third party in any form, manner, or method, creating disclosure of important technical trade secrets of the plaintiff company. Also, with the lapse of time, the defendants could no longer remember which files were sent home for work on which dates during their employment. The plaintiff compiled the proclaimed external transmission into the "Investigation Report by Claimant Himax Technologies, Inc." ("Investigation Report") and attachments, listing the time at which the emails were sent and the external mailboxes as evidence. However, the defendants were unable to learn the contents of the Investigation Report. The plaintiff did not provide proof about whether the two defendants disclosed the plaintiff's secrets, to whom the secrets were disclosed, what the actual damages were, or how much they were. The claims were thus not credible.

4.4. *Reasoning of the Courts*

The decision dealt with four issues[56]. This case report discusses only the issue regarding the burden of proof during the trial.

4.4.1. Lower Courts: The Plaintiff Bears the Burden of Proof When the Defendant Denies Wrongdoing

On the plaintiff's claim that the information sent out by the two defendants was the plaintiff's trade secrets, the Tainan District Court ruled that the plaintiff bore the burden of proof, but failed to provide proof to substantiate facts that worked to its benefit[57]. On the plaintiff's claim that many parts of the attachments to the electronic records sent out by the two defendants had been leaked to third parties, which was denied by the latter, the court ruled that the plaintiff bore the burden of proving facts that work to their favor, but failed to do so. Even assuming that the defendants intentionally refused to decode the encrypted or scrambled attachments, the most one can infer is that the attachments were indeed the plaintiff's trade secrets, but not that the defendants have leaked such trade secrets to third parties[58]. The court further reasoned that it was incumbent on the plaintiff to prove otherwise when the defendants asserted that they had deleted all the information upon leaving their employment with

56. The first two issues are less relevant to trade secret law, and rather pertain to the general contract law discussion. The last one regards the prevention measure.
57. Tainan District Court, 102 (2013) Zhi-Zi No. 4 civil decision, p. 13.
58. Tainan District Court, 102 (2013) Zhi-Zi No. 4 civil decision, p. 14.

the plaintiff, a burden the plaintiff failed to discharge[59]. Therefore, the first instance court dismissed the plaintiff's claim. Himax appealed.

The second instance affirmed the first instance court judgment. The Taiwan IP and Commercial Court reasoned that according to the Agreements, the appellee shall not be liable for damages if his copying, keeping, and using of trade secrets is "not for his personal or any third party's interests" or his taking trade secrets outside of Himax' premises was due to "the needs of business." According to the court, Himax failed to prove the appellee's acts were for his or any third party's interests or not based on "the needs of business;" although Himax questioned the appellee's claim that his use of the information at dispute was for the purpose of overtime work, Himax's assertion was not proven by evidence and was nothing but subjective speculation[60]. Furthermore, in the appendix compiled, Himax simply explained the original content of 6 of the 18 emails sent out by the appellees, and did not explain the content of the remaining 12 emails indicating that they could not be decoded. In relation to the 6 emails, Himax was unable to prove whether they were indeed "original contents of the attachments to the mails sent" as compiled by Himax or whether the contents were genuine. Therefore, the Court agreed with the appellees' claim that Himax should specifically identify which information had been disclosed by the appellees and provide proof that such information constituted trade secrets defined under the TSA. The court concluded that based on the appendix it could not know the specific contents of the allegedly infringed trade secrets, not to mention to determine whether they had actual economic value[61].

4.4.2. *The Supreme Court*[62]

The Supreme Court first referred to Article 10-1(1) and (2) of the IPCAA and pointed out that its legislative reasons was on the one hand to lower the plaintiff's burden of proof (or reduce the degree of proof) and on the other to impose an obligation on the opposing party to provide specific defense against the former's explained assertions.

The Supreme Court then questioned whether the acts of the defendants were for overtime work at home, which was only reasonable if the results of the work had been sent back to Himax (which did not happen—added by the author). It continued to ask whether Himax had failed to discharge its obligation of providing explained assertions, given that in the Investigation Report Himax had reinstated six emails, alleged that they were trade secrets, and requested that the court subpoena witnesses show the process of reinstatement. The Apex court then reasoned that presuming Himax had discharged its obligation, upon the defendants' denial, the prior court should order the defendants to reinstate the files at dispute and describe how they worked during overtime, to discharge their obligation of providing a specific defense.

The Supreme Court also pointed out that according to Article 286 of the CCP, when a party petitions evidence, unless it is deemed unnecessary, the court should

59. *Ibid.*
60. Taiwan IP and Commercial Court, 103 (2014) Ming-Ying-Shang-Zi No. 3 civil decision, p. 10.
61. Taiwan IP and Commercial Court, 103 (2014) Ming-Ying-Shang-Zi No. 3 civil decision, p. 11.
62. Supreme Court 106 (2017) Tai-Shang-Zi No. 55 civil decision, p. 3.

conduct an investigation. However, the prior court failed to subpoena witnesses and wrongly concluded that Himax failed to prove that the files were trade secrets and not used for the purpose of overtime work. In addition, the Supreme Court determined that whether the defendants had deleted the sent files was a positive fact, and the defendants should bear the burden of proving their deletion.

4.4.3. *The Retrial Court*

The Taiwan IP and Commercial Court in the retrial proceeding conducted an investigation in accordance with the instructions of the Supreme Court.

4.4.3.1. The Defendants Had Violated Himax's Confidentiality Rules

The court accepted the testimony of two witnesses from the Himax Information Security Department. Himax allowed the sending of emails only via internal email mailboxes, not via external mailboxes, required that the sending of outbound emails containing work-related documents be approved by supervisors, forbade adding attachments and allowed employees to bring laptops home to work overtime after filing an application with the supervisor in charge and being approved by the department head. The department head supervising the defendants had never allowed design personnel to access Himax's workstation from external computers.

The court then concluded that Himax had adopted multiple strict control mechanisms concerning the transmission of work-related information by employees at the design department. It was impossible that the defendants were unaware of the control mechanisms, the rules against unauthorized taking out of internal information from Himax's premises, and the value and sensitivity of source codes, as they had worked nine months and six months respectively for Himax as IC design personnel[63].

4.4.3.2. The Defendants Could Not Use "Business Needs" as a Defense

According to the contents of the emails that were sent out, as submitted by the appellant, as well as the contents of the CDs reviewed and witness testimonies given during preparatory court hearings, it can be determined that the contents of the identifiable emails included the source codes of key programs for the internal projects. In addition, the two appellees were only responsible for lower-level tasks such as testing and verification, without the authority to revise the programs, and certainly without the authority to send source codes elsewhere. The two appellees violated the company regulations and sent the source codes through email attachments to their external mailboxes without the consent of their supervisors, clearly breaching Article 1(1) of the Agreements, and exposing the appellant's trade secrets to risk. Also, the two appellees were aware that the appellant had undertaken various control measures to prevent disclosure of trade secrets. After the evidence discovery, the two appellees

63. Taiwan IP and Commercial Court, 106 (2017) Ming-Ying-Shang-Geng-(I)-Zi No. 1 civil decision, p. 15.

certainly could not use the subjective and unilateral excuse of "business needs" to avoid their liabilities for trade secret infringement[64].

4.5. *Legal Analysis*

4.5.1. *Legislative Background of Article 10-1 of the IPCAA*

The legislative rationale expressly indicated that Article 10-1 was taken reference from Article 79(3) of the CCP of Japan, which requires that, in preparatory documents, if a fact claimed by one party was denied by the other party, the denial grounds must be stated. In other Japanese intellectual property laws such as the Patent Act, Design Act, Trademark Act, Copyright Act, and Crops and Seeds Act, there exist similar specific defense obligations. Therefore, when Japan amended its Unfair Competition Act in 2003 to deal with the protection of trade secrets, an obligation for the defendant to provide specific defense was added. The defendant can refuse to provide such grounds only with justified good cause. However, whether the reason is justified is determined by the court on a case-by-case basis.

Following the introduction of Article 10-1 of the IPCAA, a new Article 19-1 was added to the Enforcement Rules of the IPCAA. It stipulates that the plaintiff (trade secret holder) must make a preliminary showing of the infringement or high likelihood of infringement of its trade secrets if it is to apply Article 10-1(2) of the IPCAA and that the court may, subject to the circumstances, then find its preliminary showing true. Where the other party denies the claim of which a preliminary showing has been made under the preceding paragraph, the court shall order it to raise a specific defense in regard to its denial within a prescribed time limit.

4.5.2. *Lower Courts Failed to Apply Article 10-1 of the IPCAA*

The amendment to the IPCAA, which introduced Article 10-1 among others, was announced by the President in a gazette on June 4, 2014, which completed the legislative process. The amendment took effect on the same date. Article 38 of the IPCAA delegates the Judicial Yuan the power to decide the date the amendment shall be implemented. The Judicial Yuan exercised its mandate in two days, namely June 6, 2014 and decided on the same day as its implementation date. That suggests the Judicial Yuan was certain that courts know about and are prepared and ready to apply Article 10-1 of the IPCAA from June 6, 2014 onwards.

The first instance court concluded the oral argument on May 26, 2014, ten days before Article 10-1 of the IPCAA was implemented. It rendered its decision on June 23, 2014, seventeen days after Article 10-1 of the IPCAA was implemented. Given the importance of this new article, which might affect the result of its decision, the Tainan District Court should have reopened the oral argument as Article 210 of the CCP mandates: "The court may, if necessary, order the concluded oral argument to be reopened before announcing the decision." However, it failed to do so.

64. Taiwan IP and Commercial Court, 106 (2017) Ming-Ying-Shang-Geng-(I)-Zi No. 1 civil decision, pp. 15-16.

The second instance court, when trying the appeal, should have spotted this legal error made by the first instance court and revoked its decision. However, it did nothing of this sort and decided to side with the first instance court's decision. The wrong was ultimately addressed by the Supreme Court and corrected by the retrial court.

4.5.3. *Preliminary Showing of Infringement or Possible Infringement by the Plaintiff*

Preliminary showing of infringement or possible infringement by the plaintiff does not mean the traditional proof by evidence. It must also be taken into consideration that asking the holder to specify the contents of trade secrets will possibly lead to further disclosure of secrets during the proceedings. Therefore, the plaintiff is only expected to make its best efforts in showing the existence of trade secrets and the infringement or possible infringement thereof. Otherwise, how can the defendant be asked to prove something that did not exist?

According to Article 284 of the CCP, to make a preliminary showing of a factual allegation, all kinds of evidence may be used to establish the truthfulness of such allegation to the belief of the court, except for the kind of evidence which cannot be submitted immediately.

Therefore, "preliminary showing" means to use all evidence that is available for an immediate investigation to persuade the court that the claim is truthful, including witnesses, documents, appraisals, examinations, interrogations of the party, etc. The evidence provided by the party does not need to convince the court thoroughly, but needs to allow the court to form a weak conviction, believing that the claim may be the approximate truth; the party should then be deemed to have fulfilled the obligation of preliminary showing[65].

In the present case, the 18 emails that the defendants had sent out were encrypted and not readable. The plaintiff had managed to decode seven of them (some entirely and some partially). It revealed that the files at dispute did contain compression mode of the PA5384 Color Enhancement Project, which belong to the top secrets of Himax, and the source codes of MIPI (Mobile Industry Processor Interface) and DSI (Display Serial Interface). This has satisfied the retrial court as an acceptable preliminary showing.

In a trade secret infringement case, the court and the two parties usually start to confirm the scope and contents of trade secrets through attack and defense in the litigation proceeding[66]. Therefore, it must be analyzed through the collection and discovery of evidence in the course of litigation to slowly substantiate the claimed contents. It was also for this reason that, in the retrial, the Taiwan IP and Commercial Court examined carefully the data and emails sent out by the appellees (defendants), and found them

65. Supreme Court 96 (2007) Tai- Kang -Zi No. 849 civil ruling. *See also* Shyh-Ming Chiang, *A Study on the "Glaubhaftmachung": Focus on the Standard of Proof (in Chinese)*, 20(1) Soochow L. Rev. 61-105.
66. Hung-Ying Peng, Calculation of Damages for Intellectual Property Infringements: With a focus on Intellectual Property Court's Decisions over Trade Secret Litigations (in Chinese), presented at the Workshop held by the Taiwan IP and Commercial Court on July 26, 2019, p. 6.

to have breached the confidentiality agreement and misappropriated Himax's trade secrets.

4.5.4. *Obligation of Specific Defense Does Not Transfer Burden of Proof*

It should be noted that the obligation of specific defense under Article 10-1 of IPCAA does not transfer the burden of proof to the defendant. The defendant is obliged to make a specific defense to deny the existence of trade secrets and the infringement thereof. In other words, the defense must be substantiated by facts and plausible explanations. Simple denial does not suffice. The more the defendants have acted in culpa ways, the more specific defense will be expected of him.

In the past, the Taiwan IP and Commercial Court did not apply this "obligation to provide specific defense" very often. In its Mediatek case 103 (2014) Ming-Ying-Su-Zi No. 3, in determining that the defendant may have infringed upon the plaintiff's trade secret, the Taiwan IP and Commercial Court pointed out: "Trade secret infringement civil cases often involve commercial competition in the high-tech industry ... Thus, in a trade secret infringement civil case, the victim should first provide evidence about the infringement or potential infringement against its trade secrets (mostly circumstantial evidence) to show grounds and give the court an approximately justified weak belief about the existence of such fact. If the other party still denies the claim, the court should order the other party to provide a specific defense for the grounds of the denial, in order to balance the burden of proof between the parties and to discover the truth. If the other party fails to provide defense before the deadline without justification or if the defense provided is not specific, the court should allow the two parties to engage in debate about the veracity of the fact to determine the grounds shown by the party as true." The view taken in this case is thus supported by the present Supreme Court judgment.

4.6. ***Commercial or Industrial Significance***

The decision rendered by the retrial court duly reduces the plaintiff's burden of proof in order to avoid the dilemma of "where the burden of proof lies, the loss of the case lies" due to the uncertainty of the trade secret contents. However, it must be also pointed out that the trade secret holders still need to convince the court to the extent of producing a weak conviction to fulfill the obligation of preliminary showing.

The importance of trade secrets management inside companies, high-tech companies, in particular, must be borne in mind. Trade secrets should be managed systematically to ensure that any leak of information will be minimized or discovered and its contents ascertained in the shortest time to help the Court form its conviction of a possible infringement.

TOPIC 4 ORDERS BY COURTS OR PROSECUTORS TO PROTECT TRADE SECRETS

Kung-Chung Liu

1. Legal Issues

Courts in Taiwan and across jurisdictions can order closed-door trials and partial publication of court decisions, as well as issuing confidentiality preservation orders to protect trade secrets from being leaked again during court proceedings. However, Taiwan leads the rest of the world by having enacted the so-called investigation confidentiality protective order by prosecutors on January 15, 2020. How has the judicial practice been implementing these orders? Does the investigation confidentiality protective order not violate the legal principle of equality of arms among parties and tip the scale against the accused defendant? Some academic discussion about these issues is warranted.

2. The Statutory Law

2.1. Court Orders

Courts can issue at least three types of orders, i.e., closed-door trial orders, partial publication of decision orders, and confidentiality preservation orders.

2.1.1. The Closed-Door Trial Order

Open court is the general rule in Taiwan, as Article 86(1) of the Court Organization Act (COA) mandates: "The argument of a suit and the pronouncement of a judgment shall be conducted in a public court session." However, its proviso states "when there are issues that may hinder national security, public order, or social values, a court may decide to deny public access." Article 87 continues by requiring that "(1)When a closed court is required, the presiding judge shall declare the reasons for such a closure. (2)In such a case, as mentioned in the preceding paragraph, the presiding judge may still allow the attendance of individuals who do not impede the case."

Article 9(1) of the IPCAA is *lex specialis* of the COA, and provides that when a party's means of attack or defense involves its own trade secrets or those of a third party, the trial may be held in private upon motion of the party and approval of the court; the same applies where both parties have agreed to have a private trial.

2.1.2. The Partial Publication Order

Article 83 (Publication of the Gazette) of the COA mandates that "All levels of courts and their branches shall issue periodical gazettes or use other appropriate methods to publish judgments. However, if it is stipulated otherwise by laws, such other provisions shall apply." As a matter of fact, neither the IPCAA nor the TSA has provisions that stipulate otherwise. The Judicial Yuan has issued Guidelines on District Courts' Handling of Trade Secret Cases on January 28, 2021 and allows courts not to publish the parts of the decisions that involve trade secrets of the parties or third parties. When courts publish decisions, they must blacken out or de-identify those parts.

2.1.3. The Confidentiality Preservation Order

Articles 11-15 of the IPCAA allow courts to issue confidentiality preservation orders when requested, but not ex officio, during the trial of trade secret infringement cases. Article 11 provides "(1) Where any one of the following situations occurs with respect to trade secrets held by a party or a third party, the court may, upon motion along with preliminary proof by such party or third party, issue a confidentiality preservation order upon the other party, agent, assistant *ad litem*, or other related party to the action: 1. Contents of a party's pleadings disclose its own trade secrets or those of a third party, or evidence-taking that has been or is to be made involves trade secrets of a party or a third party. 2. Limitation on discovery or use is required so as to prevent the discovery or use of the trade secrets in the preceding paragraph being intended for purposes other than those related to the case, and there are concerns of obstruction to the party's or the third party's business operation as a result of the disclosure of the trade secrets. (2) The preceding paragraph does not apply where the other party, agent, assistant *ad litem*, or other related party has obtained or possessed such trade secrets through means other than the document review or evidence-taking prescribed in the Paragraph 1 of the preceding paragraph. (3) The person subject to a confidentiality preservation order shall not use the trade secrets for purposes other than those related to the case, nor shall he disclose said trade secrets to those not subject to the order."

Article 12 requires that any motion seeking a confidentiality preservation order shall be in writing. Article 13 requires a ruling granting a confidentiality preservation order to specify the trade secrets to be protected, grounds for such protection, and content of the prohibition; a confidentiality preservation order shall become effective upon being served to the person subject thereto; an appeal may be filed if a motion for a confidentiality preservation order is denied by the court.

Article 14 foresees the revocation of a confidentiality preservation order: "(1) A person subject to a confidentiality preservation order may file a motion to revoke such order with the court at which the action is pending when the requirements specified in Article 11(1) are not met, or when the situation described by Article 11(2) occurs, or when the grounds of such order no longer exist. However, when a judgment of the principal case becomes final, the motion to revoke the confidentiality preservation order shall be made to the court that grants the order. (2) Movant of a motion to preserve confidentiality may file for the revocation of such order. (3) The ruling revoking a confidentiality preservation order shall be served to the movant and the opposing party. (4) An appeal may be filed against the ruling in the preceding paragraph. (5) A confidentiality preservation order shall become void when the ruling revoking such order becomes final. (6) When a ruling revoking a confidentiality preservation order becomes final, the court shall notify, in addition to the movant and the opposing party, any other persons subject to the confidentiality preservation order of the revocation of such order."

2.2. *The Investigation Confidentiality Protective Order by Prosecutors*

2.2.1. *When and to Whom Can the Order Be Issued?*

If a prosecutor investigating a trade secret case deems necessary, he may issue an investigation confidentiality protective order to the suspects, defendants, victims, complainants, agents *ad litem*, defense attorneys, expert witnesses, witnesses, or other associated persons having access to the investigation contents (Article 14-1 of the TSA(1)). Persons who are subject to such an order must not engage in the following acts in respect of the investigation contents: (1) usage for purposes other than the investigation procedures; and (2) revealing contents to person(s) not subject to the investigation confidentiality protective order. However, the provisions as set forth in the preceding paragraph shall not apply to any person(s) subject to the investigation confidentiality protective order who has already acquired or possessed the investigation contents prior to the investigation (Article 14-1 of the TSA(2)(3)).

2.2.2. *Forms and Taking Effects of the Order*

An investigation confidentiality protective order shall be issued in writing or verbally. Before issuing the order, a trade secret owner shall be afforded an opportunity to express opinions. Where the order is issued verbally, the person(s) it is issued to shall be notified in person, a recordation thereof shall be made, and the order takes effect at the time the notification thereof is made. The order in writing shall be produced within seven days, and takes effect on the day it is served upon the person(s) subject to the investigation confidentiality protective order (Article 14-2 of the TSA).

2.2.3. *Cancelation or Amendment of the Order*

Article 14-3 of the TSA stipulates the cancelation and amendment of the order by prosecutors and courts.

2.2.3.1. By Prosecutors

During the investigation, if the duty of confidentiality is extinguished or if it is necessary to amend the contents of the order, the prosecutor may ex officio cancel or amend the investigation confidentiality protective order. If the deferred prosecution or non-prosecution is finalized for a case or if part of the investigation confidentiality protective order is not within the scope of the prosecution, the prosecutor may ex officio or upon request by the person(s) subject to the order, cancel or amend the investigation confidentiality protective order.

The prosecutor canceling or amending the investigation confidentiality protective order may afford the person(s) subject to such order and the trade secret owner(s) opportunities to express opinions. The canceling or amending disposition shall be made in writing and served upon the person(s) subject to the order and the trade secret owner(s).

After a case is being prosecuted, the prosecutor shall notify the trade secret owner(s) and the person(s) subject to the investigation confidentiality protective order of the order's involvement in the effect of the prosecution and its scope, as well as of the rights and interests associated with the confidentiality preservation order and the investigation confidentiality protective order. The trade secret owner(s) or the prosecutor may file a request with the court for the issuance of a confidentiality preservation order. The investigation confidentiality protective order within the scope of the prosecution shall, within the scope of a motion, lose its effectiveness on the date a ruling granting a confidentiality preservation order becomes final.

2.2.3.2. By Courts

After a case is being prosecuted, if the trade secret owner(s) or prosecutor does not file a request with the court for the confidentiality preservation order within 30 days from the day the case has been pending to court, the court may, upon request by the person(s) subject to the confidentiality protective order or the prosecutor, cancel the investigation confidentiality protective order. The investigation confidentiality protective order that is involved in the effect of the prosecution and its scope shall, within the scope of cancellation allowed for by the court, lose its effectiveness starting from the date on which a court ruling becomes final.

Prior to finalizing its ruling, the court shall consult the trade secret owner(s) and prosecutor. The ruling shall be served upon the trade secret owner(s), the person(s) subject to the investigation confidentiality protective order, and the prosecutor.

2.2.4. Criminal Punishment for Violating an Investigation Confidentiality Protective Order

"(1) A person violating an investigation confidentiality protective order shall be punished by imprisonment for up to three years, short-term imprisonment, and/or a fine of up to NT$1 million. (2) The preceding paragraph shall apply where the violation of the investigation confidentiality protective order occurs in other countries, mainland China, Hong Kong, or Macau, regardless of whether the offense is punishable or not under the law of the land where the crime is committed." (Article 14-4 of the TSA)

3. The Judicial Practice

According to the Statistics Report, between July 2008 and June 2019, in more than 50% of each type of cases it received, the Taiwan IP and Commercial Court has held a closed-door trial: 40 civil cases and 20 civil cases in its capacity as the first instance and the second instance court respectively, and 12 criminal cases in its capacity as the second instance court[67].

With regards to confidentiality preservation orders, between July 2008 and June 2019, 187 applications for a confidentiality preservation order in civil first-instance cases were filed to the Taiwan IP and Commercial Court. Among the cases closed, 34 cases were

67. The Statistics Report, III.

withdrawn and 143 cases were approved, with an approval rate of 94% (109 cases entirely approved (approximately 59%), and 34 cases partly approved). In addition, 65 applications for a confidentiality preservation order in civil second-instance cases were filed to the Taiwan IP and Commercial Court. Among the cases closed, 6 cases were withdrawn and 49 cases were approved, with an approval rate of 85% (43 cases were entirely approved, approximately 67%, and 6 cases were partly approved). 47 applications for a confidentiality preservation order in criminal first-instance cases were filed to the Taiwan IP and Commercial Court. 36 cases were approved, leading to an approval rate of 84% (20 cases entirely approved, approximately 43%, and 16 cases partly approved). Five applications for a confidentiality preservation order in criminal second-instance cases were filed to the Taiwan IP and Commercial Court. Three cases were withdrawn and two cases partly approved, with an approval rate of 100%[68].

4. The Notorious Case

Due to the practice of courts not publishing every procedural ruling in Taiwan, and the Judicial Yuan not requiring courts to submit their procedural rulings for compilation and publication at its database, there is simply no way for the outside world to know what orders courts have awarded to protect trade secrets in what cases. As a result, no meaningful research on the merits or necessity of these orders can be conducted. It was reported by the media that the Taichung District Court in its 106 (2017) Zhi-Su-Zi 11 criminal decision (decided on June 12, 2020) held all 13 trial sessions behind closed doors and issued 13 confidentiality preservation orders in total, both being the greatest number to date[69].

5. Critique of the Investigation Confidentiality Protective Order by Prosecutors

The order was introduced in 2020 as proposed by some members of the parliament (MPs) from the ruling party. This is an unusual move, as in Taiwan legislative proposals come from competent ministries as a matter of principle. Initiatives from MPs reflect more the interests of lobbying. The Ministry of Justice (MOJ) had been rather doubtful about the necessity and appropriateness of this order, but these doubts were ignored by the legislature.

5.1. It Expands the Power of Prosecutors and Poses a Threat to the Rule of Law Principle

If a prosecutor investigating a trade secret case deems necessary, he or she may issue in writing or verbally an investigation confidentiality protective order to a wide range of parties involved. He may ex officio cancel or amend the investigation confidentiality

68. *Ibid.*
69. "The Control Yuan Should Investigate Why Taichung District Court and the Judicial Yuan Did Not Publish the Decision," the editorial of the Commercial Times (published in Taiwan in Chinese) of October 8, 2020.

protective order later. Worst of all, there is no oversight of this order, with neither court control nor administrative review, whether *ex ante* or *ex post*. Court control ensues only when the prosecutor has indicted the defendant and transferred the case to the trial court.

This is a worrying development, as we look back on the young democracy in Taiwan in the last thirty years; one key feature of democratization since the cessation of the martial law in 1987 is the separation of prosecutors from judges and putting the former's exercise of power under the latter's control. Search warrants, tapping, and arrest are not allowed anymore without a court's prior approval. Prosecutors are duly returned to their role as one of the equal parties of the adversarial criminal litigation system. With the investigation confidentiality protective order in hand, the prosecutor is restored to a pre-democratization position as an overly powerful "judiciary institution." This clearly poses a serious threat to Taiwan's fledgling democracy and the underlying rule of law principle.

5.2. *It Is Not Necessary*[70]

The MOJ had been of the opinion that the complainant and relevant third parties could be asked by the prosecutor or the search warrant issued by courts to identify trade secrets during the prosecution process, and therefore this order was not necessary. The MOJ had also pointed out that this kind of order or the so-called pre-trial protective order is issued only by courts in Korea, Japan, and the US. The MOJ had further suggested that in case the legislator still decided to introduce this order as a matter of legislative policy, the power to issue this order should be limited to judges.

5.3. *Trade Secret Cases Should Be Reserved for Judges*[71]

The MOJ had been of the opinion that the trade secrets are property rights protected by Article 15 of the Constitution, so reserving trade secret cases for judges can better protect this fundamental right: trade secrets often involve economic value of greater than tens of billions of dollars, leading or unique information, industrial competition across nations, and national security; the leakage of trade secrets, especially when competition exists between holders of trade secrets and their opposing parties, will gravely affect the property rights of holders of trade secrets. Therefore, trade secret cases should be reserved for judges, so as to be in line with the trend of protecting human rights under Taiwan's criminal procedures.

5.4. *Prosecutors Lack the Technical Capability*[72]

The MOJ had further pointed out that the determination of trade secrets always requires high professional skills which prosecutors and judges normally lack.

---

70. 108 Gazette of the Legislative Yuan No. 106, Minutes of the General Assembly (December 31, 2019), 82-83.
71. *Ibid.*
72. *Ibid.*

However, judges are now being assisted by technical examiners and are more capable. In contrast, prosecutors are not supported by technical examiners and cannot provide comprehensive protection to trade secrets when they have to issue the order within a short time period.

6. Can Confidentiality Preservation Orders and Investigation Confidentiality Protective Orders Be Applied to General Civil and Commercial Cases?

According to the general provision under Article 1 of the IPCAA, "intellectual property cases shall be adjudicated in accordance with this Act." Therefore, confidentiality preservation orders and investigation confidentiality protective orders can only be granted under Articles 11 and 14-1 of the IPCAA. However, when a non-intellectual property case involves trade secrets (such as a dispute of general contract performance or labor dispute involving internal sensitive information of an enterprise), it is doubtful whether the parties can petition for a confidentiality preservation order.

Taipei District Court in two civil decisions took a negative view. In one case, the document involved Sony Taiwan's product sale amount, meeting materials, etc. The Court pronounced that "This case (which involves confirmation of an employment relationship) is not an intellectual property right case and is not governed by the IPCAA, nor should procedural supplementation be allowed through mutatis mutandis application."[73] In another case, involving Taiwan Mobile's operating turnover, cost of telecommunications equipment, operating cost, etc., the court ruled that "However, a confidentiality preservation order is a provision under the IPCAA that restricts the publication or use of trade secrets held by parties to the case or third parties. Thus, in a general case that is not an intellectual property right lawsuit, the viewing, transcription, or photographing of evidence by the parties cannot be restricted through a confidentiality preservation order. Therefore, the petition lacks legal grounds and cannot be granted."[74]

With regard to the investigation confidentiality protective order, application to general civil and commercial cases should not be allowed, given its many drawbacks.

73. Taipei District Court 106 (2017) Lao-Su-Zi No. 200 civil decision.
74. Taipei District Court 104 (2015) Su-Zi No. 3008 civil decision (for contract performance).

TOPIC 5 A NEW DIRECTION FOR CALCULATING DAMAGES FOR TRADE SECRET INFRINGEMENT?

Kung-Chung Liu

1. Legal Issues

In addition to the usual ways of calculating damages for the owner of an infringed trade secret, i.e., his actual loss or the infringer's net profits as a result of infringement, whether and under what circumstances can courts resort to R&D costs as a proxy for damages, if at all? How may courts determine the R&D costs for a specific trade secret? What factors shall a court take into consideration when awarding punitive damages?

2. The Statutory Law

The TSA provides two civil remedies for trade secret owners whose secrets were misappropriated, namely monetary damages for restoration of the *status quo ante* and punitive damages that would have some deterrent effects on preventing future infringement.

Article 13 of the TSA stipulates:

> (1) An injured party may choose any of the following provisions to request damages in accordance with the preceding Article:
> 1. To make a claim based upon Article 216 of the Civil Code[75]. However, if the injured party is unable to prove the amount of damages, the party may take as damages the amount of profits normally expected from the use of the trade secret minus the amount of profits earned after the misappropriation; or
> 2. To request the profits earned through the act of misappropriation from the one who misappropriated. However, if the one who misappropriated is unable to prove the costs or the necessary expenses, the total income gained from the act(s) of misappropriation shall be deemed the profits.
>
> (2) Based on the provisions set forth in the preceding paragraph, if an act of misappropriation is found to be intentional, the court may, at the request of the injured party and by taking into consideration the circumstances of the misappropriation, award an amount greater than the actual damages, provided that the amount shall not exceed three times the amount of the proven damages.

There are two proxies for damages for restoration of the *status quo ante*. One is the difference between the plaintiff's expected profit and actual profit. The other is the misappropriator's net profits.

If two or more parties jointly misappropriate trade secrets, they shall be jointly and severally liable for monetary damages under Article 12 of the TSA.

75. Article 216 of the Civil Code provides: (1) Unless otherwise provided by the act or by the contract, the compensation shall be limited to the injury actually suffered and the interests which have been lost. (2) Interests which could have been normally expected are deemed to be the interests which have been lost, according to the ordinary course of things, the decided projects, equipment, or other particular circumstances.

3. The Case Law

According to the statistics of the Taiwan IP and Commercial Court, between July 2008 and December 2017, the plaintiff's claim for damages averaged TWD 4.47 million (approximately USD 140,000) in district courts and TWD 68 million (approximately USD 2.26 million) in Taiwan IP and Commercial Court. The damages rendered by the Taiwan IP and Commercial Court averaged TWD 54 million (approximately USD 1.8 million), which is roughly 80 % of the plaintiff's claim[76].

4. The Leading Case

The decision discussed here is recognized by the IP community as the Taiwan IP and Commercial Court's leading case, not only because it awarded by far the largest damages for a trade secret misappropriation case in the IP Court's history but also because it addresses many legal issues that are unique in trade secrets misappropriation cases; this is why this decision deserves close attention. Taiwan IP and Commercial Court in its capacity as the second instance court has entirely upheld the present decision[77].

4.1. Case Information

Taiwan IP and Commercial Court 102 (2013) Min-Yin-Su-Zi No. 6 concluding civil decision (decided on December 6, 2017).

4.2. Summary

The plaintiff Largan Precision Co. Ltd. (Largan) in 2011 sued the defendants Ability Opto-Electronics Technology Co. Ltd. (AOET) and four other individual defendants over infringement of its trade secrets. In calculating the actual loss caused, Largan claimed that the damages should include the value of two utility model patents, i.e., the costs invested and spent in research and development of the trade secrets. Apart from the actual loss, Largan also requested that the Taiwan IP and Commercial Court consider the benefits, profits, and advantages gained by the defendants through the misappropriation of the trade secret. Lastly, Largan asked the Court to award punitive damages because the defendants willfully misappropriated Largan's trade secrets.

The one-man bench, Judge Hung-Ying Peng, issued on October 30, 2015 an interlocutory decision[78], finding infringement of the plaintiff's trade secrets[79]. The Court also held that Largan has grounds to claim the right to patent application and

76. The Statistics Report, I.
77. Taiwan IP and Commercial Court criminal decision 107 (2018) Min-Yin-Shang-Zi No. 1 (decided on January 28, 2021).
78. According to Article 383 of Taiwan's Code of Civil Procedure (CCP), where one of the grounds of attack or defense presented separately is mature for decision, the court may enter an interlocutory judgment.
79. Only some 76 lines of Taiwan IP and Commercial Court 2013 Min Yin Su Zi No. 6 interlocutory civil decision are published on the website of the Judicial Yuan due to concerns over trade secret protection. This happens often as a result of automatic decision by algorithm. Readers can ask the system to change its decision by sending an email to the Judicial Yuan. However, it is time-consuming and

ownership over the two utility model patents at dispute, although they were issued to AOET, developed based on two of Largan's trade secrets. Twenty-six months later, the Court awarded monetary damages of TWD 1,522,470,639 against AOET and four other individual defendants in the concluding decision, which is exactly the amount that the plaintiff requested in its claim.

4.3. *Facts*

Largan is a Taiwanese lens manufacturer and has long occupied a large world share of the smartphone lens market. The secrets at issue involve Largan's lens manufacturing processes. The key to Largan's success in manufacturing and selling smartphone lenses is its automated manufacturing process and tools used therein. Largan developed its manufacturing processes and technologies independently and has no intention of disclosing, selling, or licensing them, and has always kept them as trade secrets. The manufacturing technologies have allowed Largan to reduce its reliance on human resources and improve its capacity to auto-manufacture smartphone lenses, which requires extreme precision.

Largan became aware of AOET's misappropriation of its trade secrets when it learned that AOET applied for the two utility model patents which were granted by Taiwan Intellectual Property Office (TIPO). In these two utility model patents, four of Largan's former employees and AOET's then-general manager were named inventors. Largan believed that the four employees had leaked Largan's trade secrets to AOET, as these two utility model patents were identical to two pieces of Largan's critical know-how concerning its manufacturing processes. One of the utility model patents, pat. No. M438469, is a device that picks and places a small component that is installed into a smartphone lens to improve the lens's precision. The other utility model patent, pat. No. M438320, is a gluing needle that plays an essential role in the smartphone lenses' gluing process. The two pieces of know-how were created by Largan's engineers and used exclusively for Largan's manufacturing process of its smartphone lenses. The four employees left Largan and moved to AOET in 2011 for new positions. Largan believed that AOET established its auto-manufacturing operations based on Largan's trade secrets acquired through these four employees. Largan then filed a civil lawsuit, suing AOET, AOET's then-general manager, and the four former employees for trade secrets misappropriation. Largan later pressed criminal charges against the same defendants and asked for damages of TWD 14 billion[80].

Largan requested the Court to: (1) grant a permanent injunction preventing the named defendants (including AOET) from using Largan's trade secrets; (2) declare that

sometimes leads to no change of the non-publication decision, as some courts insist on keeping their decisions not public at all or only partially public.

80. Only the copyright infringement part of the criminal case was adjudicated by the Taichung District Court (on January 16, 2021) and the defendants were fined TWD 600,000 for illegal reproduction of Largan's protected works (https://tw.stock.yahoo.com/news). The trade secret infringement part was not decided. However, the criminal case was later dropped due to settlement of the parties (*see infra* 4.6.)

Largan shall be entitled to the ownership of the two utility model patents; and (3) award Largan damages of TWD 1,522,470,639 plus interest.

The Court held in the interlocutory decision that Largan unlawfully reproduced the two utility model patents' figures in the drawings of the two devices at dispute. It further held that, except for one particular device, Largan established that AOET did misappropriate the secret manufacturing technologies alleged by Largan. The Court then continued its proceeding to award the exact damage amount that Largan requested.

4.4. *Reasoning of the court*

4.4.1. *Resorting to Discretionary Power Recognized by the CCP*

The present decision did not rely on Article 13 of the TSA to determine the damages to be awarded to the plaintiff. Rather, it turned to Article 222(1) of the CCP, which allows the courts to exercise discretionary power: "Where a party has proved injury but is unable to or is under great difficulty to prove the exact amount, the court shall, taking into consideration all circumstances, determine the amount by its conviction." It then went to great lengths to explain why the plaintiff was unable to or under great difficulty to prove the amount of damages and why it chose the R&D costs as the correct proxy.

4.4.2. *The Plaintiff Was Unable to or under Difficulty to Prove the Damages Amount*

After reciting Article 222(1) of the CCP and its legislative reasons, the present decision turned to the fact that the trade secrets at dispute were automated production technology for plastic lenses that the plaintiff has independently developed over the years, for which the plaintiff has never granted others the license, that other lens component companies treat their automated production technology as trade secrets and rarely grant others license to use such technology, and that it is difficult to reference any objective transaction value for such technology. It then acknowledged that the plaintiff spent over ten years to research and develop the trade secrets at dispute and that the investment items (such as capital, equipment, and human power) are extremely diverse and detailed so that an item-by-item calculation of damages as a result of trade secret infringement was indeed difficult. It concluded that it was therefore legitimate for this court to resort to Article 222(1) of the CCP to arrive at an amount according to its discretion[81].

4.4.3. *Using the R&D Costs as Proxy for Damages*

The present decision first rejected using the misappropriator's net profits as damages, based on two reasons. First, it was questionable for the plaintiff to include AOET's net revenues of 2013 and 2014 as its profits, as AOET had already ceased to use the trade

81. Lines 582-591 of Taiwan IP and Commercial Court 2013 Min Yin Su Zi No. 6 concluding civil decision.

secrets. Second, AOET has three major product lines, i.e., glass lens, glass focus, and plastic focus, whereas the trade secrets concerned only the production process of the plastic focus. It was therefore unacceptable to include all of AOET's net revenues as AOET's profits resulting from infringement[82].

Then the present decision accepted the expert report (Evidence 100) presented by Largan, which was done by a CPA commissioned by Largan. The Court noticed that the CPA based its assessment on the information of Largan, which was in compliance with the accountancy guidelines and relevant government regulations, openly available and certified by CPAs, who went through a compliance test, sampling, and tracking of the original receipts ensured the departmental allocation of costs principle was upheld by Largan and interviewed financial and management department staff and section chefs who later appeared before the Court and made testimony concerning the basis for cost allocation, judgment, etc. The decision found that there was no unreasonableness or contradiction in the report and that it was a credible method to adopt a fixed percentage to allocate costs to a certain technology, as original receipts are directed at departments and not any specific technology. The present decision concluded that the estimated R&D costs for the period between xx year and 2013 were credible, as it was expected that Largan would have made substantial R&D investment for the trade secrets, the estimated R&D costs were only xx%[83] of its total R&D costs of TWD 5,732,260,000 during the period and not overly high, and was only xx% of Largan's 2014 market value of TWD 162.9 billion and therefore reasonable[84].

On the issue of whether the Court should consider the actual loss of Largan to calculate its damages, the present decision feared that might lead to too high an amount, as "the trade secrets at dispute not only enabled Largan to be leading in R&D, but also brought Largan huge economic interests." The present decision therefore preferred using the R&D costs as proxy for damages[85].

4.4.4. *Punitive Damages*

The interlocutory decision has found the defendants had intentionally infringed upon Largan's trade secrets. The present decision further awarded Largan the maximum punitive damage of three times. It was based on the following considerations: (1) AOET poached the four individual defendants to work for it, knowing that they worked at Largan as R&D personnel. (2) The four individual defendants stole, through large-scale reproduction and taking away in packages, Largan's trade secrets and delivered them to AOET during and after their work for Largan, and the theft was on the R&D result that Largan had accumulated over many years. (3) The four individual defendants filed for utility models over part of the xx and xx technologies, which led to further disclosure of the two technologies to the public and other plastic lens manufacturers who can study, exploit and improve them. (4) AOET has applied the stolen trade

82. Lines 615-638 of Taiwan IP and Commercial Court 2013 Min Yin Su Zi No. 6 concluding civil decision.
83. X's are used for content blacked out in the released decision.
84. Lines 1000-1032 of Taiwan IP and Commercial Court 2013 Min Yin Su Zi No. 6 concluding civil decision.
85. Lines 1172-1180 of Taiwan IP and Commercial Court 2013 Min Yin Su Zi No. 6 concluding civil decision.

secrets to its automated manufacturing process, not only internally but also by commissioning outside contractors to manufacture xx and apply xx onto xx device. (5) The trade secrets at issue enabled Largan's profitability and market share to exceed that of its competitors by far and boosted its market value to rise continuously, reaching TWD 500 billion, TWD 413 billion more than its registered capital. (6) The stolen trade secrets covered most of Largan's automated production technology and the theft was indeed able to affect Largan's market position, and gravely endanger numerous shareholders and employees[86]. In conclusion, the present decision awarded the claimed amount of damages of TWD 1,522,470,639, as it did not exceed three times the determined amount of R&D costs of xxx.

4.5. *Legal Analysis*

4.5.1. *Two Peculiarities of the Present Case*

There are at least two peculiarities of the present case. For one, according to the Taiwan IP and Commercial Court report, between July 1998 and June 2019, while the average monetary damages claimed by the plaintiff in district courts is TWD 4.47 million, TWD 68 million is the average claim in the Taiwan IP and Commercial Court in its capacity as the first instance court[87]. The Taiwan IP and Commercial Court awarded on average 80% of those claims, which is approximately TWD 54 million[88]. However, the present decision awarded a staggering amount of TWD 1,522,470,639 in damages, exactly as Largan had claimed, not a dollar less. This is indeed a rarity in Taiwanese judicial practice.

For another, Largan was set up in 1987 and became a publicly listed company in 2002. Especially after being publicly listed, it became famous for its excellent financial performance, as it managed to become the highest-priced stock on the Taipei Stock Exchange since 2014, with registered capital of only TWD 1.34 billion. Its current stock price is about TWD 3 million a share, 30 times higher than its net worth. As the longest-surviving "King of the Stock Market," it is extremely difficult for Largan to prove that it has suffered any loss as a result of the trade secret theft.

4.5.2. *Using R&D Costs as a Proxy for Damages Is Acceptable, but ...*

This is probably the first court decision in Taiwan that advocates the use of R&D costs as a proxy for damages. The present decision seems to be concerned about the danger of over-calculating damages and therefore avoids using AOET's net profits as damages and Largan's actual loss. This approach is not without merits. Comparative study shows that the Supreme People's Court (SPC) in China instructs Chinese courts to take into consideration the R&D costs, among other factors (such as revenues and profits

86. Lines 1573-1605 of Taiwan IP and Commercial Court 2013 Min Yin Su Zi No. 6 concluding civil decision.
87. Statistics Report, at 9.
88. *Ibid.*

derived from the commercialization of the trade secrets, and the lead time in maintaining a competitive edge) when assessing "the commercial value of the trade secrets" if the infringement has led the trade secret to be known to the public[89].

However, the present decision relied completely on the expert report (Evidence 100) done by a CPA commissioned by Largan to assess Largan's R&D costs. This is less acceptable from the perspective of due process of law, as no CPA can risk offending the King of the Stock Market, not to mention the one paid by Largan. This will seriously affect the creditability of this report.

4.5.3. *The Estimated R&D Costs Seem Unreasonably High*

According to the press release of the Taiwan IP and Commercial Court of January 28, 2021[90], the estimated R&D costs for the two utility model patents were some TWD 510,321,123, meaning each utility model patent costs TWD 250 million to research and develop. However, the figure seems unreasonably high and runs against common sense in patent law. Anyone who knows the basics of patent practice will know that invention patents are much more valuable than utility model patents, as the latter do not go through substantive examination, while the former do. That is why high-tech companies almost always file only for invention patents. A patent search at the TIPO website[91] also shows that Largan has 90% of its IP portfolio as invention patents and only 10% as utility model patents: 648 invention patents and 64 utility model patents respectively[92]. According to the "Top 100 Patent Filers and Receivers" compiled and published by the TIPO, Largan started to be among the top 100 patent receivers in 2013, the year when it sued AOET, and since then has acquired 463 invention patents and 38 utility model patents. That means Largan had accumulated some 185 invention patents and 26 utility models before the litigation broke out. Therefore, if Largan spent TWD 250 million to develop one utility model patent, the total R&D costs of these 185 inventions and the other 24 utility model patents must be far above the amount of TWD 5.73 billion that the present decision recognized Largan as having spent during the year xx[93] and 2013. In other words, TWD 500 million seems unreasonably high.

In this context, it is worth pointing out that the present decision came to the conclusion that "The stolen trade secrets covered most of Largan's automated production technology and could indeed affect Largan's market position," which is technologically not possible. Rather, the 185 invention patents are more likely to cover most of Largan's automated production technology at the time.

89. *See* Article 19, SPC, Provisions on Several Issues concerning the Application of Law in the Trial of Civil Cases involving Infringement of Trade Secrets, Fa-Shi [2020] No. 7.
90. Available at: https://www.judicial.gov.tw/tw/cp-1888-366268-71ab8-1.html.
91. https://gpss4.tipo.gov.tw/.
92. https://topic.tipo.gov.tw/patents-tw/lp-781-101.html.
93. It is indeed a puzzle as to why the starting year of the R&D period is blacked out.

4.6. *Commercial or Industrial Significance*

When determining the damage amount for an intellectual property infringement, the Taiwan IP and Commercial Court's case law indicates a trend of focusing on the actual loss of the right owners or the infringers' net profits derived from the infringing activities. However, the present decision suggests a different approach to calculating the damage amount, namely to focus on the right owner's investment in the research and development of the technologies. On the positive side, the decision might provide a more adequate remedy to owners of trade secrets to recuperate their R&D investment in new technologies. However, on the negative side, the huge damage award might send out a message to innovators that perhaps they should reconsider their IP strategy and portfolio management by relying more on trade secret protection, rather than on patents. This could lead to fewer patents, and thus less disclosure and inspiration.

On a separate note, on March 5, 2021, some 36 days after Taiwan IP and Commercial Court in its capacity as the appellate court ruled entirely in Largan's favor, Largan settled all its civil and criminal cases with AOET. However, the terms and conditions of the settlement have not been disclosed but withheld as trade secrets. Just as the market was surprised by this sudden move and speculating why, Largan bought in a 15.2% share of AOET on March 9, 2021 through a private placement with a total purchase price of TWD 598 million[94]. Several days later, AOET was reported to have made a loss of TWD 1 billion and TWD 6.43 million in December 2020 due to legal costs[95].

94. Available at https://udn.com/news/story/7253/5305497.
95. Available at https://www.cna.com.tw/news/afe/202103150110.aspx.

TOPIC 6 THE CRIMINAL PUNISHMENT OF TRADE SECRET THEFT AND ECONOMIC ESPIONAGE IN TAIWAN

Kung-Chung Liu

1. Legal Issues

By resorting to (increased) criminal punishment, it is hoped that real perpetrators will be deterred from committing trade secret theft and economic espionage, while at the same time the environment will be friendly towards employee mobility and the setting up of new start-ups. The legal issues involved are how to determine the requirement "with the intention of using the trade secret abroad" in order to find economic espionage and the extent to which corporations should be held liable for employees who have taken their former employers' trade secrets inadvertently or carelessly along with them.

2. The Statutory Law

The TSA had "no teeth" until the 2013 amendment, which introduces criminal sanctions. Article 13-1(1) foresees criminal liabilities for trade secret theft: Any person committing any of the following acts with the intention of illicitly gaining for himself or a third person, or inflicting a loss on the holder of a trade secret, shall be sentenced to a maximum of five years imprisonment or detention, and a fine between TWD 1 million and TWD 10 million[96].

In addition, following the US, Japanese and Korean trend to meet the need to deter cross-border infringement of trade secrets, Article 13-2 of the TSA doubles the criminal punishment for economic espionage. It provides that any person committing a crime of infringing a trade secret with the intention of using it in foreign jurisdictions, Mainland China, Hong Kong, or Macau shall be sentenced to imprisonment between one year and ten years, and a fine between TWD 3 million and TWD 50 million (Article 13-2(1)). An attempt to commit such a crime is punishable (Article 13-2(2)). Article 13-2(3) raises the fine to an unprecedented level of "two to ten times the illicit gain" by

96. Article 13-1 of the TSA, provides, "Any person committing an act falling under any of the following circumstances for the purpose of an illicit gain for himself/herself or for a third person, or inflicting a loss on the holder of a trade secret, shall be sentenced to a maximum of 5 years' imprisonment or short-term imprisonment, and in addition thereto, a fine between NT$1 million and NT$10 million may be imposed: 1. Acquiring a trade secret by an act of theft, embezzlement, fraud, threat, unauthorized reproduction, or other wrongful means, or using or disclosing a trade secret so acquired. 2. Committing an unauthorized reproduction, usage, or disclosure of a trade secret known or possessed. 3. Failing to delete or destroy a possessed trade secret as the trade secret holder orders, or disguising it. 4. Any person who knowingly acquires, uses or discloses a trade secret known or possessed by others under circumstances prescribed in the preceding three subparagraphs.

An attempt to commit a crime specified in the preceding paragraph is punishable.

In case a fine is to be imposed, if the gain obtained by the offender exceeds the maximum fine, such fine may be increased within the extent of 3 times the gain."

the violator if his gain exceeds the maximum fine[97]. The juristic person shall be punished with the fine prescribed for its employee unless its representative has done his/her utmost to prevent a crime from being committed[98].

The TSA was again revised in 2020, mainly to introduce the "investigation confidentiality protective order" to be issued by a prosecutor investigating a trade secret case to the suspects, the defendants, the victims, the complainants, the agents *ad litem*, the defense attorneys, expert witnesses, witnesses, or other associated persons having access to the investigation contents (Articles 14-1 - 14-4).

3. The Case Law

District courts closed 49 first instance criminal cases under the TSA from 2013 to June 2019. The conviction rate is 30.30% among 99 defendants. However, after breaking down to cases under Article 13-1 of the TSA (trade secret crime) and Article 13-2 (economic espionage), the conviction rate is 27.14% and 70%[99]. The Taiwan IP and Commercial Court started to receive appeal criminal cases in 2016 and has since then to June 2019 closed 17 criminal cases. Ten appeal cases were dismissed for lack of merit, and seven led to revocation. 14 of the 29 defendants were acquitted, 9 defendants were found guilty, 8 of whom sentenced to imprisonment (5 defendants got less than 6 months), and one defendant was fined. The conviction rate is 31.03%[100]. Presumably, only two defendants were sentenced for economic espionage before June 2019.

We have searched the database of the Judicial Yuan as of March 25, 2021 and found three economic espionage cases. One is Taiwan IP and Commercial Court 105 (2016) Xing-Zhi-Shang-Su-Zi 35 (*Dairen Chemical Corporation, Taiwan (大連公司) v Yunnan Zheng Bang (雲南正邦)*), the Taiwan IP and Commercial Court upheld a 7.5-year imprisonment sentence based on Article 13-2 of the TSA. However, the Supreme Court (2018 Tai-Shang-Zi 2950 criminal decision) revoked the decision due to the absence of determination as to whether the information listed in Appendix 1-3 was independent or dependent and whether it possessed actual or potential economic value due to the secrecy.

---

97. Article 13-2 of the TSA provides "(1) Any person committing a crime prescribed in the first paragraph of the preceding article with the intention of using the trade secret in foreign jurisdictions, mainland China, Hong Kong, or Macau shall be sentenced to imprisonment between 1 year and 10 years, in addition thereto, a fine between NT$3 million and NT$50 million may be imposed.

    (2) An attempt to commit a crime specified in the preceding paragraph is punishable.
    (3) In case a fine is to be imposed, if the gain obtained by the offender exceeds the maximum fine, such fine may be increased within the extent of 2 to 10 times of the gain."

98. Article 13-4 of the TSA provides: "Where the representative of a juristic person, the agent, employee or any other staff of a juristic person or natural person commits any of the crimes prescribed in Article 13-1 or 13-2 in the course of business, not only the actor, but the juristic person or the natural person shall be punished with the fine prescribed in the Article. However, if the representative of a juristic person or natural person has done his/her utmost to prevent a crime from being committed, the juristic person or natural person shall not be punished."
99. Statistics Report, I and II.
100. *Ibid.*

The second economic espionage case, 106 (2017) Zhi-Su-Zi 4 criminal decision (*TSMC v Shanghai Huali Microelectronics Corporation (上海華力微電子)*) the Hsinchu District Court rendered a sentence of 18 months with four years' probation, put the defendant under protective custody during the probation, and asked the defendant to pay the public treasury TWD 300,000 within one year after the case is finalized. The case was appealed and led to 107 (2018) Xing-Zhi-Shang-Su-Zi 5 criminal decision by the Taiwan IP and Commercial Court, which only changed the terms and conditions for probation: the defendant shall pay the public treasury TWD 500,000 within one year after the case is finalized, shall report to the General Council of the accuser, TSMC, from September 25, 2017 to September 30, 2020, two years after the Taiwan IP and Commercial Court rendered the present decision, about his new employer and job title, and shall be prohibited from undertaking competitive activities, whether by working for others or by setting up his own company. The third economic espionage case is the leading case chosen by the present case report.

4. The Leading Case

This is the case with the harshest criminal sentence on defendants (three in total) without probation. It is also the first where a corporate defendant was also fined. The court rendered its decision on June 12, 2020; however, it initially refused to release it due to trade secret protection concerns. After public outcry and protest[101], the decision was released in late December 2020, with the sensitive parts blacked out.

4.1. Case Information

Taiwan Taichung District Court 2017 Zhi-Su-Zi 11 criminal decision (decided on June 12, 2020).

4.2. Summary

The decision found the defendants He Jian-Ting, Wang Yong-Ming, Rong Le-Tian, and United Microelectronics Corporation (UMC) in violation of the TSA. Defendant Mr. He was sentenced to 5.5 years in prison for violation of Article 13-2(1) by breaching Article 13-1(1) No. 2 with the intention of using the trade secret in Mainland China, a fine of TWD 5 million, and confiscation of the illicit gain of TWD 5,413,910. Defendant Mr. Wang was guilty of the same crime and sentenced to 4.5 years in prison, a fine of TWD 4 million, and confiscation of the illicit gain of TWD 1,527,812. Defendant Mr. Rong was guilty of the same crime and sentenced to 6.5 years in prison, a fine of TWD 6 million, and confiscation of illicit gain of TWD 1,610,952. Defendant UMC was sentenced to pay a TWD 100 million fine in total for its three employees, namely for Mr. He TWD 30 million, for Mr. Wang TWD 50 million, and for Mr. Rong TWD 40 million

101. Three editorials of Commercial Times (published in Taiwan in Chinese): "Control Yuan Should Investigate Taichung District Court and the Judicial Yuan For Not Publishing Decisions" (October 8, 2020), "Taichung District Court, IP Court and the Judicial Yuan and Their Joint Karma on Trade Secrets" (August 23, 2020), and "Taichung District Court Should Publish Its 2017 Zhi-Su-Zi 11 Criminal Decision With No Delay" (July 17, 2020).

respectively. Currently, the decision is being appealed to Taiwan IP and Commercial Court in its capacity as the second instance court for criminal cases.

4.3. *Facts*

UMC, headquartered in Taiwan, signed a technical cooperation agreement in January 2016 with Fujian Jinhua, a Mainland China-based and state-owned company, to develop a dynamic random-access memory (DRAM)-related manufacturing process, according to which Jinhua promised to provide USD 300 million to purchase R&D equipment, pay UMC USD 400 million, co-own the R&D results with UMC, and have the entire technology transferred for mass production of DRAM. The agreement was approved by the Investment Commission, Ministry of Economic Affairs, shortly before the current government took power, which adopted a hostile position towards Mainland China. UMC set up a "New Business Development Centre (NBDC)" to execute the technical cooperation agreement, which was headed by Chen Zheng-Kun. Chen left Micron Taiwan as a board director and joined UMC a month later as Senior Vice President. Mr. He and Mr. Wang followed a similar pattern. Mr. Rong was the Assistant Vice Presidentin charge of NBDC.

While still working for Micron Taiwan, Mr. He downloaded a DRAM-related manufacturing process from Micron Taiwan and Micron US (collectively Micron) via the intranet of Micron Taiwan, which is a trade secret belonging to Micron US (hereinafter electromagnetic record A) onto his personal mobile hard drive and Universal Serial Bus (USB) thumb drive. Mr. He took the notebook computer installed with electromagnetic record A and documents containing trade secrets of Micron US (hereinafter "paper info B") to UMC when joining it. Mr. He further used the notebook computer given to him by UMC with the USB portal control deactivated (usually activated to ban access via USB) to read and download electromagnetic record A. Mr. Wang used a notebook computer provided by Micron Taiwan to access the servers of Micron, downloaded a DRAM-related manufacturing process which is a trade secret belonging to Micron US (hereinafter "electromagnetic record C"), copied electromagnetic record C to his USB drive, and further to his two notebook computers, and uploaded it to cloud hardware of Google Drive. When asked by Mr. Rong to reference Micron Taiwan's design rules to compare them with UMC's test version on paper, and to indicate stable numbers used by Micron Taiwan's design rules, Mr. Wang downloaded electromagnetic record C from Google Drive, printed it on paper (hereinafter "paper info D"), filled in the parameters used by Micron Taiwan's design rules onto a dozen documents for UMC to finalize its design rules, modified the figures, and submitted them to Mr. Rong. UMC was therefore able to complete its design rules and forward them to a chip design company for the next stage of design, reducing UMC's costs in terms of time, money, equipment, and human capital in completing its design rules.

4.4. *Reasoning of the Court*[102]

4.4.1. *The Executives of UMC, Mr. Rong and Mr. Chen, Had Not Done Their Utmost to Prevent the Theft*

Mr. Rong was at the executive level of UMC and responsible for leading Mr. He and Mr. Wang. Mr. Rong and Mr. Wang have violated UMC's employment contract that prohibits employees from revealing trade secrets of former employers to UMC and using them at work by instructing Mr. Wang to provide Micron Taiwan's parameters for the DRAM manufacturing process. Mr. Rong instructed Mr. He and Mr. Wang to delete Micron's info when the Investigation Bureau was investigating. On top of that, the Investigation Bureau found a large amount of trade secrets held by Micron was stored in notebook computers, USB sticks, and mobile hard drives confiscated on the premises and in the dormitory of UMC. Therefore, Mr. Rong knowingly indulged Mr. He and Mr. Wang's violation of the TSA and can hardly be said to have done his utmost to prevent the crime from being committed.

In addition, UMC's security rule restricts access to all its computers via USB. However, Mr. Chen lifted the restriction on one UMC computer and gave it to Mr. He, who used it to access Micron's trade secrets and use them from UMC's office. Mr. Wang knew of Mr. He's acquisition of one such computer from Mr. Chen and borrowed it from Mr. He. Considering the abovementioned behavior of Mr. Rong and Mr. Chen as high executives of UMC, the defendant UMC has violated Article 13-4 of the TSA.

4.4.2. *Committing Trade Secret Theft with the Intention of Using it in Mainland China (Economic Espionage)*

Mr. He also received a salary from Jinhua in addition to from UMC, which clearly shows his intention of using the trade secrets in China. Mr. Wang and Mr. Rong knew that the trade secrets of Micron, namely manufacturing parameters of design rules for DRAM, were leaked to UMC, that UMC used these parameters, that files containing test results would be forwarded to a chip design company for the next stage of design, and that the ultimate R&D data would be transferred to Jinhua in China for mass production. They had, therefore, the intention of using the trade secrets in China.

4.4.3. *Mr. Rong Is the Most Reprehensible Among the Three Defendants*

Mr. Rong, as a high executive of UMC, rather than upgrading UMC's competitiveness through legitimate means, asked his subordinate Mr. Wang to provide Micron's trade secrets, which caused serious damage to the competitive advantages of Micron, and he is thus indeed culpable. Mr. Rong not only did not show any remorse but also fabricated facts to shield himself from any responsibility.

102. The present decision as published on the website of the Judicial Yuan does not contain line, paragraph or page number.

4.4.4. *UMC's Fine*

After taking into consideration the business scale, the registered capital, revenues, economic benefits derived from the theft committed by the three other defendants, and the saving on human resources, money, and time due to the shortened R&D period, UMC was assessed a fine of TWD 100 million.

4.4.5. *Confiscation of Salary as Illicit Gains*

Mr. He received a payment of TWD 5,430,910 from UMC and Jinhua, Mr. Wang received a payment of TWD 15,207,812 from UMC, and Mr. Rong received TWD 16,100,952 from UMC, all of which are considered by Taichung District Court to be remuneration for violation of the TSA and illicit gains by the defendants, and are declared to be confiscated according to the law.

4.5. *Legal Analysis*

4.5.1. *Did USDOJ's Settlement with UMC Pre-empt Taiwanese Courts' Finding of Economic Espionage?*

The case involved the semiconductor industry in Taiwan, Mainland China (aka the PRC), and the US, and is politically sensitive in the context of a heated US-China trade war[103], as the US is blocking China's access to semiconductor technology. After the Taiwanese Investigation Bureau started to investigate UMC in February 2017, the USDOJ (Department of Justice) watched the unfolding of the case carefully and dispatched US public prosecutors to Taiwan under the Taiwanese Mutual Legal Assistance in Criminal Matters Act. In October 2018, the US Commerce Department banned sales to Jinhua[104]. A federal grand jury indicted UMC for economic espionage (18 U.S.C. § 1831) in September 2018, along with Fujian Jinhua, and three individuals for conspiracy to steal, convey and possess stolen trade secrets of an American semiconductor company (Micron) for the benefit of Fujian Jinhua, a state-owned enterprise of the PRC.

However, two years later, the USDOJ announced on October 28, 2020 that UMC pleaded guilty to criminal trade secret theft and was sentenced to pay a USD 60 million fine. According to the plea agreement sanctioned by the Northern District Court of California, UMC pleaded guilty to one count of criminal trade secret theft in violation of 18 U.S.C. § 1832(a)(3) (not § 1831 economic espionage). The other criminal charges and a parallel civil suit brought by the USDOJ on behalf of the US against UMC will be dismissed[105]. However, the USDOJ vowed to continue "the criminal prosecution of Fujian Jinhua and the three individual defendants." Noteworthy is that instead of suing

103. For more analysis of the US-China trade war, *see* Kung-Chung Liu, Trade War, Big Data and Algorithm (in Chinese), The Taiwan Law Review (published in Chinese in Taiwan) No. 303 (August 2020), 74-91.
104. https://www.lawfareblog.com/sinotech-us-commerce-department-bans-sales-fujian-jinhua.
105. DOJ Press release "Taiwan Company Pleads Guilty to Trade Secret Theft in Criminal Case Involving PRC State-Owned Company," October 28, 2020, available at https://www.justice.gov/opa/pr/taiwan-company-pleads-guilty-trade-secret-theft-criminal-case-involving-prc-state-owned.

Mr. Rong, the USDOJ named Mr. Chen as the mastermind behind Mr. He and Mr. Wang.

As a matter of fact, the USDOJ has lost its battle against UMC and Jinhua. UMC conceded only to the simple trade secret theft, not economic espionage, in exchange for the USDOJ's dropping the much more severe economic espionage charge and a parallel civil suit against UMC which might have resulted in much higher damages than the USD 60 million fine. Jinhua will not surrender to US criminal law jurisdiction, and the employee defendants are either indicted in Taiwan or domiciled in Xiamen, China, all beyond the reach of the USDOJ, making the USDOJ's continued criminal prosecution impossible.

Were there ever economic espionage by UMC, the USDOJ would never have agreed to the plea bargain. Given this, it would be very difficult for Taiwanese courts to hold on to the present decision's conclusion: the defendants are guilty of economic espionage for Jinhua.

4.5.2. *Preventing Economic Espionage or Hindering Employees' Mobility?*

Taiwanese industries prize the flexibility of small and medium enterprises (SMEs), which thrive as start-ups enabled by the mobility of skilled workers and professionals. The introduction of economic espionage crime into the TSA with the vague term of "with the intention of benefitting foreign jurisdictions, Mainland China, HK, or Macau" can be very subjective and unpredictable on the one hand and can hinder employees' mobility on the other. It is also disproportionally disadvantaging mid- to low-level professional employees who really do not have a clue about where and how the finalized technology will be ultimately commercialized. To make things worse for skilled workers and professionals, criminal procedures, once started, are very damaging, as they normally drag on for years[106] and no employers will hire the defendants during that period. Even if skilled workers and professionals manage to clear their reputation and survive, they may still be an ill fit for the stern career competition. Taking the three defendants in the present case as an example, their careers came to an abrupt stop in 2017, and there is no telling when their case will be finalized and their next employment will start.

The present decision is especially harsh on the three employee defendants, as it considered the salary they received entirely as illicit gain from the crime. This can hardly be persuasive, as it is beyond imagination that they worked exclusively on

106. In Taiwan, the Criminal Speedy Trial Act was enacted in 2010 to remedy the overly long criminal procedures. According to Article 7 of the Act, for an outstanding case with no final judgment being made for more than eight years from the date the case is subject to the jurisdiction of first instance, unless a not-guilty verdict is announced in accordance with the law, the court shall reduce the sentence, upon the request of the accused or ex officio, and after considering the following circumstances which make it conclude that the right to a speedy trial of the accused is grossly violated and it is necessary to provide appropriate remedies: (1) whether the delay in litigation proceeding is caused by the accused; (2) the balance between the complication of the case in terms of legality and facts and the delay in the litigation proceeding; (3) other matters related to the speedy trial.

infringing Micron's trade secrets during their entire employment with UMC. As professional engineers, they must have also worked on other legal projects.

4.5.3. *Economic Espionage Requires Trade Secrets Held by Taiwanese*

The legislative reason for enacting Article 13-2 of the TSA clearly states that "This article is an increased punishment for committing Article 13-1 of the TSA crime with the intention of using trade secrets at issue abroad, as any perpetrator acquiring trade secrets of Taiwanese with the intention of using them beyond our national borders will gravely affect the international competitiveness of our industries and will therefore be more culpable." The purpose and justifiability of Article 13-2 lie in the protection of the trade secrets of our nationals. However, the present decision repeatedly stressed that the infringed trade secrets belong to Micron US, which is unequivocally a US and not a Taiwanese company, whose protection is under Article 13-1 TSA. One related question would be whether such an approach of punishing twice as harshly for benefitting foreign interests rather than domestic ones is in conformity with the spirit of the national treatment principle of the WTO.

4.6. ***Commercial or Industrial Significance***

The decision has drawn much attention from the semiconductor industry across the Taiwan Strait and even across the Pacific. It remains to be seen whether it represents a watershed for Taiwanese courts to take a very strict stance on the issue of economic espionage in the confrontation between the US and China and even between Mainland China and Taiwan, or whether the Taichung District Court is simply mimicking the Eastern District Court of Texas by taking an approach extremely in favor of trade secret holders. It also remains to be seen whether the appeal of the present decision can take place publicly, as the case is under thirteen protective orders. Importantly, it is worth observing whether the court's practice of keeping every trial session secret will be followed by other or higher courts.

Ultimately, the possibility of cross-strait cooperation in sensitive technology and whether Taiwanese industries will perish as collateral damage or even a casualty of the US-China trade war or will continue to prosper as a good team player in the global value chain depends heavily on the appropriate application of Article 13-1 and 13-2 of the TSA.

CHAPTER 5
Thailand

OVERVIEW AND SUMMARY

Sutatip Yuthayotin & Tosaporn Leepuengtham

1. BRIEF HISTORY

In the 1990s, trade secrets became increasingly important to a wide range of industries in Thailand,[1] as they have helped businesses obtain advantages over competitors. However, at the time, there was no specific law protecting trade secrets. Trade secret protection was available through general laws, namely the Penal Code (Title XI "Offences Against Liberty and Reputation," Chapter 2 "Offences of Disclosure of Private Secrets") and the Civil and Commercial Code. Section 323 of the Penal Code provides protection for all secrets, regardless of their nature. However, the provisions limit liability only to competent officials, medical practitioners, pharmacists, druggists, midwives, nursing attendants, priests, advocates, lawyers, auditors, or assistants of such professions, who acquire the secret by reason of their professional function. Section 324 of the Penal Code provides punishment for those who, by reason of their function, profession, or calling of trust, have acquired secrets about industry, discovery or scientific invention, and disclosed such secret for the unfair benefit of themselves or other persons. Even though trade secret protection may also be available under Thai Civil and Commercial Code, section 1169 only applies to disclosure of trade secrets by company directors who fail to act in good faith and in the best interests of the company.

As a member of the World Trade Organization, Thailand is obligated to enact laws to protect "undisclosed information" or trade secrets in order to be in compliance with Article 39 of the Agreement on Trade-Related Aspects of Intellectual Property Rights (the TRIPS Agreement). Article 39 stipulates that members must ensure effective protection of trade secrets against unfair competition as provided in Article 10 bis of the

1. Prasopsook Bundech, Trade Secret Protection in Thailand, Intellectual Property and International Trade Law Journal, 2002, https://ipitc.coj.go.th/th/content/category/detail/id/10367/iid/192643.

Paris Convention (1967). As a consequence, the Trade Secret Act (the Act) was first drafted in 1999, which was proposed by Thailand's Ministry of Commerce. The deliberation by members of the House of Representatives and the Senate was controversial. While the Senate has made amendments to the draft, the House of Representatives disagreed with the amendments.[2] It took a number of years to develop an agreed draft of the Act. On April 23, 2002, the Act was passed with the specific reasons that tortious liabilities under Thai law have not yet covered liabilities for violation of trade secrets, and the Act is needed to promote free trade and prevent unfair trade practices. The Act contains 6 Parts, 39 sections, has been in effect since July 22, 2002, and provides protection, including injunctive relief, against unauthorized use and disclosure of trade secrets. In addition, the Act provides compensation to trade secret owners of such infringement. The Act is a sui generis law and does not repeal the liabilities related to undue revealing of secrets under the Penal Code and the Civil and Commercial Code. A trade secret owner has two options to protect his trade secrets, one is under the Penal Code and the Civil and Commercial Code and the other is under the Act, which provides better protection.

The Central Intellectual Property and International Trade Court (CIPIT Court), as a specialized court, has jurisdiction over civil and criminal actions relating to intellectual property matters, including trade secret cases nationwide. The decisions made by the CIPIT Court had been directly appealed to the Intellectual Property and International Trade (IPIT) Court Division of Supreme Court until October 1, 2016, when the specialist Court of Appeals for Specialized Cases was established. Thereafter, the CIPIT Court's decisions have been appealed to the Court of Appeals for Specialized Cases, whose decision is final, unless the party wishing to appeal to the Supreme Court has obtained consent from the latter to hear the appeal. The Supreme Court will consent to hear such an appeal only if it deems the matter to be important and warrant one more opportunity for consideration.

2. THE SCOPE OF PROTECTION

Similar to the definition under Article 39(2) of the TRIPS Agreement, a trade secret eligible for protection under section 3 of the Act is:

(1) trade information that is not publicly known or must not yet be accessible by persons who normally deal with such information;
(2) trade information that has commercial value due to its secrecy; and
(3) trade information for which its lawful controller has taken reasonable measures to keep or maintain its secrecy.

In addition, section 3 of the Act defines "trade information" as any material that conveys the meaning of terms, matters, facts or other information communicated in

2. Tilleke & Gibbins International Ltd., Thailand: Trade Secrets in Thailand: New Developments on The Horizon, December 4, 2001, https://www.mondaq.com/copyright/14322/trade-secrets-in-thailand-new-developments-on-the-horizon.

whatever method and arranged in whatever form, including formulas, patterns, collected or assembled works, programs, methods, techniques or processes. In practice, these include methods of services, manufacturing information, know-how, consumer profiles, marketing plans, advertising strategies, pricing strategies, lists of suppliers and clients. Trade information can be broadly categorized into two types: industrial secrets, which are related to technical matters, such as a manufacturing process or chemical formula, and commercial secrets, which are related to sales methods, contract forms, customer lists, advertisement techniques, etc.

Some examples of appropriate measures include physical protection measures, such as setting up restricted areas, a closed distribution list, limited computer access and so on. In addition, non-disclosure and non-use clauses in relevant agreements governing the use of trade secrets can also be appropriate measures. Such agreements may be in the form of, but are not limited to, confidentiality agreements, non-disclosure agreements, employment agreements, manufacturing agreements, etc. Confidentiality provisions must carefully and precisely define confidential information that constitutes trade secret. Descriptions that are too vague or too general may not be enforceable. In addition, in case of violation of a confidentiality agreement, it will be necessary for the trade secret owner to prove that the information was carefully classified and maintained as confidential, and that disclosure was unauthorized or due to misappropriation.

3. TRADE SECRET OWNERS AND THEIR RIGHTS

Pursuant to section 3 of the Act, a "trade secret owner" is a person who has discovered, invented, collected, or created trade secret information without infringing another person's trade secret, or infringing the testing result or trade information that is a trade secret of a rightful holder. It also includes the transferee of the trade secret.

In addition, "trade secret controller" means the owner of a trade secret. It also includes the possessor, controller, or caretaker of the trade secret. Section 5 of the Act also affords protection to lawful transferees of a trade secret. Trade secret owners are exclusively entitled to disclose or use, or license someone else to disclose or use, trade secrets and to stipulate any terms and conditions for the maintenance of the secrecy. Trade secret owners can also transfer their trade secrets by juristic act or by inheritance.

4. INFRINGEMENT OF TRADE SECRET

Infringement of a trade secret includes an act of disclosing, taking, or using a trade secret without the consent of its owner and in a manner that breaches fair commercial practice. In this regard, the infringer must know, or have appropriate reason to know, that his action is contrary to fair commercial practices (section 6(1) of the Act).

Actions that are contrary to fair commercial practices include breach of contract, breach of confidence or persuasion to breach of confidence, bribery, intimidation, fraud, theft, receipt of stolen property, or espionage by electronic surveillance or any other means (section 6(2) of the Act).

The following acts shall not be considered a trade secret infringement:

(1) disclosure or use of a trade secret by a person who obtained the secret through a transaction, without awareness, or without any reason to be aware, that the other party to the transaction obtained the trade secret by violating another person's trade secret rights;
(2) disclosure or use of a trade secret by a state or government agency in charge of maintaining the trade secret when it is necessary: (a) to protect public health and security; or (b) for the benefit of other public interest with no commercial purpose. In such a case, the particular state agency which is responsible for keeping and maintaining the trade secrets, or any other state agency or person concerned who has access to such trade secrets, shall take reasonable measures or steps to protect the trade secrets from unfair use in trade;
(3) independent discovery, i.e., trade secrets discovered as a result of one's method of invention or development through expertise; or
(4) reverse engineering, i.e., discovery of trade secrets belonging to others by means of evaluation and analysis of existing products of others with the intention to study or discover the method by which such products are invented, manufactured or developed, provided that the product was obtained in good faith by the person who conducted the evaluation and analysis (section 7 of the Act). However, the exception is not applicable if the person who conducted such reverse engineering has entered into an agreement with the trade secret owner or the product seller which stipulates otherwise. Consequently, an express prohibition against reverse engineering when contracting for or licensing any technology or product can be agreed upon.

5. PRESCRIPTION PERIOD

Legal action against trade secret infringement shall not be allowed three years after the date when the controller knows of the infringement and of the wrongdoer. However, no legal action shall be allowed ten years after the date of infringement (section 10 of the Act).

6. CRIMINAL PENALTY

The Act provides broad protection, including criminal penalty, which is more severe than the Penal Code. Section 33 of the Act provides: "Whosoever discloses a trade secret of the other person to the public in the manner which causes the trade secret to cease being secret, with malicious intent to cause damage to the business of the controller of trade secrets, whether by publication through documents, audio or video broadcasting, or disclosure by any other means, shall be liable to imprisonment not exceeding one year or a fine not exceeding two hundred thousand baht, or both."

Section 34 of the Act stipulates: "Any person, by his or her position to maintain trade secrets in accordance with the rules prescribed under Section 15(1), unlawfully discloses or uses such trade secrets for his or her or other persons' benefits, shall be liable to imprisonment for a term of not more than two years or a fine not exceeding two hundred thousand baht, or both."[3]

Section 35 of the Act states: "(1) Any person disclosing certain facts about the business of the controller of trade secrets, which should normally be kept confidential and which he or she has obtained or known in the course of the performance of duties under this Act shall be liable to imprisonment for a term not exceeding one year or a fine not exceeding one hundred thousand baht, or both, except for disclosure in the course of an official duty or for the purpose of an investigation or legal proceeding. (2) Any person obtaining or knowing certain facts from the person under (1) in the course of an official duty or investigation or legal proceedings who discloses such facts shall be similarly liable. (3) Whosoever discloses facts which have been obtained or known as a result of his engagement in official duty, investigation or legal proceeding shall be subject to the same liability."[4]

Since the Act took effect, there have been only 17 criminal cases in the IPIT Court, 1 case in the Appeal Court for Specialized Cases and 19 cases in the Supreme Court.[5] Few trade secret cases have considered sections 33-35 of the Act, such that case law does not really establish any guidance beyond what is already stated in the Act. Yet of those cases, many have failed to secure criminal punishment mainly on technical issues involving incomplete indictments and insufficient evidence.[6]

Only an injured person, as legally defined, may bring a criminal case; otherwise, the case will be dismissed for lack of legal standing. A court has power to dismiss a case on this basis, irrespective of whether the defendant has raised this issue. A plaintiff must prove that the offense has been committed beyond a reasonable doubt. Thus, it is more difficult for a plaintiff to demonstrate the defendant's guilt than it is to establish liability for misappropriation under civil law. For example, while section 6 of the Act defines infringement of trade secret rights as being "the act of disclosure, deprivation or usage of trade secrets without the consent of the owner in a manner contrary to honest trade practices," for an offense to be committed under section 33 of the Act, the plaintiff must also prove that the defendant has disclosed a trade secret "with malicious intent to cause damage to his business." Clearly, evidence of the latter will be even more difficult to establish; therefore, some criminal cases have failed because the plaintiff lacks sufficient evidence to establish his case.

Though the criminalization of trade secret theft might serve as a greater deterrent than civil punitive damages, the strict test it requires makes it inevitable that fewer

3. Section 34 amended by Trade Secret Act (No. 2) B.E. 2558 (2015).
4. Section 35(1) amended by Trade Secret Act (No. 2) B.E. 2558 (2015).
5. Information received informally from the three courts on January 30, 2021.
6. For example, in Decision 4209/2561 (*Star Art Co. Ltd. v Mr. Kasem Tunyapuk, Miss Jantarat Kundee and Hit Galleria Co. Ltd.*) decided on July 4, 2018, the Supreme Court found that the plaintiff's indictment failed to include all of the essential elements of the section 33 offense, and quashed the indictment. The decision finds its basis in section 158(5) of the Criminal Procedure Code, which states that an indictment must contain all the acts alleged to have been committed by the accused, all the facts and particulars regarding the time and place of such acts, and the persons or articles concerned which are reasonably sufficient to give the accused a clear understanding of the charge.

cases will succeed. This leads one to question whether criminal punishment really is an effective legal tool. A would-be claimant should prioritize seeking civil remedies instead, given its less stringent requirements.

7. INJUNCTIVE RELIEF

The CIPIT Court has power to grant an injunctive relief order for trade secret controllers. The following injunctions may be granted if there is clear evidence that a person has committed, or is going to commit, any act in violation of a trade secret:

(1) an interim injunction ordering the violator to temporarily stop or refrain from infringing the trade secret; and
(2) a permanent injunction prohibiting the violator from infringing the trade secret;
(3) products manufactured as a result of the infringement of a trade secret that are still under the ownership of the infringer shall be vested with the state or the trade secret controller, as the Court orders. Alternatively, the Court may order their destruction (section 8 of the Act).

In the application for an injunction mentioned, a trade secret controller may also request that the Court orders the destruction or confiscation of instruments, apparatuses and accessories or other materials used in the trade secret infringement (section 11(3) of the Act).

Where the controller of a trade secret files action with the CIPIT Court requesting a preliminary injunction or permanent injunction and it is found that trade secret infringement exists but there are special circumstances which do not justify the injunction as requested, the Court may consider ordering the infringer to pay appropriate compensation and allow continued use of the trade secret within a reasonable period (section 11(1) of the Act).

In the case where the Court has granted an injunction stopping the resumption of infringement of a trade secret and it appears that the trade secret has been independently disclosed to the public and has lost its secrecy, the person subject to the injunction is entitled to file an application to revoke such injunction (section 11(2) of the Act).

8. PRESUMPTION FOR THE BENEFIT OF A TRADE SECRET CONTROLLER

Section 12 of the Act provides presumption for the benefit of a trade secret controller. In a civil infringement case involving a process for manufacturing a product, if the trade secret controller has proven that the infringer's product is of the same nature as the product manufactured by the process belonging to the controller, it shall be preliminarily assumed that the infringer has used the process belonging to the trade secret controller, unless proven otherwise by the infringer.

9. COMPENSATION AND PUNITIVE DAMAGES

In addition to taking action to obtain an injunction to stop the infringement, the Act allows compensation to the trade secret controller. The Court is empowered to determine compensation based on the actual damage suffered. In addition to actual damage suffered, the Court may order the infringer to compensate the trade secret owner for other benefits accrued from or in connection with the infringement by the wrongdoer. In case the Court is unable to measure the amount of damages just mentioned, it may allocate such amount of damage to the controller of trade secret as it deems appropriate. In cases where there is clear evidence that the infringement of a trade secret was carried out intentionally, or with the intention to maliciously cause damage, so that the trade secret creased to have the quality of secret, the Court shall have power to order the infringer pay punitive damages adding to the amounts mentioned above. However, such punitive damages shall not exceed two times the amount of compensation mentioned above (section 13 of the Act).

10. PRACTICE

In Thailand, there are only 96 trade secret cases tried by the CIPIT Court over the past 18 years, and since 2002, the majority of which were ruled against the trade secret owners. The reason for the CIPIT Court dismissing trade secret owners' claims was usually the absence of appropriate measures taken to maintain trade secrets. There are limited precedents of the Supreme Court on trade secrets, most of which considered the same issue of what protection measures are considered adequate.

On the other hand, parties may choose to settle their cases via court-organized mediation, which is much easier and convenient than litigation. In order to facilitate the mediation process, the Court provides personnel and facilities suitable for mediation. For examples, there are a number of mediators who have advanced communication skill in English, and virtual communication channels such as videoconferencing are available for the parties. This is clearly a favorable alternative dispute resolution process for parties disputing trade secrets. Court-organized mediation has proven to be highly successful and acceptable in terms of satisfactory outcomes and maintaining amicable relationships among parties.

TOPIC 1 THE REQUIREMENTS OF TRADE SECRET

Sutatip Yuthayotin

1. Legal Issues

Section 3 of the Act offers a very broad definition of "trade secret." Due to such broad wording, a review of Thai Supreme Court decisions is needed to gain a clear answer as to which information qualifies as trade secrets. However, Supreme Court has in most cases ruled against the secret owners due to their inability to prove the existence of the four elements of trade secrets.

2. The Statutory Law

Under section 3 of the Act, "Trade secret means trade information which is not widely known or not accessible among the persons who are related to such information. It is the information which is useful commercially due to its secret nature. It is the information for which a commercial trade secret controller uses appropriate measures to maintain its secrecy."

Sections 5 and 6 prescribe the rights of trade secret owners and acts which constitute violations of such rights:

> "Section 5
>
> A Trade Secret owner is entitled to disclose and use such Trade Secrets; deprive others of its use; and allow others to disclose or use such Trade Secrets. The owner may establish terms and conditions to maintain the secrecy of the Trade Secrets.
>
> A transfer of Trade Secrets under the above paragraph other than by way of inheritance shall be carried out in writing with the signatures of both transferor and transferee. If the transferring instrument does not specify the duration of the transfer, such transfer shall be deemed to be for a period of ten years."

> "Section 6
>
> Infringement of a Trade Secret right under this Act means acts of disclosure, deprivation of use, or use of Trade Secrets without the consent of the owner of such Trade Secrets, in a manner that is contrary to a good faith commercial practice. The infringer must know or have reason to know that his/her act is contrary to a good faith commercial practice.
>
> The manner that is contrary to a good faith commercial practice in the above paragraph includes breach of contract, infringement, or inducement of infringement, breach of trust, bribery, intimidation, coercion, fraud, theft, acceptance of stolen Trade Secrets, and espionage of Trade Secrets by electronics and other means."

3. The Case Law

Trade secret cases have the least number among all intellectual property cases reviewed by the CIPIT Court, as opposed to copyright, trademark and patent cases. Thirty-five trade secret cases considered by the CIPIT Court were appealed to the Supreme Court. Thirty-one of these appeals were filed directly with the Supreme Court before October 1, 2016, the date when the specialist Court of Appeals for Specialized Cases was established. Now, an intellectual property case will be appealed to this Court of Appeals for Specialized Cases, whose decision is final unless the Supreme Court agrees to hear the case. So far, there have been only four trade secret cases that went before the Court of Appeals for Specialized Cases and only one case where the Supreme Court consented to further hearing in 2019. Eighty percent of such cases involved the issue of the presence of the requirements under section 3 of the Act.

4. The Leading Cases

Two cases are chosen here as leading cases.

4.1. Supreme Court Decision 15697/2557

The decision established criteria for "not widely known," and the test for "commercial value."

4.1.1. Case Information

Supreme Court Decision 15697/2557 (decided on December 1, 2014). Presiding Justice Mitri Sutepakul, Justice Nulnoi Pholtawee and Justice Anan Wongpraparat.

4.1.2. Summary

The plaintiff, a recruitment company, sued the first defendant, an ex-employee of the plaintiff, and the second defendant, a new recruitment agency established by the first defendant which allegedly relied on the plaintiff's client list for its business. The CIPIT Court ruled that the list of customer names and other information in question were not trade secrets and that the two defendants did not violate the plaintiff's trade secret rights. The decision was upheld by the Supreme Court.

4.1.3. Facts

The plaintiff is a recruitment agency procuring candidates to fill various top executive roles in companies and government agencies. The first defendant was an employee of the plaintiff serving as recruitment manager. The first defendant signed an employment and confidentiality agreement with the plaintiff on July 27, 2009. While employed by the plaintiff, the first defendant was responsible for the recruitment services to six of the plaintiff's clients, including Property Care Services (Thailand) Co., Ltd. (PCS), Nation International Edutainment (Nine) PCL ("Nation"), Kerry Logistics Co., Ltd., Kerry Distribution Co., Ltd., Kerry Logistics (Thailand) Co., Ltd., and Kerry Siam Seaport Co., Ltd. ("KSS").

On August 5, 2010, the first defendant terminated his employment with the plaintiff and started his own recruitment agency, which was the second defendant and engaged in the same business as the plaintiff. The first defendant was the sole authorized director of the second defendant, a post which was subsequently changed to another (Mr. Charlie Vanichprapha). The second defendant then placed an announcement listing PCS, Nation and KSS as its clients, all of which were the plaintiff's clients served by the first defendant during his employment with the plaintiff.

The plaintiff's managing director (Mr. Lux Dendee) testified that the list of clients' names and information was commercially valuable in the plaintiff's business operations. This list was not available to ordinary employees of the plaintiff and the general public and was only available with the plaintiff's consent. The plaintiff claimed that the list is therefore the plaintiff's trade secret. The plaintiff had implemented appropriate security measures to protect the list by recording it in its computer system with password access restriction. Out of the plaintiff's 1,570 employees, only 90 top employees have access to the list. After the first defendant had resigned from the plaintiff, the first defendant had disclosed the list obtained in the course of employment with the plaintiff to the second defendant.

4.1.4. *The Reasoning of the Court*

A trade secret owner must have invested substantial time, effort and expense in the acquisition of the trade secret. As a result, if the secret is obtained by a competitor, the owner will suffer unfair commercial disadvantage. Despite the plaintiff having implemented an access code for its employees to access the list of customers, the information on the list is nonetheless accessible by any recruitment agencies and their staff members from public sources. Such information could not therefore be deemed a trade secret which the plaintiff is solely entitled to use and disclose pursuant to section 5 of the Act. Therefore, the defendant's publication of the names of the plaintiff's customers on its recruitment website, or recruitment of staff members for companies that are clients of the plaintiff, did not constitute violations of the plaintiff's ownership rights over trade secrets under section 6 of the Act.

4.1.4.1. The List of Customer Names and Other Information in Question Were Not Trade Secrets

The IPIT Division of the Supreme Court found that the plaintiff kept the list in the computer, like any other information. There is no special access code other than general passwords. Any employee of the plaintiff could access the list. The Court therefore deemed the plaintiff not to have taken appropriate security measures to protect the list. "The plaintiff, as the claiming party, has the burden of proof as to what information on the list was used by the defendants and how such information qualified as trade secrets."[7] On this point, the plaintiff only had its managing director testify that the information taken by the two defendants was names and other information of the plaintiff's clients. The testimony did not provide details of such information. The plaintiff's witness in responding to the cross-examination by the defendant's lawyer did not show the special qualities such information possessed which would qualify it

7. Supreme Court Decision 15697/2557, p. 9.

as not widely known trade secrets. The witness also failed to demonstrate that such information could not be accessed by other recruitment agencies. "The information could constitute trade secrets of the plaintiff if it were a list of candidates for various positions that had filed applications with the plaintiff, to be presented to the plaintiff's clients for selection, provided that the plaintiff exercised effort in acquiring and compiling such information, and kept it confidential. On the contrary, the Court learned from the plaintiff's witness that the names and other information of job candidates on the list were obtained from various media accessible to the general public, including job announcements of and websites of various companies. For this reason, the customers' names, their contact information, telephone numbers, email addresses are only general commercial information and not trade secrets."[8]

Although the information had some commercial value, it did not qualify it as trade secrets under the definition in section 3 of the Act. "To qualify as a trade secret, the information in question must be critical to the existence of the business currently existing or which will be carried out in the future; or the survival of the business must depend on such trade secret. Moreover, the trade secret owner must have invested a substantial amount of time, effort and expense in the acquisition of the trade secret. As a result, if the secret is obtained by a competitor, the owner will suffer unfair commercial disadvantage."[9] The plaintiff's requiring its staff members to use passwords to access the information indicated that it had made some attempt at keeping the information confidential. However, the fact that other recruitment agencies can easily access the information from public sources led the Court to conclude that the information, including customers' names, their contact information, telephone numbers and email addresses, was not trade secrets that the plaintiff had the sole right to use or disclose under section 5 of the Act. The second defendant's advertising of the names of the plaintiff's clients on the internet and providing recruitment services to the plaintiff's clients therefore did not constitute a violation of the plaintiff's right under section 6 of the Act.

4.1.4.2. Personal Expertise or Skill Acquired Through the Course of Employment

With respect to business contracts and strategies that the plaintiff claimed to be trade secrets, the plaintiff did not describe in its complaint and offer evidence on how they are special and different in some way from other contracts and strategies. If such strategies are the result of the first defendant's personal expertise or skill which it merely acquired through the course of its employment with the plaintiff and is not a trade secret, the first defendant is entitled to deploy such expertise and skill for another employer, unless it is otherwise restricted by the terms of its employment with the plaintiff.[10]

8. *Ibid.*, p. 10.
9. *Ibid.*, p. 11.
10. *Ibid.*, p. 12.

4.1.5. *Legal Analysis*

4.1.5.1. It Must Be Commercial Information

Trade secret must be "communication of a message or content." This can take any form, such as compilations, formulas, formats, programs, methods, techniques, and processes, as specified in the second paragraph of section 3 of the Act. Such commercial information can include names of clients, their contact information, telephone numbers, email addresses, business contracts and strategies, as they can be characterized as "communication of a message or content."[11] Moreover, Supreme Court Decision 4971/2552 similarly ruled that "customer information including names, addresses, telephone numbers, electronic mail addresses, customer interests, budgets, channels of knowing the product, customer questions and concerns" is "commercial information."[12]

4.1.5.2. The Information Is Unknown to the Public and Not Accessible by Unconnected Persons

The information must not be generally accessible or compiled from public sources, e.g., classified sections of newspapers, magazines, websites, etc.[13] For example, the formula of Coca Cola drink is only known to the top executives of the Coca Cola company, and is therefore a trade secret in this respect. The Supreme Court Decision 4971/2552 looked for the fact of whether most staff members had seen or known the information or not for determining whether "the information is unknown to the public and not accessible by unconnected persons."[14]

4.1.5.3. The Information Has Commercial Value Derived from Its Secrecy

The information must have commercial value due to its confidential nature. In other words, the value of the information is due to its not being known to others, as it grants commercial advantage to its owner. If such information becomes known to the owner's competitor, such advantage would be lost, and the owner would suffer unfair commercial disadvantage. This element requires that the information's secretive nature must afford business advantages to the owner.

4.1.5.4. The Trade Secret Controller Has Implemented Appropriate Measures to Keep the Information Confidential

The person who controls such information has implemented measures to keep the information confidential. Section 2 of the Act defines "Trade Secret Controller" as the owner who invented, compiled, discovered, received the transfer of, otherwise has a legal right, or created the trade secret. The definition also extends to employees and

11. *Ibid.*, p. 10.
12. Supreme Court Decision 4971/2552 decided on July 15, 2009, pp. 16-17.
13. Supreme Court Decision 15697/2557, p. 10.
14. Supreme Court Decision 4971/2552, pp. 16-17.

persons who have a duty to possess, control or safeguard the trade secret. Measures for the protection of the confidentiality of the trade secret vary according to the nature of the trade secret and the usage and type of the trade secret. In any case, the issue of whether protective measures are appropriate must be considered on a case-by-case basis according to facts and circumstances and may need to be used in conjunction with other measures such as contractual prohibitions against unlawful use and disclosure by employees, partners, suppliers, and service providers.

There are three common measures to maintain the confidentiality of a trade secret.

Physical measures

Many Supreme Court decisions, including the present one, recognize and accept physical protective measures such as keeping it in a designated place under lock and key; utilizing a warning system, access restriction, password access for digital storage format; and limiting access personnel.[15]

Contractual measures

This popular measure is typically utilized to supplement the physical measures. This consists of an agreement or undertaking between parties with confidentiality and/or non-competition clauses requiring the obligated party not to disclose trade secrets to a third party and/or not to use the secrets to compete in business with the owner of the secrets. Confidentiality and/or non-competition clauses are usually incorporated into an employment agreement, distributorship agreement, agency agreement or business partnership agreement.

Generally, a contractual provision for trade secret protection contains at least the following: (1) details of the trade secret; (2) circumstances where the disclosing party is permitted to disclose, and the receiving party is permitted to receive, the trade secret; (3) objectives of trade secret disclosure and scope of disclosure by the recipient of the trade secret; (4) the return and/or destruction of the trade secret after the end of use; (5) no other rights are granted beyond those set out in contract; (6) no unauthorized reversed engineering.

However, such general confidential and non-competition clauses inserted in a contract alone may not be considered an appropriate measure to maintain the secrecy required by the law. The Supreme Court Decision 10217/2553, for example, determined that a non-disclosure and non-compete clause included in an employment agreement does not yet meet an appropriate level of measure to maintain the secrecy of trade information. Therefore, the trade secret owner has to include other additional physical measures to maintain the secrecy of a trade secret.[16]

15. Supreme Court Decision 15697/2557, p. 11.
16. Supreme Court Decision 10217/2553 decided on November 9, 2010, p. 14.

Registration measures

This measure involves recording or registering trade secrets with the Department of Intellectual Property (DIP), Ministry of Commerce. Although Thai laws do not yet have a system of recording or registering as a means of trade secret protection, a trade secret owner may informally register the secret with the DIP, and use it as evidence of ownership in case of a future dispute, as well as security for capitalization under the DIP's program.

4.1.6. *Commercial and Industrial Significance*

One of the barriers for pursuing patenting is the substantial costs and time required to register patents. Such investment of expenses and time may not be difficult to justify for businesses with deep pockets, but may not be practical for start-ups or small and medium-sized companies with limited financial resources.

However, protection of trade secrets does not require registration, which eliminates the issue of expenses and time of a complex registration process. A trade secret will remain under legal protection so long as its secret status is maintained through appropriate security measures. Trade secrets have therefore become an attractive option for Small- and Medium-size Enterprise(s) to protect intellectual property. To protect their trade secrets, businesses should have a true understanding of the four elements described in this report.

4.2. *The Appeal Court for Specialized Cases, IP&IT Division Decision 165/2562*

Tosaporn Leepuengtham

The present decision concerns whether a kitchen layout, a wood-fired pizza oven and a pizza dough recipe are protected as trade secrets under the Act.

4.2.1. *Case Information*

The Appeal Court for Specialized Cases, Intellectual Property and International Trade Division Judgment 165/2562 (A.D. 2019) (decided on January 28, 2019).

4.2.2. *Summary*

The plaintiff sued the four defendants for acquiring confidential commercial information comprising of plans for a restaurant kitchen layout, the design of a wood-fired pizza oven, and a pizza dough recipe, and disclosing them to others. The CIPIT Court found that all the plaintiff claims were not qualified for trade secret protection and dismissed that case.[17] The Court of Appeal for Specialized Cases partially disagreed

17. The CIPIT Court, Black Case No. 148/2559 and Red Case No. 44/2561 (black case refers to a case that the verdict has not yet delivered. Once the verdict is delivered, it becomes a red case. Hence, depending on which process the case is in, its case numbers can be different, although it is the same case).

with that holding and found that only a pizza dough recipe in question was eligible for protection.

4.2.3. *Facts*

The plaintiff is an owner of an Italian restaurant named "Pizzeria Limoncello" as well as other Italian restaurants in the Zanotti group. The plaintiff brought a suit against the four defendants for unlawfully acquiring details of his restaurant's kitchen layout, his unique wood-fire pizza oven design and his original pizza dough recipes and using this information in their own pizza restaurant. The 1st defendant was a company; the 2nd defendant was the director of that company; the 3rd defendant was an employee of the 1st defendant and was also the director; the 4th defendant was another limited company. The plaintiff operated "Pizzeria Limoncello" out of a rental unit in a building owned by the 1st defendant. Later, the 2nd defendant opened an Italian restaurant, named "Café Milano," using decoration, operational practices and a menu identical to those in use at the plaintiff's establishment. The four defendants denied that they had stolen the plaintiff's trade secrets and claimed, *inter alia*, that as pizza is a well-known and well-established Italian national dish, the plaintiff's pizza dough recipe was not protectable as a trade secret.

4.2.4. *Reasoning of the Court*

4.2.4.1. Kitchen Design and Layout Were Not Secret

The Court found that "the plaintiff had not established that the kitchen design was entitled to trade secret protection. As the plaintiff's kitchen layout was accessible to others, its design and layout were not secret."[18] Moreover, the Court was satisfied that "the 4th defendant had employed a third party, A.J. Kitchen Service Co. Ltd., to design some aspects of its kitchen layout, including the electrical wiring and plumbing system, and the exhaust arrangements, meaning that these aspects had not been copied from the plaintiff's kitchen."[19]

4.2.4.2. No Sufficient Steps Were Taken with Regards to Wood-Fired Pizza Oven

With regard to the issue of whether reasonable steps have been taken by the plaintiff regarding a wood-fired pizza oven, the plaintiff testified that he had developed a unique design for a masonry wood-fired pizza oven, the cooking chamber and overhead insulation were of specific dimensions, and concrete was used to seal the gaps between the bricks. The plaintiff claimed that this design ensured that the oven rapidly produces a thin and crispy base of pizzas which distinguished the "Pizzeria Limoncello" product from those available in competing establishments.[20] The plaintiff

18. The Appeal Court for Specialized Cases, IP&IT Division Judgment 165/2562, pp. 35-36.
19. *Ibid.*, p. 34.
20. *Ibid.*, pp. 36-37.

claimed that he had taken steps to ensure that the oven design was kept secret, and that it was located in an enclosed area of the unit behind a wall which had been specifically constructed to hide it from public view. Access to the enclosed area was restricted to just three employees.[21] However, considering the evidence, the Court found that "these steps were insufficient because the only physical barrier in place to prevent access to the oven enclosure was a chain, which could be easily unlocked. In practice, it would be straightforward for anyone to access the oven, particularly when no one else was around."[22] Consequently, the Court ruled that the plaintiff had not taken all reasonable steps to keep the design of the pizza oven confidential, and so it did not constitute a trade secret.[23]

4.2.4.3. The Pizza Dough Recipe Is a Trade Secret

As for the pizza dough recipe, the plaintiff claimed that he had created the so-called 180 grams recipe himself in 2006, and that the exact constituents had remained confidential ever since. The plaintiff stated that products made with this secret recipe were only served to Pizzeria Limoncello's VIP customers, and had proven to be very popular among his esteemed clientele of diplomats and high-ranking foreign politicians, including Khalifa Bin Salman al-Khalifa (a former Prime Minister of Bahrain who was also related to the country's monarchy). Evidence from the plaintiff's chef, Mr. Dang, supported the plaintiff's testimony and confirmed that there were two pizza dough recipes: the one normally served in the restaurant and the VIP "180 grams recipe,"[24] which could not be tossed into the air and spun around to show to customers.[25] This testimony was further collaborated by Mrs. Jarunee, a waitress in the restaurant.[26]

The Court noted "the very many different recipes for pizza dough that were possible, and that new innovations and variations were not the sole preserve of the Italians."[27] As such, it found the defendants' argument that a recipe for such a traditional dish could not be protected to be ill-founded.[28] Rather, the Court ruled[29] that "the plaintiff's recipe was 'trade information' under Section 3 of the Trade Secrets Act which was not yet publicly known or not yet accessible by persons who are normally connected with the information. That VIP customers returned to the plaintiff's restaurant for his 'signature' pizza proved that any commercial value from the recipe derived from it being kept secret. Additionally, the plaintiff had taken all necessary measures to protect the information's secrecy, since only he knew the exact recipe and it would be

21. *Ibid.*, p. 38.
22. *Ibid.*
23. The Appeal Court for Specialized Cases, IP&IT Division Judgment 165/2562, p. 39.
24. *Ibid.*, pp. 39-40.
25. *Ibid.*, p. 40.
26. *Ibid.*
27. The Appeal Court for Specialized Cases, IP&IT Division Judgment 165/2562, pp. 40-41.
28. *Ibid.*, p. 40.
29. Since there is a dissenting opinion on this issue, this case has been reviewed by the General Meeting of the Appeal Court for Specialized Cases.

difficult for others to discover what it was. Thus, the plaintiff's recipe fell within the definition of a 'trade secret' in accordance with the Trade Secrets Act."[30]

4.2.4.4. The Second Defendant Misappropriated the Confidential Information

Having so held, the Court then had to determine whether the 2nd defendant had misappropriated the plaintiff's trade secret. The plaintiff testified that the 2nd defendant had visited him at "Pizzeria Limoncello" several times, and, on each occasion, had asked him (in vain) to share the secret recipe. Later, the 2nd defendant offered the plaintiff the opportunity to open a new restaurant in another of his buildings in exchange for the recipe. The plaintiff testified that he had accepted this offer, but this was done on the understanding that the 2nd defendant would keep the recipe secret. Subsequently, the 2nd defendant opened a new French restaurant, "Le Beaulieu," in Chiang Mai province which served pizza made according to the plaintiff's recipe in issue.

The Court considered "whether the plaintiff's disclosure of the recipe to the 2nd defendant would lead to the loss of any trade secret protection. It accepted the plaintiff's testimony that the disclosure of recipe was on the basis that its confidentiality would be respected. Therefore, the disclosure did not place the recipe at issue in public domain."[31]

"The plaintiff divulged his secret recipe to the Court, thus:[32] 1,000g bread flour; 20g salt, 0.5 teaspoon ascorbic acid, 1000g beer, 2.5 teaspoons olive oil and 416g water."[33] "This was compared to the recipe used by Mr. Veerachai, a chef at the 2nd defendant's restaurant, and this was found to be exactly the same. (Although the defendants' recipe stated use of '416ml of water', this is the same of the plaintiff's 416g of water, since 1g of water equates to 1ml.)"[34]

"In addition, the plaintiff's testimony explained how he had arrived at these specific quantities of the ingredients. (If he wants the pizzas to have a crispy base, he uses KITE brand bread flour, whereas SWAN brand flour is better for a more glutinous dough; ascorbic acid is included to preserve the dough and prolong its freshness; 416g of water is optimal for a thin and crispy pizza base; and use of more than the stated amount of olive oil or salt would mask the additional flavour provided by the beer.) This level of detail concerning the recipe's development served to convince the Court that the plaintiff was the creator and rightful owner of the recipe."[35]

This contrasted with the somewhat sketchy nature of the defendants' evidence as to the origin of their recipe, which the Court found unpersuasive. A chef working for the 2nd defendant, Mr. Veerasak, testified that he had acquired the recipe from Mr. Rosano, owner of "Lo Pera" restaurant. Not only was there was no material evidence provided to support this claim, but its veracity was brought into doubt by the testimony

30. The Appeal Court for Specialized Cases, IP&IT Division Judgment 165/2562, pp. 40-41.
31. *Ibid.*, p. 42.
32. Exhibit Number 76, pp. 10-11.
33. The Appeal Court for Specialized Cases, IP&IT Division Judgment 165/2562, p. 43.
34. *Ibid.*, pp. 43-44.
35. *Ibid.*, pp. 44-45.

from another witness for the defendants. Mr. Arkon, also employed at "Café Milano," stated that "as Mr. Veerasak is a chef involved in the preparation of the restaurant's French cuisine, he has never had any involvement in the pizza dough preparation."[36] Thus, perhaps unsurprisingly, the Court concluded that "the recipe in use in the 2nd defendant's restaurant was the plaintiff's recipe; the defendant had misappropriated the confidential information because he was using it without the plaintiff's consent."[37]

With regard to the other defendants, the Court held that there was insufficient evidence to prove that either the 1st or 3rd defendant was involved in the 2nd defendant's restaurant, or that they had received any benefit from the use of the appropriated recipe. Moreover, the plaintiff had failed to establish that the 4th defendant was using the misappropriated recipe in the "Café Milano" restaurant. Hence, only the 2nd defendant was found liable for the misappropriation.

4.2.4.5. Dissenting Opinion

In a dissenting opinion, the dissenting judge favored the defendants' line of argument. Pointing to the fact that "all pizza doughs are made by the same general method and based upon the same type of ingredients (flour, yeast, beer and oil),"[38] he did not consider that the plaintiff's specific recipe was different enough from the "norm" to be a trade secret.[39] To support his conclusion, the judge pointed to the large numbers of pizza dough recipes, which were readily accessible online[40] (a Google search by the term "pizza dough recipe" returned 72.9 million results, reducing to 17.7 million results by the term "pizza dough beer recipe").[41] In addition, he was skeptical that "a chef working in a busy restaurant kitchen would be able to keep a recipe secret from all their co-workers, given the tendency of developing recipes based upon one chef's sharing his knowledge and experience with others."[42] Thus, he concluded that it was unlikely that recipes could qualify for protection.[43]

The dissenting judge further cited US case law to support his dissent.[44] In *Buffets, Inc. v Klinke*,[45] the plaintiff was a corporation which ran a national chain of buffet restaurants under the name: "Old Country Buffet." One of the company's founders, Dennis Scott, devised "small batch cooking"—a method for cooking and storing food in small quantities which kept the food fresher than when cooked in larger quantities. Mr. Scott developed various novel recipes using this technique, which gained popularity

36. *Ibid.*, pp. 45-46.
37. *Ibid.*, p. 47.
38. The dissenting opinion, The Appeal Court for Specialized Cases, IP&IT Division Judgment 165/2562, p. 53.
39. *Ibid.*, pp. 52-53.
40. *Ibid.*
41. The dissenting opinion, The Appeal Court for Specialized Cases, IP&IT Division Judgment 165/2562, pp. 52-53.
42. *Ibid.*, pp. 59-60.
43. *Ibid.*
44. The dissenting opinion, The Appeal Court for Specialized Cases, IP&IT Division Judgment 165/2562, pp. 61-62.
45. 73 F.3d 965 (9th Cir. 1996).

from customers. Subsequently, Paul Klinke, one of the defendants, opened a competing buffet restaurant called "Granny's." His restaurant used "Old Country Buffet" recipes which he acquired from his son who worked as a chef at one of the plaintiff's establishments. When the plaintiff alleged that Klinke had misappropriated its "trade secret" recipes, the US District Court for the Eastern District of Washington dismissed the claim on the basis that the recipes were not trade secrets because they were readily ascertainable. Recipes for dishes such as BBQ chicken or macaroni and cheese were "basic American dishes served in buffet restaurants nationwide." In addition, the Court held that the plaintiff had failed to prove that it derived any benefit from keeping its recipes confidential. By analogy, the dissenting judge considered that a pizza dough recipe, such as the one in issue, was such a basic dish that it should not qualify for trade secret protection, even though a specific chef might have created a specific ratio and combination of ingredients and cooking method.[46]

4.2.5. *Legal Analysis*

Since there was agreement between the judges on the matter of kitchen layout and wood-fired pizza oven, this section will only consider the legal issues arising from the appropriation of the pizza dough recipe.

4.2.5.1. A Recipe *Is* an Eligible Subject Matter for Trade Secret Protection

The starting point is that, in principle, a recipe *is* an eligible subject matter for trade secret protection, even under US law. Indeed, in *Fast Food Gourment, Inc. v Little Lady Foods, Incs.*, a US court upheld trade secret protection for the plaintiff's pizza production process.[47] Thus, trade secret protection, or not, turns on the specifics of each recipe and the circumstances surrounding its use and alleged misuse. Under Thai law, to be eligible for protection under the Trade Secrets Act, a recipe—such as the pizza dough recipes in question—must meet all the requirements stated in that Act. The plaintiffs must satisfy the Court that the recipe in question is not publicly known, that they derive commercial value from the secret nature of the recipe, and that they have taken all appropriate measures to ensure that the recipe remains secret.

As we have seen already, the first requirement of the Trade Secrets Act is that the recipe falls within the definition of "trade information," as only this kind of secret information enjoys the protection of the Act. Section 3 defines "trade information" to mean "any medium that conveys the meaning of a statement, facts or other information irrespective of its method and form." It shall also include formulas, patterns, compilations or assembled works, program methods, techniques, or processes. In the case in issue, the pizza dough recipe consists of a unique combination of specified quantities of the ingredients selected together with a process for preparing the dough. Thus, the Court was correct to conclude that the matter constituted "trade information" which

46. The dissenting opinion, IP&IT Division Judgment 165/2562, pp. 63-64.
47. 542 F. Supp. 2d 849 (ND. III 2008).

might be eligible for "trade secret" protection, provided the additional threshold requirements are also met.

4.2.5.2. The Recipe Must Be Sufficiently Different from Similar Recipes Which Are Freely Available

Next, the plaintiff must satisfy the Court that its "recipe" is sufficiently different from similar recipes which are freely available to use. Here the plaintiff pointed to his use of two different recipes, the first being the one generally used and the second—being the recipe in issue—which was reserved for his special VIP customers, which had become the plaintiff's signature dish.

The dissenting judge's decision that the plaintiff's recipe was ineligible for protection as a trade secret was based upon the sheer volume of recipe variants for pizza dough available online and so easily discoverable by others. However, despite the vast numbers, neither the judge nor the defendants were able to point to an earlier example which disclosed the exact same combination as the plaintiff's recipe. Except for the simplest of dishes perhaps, neither the fact that recipes for the same product often share the same list of basic ingredients nor the existence of similar recipes should disqualify a secret recipe from protection. However, unless a plaintiff is able to point to some aspect of the recipe which creates a point of difference from those which are readily available, it will not constitute a trade secret. Here, it seems that the plaintiff was able to establish that there was something unique about his particular recipe which the defendants were unable to replicate using the many dough recipes which were freely available, or from their own "trial and error." Respectfully, the dissenting analysis is flawed, and the facts in the instant case are not on point with the US case it relied upon in support.

4.2.5.3. Reasonable Steps to Preserve the Secrecy

In addition, the Act requires the plaintiff to prove that: (i) they have taken all reasonable steps to preserve the secrecy of the trade information, and (ii) any commercial value attached to the information is derived from its secret status. It is in these aspects where the judges failed to reach a unanimous conclusion. In this case, the plaintiff testified that only he knew the exact recipe, and that he only allowed one chef to help him with the preparation, that the helper was not appraised with details of the exact recipe quantities. It is submitted that the majority decision of the two judges was correct that the steps taken were reasonable in the particular circumstances, since he had limited the number of people who had access to the recipe. Had the recipe been committed to writing, then a court might expect that this would be locked in a vault with restricted access.

4.2.5.4. The Recipe Would Seem to Be of Sufficient Economic Value

The final requirement requires demonstration that the information derives its economic value from its secret status. Again, the recipe in issue would seem to be of sufficient economic value to warrant trade secret protection, given its status as the plaintiff's signature dish, and responsible for repeat business from important VIPs.

4.2.6. *Commercial or Industrial Significance*

A chef's ability to create and hone a collection of recipes has long been recognized as a valuable asset, which can help create a professional reputation and set them apart from competitors. The recognition of recipes as protectable trade secret provides them with an incentive to innovate, by either developing entirely novel dishes or taking "old favorites" to a new level of perfection. It is also an efficient tool for promoting small enterprises that may have established a customer base for a particular signature dish. Without legal protection to fall back on, it is unlikely that small and medium businesses would be able to compete with big or multinational corporations.

TOPIC 2 THE VALIDITY AND SCOPE OF CONFIDENTIALITY AND NON-COMPETITION CLAUSES

Sutatip Yuthayotin

1. Legal Issues

In Thailand, confidentiality and non-competition clauses are popular means that a trade secret owner uses to protect valuable business assets.[48] The scope and extent of enforceability of confidentiality and non-competition clauses under Thai law are the legal issues that this report will deal with.

2. The Statutory Law

As in other legal systems, the scope and extent of enforceability of confidentiality and/or non-competition clauses under Thai law depend on the mutual intention of contracting parties. To be legally enforceable, such contractual intention must not serve objectives that are contrary to the law, impossible to perform, or violate the public order and good morals of the people. This requirement is set out in section 150 of the Thai Civil and Commercial Code, which states:

> An act is void if its object is expressly prohibited by law or is impossible or is contrary to public order or good morals.

Furthermore, the contractual provisions between parties must not impose an exceedingly unfair burden on a contracting party and thereby violate section 5 of the Unfair Contract Terms Act 1997, which states:

> "The terms restricting the right or freedom in professing an occupation or an execution of a juristic act related to the business, trading or professional operation which are not void, but being the terms that cause the person whose right or freedom has been restricted to bear more burden than that which could have been anticipated under normal circumstances, shall be enforceable to the extent that they are fair and reasonable according to such circumstances.
>
> In determining whether the terms under the above paragraph cause the person, whose right or freedom has been restricted, to bear more than that which could have been anticipated, consideration shall be taken as to the scope of the area and the period of restriction of right or freedom, including whose ability and opportunity to profess occupation or to execute juristic act in other forms or with other persons, as well as all legitimate advantages and disadvantages of the contracting parties" (Thai Trade Secrets Act 2002 (the Act) *is silent on* the scope and extent of enforceability of confidentiality and non-competition clauses).

48. Rattapong Chokchairittikul, What Are Trade Secret?, Executive Journal, Bangkok University, July-September 2009, available at, https://www.bu.ac.th/knowledgecenter/executive_journal/july_sep_09/pdf/Exceutive_Journal29_3_103-105.pdf, p. 2.

3. The Case Law

There are a large number of cases relating to confidentiality and non-competition clauses in Thailand. For example, the Central Labor Court—the first instance court which has jurisdiction over disputes relating to confidentiality and non-competition clauses in employment contracts—tried 51 cases in 2019 and 39 cases in 2020 (as of October) on this matter. Approximately 80% of such cases were appealed to the Supreme Court.

In the past, the Supreme Court adopted two approaches in determining the enforceability of an employment agreement containing confidentiality and/or non-competition clauses that bar employees from competing with the employer. The first approach was a strict interpretation of these contract clauses to protect employee's rights. The rationale for this was that if these clauses unfairly restrict the employees' possibility of earning a livelihood, they could be contrary to public order and good moral and thus unenforceable under Thai law. The second approach relied on the Court's interpretation of the intention of contracting parties. This approach was supported by the rationale that these clauses do not absolutely prevent the employee from earning a living, and are as such enforceable.

The two Supreme Court cases presented later follow the second approach, focusing on the intentions of the contracting parties. The two decisions lay down important and widely cited criteria for the enforceability of confidentiality and non-competition clauses, namely the scope of restrictions must be fair, reasonable and not excessively burdensome. In other words, the restrictions will be enforceable if the terms are prescribed fairly and reasonably under the circumstances. However, if the restricted party is a specialist whose expertise is limited in the restricted trade, a limitation of a wide geographical area and long duration would render him or her unable to maintain a livelihood. In such case, the Court shall void the restrictions.

4. The Leading Cases

Two cases are chosen here as leading cases.

4.1. *Supreme Court Decision 1275/2543 (Decided on March 20, 2005)*

The decision was delivered by Justices Panya Suthibhodi (presiding), Sala Theprum-pan and Rungroj Ruenrengwong.

4.1.1. Summary

The Central Labor Court, the first instance court, ruled that the agreement, which restricted the defendant from working in five countries for five years after ending employment with the plaintiff, placed excessive restriction on the defendant and was unfairly one-sided in favor of the plaintiff. The Court is also of the view that during employment the plaintiff had not trained the defendant on a specific trade which could be considered to be given in exchange for the defendant's agreeing to such employment restrictions. The Court therefore found the agreement to be unenforceable, as it was contrary to public order and good morals pursuant to section 150 of the Thai Civil and Commercial Code. The defendant was not required to pay damages to the plaintiff, and the case was dismissed. The plaintiff appealed to the Supreme Court. The Labor Division of the Supreme Court reversed the ruling of the lower court.

4.1.2. Facts

The plaintiff was engaged in moving business. On February 15, 1993, the plaintiff hired the defendant. Before the employment ended, the defendant served his final position as the branch manager of JVK Indochina Mover (Laos) Co., Ltd. The defendant was paid a monthly salary of USD 2,200 and other benefits as set out in the employment contracts dated November 26 and December 29, 1993. Through his position, the defendant had gained a great amount of information about the plaintiff's businesses, subsidiaries, and trade secrets. To protect its interests, the plaintiff and defendant entered into an agreement that provided, during the defendant's employment with the plaintiff and five years thereafter, that the defendant must not work for, or own interests in, the plaintiff's competitors in moving and storage businesses in Thailand, Vietnam, Cambodia, Laos or Myanmar. If this agreement were violated, the defendant agreed to pay THB 1,000,000 in damages to JVK Indochina Mover (Laos) Co., Ltd. Before the lapse of five years after terminating employment with the plaintiff, the defendant had entered into an employment relationship with SKO Moving Co., Ltd., a direct competitor of the plaintiff.

4.1.3. Reasoning of the Court

The present decision reconciles the two different approaches mentioned above, and establishes a clear direction for future rulings on the enforceability of confidentiality and non-competition clauses, with three factors to consider:

(1) The duration of restriction, namely whether the restriction period is excessive.
(2) The scope of restriction, namely whether the types of restricted activities are clearly defined or too broad.
(3) The restricted territory, namely whether the areas in which the employee is prohibited from engaging in activities that are deemed in competition with the employer are unreasonable.

If any of these factors is considered by the Court to have placed unfair burden on the employee versus the concerns for the protection of employer's interest, the Court may find them unenforceable.

The present decision ruled that "the agreement between the parties ... clearly defined the scope and types of businesses in which the defendant is prohibited from engaging as it is in competition with those of the plaintiff. Such restrictions did not absolutely bar the defendant from earning a living. The defendant can still pursue employment in other businesses beyond those agreed in the agreement. The geographical limitations are clearly specified as the five countries and no others. The parties voluntarily entered into such agreement, which did not completely bar the defendant from making a living. The scope of restrictions is clearly expressed as those businesses that are in competition with the plaintiff for a limited duration and within clearly specified territories. It is therefore an enforceable contractual provision, as it fairly protected the plaintiff's legitimate commercial interests without placing excessive burden on the defendant. Such provision is not contrary to public order and good morals. The defendant must pay damages to the plaintiff, as the defendant entered into an employment with the plaintiff's competitor only one year after the end of employment with the plaintiff while still in the effect of the agreed restriction period."[49]

4.2. *Supreme Court Decision 6075/2549*

4.2.1. Case Information

Supreme Court Decision 6075/2549 (decided on September 12, 2006). The decision was delivered by Justices Pongthep Siripongtikanon, Wasan Soipisut and Witawit Hirunrujipong.

4.2.2. Summary

The Central Labor Court, the first instance court, ruled on August 25, 2003, that the provision at the end of the employment contract, which stated that: "[the plaintiff] agrees not to work for any other law firm in Bangkok for two years after terminating employment with [the defendant] for any reason whatsoever. The foregoing paragraph shall not apply to lawyers employed by [the defendant] ...," was unenforceable. The Court dismissed the counterclaims by the three defendants which requested that the Court orders the plaintiff to terminate employment with another law firm in Bangkok currently employing the plaintiff, to bar the plaintiff from being employed by another law firm in Bangkok for two years as specified in the employment contract, to pay damages for breach of employment contract, and to return any client list, case files, opinions and advice to the defendants. The defendants appealed to the Labor Division of the Supreme Court, which reversed the ruling of the Central Labor Court and remanded the case back to the lower court to determine the amount of damages that the plaintiff must pay the first defendant as compensation for working for another law firm before the expiry of the agreed non-competition period.[50]

49. Supreme Court Decision 1275/2543, pp. 7-9.
50. Supreme Court Decision 6075/2549 is one of the decisions of the highest court that followed the precedent set by Supreme Court Decision 1275/2543. It confirms that an employment contract containing confidentiality and/or non-competing provisions is enforceable to the extent that such provisions only restrict an employee from competition for a certain period, e.g., two or five years from the termination of employment, and clearly define the types of business and geographical areas of such restriction, e.g., law firms in Bangkok metropolitan area, etc. So long as the employee still has some means to sustain a livelihood, the Court will uphold the enforceability of such provisions.

4.2.3. *Facts*

The three defendants employed the plaintiff on January 1, 1994, as intellectual property manager. Under the terms of the employment contract, the plaintiff agreed not to work for another law office in Bangkok for two years after ending employment with the defendants for whatever reason. The plaintiff's final position at the defendants' company was Director of Intellectual Property Division. Such positions gave the plaintiff access to trade secrets and trade information of the first defendant. Before the two-year period had lapsed, the plaintiff had entered into an employment with another law firm in Bangkok.

4.2.4. *Reasoning of the Court*

The Supreme Court ruled that the provision at the end of the employment contract, which stated that "[the plaintiff] agrees not to work for any other law firm in Bangkok for two years after terminating employment with [the defendant] for any reason whatsoever. The foregoing paragraph shall not apply to *lawyers* employed by [the defendant] ...," was enforceable (emphasis added). The Supreme Court opined that "the word 'lawyers' in that provision referred to litigators and legal counsels in specific cases. On the other hand, the plaintiff's position as Intellectual Property Manager and Director of the Intellectual Property Division was not a 'lawyer' (litigator) that had been exempted from the coverage of that contractual provision. The plaintiff's position made commercial and trade secrets of the first defendant privy to her. The non-competing provision was therefore enforceable, as it fairly protected the defendant's legitimate business rights. The provision was not void, as it was not contrary to public order and good morals. The plaintiff was therefore bound not to work for another law firm in Bangkok for two years from the end of employment with the defendant."[51]

4.2.5. *Legal Analysis*

According to laws and court precedents in Thailand, confidentiality and/or non-competition clauses are enforceable. However, there are specific criteria that such clauses must meet for them to be legally enforceable.

4.2.5.1. Form of Confidentiality and/or Non-competition Clauses

A provision which prohibits a party from engaging in employment with a competitor of the other party or engaging in competing activities can commonly be found in an employment contract[52] or in a separate non-disclosure or non-competing agreement.[53]

In analyzing the enforceability of confidentiality and non-competition clauses, one must first refer to the basic principles of contract law. For example, there must be a meeting of intentions between contracting parties (employer and employee, service

51. Supreme Court Decision 6075/2549, p. 24.
52. Supreme Court Decision 1275/2543 decided on March 20, 2000.
53. Supreme Court Decision 6075/2549 decided on September 12, 2006.

provider and service recipient, or information disclosing party and information receiving party) whereby one party agrees not to reveal received information to third parties, not to be employed by a competitor of, or otherwise compete with, the employer, the service receiver, or the information disclosing party. Such non-competition restrictions are typically subject to certain agreed conditions and are normally imposed on strategic personnel such as high-level executives, managers, heads of finance, heads of sale and marketing, heads of research and development, project heads, engineers, and researchers.

4.2.5.2. Legal Requirements

An enforceable confidentiality and/or non-competition clause must satisfy the following legal requirements:

(1) It must have a lawful objective. It must not be impossible to perform or contrary to public order and good morals. For example, it must not impose an absolute restriction such that the obliged party cannot maintain a livelihood (section 150 of the Civil and Commercial Code).
(2) It must not impose a burden on the rights and freedom of the obliged party to engage in an occupation or business excessively by going beyond what can normally be expected when entering into such an agreement (section 5 of the Unfair Contract Terms Act 1997).
(3) The restrictions must be fair and reasonable under the circumstances (section 5 of the Unfair Contract Terms Act 1997).

4.2.5.3. Criteria under the Supreme Court Precedents

In addition to the requirements set out in the codified laws, the enforceability of a confidentiality and/or non-competition clause is also influenced by criteria prescribed by precedents of the Supreme Court. The Court plays a critical role in determining whether the non-competition restriction is fair and reasonable under the circumstances. Such a determination varies from case to case, depending on the context of the case and nature of the parties involved.

The two Supreme Court cases presented above, particularly the 1275/2543 decision, lay down an important and widely cited criterion for the enforceability of a confidentiality and/or non-competition clause; namely, the scope of restrictions must be fair, reasonable and not excessively burdensome. The scope of restrictions includes types of restricted employment or business (restricting only certain types of employment, business or industry), geographical limits (restricting the locality, area, province, country or region), and time limits (restricting during employment and a certain agreed period thereafter, normally between six months and five years).

The above restrictions will be enforceable if their terms are prescribed fairly and reasonably under the circumstances. In determining fairness and reasonableness of the terms, the Court will consider various surrounding facts and factors, for example, the ability and opportunity of the restricted party to earn a living. If the restricted party is a specialist whose expertise is only in the restricted trade, a limitation of wide scope and geographical area and long duration would render him/her unable to maintain a livelihood. In such a case, the Court may void the restrictions.[54]

The Court may also consider the benefits which may be gained, and losses which may be suffered, by each respective party.[55] If the limitation affords a reasonable protection for a party's legitimate business interests, which may incur significant damage if not protected, the Court is likely to find it enforceable.[56] The examples of legitimate business interests include a case where the employer incurs substantial expenses to train the employee, high costs in transferring trade secrets from one party to the other, etc.[57] Good faith and bargaining powers of the parties at the time of entering into the agreement are also important elements in considering the enforceability. In any event, an employment contract whereby an employee agrees not to disclose trade secrets to a third party or be subject to penalties may not be sufficient to ensure that trade secrets will not be disclosed by the employee.

Although confidentiality clauses and non-competition clauses both protect legitimate business interests of the employer and owner of information, there are some differences between these two types of clauses. A non-competition clause is deemed to affect the basic rights of the restricted party to earn a living and maintain a livelihood. Therefore, it must satisfy more stringent legal criteria in order to be enforceable. On the other hand, a confidentiality clause only bars the restricted party from disclosing or using information it acquires from the protected party and is therefore not subject to legal requirements as strenuous as those for a non-competition clause.

4.2.6. *Commercial and Industrial Significance*

Trade secret is a type of intellectual property and can have substantial economic and business value. Confidentiality and non-competition clauses are common tools that have long been utilized by business owners to protect their trade secrets from unlawful use by third parties. Thai courts have accepted the enforceability of these clauses, provided that they satisfy the legal criteria established by the Supreme Court rulings, including the fairness and reasonableness tests.

Confidentiality and non-competition clauses serve to prevent unfair takeover of one's market share, and poaching of one's employees and business partners by one's competitor. Without the protection of these clauses, an employer would be hesitant to

54. Supreme Court Decision 2169/2557 decided on March 6, 2014, for example, ruled that a contractual provision prohibiting a defendant from being employed as "management" by plaintiff's competitor after terminating employment with the plaintiff must be strictly interpreted. The fact that the defendant became an "employee" of A, which is plaintiff's competitor, did not mean that the defendant is its "management" or "participating in the management" of A. As the contractual provision did not bar defendant from being a mere "employee" of a competitor, defendant had not breached the terms of the non-competition clause.
55. *Ibid.*
56. Jairak Euarchukiate, Trade Secrets Misappropriation, Central Intellectual Property and International Trade Court Law Journal (2017) (in Thai), available at, https://ipitc.coj.go.th/th/content/category/detail/id/10413/cid/10418/iid/192645, p. 164.
57. Supreme Court Decision 690/2552 decided on February 5, 2009.

invest in training its employees, as they can be easily poached by competitors without legal consequences to them and the competitors. Due to these considerations, a trade secret owner should consider utilizing confidentiality and non-competition clauses for protection, provided that the imposed restrictions on occupation, business, geographical limitation and duration are fair and reasonable in scope in light of the circumstances and context of the agreement. Decisions of the Supreme Court can be useful in providing guidelines on what terms would be deemed fair and reasonable under comparable contexts and circumstances.

TOPIC 5 CIVIL REMEDIES: INJUNCTIVE RELIEF AND DAMAGES

1. Injunctive Relief

Sutatip Yuthayotin

1.1. Legal Issues

Section 8 of the Act offers a tool for interim and permanent injunction to protect trade secrets from potential unlawful disclosure. The qualifications for such injunction are one important legal issue that must be considered under Thai law.

1.2. The Statutory Law

Under Thai law, there are two types of preliminary injunction in IP cases: the conventional type under the Civil Procedural Code; and the provisional injunction under the Court Rules of the Central Intellectual Property and International Trade Cases B.E. 2540 (1997) ("CIPIT Court Rules").

According to the Civil and Procedural Code, a conventional injunction can be applied and executed ex parte at any time before or after the filing of the complaint but before courts render judgment. Section 254(1)-(3) of the Civil and Procedural Code provides that:

> In a case other than a petty case, the plaintiff is entitled to file with the Court, together with his plaint or at any time before judgment, an ex parte application requesting the Court order, subject to the conditions hereinafter provided, all or any of the following protective measures:
> (1) the seizure or attachment before judgment, of the whole or part of the property in dispute or the defendant's property, including any money or property due to the defendant by a third person;
> (2) a temporary injunction restraining the defendant from repeating or continuing any wrongful act or breach of contract or the act complained of, or other order minimizing trouble and injury which the plaintiff may thenceforward sustain on account of the defendant's act or a temporary injunction restraining the defendant from transfer, sale, removal or disposal of the property in dispute or the defendant's property, or an order stopping or preventing the wasting or damaging of such property, until the case becomes final or until the Court has otherwise ordered;
> (3) an order directing the Register, the competent official or any other person having legal power and duty to extinguish registration, modification, or cancellation of registration appertaining to the property in dispute or the defendant's property, or concerning the act complained of temporariness until the case shall become final or the Court shall issue the order otherwise, notwithstanding, in so far as it is not contrary to or inconsistent with the provisions of law concerned.

In addition, according to section 8 of the Act, the application for provisional measure may be filed ex parte at any time before or after the filing of the complaint. It gives the authority to the Court to temporarily prohibit the party who has breached or is about to breach trade secrets from continuing or committing such breach before and during litigation:

> **Section 8** Where there is clear evidence that an infringement of trade secrets has been committed or is about to be committed, the affected or imminently to be affected controller of trade secrets has the following remedies: (1) Petition the court for an interim injunction, temporarily to stop the infringement of trade secrets; and, (2) File an action in the court for a permanent injunction, permanently to stop the infringement of trade secrets and claim damages from the wrongdoer.
>
> The petition under (1) may be filed prior to the action under (2).

The proceedings for such provisional injunction according to section 8 of the Act are governed by the CIPIT Court Rules, as trade secret litigation is under its jurisdiction. Pursuant to "Chapter 2 Proceedings: Provisional Measures of Protection Prior to Instituting an Action" of the CIPIT Court Rules, the application for provisional measure for trade secret cases may be filed ex parte at any time before or after the filing of the complaint. Further provisions can be found in Rule 12 to Rule 18:

> **Rule 12** An application for the Court order under Section 65 of the Copyright Act B. E. 2537, Section 77bis of the Patent Act B. E. 2522, Section 116 of the Trademark Act B. E. 2534 or other intellectual property legislation, shall state the facts establishing a prima facie case and the reasons sufficient for the Court to believe that it is appropriate to grant such order. The application shall also include a statement confirming the facts of a person who witnessed the cause of the application, in order to substantiate such application.
>
> **Rule 13** In considering the application under Rule 12, the Court shall grant the application if it is satisfied that:
>
> (1) There is reasonable ground for the application, as well as sufficient reasons for the Court to grant such application, and
>
> (2) The nature of the damage incurred by the application is such that the damage cannot be restituted by monetary measures or any other form of indemnity, or the prospective defendant is not in a position to compensate the applicant for his damage, or it might be difficult to enforce the judgment against the prospective defendant afterwards.
>
> In considering the application, the Court shall take into account the balance of the extent of damage that might be incurred by both parties.
>
> If the Court issues an order dismissing the application, such order shall be final.
>
> **Rule 14** In cases where the Court grants the application under Rule 13, the Court shall notify the prospective defendant of the order without delay.
>
> The order under paragraph one shall immediately bind the prospective defendant even if the prospective defendant has not been notified of the order.
>
> **Rule 15** In cases where the Court grants the application under Rule 13, taking into account any damage that the prospective defendant might incur, the Court shall order the applicant to provide security for such damage in an amount within a period and under conditions which the Court deems appropriate.
>
> **Rule 16** In cases where the Court grants the application under Rule 13, the prospective defendant may file an application requesting the Court to repeal or modify the provisional measures of protection. The order of the Court repealing or modifying the measures shall be final.
>
> In the case specified in paragraph one, the prospective defendant may make a request in the application to repeal or modify the provisional measures, or file with the Court, within thirty days from the date on which the Court issues an order

repealing or modifying the measures, a request for the Court order directing the applicant to compensate him for his damage. If the Court finds, after making an inquiry, that the order granting provisional measures of protection which has been repealed or modified was granted due to the Court's misunderstanding that there is ground for taking an action against the prospective defendant or sufficient reason to grant such provisional measures by the fault or negligence of the applicant, the Court may order the applicant to compensate the prospective defendant in the amount the Court deems appropriate. If the applicant fails to comply with such Court order, the Court may enforce such order as if the applicant were a judgment debtor.

Rule 17 In a case where the Court grants the application under Rule 13 but the applicant fails to institute an action relating to the application within fifteen days from the date on which the application was granted or within the period prescribed by the Court, the provisional measures shall lapse at the expiration of the aforesaid period.

In the case specified in paragraph one, the prospective defendant may file with the Court, within thirty days from the date on which the provisional measure is deemed to lapse, a request for a Court order directing the applicant to compensate him for his damage in an amount the Court deems appropriate. If the applicant fails to comply with such order, the Court may enforce such order as if he were a judgment debtor.

Rule 18 In cases where the Court grants the application under Rule 13 and an action is instituted in relation to the application within fifteen days from the date on which the application was granted or within the period prescribed by the Court, the provisional measures so granted or modified under Rule 16 paragraph one shall continue to be in force, unless the Court issues an order repealing or modifying the measures

1.3. The Case Law

For a period of almost 20 years since 2002, when the Act was enacted, nine injunctions have been requested in connection with trade secret cases. None of these has been successful. Four out of these nine applications were voluntarily withdrawn by the petitioners after successful settlement with the opposing parties.

1.4. The Leading Cases

Two decisions are chosen as leading cases, as they demonstrate a pre-complaint filing of the application for injunctive relief and a post-complaint filing of the application for injunctive relief, respectively. In both cases, the CIPIT Court dismissed the applications for injunctive relief for different reasons.

1.4.1. CIPIT Court Decision Tor. Por. 31/2549

1.4.1.1. Case Information

CIPIT Court Decision Tor. Por. 31/2549 (decided on March 2, 2006). The decision was rendered by Judge Therdchai Thanapongporn, Judge Wisit Sripibul and Associate Judge Pannee Supatrapan.

1.4.1.2. Summary

The plaintiff filed a petition for injunction with the complaint seeking a court order to prohibit the defendant from continuing violation of the plaintiff's rights over trade secrets and to require the defendant to hand over or destroy items, equipment and tools used by the defendant to breach the plaintiff's trade secrets. The CIPIT Court is of the view that injunctive relief will not be effective in protecting the trade secret of the plaintiff because the disclosure of the trade secret has already rendered it no longer a secret. The disclosure process is irreversible and cannot restore the confidentiality of the trade secret. Therefore, the Court dismissed the petition for injunction, and the order is final according to Rule 13 of the CIPIT Court Rules.

1.4.1.3. Facts

The plaintiff filed a petition for an injunction along with the complaint under the Act. The plaintiff filed a police report and made a criminal complaint alleging that the defendant stole designs for packaging machinery from the plaintiff. The defendant then used and disclosed the designs by selling them to the first defendant, who was a former client of the plaintiff.

Later, on January 17, 2006, the police conducted a search on the first defendant's business premises. The police discovered the machinery and equipment derived from the violation of the plaintiff's trade secrets, as well as many other documents containing industrial and commercial information of the plaintiff, including the designs for packaging machinery and information about the plaintiff's clients.

The plaintiff claimed that if the defendants continued with their actions, the plaintiff's information would lose its confidentiality and that would cause irreparable harm to the plaintiff and its business to the extent that it might go out of operation. The plaintiff petitioned the Court to order the defendants to cease their violations of the plaintiff's trade secrets and to require the defendants to destroy or hand over all machinery, equipment and documents relating to the violation of the plaintiff's trade secret.

1.4.1.4. The Reasoning of the Court

The Court held proceedings requiring the plaintiff to present evidence and witnesses to demonstrate that the defendants had violated or would violate the plaintiff's trade secret under section 8 of the Act. The Court found that the defendants constructed two super mono-lock rotary packaging machines as stated in the plaintiff's complaint. One of these machines was sold, and another was awaiting completion while the defendants were looking for necessary parts. The defendants planned to complete the second machine in 90 days from these court proceedings.

The Court found that "in respect of the first machine that had already been sold by the defendants, the injunction would not have helped the plaintiff, since the machine was already completed and sold to a third party. The plaintiff can only seek monetary recourse in respect of the first machine. For the second machine, since it would take 90 days from these proceedings to complete, it would not be harmful to the plaintiff if the court allows the defendants an opportunity to object, as the plaintiff always had monetary recourse as an option. The Court therefore dismissed the plaintiff's petition for injunction and scheduled the main litigation proceedings."[58]

1.4.2. *CIPIT Court Decision Tor. Por. 98/2552*

1.4.2.1. Case Information

CIPIT Court Decision Tor. Por. 98/2552 (decided on December 15, 2010). The decision was rendered by Judge Chankrapoeh Torsuwan-Sinthawathaworn, Judge Poomchai Panpruetpayat and Associate Judge Sudjit Pinyoying.

1.4.2.2. Summary

The plaintiff filed a petition for an injunction to prohibit the defendants from continuing to breach confidentiality and non-competition agreements with the plaintiff. The CIPIT Court dismissed the plaintiff's petition.

1.4.2.3. Facts

The two plaintiffs sued the five defendants for breach of contract and violation of trade secrets. During evidence-taking proceedings, the defendants' witnesses testified that the defendants had a plan to construct machinery and equipment for manufacturing magnetic dust. The plaintiff worried that such a plan would result in the disclosure of the plaintiff's trade secrets once engineers started to construct such machinery and equipment. However, the plaintiff was unable to present clear and convincing evidence that the defendants had infringed on the plaintiff's trade secret. The plaintiff only relied on the defendants' testimonies and the plaintiff's own speculation that the defendants would use the trade secret for their manufacturing plan. The plaintiffs claimed they would suffer irrevocable harm if the defendants disclosed the plaintiff's trade secret to third parties. These secrets included blueprints for machinery and related components for the production of magnetic dust, as well as various manufacturing processes. Disclosure of these trade secrets to third parties would irreversibly cause them to cease to be trade secrets.

During the hearing, the defendants' witnesses, specifically, the second defendant and Mr. Richard Malcavech, admitted that the five defendants planned to construct additional machinery and components for the manufacturing of magnetic dust. This led the plaintiffs to believe that the defendants would move the machinery and components, as well as transfer secret technology to third parties.

The plaintiffs therefore filed a petition for injunction prohibiting the five defendants from continuing violations by:

58. The CIPIT Court Decision Tor. Por. 31/2549, p. 1 para. 2.

(1) moving or transferring the machinery and components, technical blueprints and other related documents (whether in paper or electronic form) of the plaintiffs, which were used for the manufacturing of magnetic dust, to any third party or location outside the first plaintiff's manufacturing plant without approval from the Court;
(2) constructing or hiring any third party to construct machinery and components using the plaintiffs' trade secrets without approval from the Court; or
(3) disclosing the trade secret in dispute in any manner to any third party or company of the defendants.

1.4.2.4. The Reasoning of the Court

After reviewing evidence and witnesses presented by the two plaintiffs, the Court found that there was a possibility that the five defendants may continue their violation of the plaintiffs' trade secrets by revealing the plaintiffs' trade secrets. This finding was based on the admission by the second defendant and Mr. Richard Malcavech during the hearing that the five defendants planned to construct additional machinery and components for the manufacturing of magnetic dust, coupled with the losses suffered by the first defendant that led to the possible relocation of its manufacturing plant to the People's Republic of China (PRC), the principal source of raw materials, or the sale of its manufacturing technology to a Chinese buyer. This was because the first defendant had been engaging in a joint venture with PBA Group, a Singaporean group of companies. PBA Group members include companies from the PRC, Ningbo Jinfeng Magnets Co., Ltd. and Ningbo Konit Nihon Magnets Co., Ltd. The first defendant's witness (Mr. Richard Malcavech) additionally responded to a cross-examination by the plaintiffs' lawyer that the second defendant planned to construct new machinery to produce magnetic dust, but had not started construction.

The plaintiffs testified that the defendants had for the first time engaged in the business of magnetic dust manufacturing by using the machinery, components and processes that the plaintiff claimed to be its trade secrets. By building additional machinery and components, the defendants would inevitably need to reveal the plaintiff's trade secrets to third parties. For instance, blueprints of the machinery and components would need to be shown to them, which would result in the trade secret losing its confidentiality. Over the past two years, 95% of raw materials used in the production of magnetic dust have had to be imported from the PRC, prices of which have increased significantly. Such a factor has led to a rise in manufacturing costs of the defendants, and defendants' consequent inability to meet their sale targets. The defendants would likely need to relocate their manufacturing plant to the PRC or sell their manufacturing technology to a Chinese buyer in order to reduce production costs. The actions of the five defendants led the plaintiffs to believe that they would move the machinery and components, as well as transfer secret technology to the PBA Group or other companies from the PRC or third parties.

The CIPIT Court was not persuaded, and concluded that the plaintiffs did not offer any evidence or witness to support the allegation, and that the testimony was based solely on its own speculation. Therefore, the Court could not conclusively find that the five defendants planned to disclose the plaintiffs' trade secret as claimed by the plaintiffs. Due to this, there was insufficient justification to grant injunction as requested by the plaintiffs. The Court then dismissed the plaintiffs' petition for injunctive relief.[59]

1.4.2.5. Legal Analysis

1.4.2.5.1. Thai Courts Are Very Careful in Granting Provisional Injunction

When there is a dispute concerning unlawful use of trade secrets, the trade secret owner or injured party may seek an injunction to prevent potential disclosure of trade secrets. The injunction granted under the "Inevitable Disclosure Doctrine" of the US is a clear example, allowing an employer to petition for a court order to prohibit a former employee from working for a competitor or engaging in a competing business, as this would lead to inevitable disclosure of the employer's trade secrets. Under this Doctrine, court will grant an injunction if the petitioner proves that: (1) the role or scope of work of the employee is similar to those for which the employee was employed by the petitioner, such that it would be inevitable for the employee to use the trade secret of the petitioner in the employment; and (2) the trade secret is valuable to both the petitioner and the new employer.[60]

Although under Thai law there is no legal code or court precedents similar to the Inevitable Disclosure Doctrine of the US, the trade secret owner or injured party can still seek an injunction pursuant to section 8 of the Act. Under that Section, the Court may grant an injunction barring the party who breaches or is about to breach trade secret rights from continuing or committing breach before and during the trade secret owner's or injured party's litigation against such party. This affords the trade secret owner and injured party the preventive measures and mitigation of damages. However, the Court will be very careful in granting such injunction, as, at the time of issuing an injunction order, the Court has not yet had the opportunity to consider all the evidence and witnesses.

1.4.2.5.2. Legal Requirements for Granting Provisional Injunction

In the case of conventional interim measures under the Civil and Procedural Code, an interim injunction can be applied and executed ex parte at any time before or after the filing of the complaint but before judgment by the Court. For this, two requirements must be satisfied. First, there must be clear and convincing evidence that the party against which the injunctive relief is sought has engaged in the act of infringement; and second, there must be proof of irremediable harm if the injunction were not to be swiftly granted.

59. The CIPIT Court Decision Tor. Por. 98/2552, p. 4.
60. Kahnke E. Randall, Bundy L. Kerry and Liebman A. Kenneth, Doctrine of Inevitable Disclosure, Faegre & Benson LLP., September 2008, available at, https://ipo.org/wp-content/uploads/2013/04/DoctrineofInevitableDisclosure.pdf (accessed on December 28, 2020), pp. 1-2; Kitkuson Sarawut, Inevitable Disclosure Doctrine: Experience from USA, BU Academic Review, Vol. 2, No. 1, January-June 2003, p. 132.

Pursuant to Rule 13, the CIPIT Court Rules and the Act, the application of a provisional measure for trade secret cases may be filed ex parte at any time before or after the filing of the complaint if the following conditions are met:

- there are reasonable conditions to support the application for an interim measure and sufficient justifications for the Court to approve such an application;
- the nature of the damage incurred cannot be resituated by monetary measures or any other form of indemnity; and
- the prospective defendant is unable to compensate the applicant for the damage or it might be difficult to enforce the judgment against the prospective defendant afterward.

Generally, where a preliminary injunction is granted in an IP case, it is typically subject to a security deposit, usually set as an additional condition by the Court which issues the injunction (Rule 15, CIPIT Court Rules). The security is intended to cover potential damages to the defendant in case the injunction is later found to be unjustified.

The defendants can counter the plaintiff's application for preliminary injunction. In the event of such opposition by the defendant, the preliminary injunction is typically conditioned on the initiation of *inter partes* court proceedings within a certain time limit. Under this opposition procedure, a potential defendant files an argument with the Court explaining the reasons why such a preliminary injunction should not be granted (Rule 16, CIPIT Court Rules). In such circumstances, the Court will usually offer to hear both sides.

1.4.2.6. Commercial and Industrial Significance

The proceedings of provisional measures for trade secret cases under Thai laws are governed by the following important basic principles. First, preliminary injunctions are to be granted in cases where delayed action would likely cause irreparable harm to the claimant. Second, when preliminary injunctions are granted, their enforcement is typically subject to a security deposit set by the injunction-issuing court.

The past twenty years' experience of Thailand since the Act was enacted shows that petitions for injunctive reliefs in trade secret cases have rarely been granted, which has led to some criticism. However, given the lengthy litigation time, which could last several years from the first complaint to the judgment by the Supreme Court, the injunctive measure is one of the very important tools for protecting the rights of good faith litigating parties during the long litigation period. The petitioner must consider court precedents, ruling guidelines and reasoning, and the complexity of the litigation process, in order to have a reasonable chance of success.

2. Damages

Tosaporn Leepuengtham

2.1. *Legal Issues*

What are the methods for calculating damages? What is the required causation between an infringer's profit and infringement? Are there statutory or punitive damages?

2.2. *The Statutory Law*

Prior to the enactment of the Act in 2002, damages for this kind of activity were awarded under tort law and contract law. Section 438(1) of the Civil and Commercial Code empowers the Court to determine the manner and the extent of compensation according to the circumstances and the gravity of the wrongful act.

Section 13 of the Act stipulates that "In determining to measure of damages where an action under section 8(2) has been filed, the court is empowered to apply the following rules:

(1) In addition to the damages for the actual damages suffered, the court may include in the damages for the plaintiff account of profits accrued from or in connection with the infringement by the infringer.
(2) In case where the court is unable to measure the damages under (1), it may award such amount of damages to the controller of trade secrets, as it deems appropriate.
(3) In case where there is clear evidence that the infringement of trade secrets is conducted willfully or maliciously, causing the trade secrets to cease the quality of secrecy, the court is empowered to order the infringer to pay punitive damages in addition to the amount of damages granted under (1) and (2). However, the punitive damages shall not exceed twice the amount of damages under (1) or (2)."

Once a defendant has been held liable for trade secret misappropriation, Thai courts normally award damages under section 13(1) of the Trade Secrets Act, provided that the plaintiff can prove that they have suffered an actual loss. Punitive damages are permitted under section 13(3) of the Act, but are rarely granted. This is because, in most cases, it can be difficult for plaintiffs to demonstrate damage.

2.3. *The Case Law*

Up until this writing, there are only some 31 cases on this matter in the IPIT Court, 8 cases in the Appeal Court for Specialized Cases and 12 cases in the Supreme Court.[61] Due to the limited number of trade secret cases, the published judgments do not add

61. Information received informally from the three courts mentioned above on January 30, 2021.

much to the statutory framework, and therefore there is no leading case to be reported. The following decisions are examples of Thai courts' approach to the award of damages arising from trade secret misappropriation.

2.4. The Leading Cases

Three leading cases are chosen here.

2.4.1. Supreme Court Decision 7769/ 2557

2.4.1.1. Case Information

Supreme Court Decision 7769/ 2557 A.D. 2014 *Delmax Machinery Ltd. v Bangkok Engineering and Machinery Ltd. and others* (decided on June 17, 2014).

2.4.1.2. Summary

In the first instance, the IPIT Court found that the 1st to 4th defendants were liable for misappropriating the plaintiff's trade secret and awarded the damages for THB 1,000,000. The Court dismissed the action against the remaining defendants. Both the plaintiff and the defendants appealed to the Supreme Court. The Supreme Court affirmed the THB 1,000,000 damages awarded by the first instance court, but declined to award punitive damages.

2.4.1.3. Facts

The plaintiff was a limited company which manufactured liquid packing machines. The 2nd to 14th defendants were all ex-employees of the plaintiff. The 2nd to 11th defendants are all the shareholders of the 1st defendant, which is a limited company. The 2nd to 4th defendants are also the directors of the 1st defendant. The 15th defendant acted as an agent of the 16th defendant, who had purchased machinery from the 1st defendant.

The plaintiff developed an improved liquid packing machine, which was able to wash, fill, sort and close bottles. The plaintiff suspected that during his employment, the 2nd defendant had stolen a customer list and document containing the machine's assembly drawings with the intent to use this information in the production of his own bottling machines. The plaintiff reported his concerns to the police, who searched the 1st defendant's office and found the missing documentation. The defendants' bottled products were assembled by using the same design of machine as that of the plaintiff. Armed with this information, the plaintiff commenced proceedings under the Trade Secrets Act, alleging that the 1st to 14th defendants had acquired and used trade secrets without its consent.

2.4.1.4. Reasoning of the Court

The Supreme Court considered the plaintiff's evidence presented during the trial, which comprised testimonies from Mr. Rungroj and Mr. Chotiwut, who were both directors of the plaintiff. "They testified that the plaintiff had tendered to supply a bottling machine to the 16th defendant and another company, Thai Sun Food Ltd, at a quoted price of 30,655,945.12 baht, but that these sales had been lost to the 3rd defendant. The evidence attested that but for the defendants' use of the trade secrets, the plaintiff would have profited 18,622,770.40 baht from both sales."[62] However, the Supreme Court held that "the plaintiff failed to prove that it would have sold the machines at the quoted amount, had the 3rd defendant not submitted a lower quote. Therefore, the loss of its profit as claimed was only an expectation and not the plaintiff's actual loss."[63]

The Supreme Court affirmed the THB 1,000,000 damages awarded by the first instance court. This amount was calculated based upon the fact that the 1st defendant's machine replicated less than 20% of the layout of the plaintiff's machine.[64] However, the Supreme Court declined to award the plaintiff punitive damages since the plaintiff failed to prove that the defendants' actions had resulted in the loss of the trade secret, as required by section 13(3) of the Act.[65] The Supreme Court "noted that the plaintiff had only claimed that the 1st defendant had taken the customer list and layout of his machine part. The plaintiff had not advanced testimony asserting how the 1st to 4th defendants had acted maliciously, or caused the trade secret to lose its secret status."[66]

2.4.2. The Appeal Court for Specialized Cases Decision 185/2562 A.D. 2019

2.4.2.1. Case Information

The Appeal Court for Specialized Cases Decision 185/2562 A.D. 2019 (decided on January 28, 2019).

2.4.2.2. Summary

The Appeal Court for Specialized Cases held that only the recipe at issue was protected as a trade secret, and this had been misappropriated as the plaintiff claimed.

2.4.2.3. Facts

The plaintiff sued the four defendants for appropriating the layout of his restaurant kitchen, the design of his wood-fired pizza oven and his special pizza dough recipe, and then disclosing this information to others, causing his trade secrets to be lost. The

62. Supreme Court Decision 7769/2557, p. 28.
63. *Ibid.*, pp. 28-29.
64. The author cannot elaborate more on how the calculation was done, as it is the only reason given for calculating in the decision.
65. Supreme Court Decision 7769/2557, pp. 29-30.
66. *Ibid.*

defendants argued that: (i) the information did not satisfy the requirements for trade secret protection; and (ii) the plaintiff had not taken sufficient reasonable steps to maintain the confidentiality of that information.

2.4.2.4. Reasoning of the Court

The Appeal Court for Specialized Cases awarded damages to the plaintiff for the actual loss of the business incurred from the unauthorized use of his pizza dough recipe. The Court calculated "the amount of the award by considering the plaintiff's evidence regarding his loss of income resulting from the infringement and its impact upon his competitiveness in this field and awarded damages for 1,500,000 baht."[67] The Court denied compensation for other damages claimed, including materials the plaintiff planned to use in the restaurant, employee salaries, and design costs for the kitchen layout, "since none of these costs were relevant to the disclosure of the protected recipe which had been appropriated."[68] The Court did not grant exemplary damages to the plaintiff in this case either.

2.4.3. Supreme Court Decision 9072/2547 A.D. 2004

Prior to the enactment of the Act in 2002, the Court had certain discretion when awarding compensation, depending on the evidence of damage which the plaintiff presented. The case is an example of how damages were assessed for breach of confidence under the provisions in the Civil and Commercial Code.

2.4.3.1. Case Information

Supreme Court Decision 9072/2547 A.D. 2004 (decided on December 21, 2004).

2.4.3.2. Summary

The IPIT Court ruled in favor of the plaintiff and awarded compensation. The Supreme Court affirmed the first instance's verdict.

2.4.3.3. Facts

The plaintiff was a company engaged in the field of construction, and the defendant was a former employee of that company. The defendant's employment contract included clauses of non-disclosure of confidential information and a non-compete clause, which prohibited the defendant from working for any rival company for the period of two years after the employment ended. The contract stated that any breach of the non-compete clause would result in a liquidated fine of THB 200,000. On leaving the plaintiff's employment, the defendant immediately joined a competitor's company.

67. The Appeal Court for Specialized Cases Decision 185/2562, p. 50.
68. *Ibid.*

The plaintiff sued the defendant for damages arising from the breach of employment contract.

2.4.3.4. Reasoning of the Court

The Supreme Court held that "under the non-disclosure clause in the employment contract, the defendant was obliged to refrain from disclosing the plaintiff's business information to other companies operating in the same field for the agreed two-year period, or pay the plaintiff the amount of 200,000 baht. Thus, this amount was considered a liquidated fine under Section 379 of the Civil and Commercial Code[69] which was subject to reduction at the Court's discretion, if it exceeded a reasonable amount."[70]

2.4.3.5. Legal Analysis

2.4.3.5.1. Under Section 438 of the Civil and Commercial Code

Before awarding compensation to an injured party for a trade secret breach, a Thai court will first consider the facts of the case and determine whether a trade secret has been disclosed in bad faith. If a defendant is held liable for trade secret misappropriation, the Court will determine the monetary sum of compensation payable to the plaintiff. However, a plaintiff must prove what type of damage has incurred, and demonstrate that such losses are attributable to the misappropriation. The Court must also consider the gravity of the defendant's wrongful acts, meaning that the amount of compensation depends upon the specific circumstances of each case. The Court also has discretion to reduce the amount of damages claimed if it feels that the claim exceeds the actual loss. As there are no explicit guidelines for damage calculations, much turns upon the quality of the evidence of damage adduced by the plaintiff, although, when exercising its discretion, a court will also consider not only the plaintiff's loss but also the value of any benefit that the infringer has gained.

Under section 438 of the Civil and Commercial Code,[71] a Thai court is only empowered to award compensation to injured parties to redress harm, rather than to punish wrongdoing, meaning a compensation award cannot exceed the actual loss. Nevertheless, since the wording of section 438 refers to the exercise of a court's discretion, it is possible to misinterpret that such discretion might lead to punitive damages.

69. Section 379 of the Civil and Commercial Code states that "If the debtor promises the creditors the payment of a sum of money as penalty in case he does not perform his obligation or does not perform it in the proper manner, the penalty is forfeited if he is in default, if the performance due consists in a forbearance, the penalty is forfeited as soon as any act in contravention of the obligation is committed."

70. Supreme Court Decision 9072/2547 (A.D. 2004), pp. 5-6.

71. Section 438 of the Civil and Commercial Code provides that "(1) The Court shall determine the manner and the extent of compensation according to the circumstances and the gravity of the wrongful act. (2) Compensation may include restitution of the property of which the injured person has been wrongfully deprived or its value as well as damages be granted for any injury caused."

2.4.3.5.2. Punitive Damages

While compensation has long been recognized under Thai law, punitive damages were recognized for the first time by section 13(3) of the Act. The function of punitive damages is to punish wrongdoers and to deter future misconduct. However, there has yet to be a single case in which a court has awarded punitive damages under this provision in addition to damages covering the actual loss.

In its Decision 7769/2557, the Supreme Court did not award punitive damages because the plaintiff failed to prove that the defendants' trade secret infringement had been willful and resulted in the loss of secrecy. This holding affirms that the burden of proof for these twin requirements of the punitive damage provision of section 13(3) of the Act lies with the plaintiff. Since the purpose of punitive damages is to punish the wrongdoers and to deter future misconduct, the plaintiff is required to prove that the harm he suffered was willfully conducted by the defendant and caused the loss of his trade secret as required under section 13(3).

The Appeal Court for Specialized Cases in its Decision 185/2562 upheld a damages award based upon the evidence adduced by the plaintiff of its loss of the profit arising from the actual infringing act while discounting other costs which it considered were unconnected to the infringement. This compensation was granted in accordance with section 13(1) and (2) of the Trade Secret Act. In this case, the plaintiff did not seek an award of punitive damages in the original complaint. Yet, as the issue of punitive damages is not a question of law concerning public order, a Thai court does have discretion to raise this on its own volition, and make a punitive award in its decision.[72]

Despite rare awarding of punitive damages in trade secret litigation, punitive damages have been recognized in the following Thai legislation: Liability for Damage Arising from Unsafe Products Act B.E. 2551 (2008),[73] the Consumer Case Procedure Act B.E. 2551 (2008),[74] the Copyright Act B.E. 2537 (1994) as amended in B.E. 2558 (2015)[75] and the Gender Equality Act B.E. 2558 (2015).[76] Although award of punitive damages is also rare under these pieces of legislation, there is some case law which might provide guidance for trade secret cases.

In a case concerning a claim for unfair business practices under the Consumer Case Procedure Act,[77] the Supreme Court awarded punitive damages against a real estate company for withholding information about an apartment which it had sold. The

72. Section 142 of the Civil Procedure Code states that "A judgement or order of a Court disposing of a case shall decide on every claim in the plaint, but no judgement or order shall be given for anything in excess of or not include in such complaint, except that: (5) In the case where a point of law involving public order could have been raised, the Court may, where it thinks fit, raise it for decision and give judgement accordingly."
73. Section 11(2) of Liability for Damage Arising from Unsafe Products Act empowers the Court to award punitive damages of up to twice the amount of the actual damage.
74. Section 42 of the Consumer Case Procedure Act permits the Court to award punitive damages of up to five times of the amount of the actual damage.
75. Section 64(2) of the Copyright Act has been amended to authorize the Court to grant punitive damages up to twice the amount under para. 1 of this section.
76. Section 18(2) of the Gender Equality Act authorizes the Court to award punitive damages up to four times of the amount of the actual damage.
77. Supreme Court Decision 7567/B.E. 2562 decided on December 27, 2019.

plaintiffs bought an apartment in the defendant's condo, not knowing that a backup generator for the block was installed in a room located directly below them. The defendant's marketing material had merely indicated that the space underneath was used for residents' parking. Having moved in, the plaintiffs were disturbed by the noise, smell and vibrations emanating from the generator, especially when it operated during power cuts at night. The Supreme Court held that the defendant's business conduct ignored its corporate social responsibility. Exceptionally, it awarded punitive damages at twice the amount of the plaintiff's actual loss.

Although punitive damages are only imposed in a small number of cases in Thailand, it is submitted that they are an effective and important feature of the civil justice system, in addition to any punishment available in criminal law. Punitive damages as a civil law remedy provide an additional signal that they not only punish reckless actions but also deter potential wrongdoers from egregious actions in the future. As noted already, each piece of legislation sets a cap on the amount of punitive damages which can be awarded, based upon the plaintiff's actual loss. Therefore, a court's ability to award exemplary damages is contingent upon the plaintiff's adducing adequate evidence to show that the defendant's actions have caused a quantifiable loss.

2.4.3.6. Commercial or Industrial Significance

The purpose of damages in trade secrets law is to compensate victims for the injury arising from unfair misappropriation of their commercially important information, and to put them back to their original position, as far as is possible. In contrast, punitive—or exemplary—damages serve to punish the defendant's socially undesirable behavior, and to deter them, and others, from future misconduct. Although rarely awarded, the threat of punitive damages might tip the balance in the trade secret holder's favor and avoid the need for them to bring their case before a court, as it may seem more attractive for an appropriator to settle the dispute, rather than running the risk that a court might award damages far higher than the value of the information taken.

Part III Asian Common Law Jurisdictions

CHAPTER 6

Singapore

Ng-Loy Wee Loon

OVERVIEW AND SUMMARY

In Singapore, there is no legislation enacted specifically for the protection of trade secrets.[1] What is available is the common law action for "breach of confidence," and this is the cause of action that is invoked to deal with unauthorized use or disclosure of trade secrets.

There are, in general, three essential elements in an action for breach of confidence, namely:

(1) the plaintiff's information must qualify as "confidential information";
(2) the defendant must owe an obligation of confidentiality to the plaintiff (i.e., to keep this information confidential); and
(3) the defendant must have breached this obligation by using or disclosing this information without the authorization of the plaintiff.

If the plaintiff succeeds in establishing these three elements, the defendant would be held liable unless the defendant can show that his disclosure of the confidential information is justified by some broader public interest.

The remedies available to the plaintiff who succeeds in making out his claim for breach of confidence are civil in nature. In particular, the plaintiff may get a monetary award (damages or an account of profits) and an injunction against the defendant.

1. This is to be contrasted with the position taken in some other common law countries. For example, the U.S. has its Defend Trade Secrets Act 2016. Note, though, that there is a piece of Singapore legislation which is tangentially relevant for this topic. This is the Official Secrets Act: *see infra* note 30.

TOPIC 1 THE LEGAL CRITERIA IN AN ACTION FOR BREACH OF CONFIDENCE

This section examines more closely each of the three essential elements in the common law action for breach of confidence. There is also a brief examination of the defense of public interest.

1. First Element: The Plaintiff's Information Must Qualify as Confidential Information

The first point to note is that the term used in the action for breach of confidence is not "trade secret," but "confidential information." Trade secrets are but an example of the different types of confidential information which are covered by this cause of action.[2] In fact, the term "trade secret" has a very special meaning in this area of the law when former employees are involved.[3]

1.1. The Requirement for *Relative* Secrecy

For a piece of information to qualify as "confidential information," there is only one criterion which it must satisfy; namely, the information must "not [be] freely available in the public domain."[4] This criterion is not particularly difficult to satisfy. Case law has made it clear that all it requires is for the plaintiff to show that the information has *relative* secrecy. What this means is that even when the information is known to some members of the public, the court may still conclude that the information has not entered the public domain, hence qualifies as confidential information. The following two cases illustrate the significance of this principle.

The first case is *PH Hydraulics & Engineering Pte Ltd v Intrepid Offshore Construction Pte Ltd*:[5]

- Facts: The plaintiff, a manufacturer of hydraulic winches, had made drawings of its design of winches which were developed in response to its customers' needs and required specifications. These drawings were published in operating manuals which were sent to the customers. The 1st defendant was a rival of the plaintiff, while the 2nd defendant was an ex-employee of the plaintiff. The plaintiff sued these two defendants when it discovered that copies of its drawings of the winches were taken by the 2nd defendant with him when he left the plaintiff's employment to join the 1st defendant. The defendants argued that the information relating to the winches as contained in the

2. The following are some examples of non-trade-related confidential information that are covered by the action for breach of confidence: a secret extramarital affair (*X Pte Ltd v CDE* [1992] 2 SLR(R) 575); a teacher's confidential report on a student's progress (*Total English Learning Global Pte Ltd v Kids Counsel Pte Ltd* [2014] SGHC 258); and a doctor's confidential report on a patient's medical condition (*Mykytowych, Pamela Jane v V I P Hotel* [2016] 4 SLR 829).
3. *See* further, *infra* notes 12-13 and the accompanying main text.
4. *Stratech Systems Ltd v Guthrie Properties (S) Pte Ltd* [2001] SGHC 77 at [37].
5. [2012] 4 SLR 36.

drawings became public knowledge when the drawings were made available to the customers via the operating manuals.

- Reasoning and conclusion of the court: The defendants' argument was misconceived. The first element of the action for breach of confidence merely required that the information has "relative secrecy,"[6] and therefore it was possible for the information to qualify as confidential information even though it was known to a limited circle of people outside of the plaintiff's organization. As to how limited or small this circle of people must be, it depended on the facts of each case. In this particular case, the drawings were given to the customers for a specific purpose (namely, for their consideration and own internal use). Further, there was no evidence that the customers had disseminated the drawings to others. Based on these facts, the High Court came to the conclusion that the information in the drawings still retained its confidential nature despite its distribution to the customers.

The second case is *Wee Shuo Woon v HT SRL*:[7]

- Facts: The plaintiff and the defendant were involved in a breach of contract dispute. While this dispute was ongoing, the plaintiff's computer system was hacked by an unknown third party. This third party extracted a copious amount (about 500 GB) of data from the plaintiff's computer system and uploaded this data onto the *WikiLeaks* website. When the defendant learnt of this hacking, he searched the *WikiLeaks* website and found among the hacked data certain emails containing confidential information that was relevant to the ongoing breach of contract dispute between him and the plaintiff. The defendant then sought to use these emails in the legal proceedings relating to this breach of contract dispute. This prompted the plaintiff to immediately commence an action for breach of confidence against the defendant, and to apply for an interim injunction to restrain him from using the confidential information in the leaked emails. The defendant argued that the information in the emails had lost its confidential nature once these emails became available on the *WikiLeaks* website for any Internet surfer in Singapore to access. The crux of the defendant's argument was that everything that could be found on the Internet was public domain material.
- Reasoning and conclusion of the court: The defendant's argument was misconceived. Information that had been accessed by "a limited segment of the public" could still qualify as confidential information.[8] The court emphasized that the size of this limited segment of the public was a very fact-sensitive issue. The court gave the following guideline to use in this inquiry: having regard to all the circumstances of the case, would it be just to require the defendant to treat the information as confidential?[9] In this particular case, the

6. *Ibid.*, at [46].
7. [2017] 2 SLR 94.
8. *Ibid.*, at [39].
9. *Ibid.*, at [31] and [35].

Court of Appeal took note of the following matters: the emails constituted a minute portion of the 500 GB of hacked data and it would have taken many hours to trawl through this data to find these emails; few people knew about or suspected the existence of the emails in the hacked data, and it was not likely that these few would have had the inclination or interest to spend hours trawling through the data to locate these emails. These matters allowed the Court of Appeal to find that, even though the emails were available on the *WikiLeaks* website, these emails had not in fact been accessed by many others (apart from the defendant). Unspoken in this finding was the sentiment that the plaintiff was the hapless victim of illegal hacking, and it would not be fair for the defendant to benefit from this misfortune suffered by the plaintiff. The Court of Appeal concluded that the confidential nature of the information in these emails had not been destroyed by the hacker putting them up on the *WikiLeaks* website.

1.2. The Requirement to Assess the Information *as a Whole*

Case law has also made it very clear that when determining if the information is freely available in the public domain (i.e., whether the information has relative secrecy), the information must be assessed *as a whole*. This means that even when the individual components within the information are already in the public domain, it is possible for the court to find that the information as a combined package is not yet in the public domain. The following two cases illustrate the operation of this principle.

The first case is *Stratech Systems Ltd v Guthrie Properties (S) Pte Ltd*:[10]

- The plaintiff, the designer of a "ticket-less" and "cash-less" car park system, had entered into negotiations for the installation of this car park system at the defendant's building. To this end, the plaintiff disclosed to the defendant the technical information relating to the functionality of the system. The defendant argued that there was nothing confidential in the technical information disclosed by the plaintiff because the distinct components in this technical information (e.g., the type of software used in the system) were already practiced by persons skilled in this area.
- Reasoning and conclusion of the court: The defendant's argument was misconceived. It was irrelevant that the individual components in the plaintiff's technical information were in the public domain. What was relevant and critical was the way in which the plaintiff had combined these components to work as an integrated unit. The High Court assessed the plaintiff's technical information *as a whole* and found that, as an integrated unit, it was not available in the public domain. Thus, the court concluded that the plaintiff's technical information qualified as confidential information for the purposes of the first element.

10. [2001] SGHC 77.

The second case is *Adinop Co Ltd v Rovithai Ltd*:[11]

- Facts: The plaintiff was a distributor of the defendant's products which were used in the F&B sector. The dispute related to a list called the "Key Customers List" compiled by the plaintiff. This list contained the identities of the customers who bought the defendant's products through the plaintiff, as well as other customer-related information (e.g., how these customers used the defendant's products in their F&B business). The plaintiff made available a copy of the Key Customers List to the defendant. When the distributorship arrangement ended, the defendant made use of this list to reach out to the customers to inform them that the plaintiff was no longer its distributor. This prompted the plaintiff to sue for breach of confidence. The defendant argued that there was no confidential information in the Key Customers List because much of this information was available in the public domain. More specifically, the defendant argued that it would have been possible for the defendant either on its own or through third parties who provided market intelligence services, to conduct investigations in the F&B sector and in this way to construct its own list.
- Reasoning and conclusion of the court: The defendant's arguments were misconceived. The focus of the inquiry was not on whether the bits of information in the Key Customers List (e.g., who in the F&B sector bought the defendant's products, and for what purpose) were in the public domain. Instead, the focus must be on whether the *assembly* of the information *as a whole* was in the public domain. In this case, there was no evidence that the information in the Key Customers List assessed *as a whole*, i.e., as a compilation, was readily available in the public domain. The evidence revealed that it would have taken a long time for the defendant or a market intelligence service provider to come up with its own list and, even then, this list would not be as comprehensive as the plaintiff's Key Customers List. This evidence led the High Court to conclude that the information in the Key Customers List assessed *as a whole* qualified as confidential information. This finding of fact was upheld by the Court of Appeal.

2. Second Element: The Defendant Must Owe an Obligation of Confidentiality to the Plaintiff (To Keep the Information Confidential)

The obligation of confidentiality may arise by way of contract or it may be imposed by equity.

11. The High Court's decision is unreported: [2018] SGHC 129. The Court of Appeal's decision is reported as [2019] 2 SLR 808. There is a further discussion of this case at, *infra*, note 17.

2.1. *Contractual Obligations of Confidentiality*

In some cases, the obligation of confidentiality is explicitly provided for in a contract between the parties. For example, the plaintiff and the defendant may have signed a Non-Disclosure Agreement (NDA) before they commenced discussions on a joint venture to commercially exploit the plaintiff's confidential information, and the NDA contains an express confidentiality clause. Another example is where the defendant is an employee of the plaintiff and there is an express confidentiality clause in the defendant's contract of employment. It should be noted that where the contract provides for these confidentiality clauses, there is the issue of enforceability of these clauses (whether the clause offends the doctrine of restraint of trade). This issue will be examined later in Topic 2.

Where the parties have a contract but this contract does not contain any express confidentiality clause, it is still possible for an obligation of confidentiality to arise by reason of an *implied term* in the contract. A classic example of such scenario is where the defendant is an employee of the plaintiff but the contract of employment has not expressly provided for a confidentiality clause. In such cases, the Singapore courts have readily held that the defendant has impliedly agreed in the contract of employment to be bound by an obligation of confidentiality during, and after the termination of, his employment. During the employment, this implied obligation takes the form of a very high duty of fidelity: the obligation is not to use or divulge *any* of the plaintiff's confidential information except in the discharge of the defendant's duties as an employee. After the termination of the employment, the scope of this implied obligation is a more limited one: the obligation is not to use or divulge a specific subcategory of the plaintiff's confidential information, namely, information that possesses a sufficiently high degree of confidentiality as to qualify as "trade secrets."[12] This post-employment implied obligation of confidentiality is far more limited in order to promote labor mobility.

When the court determines if the plaintiff's information qualifies as "trade secret," it will consider the following factors:[13]

(a) The nature of the employment—The person who was employed in a capacity where he habitually handled confidential material is more likely to be dealing with "trade secrets" than another employee in the lower ranks of the organization.
(b) The nature of the information itself—Information which was circulated widely within the organization is less likely a "trade secret," compared with information which is accessible only to a few selected individuals. Obvious examples of "trade secrets" are secret manufacturing processes and secret chemical formulae.
(c) Whether the employer impressed on the employee the confidentiality of the information.

12. *See*, e.g., *Tang Siew Choy v Certact Pte Ltd* [1993] 1 SLR(R) 835 at [16].
13. *Ibid.*

(d) Whether the information can be easily isolated from other information which the employee is free to use or disclose.

The case *Asia Business Forum Pte Ltd v Long Ai Sin*[14] will be used as an example to illustrate how the court determines the status of the information by reference to the above factors:

- Facts: The plaintiff, a conference organizer, had developed a training manual which was a comprehensive compilation describing in detail the concept, approach and method on how the plaintiff went about organizing its conferences. This training manual was made available to an employee of the plaintiff (the 1st defendant). After leaving the employment of the plaintiff, the 1st defendant took on several other jobs before she set up a rival company (the 2nd defendant) to provide conference organizing services. The plaintiff sued the two defendants for breach of confidence, alleging that the 1st defendant had used the confidential information in the training manual for the benefit of the 2nd defendant's business. For the plaintiff to succeed, it had to show that the confidential information in the training manual amounted to "trade secrets." The plaintiff relied on the fact that the manual had been painstakingly created, compiled and arranged over many years.
- Reasoning and conclusion of the court: The defendant's argument was misconceived. The effort and expense in developing a piece of information in itself were not conclusive in the question whether the information qualified as a "trade secret" which an employee would not be permitted to use or disclose after his employment. Instead, the court would have regard to the factors listed above. In this case, the 1st defendant was a group manager and hence relatively senior in the plaintiff's organization. However, the nature of the plaintiff's training manual was not so significantly different from that of other conference organizers. Further, the plaintiff had never impressed on the 1st defendant that the information in the training manual was highly confidential, and the manual was not marked "confidential." Based on these facts, the High Court found that the information in the training manual was not "so sensitive or fragile"[15] as to need special protection as trade secrets.

It should also be noted that, where the obligation of confidentiality arises by way of a contractual term (express or implied), the plaintiff's action against the defendant usually has two claims: breach of confidence and breach of contract.

2.2. *Equitable Obligations of Confidentiality*

In the absence of a contract between the parties, the court may invoke equity to impose an obligation of confidentiality on the defendant. Equity is all about "good faith and

14. [2003] 4 SLR(R) 658.
15. *Ibid.*, at [22].

conscience."[16] Thus, the court is primarily concerned with whether the defendant received or took the confidential information in circumstances which would make it unconscionable for him to divulge or use the information. More specifically, the court uses the following test in this inquiry: did the defendant receive or take the confidential information in circumstances where he knew or ought to know that the information is confidential? If so, the court would regard the defendant's conscience as having been tainted and, accordingly, impose an equitable obligation of confidentiality on the defendant.

This test applies whether the defendant is: (i) a *direct* recipient of confidential information (i.e., where the defendant received the confidential information from the plaintiff); or (ii) an *indirect* recipient of confidential information (i.e., where the defendant received the information from a third party to whom the plaintiff imparted the information); or (iii) a *taker* of confidential information (i.e., where the defendant surreptitiously took or acquired the information from the plaintiff without the latter's knowledge/consent). It should be evident that the third category of defendants (the takers of confidential information) is particularly important in the context of industrial espionage.

The following three cases are examples to show how this test has been applied by Singapore courts in each of the three categories (direct recipient; indirect recipient; and taker of confidential information).

The first case (involving a direct recipient of the confidential information) is *Adinop Co Ltd v Rovithai Ltd*:[17]

- Facts: The plaintiff was the distributor of the defendant's products. The plaintiff had complied confidential client-related information in the form of a list known as the "Key Customers List." The defendant requested for, and was given, a copy of the Key Customers List by the plaintiff. When the distributorship arrangement between the parties ended, the defendant made use of the information in the Key Customers List to reach out to the customers to inform them that the plaintiff was no longer its distributor.
- Reasoning and conclusion of the court: When information of commercial or industrial value was given to a party on a "business-like basis,"[18] the court would readily infer that the party knew that the information was being imparted to him in confidence. This was exactly the position of the defendant in this case: it received very useful client-related information in a business context. Thus, the Court of Appeal concluded that the defendant was bound by an equitable obligation not to use the information, and this means that the defendant was not at liberty to use the information to contact the customers after the termination of the distributorship arrangement.

16. *Invenpro (M) Sdn Bhd v JCS Automation Pte Ltd* [2014] 2 SLR 1045 at [131].
17. [2019] 2 SLR 808. There is also a discussion of this case at, *supra*, note 11.
18. *Ibid.*, at [88].

The second case (involving an indirect recipient of the confidential information) is *Clearlab SG Pte Ltd v Ting Chong Chai*:[19]

- Facts: Four of the plaintiff's employees in its R&D department had access to the plaintiff's confidential information relating to a technology developed by the plaintiff. When these employees left the plaintiff to join a rival company, they brought along with them documents containing this confidential information. The plaintiff brought an action for breach of action against these ex-employees, the rival company as well as the rival company's director (the 9th defendant). As far as the 9th defendant was concerned, he was an indirect recipient of the confidential information in that he received the information, not directly from the plaintiff, but from the plaintiff's ex-employees.
- Reasoning and conclusion of the court: The High Court found that the 9th defendant knew, from the presence of the plaintiff's name and a confidentiality warning on the documents brought over by the ex-employees of the plaintiff, that the contents therein were confidential information belonging to the plaintiff. The court concluded that the 9th defendant owed an equitable obligation of confidentiality to the plaintiff not to use this information.

The third case (involving a taker of the confidential information) is *Vestwin Trading Pte Ltd v Obegi Melissa*:[20]

- Facts: The 9th defendant was a private investigator who was engaged by the other defendants to find out certain financial information relating to the plaintiff's business. The 9th defendant went to the trash collection bin in the building where the plaintiff's office was located, and found in the bin some documents which had been thrown out by the plaintiff as trash. These documents contained the plaintiff's confidential financial information. When the plaintiff discovered the activities of the 9th defendant, the plaintiff commenced an action for breach of confidence and applied for an injunction to restrain use of its confidential financial information by all the defendants. As far as the 9th defendant was concerned, he was a taker of confidential information since he took the information without the knowledge and consent of the plaintiff.
- Reasoning and conclusion of the court: The second element in the action of breach of confidence did not require that there must be an "intentional communication" of the confidential information by a plaintiff to the defendant.[21] In this case, the High Court found that the 9th defendant had surreptitiously acquired the plaintiff's documents knowing full well that the information in these documents was confidential in nature. This fact led the court to conclude that the 9th defendant must be bound by an equitable obligation of confidentiality.

19. [2015] 1 SLR 163. There is a further discussion of this case at, *infra*, note 22.
20. [2006] 3 SLR(R) 573.
21. *Ibid.*, at [45].

3. The Third Element: The Defendant Must Have Breached the Obligation of Confidentiality by Using or Disclosing the Information Without the Authorization of the Plaintiff

The presence of this third element does not mean that the plaintiff has to wait until there has been actual unauthorized use/disclosure of the confidential information by the defendant before commencing the action for breach of confidence. The breach of confidence may take the form of a serious *threat* of an unauthorized use/disclosure of the information by the defendant. It may also be possible for the breach of confidence to take the form of the defendant's wrongful acquisition of the information per se. These two points were made in the following two cases.

The first case is *Clearlab SG Pte Ltd v Ting Chong Chai:*[22]

- Facts: Four employees in the plaintiff's R&D department left to join a rival of the plaintiff. These employees brought along with them copies of a large number of documents containing confidential information relating to a technology developed by the plaintiff. The evidence showed that these ex-employees had used some, but not all, of this confidential information for the benefit of their new employer (the plaintiff's rival). The plaintiff commenced an action for breach of confidence against *inter alia* these ex-employees. The defendants argued that they had not breached their obligation of confidentiality in relation to the information that had not been used. The crux of this argument was that the third element in the action was satisfied only when the defendants had actually used the confidential information, or disclosed the confidential information to a third party to the detriment of the plaintiff.
- Reasoning and conclusion of the court: The defendants' argument was misconceived. The third element in the action for breach of confidence was not limited to the situation where there had been actual use or disclosure of the confidential information; it sufficed for the plaintiff to show that there was a *threatened* use or disclosure of the information. In this case, the High Court assessed that the unused information could potentially be used by the ex-employees at their new place of employment. Thus the court concluded that the third element was satisfied in relation to *all* of the confidential information taken by these ex-employees (whether the information had actually been used or not). This conclusion had a significant impact on the remedies ordered against the defendants: *all* the confidential information (whether used or unused) fell within the scope of the injunction and the delivery-up order granted by the court.

The second case is *I-Admin (Singapore) Pte Ltd v Hong Ying Ting:*[23]

- Facts: The plaintiff, which was in the business of providing payroll administrative services to businesses, had developed a software and data processing

22. [2015] 1 SLR 163. There is also a discussion of this case at, *supra*, note 19.
23. [2020] 1 SLR 1130 (CA); [2020] 3 SLR 615 (HC).

system. The 1st and 2nd defendants were the employees of the plaintiff or its subsidiary. They left to set up a rival company (the 3rd defendant). Subsequently, *X* who was another employee of the plaintiff surreptitiously copied the plaintiff's confidential information such as its software source code, and passed this information to the 1st and 2nd defendants. The evidence showed that these defendants reviewed and referenced the plaintiff's confidential information, but eventually they did not use the plaintiff's confidential information in the development of a source code for use in the 3rd defendant's business.[24] The defendants thus argued that they had not used the confidential information, and further, there was no risk that they would ever use this information since they had already developed their own software. For these reasons, the defendants took the position that the third element had not been satisfied.

- Reasoning and conclusion of the court: The defendants' argument was misconceived. To ensure that the action for breach of confidence would adequately protect the legitimate interests of the plaintiff, it was necessary to extend the notion of unauthorized "use" in the third element to include the unauthorized *acquisition* of the confidential information by the defendant. In other words, the breach of confidence had occurred at the point of the defendant's act of acquiring the confidential information without the plaintiff's knowledge or consent, and thus it was immaterial that there was no actual or threatened use of the information by the defendant. In such cases, once the plaintiff was able to prove the first and second elements, this would give rise to a presumption that the breach of confidence (the third element) had occurred. This presumption was a rebuttable one: it was for the defendant to rebut this presumption by showing that his acquisition of the information was not unconscionable. In this case, the defendants were not able to rebut the presumption. Therefore, the Court of Appeal held that the third element had been satisfied and accordingly concluded that the defendants were liable for breach of confidence.

4. Defense of Public Interest

If the three essential elements (confidential information; obligation of confidentiality; breach of this obligation) are established, the defendant would be held liable to the plaintiff for breach of confidence unless the defendant can make out the defense of public interest. This defense, in essence, exonerates the defendant from his breach of confidence because some broader public interest is served by the defendant's unauthorized use or disclosure of the confidential information. For example, if the confidential information relates to the unsafe nature of the plaintiff's technology, it would

24. The plaintiff's software and the defendant's software were substantially different. This was a finding of fact made by the High Court: *see* [2020] 3 SLR 615 at [59]. There was no appeal against this finding: [2020] 1 SLR 1130 at [36].

arguably be in the interest of the public for the defendant to disclose this information to the relevant authority or even to the general public.

There is no Singapore case involving trade secrets where this defense of public interest has been raised. For illustrative purposes, reference will be made to a U.K. decision, *Lion Laboratories Ltd v Evan*.[25] The plaintiff in this case was the manufacturer of a breath analyzer which was used by the police for measuring the level of alcohol in drivers of motor vehicles. The plaintiff had certain confidential documents containing information that suggested that the readings given by the plaintiff's product were inaccurate. The defendants came into possession of this confidential information, and sought to have this confidential information published by some newspapers. The plaintiff applied for an injunction to restrain this publication, arguing that it would amount to a breach of confidence. The U.K. Court of Appeal refused to grant the injunction because, in its assessment, it was very important for the general public to be informed of the product's inaccurate readings. This was because the police used these readings as the basis for charging drivers with the offense of drunken driving, and these members of the public needed to know this information in order to be able to properly defend themselves against such charges.

25. [1985] QB 526.

TOPIC 2 THE ENFORCEABILITY OF CONFIDENTIALITY AND/OR NON-COMPETE CLAUSES

Where there is a contract between the parties, the contract often contains a confidentiality clause and/or non-compete clause which has the effect of restricting use of confidential information post-contract (e.g., after the termination of the defendant's contract of employment). In such cases, it is possible that the clause would not be enforced by the courts on the ground that it offends the common law doctrine of "restraint of trade." This doctrine is based on public policy; namely, it is against the public's interest for a party to use contract to bind another in ways that unreasonably restrict the latter's right to freedom of trade.

To counter the defendant's claim that the confidentiality clause amounts to a restraint of trade, the plaintiff must be able to show that: (i) he has a legitimate proprietary interest in restricting the defendant's freedom to trade, and (ii) the restriction on the defendant is reasonable.[26]

On (i), a legitimate proprietary interest can take the form of confidential information that has a sufficiently high degree of confidentiality as to qualify as a "trade secret." This issue has already been discussed earlier.[27]

On (ii), the factors that are taken into account in determining the reasonableness of the restriction: the duration of the restriction to use the plaintiff's confidential information; the geographical area covered by the restriction; and the nature of the confidential information.

26. *Man Financial (S) Pte Ltd v Wong Bark Chuan David* [2008] 1 SLR(R) 663.
27. *See supra* notes 13-15 and the accompanying main text.

TOPIC 3 THE BURDEN OF PROOF

The general rule is that the plaintiff bears the burden of proving all the three essential elements of the action for breach of confidence. There is an exception to this general rule: in cases where the defendant is a taker of the confidential information, that is, the defendant acquired the information surreptitiously without the consent or knowledge of the plaintiff, once the plaintiff has proved the first and second elements, there is a rebuttable presumption that the third element has also been satisfied and it is the defendant who bears the burden of rebutting this presumption.[28]

Where the defendant invokes the defense of public interest, the burden of establishing this defense is borne by the defendant.

28. *I-Admin (Singapore) Pte Ltd v Hong Ying Ting* [2020] 1 SLR 1130. This case is discussed at, *supra*, note 23.

TOPIC 5 MONETARY AWARDS

The court may make the following monetary awards against the defendant found liable for breach of confidence: an account of profit or damages. These are non-cumulative remedies, and so the plaintiff must elect between these two monetary awards.

When an account of profits is ordered, the computation of the quantum of profits is guided by the aim of depriving the defendant of the benefit acquired by him as a result of his breach of confidence. The focus is on the actual profit earned by the defendant from the sale of his products/services made possible by his breach of confidence.

Where an award of damages is made for a breach of a contractual obligation of confidentiality, the computation of the quantum of damages is guided by the aim of putting the plaintiff as far as possible in the same position he would have been if the breach of confidence had not occurred. The focus is on the loss suffered by the plaintiff sustained as a result of the defendant's breach of confidence. The quantum of this loss could be the plaintiff's loss of sales or loss of license fees.

It should be noted that if the defendant has breached an equitable obligation of confidentiality (as opposed to a contractual obligation of confidentiality), the Singapore court has jurisdiction to award *equitable* damages. In determining the quantum of equitable damages, the court has far more flexibility.[29] For example, the court may decide that the quantum is the cost that the defendant would have incurred by engaging a third party to develop the confidential information.

29. *Ibid.*, at [77].

TOPIC 6 CRIMINAL SANCTIONS

In Singapore, criminal liability can only be imposed by a statute. Therefore, where the protection of confidential information/trade secrets is sought via the common law action for breach of confidence, the defendant will not and cannot be subject to any criminal sanction.

There is one particular set of statutory criminal offenses that merits a brief mention. These are the criminal offenses created by the Official Secret Act.[30] For example, a person to whom "secret official" information has been entrusted in confidence by a person holding office in the government shall be guilty of an office if he communicates this information without the proper authorization. Thus, a person who comes into possession of any trade secret that is related to government work should proceed with caution. If the information falls within the ambit of the Official Secrets Act, a conviction for a wrongful communication of this information subjects the person to a fine of not exceeding SGD 2,000 and to imprisonment for a term not exceeding two years.[31]

30. Cap. 213, 2012 Rev. Ed.
31. *See* section 5 read with section 17(2) of the Official Secrets Act.

CHAPTER 7

Hong Kong

Jyh-An Lee & Jingwen Liu

OVERVIEW AND SUMMARY

Inherited from the common law tradition, Hong Kong has no statutory protection for confidential information and trade secrets.[1] Instead, confidential information is protected by the common law practice of breach of confidence. The breach of confidence claim covers a wide range of confidential information, including but not limited to technical know-how, commercial records, and government or even personal information.[2] For a breach of confidence claim to be established, three elements must be found. First, the subject information must have the necessary quality of confidence. Second, that information must have been imparted in circumstances importing an obligation of confidence. Third, there must be an unauthorized use of that information to the detriment of the party communicating it.[3] Once a breach of confidence has been found, the aggrieved owner of the information is entitled to the equitable remedy of injunction. Damages, including exemplary damages, are also available according to the principles set down in *China Light & Power Co Ltd v Ford*.[4] It is noteworthy that Hong Kong has hesitated to introduce criminal liabilities to breach of confidence. In spite of the global tendency towards criminalisation of trade secret infringement, a consultation paper issued by Hong Kong Bar Association (HKBA) in 2001 explicitly voiced against adopting such legislation in Hong Kong.[5]

1. Angus Phang, Ling Ho and Mena Lo, 'Hong Kong', in Melvin F. Jager (ed.), *Trade Secrets Throughout the World* (Clark Boardman Callaghan 2019) § 17:6.
2. David Llewelyn and Tanya Aplin, *Intellectual Property: Patents, Copyright, Trade Marks and Allied Rights* (9th edn, Sweet & Maxwell 2019) 319.
3. *Coco v A.N. Clark (Engineers) Ltd* [1969] RPC 41.
4. *China Light & Power Co Ltd v Ford* [1996] 1 HKLRD 57.
5. Hong Kong Bar Association, *Consultation Paper on Unfair Competition and Intellectual Property Rights* (11 May 2001).

1. THE EQUITABLE ACTION FOR BREACH OF CONFIDENCE

1.1. The Necessary Quality of Confidence

In the commonwealth world, information is traditionally divided into three categories according to the principles laid down in *Faccenda Chicken Ltd v Fowler*: (i) information that is trivial or in the public domain; (ii) confidential information; and (iii) specific trade secrets.[6] For a breach of confidence to be found, the subject information cannot be trivial or easy to access from public sources. Information from both categories (ii) and (iii) is eligible subject matter for a breach of confidence cause of action. The main feature that distinguishes a trade secret from confidential information is that, in the employment sphere, a trade secret of the employer cannot be utilised by a departing employee even after the termination of his employment contract, whereas ordinary confidential information is free to be used by an ex-employee, absent an express obligation imposed by an enforceable restrictive covenant governing his post-employment behaviour.[7]

Topic 1 of this chapter provides some insights on what might constitute a trade secret, as opposed to ordinary confidential information, in Hong Kong. Based on English case law, the court in *AXA China Region Insurance Co Ltd and Another v Pacific Century Insurance Co Ltd and Others* listed the following qualities essential for a trade secret:

(1) it is used in a trade or business (*Lansing Linde* and *Faccenda Chicken* 5(b));
(2) it is confidential, i.e., not already in the public domain (*Thomas Marshall v Guinle* and *Faccenda Chicken*);
(3) it can be easily isolated from other information which the employee is free to use so that any man of average intelligence and honesty would think it is improper to use the information at the disposal of his new employer (*Faccenda Chicken* 5(d) and *Printers & Finishers*);
(4) it would be liable to cause real or significant harm to the owner if disclosed to a competitor (*Lansing Linde* and *Thomas Marshall v Guinle*); and
(5) the owner of the information must limit its dissemination or at least not encourage or permit its widespread publication or otherwise impress upon the employee the confidentiality of the information (*Lansing Linde* and *Faccenda Chicken* 5(c)).[8]

1.2. Circumstances Importing an Obligation of Confidence

When illustrating what circumstances would give rise to an obligation of confidence, the presiding judge, Mr Justice Megarry ('Megarry J'), developed the so-called reasonable man test in *Coco v A. N. Clark (Engineers) Ltd.*, ruling that 'if the circumstances are

6. *Faccenda Chicken Ltd v Fowler* [1987] Ch 117.
7. *Ibid.*
8. *AXA China Region Insurance Co. Ltd. and Another v Pacific Century Insurance Co. Ltd. and Others* [2003] 3 HKC 1 [38].

such that any reasonable man standing in the shoes of the recipient of the information would have realised that upon reasonable grounds the information was being given to him in confidence, then this should suffice to impose upon him the equitable obligation of confidence'.[9] This is thus viewed as an equitable root of a binding obligation of confidence.

Confidentiality can also arise from a binding contractual obligation. In *Akihiro Oba and Others v Kishimoto Sangyo Co. Ltd. and Another*,[10] the Court of Appeal in Hong Kong specifically pointed out the different legal effects arising from a breach of contractual obligation and that of an equitable one. Because the 1st defendant, Mr Oba, was holding the concurrent positions of a senior manager at the plaintiff's company in Japan and a director of its Hong Kong subsidiary, his alleged misappropriation of the plaintiff's confidential information had simultaneously resulted in a breach of fidelity duty and breach of fiduciary duties. When hearing the dispute, the Court of Appeal pointed out that:

> Breach of the duty of fidelity results in the common law remedy of damages; breach of fiduciary duties calls for remedies in equity. Although, since the Judicature Act of 1873, the streams of common law and equity have merged, there are essential differences in remedies which must be recognised.[11]

The duty of fidelity arises by implication from an employment contract. 'For breach of this duty damages are recoverable at common law.'[12] On the other hand, 'breach of fiduciary duty imports wider considerations'. Equitable relief for such breach is founded on the commonwealth legal tradition.[13]

1.3. Unauthorized Use to the Detriment of the Plaintiff

The third element put forward in *Coco v Clark* is that the defendant must have misused the information to the detriment of the plaintiff. First of all, there must be an unauthorized use of the subject information by the defendant. In Hong Kong, unauthorized use was sometimes found by way of drawing inference in case law, such as the leading cases of **Topic 3** and **Topic 5** of this chapter. To be specific, in both cases, since the plaintiff had adduced evidence to prove the confidentiality of the subject information and the defendant's duty of confidence, the burden shifted to the defendant to prove that he had not misused or disclosed the subject information. Given the defendant failed to discharge this burden, the court drew an inference in favour of the plaintiff to find a breach of confidence established.

With regard to the detriment, Megarry J himself questioned whether it was necessary in the establishment of a breach of confidence:[14]

9. *Coco v Clark*, *supra* note 3, 420-421.
10. *Akihiro Oba and Others v Kishimoto Sangyo Co. Ltd. and Another* [1996] 1 HKLRD 196.
11. *Ibid.*, [33].
12. *Ibid.*, [34].
13. *Ibid.*, [42].
14. Llewelyn and Aplin, *supra* note 2, 346.

> At first sight, it seems that detriment ought to be present if equity is to be induced to intervene; but I can conceive of cases where a plaintiff might have substantial motives for seeking the aid of equity and yet suffer nothing which could fairly be called detriment to him, as when the confidential information shows him in a favourable light but gravely injures some relation or friend of his whom he wishes to protect. The point does not arise for decision in this case, for detriment to the plaintiff plainly exists. I need therefore say no more than that although for the purposes of this case I have stated the proposition in the stricter form, I wish to keep open the possibility of the true proposition being that in the wider form.[15]

2. CIVIL REMEDIES

2.1. Injunctions

Injunctions, as a category of equitable remedy, are a common remedy in cases involving breach of confidence. Because the leakage of confidential information normally concerns significant commercial value and irreparable economic loss, applications for interlocutory reliefs are frequently brought by plaintiffs before a final decision is reached. A random search at Westlaw Asia with keywords 'breach of confidence' and 'interlocutory injunction' revealed 67 results in Hong Kong as of 17 March 2021. Special forms of injunctions such as Mareva injunctions and Anton Piller orders are frequently sought as well. As illustrated further in **Topic 1** of this chapter, the rules governing the granting of interlocutory injunctions in Hong Kong were set down in the English case *American Cyanamid Co v Ethicon Ltd.*[16] In short, the court must be satisfied that, having taken into account all prima facie evidence and the balance of convenience, etc., there is a serious issue to be tried and the plaintiff has a good prospect of success at trial, before an interlocutory injunction will be granted.

Under certain circumstances, a springboard injunction is applicable. A springboard injunction is usually applied by an ex-employer to prevent its ex-employee from obtaining a head start in a competing business by misusing the former's confidential information.[17] The concept arose in the area of confidential information misappropriation,[18] but is not confined to breach of confidence cases.[19] The basic idea is 'to erase any artificial advantage a confidant might derive from being privy to confidential information which later becomes public'.[20] Unlike an ordinary injunction for breach of confidence, a springboard injunction can still be claimed even when the confidential information later becomes publicly accessible.[21] Moreover, a springboard injunction is typically applied in the absence of an express restrictive covenant between the

15. *Coco v Clark, supra* note 3, 421.
16. *American Cyanamid Co v Ethicon Ltd* [1975] AC 396, at 407-409.
17. Gareth Edwards, 'Springboard Injunctions' (2012) Credit Management 41.
18. *See*, e.g., *Terrapin Ltd v Builders' Supply Co (Hayes) Ltd* [1960] RPC 135.
19. *QBE Management Services (UK) Ltd v Dymoke* [2012] IRLR 458. However, it was at one time limited to cases involving misuse of confidential information both in the UK and in Hong Kong.
20. *ICAP (Hong Kong) Ltd v BGC Securities (Hong Kong) LLC & Others* [2005] 2 HKLRD 349, citing John Hull, *Commercial Secrecy: Law and Practice* (1997) at p. 63 para. 3.42.
21. Jeffrey Pinsler, 'The Springboard Injunction and Its Future Potential in Singapore' (2017) The Singapore Law Gazette https://v1.lawgazette.com.sg/2017-09/1954.htm, accessed 19 March 2021.

parties.[22] In the recent case *McLarens Hong Kong Ltd v Poon Chi Fai Corey*,[23] the Court of First Instance clarified that five issues must be considered when determining whether a springboard injunction should be granted:

(1) whether there was unlawful use of the plaintiff's confidential information and/or breach of fiduciary duties by the defendants;
(2) whether by reason of such breaches of confidence and/or fiduciary duties, the defendants have obtained an unfair competitive edge or 'head start' over the plaintiff;
(3) whether the unfair advantage still exists at the date when the springboard injunction is sought and that it will continue to have such effect unless the relief sought is granted;
(4) whether damages are an adequate remedy to the plaintiff; and
(5) in deciding whether to grant any interlocutory injunction, including a springboard injunction, the court must take whichever course appears to carry the lower risk of injustice if it should turn out that it was wrong.[24]

As of 19 March 2021, search at Westlaw Asia with keywords 'breach of confidence' and 'springboard injunction' revealed seven results, in six of which the court decided the springboard doctrine should not be applied.

2.2. Damages

As illustrated in **Topic 5** of this chapter, there had been disputes among commonwealth jurisdictions with regard to whether damages, as a classical legal remedy, could be applied to address an equitable wrong. Though inconsistency occurs occasionally, an overall investigation into the pre-1873 case law of England virtually supports the proposition that damages could not be awarded for infringement against purely equitable rights.[25] The principle was not overhauled until the Chancery Amendment Act 1858 ('Lord Cairns' Act').[26] Section 2 of the Act stipulated that in any case where the Court of Chancery had jurisdiction to entertain an application for an injunction or specific performance, the court could award damages in addition or substitution therefor.[27] Although having been repealed for decades, the very essence of this section can still be traced in today's statutory enactment of the United Kingdom (UK): section 50 of the Senior Courts Act 1981, which provides that '[w]here the Court of Appeal or the High Court has jurisdiction to entertain an application for an injunction or specific performance, it may award damages in addition to, or in substitution for, an injunction

22. Paul Goulding, 'Commentary: Springboard Injunctions in Employment Law' (1995) 24(2) Industrial Law Journal 152.
23. [2019] 3 HKLRD 403.
24. *Ibid.*, [19].
25. David Capper, 'Damages for Breach of the Equitable Duty of Confidence' (1994) 14 Legal Stud 313, 317-319.
26. The Chancery Amendment Act 1858 (UK).
27. *Ibid.*, section 2.

or specific performance'.[28] As such, it is clear that in both legislation and case law, damages can be awarded against equitable wrongs.[29] Such damages are usually referred to as 'equitable damages'. The difference between equitable damages and common law damages is less significant; insofar, it has been described as 'a difference without a distinction'.[30]

The provision of Lord Cairns' Act and its successors have also been imparted to Hong Kong legislations. Section 17 of the High Court Ordinance provides that '[w]here the Court of Appeal or the Court of First Instance has jurisdiction to entertain an application for an injunction or specific performance, it may award damages in addition to, or in substitution for, an injunction or specific performance'.[31] In Hong Kong, the binding authority on this issue is *China Light*.[32] As the presiding judge, Mr Justice Godfrey JA, stated in the judgment:

> '[a]s a matter of history, the common law provided no protection against the misuse of confidential information. No action for damages (the only remedy available for any wrongful act at common law) would lie. Eventually, equity, true to form, stepped in to supplement this deficiency of the common law; it made available the equitable remedy of an injunction to restrain such misuse. Now, however, under the Chancery Amendment Act 1858 (Lord Cairns' Act), damages may be granted in certain cases in lieu of an injunction'.[33]

More importantly, the decision has made it clear that exemplary damages are also available to a breach of confidence case.[34] However, as the purpose of exemplary damages is to punish rather than to compensate, they should only be applied where basic and aggravated compensatory damages are both inadequate.

3. EFFORTS TOWARDS CRIMINALIZATION

Treating trade secret misappropriation as a criminal offence has become an increasingly common practice worldwide.[35] Notwithstanding the global trend, in 2001, the HKBA published a Consultation Paper on Unfair Competition and Intellectual Property Rights, which explicitly voiced against the criminalization of trade secret misappropriation in the foreseeable future. Specifically, the paper pointed out that:

> As with the tort of passing off, the action for breach of confidence has been developed gradually by the courts. Although there is some uncertainty as to the

28. Senior Courts Act 1981, section 50 (UK).
29. Capper, *supra* note 25, 320.
30. *Ibid.*, 323.
31. High Court Ordinance (Cap. 4) section 17.
32. *China Light*, *supra* note 4.
33. *Ibid.*
34. *Ibid.*, at 30D-30E, 34H-34I and 38H.
35. According to a proposal submitted by the United States to the Asia-Pacific Economic Cooperation (APEC) at the 40th Intellectual Property Rights Experts' Group Meeting, about two-thirds of the participating economies had offered criminal prosecution of trade secret misappropriation. *See* U.S.-APEC Technical Assistance to Advance Regional Integration (US-ATAARI), *Trade Secret Protection in the APEC Economies* http://mddb.apec.org/Documents/2015/IPEG/IPEG1/15_ipeg1_027.pdf accessed 20 March 2021.

> scope of the cause of action, for example as to the circumstances in which someone not in a relationship with the owner of the information can nevertheless be subject to an obligation of confidence, the Bar believes that it is sufficiently flexible to be adapted and developed by the courts as necessary. The Bar sees no need to criminalise misuse of trade secrets in Hong Kong.[36]

The HKBA trusted that the judge-made law of confidence provided the flexibility and emphasized equitable doctrines in regulating misuse of trade secrets, rather than the textual content of a pre-made criminal ordinance.

36. HKBA Consultation Paper, *supra* note 5.

TOPIC 1 THE REQUIREMENTS OF TRADE SECRET IN HONG KONG

Jyh-An Lee & Jingwen Liu

1. Legal Issues

What are the requirements of a protectable trade secret?
How to distinguish a trade secret from other forms of confidential information?
Is customer information a protectable trade secret?
What constitutes duty of fidelity and obligation of confidence?

2. The Statutory Law

There is no statutory protection for trade secrets in Hong Kong.[37]

3. The Case Law

As of 15 February 2021, a search of cases at Westlaw Asia with keywords 'trade secret' and 'confidential information' revealed 159 results in Hong Kong. However, most of the decisions did not define what constituted a protectable 'trade secret'. Among the five judgments decided after 2001, which clearly defined 'trade secrets', four of them cited *AXA* and accordingly held that there were five elements constituting a trade secret, which will be introduced below. The only decision among these five cases that did not cite the *AXA* case was made around the same time as *AXA*. The judicial practice in Hong Kong indicates the different levels of protection for confidential information and trade secrets. As explained by the court in *Willwin Development (Asia) Co Ltd v Wei Xing*, '[m]ere confidential information will only be protected during employment and not thereafter, in the absence of any express covenant from the employee ... This is as opposed to trade secrets of the employer, which will be protected even after termination of employment of the employee'.[38]

4. The Leading Case(s)

4.1. Case Information

The High Court of the Hong Kong Special Administrative Region Court of First Instance, HCA 9093/2000, *AXA China Region Insurance Co Ltd and Another v Pacific Century Insurance Co Ltd and Others* [2001] HKCFI 912 (24 July 2001) – While this judgment only concerned plaintiffs' application for interlocutory injunction, delivery up order and disclosure order, it provided the most comprehensive explanation regarding the definition and scope of trade secrets among all court decisions in Hong Kong.

37. Phang, Ho and Lo, *supra* note 1.
38. *Willwin Development (Asia) Co Ltd v Wei Xing* [2016] HKEC 554 [101].

4.2. Summary

An insurance company had poached a large group of individual agents previously working for a competing company in the same industry and at around the same time launched a policy matching scheme specifically targeting policyholders of the latter. The second company subsequently found out that the client information, containing the personal particulars of its policyholders as well as the details of the sold policies stored in its internal electronic system, the access to which was strictly restricted even within the firm itself, had been carried away by those departing agents, who had subsequently joined the competitor. It therefore initiated the current action in court, seeking to enjoin both the individual agents and the competing firm from utilising its confidential information or dealing with its policyholders, on the basis of breach of implied duty of fidelity and breach of confidence, respectively. To make a decision for the current dispute, the court needed first to decide the nature of the client information in question, i.e., whether it had amounted to a protectable trade secret of the plaintiffs. After pondering on the factual grounds of the case, the court concluded that the client information in issue had met all requirements of a trade secret, and thus there was at least a serious issue to be tried as to whether it could be protected as a trade secret. Ultimately, an interlocutory injunction, among others, was granted by the court.

4.3. Facts

Both plaintiffs ('AXA') were under the AXA insurance group, carrying on the business of insurance underwriting. Like most of the insurance companies in Hong Kong, AXA sold insurance policies mainly through the insurance agents appointed by AXA under contracts called 'Agent's Contract'. It was indisputable that these agents, who did not get a basic salary from AXA but rather earn commissions out of the policies they had sold, were not employees of AXA. Each agency was run in a pyramidal structure. From bottom to top, there were agents, managers, senior managers, directors, senior directors and regional directors of the agency. AXA had an internal electronic Sales and Marketing System (SAMS), where the particulars of their policyholders and details of policies, including name, telephone number, address, policy number, expiry date, currency of account, sum insured, amount of premium, cash value, dividend, loan balance and interest thereon, payment mode and the underwriters (if any) were stored. Access to SAMS was restricted to senior branch managers and above and could only be achieved through using a designated personal computer at each agency office. Persons who were allowed access would be given a password and required to sign a Hardware Rental Agreement and Software Licence, which had made express the licensee's obligation of confidentiality.

AXA claimed that the above particulars of their policyholders and details of policies ('Client Data') were its trade secrets. Client Data include any information obtained or derived by an agent in the course of his agency with AXA, not being information known to the agent prior to such obtaining or derivation, and contained in SAMS, and any documents whether in hard copy or electronic form containing such information and any of the documents listed in Schedule C to the Statement of Claim, whether in hard copy or electronic form.

The first defendant Pacific Century Insurance Company (PCI) was also an insurance company and AXA's major competitor. The other defendants ('the Individual Defendants') were insurance agents appointed by AXA. PCI launched a policy matching scheme in March 2000 specifically targeting AXA policyholders so that they may surrender their AXA policies and switch to PCI policies. PCI also approached AXA agents and offered them a 'hefty welcome bonus' to join PCI. As a result, a large number of AXA agents terminated their Agent's Contracts with AXA and joined PCI. Consequently, many of AXA's policyholders who were served by these agents surrendered their AXA policies and switched to PCI policies. At about the same time, AXA noticed that an unusually large amount of their client information from their SAMS had been printed out under the passwords assigned to several Individual Defendants prior to the termination of their agency with AXA.

AXA thus applied to court for interlocutory injunction to: (1) restrain PCI from disclosing, divulging or otherwise using any of AXA's Client Data, restrain PCI from accepting any application for a life insurance policy by persons whose names appeared in AXA's Client Data and who had been approached by any agent of PCI at a time when any of the Client Data were in the possession or under the control of PCI, restrain PCI from soliciting any business by representing that certain specified life insurance products of PCI match or are comparable with the corresponding AXA product and restrain PCI from accepting any application for certain specified life insurance product from any person holding a life insurance product issued by AXA and (2) restrain the Individual Defendants from disclosing, divulging or otherwise making use of any of AXA's Client Data. Specifically, the plaintiffs sought to restrain the Individual Defendants from accepting any life insurance policy application by AXA's ex-clients who had been approached by PCI, as well as those holding an AXA policy, soliciting business by representing that certain life insurance products of PCI match or are comparable with the corresponding AXA product and disclosing, divulging or otherwise making use of any of AXA's Client Data.

4.4. *Reasoning of the Court*

4.4.1. *The General Principle Applicable to the Grant of Interlocutory Injunctions*

The court first applied the *American Cyanamid* Principle, the general principle applicable to the grant of interlocutory injunctions, which had been well settled since the House of Lord's decision in *American Cyanamid Co v Ethicon Ltd.*[39] As established by *American Cyanamid*, '[i]n order for an interlocutory injunction to be granted, the plaintiff's first hurdle is to satisfy the court that the claim is not frivolous or vexatious; in other words, that there is a serious question to be tried … Second, if satisfied that there is a serious question to be tried, the court shall go on to consider whether the

39. *American Cyanamid, supra* note 16, at 407-409.

balance of convenience lies in favour of granting or refusing the interlocutory relief that is sought. In the balancing exercise, the court shall consider whether damages would be an adequate remedy and whether the unsuccessful party would be in a financial position to pay them ... Third, where there is doubt as to the adequacy of the respective remedies in damages available to either party or to both, then the question of balance of convenience arises. Fourth, where other factors appear to be evenly balanced it is a counsel of prudence to take such measures as are calculated to preserve the status quo'.[40]

4.4.2. Five-Step Test for Determining Whether There Is a Serious Question to Be Tried

Based on the above principle, the court needed to first decide whether the plaintiffs had established that there was a serious issue to be tried. Notably, the plaintiffs' case against the Individual Defendants was based on the breach of implied duty of fidelity, whereas that against PCI was based on its breach of confidence. To answer both the questions of whether there was a duty of fidelity on the part of the Individual Defendants and whether there was a duty of confidence on the part of PCI with respect to the use of AXA's Client Data, an antecedent issue would be to determine the nature of the 'Client Data' in dispute, i.e., whether the Client Data were a trade secret or confidential information equivalent to trade secret.

After a thorough examination into the English cases concerning the definition of trade secret, the court concluded that 'a trade secret or its equivalent must be information: –

(1) used in a trade or business (*Lansing Linde* and *Faccenda Chicken* 5(b));
(2) [which] is confidential, i.e. not already in the public domain (*Thomas Marshall v. Guinle* and *Faccenda Chicken*);
(3) [which] can be easily isolated from other information which the employee is free to use so that any man of average intelligence and honesty would think it is improper to use the information at the disposal of his new employer (*Faccenda Chicken* 5(d) and *Printers & Finishers*);
(4) which, if disclosed to a competitor, would be liable to cause real or significant harm to the owner (*Lansing Linde* and *Thomas Marshall v. Guinle*); and
(5) for which the owner of the information must limit its dissemination or at least not encourage or permit its widespread publication or otherwise impress upon the employee the confidentiality of the information (*Lansing Linde* and *Faccenda Chicken* 5(c))'.[41]

Based on the above five-step test, the court found that, first of all, the Client Data were undoubtedly used in trade or business. Second, the Client Data included the personal particulars of AXA's policyholders, which were not in the public domain.

40. *AXA China, supra* note 8, [24]-[27].
41. *Ibid.*, [38].

Third, because each agent handled approximately three-hundred policyholders, the court was far from convinced that the contact details of all these policyholders could be recalled or innocently carried away in the head of an agent. Further, there was no difficulty in finding that the disclosure of the Client Data to PCI would almost certainly cause significant harm to AXA's business because PCI would thus be able to contact AXA's policyholders directly. Last but not least, with the password system and the SAMS, AXA had effectively limited the dissemination of the information and did not encourage its widespread publication. Therefore, AXA's Client Data fulfilled all requirements of a trade secret in Hong Kong. Additionally, the court explained that trade secrets include not only secret formulae for the manufacture of products but also, in an appropriate case, the names of customers and the goods which they buy.

On the premise that the subject information has amounted to trade secrets or confidential information that is equivalent to trade secrets of the plaintiffs, the court could easily find the existence of the Individual Defendants' implied duty of fidelity as well as the PCI's duty of confidence in the given scenario. Further, the court was satisfied that the plaintiffs had established a serious issue to be tried as to whether the defendants had breached their respective duties owed to the plaintiffs. As a result, all orders, including the injunction sought by the plaintiffs, were granted by the court with the amendment made in respect of the coverage of Client Data.

4.5. Legal Analysis

4.5.1. Trade Secrets Enjoy Stronger Protection than Confidential Information

In the English case *Faccenda Chicken*, Goulding J, the presiding judge at the first-instance trial, defined three classes of information: '(i) information which, because of its trivial character or its easy accessibility from public sources of information, cannot be regarded by reasonable persons or by the law as confidential at all; (ii) information which the servant must treat as confidential ... but which once learned necessarily remains in the servant's head and becomes part of his skill and knowledge; (iii) specific trade secrets so confidential that, even though they may necessarily have been learned by heart and even though the servant may have left the service, they cannot lawfully be used for anyone's benefit but the master's'.[42]

Goulding J distinguished trade secrets (category-iii) from other confidential information (category-ii) in the sense that the servant cannot lawfully use trade secrets even if he or she has left the service. However, a servant can use other confidential information after he or she left the service unless there is an express covenant or if the servant deliberately memorizes the confidential information during the employment.[43] Confidential information other than a trade secret enjoys a weaker degree of protection. The main difference lies in the post-employment protection: absent a contractual obligation, trade secrets are still to be protected by the implied duty of fidelity, while confidential information would not be similarly protected. The *Faccenda Chicken* court

42. [1984] I.C.R. 589.
43. *Ibid.*

ruled that a customer name list was neither trade secret nor its equivalent; instead, it was category-ii confidential information. Based on *Faccenda Chicken*, the defendants in this Hong Kong case argued that the Client Data were confidential information but not trade secrets; therefore, an agent's duty of fidelity ceased upon termination of agency.

However, in the present case, the court held that the finding in *Faccenda Chicken* that a customer name list was not a trade secret or its equivalent should be limited to its facts.[44] *Faccenda Chicken* did not lay down any principle that neither customer lists nor customer information amount to trade secret or are equivalent to a trade secret.[45] Instead of following the trichotomy of information in *Faccenda Chicken*, the court cited two other English cases, *SBJ Stephenson Ltd v Mandy* [1999] EWHC 277 (QB) and *Lansing Linde Ltd v Kerr* [1991] 1 WLR 251, to explain that:

> by whatever name the information is called, if it is material which in all the circumstances of the case is of such a highly confidential nature as to require the same protection as a trade secret *eo nomine*, then the law gives it the same protection as a trade secret. It is all a matter of fair and honourable dealing which a person in a fiduciary position must maintain in respect of the information he received in the course of his agency or employment.

In summary, the court did not entirely follow the *Faccenda Chicken* definition of trade secrets, which is information being 'so confidential that, even though they may necessarily have been learned by heart and even though the servant may have left the service, they cannot lawfully be used for anyone's benefit but the master's'. Instead, based on a different line of English case law, the court established its own definition of trade secrets with five elements mentioned above. Nonetheless, the court did not disrupt the common law tradition in the distinction between trade secret and confidential information.

4.5.2. PCI's Breach of Confidence

The plaintiffs' case against the Individual Defendants was based on the breach of implied duty of fidelity, whereas that against PCI was based on its breach of confidence. Duty of fidelity may be created by express terms in a contract or by necessary implication so as to give to a transaction the effect which must have been in contemplation of the parties when they entered into the contract. The duty is readily implied to parties in a fiduciary relation, such as trustee and beneficiary, principal and agent, master and servant and solicitor and client. As Megarry J explained in *Coco v Clark*, the employees had implied obligation of confidence on the basis that 'the circumstances are such that any reasonable man standing in the shoes of the recipient of the information would have realized that upon reasonable grounds the information was being given to him in confidence'.[46] The court in this case ruled that the Agent's Contract imposed on the Individual Defendants an obligation of secrecy in relation to the business of AXA. Therefore, Individual Defendants were in breach of their duty of

44. *AXA China, supra* note 8, [48].
45. *Ibid.*, [44].
46. *Coco v Clark, supra* note 3.

fidelity by making copies of AXA's Client Data during the subsistence of their agency for use in competition with AXA after their agency ended.

The court cited the English case *Coco v Clark* to determine whether PCI was in breach of confidence.[47] The court ruled that AXA's claim of breach of confidence against PCI was substantiated according to the principle in *Coco v Clark* because AXA had proved that: (1) the Client Data which AXA sought to protect have the necessary quality of confidence about them; (2) PCI must know that the information was confidential; (3) it must have been imparted in circumstances importing an obligation of confidence; (4) there must have been an unauthorized use of the information to the detriment of AXA; and (5) PCI must have been dishonest in using the information.[48]

4.6. *Commercial or Industrial Significance*

Confidential information and trade secrets are subject to different levels of protection in Hong Kong. Absent contractual arrangements, the protection of confidential information exists during the employment relation, whereas trade secrets protection through the implied duty of fidelity still exists after the relationship ends. Although this decision set forth the standard for determining what constitutes a trade secret, there will still be room for argument in defining confidential information and trade secrets between parties in litigation. For example, whether 'any man of average intelligence and honesty would think it is improper to use the information at the disposal of his new employer' and whether the disclosure of the subject information will cause 'real or significant harm to the owner' are always debatable. Therefore, to obtain more comprehensive protection over valuable information, businesses are advised to impose more confidence obligations on their employees and partners in the contracts.

The judgment made it clear that a wide range of commercially valuable information is trade secrets, including but not limited to secret formulae for manufacture of products, names of customers and goods they buy, designs or special methods of construction, etc.[49] This case also concerns the use of digital technology and database process to preserve confidential information. As the court required that 'the owner of the information must limit its dissemination or at least not encourage or permit its widespread publication or otherwise impress upon the employee the confidentiality of the information', it is now crucial for the proprietor of confidential information or trade secrets to adopt more encryption technologies in their database. These new technologies can not only reduce the possible leakage of confidential information or trade secrets but also help the information proprietor more easily claim trade secret protection in court. In this case, AXA requires passwords assigned only to senior branch managers and above as a prerequisite to access the SAMS. Other common measures include software automatically screening outgoing electronic files for sensitive keywords that may indicate trade secret leakages, automatic alerts to the system administrator to monitor abnormal internet traffic, etc.

47. *AXA China, supra* note 8, [134].
48. *Ibid.*
49. *Ibid.*, [67].

In another Hong Kong case, *Deacons v White & Case Ltd Liability Partnership and Others*,[50] an equity partner of a law firm switched to another together with almost all of the core members of his team. When seeking career advancement, he provided his prospective employer with a business plan incorporating the work and billing amount undertaken by him and by the entire department. In deciding whether the figures constituted the ex-employer's trade secret, the court considered the fact that such information was stored in the second highest level of access in the plaintiff's intranet, which was restricted to equity partners only, and the information system consisting of various levels of access corresponding with the seniority of employees had secured the secrecy or confidentiality of such financial information.[51] Therefore, businesses are advised to design their network system governing access to confidential information according to the ranks and need of individual employees.

50. [2003] 3 HKLRD 670.
51. *Ibid.*, [137].

TOPIC 2 THE VALIDITY AND SCOPE OF CONFIDENTIALITY AND/OR NON-COMPETITION TERMS

Jyh-An Lee & Jingwen Liu

1. Legal Issues

Is a confidentiality or non-competition clause in an employee's employment contract valid and enforceable after the termination of employment?
Under what circumstances will such restrictive covenants be deemed reasonable and necessary in protecting the former employer's legitimate interests?
Under what circumstances will the scope of the restraint be deemed too wide to be enforceable?
Who shall bear the burden to prove the reasonableness of such restrictive covenants?

2. The Statutory Law

There is no statutory protection for trade secrets in Hong Kong. Nor is there any statute governing non-competition agreement therein.

3. The Case Law

As of 19 February 2021, a search of cases at Westlaw Asia using the keywords 'confidential information', 'restrictive covenant' and 'non-competition' revealed 20 results. There were 11 decisions which specifically touched upon the enforceability of a particular non-competition covenant. Among all covenants in these 11 decisions, only 1 was acceptable to the court, while all others were viewed as unenforceable (or at least without a good prospect of success where the action was in an interim stage). A glance at the case law demonstrates the hardship facing employers in enforcing covenants of the kind.

The present case, *Degreeasia Ltd t/a Hong Kong Institute of Continuing Education v Paules Lee Siu Yuk and Others*,[52] has been widely cited in subsequent judgments relevant to restrictive covenants in Hong Kong. The principle set forth in the case is as below:

(1) If the court is to uphold the validity of any covenant in restraint of trade, the covenantee must show that the covenant is both reasonable in the interests of the contracting parties and reasonable in the interests of the public.
(2) A distinction is, however, to be drawn between (a) a covenant against competition entered into by a vendor with the purchaser of the goodwill of a business, which will be upheld as necessary to protect the subject-matter of the sale, provided that it is confined to the area within which competition on the part of the vendor would likely injure the purchaser in the enjoyment of goodwill he has bought, and (b) a covenant between master and servant

52. *Degreeasia Ltd t/a Hong Kong Institute of Continuing Education v Paules Lee Siu Yuk and Others* (25/06/2010, HCA1686/2006).

designed to prevent competition by the servant with the master after the termination of his contract of service.

(3) In the case of contracts between master and servant, covenants against competition as such are never upheld by the court.

(4) The subject-matter in respect of which an employer may legitimately claim protection from an employee by a covenant in restraint of trade was further identified by Lord Wilberforce in *Stenhouse Ltd v. Phillips* [1974] AC 391, at 400, as follows: 'The employers' claim for protection must be based upon the identification of some advantage or asset inherent in the business which can properly be regarded as, in a general sense, his property, and which it would be unjust to allow the employee to appropriate for his own purposes, even though he, the employee, may have contributed to its creation.'

(5) If the court is to uphold restrictions which a covenant imposes upon the freedom of action of a servant after he had left the service of the master, the master must satisfy the court that the restrictions are no greater than are reasonably necessary for the protection of the master in his business. For any covenant in restraint of trade to be treated as reasonable in the interests of the parties, it must afford no more than adequate protection to the benefit of the party in whose favour it is imposed.[53]

4. The Leading Case(s)

4.1. Case Information

The High Court of the Hong Kong Special Administrative Region Court of First Instance, HCA 1686/2006, *Degreeasia Ltd t/a Hong Kong Institute of Continuing Education v Paules Lee Siu Yuk and Others* [2010] HKCFI 567 (decided on 25 June 2010).

4.2. Summary

Two ex-employees joined a competing company, and nine customers followed them to join the company as well. The ex-employer sued the ex-employees for, *inter alia*, breach of restrictive covenant and misappropriation of trade secrets and confidential information. The court held that: (1) the one-year restraint after employment was too wide to be enforceable, and the ex-employer failed to demonstrate that such a restraint was reasonable and necessary for protecting its legitimate interests; and (2) isolated telephone numbers of customers did not constitute trade secrets. All claims of the plaintiff were therefore rejected by the court.

4.3. Facts

The plaintiff, Degreeasia Limited ('Degreeasia'), was a company offering overseas universities' degree courses to students in Hong Kong via its Hong Kong Institute of Continuing Education. The 2nd defendant, Institute of Advanced Learning, offered similar courses in Hong Kong. The 1st and 3rd defendants, both ex-employees of Degreeasia, joined the 2nd defendant after their employment with Degreeasia.

53. *Ibid.*, [33].

The 1st defendant, Ms Paules Lee, was employed by Degreeasia as an 'education consultant' since 25 June 2005. The employment contract included a confidentiality clause, which prohibited her from disclosing any 'information, operation procedures, [or] business practice secrecy' of Degreeasia at any time. On 1 September 2005, her position at the company was changed to a 'student services coordinator' in a new employment contract. The new contract imposed a time limit to the original confidentiality clause, which was during the time of the employment and two years after its termination. Meanwhile, a restrictive clause was added to the new employment contract, prohibiting her from enticing away any staff or clients of Degreeasia, or being employed or enticed to 'any consultancy position for salaried or non-salaried, to any relevant company, entity, association or organization in the education, training & development or whatsoever industry' within one year after leaving the company. Lee was dismissed by Degreeasia on 10 June 2006. On 4 July 2006, Lee, introduced by the 3rd defendant, joined the 2nd defendant as a 'part-time, temporary receptionist'. Lee's job at the Institute of Advanced Learning was in nature close to an education consultant, who was responsible for the promotion of the courses and recruitment of students.

The 3rd defendant, Mr Kenny Suen, had first been employed by Degreeasia as a marketing manager since 6 May 2003. The employment contract at the time did not include any confidentiality clause or restrictive covenant. On 1 February 2005, Degreeasia offered Suen another employment contract, which included restrictive clauses similar to those imposed on Lee. However, this contract was never signed by Suen. Suen decided to leave Degreeasia on 27 January 2006 and joined the 2nd defendant on 13 March 2006 as a programme manager.

During her employment at Degreeasia, Lee served as the class mistress of Class A3, the students of which were enrolled in the Benedictine College programme. Lee had access to information such as the name list, timetable, transcripts, addresses and telephone numbers of the students. According to Lee, she maintained good relationships with some students; therefore, they contacted her from time to time outside of office hours. In July 2006, after Lee switched to the 2nd defendant, she and Lam Yiu, a student from Class A3, had a telephone conversation. Over that phone call, Lee mentioned to Lam Yiu that Benedictine College had dropped in ranking and invited her to pay a visit to the 2nd defendant to explore more study possibilities. After the phone call, Lam Yiu shared what she had heard with some other students in Class A3, who were all worried about Benedictine College's dropping in ranking. Consequently, a batch of seven students ended up visiting the 2nd defendant's premises, with several other batches following. Both Lee and Suen were present during the students' visits, and Suen introduced them to a course of Utah State University (USU) offered at the 2nd defendant. Eventually, nine students previously enrolled in the Benedictine College course transferred to the USU programme.

The plaintiff claimed that both individual defendants were bound by the restrictive covenant and confidentiality clause in their respective contracts. The plaintiff also argued that in any event, both individual defendants were subject to the implied duties of fidelity during and after the employment. The plaintiff's claims against the two individual defendants were, *inter alia*, for breaching their restrictive covenants by assuming duty at the 2nd defendant during the restrictive period and enticing students away from the plaintiff to the 2nd defendant, and that Lee had, during her employment with Degreeasia, 'compiled, duplicated or made a copy of a confidential student list containing the names, telephone numbers, contact details and addresses of Degreeasia's students and had kept it' when she moved to the 2nd defendant. The 2nd defendant was alleged by the plaintiff to have, among others, knowingly and dishonestly committed this breach by employing the Individual Defendants and misappropriated the plaintiff's confidential information and trade secrets. All allegations were denied by the respective defendants.

4.4. ***Reasoning of the Court***

4.4.1. *The Validity and Enforceability of the Restrictive Covenant*

In deciding the validity of the restrictive and confidentiality clauses, the court first set out that '[t]he basic rule is that covenants in restraint of trade are unenforceable unless they can be shown to be reasonable in the interests of the parties and in the public interest (see *Bridge v Deacons* [1984] 1 AC 705 at 713A–B per Lord Fraser of Tullybelton). It is trite that the burden of demonstrating the reasonableness of a covenant is on the party seeking to enforce it, in this case Degreeasia'.[54] Citing Hoffman LJ in *Steiner (UK) Ltd v Spray*, the court pointed out that '[i]t is clearly established that the employer is not entitled to protect himself merely against competition. The only legitimate interests which, as against a former employee, he is entitled to protect are his trade secrets and customer connections to the extent that the employee may have gained influence over the customer so they would be likely to follow the employee to his or her new employment'. It further went on to apply this principle to the present case to examine whether the restrictive covenants were valid.

In the case of Lee, the restrictive covenant included two types of prohibition: non-employment and non-solicitation restrictions. The court ruled that these restrictive covenants were unenforceable since they failed the reasonableness test. First, Lee's last position at Degreeasia was a student services coordinator, which was purely administrative, not academic, in nature. The court questioned whether there should be a post-employment restraint at all. Normally students choose to enrol in a course because of the education quality, rather than their relationship with someone like Lee. Furthermore, even if the existence of a restrictive covenant were justifiable, the language of the clause was too wide to be enforceable. The court explained that the phrase 'or whatsoever industry' was undoubtedly too wide. Additionally, the judge Mr Recorder Shieh, SC found the one-year period unreasonable because little training was provided to Lee when she took up the position in the first place. Accordingly, Degreeasia needed no such period as long as one year to locate and train a backup to replace her. Moreover, the ambit of restriction was too wide because 'consultancy' was not properly defined and could potentially cover industries remote to the plaintiff's business interests. Third, the court applied the principle of proportionality and held

54. *Ibid.*, [32].

that enforcing the restrictive clause would essentially 'deprive Paules Lee's ability to earn a living in a way which is wholly disproportionate to any legitimate interest of Degreeasia'.[55]

With regard to the plaintiff's claim against Suen, as an antecedent issue, the court ruled that absent the signature of Suen, the default position of law provided that the unsigned contract incorporating the restrictive and confidentiality clauses was not binding on him, unless Degreeasia could adduce evidence for a rebuttal, which it had failed to do. The court further explained that even if such clauses were binding on Suen, the validity of such clauses would still fail the reasonableness test. As a marketing manager, Suen's position was a salesperson in nature and he did not have influence over students regarding the choice of courses. Therefore, his position did not justify a post-employment restraint.

In summary, the plaintiff's breach of restrictive covenant claims against both individual defendants failed because the restrictive covenants in question per se were unreasonable and thus unenforceable.

4.4.2. Misappropriation of Trade Secrets and Confidential Information

The plaintiff's claim against Lee for misusing the former's confidential information or trade secrets to solicit students also failed. The court cited the threefold classification in *Faccenda Chicken* to categorise information acquired during employment as below:

(1) information which is trivial, or accessible from public sources;
(2) information which is confidential, either because the employee was expressly told so or because of its character, but which once learned necessarily remains in the employee's head and becomes part of his own skill and knowledge applied in the course of his employer's business; and
(3) specific trade secrets.

For the first category (i.e., information that is trivial or publicly accessible), the use of information is not restricted, whether during or after the employment relationship. For the third category (i.e., trade secrets), no one other than the owner could legitimately use such information, no matter whether during or after the employment relationship. The rule for the second category is more complicated. During the employment period, the employee is subject to a confidentiality obligation in the employment contract. Even in the absence of an expressed obligation, the employee still bears the implied duty of good faith or fidelity during the employment. To obtain post-employment protection for information falling under this category, the employer could only rely on an express term in the form of a written contract. Nevertheless, Mr Recorder Shieh, SC made clear that a covenant explicitly prohibiting the post-employment use of 'all confidential information' of the ex-employer was invalid and therefore unenforceable. The employer could only adopt a 'suitably worded restrictive

55. *Ibid.*, [58].

covenant against working for particular persons in particular localities and within particular timeframes'.[56]

Based on the above principle, Mr Recorder Shieh, SC reasoned that Lee would only be liable if she had either: '(a) utilized Degreeasia's trade secrets in approaching and soliciting Lam Yiu and her group; or (b) "stolen" Degreeasia's confidential information during her employment and used it for the purpose of approaching and soliciting Lam Yiu and her group'. In the present case, the evidence was insufficient to support Degreeasia's claim that Lee made a wholesale copy of student lists consisting of their relevant information, but only sufficient to the extent that Lee had exchanged telephone numbers with a number of students in her class. In deciding whether these contact numbers had amounted to Degreeasia's trade secrets, Mr Recorder Shieh, SC opined that '[t]hough trade secret is not limited to things such as a secret trade process or formula, I refuse to accept any suggestion that it could cover a telephone number (which belongs to the owner of the telephone, not to Degreeasia) which the owner thereof is free to give out to other people'.[57] Furthermore, although the collection of customer information including their telephone numbers might be regarded as confidential information or trade secrets, such protection was for the efforts in the compilation rather than the telephone numbers per se. Therefore, the isolated telephone numbers given to Lee in a social context did not even qualify as confidential information, not to mention trade secrets. Therefore, the above-mentioned telephone numbers were neither confidential information nor trade secrets.

4.5. *Legal Analysis*

A restrictive covenant is a clause in the employment contract governing the employee's post-employment behaviours.[58] The restrictive covenant may take the form of a non-competition, non-solicitation, non-dealing, non-poaching or non-disclosure clause.[59] The general principle in Hong Kong and many other common law jurisdictions is that such a post-employment restrictive covenant is invalid and unenforceable, unless it can be proven to be reasonable, not only in the interest of the contracting parties but also in terms of public interests.[60] The principles governing the validity and enforceability of a post-employment restrictive covenant were well illustrated in another Hong Kong case, *Natuzzi Spa v De Coro Ltd*, as below:

56. *Ibid.*, [123].
57. *Ibid.*, [143].
58. Richard E. Kaye, 'Cause of Action to Enforce Noncompetition Covenant in Employment Contract', in Thomson Reuters and West (eds), *Causes of Action (Second)* (Thomson Reuters 2019).
59. Pattie Walsh, Alison Smith and Minter Ellison, 'Protecting Business, Customer and Client Relationships from Competitors and Departing Employees in Hong Kong' (2008) 18(2) Employment & Industrial Relations Law 22, 23.
60. *Herbert Morris Ltd v Saxelby* [1916] AC 688; *Bridge v Deacons* [1984] 1 AC 705; *Office Angels Ltd v Rainer-Thomas and O'Connor* [1991] IRLR 214.

(a) No employer is entitled to make use of a restrictive covenant to protect himself against competition per se. A covenant against competition per se is not reasonable and accordingly void.
(b) An employer is not entitled to prevent his ex-employee from using the skill and knowledge in his trade or profession which he learnt in the course of his employment. Nor is he entitled to prevent his ex-employee from using in the service of some person other than the employer the general knowledge the employee has acquired of the employer's scheme of organisation and methods of business.
(c) An employer is entitled to make use of a restrictive covenant to protect his interests in his trade secrets and in his trade connections. However, the restrictive covenant, to be valid, must afford no more than adequate protection to the party in whose favour it is imposed. It must be reasonable not only in reference to the interests of the parties concerned but also in reference to the interests of the public.
(d) The onus of proving the reasonableness of the restriction rests on the party who seeks to enforce the restriction. The more onerous the restriction, the heavier the weight of the onus.[61]

Similarly, in this case the restrictive covenant between Degreeasia and Lee was unenforceable, unless Degreeasia could demonstrate the scope of the restriction was reasonable and necessary to protect its interests. Decisive factors in the reasonableness test included the nature of the employment, the duration and ambit of the restriction, the principle of proportionality, etc.[62]

4.6. *Commercial or Industrial Significance*

Restrictive covenants have been widely adopted in employment agreements to manage the risk relevant to confidential information and labour turnover. However, this case reveals that a blind inclusion of such covenants to the maximum degree may turn out to be an unfavourable legal and business arrangement. Put differently, despite the employers' ambition to maximise the protection for its confidential information, an overly broad covenant may cause its invalidity.

To be legally enforceable in Hong Kong, a covenant needs to be reasonable in its restriction of duration, geography, and scope of work. Although the court in *Degreeasia* held that the duration of one year is too long for the covenant to be enforceable, this does not mean that all covenants of more than one year are unenforceable. The determination of reasonableness is made on a case-by-case basis and concerns the role, responsibility and seniority of the employee, the nature of the employment, and the norm in the industry. In another Hong Kong case, *Rever (AMA) Salon Ltd v Kung Wai For & Others*,[63] the court ruled that a one-year restraint was necessary to protect the

61. *Natuzzi Spa v De Coro Ltd* (16/06/2006, HCA4166/2003) [44].
62. *Degreeasia, supra* note 52.
63. *Rever (AMA) Salon Ltd. v Kung Wai For, Danny and Others* (24/10/2001, HCA10399/2000).

interests of the plaintiff, an A-grade hair salon[64] practising in the commercial area of Tsim Sha Tsui in Hong Kong. The court reached this conclusion after considering the dependence of a hair salon on its regular customers, the ease with which a customer may be persuaded to follow an employee who leaves, the difficulty in policing and enforcing a non-soliciting provision, and the number of salons and number of A-grade salons in Hong Kong and in Tsim Sha Tsui specifically.[65]

There was no geographic limit in the restrictive covenant in *Degreeasia*. Generally speaking, an unlimited covenant in geography is not per se invalid, but the employer must show a business presence of an international character and the reasonableness of the restraint in light of its worldwide competition.[66] Degreeasia clearly did not fall into this kind, as its services specifically targeted local students in Hong Kong. Therefore, another takeaway from this case is that to play safe, local businesses may wish to tailor a precise locality term, taking into account the reach of its business and the characters of its industry. In *Rever (AMA) Salon*, the scope of the restraint was precisely defined to 'a radius of 1 mile of the premises of the Company ... where such premises were on Hong Kong Island and within a radius of 3/4 mile of the premises of the Company ... where such premises were on Kowloon'.[67] Additionally, the ambit of works prohibited by the restrictive covenant is also subject to the reasonableness test. Overly broad terms such as 'whatsoever industry' are highly likely to be void. Additionally, other considerations such as the hardship on the employee and public interest may also affect the reasonableness determination.

In summary, business and legal professionals are advised to consider a variety of factors relevant to the subject employment when drafting a restrictive covenant.

64. At the time of the litigation, the grade of hair salons was determined by the charge of a basic shampoo and cut. The salon was categorised as A grade if it charged more than HKD 350, B grade if the charge was between HKD 250 and HKD 350, and C grade if it was below HKD 250. *See Rever (AMA) Salon, supra* note 63.
65. *Rever (AMA) Salon, supra* note 63.
66. *Cranston Print Works Co. v Pothier*, 848 A.2d 213, 220 (R.I. 2004).
67. *Rever (AMA) Salon, supra* note 63.

TOPIC 3 THE BURDEN OF PROOF AND ITS REVERSAL

Jingwen Liu & Jyh-An Lee

1. Legal Issues

On what evidential grounds can a breach of confidence claim be established?
Who shall bear the burden of proof in a breach of confidence claim?
When will the burden shift to the defendant in a breach of confidence case?

2. The Statutory Law

There is generally no statutory protection for trade secrets in Hong Kong.[68]

3. The Case Law

As of 8 March 2021, search for cases with keywords 'duty of confidence' and 'inference' at Westlaw Asia revealed 38 results in Hong Kong. Although most of the cases do not directly deal with the issue of who shall bear the burden of proving a misappropriation, an inference has been drawn in five of the above cases against the defendants, whose breach was either established by the court or at least considered as raising a serious issue to be tried.

An inference to be drawn, despite not being a complete reversal of burden of proof, allows the burden to be partly shifted to the defendant when prima facie evidence has been adduced on the part of the plaintiff. When it comes to a breach of confidence cause of action in particular, the case law in Hong Kong has made clear that even though the legal burden of proving breach is on the plaintiff, once he has proved the confidential nature of the information and the duty of confidence on the part of the defendant, the burden then shifts to the defendant to adduce evidence to show that he had not misused or disclosed the information which is confidential in nature.[69]

That said, in most cases, the finding of a breach of confidence by way of inference is not common. As the court in *Devere Group Hong Kong Ltd v Nicholas Edward John Smith* put it, when reaching a conclusion of breach of confidence as an inference to be drawn, '[a]ny such inference must be properly grounded in the primary facts of this case'.[70] The general principles guiding the drawing of an inference in Hong Kong can be found in *Nina Kung v Wong Din Shin*.[71] In particular, the said decision warned against the risk of courts 'indulging in conjecture under the guise of drawing an inference where the primary evidence does not logically and reasonably justify the particular inference in question. It is not permissible merely to choose what may be the more likely of two guesses if neither was properly justified by the primary facts'.[72]

68. Phang, Ho and Lo, *supra* note 1.
69. *William Allan v Messrs Ng & Co. (A Firm) and Another* [2012] 2 HKLRD 160 [150].
70. *Devere Group Hong Kong Ltd v Nicholas Edward John Smith* [2014] HKEC 570 [33].
71. *Nina Kung v Wong Din Shin* (2005) 8 HKCFAR 387.
72. *Ibid.*, [185]-[187].

4. The Leading Case(s)

4.1. *Case Information*

The District Court of the Hong Kong Special Administrative Region, DCCJ 1178/2009, *Dunamis International Co Ltd v Chan Hong Kit and Others* [2010] HKDC 242 (20 October 2010).

4.2. *Summary*

Ex-employees started their own business in competition with the plaintiff. Ex-employees used acquired customer information and a price list compiled by the plaintiff and stored in the plaintiff's internal databases to solicit customers away from the plaintiff by offering better prices. The plaintiff sued for, *inter alia*, breach of confidence for misusing the confidential information contained in these databases. The court held that when it came to breach of confidence, it was always a matter of inference as to whether the subject information was utilised by the defendants, given the envisaged difficulty for the plaintiff to adduce direct evidence to prove such breach. Because it was not likely to be a coincidence that the defendants' company had traded with numerous customers of the plaintiff located in different regions around the globe whose information was hard to find through the internet, the defendants' failure to offer a reasonable explanation aided the inference to be drawn in favour of the plaintiff.

4.3. *Facts*

The plaintiff was a wholesaler of mobile phones and mobile phone accessories incorporated in Hong Kong with customers around the world. All three defendants were former employees of the plaintiff. The 1st defendant, Mr Chan Hong Kit, had been employed by the plaintiff since 25 April 2005 as a salesperson. The 2nd defendant, Mr Wong Kwok Man, was employed as a sales coordinator by the plaintiff on 24 April 2007, and the 3rd defendant, Mr Sham Lai Kam, first came on board as the plaintiff's IT technician on 25 June 2007. The court found that all three defendants were governed by the plaintiff's 'Internal Rules and Regulations', which provided that, without the company's consent, an employee should not, within six months after resignation, take up occupation at any companies of the same kind; otherwise, the company reserves the right to claim compensation for all its loss.

The plaintiff had complied the information of all its clients or potential clients in its customer database. The entries therein included the names, addresses, email addresses, phone numbers, contact persons, the passwords assigned to the customers for their access to the plaintiff's website for price quotation, the models which the customers had previously ordered and the special pricing codes which represent the gap between the price and the cost of each product sold, etc. Together with the customer database was a price list consisting of particulars and descriptions of the products, costs it secured from its suppliers and prices it offered to different customers. Both the customer database and the price list were considered sensitive in nature, and thus their internal access was restricted to the sales and IT persons of the plaintiff exclusively. Meanwhile, for the sake of smooth communication with clients, each of the plaintiff's staff members was provided with a company email address as well as a Hotmail account with the sole purpose of setting up an MSN account to keep contact with the clients. The plaintiff, however, stressed internally to its employees that any order from clients should be placed through the company account, whereas Hotmail was not an official work email account.

On 7 April 2008, the director and founder of the plaintiff, Mr Lee, decided to dismiss the 1st defendant Chan due to his unsatisfactory performance. Prior to informing Chan about the decision, Lee instructed the plaintiff's sales manager, Mr Fung, to log into Chan's Hotmail account and check his MSN records. Mr Fung then found that the password to Chan's Hotmail account had been changed. He subsequently requested Chan to provide the new password, and the request was refused by Chan. It was not until the next day when Chan was formally discharged by Lee did he agree to cooperate and provide the new password to the plaintiff. By that time, it was discovered that most of the emails in his Hotmail account and MSN records had been deleted.

Since the departure of Chan, the 3rd defendant Mr Sham had taken up a concurrent position of a sales coordinator to fill Chan's shoes. However, given the close friendship among the three defendants, Mr Lee specifically warned Wong and Sham that they should never share any plaintiff's information with Chan since the latter was no longer an employee of the company. However, Mr Fung logged into Wong's Hotmail account in around early June 2008 and discovered that there was a chat history between Wong and 'Peter (UK)', whose registered email address happened to be the same one appearing on Chan's resume. In their conversation, the price list was imparted to this 'Peter (UK)' as requested. Because the plaintiff became suspicious and particularly concerned about the close relationship among the three defendants, both the 2nd and 3rd defendants were dismissed on 15 June 2008.

On 11 June 2008, a company named 'Masterfone' was incorporated in Hong Kong, with a registered business scope of 'trading and entertainment production'. Under cross-examination, it was conceded that the four shareholders of Masterfone were actually the respective parents of the three defendants and a common friend of the three. All three defendants had helped set up the business and were engaged in its operation after their dismissal at the plaintiff.

The plaintiff alleged that some of its customers to which the 1st and 2nd defendants were the responsible sales and contact person while they were working at the plaintiff had been doing business with Masterfone, and as a result, they did not place orders with the plaintiff as frequently as they had before. Five such customers were enumerated by the plaintiff, and one of them had even explicitly confessed to the plaintiff that they had been doing business with Masterfone because it had offered better prices. According to the plaintiff, all of these customers were small- or medium-sized companies based in North America or Europe. Some of them might not even have an official website and thus it was difficult to locate their information online. The plaintiff therefore brought this suit to the court, alleging the defendants had, *inter alia*, breached their duties of fidelity owed to the plaintiff, the relevant clauses in their employment contracts, and duties of confidence.

4.4. *Reasoning of the Court*

4.4.1. *Whether the Customer Database and the Price List Were Trade Secrets of the Plaintiff*

When determining the confidentiality of the subject information contained in the databases, the court cited several English cases and laid down the following principles:

(i) A trade secret is information which, if disclosed to a competitor, would cause real harm to the owner of the secret. It must be information used in a trade of business, and the owner must limit the dissemination of it or at least not encourage or permit its widespread publication. It includes not only secret formulae for the manufacture of products but also, in an appropriate case, the names of customers and the goods which they buy.[73]

(ii) To determine whether a particular piece of information is a trade secret or equivalent to a trade secret, it is necessary to consider: (a) the nature of the employment, for example, whether the status of the employee was such that he regularly handled confidential information and recognised it as such or whether the information was only handled by a restricted number of employees; (b) the nature of the information itself; (c) whether the employer had stressed the confidentiality of the information to the employee; and (d) whether the information could be easily isolated from other non-confidential information which was part of the same package of information.[74]

Having regard to the above criteria, the court concluded that the customer database and the price list at issue constituted not only confidential information but also trade secrets of the plaintiff. Specifically, the court took into account the following factors:

(i) the information contained in the customer database and the price list was used in the plaintiff's business;

(ii) only a limited number of employees who had been designated as 'authorized persons' could have access to the customer database and the price list;

(iii) if the information contained in the customer database and the price list was disclosed to the plaintiff's competitor, real or significant harm would be caused to the plaintiff. Lists of customers, their contact information, their record of past purchases and the prices offered are no doubt valuable items of information which, if disclosed to competitors, would enable those competitors to lure the plaintiff's customers away;

(iv) the 1st defendant admitted during cross-examination that the information contained in the customer database was sensitive information, and himself would never give away Masterfone's list of customers to its competitors because if that were done, Masterfone's business might well be adversely affected; and

73. *Lansing Linde Ltd. v Kerr* [1991] 1 WLR 251 at 260.
74. *Faccenda Chicken Ltd. v Fowler* [1986] 1 All ER 617 at 626e-627g.

(v) as some of the customer companies do not have their own website, it was difficult for the plaintiff's competitors to find out information about them.[75]

Notably, one of the arguments put forward by the defendant's counsel was that there was no evidence showing that the plaintiff had impressed the defendants on the confidential nature of the customer database and the price list. This argument was rejected by the court, on the grounds that the said information was restricted to only limited members of the plaintiff, a password was required to get access, the 1st defendant acknowledged that he would deem such customer information of Masterfone to be sensitive himself, and the confidential nature of such information would be recognised by 'a man of ordinary honesty and intelligence'.[76] As a result, the information contained in the customer database and price list was categorised by the court as trade secrets.

4.4.2. *Whether the Defendants Had Breached Their Duties of Confidence*

Although some of the plaintiff's claims were dismissed by the court because of inadequate evidence, inference was drawn in favour of the plaintiff regarding the defendants' breach of confidence by the defendants' providing of the customer database and price list to Masterfone. In particular, the court agreed with the plaintiff's counsel and held that 'it is always a matter of inference as to whether a company had made use of the confidential information of a plaintiff because the plaintiff will seldom be able to have direct evidence of a defendant using such confidential information'.[77] In the present case, the plaintiff had adduced evidence (e.g., the MSN records) to show that Masterfone had done business with quite a few small- and medium-sized enterprises located in the US, Poland, Canada, Slovakia, etc., which were all previous clients of the plaintiff with their information stored in the customer database. Further, there was also evidence from one of these client companies stating that they had been placing orders from Masterfone since June 2008 because the latter had offered a more competitive price to them.

The court held that although the burden was always on the plaintiff to prove its case, the circumstances in this case required the defendants to bear certain burden of proof as well. Since the defendants failed to explain why Masterfone transacted with a large number of the plaintiff's previous customers, it could be inferred that those business transactions were not mere coincidence. Instead, what could be inferred here was that the defendants utilised the plaintiff's customer database as well as the price list to divert business away to Masterfone. Therefore, it was unproved how the subject information was disclosed, misappropriated, or utilised by the defendants, but considering their previous positions at the plaintiff, their access to the subject information, and their clinging relationship with Masterfone (that Masterfone was indeed set up by them), the court found as a matter of inference that the three defendants had provided

75. *Dunamis International Co Ltd v Chan Hong Kit and Others* (DCCJ1178/2009, unreported, 20 October 2010) [153].
76. *Ibid.*, [156].
77. *Ibid.*, [232].

the customer database and price list to Masterfone and thus breached their respective duties of confidence.

As a result, the court ordered against the defendants, restraining them from relying on and/or making use of the customer database (or any part thereof) and from disclosing the customer database (or any part thereof) to any third party until further order.[78]

4.5. *Legal Analysis*

In a case concerning a breach of confidence claim, onerous burden of proof is on the plaintiff with respect to the confidentiality of the subject information, the importation of a duty of confidence, and the occurrence of the alleged breach to the detriment of the plaintiff.[79] If any compensatory damages are claimed, the plaintiff also has to prove it has suffered actual loss due to the misconduct and to quantify the loss in sum.[80] If the plaintiff has adduced sufficient evidence on the confidentiality of the information and there exists a contractual or equitable duty of confidence, the burden will shift to the defendant to prove it did not commit the alleged breach, to the extent that, had the defendant failed to discharge its burden of proof, an inference may be drawn at the discretion of the judge in favour of the plaintiff, given the anticipated hardship faced by the plaintiff to adduce direct evidence to prove a breach.[81] Yet, it should not be regarded as a total reversal of the general position of law, as the drawing of inference is always subject to the factual circumstances and judges' discretion, and consequently less certain than a statutory presumption.

In *Coco v Clark*, Megarry J identified three elements in establishing a breach of confidence claim.[82] To substantiate a claim based on breach of confidence, all three elements must be proven to the court's satisfaction. The burden of proof of each element is analysed below.

4.5.1. *Confidentiality and Relevance of the Information*

In any breach of confidence litigation, the plaintiff needs to prove that the subject information is used in trade or business,[83] it is confidential and not in public domain,[84] it is easily separated from other information which an employee is free to utilise,[85] it will be detrimental to the owner if disclosed to a competitor,[86] and it has been in limited circulation due to the precautions taken by the owner.[87] The plaintiff also has to prove

78. *Ibid.*, [243].
79. *Coco v Clark, supra* note 3.
80. *William Allan, supra* note 69.
81. *Dunamis, supra* note 75, [232].
82. *See* text accompanied by *supra* note 3.
83. *Lansing Linde, supra* note 73; *Faccenda Chicken, supra* note 74, 5(b).
84. *Thomas Marshall (Exports) Ltd v Guinle* [1979] Ch 227; *Faccenda Chicken, supra* note 74.
85. *Faccenda Chicken, supra* note 74, 5(d); *Printers & Finishers Ltd. v Holloway* [1965] R.P.C. 239.
86. *Lansing Linde, supra* note 73; *Thomas Marshall, supra* note 84.
87. *Lansing Linde, supra* note 73; *Faccenda Chicken, supra* note 6, 5(c).

that precautionary measures have been taken to maintain the secrecy of the subject information.

In the present case, witnesses were called upon by the plaintiff to demonstrate that the latter relied heavily upon the customer database and price list in its daily operation, and the plaintiff had limited their access to only staff members in the sales and IT departments, to each of whom a password was assigned to prevent the leakage of confidential information. The plaintiff also illustrated that once the information stored in the databases was leaked, significant harm would be caused to its business because its competitors would be able to seduce its customers away by offering better prices, as price was highly sensitive in the mobile wholesale businesses.

4.5.2. *An Express or Implied Duty of Confidence*

An express clause of confidentiality in a contract is normally a proper documentary proof of the confidence obligation.[88] Absent an explicit agreement, whether the implied duty of confidence will survive the expiration of the contract and impose a post-termination obligation depends on factual circumstances.[89] While a non-contractual obligation of confidence arises from equity, the finding of the obligation by equity normally involves judges' discretion.[90] Little guidance has been provided to aggrieved plaintiffs as to how the 'circumstances importing an obligation of confidence' could be proved on evidence. The plaintiff may alternatively claim a breach of fiduciary duty by proving the fiduciary relationship between the parties.[91]

4.5.3. *The Misuse of the Information to the Detriment of the Plaintiff*

While the burden is always on the plaintiff to prove its case in a civil dispute,[92] *Dunamis* has made clear that when it comes to breach of confidence, inference can be drawn in determining whether the confidential information has been utilised. Inference, as classically defined, is 'the link by which an evidentiary fact is connected with the principal, which latter is said to be inferred or deduced from the evidentiary one, or to be a conclusion from it'.[93] As supported by the *Dunamis* court, the rationale behind the inference is the anticipated difficulties for the plaintiff to adduce direct evidence proving such breach.[94]

---

88. Emir Crowne and Tasha De Freitas, 'Canada's Inadequate Legal Protection Against Industrial Espionage' (2013) 13 Chicago-Kent Journal of Intellectual Property 192, 204.
89. In the employment context, this may include: (i) the nature of the employee's employment; (ii) the nature of the information itself (whether or not the information can be classified as a trade secret or requires the level of protection of a trade secret); (iii) whether the employer impressed upon the employee the confidentiality of the information (not only in words but also in attitude towards the information); and (iv) whether the relevant information could be easily isolated from other information the employee is allowed to disclose. *See Faccenda Chicken, supra* note 6.
90. Crowne and Freitas, *supra* note 88, 203.
91. *Ibid.*
92. *Dunamis, supra* note 75, [237].
93. John Reynolds Gulson, *Philosophy of Proof in Its Relation to the English Law of Judicial Evidence* (G. Routledge 1905).
94. *Dunamis, supra* note 75, [232].

A similar approach was adopted in the High Court decision *William Allan v Messrs Ng & Co. (A Firm) and Another*,[95] in which a solicitor's firm had acquired confidential information from its quasi-client from a general and informal consultation and subsequently misused that information to represent the opposite party in a parallel suit. The court held that once the plaintiff has proved to the satisfaction of the court that: (1) the subject information had been imparted to the defendants; (2) the subject information was confidential in nature; and (3) the subject information was relevant to the parallel proceedings, 'the burden shifted to the defendants to adduce sufficient evidence to show that they had not made use of the confidential information or disclosed the same'.[96] The shift of burden of proof was not disputed in the appeal to the Hong Kong Court of Appeal.[97]

4.5.4. *The Validity of a Covenant in Restraint of Trade*

Like in many other common law jurisdictions, the general principle in Hong Kong provides that a covenant in restraint of trade is generally unenforceable, unless it can be shown to be reasonable in the interests of the parties and the public.[98] The onus of proving the reasonableness of such restrictions is on the party who seeks to enforce the covenant, i.e., the plaintiff.[99] A plaintiff has to demonstrate that the duration, geographic range and type of work restricted by the relevant clauses are necessary to protect its legitimate interests. In the present case, the court held that a six-month restriction was reasonable in protecting the plaintiff's sensitive information in the mobile industry. The court also ruled that the term 'any companies of the same kind' was a reasonable restriction. However, the court ultimately decided that the restrictive covenant was unenforceable because it imposed no geographic limit.

4.5.5. *The Damage Caused to the Plaintiff*

Lastly, the burden to prove the actual damage suffered by the plaintiff as a result of the defendant's wrongdoing is on the plaintiff as well. The plaintiff is obliged to prove both the existence and the amount of such damage caused by the defendant's breach of confidence and their causal relationship. In the event that the causation between the wrong and the damage cannot be established or the amount of damage cannot be specified on evidential grounds, the court would grant nominal damages,[100] which only consist of a trivial sum of money, as a symbolic recognition of the harm caused to the plaintiff by such condemned wrongdoing. The allocation of the burden to the plaintiff seems reasonable insofar it is only at the plaintiff's convenience to collect evidence to prove the actual loss suffered by it in a specified period of time.

95. *William Allan*, *supra* note 69.
96. *Ibid.*
97. *Ibid.*
98. *Bridge v Deacons* [1984] 1 AC 705 at 713A–B *per* Lord Fraser of Tullybelton.
99. *Degreeasia*, *supra* note 52, [32].
100. *Ibid.*, [58].

4.6. *Commercial or Industrial Significance*

Preventing sensitive business information from being unduly disclosed to competitors has become a common concern of entities of all sizes. However, when such proprietary information was misappropriated, not all proprietors have the necessary resources to bring a legal action to court or substantiate their claims with adequate evidence. An unduly onerous burden of proof allocated to the plaintiff may cause the wrongdoer as well as the downstream recipient of such information to escape liabilities.[101]

In this regard, it was exemplified in *Dunamis* that as long as the plaintiff can prove that the information itself has the necessary quality of confidence and it has been imparted in circumstances importing an obligation of confidence, the burden will then shift to the defendant to show that it did not misuse the information. If the defendant fails to provide a reasonable explanation, an inference would likely be made by the court in favour of the plaintiff.

Understanding the allocation of burden of proof is critically important for both plaintiffs and defendants in litigation concerning breach of confidence. Parties that are not able to bear the burden of proof stand slim chance to win the litigation. Therefore, the rule governing burden of proof in lawsuits concerning breach of confidence plays a decisive role in the outcomes of their litigation.

101. Crowne and Freitas, *supra* note 88, 212.

TOPIC 5 THE DAMAGES

Jingwen Liu & Jyh-An Lee

1. Legal Issues

What are the available remedies for a breach of confidence claim? Under what circumstances shall nominal damages, aggravated damages, or exemplary damages be granted in a breach of confidence case?
How is the amount of compensatory damages to be measured? What is the relationship between a loss of profit and account of profit claim?

2. The Statutory Law

Section 17 of the High Court Ordinance of Hong Kong provides that '[w]here the Court of Appeal or the Court of First Instance has jurisdiction to entertain an application for an injunction or specific performance, it may award damages in addition to, or in substitution for, an injunction or specific performance'.[102]

3. The Case Law

The general principle in Hong Kong is that the compensatory damages payable to a plaintiff are subject to the actual loss suffered by the plaintiff. However, as pointed out by *William Allan*,[103] exemplary damages remain one of the remedies and should be applied where compensatory damages are deemed inadequate. That said, the use of such punitive damages is extremely exceptional. When the Court of the Appeal delivered the judgment of the present case in 2012, there were merely 13 cases in Hong Kong since 1976 in which exemplary damages were granted.[104] When it comes to a breach of confidence cause of action in particular, a search for cases at Westlaw Asia with keywords 'breach of confidence' and 'exemplary damages' revealed 23 cases in Hong Kong as of 9 March 2021. In five of the above cases, the plaintiff has claimed damages, including exemplary damages, in its summons, for the defendant's breach of confidence. Nevertheless, the present case was the only one in which exemplary damages were granted. In *China Light*,[105] the court, despite having recognised the appropriateness of awarding exemplary damages in breach of confidence cases, refused to grant such a remedy in this very decision, given that the factual situation did not fall into the scope of exemplary damages. Moreover, in *Deacons v White & Case*,[106] the court, citing the English precedent *A v Bottrill*,[107] developed a 'test of outrageousness' in deciding whether to award exemplary damages. Following such strict criteria, the claim against the defendants failed, for their conduct, despite having amounted to

102. High Court Ordinance (Cap. 4) section 17.
103. *William Allan, supra* note 69.
104. *Ibid.*, [70].
105. *China Light, supra* note 4.
106. *Deacons v White & Case, supra* note 50.
107. *A v Bottrill* [2002] UKPC 44.

a cynical disregard for the rights of the plaintiff, was not vindictive or malicious or so outrageous that nothing less than an award of exemplary damages would have achieved justice.[108] Overall, the case law seems to suggest that exemplary damages, although available, are not common remedies for breach of confidence in Hong Kong.

4. The Leading Case(s)

4.1. Case Information

The High Court of the Hong Kong Special Administrative Region Court of Appeal, CACV 13/2011, *William Allan v Messrs Ng & Co. (A Firm) and Another* [2012] HKCA 119; [2012] 2 HKLRD 160; [2012] 2 HKC 266 (6 March 2012).

4.2. Summary

The 2nd defendant, Mr Christopher Erving, was a partner at the 1st defendant, Messrs Ng & Co., a solicitor's firm in Hong Kong ('the firm'). The plaintiff, Mr William Allan, was a practising barrister while his ex-wife ('the wife') was in medical practice.

The 2nd defendant, who had previously handled the plaintiff's consultation pertaining his divorce proceedings, ended up representing the opposite party, i.e., the wife in the said proceedings. The husband sued the solicitor together with the firm for, *inter alia*, breach of fiduciary duty and breach of confidence and sought exemplary damages. The trial judge supported the husband's claims and granted exemplary damages in the amount of HKD 2.14 million, consisting of the commission fees payable to the firm by the wife in the divorce proceedings and the costs ordered against the husband in the interlocutory proceedings relating to the divorce procedures as well as the present case, with both pre- and post-judgment interest to run from the date of the writ. The Court of Appeal upheld the decision that the solicitor and the firm were jointly and severally liable for damages, including exemplary damages. However, it disagreed with the trial judge on the amount. Specifically, the Court of Appeal pointed out that when assessing damages in general, it was important to distinguish between the different headings of damages to be awarded, be they compensatory, aggravated, or exemplary. As a result, the Court of Appeal held that the plaintiff should only be entitled to a nominal sum of HKD 100 for compensation because he failed to prove the actual loss caused by the defendants' conduct. As for exemplary damages, the court investigated the precedents in Hong Kong and agreed on an amount of HKD 400,000. Additionally, the court ruled that for the amount of HKD 100, there was no need to award interest, while for the amount of HKD 400,000, interest should only run from the day of the judgment.

108. *Deacons v White & Case*, *supra* note 50.

4.3. *Facts*

On 29 April 1994, the wife filed a petition for divorce against the plaintiff. However, in the following days, both the wife's solicitor at the time and herself wrote to the plaintiff, stating her intention to pursue no further in the divorce proceedings if the plaintiff agreed to a settlement. On 12 or 13 May 1994, authorised by the plaintiff, the plaintiff's sister Alison approached the 2nd defendant through phone, with a hope to retain him as the plaintiff's solicitor in the divorce proceedings. During the 45-minute conversation, confidential information pertaining to the personal details, occupation and financial income of the plaintiff and the wife, the assets of the plaintiff and means of acquisition, the wife's grounds for divorce, the plaintiff's stances, bottom lines, and tactics in relation to the custody and financial issues in the divorce proceedings was imparted. Alison also mentioned that she was deeply concerned with confidentiality given the delicate situation in the divorce proceedings and was assured by the 2nd defendant that the information would be kept confidential. The telephone call resulted in a meeting arrangement for the plaintiff and the 2nd defendant. However, the meeting was postponed by the plaintiff himself on the morning of the agreed date, as he received a message from the wife and sensed an amicable settlement was possible. No retainer was paid to engage the 2nd defendant for the subject matter.

At around the same time, the wife started to be suspicious of the billing of her own solicitors. On 17 May 1994, she also approached the 2nd defendant, recommended by a friend, for general advice. After several meetings, she orally instructed the firm to act for her. On 26 May 1994, a Notice of Change of Solicitors was filed on behalf of the wife by the firm and delivered to the plaintiff thereafter. Upon receiving the Notice, the plaintiff and Alison both called the 2nd defendant to condemn his behaviour and urge him to cease representing the wife. On 8 July 1994, both the wife and the firm wrote to the plaintiff, informing him of her decision to proceed with the divorce. On 12 July 1994, the plaintiff engaged another firm to act for him in the proceedings.

While the divorce matters intensified, the plaintiff brought suit against the defendants in the present case on 28 October 1994 and applied for an interlocutory injunction prohibiting the defendants from acting for the wife, which was dismissed by Justice Sears on 10 November 1994, with costs against the plaintiff. However, at that time, his bank accounts were all frozen as requested by the wife and he was evicted from the matrimonial home. Given his mental collapse and inability to pay outstanding debts owed to both his own solicitors and the defendants arising from the interlocutory injunction proceedings, he wrote to his own solicitors hoping to withdraw the current action. On the other hand, a bankruptcy application was filed by the defendants against him. At the hearing of the plaintiff's application for stay of the bankruptcy on 22 July 1996, Justice Patrick Chan advised the wife to 'make a conscious decision to retain a solicitor' and 'consider the interest of the child'. It was not until then that the wife replaced the defendants and retained another firm as her solicitors. The divorce proceedings had been extremely protracted and not concluded until 21 July 2001. Nevertheless, the present case was not withdrawn eventually, as the plaintiff secured legal aid. In front of the Court of First Instance, the plaintiff sued for, *inter alia*, exemplary damages for breach of confidence.

4.4. *Reasoning of the Court*

4.4.1. *The First-Instance Decision*

At first trial, the trial judge, Justice To ('To J'), confirmed the confidentiality of the subject information, being the stances, bottom lines and tactics imparted to the 2nd defendant by Alison on behalf of the plaintiff during the phone call. He defined the relationship between the plaintiff and the 2nd defendant as a quasi-client-solicitor relationship, which indisputably gave rise to a duty of confidence. Moreover, the court supported the argument that once the confidentiality of the subject information had been established, the burden shifted to the defendants to prove they never disclosed or misappropriated such information. In particular, To J pointed out that under the Hong Kong Solicitors' Guide to Professional Conduct, a solicitor was bound by both a duty to hold in confidence all information of his client acquired in the course of the professional relationship[109] and a duty to pass on to his client all material information relevant to the subject matter regardless of the source.[110] A solicitor was in breach of these duties if he acquired the information from a former client and used that information to act for a present client.[111] In the present case, the 2nd defendant's duty owed to his present client would require his breach of confidence owed to his former quasi-client, i.e., the plaintiff.

At trial, both the parties and the court agreed that it was extremely difficult to prove the actual damages suffered by the plaintiff since there was no knowing how the divulged information had shaped the direction of the divorce proceedings. Hence, the plaintiff abandoned the compensatory claim and opted to concentrate on exemplary damages. Nevertheless, To J found that although the amount of the damages could not be specified, the damages could be readily presumed, as if it were not for the divulged information, the divorce proceedings would have at least 'proceeded more smoothly, incurring less time and costs', and the current litigation, the interlocutory proceedings and the costs incurred therefrom would have been avoided, nor would the plaintiff have suffered the bankruptcy crisis. Therefore, although there was no sufficient evidence to support the compensatory damages claim, To J held that the plaintiff was still entitled to at least nominal damages, in addition to the exemplary damages being sought. Based on the findings of the defendants' conduct being 'extremely outrageous' and 'utterly unreasonable', the judge felt it necessary to display the court's firm disapproval of such behaviours by granting exemplary damages. Taking into consideration: (1) the blameworthiness of the defendants' conduct; (2) the degree of vulnerability of the plaintiff; (3) the harm or potential harm directed specifically at the plaintiff; (4) the need for deterrence; and (5) the advantage wrongfully gained by the defendants from the misconduct, To J ordered exemplary damages including the following components:

109. Law Society of Hong Kong, *The Hong Kong Solicitors' Guide to Professional Conduct* http://www.hklawsoc.org.hk/pub_e/professionalguide/volume1/default.asp (1998) Vol. 1 para. 8.01.
110. *Ibid.*, para. 8.03.
111. *William Allan, supra* note 69.

(1) the profits the defendants made from acting for the wife, at $1.19 million (having regard to the costs incurred by the wife of $2.38 million and, on a 'rough assessment', assumed half of that represented the defendants' gross profits);
(2) the costs the defendants were awarded in successfully opposing the interlocutory injunction application and the costs the defendants should have paid the plaintiff in that application, at $750,000 (taking the agreed costs of $375,000 awarded to the plaintiff, which the judge assumed to have been paid by the plaintiff with interest, and awarded a like amount to the plaintiff as the plaintiff's own costs); and
(3) the miscellaneous costs orders the defendants were awarded in the bankruptcy proceedings and charging order over the matrimonial property, at $200,000 (this was a 'notional sum' allowing for the plaintiff's costs in the bankruptcy proceedings and the costs incurred in the charging order).

The total amount had arrived at $2.14 million, with interest to run on the first and third items from the date of the writ in the current action (i.e., 28 October 1994), and on the second item from the date for judgment of agreed costs (i.e., 29 November 1995).[112] Moreover, the judge directed the Law Society to commence disciplinary proceedings against the 2nd defendant and consider removing him from the rolls of solicitors. The dispute was then brought to the Court of Appeal.

4.4.2. *The Court of Appeal Decision*

Based on the finding that the 2nd defendant's wrongdoing was 'reasonably incidental' to the firm's business, the court found the firm and the 2nd defendant jointly and severally liable for whatever damages would be decided for the 2nd defendant's breach of confidence. The court also considered whether exemplary damages were applicable at all and whether the amount was reasonable.

4.4.2.1. The Applicability of Exemplary Damages in General

With reference to the authority of *A v Bottrill*,[113] the presiding judge of appeal, Justice Kwan JA ('Kwan JA'), concluded that the rationale for exemplary damages was to punish rather than to compensate. They were intended to be additional to compensatory damages, which were to make up for the pecuniary and non-pecuniary loss suffered by a plaintiff.[114] Citing Lord Nicholls in *A v Bottrill*, the court explained that:

> In the ordinary course the appropriate response of a court to the commission of a tort is to require the wrongdoer to make good the wronged person's loss, so far as a payment of money can achieve this. In appropriate circumstances this may include aggravated damages. Exceptionally, a defendant's conduct in committing a civil wrong is so outrageous that an order for payment of compensation is not an adequate response. Something more is needed from the court, to demonstrate that

112. *Ibid.*, [26]-[28].
113. *A v Bottrill*, *supra* note 107.
114. *William Allan*, *supra* note 69, [52].

> such conduct is altogether unacceptable to society. Then the wrongdoer may be ordered to make a further payment, by way of condemnation and punishment.[115]

As such, there was a clear distinction between compensatory and exemplary damages. Kwan JA warned against the possibility of the boundary becoming less obvious, were a combined award to be made.[116]

Meanwhile, the court made it clear that exemplary damages should be considered 'a remedy of last resort'. It is only if the available remedies are inadequate to punish and deter the defendant that exemplary damages should be considered.[117]

4.4.2.2. The Applicability of Exemplary Damages Against Equitable Wrongs

The defendants' counsel argued that damages, including exemplary damages, as a common law remedy, should not be misused in correcting an equitable wrong, being the breach of confidence claim under the current circumstance. The counsel cited a classic case of 1872 in England[118] as well as a subsequent judgment in Australia[119] to demonstrate that a court of equity had no jurisdiction to grant punitive monetary awards for breach of fiduciary duties. However, Kwan JA pointed out that the same practice was not followed by courts in Canada[120] and New Zealand,[121] and had caused confusion and inconsistency among commonwealth jurisdictions. To address the contradicting approaches, the Law Commission of England issued a Report on Aggravated, Exemplary and Restitutionary Damages in 1997 ('Law Commission Report'), which recommended that 'exemplary damages should be available for equitable wrongs' to pave way for a uniform resolution.[122] In Hong Kong, the widely cited case law *China Light* explicitly stated that 'exemplary damages are available in cases of breach of confidence'.[123]

4.2.2.3. The Assessment of Exemplary Damages

The Court of Appeal disagreed with the trial court's calculation of damages. Specifically, the trial judge had erred in his calculation in three ways: he had included what was in essence compensatory damages in the sum of exemplary damages, being the second and third components of the amount ($750,000 for costs of both parties in the interlocutory injunction proceedings and $20,000 for costs in the bankruptcy proceedings and charging order over the matrimonial home) that had been granted to the plaintiff. Meanwhile, the first component of $1.19 million, being the fees incurred for representing the wife in the divorce case, was actually an account of profits. It was not

115. *A v Bottrill, supra* note 107, [20].
116. *William Allan, supra* note 69, [53].
117. *Ibid.*, [55].
118. *Vyse v Foster* (1872) LR 8 LRCh App 309.
119. *Harris v Digital Pulse Pty Ltd* (2003) 56 NSWLR 298.
120. *Norberg v Wynrib* [1992] 2 SCR 226.
121. *Aquaculture Corporation v New Zealand Green Mussel Ltd* [1990] 3 NZLR 299.
122. Law Commission, *Report on Aggravated, Exemplary and Restitutionary Damages* (Law Com No. 247, 1997) paras 5.54-5.56.
123. *China Light, supra* note 4, at 29C to F, 30C to E, 34H to I and 38H.

proper for either form to be included in the calculation of exemplary damages, which was aimed to be punitive and should be applied in addition to, not in replacement of, compensatory damages or restitution of enrichments. Furthermore, even if the three components were deemed individually acceptable, the plaintiff should have only been awarded either the sum of the first item or the other two since compensatory damages and an account of profits were meant to be alternative rather than cumulative. In any event, the total amount of $2.14 million was deemed 'unreasonable and wholly excessive'.

Kwan JA first acknowledged To J's decision that the plaintiff was entitled to a nominal sum of compensatory damages and ordered an amount of $100 to be paid under this heading. Next, although not satisfied with the amount decided in the first trial, he explained that this was 'an appropriate case for an award of exemplary damages'. Had the plaintiff relied on either a loss or an account of profit claim and adduced evidence thereof, he would still find the compensation or the quantum of restitution inadequate to punish and deter the defendants, and order exemplary damages to be paid. As neither the compensation payable nor the account of profits was a proper method to calculate exemplary damages, the final figure was determined by the judge's discretion. Kwan JA referred to previous cases in Hong Kong where exemplary damages were applied, among which the highest sum was set at $200,000. However, given that the said decision had been 12 years old at the time of the appeal, inflation was taken into account, as were the disciplinary proceedings against the 2nd defendant at the Law Society, the defendants' undertakings not to enforce their rights acquired in the previous court proceedings against the plaintiff, and the general principle of proportionality. Overall, he deemed $400,000 would be a proper amount under this heading.

The last issue was to decide whether it was reasonable to order the defendants to pay interest on the determined amount over a 15-year period, starting from the date of the writ of this protracted litigation. Citing multiple common law precedents, Kwan JA held that unlike compensatory damages, on which interest may be awarded to run from the date of the writ, '[i]nterest before judgment should not be awarded on exemplary damages, as the function of this kind of award is to punish and deter the defendant and the plaintiff is not being kept out of money which should have been paid to him'.[124]

4.5. *Legal Analysis*

4.5.1. *The Availability of Damages in Breach of Confidence Cases*

In common law jurisdictions, there has been a long-established distinction between legal and equitable remedies, alongside the ancient distinction in England between courts of law and courts of equity.[125] Though courts of the two kinds have merged since

124. *William Allan*, *supra* note 69, [76].
125. Tyler J. Bowies, 'Employment Discrimination: Distinguishing Between Equitable Remedies and Compensatory Damages' (2008) 15 The Journal of Law and Economics 11, 12.

the late nineteenth century,[126] the concepts of legal and equitable reliefs are retained.[127] The most typical legal remedy is an award of monetary damages,[128] while equitable remedies include injunctions, specific performance, reformation, quiet title, reinstatement, equitable rescission, equitable lien, constructive trust, subrogation and accounting for profits, etc.[129]

In Hong Kong, the most important case law is *China Light*,[130] in which the court cited Lord Cairns' Act in the UK and stated that:

> As a matter of history, the common law provided no protection against the misuse of confidential information. No action for damages (the only remedy available for any wrongful act at common law) would lie. Eventually, equity, true to form, stepped in to supplement this deficiency of the common law; it made available the equitable remedy of an injunction to restrain such misuse. Now, however, under the Chancery Amendment Act 1858 (Lord Cairns' Act), damages may be granted in certain cases in lieu of an injunction, and this has caused some confusion.[131]

In the present case, the defendants' counsel argued that since exemplary damages were designed to be punitive, the court had no power to grant a punitive monetary award against such breach of fiduciary duty.[132] Kwan JA disagreed and explained that the practices were inconsistent among commonwealth jurisdictions and some of them not only contradicted the Law Commission Report but also ran against the principle set down in *China Light*, in which the Court of Appeal had concluded that exemplary damages were available in cases of breach of confidence.[133]

4.5.2. *Different Types of Damages*

The error of the trial judge's calculation of damages derived from his fusion of compensatory and exemplary damages. In hearing the appeal case, Justice Fok JA added to Kwan JA's judgment that '[i]t is important to keep in mind some basic distinctions between compensatory (or basic) damages, aggravated damages and exemplary damages as these differences are significant both in terms of substance and procedure'.[134] When assessing the amount of the damages to be awarded, it is material to first find out what types of damages are to be awarded, be they special, general, aggravated or exemplary. The qualitative characterisation would have a significant impact on the quantitative determination.

---

126. Samuel L. Bray, 'The Supreme Court and the New Equity' (2015) 68 Vanderbilt Law Review 997, 1046, 1054; *Franks v Bowman Transp. Co.*, 424 U.S. 747, 763 (1976); Samuel L. Bray, 'The System of Equitable Remedies' (2016) 63 UCLA Law Review 530, 537.
127. Gaylord A. Jentz, Kenneth W. Clarkson and Roger LeRoy Miller, *West's Business Law: Alternative UCC Comprehensive Edition* (3rd ed., West Publishing Company 1987).
128. Alexander J. Black, 'Undue Influence and Unconscionability in Contracts and the Equitable Remedy of Rescission in Canada' (2011) 17 New England Journal of International and Comparative Law 47, 48.
129. Bray, 'The System of Equitable Remedies', *supra* note 126, 541-542.
130. *China Light, supra* note 4.
131. *Ibid.*
132. *William Allan, supra* note 69, [38].
133. *China Light, supra* note 4.
134. *William Allan, supra* note 69, [81].

4.5.2.1. Compensatory Damages

Compensatory damages are awarded to make up for the loss suffered by a victim as a result of wrongdoing. Compensatory damages can be further divided into specific damages and general damages. The former refers to the quantifiable pecuniary loss sustained by the plaintiff and will be decided by the court based on different metrics, such as cost for medical treatment, while the latter reflects the non-pecuniary loss such as damages for pain, suffering, loss of amenities and injury to reputation, etc., on which the court will have to show some discretion to quantify with reference to the special circumstances.[135]

When establishing his claim for compensatory damages, a plaintiff will have to prove the wrongdoing of the defendant, the loss suffered by itself, and the causal link between the act complained of and the loss alleged. For equitable damages, it requires no less than ordinary common law damages for the causation and remoteness evaluation to be passed.[136] A plaintiff will also have to prove, on the balance of probabilities, both the fact and the amount of the damage. 'If the fact of damage is shown, but no evidence is given as to its amount so that it is virtually impossible to assess damages, this will generally permit only an award of nominal damages.'[137]

When calculating the compensatory damages payable to the plaintiff, a loss of profit claim is one of the typical options. A loss of profit claim is a method for a plaintiff to quantify and justify its claim for a fixed-amount compensation. It provides a method of calculating compensatory damages, being the profits a plaintiff could have made if it were not for the defendant's misbehaviour. This is to be distinguished from an account of profit claim, which, in contrast, is a classical equitable remedy seeking to restitute the unjust enrichment from the wrongdoer.

4.5.2.2. Nominal Damages

By definition, nominal damages are 'a trivial sum of money awarded to a litigant who has established a cause of action but has not established that he is entitled to compensatory damages'.[138] Nominal damages usually come into play and fill compensatory damages' shoe when the claimant is entitled to compensation as a general matter of law, but there is simply no actual loss caused by the alleged breach or no sufficient evidence to prove the same. In this regard, nominal damages serve as a symbolic recognition of the harm of the wrongdoing with only a declaratory effect.[139] Though some have been arguing that nominal damages are to be divorced from compensatory damages,[140] they are still compensatory in nature.[141] In the present case, both the trial judge and judges of appeal had recognised the plaintiff's entitlement to

---

135. *Ibid.*, [82].
136. *Akihiro Oba, supra* note 10, [48].
137. *ICI Swire Paints Ltd v Techni Motor & Engineering & Trading Co* (HCA 7251/1995, 29 January 2003).
138. The Restatement (Second) of Torts, section 907.
139. 25 C.J.S. Damages § 17.
140. *See*, e.g., Jacob A. Stein, *1 Stein on Personal Injury Damages Treatise* (3rd ed., Clark Boardman Callaghan 1997) § 1:3.

nominal damages given his failure to prove the actual loss caused by the defendants' misuse of confidential information.

4.5.2.3. Aggravated Damages

Non-pecuniary loss in a tort claim sometimes involves hurt feelings or mental distress. Where such feelings are involved, aggravated damages over and above the normal range of general damages may be granted, as a compensation to the injury caused to the plaintiff's pride, dignity and such as a consequence of the defendant's conduct.[142] The idea of aggravated damages was first laid down by *Rookes v Barnard*, where Lord Devlin stated that 'the manner of committing the wrong may be such as to injure the plaintiff's proper feelings of dignity and pride. These are matters which the jury can take into account in assessing the appropriate compensation'.[143] According to Lord Devlin, aggravated damages are still compensatory in nature, the application of which is because of the increase of the injury caused to the plaintiff due to the mental suffering, rather than to be punitive.[144] In this regard, aggravated damages are to be distinguished from exemplary damages, the application of which would go through a stricter scrutinization insofar as basic and aggravated damages are deemed inadequate.

4.5.2.4. Exemplary Damages

Unlike the typical purpose of damages, which is to compensate, the purposes of exemplary damages are to punish and to deter. This facet of exemplary damages has made it an anomaly in the civil sphere since it has more or less blurred the functions of civil and criminal laws.[145] Nevertheless, as pointed out by Fok JA in the present case, they remain a part of the common law of England as well as that of Hong Kong.[146] In *Rookes*, Lord Devlin strictly restricted the use of exemplary damages to three categories of cases: (1) oppressive, arbitrary or unconstitutional action by the servants of the government; (2) where the defendant's conduct has been calculated by him to make a profit for himself which may well exceed the compensation payable to the plaintiff; and (3) where exemplary damages are expressly authorized by statute.[147] In the present case, both the trial judge and the judges of appeal agreed on the notion that the behaviour of the defendants, as professional solicitors, was so disgraceful that it deserved the court's express disapproval by way of awarding exemplary damages.

141. *See, e.g.*, *Fairfield v American Photocopy Equipment Co.*, 138 Cal App 2d 82, 291 P2d 194; *Booth v Quality Dairy Co.*, 393 SW2d 845 (Mo App); Allan, *supra* note 2, [84].
142. *William Allan, supra* note 69, [83].
143. *Rookes v Barnard* [1964] AC 1129, [1964] 1 All ER 367.
144. *Ibid.*, at 407; Hardinge Stanley Giffard Halsbury, *Halsbury's Laws of England* (3rd edn, 1969) Vol. 12 para. 1189, at 472-473.
145. Harvey McGregor, *McGregor on Damages* (18th edn, Sweet and Maxwell 2009) at §11-001.
146. *William Allan, supra* note 69, [85].
147. *Rookes, supra* note 143.

4.6. *Commercial or Industrial Significance*

Under some circumstances, the existence of exemplary damages has made Hong Kong an ideal forum for owners of confidential information to take actions against wrong-doers. For example, in *Shenzhen Futaihong Precision Industry Co Ltd v BYD Co Ltd*, BYD asked the court to stay an action brought by its business rival because there was a parallel suit between the parties at Shenzhen Intermediate People's Court of the People's Republic of China. The court rejected BYD's request, on the basis that should the dispute be stayed for the Shenzhen action, the plaintiff would be deprived of the potential advantages of exemplary damages, as well as other forms of equitable remedies.[148] In this regard, the significance of the present case is that it clarified that an award of exemplary damages was applicable to a breach of confidence claim, and meanwhile explained its interrelation with compensatory, nominal and aggravated damages. Moreover, in addition to illustrating the correct way to consider various factors for damage assessment, this judgment exemplified the methods to calculate different types of damages, including compensatory damages, nominal damages, and aggravated damages, in a breach of confidence case.

148. *Shenzhen Futaihong Precision Industry Co Ltd v BYD Co Ltd* [2008] HKEC 1093.

CHAPTER 8
Malaysia

OVERVIEW AND SUMMARY

Lim Heng Gee

1. INTRODUCTION

The obligation to respect the confidentiality of certain information can arise from contract, normally in the form of a confidentiality clause in the contract of employment. However, even absent such express term, there may be read into the contract an implied obligation of confidence. In *Engineered Products & Services v Ku Meng Choon*, the judge said, 'However, in the absence of any express terms, the obligations of the employee in respect of the use and disclosure of information are the subject of implied terms.'[1]

Further, even in the absence of any contractual relationship, the obligation of confidence could arise under equitable obligations.[2] This is because 'The law on this subject does not depend on any implied contract. It depends on the broad principle of equity that he who has received information in confidence shall not take unfair advantage of it.'[3]

There is no statute protecting confidential information, including trade secrets. Most common law countries follow the United Kingdom in relying on the equitable remedy of breach of confidence. Section 3(1) of the Civil Law Act 1956 provides that in the absence of local statutes, English common law and the rules of equity will continue to apply. By virtue of this section, the English tort of breach of confidence would be available in Malaysia.[4]

During his employment, an employee may acquire further skills, techniques or information which may make him an even better technician, technologist, scientist or

1. [2015] 2 AMCR 219, para. 123.
2. *See Electro Cad Australia Pty Ltd & 2 Ors v Mejati RCS Sdn Bhd* [1998] 3 AMR 2555, pp. 2576-2577.
3. *See Motordata Research Consortium Sdn Bhd v Ahmad Shahril bin Abdullah* [2017] 7 AMR 560, para. 62.
4. *See Regent Decorators (M) Sdn Bhd v Michael Chee* [1984] 2 CLJ (Rep) 441.

whatever. Since he has acquired these skills and knowledge by his own effort he would consider that they are essentially something to which he is personally entitled. The problem is how to demarcate information which the employee is entitled to call his own, to do as he wishes, and that information which the employer is entitled to deem confidential and not in any way usable by the employee outside the confines of the workplace, or when such employment has ended? To overcome this problem, many employers require their employees to sign confidentiality agreements. In Malaysia, such agreements are enforceable if they are not construed as contracts in restraint of trade. Section 28 of the Contracts Act 1950 (the provision of section 28 has been fully set out in the case report on Topic 2) essentially provides that every agreement in restraint of trade is void. There are three exceptions relating to the sale of goodwill and agreements relating to partnership matters.

In Malaysia, there is no statute relating to the burden of proof. There are three statutory bases for the courts to grant ex parte interlocutory orders: the Courts of Judicature Act 1964, the Specific Relief Act 1950 and Rules of Court 2012 (a brief outline of the statutes and the Rules of Court has been provided in the case report for Topic 4). Lastly, there is no criminal punishment for trade secret infringement in Malaysia. There has also been no call from the industry to impose criminal liability for breach of confidence.

2. THE ELEMENTS ESSENTIAL TO A CAUSE OF ACTION FOR BREACH OF CONFIDENCE

In *Schmidt Scientific Sdn Bhd v Ong Han Suan & Ors*,[5] the court, following the English case of *Coco v AN Clark (Engineers) Ltd (No 2)*, held that in order to succeed in an action for breach of confidence, the plaintiff must establish to the satisfaction of the court three elements, namely:

(a) the information which the plaintiff is seeking to protect is of a confidential nature;
(b) the information in question was communicated in circumstances importing an obligation of confidence; and
(c) there must be an unauthorized use of that information to the detriment of the party communicating it.

Following *Schmidt Scientific*, other courts have consistently applied these three elements.[6] The *Coco v Clark* test was given its imprimatur by the Court of Appeal in *Seven Seas Industries Sdn Bhd v Phillips Electronic Supplies (M) Sdn Bhd & Anor*.[7] For more details, refer to the case report on Topic 1.

5. [1998] 1 CLJ 685, p. 693.
6. *See*, for example, *Yeohata Industries Sdn Bhd v Coil Master Sdn Bhd* [2001] MLJU 281, *Ku Pon & Ors v Pemandangan Sinar Sdn Bhd & Ors* [2004] 6 MLJ 253 and *Svenson Hair Center Sdn Bhd v Irene Chin Zee Ling* [2008] 8 CLJ 386.
7. [2008] 3 AMR 393; [2008] 5 MLJ 157.

3. THE VALIDITY AND SCOPE OF CONFIDENTIALITY AND/OR NON-COMPETITION CLAUSES

3.1. The Distinction Between Confidential Information and the Employee's General Stock of Knowledge

The cases have shown that courts are alert to the need to maintain a proper balance between the rights of the employers to protect their confidential information and the rights of the employees to take along and use certain information needed to enable them to be a useful addition to his new employers. According to the Court of Appeal, 'If the impugned "information" was from within the general fund of the defendant's own knowledge, exposure and experience accumulated in the diecast industry over the years ..., there was definitely not grounds, ... to hold that there had been a breach of fiduciary duty or even a breach of confidentiality by defendant ... .'[8]

In *Optotronic Semiconductors Sdn Bhd v Chan Ah Chyoo*, the court held that to establish whether the information received was a trade secret, the following factors would have to be considered:[9]

(i) the nature of employment;
(ii) the nature of information received;
(iii) whether the plaintiff had stressed the confidentiality of the information to the defendant; and
(iv) whether such information could be isolated from other non-confidential information within the same package of information.

For more details, refer to the case report on Topic 2.

3.2. Section 28 of the Contracts Act and Restraint of Trade

Svenson Hair Center Sdn Bhd v Irene Chin Zee Ling is the first reported case where the intersection between the protection of confidential information and section 28 of the Contracts Act was fully argued. The court stressed that 'the law does not debar an ex-employee from making any use of or drawing on a fund of knowledge and experience or skills that he had acquired while working for the employer. That would be tantamount to depriving him of his livelihood'.[10] The law only imposes on the employee a general duty to act in good faith. Clearly, acts such as memorizing a formula or a list of the employer's customers or taking away such list by an employee for his use were improper and would constitute acting in bad faith. The court rejected the defendant's argument that the clause in issue should be limited to a reasonable period of time from the termination of her employment. The court stressed that the plaintiff's right to protect its confidential information in the clause did not have any time limit. Accordingly, reading the employment agreement as a whole, it was clear that while there was no general restriction on the defendant from soliciting and or

8. *Vision Cast Sdn Bhd & Anor v Dynacast (Melaka) Sdn Bhd & Ors* [2015] 1 MLJ 424, para. 54.
9. [2013] 2 AMCR 267, p. 271.
10. *Svenson Hair Center Sdn Bhd v Irene Chin Zee Ling* [2008] 8 CLJ 386, para. 15.

competing with the plaintiff, this did not apply where such soliciting or competition was effected through the use of the plaintiff's confidential information.[11] The court then stressed that 'If a contrary view is taken by this court in the current case, it would mean that the defendant, notwithstanding her blatant breach of contract and trust in wrongfully obtaining the confidential information, needs only wait for the 12 months period to expire before she could exploit such information with impunity.'[12]

In *Worldwide Rota Dies Sdn Bhd v Ronald Ong Cheow Joon*,[13] the plaintiff successfully claimed an order injuncting the defendant from enticing the plaintiff's customers to the defendant or to any other company. As to the restraint of trade and contravention of section 28 arguments, the court reiterated the principle that 'Restraint against competition is justifiable if its object is to prevent the exploitation of trade secrets learned by the servant in the course of his employment.'[14]

In *Lim Yoke Lin v Roy Hong Ping Wei & Ors*,[15] the court stressed that 'it is imperative upon this Court to scrutinise the impugned clause whether it amounts to restraint of trade and if so, whether the exceptions apply. Reasonableness is not recognised under our Contracts Act as far as section 28 is concerned'.[16] As the plaintiff was unable to demonstrate how Clause 3.8 could escape from being caught under section 28 of the Contracts Act, and as no confidential information was alleged to have been taken away by the defendant, the court held that the impugned clause was void.[17]

Finally, the Federal Court in *Dynacast (Melaka) Sdn Bhd & Ors v Vision Cast Sdn Bhd & Anor*[18] held that 'The proposition of law in *Svenson Hair Centre* ... should be considered in the context of the facts and circumstances of each case. In that case, the protection of confidential information did not have any time limits. The proposition of law was a settled principle.'[19]

4. THE BURDEN OF PROOF FOR TRADE SECRET AND INFRINGEMENT AND ITS REVERSAL

4.1. The Legal Burden of Proof for Establishing the Cause of Action

Just like any other tort actions, the legal burden in an action for breach of confidence lies on the plaintiff. The plaintiff has to discharge the onus of establishing his pleaded case, i.e., that the defendant breached his duty of confidentiality on the balance of probabilities.[20]

In *Risk – X Sdn Bhd v Capital Market Risk Advisor Sdn Bhd*, the court held that the plaintiff has failed to prove its case on the balance of probabilities against the

11. *Ibid.*, para. 16.
12. *Ibid.*, para. 17.
13. [2010] 8 MLJ 297.
14. *Ibid.*, para. 109.
15. [2019] 1 LNS 1439.
16. *Ibid.*, para. 18.
17. *Ibid.*, para. 20.
18. [2016] 6 CLJ 176.
19. *Ibid.*, paras 19-20.
20. *See*, for example, *Ecooils Sdn Bhd v Raghunath Ramaiah Kandikeri* [2014] 7 MLJ 309, para. 67 and *Ampledeal (M) Sdn Bhd & Ors v Laponie (M) Sdn Bhd & Ors* [2015] MLJU 1933.

defendants on the claim as pleaded. This was because the plaintiff had not identified what the information which was deemed to be confidential was.[21]

Similarly, in *Vision Cast Sdn Bhd & Anor v Dynacast (Melaka) Sdn Bhd & Ors*, the Court of Appeal allowed the respondents' appeal against the High Court decision on the grounds, *inter alia*, that the details of the confidential information sought to be protected were not pleaded with specificity by the plaintiffs,[22] The Court of Appeal decision was upheld on appeal to the Federal Court.[23] The Federal Court was of the view that more specifications should have been provided on the claimed misappropriation of private and confidential information. This is crucial to defendants in breach of confidence cases as they are entitled to know what were the private and confidential information alleged to have been misappropriated so as to enable them to contest the claim.[24] For more details, refer to the case report on Topic 3.

4.2. The Legal Burden of Proof for the Remedies Sought

The same burden of proof is borne by the plaintiff in relation to the remedies sought. For example, if the plaintiff is claiming damages, the onus is on the plaintiff to prove his actual loss or damages, supported by evidence or supporting documents.[25]

4.3. Interlocutory Applications

The plaintiff needs to prove to the satisfaction of the court that it is entitled to the grant of interlocutory orders. Failure to do so would result in the application being refused or the orders granted being set aside and the plaintiff subject to pay damages on its undertaking. For example, in *Niro Ceramic Sales & Services (M) Sdn. Bhd & Anor v Low Chin Guan & Ors*, the plaintiff applied for an interim injunction to restrain the defendants from doing various acts and an order directing the defendants to deliver up to the plaintiffs various documents purportedly containing confidential information and trade secrets obtained from the latter. The application was rejected on the ground that the evidence relied upon by the plaintiffs was clearly insufficient to establish any of the pleaded causes of action on a prima facie basis.[26]

In *Regent Decorators (M) Sdn Bhd & Anor v Michael Chee & Ors*,[27] the plaintiffs obtained an ex parte Mareva injunction against the defendants as a result of which the 4th defendant was restrained from dealing with its assets generally including and in

21. *Risk – X Sdn Bhd v Capital Market Risk Advisor Sdn Bhd* [2016] 2 AMCR 745, paras 42-43.
22. [2015] 1 MLJ 424, paras 18 and 39.
23. *Dynacast (Melaka) Sdn Bhd & Ors v Vision Cast Sdn Bhd & Anor* [2016] 3 MLJ 417; [2016] 6 CLJ 176, para. 30.
24. [2016] 6 CLJ 176, para. 29.
25. *See*, for example, *Ampledeal (M) Sdn Bhd & 3 Ors v Laponie (M) Sdn Bhd & 3 Ors* [2015] MLJU 1933 (no pagination provided) where the plaintiffs failed to obtain damages for the loss they claimed amounting to MYR 15.9 million as it was unsupported by evidence or any supporting documents. *See also ZY Phyto Tech Industries (M) Sdn Bhd & Anor v Nazri bin Zakaria & Ors* [2018] 11 MLJ 110, para. 7. *infra*, at Topic 5, para. 4.5.2.
26. *Niro Ceramic Sales & Services (M) Sdn. Bhd. & Anor v Low Chin Guan & Ors*, Suit No. 22NCVC-695-11/2017, 4 October 2018, para. 30.
27. [1984] 2 CLJ (Rep) 441, p. 443.

particular any money standing to the credit of the 4th defendant in its account with its bankers. The court held that there had been no evidence that there was a danger that the available assets of the defendants would be dissipated to prejudice the plaintiffs' claim. The court, therefore, lifted the Mareva injunction.[28] In *Niro Ceramic Sales & Services (M) Sdn. Bhd. & Anor v Low Chin Guan*,[29] the application for interim spring board injunction and delivery up of documents was rejected because of the total lack of evidence to support the alleged usage of the plaintiff's confidential information and trade secrets and/or unlawful acts by the defendants to obtain a head start.

The plaintiff in *Apparatech (M) Sdn Bhd v Ng Hock Chong & Anor*[30] sued the first defendant for breach of his duty not to misuse any information confidential of the plaintiff. The plaintiff had obtained an ex parte Anton Piller order to permit an entry at the second defendant's premises in order to search, inspect, photograph or photocopy and deliver into safe keeping of the plaintiff's solicitors all documents and articles which were listed in the list of items annexed to the order. The court set aside the order on the ground, *inter alia*, that the plaintiff had failed to provide evidence that there was a real possibility that relevant materials may be destroyed.[31]

5. THE ORDER FOR PROTECTING THE SECRECY OF TRADE SECRET DURING PROSECUTION AND TRIAL

The basic rule is that a plaintiff must satisfy all the essential requirements for the grant of such orders. As these orders are regarded to be 'draconian', non-compliance with the requirements would result in the order being set aside and the plaintiff punished with damages.

5.1. Anton Piller Order

An Anton Piller order is basically the civil equivalent of a search warrant. It permits the plaintiff, without prior notice, to search and take possession of the records or other items of the defendant. In *Apparatech (M) Sdn Bhd v Ng Hock Chong & Anor*, the plaintiff's granted ex parte Anton Piller order was set aside on the ground, *inter alia*, that the plaintiff had failed to provide evidence that there was a real possibility that relevant materials may be destroyed.[32]

---

28. *Regent Decorators (M) Sdn Bhd & Anor v Michael Chee & Ors* [1984] 2 CLJ (Rep) 441, pp. 442-444.
29. Suit No. 22NCVC-695-11/2017, 4 October 2018, para. 21.
30. [2006] 2 MLJ 61.
31. *Apparatech (M) Sdn Bhd v Ng Hock Chong & Anor* [2006] 2 MLJ 61, para. 50. *See also Pentamaster Instrumentation Sdn Bhd v QAV Technologies Sdn Bhd* [2017] 5 CLJ 736 and *Sigma Glove Industries Sdn Bhd & Ors v Ong Chin Kok & Anor* [2018] 8 MLJ 481.
32. [2006] 2 MLJ 61, para. 50. *See also Pentamaster Instrumentation Sdn Bhd v QAV Technologies Sdn Bhd* [2017] 5 CLJ 736 and *Sigma Glove Industries Sdn Bhd & Ors v Ong Chin Kok & Anor* [2018] 8 MLJ 481, where the risk of destruction requirement was not satisfied by the plaintiffs.

5.2. Mareva Injunction

A Mareva injunction 'is an injunction granted ex parte against a defendant in a pending action to restrain him from removing assets from and now even dissipating them within the jurisdiction and so stultifying any judgment in favour of the plaintiff'.[33] In *Regent Decorators (M) Sdn Bhd & Anor v Michael Chee & Ors*, the court lifted the Mareva injunction as there was no evidence the available assets of the defendants would be dissipated to prejudice the plaintiffs' claim.[34]

5.3. Interim Injunction and Interlocutory Injunction

The law relating to the grant of an interlocutory injunction in Malaysia is based on the principles enunciated by the House of Lords in *American Cyanamid v Ethicon*[35] (for more details, refer to the case report on Topic 4). In *Associated Tractors Sdn Bhd v Chan Boon Heng & Anor*, the Supreme Court (now the Federal Court) had held that 'the most important factor to consider as a matter of principle is the question of whether in lieu of the injunction, damages would be an adequate and proper remedy because in the matter of injunctions and exercising its jurisdiction the court acts upon the principle of preventing irreparable damage'.[36]

The plaintiff in *Agensi Pekerjaan Talent2 International Sdn Bhd v Kenneth Yong Fu* Loong sued the defendant for breach of his employment contract and use of the plaintiff's confidential information.[37] Following this, the plaintiff filed for an interlocutory injunction to prevent the defendant from soliciting the plaintiff's present employees to leave their employment with the plaintiff and that he be injunct from disclosing and using confidential information belonging to the plaintiff. The court held that there were serious questions of law and fact in dispute between the parties that had to be addressed. The balance of convenience clearly favoured the plaintiff because the injunction only sought to restrain the defendant from doing what he had covenanted not to do. In relation to whether damages would be an adequate remedy, the court held that 'If an injunction is not granted, the loss suffered by the plaintiff would be irreparable and incalculable in terms of losing its market share for which it had expended significant time and money to develop its customer and candidate lists. If the defendant subsequently succeeded in his defence, damages would be an adequate remedy.'[38] The *Agensi Pekerjaan* court followed the approach in *Svenson Hair Centre Sdn Bhd v Irene Chin Zee Ling*, where the court held as follows:

> I hold that damages will not be an adequate compensation for the plaintiff in view of the very nature of the breach of contractual prohibition and confidence, which make it difficult for the plaintiff to quantify monetarily its loss of patronage of

33. *Zainal Abidin bin Haji Abdul Rahman v Century Hotel Sdn Bhd* [1982] 1 MLJ 260, p. 262.
34. [1984] 2 CLJ (Rep) 441, pp. 442-444.
35. *American Cyanamid v Ethicon* [1975] 1 All ER 504. *See Keet Gerald Francis Noel John v Mohd Noor @ Harun bin Abdullah* [1995] 1 CLJ 293 and *Svenson Hair Centre Sdn. Bhd. v Irene Chin Zee Ling* [2008] 7 MLJ 903.
36. *Associated Tractors Sdn Bhd v Chan Boon Heng & Anor* [1990] 1 CLJ (Rep) 30.
37. [2011] 4 AMR 814.
38. *Ibid.*, paras 21-24, 28 and 33.

customers and/or the long term loss and damage to the Bella Beauty Business' business, strategies and competitiveness.[39]

Yeohata Industries Sdn. Bhd & Anor v Coil Master Sdd Bhd & Ors[40] involves an application for both a prohibitory injunction and a mandatory injunction against the defendants to, *inter alia*, restrain them from using the plaintiffs' confidential information until disposal of the suit and also that the defendants deliver to the plaintiffs documents relating to the manufacture, production and marketing of both 'YEOHATA' and 'COILMASTER MK 1' within seven days from the date of service of the order.

In relation to the question as to whether damage would be an adequate remedy if the plaintiff were to succeed at trial, the court took into consideration the fact that the plaintiff will suffer irreparable damages to their business and reputation in that the defendants would continue to make false claim, fraudulent misrepresentations to third parties and to injure the name and business of the plaintiffs, resulting in the plaintiffs having to rebuild their marketing network to prevent further sabotage. All these damages were extremely difficult to be assessed. In addition, the first defendant company had just been incorporated in July 1999 (less than two years before the present suit) and the paid-up capital was MYR 500,000.00. The court concluded that there were no substantial grounds for supposing that the first defendant company would be in a position to pay substantial damages to the plaintiffs in the event the plaintiffs succeeded during the trial. In contrast, the plaintiffs were in the business for over 25 years and had experience and reputation in the industry all along the period. Based on all these considerations, the court granted both the prohibitory and mandatory interim injunction as prayed.

In contrast to the above cases, in *Horizon Film Entertainment Sdn Bhd v Mohamad Azlan Norani*, the application for interlocutory injunction was rejected, even though there were serious bona fide issues to be tried among the parties. This was because the court was satisfied that the movie film production in issue was largely a commercial undertaking with a view to profit. In this respect, damages would definitely be an adequate remedy. The plaintiffs have not shown that damages would be difficult to assess here.[41]

6. THE DAMAGES

The burden of proving the loss or damage lies on the party who is entitled to damages.[42] If the successful plaintiff is unable to prove his actual loss, he may opt to claim for an account of profits made by the defendant as a result of his breach of confidence.[43]

Lord Wilberforce in the House of Lords' decision in *General Tire v Firestone* identified the following general principles in relation to the award of damages:

39. *Agensi Pekerjaan Talent2 International Sdn Bhd v Kenneth Yong Fu Loong* [2011] 4 AMR 814, para. 33, following *Svenson Hair Centre Sdn Bhd v Irene Chin Zee Ling* [2008] 8 CLJ 386.
40. [2001] MLJU 281.
41. Civil Suit No. 22IP-32-04/2019, 25 July 2019, paras 16 and 21.
42. *Lim Tze Sian v Coverright Surface Malaysia Sdn Bhd* [2017] 1 MLJ 418, para. 32.
43. *See*, for example, *Juris Technologies v Foo Tiang Sin and 5 Others* [2020] 3 AMR 36, para. 75.

i) As in the case of any other tort ... the object of damages is to compensate for loss or injury.
ii) The general rule ... is that the measure of damages is to be, so far as possible, that sum of money which will put the injured party in the same position as he would have been in if he had not sustained the wrong.
iii) The plaintiffs have the burden of proving their loss.
iv) Damages should be liberally assessed but that the object is to compensate the plaintiffs and not punish the defendants.[44]

The above principles have been reiterated by the Federal Court in *Taiping Poly (M) Sdn Bhd v Wong Fook Toh and Ors.*[45] In *ZY Phyto Tech Industries (M) Sdn Bhd & Anor v Nazri bin Zakaria & Ors,*[46] the defendants were ordered to pay damages for the wrongful use of the plaintiff's confidential information. The court ordered that damages will be assessed by reference to an account of profits from the plaintiff. Despite this order, the plaintiff adduced projected losses based on historical trends and sales estimates without presenting a profit and loss account. It was held that the plaintiff had failed to discharge the burden of proving the loss or damage it suffered.

Besides compensatory damages, the plaintiff could also seek aggravated damages and exemplary damages. Aggravated damages are determined with reference to the defendant's motive as well as the plaintiff's good reputation, whereas the purpose of exemplary damages is to punish. The court in *Worldwide Rota Dies Sdn Bhd v Ronald Ong Cheow Joon* held that 'Whenever the defendant's conduct is sufficiently outrageous to merit punishment in situations where the defendant's conduct discloses malice, fraud, cruelty, insolence or the like, then exemplary damages would be granted.'[47]

In *Lim Tze Sian v Coverright Surface Malaysia Sdn Bhd,* the plaintiff-respondent claimed damages in the form of loss of profits. The Court of Appeal held that 'There must be a causal link or nexus between the loss claimed and the act of the appellant.'[48] As the respondent was not able to prove that its loss was attributable to the defendant-appellant, it was not entitled to any compensation, including a claim for loss of profits. For more details, refer to the case report on Topic 5.

44. *General Tire v Firestone* [1975] 1 WLR 819, p. 824.
45. Civil Appeal No. J-03-142-2004, para. 18.
46. [2018] 11 MLJ 110.
47. [2010] 8 MLJ 297, para. 154.
48. [2017] 1 MLJ 418, para. 31.

TOPIC 1 THE REQUIREMENTS OF TRADE SECRET

Farizah Mohamed Isa

1. Legal Issues

In Malaysia, trade secrets are protected under an area of law called breach of confidential information which is a common law tort. It generally protects both trade secrets and private information conveyed in confidence usually in the course of employment. The rules on protection include ideas, information, technology or 'know-how' not known to the public, and as such, the unauthorized disclosure of this information or trade secret is considered a breach of confidence and may give rise to a civil liability.

The relationship between employers and employees commonly gives rise to an automatic 'duty of confidentiality', which is within the scope of a 'duty of fidelity'. This duty prescribes that the employee must act in the employer's best interest at all times, which includes the protection of confidential information and trade secrets of the employer. Not only that, once an employee leaves employment, he or she is still obliged to keep confidential all information and trade secrets which he/she was exposed to in the course of the employment. This is especially relevant and significant when the employee leaves and is involved in the same field of his previous employer.

2. The Statutory Law

As stated above, this area of law is governed by common law and equitable principles. There are no specific statutes pertaining to the protection of trade secrets. Hence, there is no statutory definition of what a trade secret encompassed. However, guidance can be obtained from Article 39 of the Agreement on Trade-Related Aspects of Intellectual Property Rights. This provision states the following:

(i) The information must be secret (i.e., it is not generally known among, or readily accessible to, circles that normally deal with the kind of information in question).
(ii) It must have commercial value.
(iii) It must have been subject to reasonable steps by the rightful holder of the information to keep it secret (e.g., through confidentiality agreements).

3. The Case Law

Cases that have been decided in the Malaysian courts seem to be in line with this provision and also follow principles of leading cases in the United Kingdom on the requirements of trade secrets and what gives rise to a civil action.

The cases on trade secrets and breach of confidential information in Malaysia mostly relate to employer-employee contracts and duties owed by an employee in relation to unauthorized use of the information in question.

4. The Leading Case

The case below was chosen because this was the first case in Malaysia where the principles in the landmark case of *Coco v AN Clark (Engineers) Ltd* [1969] RPC 41 were applied.

4.1. Case Information

Schmidt Scientific Sdn Bhd v Ong Han Suan & Ors [1997] 5 MLJ 632; [1998] 1 CLJ 685. High Court Malaya, Kuala Lumpur, Civil Suit: D5-22-410-1994, 26 June 1997. RK Nathan, JC.

4.2. Summary

This case deals with issues of contract, whether there is a breach of a 'duty of fidelity' between the plaintiff employer and his former employees which was encompassed in a confidentiality clause in the contract of employment. The plaintiff brought an action to stop the defendants from further using the confidential information obtained while the defendants were in his employment. The defendants contended that the duty of fidelity or good faith was not enforceable after the employment ends, as this would amount to a restraint of trade. The defendants also questioned the nature of the confidential information, as, according to them, trade secrets or confidential information applied only to secret formulas and manufacturing processes or 'unique intellectual work' which in this case were not. The elements required to show breach of confidence were also described in detail by the learned judge in this case.

4.3. Facts

The plaintiff was the employer of the 1st to 4th defendants and dealt in the sale of certain scientific equipment for which it was the exclusive distributor in Malaysia. The 1st to 4th defendants left the employment of the plaintiff and started their own company, which was the 5th defendant, in December 1993. On 1 April 1994, the 5th defendant was appointed a distributor of certain products for which the plaintiff had earlier been the sole distributor. The contracts of employment between the plaintiff and the 2nd to 4th defendants contained a fidelity clause which imposed an obligation on the 2nd to 4th defendants not to have any interest in any business similar to the plaintiff's business and to keep confidential all information about the plaintiff's dealings, transactions, and financial matters.[49] The 5th defendant approached several existing customers of the plaintiff and secured certain sales which affected the plaintiff in terms of profits and loss of sales.

49. Between December 1993 and January 1994, the 5th defendant had approached three existing customers of the plaintiff regarding the sale of products sold by the plaintiff at a time when the 5th defendant was not yet an authorized distributor and managed to secure a sale whereby the 5th defendant made a profit of MYR 26,000.

The plaintiff applied for, *inter alia*:[50]

(i) an injunction to restrain the 5th defendant from using or disclosing any trade secrets and soliciting orders from the plaintiff's customers;
(ii) an injunction to restrain the 1st to 4th defendants from disclosing to the 5th defendant any confidential information and/or trade secrets of the plaintiff; and
(iii) an order that the defendants deliver up the confidential documents of the plaintiff in the possession of the defendants.

In their defence, the defendants contended, *inter alia*, that the confidential documents, in order to be protected, must be the product of unique intellectual work by the plaintiff or its employees, which in this case were not classified in such a category.

RK Nathan JC decided in favour of the plaintiff and allowed the plaintiff's application.

4.4. *The Reasoning of the Court*

4.4.1. *Duty of Fidelity*

The duty of good faith or fidelity does not only prohibit an employee from misusing or disclosing information while still in the employer's employment but also prohibits the employee from using any confidential information obtained during his employment without the employer's consent for his own or someone else's use after the employment contract ends. Where the court finds that there exists a confidential relationship between two parties, it can infer an implied contract arising out of that confidential relationship. The fidelity clause in the employment contract read as follows:

> Fidelity: During the employment with the company you shall not have any direct or indirect interest in any business similar to the company's business and you shall direct all your efforts, duties and responsibilities to further the interests of the company. Any information about the company, its dealings, transactions and financial matters are regarded as confidential and are not allowed to be divulged to any person whatsoever.[51]

The judge found that this duty of good faith or fidelity did not just require that the employee refrains from misuse or from disclosing information while still in the employment of the plaintiff; there is also an implied duty that prohibits the employee from using any confidential information obtained during his employment, without the employer's consent, after the employment contract ends. Thus, it was a breach of the fidelity clause and the implied duty to remove a customer list or to deliberately set out to memorize the said list with the intention of using it later, even though it was used post-employment.[52] RK Nathan JC referred to and agreed with the decision of the

50. *Schmidt Scientific Sdn Bhd v Ong Han Suan & Ors* [1998] 1 CLJ 685, p. 686.
51. *Ibid.*, p. 689.
52. *Ibid.*, p. 691.

English case of *Robb v Green*[53] where the Court of Appeal held that the employee was in breach of an implied term of the contract of service in making copies of his employer's list of customers' names and addresses, with the intention of using it for the purpose of soliciting orders from them after he had left his employer's service and set up a similar business on his own account.[54]

RK Nathan JC also referred to another English case which bears some resemblance to the case in hand. In *Merryweather v Moore,*[55] the defendant, upon completing a term of apprenticeship with the plaintiffs, a firm of engine-makers, was retained in their employment as a paid clerk, but he ultimately left their service for that of another firm of engine-makers. Two days before leaving the plaintiffs' service, he compiled for his own purposes, and without their knowledge or consent, a table of dimensions of various types of engines made by them, and this table he had in his possession when he entered the service of his new employers. The new employers subsequently exposed for sale an engine which corresponded to the dimensions given in the table. The court held that in compiling and retaining the table for his own purposes, the defendant had committed an abuse of the confidence ordinarily existing between a clerk and his employer, or a breach of the implied contract arising from that confidence. The plaintiffs were entitled to an interim injunction restraining the defendant from publishing or communicating the table or its contents to any person.

Accordingly, in this case, RK Nathan JC stressed that apart from the general duty of good faith and fidelity, the 1st to 4th defendants, and through them the 5th defendant, as ex-employees of the plaintiff were also under an implied duty not to use, divulge and/or disclose to whomsoever, any confidential information and/or trade secrets obtained during the course of their employment with the ex-employer after the employment had ceased for their own or the 5th defendant's benefit to the detriment of the plaintiff. He found that the defendants had used, divulged and/or disclosed confidential information and/or trade secrets of the plaintiff. Another English case that was referred to by RK Nathan JC was *Seager v Copydex, Ltd.*[56] He quoted Lord Denning MR, where His Lordship in that case did not even want to consider the question of an implied contract but relied on equity.[57]

From the facts of this case, RK Nathan JC held that the plaintiff had satisfied all three aspects of the cases referred to against all the defendants. Hence, the defendants, who came into possession of confidential information, knowing it to be such, were under a duty not to take unfair advantage of it or to make use of it to the prejudice of the plaintiff. The 5th defendant to whom the information has been wrongfully revealed also was under a duty of confidence to the plaintiff. As such, the Court granted the

---

53. *Robb v Green* [1895] 2 QB 315.
54. Justice Nathan quoted Lord Esher MR in this case, where His Lordship stated among other things that the duty of good faith by an employee towards his employer must be implied. 'I think that in a contract of service the court must imply such a stipulation as I have mentioned, because it is a thing which must necessarily have been in view of both parties when they entered into the contract ...' pp. 316-317.
55. *Merryweather v Moore* [1892] 2 Ch 518.
56. *Seager v Copydex, Ltd.* [1967] 2 All ER 416.
57. *Ibid.*, p. 417.

equitable relief of an injunction against the 5th defendant as well as against the rest of the defendants.

4.4.2. *Requirements of an Action for Breach of Confidence*

In the instant case, RK Nathan JC stated the plaintiff had satisfied all three elements and was entitled to an injunction against all the defendants. He referred to the case of *Coco v A.N. Clark (Engineers) Ltd (No. 2)*[58] and quoted Megarry J where he held that in order to succeed in an action for breach of confidence, the plaintiff must establish to the satisfaction of the court three elements, namely:

(i) the information which the plaintiff is seeking to protect is of a confidential nature;
(ii) the information in question was communicated in circumstances importing an obligation of confidence; and
(iii) there must be an unauthorized use of that information to the detriment of the party communicating it.[59]

4.4.3. *The Confidential Nature of the Information*

As for this issue, there was evidence on the plaintiff's behalf that the 4th defendant had printed out information relating to, *inter alia*, the plaintiff's customer database, suppliers and cost prices. RK Nathan JC explained that, in the light of the particular nature of the plaintiff's business, trade secrets were not limited to manufacturing processes or secret formulas but extended also to information relating to customers, suppliers, cost prices and the specific needs and requirements of the customers. The compilation of the lists of customers, their specific needs and cost prices were confidential even if the method of arriving at the selling price of the equipment was neither a unique intellectual work nor ingenious.[60]

From the evidence given by the plaintiff in this case, it was obvious to the Court that prior to the 1st to the 4th defendants leaving the employment of the plaintiff, there were no other competitors in the market for the Tabai and Suga products and that the plaintiff was the only agent in Malaysia.[61] The defendants had access to confidential information and/or trade secrets of the plaintiff. There was information relating to cost prices, quoted prices, specific needs and requirements of the customers and suppliers, status of all ongoing negotiations with the customers, and price list. This information was highly confidential in nature, and not generally known in the market. The disclosure of this information would no doubt cause detriment to the plaintiff in terms of business and reputation.

Based on these, RK Nathan JC held that the nature of the information, in the light of the plaintiff's business and its trade practice, compelled the court to grant the

58. *Coco v A.N. Clark (Engineers) Ltd (No. 2)* [1969] RPC 41.
59. *Schmidt Scientific Sdn Bhd v Ong Han Suan & Ors* [1998] 1 CLJ 685, p. 693.
60. *Ibid.*, p. 696.
61. The Tabai and Suga products were the scientific equipment which the plaintiffs were initially the exclusive distributor of, in Malaysia.

protection the plaintiff applied for. In this judgment, he held that trade secrets are not limited to manufacturing processes or secret formulae but extended to information relating to the list of names and addresses of the customers and suppliers, specific questions sent to the customers, cost prices, specific needs and requirements of the customers and status of the ongoing negotiation with the customers. Therefore, the above-mentioned information had the necessary quality of confidentiality.

4.4.4. *That the Information in Question Was Communicated in Circumstances Importing an Obligation of Confidence*

From the discussion relating to the duty of confidence and duty of fidelity and good faith between employers and employees in the first issue above, this requirement was duly met.

4.4.5. *Unauthorized Use of That Information to the Detriment of the Party Communicating It*

In view of the senior positions held by the 1st to the 4th defendants in the plaintiff's employment, it cannot be denied that they had access to a great deal of confidential information and/or trade secrets of the plaintiff. RK Nathan JC inferred that the defendants, in approaching the customers of the plaintiff for the sale of the same equipment, must have made use of or taken and/or made copies of the confidential information and/or trade secrets of the plaintiff. This was a matter which was strictly within the specific knowledge of the plaintiff alone and no one else. In his view, the plaintiff was entitled to rely on an inference that the defendants had made use of the confidential information and/or trade secrets of the plaintiff because of the admitted similarity of the quotation sent out by the plaintiff and the 5th defendant to Sharp Roxy Corporation (M) Sdn Bhd and the other so-called coincidences of the 5th defendant approaching the other customers of the plaintiff for the sale of an identical equipment with the exact specifications, except for a lower price. There was sufficient evidence in this case to prove on a balance of probabilities that the defendants had taken or made copies of confidential documents from the plaintiff and used them for the benefit of the 5th defendant.[62]

Upon close examination of the 5th defendant's letter of offer, it was discovered that the documents contained specific information relating to a particular Tabai equipment, and that one of which corresponded exactly in fact and content with that of the plaintiff's earlier letter of offer dated 28 October 1993. The question was where did the 5th defendant obtain the information relating to the specification of the particular equipment, since the 5th defendant was not the authorized agent, at the material time. No evidence was led by the defendants to show the source of the information, apart from stating standard model and market information. Certainly, such detailed information could not possibly be obtained from any other source, except from the plaintiff.

62. *Schmidt Scientific Sdn Bhd v Ong Han Suan & Ors* [1998] 1 CLJ 685, p. 698.

The information relating to the specific requirements and needs of the customers in respect of the particular equipment was highly confidential in nature and sensitive to its competitor. Apart from the specification of the equipment which was identical, RK Nathan JC concluded that the net selling price could only have been configurated after obtaining the costs price from the principal/supplier, and at that time the plaintiff was the exclusive agent/distributor for Tabai products. He had no hesitation in concluding that the 5th defendant had in all probability received and/or obtained the information from the documents belonging to the plaintiff. Hence, the requirement of unauthorized use of the information belonging to the plaintiff was satisfied.[63]

RK Nathan JC stated that in his judgment where he considered the implied duty of fidelity and also Lord Denning's view that equity is to be applied in this situation, as illustrated in the case of *Seager v Copydex*. He was of the view that a breach of confidence should also be regarded as a tort with damages to be awarded to the successful plaintiff. In his opinion, since the categories of tortious liability remain open, the ingenuity and resourcefulness of the human mind can and ought to lead to fresh categories of tort being established and breach of confidence should be included in the list.[64]

4.5. *Legal Analysis*

4.5.1 *A Trade Secret Extends to Information Which Would Prejudice Its Owner When Used Without His Consent or Knowledge*

In the present case, the High Court was faced with several issues in determining the scope and nature of confidential information/trade secrets. As there are no statutory interpretation or definition of confidential information/trade secret and what they should comprise, the scope and nature of it must be examined on a case-by-case basis. What should be considered as a trade secret would differ depending on the nature and field of the business. The defendants in this case contended that the documents referred to by the plaintiff as being confidential must be the product of unique intellectual work and ingenuity. Since the information was merely a 'configuration' of data supplied by the manufacturers for the purpose of arriving at the selling price, it was neither unique intellectual work nor ingenious. The defence argued that every trader in its normal course of business fixes a price for a product sold to customers in the same way as the 'configuration' referred to by the plaintiff.[65]

The judge in this case rightfully rejected this argument. According to him, there is no doubt that the method of configuration is not confidential, but what makes it confidential was the compilation of lists of the names and addresses of customers, specific needs and requirements of the customers and their budget and the costs and prices of the equipment obtained from the overseas principal/supplier. The defendants had saved themselves the time and trouble of having to go through laborious discussions and negotiations with the customers, the effort put in to compile the list of

63. *Ibid.*, p. 700.
64. *Ibid.*, p. 702.
65. *Ibid.*, p. 700.

names and addresses of customers and suppliers and above all the costs and prices which are only available from the overseas principal/supplier.

This established that in Malaysia, a trade secret is not confined to technology, know-how or a secret formulation only. It extends to any information which would prejudice the owner of the information when used without its consent or knowledge.

4.5.2. *Duty of Fidelity after the Employee Leaves His/Her Employment*

As to the obligation of confidence, it was clear in this case that the parties were under an obligation of confidence stipulated in their employment contract. What was in issue was whether this obligation also gave rise to a duty of fidelity to an employer which would bind the employee even after the employee leaves his/her employment. This case illustrated that this duty of fidelity must be implied from the expressed duty of confidentiality in the contract, and it continues to bind the employees even after employment, especially so if the said ex-employee enters into a similar field of employment or starts his or her own business in a similar field as their ex-employer. This was in line with the decisions of leading English cases in this matter.[66]

4.5.3. *Unauthorized Use*

On the requirement of unauthorized use, in this case, the plaintiff had clearly established that the information relating to the current sales status of its products to the customers was highly confidential in nature; hence, it was reasonable to infer that the defendants had used, without consent, the plaintiff's information in approaching the plaintiff's existing customers offering the same equipment. No plausible explanation was given by the defendants in respect of such coincidences within such a short time, after the 5th defendant was incorporated. The 5th defendant had approached these customers for the sale of Tabai and Suga products in which the plaintiff had an ongoing negotiation with the said customers for the same equipment/instrument at that time. No evidence was led to show that the 5th defendant knew of the customers' needs and requirements through negotiations/discussions with them.[67] Further, the plaintiff showed that the use of this information had caused them to suffer loss of sales and profits.

4.5.4. *Restraint of Trade?*

On the issue of restraint of trade that was also argued by the defendants, the High Court found that it was not the plaintiff's case to restrain the defendants from entering into the same trade as the plaintiff. The plaintiff's case was to restrain them from using, disclosing and/or divulging confidential information and/or trade secrets of the plaintiff to the detriment of the plaintiff. Therefore, it was clear that the allegation of restraint of trade had no significance in this case.

---

66. *See* the cases in notes 54, 55 and 56.
67. *Schmidt Scientific Sdn Bhd v Ong Han Suan & Ors* [1998] 1 CLJ 685, p. 699.

4.6. *Commercial or Industrial Significance*

The protection of confidential information/trade secrets is crucial against misappropriation or theft of trade secrets and corporate espionage. It would threaten innovation, growth, development and investment of business entities and national economy globally.[68] Such acts would have a tendency to kill a business and stop it from developing further. Measures must be taken to minimize the incidences of trade secret thefts and breaches of confidential information. In various businesses, trade secrets are crucial compared to patents; hence a watertight contract and technical measures to protect trade secret are crucial for the survival of such businesses.

A trade secret is essential to brand value and corporate strategy. Therefore, a trade secret is a growing commercial power that gives a business entity a competitive edge and thus must be protected. In short, protecting a trade secret is protecting the business. As seen in the case discussed above, a business that was built and established by the plaintiff was affected when confidential information was used in an unauthorized manner by ex-employees. Although the information concerned was just customer lists, pricing and data which can be regarded as customary in a business or without any uniqueness or not an intellectual creation, the repercussions of its unauthorized use was damaging and could kill a business that took years to build and establish.

It was suggested that the protection of trade secrets by a company against the employee and competitors requires an integrated approach. The legal approach alone is not sufficient to protect the trade secrets from theft and corporate espionage by the employee. It must be combined with administrative measures to ensure comprehensive protection. While the law provides the foundation for the company to protect their trade secrets through contractual obligation, the administrative approach will monitor adherence and compliance of the obligation through the code of conduct and business ethics. Such integrated approaches will create a culture of confidentiality, compliance and respect within the organization and promote healthy competition within the industry.[69]

Also, instead of just a civil liability imposed against a defendant, the theft of trade secret committed by an ex-employee or persons having that obligation of confidence should also be a criminal offence and punished according to criminal sanctions. This would invariably strengthen the protection of trade secret and confidential information which is crucial to the business.

68. Organisation for Economic Co-operation and Development (OECD) report on Enquiries into Intellectual Property Economic Impact: Approaches to the Protection of Trade Secrets, Elsevier (2016).
69. Jalil J. & Hassan H., *Protecting Trade Secret from Theft and Corporate Espionage: Some Legal and Administrative Measures*, International Journal of Business and Society, Vol. 21(S1), 2020, 205-218.

TOPIC 2 THE VALIDITY AND SCOPE OF CONFIDENTIALITY AND/OR NON-COMPETITION CLAUSES

Lim Heng Gee

1. Legal Issues

The issue discussed here is the relationship between protections of confidential information and restrictive covenants in employment contracts and whether the contractual restrictions constitute a restraint of trade and are, therefore, void and unenforceable.

2. The Statutory Law

The applicable statute is the Contracts Act 1950 (Revised 1974). This statute governs the rules relating to the making of valid contracts, what contracts are voidable or void, the legal consequence of a voidable or void contract, the duties of parties to a contract, and the consequences of breach of contract.

3. The Case Law

All the cases decided under this topic were decided in the High Court, except for one which went on appeal to the Court of Appeal and finally to the Federal Court. Summaries of some of the important case on this topic are found in the Overview and Summary.

4. The Leading Case

Svenson Hair Center is the leading case on this topic as it discusses the relationship between non-solicitation clauses, non-compete clauses and confidentiality clauses in employment contracts, and section 28 of the Contracts Act, which declares contracts in restraint of trade void.

4.1. Case Information

Svenson Hair Center Sdn Bhd v Irene Chin Zee Ling [2008] 8 CLJ 386. Civil Suit No: D1-22-284-2006, High Court Malaya, Kuala Lumpur, Malaysia, 31 January 2008. Vincent Ng J.

4.2. Summary

This case deals with an application for an injunction to restrain an ex-employee from contacting any of the present customers of the plaintiff until judgment in the action. The defendant had been employed by the plaintiff, whose business was in providing skin and beauty care, products and services. On leaving her employment with the plaintiff, she had allegedly been contacting the plaintiff's customers to entice them to patronize the business in which she was currently employed. This was alleged to be a contravention of certain express prohibitions regarding confidentiality, non-solicitation and non-competition in the employment contract. The court held that the restrictions were meant to protect the confidential information of the plaintiff and hence not void as a restraint of trade. An interim injunction was granted against the defendant. There was no appeal from this decision.

4.3. *Facts*

The defendant, Irene Chin, had been employed by the plaintiff, Svenson Hair Center, since 24 February 1999. She resigned in June 2005. She then joined a competing business, Marique Wellness, which commenced business in October 2005.

It was alleged that the defendant, during the period of her termination notice, took possession of several boxes containing the plaintiff's customer treatment cards. It was further alleged that the defendant, after leaving the plaintiff's employment, had been contacting the plaintiff's customers. The defendant admitted that she did contact some of the plaintiff's customers named, but she had only contacted them to advise them that she was no longer working for the plaintiff. However, one of the plaintiff's customers had testified that she was contacted by the defendant who had informed her that another beauty wellness centre, Marique Wellness, had opened and had asked her to go over there.

In the course of her employment with the plaintiff, the defendant had executed a total of three employment agreements which contained express and specific prohibitions regarding confidentiality, non-solicitation and non-competition. The material clauses in the said agreements are reproduced below:

> Clause 7.01: Confidentiality
>
> The employee acknowledges that during the course of the employment he may receive special training from the company and may have access to:
>
> (i) ...;
> (ii) lists or details of customers of the company or other member of the group;
> (iii) ...; and
> (iv) ...;
>
> (all such information hereinafter referred to as 'confidential information').
>
> Clause 7.02:
>
> The employee agrees that he shall not whether during or after the termination of this agreement without limit in point of time (except as authorized or required by his duties hereunder or to the extent required by law or by an order from a court of competent jurisdiction):
>
> (i) divulge or communicate to any person any of the confidential information;
> (ii) use any such confidential Information for any purpose other than that of the company or other member of the group and in the performance of his duties hereunder; and
> (iii) ... .

According to the plaintiff, the evidence mentioned above was sufficient to show that the defendant did contact the plaintiff's customers after the cessation of her employment, to ask them to go over to the competing business and that it would appear that the defendant may have taken and utilized the plaintiff's confidential information against its interest.

The defendant, however, contended that there were no bona fide serious issues to be tried to warrant the grant of an injunction, as: (i) the plaintiff's alleged confidential information, which comprised of the customer list, customer preferences and business know-how, could not be considered confidential information; (ii) the defendant had not taken copies of the plaintiff's customer treatment cards, or divulged or exploited the same; and (iii) the contractual prohibition was void for illegality.

4.4. *The Reasoning of the Court*

4.4.1. *The Customer List, Customer Preferences and Business Know-How Are Considered to Be Confidential Information*

The court first dealt with the defendant's contention that the plaintiff's alleged confidential information, which comprised the customer list, customer preferences and business know-how, could not be considered confidential information. Citing English authorities,[70] the court held that 'the confidentiality of the said confidential information could not be seriously disputed as this has been expressly mentioned in cl. 7.01(ii) of the employment agreement'.[71] The court also relied on the Malaysian case of *Schmidt Scientific Sdn Bhd v Ong Han Suan & Ors*[72] where even the 'list of names and address of customers and suppliers' were classified as trade secrets.[73]

The court rejected the defendant's contention that the plaintiff's customer's names, lists and details were part of the defendant's own skill, knowledge and business experience. The court again referred to *Faccenda Chicken* where Neill LJ said:

> The duty of good faith will be broken if an employee makes or copies a list of the customers of the employer for use after his employment ends or deliberately memorizes such a list, even though, except in special circumstances, there is no general restriction on an ex-employee canvassing or doing business with customers of his former employer.[74]

The court stressed that 'the plaintiff has, *prima facie*, shown in Penny's affidavit that the defendant had taken possession of the plaintiff's customer treatment cards during the period of her termination notice'.[75]

70. *Faccenda Chicken Ltd v Fowler and Others* [1986] 1 All ER 617 and *Thomas Marshall (Exports) Ltd v Guinle* [1978] 3 All ER 193.
71. *Svenson Hair Center Sdn Bhd v Irene Chin Zee Ling* [2008] 8 CLJ 386, para. 10.
72. [1998] 1 CLJ 685.
73. *Ibid.*, para. 10.
74. *Ibid.*, para. 11.
75. *Ibid.*

4.4.2. The Contractual Prohibitions Do Not Contravene Section 28 of the Contracts Act 1950

The court next considered the defendant's submission that the contractual prohibition was void under section 28 of the Contracts Act 1950.

Section 28 of the Contracts Act 1950 provides:

> 28. Agreement in restraint of trade void
>
> Every agreement by which anyone is restrained from exercising a lawful profession, trade, or business of any kind, is to that extent void.
>
> Saving of agreement not to carry on business of which goodwill is sold
>
> *Exception 1* – One who sells the goodwill of a business may agree with the buyer to refrain carrying on a similar business, within specified local limits, so long as the buyer, or any person deriving title to the goodwill from him, carries on a like business therein:
>
> Provided that such limits appear to the court reasonable, regard being had to the nature of the business.
>
> of agreement between partners prior to dissolution
>
> *Exception 2* – Partners may, upon or in anticipation of a dissolution of the partnership, agree that some or all of them will not carry on a business similar to that of the partnership within such local limits as are referred to in exception 1.
>
> or during continuance of partnership
>
> *Exception 3* – Partners may agree that some one or all of them will not carry on any business, other than that of the partnership, during the continuance of the partnership.

The court held that the *dicta* of Neill LJ in *Faccenda Chicken* 'clearly lays down the law, which is equally applicable in Malaysia, that there is generally no restriction to an ex-employee competing with his ex-employer by canvassing or doing business with the latter's former customers'.[76] The court continued that 'This is certainly in line with general principles which allows competition and is consonant with section 28 of the Contracts Act.'[77]

After reciting section 28, the court emphasized that 'Notwithstanding this provision, what is in my view not permissible, is for such competition to be pursued by wrongfully utilizing the confidential information, eg, list of customers belonging to the ex-employer; and the courts have been vigilant to protect the employer's interest in this regard.'[78] The court then referred to a statement in *Faccenda Chicken* where Neill LJ held that 'The restrictive covenant cases demonstrate that a covenant will not be upheld on the basis of the status of the information which might be disclosed by the

76. *Svenson Hair Center Sdn Bhd v Irene Chin Zee Ling* [2008] 8 CLJ 386, para. 12.
77. *Ibid.*, para. 12.
78. *Ibid.*

former employee if he is not restrained unless it can be regarded as a trade secret or the equivalent of a trade secret.'[79]

The court proceeded to 'unravel the subtle and delicate underlying basis of several court decisions which formulated the principles governing restraint of trade'.[80] The court stressed that 'the law does not debar an ex-employee from making any use of or drawing on a fund of knowledge and experience or skills that he had acquired while working for the employer. That would be tantamount to depriving him of his livelihood'.[81] The law only imposes on the employee a general duty to act in good faith, such as a man of average intelligence and honesty would think proper. Clearly, acts such as memorizing a formula or a list of the employer's customers or taking away such list by an employee for his use is improper and would constitute acting in bad faith. In this context, the court pointed out that 'It is wholly pertinent to observe that cl. 7.01(ii) and cl. 7.02(i) and (ii) of the employment agreement expressly proscribes the "use of any confidential information" as well as the disclosure of information.'[82]

4.4.3. *The Restriction in Perpetuity Was Reasonable and Thus Valid*

The court rejected the defendant's argument that Clause 7.02 should be limited to a reasonable period of time from the termination of her employment. The court stressed that the plaintiff's right in law to protect its confidential information was premised on Clause 7.02, which did not have any time limit. Accordingly, reading the employment agreement as a whole, it was clear that while there was no general restriction on the defendant from soliciting and or competing with the plaintiff after 12 months,[83] this did not apply to situations where such soliciting or competition was effected through the use of the plaintiff's confidential information. In the latter situation, Clause 7.02 provided the plaintiff with the contractual right to restrain such breaches, while the law itself would enforce such contractual rights by the granting of an injunction.[84] The court then stressed that 'If a contrary view is taken by this court in the current case, it

79. *Faccenda Chicken Ltd v Fowler and Others* [197] Ch 117, p. 137, CA, citing *Herbert Morris Ltd v Saxelby* All ER Rep 305 at 317, per Lord Parker and *Littlewoods Organisation Ltd v Harris* [1977] 1 WLR 1472 at 1484, per Megaw LJ.
80. *Svenson Hair Center Sdn Bhd v Irene Chin Zee Ling* [2008] 8 CLJ 386, para. 15. As there were no relevant Malaysian cases relating to confidential information and restrictive covenants, the court referred to *Drake Personnel Ltd v Beddison* [1978] VIC Lexis 101 [1979] VR 13; *Faccenda Chicken Ltd v Fowler and Others CA* [1986] 1 All ER 617; *Saltman Engineering Co Ltd v Campbell Engineering Co Ltd* [1963] 3 All ER 413; *Stepheson Jordan & Harrison Ltd v MacDonald & Evans* [1952] RPC 10; *Thomas Marshall (Exports) Ltd v Guinle* [1978] 3 All ER 193.
81. *Svenson Hair Center Sdn Bhd v Irene Chin Zee Ling* [2008] 8 CLJ 386, para. 15.
82. *Ibid.*, para. 15.
83. Note that Clauses 8 and 9, which were not fully set out in the judgment, precluded the defendant from soliciting and/or competing with the plaintiff within 12 months from her termination of employment. However, as the 12-month period had already expired at the date of the judgment, nothing turned on this point.
84. *Svenson Hair Center Sdn Bhd v Irene Chin Zee Ling* [2008] 8 CLJ 386, para. 16. The court quoted a passage in *Thomas Marshall (Exports) Ltd v Guinle* [1978] 3 All ER 193 where Megarry VC said at p. 199, 'The case is not one, of course, in which the company seeks to restrain the defendant from engaging in any competing work, but one in which the company merely seeks restraints in terms of what I have called the soliciting order and the breach of confidence order.'

would mean that the defendant, notwithstanding her blatant breach of contract and trust in wrongfully obtaining the confidential information, needs only wait for the 12 months period to expire before she could exploit such information with impunity.'[85]

4.4.4. *Defendant's Livelihood and Access to Customers Would Not Be Affected*

As to the defendant's contention that the injunction, if granted, would affect her livelihood and her customer access right, the court stressed that the injunction was merely to stop her from calling, approaching or contacting the plaintiff's customers that appeared in the customer list, as opposed to stopping her from working with the competing business.[86]

4.5. *Legal Analysis*

4.5.1. *The Validity and Scope of Confidentiality and/or Non-competition Clauses*

Svenson Hair Center is the first reported case where the intersection between the protection of confidential information and section 28 of the Contracts Act was fully argued. In an earlier case, *Schmidt Scientific Sdn Bhd v Ong Han Suan & Ors*,[87] the defendants, ex-employees of the plaintiff, had attempted the restraint of trade argument against an application for an injunction to restrain them from disclosing to the 5th defendant any confidential information of the plaintiff. The court held that the allegation of restraint of trade failed as the plaintiff was not attempting to restrain the defendants from entering into the same trade but from using or disclosing confidential information of the plaintiff.[88] The court stated that 'To my mind, there is also an implied duty that prohibits the employee from using any confidential information obtained during his employment, without the employer's consent, for his own or someone else's use after the employment contract ends.'[89] However, the court made no reference to section 28 of the Contracts Act in arriving at its decision.

The next case where restraint of trade was relied on is *Worldwide Rota Dies Sdn Bhd v Ronald Ong Cheow Joon*.[90] Here the plaintiff successfully claimed an order injuncting the defendant from enticing the plaintiff's customers to the defendant or to any other company unless the plaintiff's customers willingly and on their own accord contacted the defendant.

Clauses 9 and 10 in the letter of offer provided as below:

> Cl. 9: All information learned or obtained in the course of work in the Company shall be deemed to be strictly confidential. No such information shall be divulged to any outside party.

85. *Ibid.*, para. 17.
86. *Svenson Hair Center Sdn Bhd v Irene Chin Zee Ling* [2008] 8 CLJ 386, para. 18.
87. [1998] 1 CLJ 685.
88. *Schmidt Scientific Sdn Bhd v Ong Han Suan & Ors* [1998] 1 CLJ 685, p. 700.
89. *Ibid.*, p. 691, referring to *Robb v Green* [1895] 2 QB 315.
90. [2010] 8 MLJ 297.

> Cl. 10: Upon your resignation before or after being confirmed, you shall not be engaged in work or own the same trade as the Company in Malaysia, Singapore, Thailand, Indonesia, Philippines and Taiwan for an immediate period of three years from the date of resignation.

It was alleged that the defendant had in breach of these provisions, after joining Alpha Mould Sdn Bhd, a company set up to compete against the plaintiff, sent quotations to the customers of the plaintiff at a lower price in order to lure away the plaintiff's customers. The confidential information pertaining to the list of customers and the quotation list of the plaintiff was obtained by the defendant while employed with the plaintiff. This was not denied by the defendant.[91] After going through the authorities, the court concluded that the defendant was in breach of confidence.[92]

The court then considered the defendant's argument that the restraint of trade clause in Clause 10 contravened section 28 of the Contracts Act. The court stressed that the defendant had agreed that he would not compete against his former employer either to work or own the same trade as the employer in specified countries for a period of three years from the date of his resignation.[93] The court reiterated the principle that 'Restraint against competition is justifiable if its object is to prevent the exploitation of trade secrets learned by the servant in the course of his employment.'[94] The court then opined that 'A restraint is permissible if it is fashioned in such a way as to prevent a misuse of trade secrets or business connexion.'[95] This aspect of the *Worldwide Rota Dies* case is unremarkable in view of the *Svenson Hair Center* case and the authorities cited therein. As to the reasonableness of the geographical extent of the restraint, the court said that 'The geographical area of the restraint must be viewed in the context of the ease of travel and the character of the business that is under scrutiny. ... Here, the plaintiff's pioneering status has gone across South East Asia and the restraint to those countries mentioned in clause 10 of the letter of offer would be reasonable.'[96]

The court then considered the contention that the restraint of trade clause contravened section 28 of the Contracts Act. The court remarked that in considering section 28 of the Contracts Act, there must be some measure of flexibility. According to the court, 'the commercial reality of the matter dictates this kind of approach. ... The test of reasonableness must be applied in construing a restraint of trade clause'.[97] The court justified this approach by relying on section 1(2) of the Contracts Act which provides that:

> Nothing herein contained shall affect any written law or any usage or custom of trade, or any incident of any contract, not inconsistent with this Act.

91. *Ibid.*, para. 72.
92. *Ibid.*, paras 95-97.
93. *Ibid.*, para. 109.
94. *Worldwide Rota Dies Sdn Bhd v Ronald Ong Cheow Joon* [2010] 8 MLJ 297, para. 109, citing *Hagg v Darley* [1878] 47 LJ Ch 567; *Caribonum Company Limited v Le Couch* [1913] 109 L.T. 587; and *Haynes v Doman* [1899] 2 Ch 13.
95. *Worldwide Rota Dies Sdn Bhd v Ronald Ong Cheow Joon* [2010] 8 MLJ 297, para. 116.
96. *Ibid.*, para. 119.
97. *Worldwide Rota Dies Sdn Bhd v Ronald Ong Cheow Joon* [2010] 8 MLJ 297, para. 126.

According to the court, 'All that section 1(2) ... says is that the legal consequences of a contract which ensue at common law are to continue to apply unless some different legal consequences are spelt out in the Act.'[98] Applying English authorities,[99] the court ruled that the reasonableness of the restraint of trade in the context of the interests of the parties as well as the public must be considered,[100] and that in considering what is said to be reasonable between the parties, the parties are usually the best judges of what is reasonable.[101] Further, in determining the importance of public interest in the restraint of trade doctrine, 'It is in the interests of the public policy not to interfere with the freedom of contract of the parties.'[102] As the defendant had agreed to the contents of the letter of offer which incorporated Clauses 7, 8, 9 and 10, he must be bound by it. The court in *Worldwide Rota Dies* concluded that on the facts of the case, section 28 of the Contracts Act did not apply, remarking that it would 'apply generously the common law regime in construing the restraint of trade in this case'.[103]

4.5.2. *Section 28 Is Indeed Inconsistent with the Common Law Doctrine of Restraint of Trade*

With respect, it would appear that the *Worldwide Rota Dies* court had been overenthusiastic in relying on section 1(2) of the Contracts Act to justify the adoption of the common law doctrine of reasonableness in construing restraint of trade clauses. Section 1(2) only applies in the absence of anything 'not inconsistent with this Act'. Section 28, which makes agreement in restraint of trade void except in the three specified circumstances, is indeed inconsistent with the common law doctrine of restraint of trade.

With that, we turn to the case of *Lim Yoke Lin v Roy Hong Ping Wei & Ors*.[104] At issue was the defendant's contention that Clause 3.8 of the Sale of Shares Agreement, which provided that 'The vendor hereby agreed not to conduct or operate any business similar to, or competitive with, the Company worldwide for a period of ten years', was void pursuant to section 28 of the Contracts Act. Although this case did not involve any issues relating to the protection of confidential information, it is instructive as the court reviewed previous decisions relating to the application of section 28.[105] The *Lim Yoke Lin* court concluded that 'Thus, it is imperative upon this Court to scrutinise the impugned clause whether it amounts to restraint of trade and if so, whether the

98. *Ibid.*, para. 126.
99. *Esso Petroleum Co. Ltd. v Harper's Garage (Stourport) Ltd.* [1968] AC 269, H.L and *North Western Salt Company, Limited v Electrolytic Alkali Company, Limited* [1914] AC 461. *Worldwide Rota Dies Sdn Bhd v Ronald Ong Cheow Joon* [2010] 8 MLJ 297, paras 129-130.
100. *Worldwide Rota Dies Sdn Bhd v Ronald Ong Cheow Joon* [2010] 8 MLJ 297, para. 128.
101. *Ibid.*, para. 129.
102. *Ibid.*, para. 131.
103. *Ibid.*, para. 133.
104. [2019] 1 LNS 1439.
105. *Polygram Records Sdn Bhd v Hillary Ang & 4 Ors & Anor* [1994] 3 CLJ 806; *Worldwide Rota Dies Sdn Bhd v Ronald Ong Cheow Joon* [2010] 8 MLJ 297; *Nagadevan Mahalingam v Millennium Medicare Services* [2011] 3 CLJ 529; *Vision Cast Sdn Bhd & Anor v Dynacast (Melaka) Sdn Bhd & Ors* [2014] 8 CLJ 884; and *Millennium Medicare Services v Nagadevan Mahalingam* [2016] 2 CLJ 36. *Lim Yoke Lin v Roy Hong Ping Wei& Ors* [2019] 1 LNS 1439, paras 15-19.

exceptions apply. Reasonableness is not recognised under our Contracts Act as far as section 28 is concerned.'[106] As the plaintiff was unable to demonstrate how Clause 3.8 could escape from being caught under section 28 of the Contracts Act, and as no confidential information was alleged to have been taken away by the defendant, the court had no option but to hold that Clause 3.8 was void and the plaintiff could not enforce it.[107]

In the final analysis, it is clear that the approach adopted by the court in *Worldwide Rota Dies* is contrary to the approaches adopted by other courts as regards the effect of section 28 on restraint of trade clauses. It is accepted now that the common law regime of reasonableness in the determination of the validity of restraint of trade clauses has no application as far as the strict terms of section 28 of the Contracts Act are concerned. To quote *Polygram Records Sdn Bhd v Hillary Ang & 4 Ors*, 'Once the Malaysian Courts take the view that a particular covenant is a covenant in restraint of trade, the Courts have no discretion but to declare it to be void under s. 28 of the Contracts Act, subject to the three exceptions provided for by the said section.'[108]

Finally, it is worth noting the decision of the Federal Court in *Dynacast (Melaka) Sdn Bhd & Ors v Vision Cast Sdn Bhd & Anor*[109] which held that 'The proposition of law in *Svenson Hair Centre* ... should be considered in the context of the facts and circumstances of each case. In that case, the protection of confidential information did not have any time limits. The judge rationalised that a contrary view would mean an ex-employee could exploit confidential information with impunity. All that was needed to do was to wait until the expiry of the restriction period. Such an outcome could not have been intended by any of the contracting parties as it would defeat the very purpose of having a confidentiality provision in an employment agreement. This court agreed with the rationale. The proposition of law was a settled principle.'[110]

4.6. *Commercial or Industrial Significance*

To protect confidential information from being misused or divulged by their employees, it is usual for employers to require that employees enter into confidentiality, non-solicitation and non-competition agreements. These obligations could also extend to the post-employment period, whether for a specified time or indefinitely. An ex-employee cannot be prevented by his employer from making any use of, or drawing on, the fund of knowledge and experience or skills that he had acquired while working for the employer. The general rule is that any form of restraint of trade is void unless it falls under the exceptions provided in section 28 of the Contracts Act. However, while there can be no general restriction on the ex-employee from soliciting and or competing with the ex-employer after termination of his employment, this does not apply to situations where such soliciting and or competition is effected through the use of the employer's confidential information.

106. *Lim Yoke Lin v Roy Hong Ping Wei & Ors* [2019] 1 LNS 1439, para. 18.
107. *Ibid.*, para. 20.
108. [1994] 3 CLJ 806 at p. 807.
109. [2016] 6 CLJ 176.
110. *Ibid.*, paras 19-20.

Such restraint is permissible if it is fashioned in such a way as to prevent a misuse of trade secrets or business connexion of the ex-employer. As long as it is not used to place fetters on ex-employees' ability to compete, it would not be a void restraint. Care must be taken, however, to identify the specific confidential information sought to be protected in the agreement and that these restrictions shall cease to apply to any such confidential information which may have come into the public domain otherwise than through any unauthorized disclosure by the employee.

TOPIC 3 THE BURDEN OF PROOF FOR TRADE SECRET AND INFRINGEMENT AND ITS REVERSAL

Sik Cheng Peng

1. Legal Issues

A plaintiff in a claim for breach of confidence is obliged to fulfil three elements: the information that the plaintiff seeks to protect is of a confidential nature; the said information was communicated in circumstances importing an obligation of confidence; and there must be an unauthorized use of the said information to the detriment of the party communicating it.

The burden of proof for the above-mentioned elements lies on the plaintiff to establish them to the satisfaction of the court on balance of probabilities. Accordingly, a plaintiff must identify with sufficient particularity as to what was the confidential information that allegedly has been used without authorization. If the plaintiff fails to discharge this burden, the plaintiff's case must fail.

2. Statutory Law

The law on the burden of proof in Malaysia is governed under Chapter VII of Part III of the Evidence Act 1950 (Act 56). According to section 101(1) of the Evidence Act 1950, a plaintiff seeking a judgment as to any legal right or liability which depends on the existence of facts asserted must prove that the facts exist. Section 101(2) of the same Act makes it clear that the burden of proof lies on a person who must prove the existence of any fact. In addition, section 102 of the Act provides that the burden of proof lies on the person who would fail if no evidence at all was given on either side. Section 106 of the Act, on the other hand, deals with burden of proving facts especially within knowledge of any person. In such circumstances, the burden of proof is placed on that person with the knowledge.

3. Case Law

There are several High Court decisions in which the court laid down the general principles on the burden of proof in claims on breach of confidence. They are *Repco (M) Sdn Bhd v Tan Toh Fatt & Ors* in which the above-mentioned provisions of the Evidence Act 1950 were cited;[111] *Niro Ceramic Sales & Services (M) Sdn Bhd & Anor v Low Chin Guan & Ors* in which the court stated that the onus is on the plaintiff to establish a prima facie basis for the cause of action pleaded against the defendants,[112] and *BM Trada (Penang) Sdn Bhd v Hong Beng Kiong & Ors* where the court reiterated the well-established principle that where the plaintiff fails to discharge the burden of proof, the plaintiff's case must fail.[113]

111. [2013] 7 MLJ 408, paras 19-20.
112. [2018] MLJU 1868, para. 17.
113. [2018] MLJU 1724, paras 43-44.

The plaintiffs in various High Court cases had failed to discharge the burden of proof, including *Navi & Map Sdn Bhd v Twinice Sdn Bhd & Ors*[114] and *Dr HK Fong BrainBuilder Pte Ltd v SG-Maths Sdn Bhd & Ors.*[115] In these cases, the issue was not with the identification of the alleged confidential information in pleadings but with failure on the part of the plaintiffs to satisfy the court that the information was confidential in nature and/or there was unauthorized use of the information by the defendants.

The High Court decision in *Ampledeal (M) Sdn Bhd & 3 Ors v Laponie (M) Sdn Bhd & 3 Ors*[116] is a case where the court found that the plaintiff failed to state or disclose the particulars of the confidential information. The High Court stressed on the obligation of the plaintiff to identify with sufficient particularity in their pleadings as to what was the confidential information that they claimed had been misused. Around the same time, the same legal issue was addressed by the Court of Appeal in *Vision Cast Sdn Bhd & Anor v Dynacast (Melaka) Sdn Bhd & Ors*[117] and an appeal was made to and heard by the Federal Court in 2016 in *Dynacast (Melaka) Sdn Bhd & Ors v Vision Cast Sdn Bhd & Anor.*[118] In 2017, the Court of Appeal emphasized the importance of the rules of pleadings in claiming reliefs for breach of confidence. In 2018, the High Court in *Niro Ceramic Sales & Services (M) Sdn Bhd & Anor v Low Chin Guan & Ors*[119] held that the plaintiff failed to prove to the court's satisfaction of its claim and one of the main reasons was the particulars of the documents were not disclosed to the court for consideration.

4. The Leading Case

The Federal Court decision in *Dynacast (Melaka) Sdn Bhd & Ors v Vision Cast Sdn Bhd & Anor*[120] is selected as the leading case since it is the only judgment delivered by the highest court in Malaysia on the issue relating to identification with sufficient particularity the alleged confidential information in proving a case for breach of confidence. The decision has been applied and followed in the High Court decisions of *Ganesh Raja a/l Nagaiah & Ors v NR Rubber Industries Sdn Bhd*[121] and *Dr HK Fong BrainBuilder Pte Ltd v SG-Maths Sdn Bhd & Ors.*[122]

4.1. Case Information

Dynacast (Melaka) Sdn Bhd & Ors v Vision Cast Sdn Bhd & Anor [2016] 3 MLJ 417; [2016] 6 CLJ 176. Civil Appeal No 02(f)-95-12 of 2014 (J), Federal Court, Putrajaya,

114. [2010] MLJU 1210.
115. [2018] 11 MLJ 701.
116. [2015] MLJU 1933.
117. [2015] 1 MLJ 424.
118. [2016] 3 MLJ 417; [2016] 6 CLJ 176.
119. [2018] MLJU 1868.
120. [2016] 3 MLJ 417; [2016] 6 CLJ 176.
121. [2017] 2 MLJ 396; [2017] 4 CLJ 420.
122. [2018] 11 MLJ 701.

Malaysia, 16 May 2016. Arifin Zakaria Chief Justice, Zulkefli CJ (Malaya), Richard Malanjum CJ (Sabah and Sarawak), Abdull, Hamid Embong And Zainun Ali FCJJ.

4.2. *Summary*

The case concerned a claim brought by the appellants against their former employee on the ground of breach of confidence. The High Court ruled in favour of the appellants and the respondents appealed to the Court of Appeal. The Court of Appeal allowed the appeal as it found that the appellants did not specify what was the private and confidential information that they claimed to have been misappropriated by the respondents. The Court of Appeal also found that there was insufficient evidence to establish the alleged breach of confidence by the respondents. The appellants appealed to the Federal Court which agreed with the Court of Appeal's findings.

4.3. *Facts*

The third appellant, a multinational company incorporated in the United Kingdom, was involved in the business of die-casting components. The first appellant and the second appellant were wholly owned subsidiaries of the third appellant in Malaysia and Singapore, respectively. The second respondent was a former employee of the second appellant since 1980 and eventually became the regional director of the third appellant's group of companies. The letter of appointment of the second respondent as a quality control engineer at the second appellant contained an undertaking by the second respondent agreeing to keep the secrets of the company throughout his employment and at all times after the termination.[123] The second respondent had also signed a confidentiality agreement and a deed of restrictive covenant on any trade secret or other confidential information of the companies.[124]

During the six months before the second respondent left the appellants, he was responsible for the appellants' four product lines of die-cast component manufactured for Motorola, namely, Guppy, Waris, Piranha, and Malin. After his resignation in April 2002, the second respondent joined a company from July 2002 until September 2003. Later he left the company and set up his own company, the first respondent, in October 2003. The first respondent was engaged in a similar die-casting business.

The appellants claimed that the second respondent had misappropriated private and confidential information and thus breached the terms of his employment contract, employee confidentiality agreement, and the deed of restrictive covenant and/or his duties imposed by law and equity. The High Court held that the second respondent breached his obligations of confidentiality by soliciting for business from the appellants' customers and using information he obtained from his previous employment with the appellants.

---

123. *Dynacast (Melaka) Sdn Bhd & Ors v Vision Cast Sdn Bhd & Anor* [2016] 3 MLJ 417; [2016] 6 CLJ 176, para. 14.
124. *Ibid.*

The respondents appealed to the Court of Appeal on the grounds, *inter alia*, that the details of the confidential information sought to be protected were not pleaded by the appellants, that there shall be clear and precise identification of such information in the pleadings, and that an averment in wide and general terms was not acceptable in law.[125] Clause 2.1(d) of the deed of restrictive covenant in dispute referred to 'trade secret or other confidential information concerning the businesses, finances, dealings, transactions or affairs of the Group or any of its customers to clients', which the Court of Appeal found 'a broad-brush sweep of matters intended to be encompassed'.[126] The scope was too broad and general for any relief to be granted.[127] The appeal was allowed as the Court of Appeal found the appellants' claim failed on the pleadings, the facts, and evidence.

The appellants appealed to the Federal Court and contended that their claim was only to enforce the contractual clauses relating to confidential information agreed upon by the second respondent. Essentially, the key questions centred on the question of the enforceability of confidentiality clauses in the second respondent's contract of employment and a further question of whether the confidentiality clauses were void as a restraint of trade.[128]

4.4. *The Reasoning of the Court*

The Federal Court first noted that the law as laid down in *Svenson Hair Center Sdn Bhd v Irene Chin Zee Ling*[129] should be considered in the present case. In that case, the protection of confidentiality information was not subject to any time constraints due to an express clause in the employment agreement, which provided for the duty of confidence during and after the termination of the agreement. The respondents submitted that the question of the enforceability of the restrictive covenants had no bearing on the appeal in view of the Court of Appeal's holding that the appellants' claim failed on the pleadings, the facts and evidence. The Federal Court, therefore, begun by considering if such submission has any merit.

4.4.1. *Lack of Sufficient Particularity in the Claim*

The Federal Court scrutinized the appellants' claim in their statement of claim which referred to the information in question as follows:

(i) 'documented information on drawings, reports, data held on computer discs, software etc including but not limited to materials, tooling, machines, equipment, designs, processes, formulae, projects, products, costs, financial data, marketing plans, customer and supplier lists or business projections' as in the employee confidentiality agreement;

125. *Vision Cast Sdn Bhd & Anor v Dynacast (Melaka) Sdn Bhd & Ors* [2015] 1 MLJ 424, para. 17.
126. *Ibid.*, para. 39.
127. *Ibid.*, para. 56.
128. *Dynacast (Melaka) Sdn Bhd & Ors v Vision Cast Sdn Bhd & Anor* [2016] 3 MLJ 417; [2016] 6 CLJ 176, para. 18.
129. [2008] 7 MLJ 903; [2008] 8 CLJ 386.

(ii) 'the publication or disclosure of any trade secret or confidential information concerning the businesses, finances, dealings, transactions or affairs of the Group of any of its customers or clients entrusted to him' as in a deed of restrictive covenant;
(iii) 'all confidential information which include but not limiting to the clientele and business development' of the appellants as stated in paragraph 12 of the statement of claim; and
(iv) 'the knowledge and confidential information he [the second respondent] had obtained during his tenure' with the appellants as stated in paragraph 18 of the statement of claim.

Upon the perusal of the statement of claim, the Federal Court found nothing in it confining the appellants' claim to only four of their product lines. On the contrary, the Federal Court found that their claim was vouched 'in the broadest terms possible', including the several purported acts committed by the second respondent allegedly in breach of his covenants with the appellants.[130] It held that even where the appellants sought to only enforce the contractual clauses, it was insufficient to merely state that the second respondent had 'misappropriated the private and confidential information' of the appellants.[131]

The Federal Court was of the view that more specifications should have been provided on the claimed misappropriation of private and confidential information. This is crucial to defendants involved in breach of confidence cases as they are entitled to know what are the private and confidential information allegedly to have been misappropriated so as to contest the claim.[132] The Federal Court referred to the cases of *Faccenda Chicken Ltd v Fowler*[133] and *Ixora Trading Incorporated and another v Jones and another*[134] which expounded that information will only be protected if it can be properly classed as trade secret, or as material which may not be properly described as a trade secret but is in all the circumstances of such a highly confidential nature as to require the protection as a trade secret *eo nominee*.[135]

Accordingly, the Federal Court agreed with the Court of Appeal which found that the appellants' claim was that the second respondent had 'stolen' information, in general terms, and used it for his own benefit through the first respondent. It follows that the appellants had failed to identify with sufficient particularity in their pleading what was the confidential information that had been misappropriated.[136] The Federal Court opined that the Court of Appeal was justified in holding that if the 'information'

130. *Dynacast (Melaka) Sdn Bhd & Ors v Vision Cast Sdn Bhd & Anor* [2016] 3 MLJ 417; [2016] 6 CLJ 176, para. 27.
131. *Dynacast (Melaka) Sdn Bhd & Ors v Vision Cast Sdn Bhd & Anor* [2016] 3 MLJ 417; [2016] 6 CLJ 176, para. 28.
132. *Dynacast (Melaka) Sdn Bhd & Ors v Vision Cast Sdn Bhd & Anor* [2016] 3 MLJ 417; [2016] 6 CLJ 176, para. 29.
133. [1987] Ch 117.
134. (1989) IP & T Digest 11; [1990] FSR 251.
135. *Dynacast (Melaka) Sdn Bhd & Ors v Vision Cast Sdn Bhd & Anor* [2016] 3 MLJ 417; [2016] 6 CLJ 176, para. 29.
136. *Dynacast (Melaka) Sdn Bhd & Ors v Vision Cast Sdn Bhd & Anor* [2016] 3 MLJ 417; [2016] 6 CLJ 176, para. 30.

in question was from within the general domain of the second respondent's own knowledge, exposure, and experience accumulated in the industry over the years, which would include potential customers and price trends in the market, there was absolutely no basis to hold a breach of fiduciary duty or a breach of confidence.[137]

4.4.2. *Enforcement of Contractual Covenants on Confidentiality*

However, the appellants argued that the rule that information sought to be protected as confidential information must have the essential quality of confidence only applies where there is no applicable confidentiality clause between the parties, unlike the present case where there was an express clause agreed upon by the parties.[138] The appellants contended that it was only an enforcement of a contractual clause in the present case, referring to the statements by Megarry J in *Coco v AN Clark (Engineers) Ltd*[139] listing down the three elements for a case of breach of confidence to succeed, apart from contract. The appellants argued that in cases of contract, the main question is that of interpreting the contract and any terms implied in it. While the Federal Court accepted Megarry J's statements, it went on to explain that it was absolutely another matter where the details of the private and confidential information allegedly misappropriated were absent and thus disabled the respondents from defending the case.[140]

The Federal Court went on to accentuate the need for a clear case before the doctrine of confidential information by employers may be invoked by employers as well as the perils of its abuse.[141] Scott J's statements in *Balston Ltd v Headline Filters Ltd*[142] were quoted which in essence stressed on the harmful effects of employers' abuse of the doctrine of confidential information, including restricting the ability of ex-employees to use their skills and experience after the end of their employment to compete with their ex-employer, which would in turn produce a new form of servitude or serfdom on technologically qualified employees.

4.4.3. *Lack of Evidence on the Alleged Breach*

The Federal Court also refused to interfere with the Court of Appeal's factual findings on the evidence adduced by the appellants to establish their claim for breach of the confidentiality clause.[143] The Court of Appeal found that the High Court made conclusions without proper and sufficient appreciation of the totality of the evidence

137. *Ibid.*
138. *Dynacast (Melaka) Sdn Bhd & Ors v Vision Cast Sdn Bhd & Anor* [2016] 3 MLJ 417; [2016] 6 CLJ 176, para. 31.
139. [1969] RPC 41, pp. 46-47.
140. *Dynacast (Melaka) Sdn Bhd & Ors v Vision Cast Sdn Bhd & Anor* [2016] 3 MLJ 417; [2016] 6 CLJ 176, para. 32 where the Federal Court quoted Mummery J's statements in *Ixora Trading Incorporated and another v Jones and another* (1989) IP & T Digest 11; [1990] FSR 251, pp. 261-262, which also involved the enforcement of confidentiality clause.
141. *Dynacast (Melaka) Sdn Bhd & Ors v Vision Cast Sdn Bhd & Anor* [2016] 3 MLJ 417; [2016] 6 CLJ 176, para. 33.
142. [1987] FSR 330, at 351.
143. *Dynacast (Melaka) Sdn Bhd & Ors v Vision Cast Sdn Bhd & Anor* [2016] 3 MLJ 417; [2016] 6 CLJ 176, para. 35.

placed before the court, particularly the finding that the respondents had breached confidential obligations.[144] The Court of Appeal also found insufficient evaluation of the evidence at the trial, including that the appellants' main witness failed to pinpoint the 'documented information' which was stolen or misused by the second respondent.[145] Hence, the Federal Court held that the appellants' claim for breach of confidentiality must fail on account of vague and insufficient pleadings as well as from the evidential aspect.[146]

4.5. *Legal Analysis*

4.5.1. *Careful Pleading*

The rules of pleadings and proof are crucial in cases involving confidential information. The principles require that the pleadings must clearly identify the information alleged to have been conveyed in confidence and claimed to have been misappropriated.[147] In *Manderson M and F Consulting v Incitec Pivot Ltd (No 2)*,[148] Croft J held that the pre-eminent element in the pleading of a claim on breach of confidence is the identification or definition in specific, in contrast to merely general, global terms, or some inferential basis of what is claimed to be confidential information.

Likewise, the Supreme Court of Australia in *GlaxoSmithKline Australia Pty Ltd v Ritchie & Anor*[149] placed emphasis on careful pleading. 'It ought not be the judge who is left to identify that which, in a breach of confidence case, the plaintiff contends has been misused'. The Supreme Court of Australia followed the judgment of Laddie J in *Ocular Sciences v Aspect Vision Care Ltd*[150] that if a plaintiff seeks relief against a defendant for misuse of confidential information, the burden lies on him to ensure that the defendant knows what information is in dispute.

Malaysian courts have endorsed this requirement as well. In *Tracerco Asia Sdn Bhd v Nor Hisham Mohd Nordin & Ors*,[151] for instance, the court highlighted the need to identify and plead clearly matters of importance, including the confidential information on which the plaintiff bases his case. The Court of Appeal explained in *Ganesh Raja a/l Nagaiah & Ors v NR Rubber Industries Sdn Bhd* that 'when equitable relief as opposed to contractual relief are sought, the threshold for the former is high'.[152] Nonetheless, the courts in either contractual or equitable claims on confidential information stress on the nature of information and breach of confidence, making

144. *Dynacast (Melaka) Sdn Bhd & Ors v Vision Cast Sdn Bhd & Anor* [2016] 3 MLJ 417; [2016] 6 CLJ 176, para. 34.
145. *Ibid.*
146. *Dynacast (Melaka) Sdn Bhd & Ors v Vision Cast Sdn Bhd & Anor* [2016] 3 MLJ 417; [2016] 6 CLJ 176, para. 36.
147. *Ganesh Raja a/l Nagaiah & Ors v NR Rubber Industries Sdn Bhd* [2017] 2 MLJ 396; [2017] 4 CLJ 420, para. 5.
148. [2011] VSC 205.
149. [2008] VSC 164.
150. [1996] RPC 289; [1996] EWHC Patents 1.
151. [2013] 7 MLJ 75.
152. [2017] 2 MLJ 396; [2017] 4 CLJ 420, para. 6.

reference to cases including *Dynacast (Melaka) Sdn Bhd & Ors v Vision Cast Sdn Bhd & Anor.*[153]

4.5.2. *The Rationale of Detailed Specifications*

The rationale of specifying what is the information sought to be protected was explained by the Court of Appeal in *Vision Cast Sdn Bhd & Anor v Dynacast (Melaka) Sdn Bhd & Ors.*[154] Such requirement is necessary so that a defendant would know the actual complaint made and answer it. It is also crucial to enable the court to strike a balance between two competing interests. The gravity of failure to identify the nature of information in the pleadings was described by the Court of Appeal in *Ganesh Raja a/l Nagaiah & Ors v NR Rubber Industries Sdn Bhd* as a grave omission which does not only compromise the integrity of the decision-making process but also renders the judgment sterile.[155]

In *Ganesh Raja a/l Nagaiah & Ors v NR Rubber Industries Sdn Bhd,* the court also explained that prayers which are too wide may encroach on the doctrine of restraint of trade.[156] As the Federal Court remarked in *Dynacast (Melaka) Sdn Bhd & Ors v Vision Cast Sdn Bhd & Anor* above, the need for a clear case and the harmful effect of abuse are even more apparent in cases involving the use of the doctrine of confidential information by employers.[157] Abuse of the doctrine of confidential information by employers may result in stifling fair and healthy competition in the market.

An example of a successful claim on confidential information may be seen in the case of *Ecooils Sdn Bhd v Raghunath Ramaiah Kandikeri,*[158] which involved breach of confidence claims on several grounds including the confidentiality clause in the letter of appointment. In this case, the plaintiff specifically pleaded that it had developed a confidential technology of using spent bleaching earth as fuel to generate energy and steam in a custom-made boiler as well as trade secret in the form of confidential information on the cost, benefits, pricing, cost-saving benefits, specific requirements of the specially designed boiler. After considering the evidence, the court held that the plaintiff had proved on balance of probabilities that such information was a highly confidential information. By way of contrast, despite the plaintiff had identified the peculiarity of the information claimed to be confidential in *BM Trada (Penang) Sdn Bhd v Hong Beng Kiong & Ors,*[159] namely, information relating to telephone and facsimile numbers, addresses, email address, and business details of the plaintiff's clients, the plaintiff failed to establish the alleged confidential nature of the information on the balance of probabilities.[160]

153. [2017] 2 MLJ 396; [2017] 4 CLJ 420, para. 7.
154. [2015] 1 MLJ 424, para. 56.
155. [2017] 2 MLJ 396; [2017] 4 CLJ 420, para. 11.
156. [2017] 2 MLJ 396; [2017] 4 CLJ 420, para. 16.
157. [2017] 2 MLJ 396; [2017] 4 CLJ 420, para. 33, quoting Scott J's words in *Balston Ltd v Headline Filters Ltd* (1987) FRS 330, p. 351.
158. [2014] 7 MLJ 309.
159. [2018] MLJU 1724.
160. *Ibid.*, paras 41, 43.

4.6. Commercial or Industrial Significance

The requirement of identifying with sufficient details in pleadings what was the confidential information alleged to have been misused is given emphasis since failure to do so may unfairly prevent employees from making use of their own knowledge, exposure, and experience accumulated in the relevant industry over the years of their service.[161] A clear distinction should be made between genuine trade secret and knowledge that employees may take away with them.[162] The requirement is also necessary to ensure that no one is to enjoy monopoly or secrecy in publicly available information.[163]

The appellants in *Dynacast (Melaka) Sdn Bhd & Ors v Vision Cast Sdn Bhd & Anor* contended that the thrust of their claim was merely to enforce contractual covenants on confidentiality.[164] Nonetheless, as commented by Lai Kew Chai J in *Tang Siew Choy & Ors v Certact Pte Ltd*,[165] a lack of particularity about the precise nature of the trade secret usually indicates an attempt to prevent the employee from making legitimate use of the knowledge and skills they gained in their previous employment. Whereas Cross J expounded in *Printers and Finishers Ltd v Holloway*[166] that not all information given to employees in confidence is a trade secret, even where there is an express covenant on the matter.

A court in hearing claims on trade secrets in employer-employee relationships has to uphold the contracting parties' obligations to honour a contract of service while at the same time to respect employees' legitimate interests in advancing their career or profession. This would ultimately serve the public interest by better and more efficient use of employees' aptitudes, skills, knowledge, and experience.[167] The disastrous effect of a wide and vague statement of claim on breach of confidence was well explained by Templeman J in *Zink Co Ltd v Lloyd's Bank Ltd and Airoil Burner Co (GB) Ltd*.[168] Templeman J described that the life of an ex-employee becomes intolerable if an employer is allowed to allege that he has trade secrets of the broadest nature and that the employee had learned them. According to the learned judge, this would lead to oppression.

Apparently, the requirement of identifying with particularities places plaintiffs alleging breach of confidence in a 'damned if I do, damned if I don't' situation. The predicament was splendidly described by Graham J in *Diamond Stylus Co Ltd v Bauden Precision Diamonds Ltd & Ors*[169] as that if a plaintiff in a claim for breach of confidence discloses in detail the confidential information, he destroys the secrecy of the information; whereas if he is not ready to do so, he faces tremendous difficulty in showing that

161. *See Ampledeal (M) Sdn Bhd & 3 Ors v Laponie (M) Sdn Bhd & 3 Ors* [2015] MLJU 1933.
162. *Tang Siew Choy & Ors v Certact Pte Ltd* [1993] 3 SLR 44.
163. *See Faccenda Chicken v Fowler* [1985] FSR 105, p. 114.
164. *Dynacast (Melaka) Sdn Bhd & Ors v Vision Cast Sdn Bhd & Anor* [2016] 3 MLJ 417; [2016] 6 CLJ 176, para. 25.
165. [1993] 1 SLR 44.
166. [1964] 3 All ER 731; [1965] 1 WLR 1.
167. *GD Searle & Co Ltd v Celltech Ltd* [1982] FSR 92, p. 99.
168. [1975] RPC 385, p. 392.
169. [1973] RPC 675.

the defendant has stolen or abused the secret.[170] Yet, it remains imperative for plaintiffs to provide sufficient details on the information they seek to protect. The plight can be avoided since the court has the means of safeguarding the secrecy of the information in question.

170. *Ibid.*, p. 676.

TOPIC 4 THE ORDER FOR PROTECTING THE SECRECY OF TRADE SECRET DURING PROSECUTION AND TRIAL: INTERLOCUTORY INJUNCTION

Farizah Mohamed Isa

1. Legal Issues

In Malaysia, one of the remedies available for a plaintiff to stop or restrict further unauthorized use of trade secrets pending a trial would be an order for an interim or an interlocutory injunction.[171] It is generally issued by the courts to ensure both parties' status quo is maintained. This order is issued to stop either party from acting in a particular manner during the pendency of the civil action.

2. The Statutory Law

Order 29 of the Malaysian Rules of Court 2012 has a specific provision to guide judges and lawyers on the procedure to apply for an injunction. In essence, Rule 1 of this Order provides that an application for the grant of an injunction may be made by any party to a cause or matter before or after the trial of the cause or matter, whether or not a claim for the injunction was included in the party's originating process, counterclaim or third-party notice, as the case may be. In an action for breach of confidential information, these measures are often used to ensure that the defendant is prevented from continuing to do something, in this context, to further use the trade secret or confidential information.

3. The Case Law

The rules the courts in Malaysia often refer to in deciding whether this order is to be given are the test based on the principles governing the grant or refusal of an interlocutory injunction which were expounded by the House of Lords in *American Cyanamid Co. v Ethicon Ltd* [1975] 1 All ER 504. These principles are not exclusive to cases on trade secrets or breach of confidential information; it is applied to all cases where the plaintiff seeks an order for an interim or an interlocutory injunction.

4. The Leading Case

This case is chosen because it illustrates the application of the principles in *American Cyanamid* in great detail, and specifically when a breach of confidential information is alleged by the plaintiff.

171. Although often used interchangeably, there is a difference between an interlocutory injunction and an interim injunction. An interlocutory injunction is obtained prior to, and remains in force until trial, whereas an interim injunction is obtained ex parte for a very limited time until each party can attend court for the application of an interlocutory injunction.

4.1. *Case Information*

Niro Ceramic Sales & Services (M) Sdn. Bhd. & Anor v Low Chin Guan & Ors. [2018] 1 LNS 1982; [2018] MLJU 1868, High Court of Malaya, Shah Alam, Selangor; Civil Suit No: 22NCVC-695-11/2017 (decided on 4 October 2018). Gunalan Muniandy J.

4.2. *Summary*

The plaintiffs being previous employers of the defendants applied for an interim injunction to restrain the defendants (D1-D4) from doing various acts and an order directing D1-D4 to deliver up to the plaintiffs documents purportedly containing confidential information and trade secrets obtained from the latter. The grounds in support of the plaintiff's application were, *inter alia,* that D1 and D2 were former employees of the plaintiffs and hence both D1 and D2 owed contractual duties, duty of fidelity, fiduciary duties, duty of confidence and statutory duties to the plaintiffs. The plaintiffs also contended that without the knowledge nor approval of the plaintiffs, D1 and D2 caused the incorporation of D3 and D4 to market, sell and distribute tiles in competition with the plaintiffs, and at all material times, D1 was the person behind and in control of D3 and D4. Further, there were serious issues to be determined in this action and there was a strong prima facie evidence in favour of the plaintiffs against the defendants. The plaintiff also pleaded that monetary awards were not an adequate remedy if the plaintiffs succeed in their claim. Lastly, the balance of convenience weighs in favour of the plaintiffs being granted the injunction.

4.3. *Facts*

The plaintiffs (P1 and P2) were members of the Niro Ceramic Group of Companies. P1 was in the business of marketing, sales and distribution of ceramic tiles (NIRO Tiles) manufactured by P2. D1 and D2 were employees of the plaintiffs. From 23 November 2009 until his termination on 27 November 2017, D1 held the position of General Manager for the Domestic Sales Division and headed that division which comprised of 37 subordinates. Until his resignation on 31 January 2017, D2 held the position of Sales Manager – Project. He was first employed on 1 February 2002. D3 and D4 were companies incorporated by D1 to sell Dongpeng Tiles manufactured by Dongpeng Holdings Company Ltd. of China. The interim injunction against D1 and D2 arose from their breaches of contractual duties, duty of fidelity, fiduciary duties, duty of confidence and also statutory duties.[172]

The defendants laid out several arguments. D1 contended that, first, when the documents were handed to employees of the plaintiffs (including the 1st defendant), there was no classification that such documents contained confidential information or trade secret. D1 also specifically averred that two senior managers who previously resigned from the plaintiffs and had access to the same documents were never asked to return the documents in their possession when the plaintiffs knew at that time that the

172. *Niro Ceramic Sales & Services (M) Sdn. Bhd. & Anor v Low Chin Guan & Ors* [2018] 1 LNS 1982, p. 2.

two senior managers were going to join the competitors of the plaintiffs. Although these documents were said to have been retracted from the Court records and hidden by the plaintiff, D1 argued that if the same had been disclosed, they would have revealed that the information was readily available in the public domain and obtainable by subscribing to or purchasing from a trade information service provider or by googling and following up with phone calls. There was no evidence adduced by the plaintiffs showing that D1 had utilized the information after he was fired or terminated by the plaintiffs from their employment.[173]

As to the plaintiffs' allegation of breach of confidential information and disclosure of trade secrets, D1 argued that it was a blatant attempt at restraint of trade and to prevent healthy competition in the market. In support of this contention, D1 cited the Court of Appeal case of *Ganesh Raja a/l Nagaiah & Ors v NR Rubber Industries Sdn. Bhd.*, where the Court of Appeal held that the respondents' claims did not identify the nature of the information which the respondents sought to seek injunction. The prayers of the respondents were said to be too wide and sufficient to impinge the doctrine of restraint of trade.[174] The Court of Appeal further stated that the customers, suppliers and forwarders list together with their contact numbers must be established to be information of confidential in nature. Even access to the information in the company must have been limited only to certain persons. General information available to all employees or public per se cannot be said to give rise to the doctrine of confidentiality.

To further support their arguments, D1 also referred to the Federal Court case of *Dynacast (Melaka) Sdn. Bhd. v Vision Cast Sdn. Bhd. & Anor.*, where it was pronounced, *inter alia*, that there must be a clear case of a breach of confidence by employers before its invocation to ensure that the use of this doctrine is not abused by employers.[175] D1 also contended that the plaintiffs' prayers were an attempt to obtain what the plaintiffs were not able to obtain by contract because such terms, if placed in a contract, will be against section 28 of the Contracts Act 1950 that renders any provision restraining trade or competition as void. As such, in the context of D1's termination from the plaintiffs' employment, any attempt to restrain D1 from utilizing the knowledge and skills that he obtained during his years of employment with plaintiffs in the tiles trading industry will be denying D1 of his livelihood and infringe section 28 of the Contracts Act 1950.[176] Reference was also made to the Court of Appeal case of *Millennium Medicare Services v Nagadevan Mahalingam.*[177]

Finally, D1 contended that no confidential information or trade secret existed in this case as alleged by the plaintiffs. The orders sought were to stifle competition and deny D1 his livelihood based on the knowledge and skills that he had gained during his past working years.

173. *Ibid.*, p. 7.
174. *Ganesh Raja a/l Nagaiah & Ors v NR Rubber Industries Sdn. Bhd.* [2017] 2 MLJ 396 (CA) paras 2, 16.
175. *Dynacast (Melaka) Sdn. Bhd. v Vision Cast Sdn. Bhd. & Anor* [2016] 3 MLJ, p. 417.
176. Section 28 Contracts Act 1950 provides that, 'Every agreement by which anyone is restrained from exercising a lawful profession, trade, or business of any kind, is to that extent void.'
177. *Nagadevan Mahalingam v Millenium Medicare Services* [2011] 3 CLJ 529; [2011] 4 MLJ 739.

As for D2, D3 and D4, their contentions were:

(a) D2 had tendered a notice of resignation on 30 November 2016 which took effect two months thereafter. D2 had attempted to tender his notice of resignation in July 2016 but was persuaded by his immediate superior to withhold his resignation due to shortage of manpower at the plaintiffs' companies at that material time. Apart from the contractual duties and the duty of fidelity during his employment with the plaintiffs, D2 argued that he did not owe any other duties such as fiduciary duties to the plaintiffs.

(b) D2 also confirmed under oath that he did not have in his possession any of the documents referred to by the plaintiffs and the plaintiffs' allegation of diverting business opportunity on or around 2015 was baseless as D3 and D4 had not even been incorporated at the material time and he (D2) was only appointed as a director to D3 and D4 respectively in July and October 2017. D2 further submitted that all the correspondence addressed to and/or copied to D2 could not in any way have indicated that D2 had diverted any business opportunity of the plaintiffs and/or that he had also divulged or disclosed the purported confidential information and trade secrets of the plaintiffs and finally the plaintiffs had not produced any document indicating that D2, D3 and D4 had caused the plaintiffs to suffer any loss which would justify the order pleaded.[178]

On the facts and evidence, the High Court found that the plaintiffs had failed to satisfy the established test propounded in the *American Cyanamid* case for the grant of an interlocutory injunction and the consequential reliefs applied for. Gunalan Muniandy J rejected and dismissed the plaintiffs' application with costs.

4.4. *The Reasoning of the Court*

4.4.1. *Principles Applicable to Interim Injunctions*

In coming up with this decision, Gunalan Muniandy J first explained the principles applicable to interim injunctions. He referred to the English landmark case of *American Cynamid Co. v Ethicon Ltd.*[179] as the leading authority on this aspect of the law. The guiding principles for the granting of interlocutory injunctions were clearly enunciated by the House of Lords and have been adopted by the Malaysian courts. Muniandy Gunalan J quoted the case of *Keet Gerald Francis Noel John v Mohd Noor @ Harun bin Abdullah & 2 Ors,*[180] where the Court of Appeal in adopting the *American Cynamid Co.*

178. *Niro Ceramic Sales & Services (M) Sdn. Bhd. & Anor v Low Chin Guan & Ors* [2018] 1 LNS 1982, p. 10.
179. *American Cynamid Co. v Ethicon Ltd.* [1975] 1 All ER 504.
180. *Keet Gerald Francis Noel John v Mohd Noor @ Harun bin Abdullah & 2 Ors* [1995] 1 MLJ 193.

case laid down the principles as to the approach that the Court should adopt in deciding an application for an interim injunction. It is as follows.[181]

First, a judge must ask himself whether the totality of the facts presented before him discloses a bona fide serious issue to be tried. Then, when considering this question, he must bear in mind that the pleadings and evidence are incomplete at that stage. Above all, he must refrain from making any determination on the merits of the claim or any defence to it. It is sufficient if he identifies with precision the issues raised on the joinder and decides whether these are serious enough to merit a trial. If, after considering all relevant material before him, that no serious question is disclosed, that is an end of the matter and the relief is refused. On the other hand, if he does find that there are serious questions to be tried, he should move on to the next step of his enquiry.

Second, having found that an issue has been disclosed that requires further investigation, he must consider where the justice of the case lies. In making his assessment, he must take into account all relevant matters, including the practical realities of the case. He must weigh the harm that the injunction would produce by its grant against the harm that would result from its refusal. He is entitled to take into account, *inter alia*, the relative financial standing of the litigants before him. If after weighing all matters, he comes to the conclusion that the plaintiff would suffer greater injustice if relief is withheld, then he would be entitled to grant the injunction especially if he is satisfied that the plaintiff is in a financial position to meet his undertaking in damages.

Third, if he concludes that the defendant would suffer the greater injustice by the grant of an injunction, he would be entitled to refuse relief. Of course, cases may arise where the injustice to the plaintiff is so manifest that the judge would be entitled to dispense with the usual undertaking as to damages. Apart from such cases, the judge is entitled to take into account the plaintiff's ability to meet his undertaking in damages should the suit fail, and, in appropriate cases, may require the plaintiff to secure his undertaking, for example, by providing a bank guarantee, and the judge must have in the forefront of his mind that the remedy that he is asked to administer is discretionary, intended to produce a just result for the period between the date of the application and the trial proper and intended to maintain the status quo. This was an expression explained by Lord Diplock in *Garden Cottage Foods Ltd v Milk Marketing Board*.[182] This order is a judicial discretion and capable of correction on appeal.

Accordingly, the judge would be entitled to take into account all discretionary considerations, such as any adequate alternative remedy that would satisfy the plaintiff's equity, public interest and any other factors when arriving at his conclusion.

In applying these approaches to the present case, Muniandy Gunalan J stated that, first and foremost, the onus was on the plaintiffs to establish on a prima facie basis one or more of the causes of action pleaded against the defendants to restrain them via

181. *Niro Ceramic Sales & Services (M) Sdn. Bhd. & Anor v Low Chin Guan & Ors* [2018] 1 LNS 1982, pp. 4-6.
182. *Garden Cottage Foods Ltd v Milk Marketing Board.* [1984] AC 130; [1983] 2 All ER 770; [1983] 3 WLR 143.

the injunction. If they failed to do this, then the question of there being a serious question to be tried would not arise. The dispute pertaining to the nature of the information possessed by D1 and D2 was a serious matter; were they confidential information or trade secrets as alleged by the plaintiffs? The judge referred to the decision of the Court of Appeal in *Vision Cast Sdn. Bhd. & Anor v Dynacast (Melaka) Sdn. Bhd. & Ors* where it was pronounced that:[183]

> If the impugned 'information' was from within the general fund of the second defendant's own knowledge, exposure and experience accumulated in the diecast industry over the years as was the case here (and this would include potential customers, price trends in the market/public domain etc.), there was definitely not grounds, in our assessment to hold that there had been a breach of fiduciary duty or even a breach of confidentiality by the second defendant in this case.

Muniandy Gunalan J confirmed that the defendants were not in possession of the said documents and information. Hence, there was no basis to seek an injunctive relief against D2-D4 for the alleged dissemination of the purported confidential information and trade secrets. On his evaluation of the evidence presented on the nature of the confidentiality of the information, he said that the plaintiffs have failed to prove that the documents that D1 and D2 were privy to were classified as confidential information or amounted to trade secrets. More importantly, the particulars of the documents were not disclosed to the Court for consideration of their true nature. Furthermore, most of the information appeared to be available in the public domain and accessible online.[184] Furthermore, there was no evidence that D1-D4 had utilized the information and documents in question to the detriment or disadvantage of the plaintiff to justify the relief sought.

4.4.2. The Springboard Doctrine/Injunction

In view of the total lack of evidence to support the alleged usage of the plaintiffs' confidential information and trade secrets and/for unlawful acts by the defendants to obtain a head start, Muniandy Gunalan J applied the 'springboard doctrine/ injunction'. He explained that the circumstances of the instant case did not satisfy the legal test for a springboard injunction as laid down by Haddor Cave J in *QBE Management Services (UK) Ltd. v Dymoke & Ors.*[185] The test enunciated was as follows:

(1) Where a person has obtained a head start as a result of unlawful acts, the Court has the power to grant an injunction which restrains the wrongdoer so as to deprive him of the fruits of his unlawful acts. This is what is known as the 'springboard' relief.

---

183. *Vision Cast Sdn. Bhd. & Anor v Dynacast (Melaka) Sdn. Bhd. & Ors* [2015] 1 MLJ 424.
184. *Niro Ceramic Sales & Services (M) Sdn. Bhd. & Anor v Low Chin Guan & Ors* [2018] 1 LNS 1982, p. 7.
185. *QBE Management Services (UK) Ltd. v Dymoke & Ors* [2012] IRLR 458, pp. 240-247.

(2) The purpose of a springboard order is 'to prevent the defendants from taking unfair advantage of the springboard which [the Judge] considered they must have built up by their misuse of the information in the card index'.[186]
(3) A springboard relief is not confined to cases of breach of confidence. It can be granted in relation to breaches of contractual and fiduciary duties and flows from a principle that the court may grant an injunction to deprive a wrong-doer of the unlawful advantage derived from his wrongdoing.
(4) A springboard relief must, however, be sought and obtained at a time when any unlawful advantage is still being enjoyed by the wrongdoer.
(5) A springboard relief should have the aim of 'simply restoring the parties to the competitive position they each set out to occupy and would have occupied but for the defendant's misconduct'.[187] It will not be fair and just if it has a much more far-reaching effect than this, such as driving the defendant out of business.
(6) A springboard relief will not be granted where a monetary award would have provided an adequate remedy to the claimant for the wrong done to it.
(7) A springboard relief is not intended to punish the defendant; it is merely to provide fair and just protection for unlawful harm on an interim basis. What is fair and just in any circumstances will be measured by:
    (i) the effect of the unlawful acts upon the claimant; and
    (ii) the extent to which the defendant has gained an illegitimate competitive advantage.
(8) Lastly, the burden is on the claimant to spell out the precise nature and period of the competitive advantage. An 'ephemeral' and 'short term' advantage will not be sufficient.

In line with the above, Muniandy Gunalan J found that the plaintiffs failed to show that the defendants were using or intended to use the information as a springboard to the detriment of the plaintiffs. In addition to that, Muniandy Gunalan J further stated that several of the orders sought by plaintiffs appeared prima facie to be in reality, a restraint of trade against the defendants and thereby was in conflict with section 28 of the Contracts Act, 1950. The Court would not, in principle, grant an order that is against the law.[188]

In view of the terms of section 28, of the Contracts Act 1950, D2 should be free to run the operations of D3 and D4 upon the expiration of his employment contract with the plaintiffs. D2, D3 and D4 had also demonstrated that, on this score, the plaintiffs have been unable to show that their claim is prima facie sustainable for an interlocutory injunction to be granted.[189]

---

186. Nourse LJ in *Roger Bullivant v Ellis* [1987] ICR 464, p. 476G.
187. Per Sir David Nicholls VC in *Universal Thermosensors v Hibben* [1992] 1 WLR 840, p. 855A.
188. *Niro Ceramic Sales & Services (M) Sdn. Bhd. & Anor v Low Chin Guan & Ors* [2018] 1 LNS 1982, p. 16.
189. *Ibid.*

On the issue of breach of fiduciary duties, Muniandy Gunalan J stressed that there was clearly no case of any fiduciary duty due and owed by D2 to the plaintiffs. Neither was there any evidence adduced which showed that D2, D3 and D4 had dishonestly assisted D1 as a director of the plaintiffs' companies in breach of his fiduciary duties towards the plaintiffs and/or breach of trust that resulted in loss to the plaintiff. Nowhere in the evidence produced by the plaintiffs was it even suggested that there was in fact any illegal activity having been carried out by D2, D3 and D4 together with D1 while D2 was still under the employment of the plaintiffs.[190]

Upon evaluation of the whole spectrum of the instant case, Muniandy Gunalan J was of the view that the evidence relied upon by the plaintiff was clearly insufficient to establish any of the pleaded causes of action on a prima facie basis. The plaintiffs' application was based on allegations and contentions as to the several breaches of confidentiality, fiduciary duties and fidelity by D1 and D2, who had since left the employment of the plaintiff. In other words, these duties were no longer binding on the defendants. Further, the plaintiffs' application and the grounds to support their application for the interim injunction were in its scope far too wide, excessive and unreasonable to be considered and amounted to unfair protection of the plaintiff's business.[191]

4.5. *Legal Analysis*

4.5.1 *No Bona Fide Serious Matter to Be Tried*

It can be adduced from the above case that the discretionary power of the courts to grant an interim or an interlocutory injunction must meet the principles enunciated by the *American Cynamid* case. This equitable remedy is highly effective as a measure to restrict a defendant using the confidential information as a springboard to gain a wrongful advantage over the plaintiff where the plaintiff would suffer loss and damage as a consequence. The learned judge, in coming to his decision, considered the first approach of the principle by investigating whether the plaintiff had a bona fide serious matter to be tried. The plaintiffs claimed that the defendants had breached several duties by using certain information belonging to the plaintiffs. This information was obtained while the defendants were employees of the plaintiffs. The evidence showed that first, the information in question was information that was in the public domain and easily available. Further, the plaintiffs had never indicated to the defendants that they were confidential in nature and must be treated as such. It was also shown that the defendants did not have in their possession the alleged documents which were to be returned to them. Whatever duties that the plaintiffs claimed was breached by the defendants were found to be irrelevant as the duties were non-existent because the defendants were no longer employees of the plaintiffs.

The judge further examined whether the defendants gained a competitive advantage over the plaintiffs through the springboard doctrine. Due to the fact that the

190. *Niro Ceramic Sales & Services (M) Sdn. Bhd. & Anor v Low Chin Guan & Ors* [2018] 1 LNS 1982, p. 18.
191. *Ibid.*, p. 19.

information in question was normal public information, the springboard issue could not arise. Therefore, it can be seen that in this case, the judge considered the nature of the information, the relationship between the plaintiffs and the defendants and whether any wrongful act was committed by the defendants that would affect the plaintiffs' pending trial. After careful deliberation, it was decided that the plaintiff failed to show that there was a serious matter to be tried and as such the other two steps in the *American Cynamid* principles need not be considered further.

4.5.2. The Restraint of Trade Provision

The judge also agreed that by restraining the defendants from embarking on a similar business as their ex-employer would invoke the restraint of trade provision which is forbidden by virtue of section 28 of the Malaysian Contracts Act 1950. This provision states that every agreement by which anyone is restrained from exercising a lawful profession, trade, or business of any kind, is to that extent void, except, agreements involving sales of goodwill of a business; partners prior to dissolution; and continuance of the partnership.

4.6. Commercial or Industrial Significance

To maintain the confidential nature of trade secrets, employers or owners of such secrets can take several measures to ensure that their employees will not become 'insider threats' while in employment or after they have left their employment with their employers. A usual way is by contract of non-disclosure or a non-disclosure agreement which sometimes is detailed in the employment contract. In cases where these contracts are breached, a remedy such as an interim or interlocutory injunction is effective in ensuring that no further damage can be done to the employer's business.

In a highly competitive business environment, an order from the court would be useful weapon that a business could rely upon. As such, the courts must tread carefully when granting or refusing the application for this order. On the one hand, the sanctity of the trade secret must be preserved and protected; on the other hand, there must be healthy competition among businesses which would promote economic growth in a country. Therefore, the courts must use this discretionary power with utmost caution. The rules and guidelines relating to this remedy must be interpreted in line with the nature of the business involved and the impact this remedy would have on the said business.

TOPIC 4 THE ORDER FOR PROTECTING THE SECRECY OF TRADE SECRET DURING PROSECUTION AND TRIAL: ANTON PILLER ORDER

Lim Heng Gee

1. Legal Issues

The issue here is what are the requirements to be fulfilled before a plaintiff is entitled to get an ex parte Anton Piller order against the defendants to assist him in his litigation against the defendant.

2. The Statutory Law

The applicable statutes are the Courts of Judicature Act 1964, the Specific Relief Act 1950 and Rules of Court 2012. The Courts of Judicature Act essentially set out the powers and jurisdictions of the Superior Courts in Malaysia, i.e., the High Court, the Court of Appeal and the Federal Court. The Specific Relief Act is a statute of general application which sets out the equitable remedies available to parties whose contractual or civil rights have been infringed, like specific performance, rectification of documents, declaratory decrees and the grant of the various types of injunction. The Rules of Court 2012 set out procedural rules, made in the exercise of the powers conferred by the Courts of Judicature Act 1964 and the Subordinate Courts Rules Act 1955, to apply to all proceedings in the Magistrates' Court, the Sessions Court and the High Court.

3. Case Law

All the cases on the Anton Piller order relating to breach of confidence suits were decided and ended at the High Court level. As the order is draconian in nature, it is not surprising that there were only three cases involving the grant of the Anton Piller order in relation to breach of confidence. In all these cases, the defendants had applied to set aside the Anton Piller granted ex parte.

4. The Leading Case

The leading case is *Apparatech (M) Sdn Bhd v Ng Hock Chong & Anor* [2006] 2 MLJ 61. It is the first case where an Anton Piller order was granted ex parte in a breach of confidence case and subsequently set aside for non-compliance with procedural and substantive requirements for obtaining such an order. It highlights that strict compliance with the rules to obtain and execute the ex parte Anton Piller order is vital. Any non-compliance would result in the order being set aside and the plaintiff would be liable for damages.

4.1. *Case Information*

Apparatech (M) Sdn Bhd v Ng Hock Chong & Anor [2006] 2 MLJ 61. Civil Suit No: D4-22-1442-2002, High Court Malaya, Kuala Lumpur, Malaysia, 10 October 2005. Dato' Hj Abdul Malik bin Hj Ishak J.

4.2. *Summary*

This case is a continuation of the plaintiff's earlier successful application for an ex parte Anton Piller order against the defendants to permit the plaintiff to enter the second defendant's premises in order to search, inspect, photograph or photocopy and deliver into safekeeping of the plaintiff's solicitors all documents and articles which were listed in the application. The present case relates to the plaintiff's application for committal proceeding against the director of the second defendant for non-compliance with the order. The defendants, in turn, applied to set aside the Anton Piller order. The court dismissed the plaintiff's application for committal proceeding and allowed the defendants' application to set aside the Anton Piller order. There was no appeal from this decision.

4.3. *Facts*

The plaintiff, Apparatech (M) Sdn Bhd, carries on business as supplier and technical consultant of scientific and educational equipment and apparatus imported from overseas for universities, polytechnics and technical colleges as well as to various Ministries.

The first defendant, Ng Hock Chong, was employed by the plaintiff in 1992. He was entrusted by the plaintiff to fully take charge of the plaintiff's operational and financial matters as well as the day-to-day operations of the plaintiff. He was also entrusted to deal with the overseas principals and to prepare and submit tender documents for the projects of the Ministries, universities, polytechnics and all other government and private colleges.

The plaintiff sued the first defendant for, *inter alia*, breach of his duty, both during and after his employment, not to misuse any information confidential of the plaintiff or to disclose such information to any third party. The confidential information included all documents and records pertaining to the tender strategy, the principals' price list of the equipment and apparatus, numerous private and confidential documents and computer data relating to various projects of the Ministry of Education, Ministry of Labour, Ministry of Defence, Ministry of Youth and Sports, all UITMs, University Technology Petronas, Polytechnics at Tanjung Malim and Kulim, other universities and colleges.

The first defendant resigned from the plaintiff's employment on 30 June 2002. It was alleged that he, while still an employee of the plaintiff, had on 1 March 2002 joined the second defendant, Selamat Ekuiti Sdn Bhd, as a director. It was also alleged that the first defendant had removed the confidential information from the plaintiff's office and was making use of the same for his own purposes and for the purposes of the second defendant.

The plaintiff had obtained an ex parte Anton Piller order on 20 September 2002. The ex parte Anton Piller order permitted an entry at the second defendant's premises in order to search, inspect, photograph or photocopy and deliver into safekeeping of the plaintiff's solicitors all documents and articles which were listed in the list of items annexed to the order.

The plaintiff now sought committal proceeding against Koay Chee Hong (Koay), the director of the second defendant, for contempt in that he had 'deliberately and/or intentionally and/or wilfully refused to allow the named persons to carry out the execution of the Anton Piller order on 23 September 2002 at or about 5pm at the first floor of the premises'. The defendants, in turn, applied to set aside the ex parte Anton Piller order.

4.4. *The Reasoning of the Court*

The court has to deal with the defendants' grounds to set aside the ex parte Anton Piller order for non-compliance of the rules governing the grant of an ex parte Anton Piller order, among other issues.

4.4.1. *The Plaintiff Failed to Make a Full and Frank Disclosure When Applying for the Order*

The defendants contended, *inter alia*, that there was non-compliance with O 29 rule 1(2A) of the Rules of the High Court 1980.[192]

Order 29 rule 1(2A) states:

> (2A) The affidavit in support shall contain a clear and concise statement:
> (a) of the facts giving rise to the claim against the defendant in the proceedings;
> (b) of the facts giving rise to the claim for the interlocutory relief;
> (c) ...;
> (d) ...;
> (e) of any facts known to the applicant which might lead the court not to grant relief *ex parte*;
> (f) ...; and
> (g) of the precise relief sought.

In dealing with this ground, the court referred to the statement made by His Lordship Gopal Sri Ram JCA, speaking for the Court of Appeal in *Motor Sports International Ltd (servants or agents at Federal Territory of Labuan) & Ors v Delcont (M) Sdn Bhd*, where His Lordship said:

> The provisions of O 29 r 1(2A) were introduced ... to ensure that *ex parte* injunctions of any sort were not granted willy-nilly, but only in cases where they were truly called for. In order to ensure that the policy behind the introduction of r 1(2A) is not defeated, High Courts must demand strict compliance with its terms.

192. Now Order 29 rule 1(2A)(a)-(g) of the Rules of Court 2012.

> More so, when the relief applied for is in the nature of a Mareva or an Anton Piller type of injunction because of the incalculable harm and damage that may be caused to a defendant by the grant of either of these orders.[193]

The court then examined whether there was any failure of the plaintiff to make a full and frank disclosure when applying for the order. It answered this in the affirmative as the evidence showed the plaintiff had suppressed material facts known to the plaintiff which might lead the court not to grant the Anton Piller order. Among them were that David Ng Hock Heng (the Managing Director of the plaintiff) knew but did not reveal to the court; that there were other third parties that were sharing the premises in issue; that third parties were also involved in the same business and that they were competing with each other and against the plaintiff and that the list of documents annexed to the Anton Piller order also included documents from the third parties; and that the rights of third parties to protect their own properties might be infringed if the Anton Piller order was executed.[194]

The court stressed that an Anton Piller order was a very harsh remedy and was just like a search warrant which allowed entry into the defendants' premises to search, inspect and remove documents and materials which were relevant to the litigation. Thus, there was a strict duty imposed on the plaintiff to make a full and frank disclosure. On the facts, the court held that there was not only an inadequate disclosure, but there were also misrepresentations which ultimately led the court to grant the Anton Piller order on an ex parte basis. There were also contradictory versions between the documents in two different affidavits deposed to be David Ng relating to the function and scope of duties of the first defendant and also the business activities and financial standing of the plaintiff.[195]

The court concluded that as the duty of full and frank disclosure was not observed by the plaintiff and that there were misleading averments advanced by the plaintiff, it was entitled to discharge the Anton Piller order. The court stressed that 'this would even be so if, after a full enquiry, the view taken was that it was just and convenient that the Anton Piller order would probably have been made even if there have been a full disclosure'.[196] Stressing that the non-disclosure and suppression of material facts and misleading facts asserted by the plaintiff in obtaining the order constituted a serious breach which, had it been disclosed or had the facts been properly presented, the court would not have granted the Anton Piller order, the court acceded to the defendants' application to discharge the order.[197]

193. [1996] 2 MLJ 605, p. 611, referred to by Clement Skinner J in *UMAS Sendirian Berhad v RHB Bank Berhad & Anor* [2001] 1 AMR 1024, p. 1042. *See Apparatech (M) Sdn Bhd v Ng Hock Chong & Anor* [2006] 2 MLJ 61, para. 40.
194. *Apparatech (M) Sdn Bhd v Ng Hock Chong & Anor* [2006] 2 MLJ 61, para. 41.
195. *Ibid.*, at para. 42, citing the English cases of *EMI Ltd v Pandit* [1975] 1 All ER 418 and *Columbia Picture Industries Inc v Robinson* [1986] 3 All ER 338.
196. *Ibid.*, para. 43, referring to, among others, *Siporex Trade SA v Comdel Commodities Ltd* [1986] 136 LJ 538 and *R v Kensington Income Tax Commissioners* [1917] 1 KB 486 and *PMK Rajah v Worldwide Commodities Sdn Bhd & Ors* [1985] 1 MLJ 86.
197. *Apparatech (M) Sdn Bhd v Ng Hock Chong & Anor* [2006] 2 MLJ 61, para. 43.

4.4.2. *The Anton Piller Order Was Too Wide, Imprecise, Vague and Oppressive*

The court then perused the Anton Piller order granted to the plaintiff to decide on the veracity of the defendants' allegations. The defendants were ordered to surrender to the plaintiff the following:

(1) Any and all information, documents, records or otherwise pertaining to the tender strategy for various projects of the Ministry of Education, Ministry of Labour, Ministry of Defence, Ministry of Youth and Sports, all UITMs, University Technology Petronas, Polytechnics Merlimau, Tanjung Malim and Kulim, universities, polytechnics and colleges.
(2) Any and all information, documents, records or otherwise pertaining to the principals' price list of the scientific and educational equipment and apparatus for various projects of the Ministry of Education, Ministry of Labour, Ministry of Defence, Ministry of Youth and Sports, all UITMs, University Technology Petronas, Polytechnics Merlimau, Tanjung Malim and Kulim, universities, polytechnics and colleges.
(3) Any and all information, documents, records or otherwise pertaining to the private and confidential documents and records of the plaintiff.[198]

On this issue, the court referred to the English case of *Garden Cottage Foods Ltd v Milk Marketing Board*, where the House of Lords held that all orders of the court should be expressed in clear and unambiguous terms especially where (as in the case of injunctions) the failure to comply will constitute contempt of court.[199] The court also referred to three other English cases which emphasized that 'an injunction should be framed so as to make it plain to those to whom it is directed, and to those who may be affected by it, the nature of the obligation arising from the order, so that they may know precisely what they are required to do or abstain from doing'.[200] The court concluded that these principles of law, when applied to the facts of the present case, weighed heavily in favour of the defendants. The Anton Piller order was too wide, imprecise, vague and oppressive in the extreme, and the defendants were put in a dilemma as to what documents were covered under the order.[201]

4.5. ***Legal Analysis***

4.5.1. *Three Essential Preconditions for the Making of Anton Piller Order*

An Anton Piller order can be applied for in all kinds of cases, although *Apparatech (M) Sdn Bhd* is the first reported case relating to the protection of confidential information

198. *Ibid.*, para. 54.
199. [1984] 1 AC 130 (HL). *Apparatech (M) Sdn Bhd v Ng Hock Chong & Anor* [2006] 2 MLJ 61, para. 54.
200. *Apparatech (M) Sdn Bhd v Ng Hock Chong & Anor* [2006] 2 MLJ 61, para. 54, citing *Attorney-General v Staffordshire County Council* [1905] 1 Ch 336, p. 342; *Morris v Redland Bricks Ltd* [1970] AC 652, pp. 666-667; and *Collins v Wayne Iron Works* (1910) 76 Atl 24, p. 25.
201. *Apparatech (M) Sdn Bhd v Ng Hock Chong & Anor* [2006] 2 MLJ 61, para. 54.

where such an order was issued. The Anton Piller order is a very powerful and effective tool in the arsenal available for use by plaintiffs. '[It] is very draconian and it carries with it a very drastic effect when it is executed. It is for these salient reasons that an Anton Piller order should only be granted in very exceptional cases.'[202] For that reason, stringent conditions have to be satisfied before a court would grant such an order.

The Anton Piller order derives its name from the case of *Anton Piller KG v Manufacturing Processes Ltd & Ors*, a decision of the Court of Appeal.[203] It received the approval of the House of Lords in the case of *Rank Film Distributors Ltd & Ors v Video Information Centre & Ors*.[204] In Malaysia, the courts have granted Anton Piller orders starting with the case of *Lian Keow Sdn Bhd v C Paramjothy & Anor* and it is now a common feature in the Malaysian courts.[205]

The power to grant an ex parte Anton Piller order in the United Kingdom is based on the inherent power of the court.[206] In Malaysia, there appears to be three statutory bases for the Malaysian courts to grant ex parte Anton Piller order, ad interim Anton Piller order and inter partes Anton Piller order. They are section 25(2) of the Courts of Judicature Act 1964 and paragraph 6 of the Schedule to the Courts of Judicature Act,[207] Order 29 rule 1 of the Rules of Court 2012 and section 51(1) of the Specific Relief Act 1950.[208] In view of the above provisions, there is thus no need to resort to the court's inherent jurisdiction to grant an Anton Piller order.[209]

In the seminal case of *Anton Piller KG v Manufacturing Processes Ltd*, Ormrod LJ held that:

> There are three essential pre-conditions for the making of such an order, in my judgment. First, there must be an extremely strong *prima facie* case. Secondly, the damage, potential or actual, must be very serious for the plaintiff. Thirdly, there must be clear evidence that the defendants have in their possession incriminating documents or things, and that there is a real possibility that they may destroy such material before any application *inter partes* can be made.[210]

202. *Ibid.*, para. 7, citing *Thermax Ltd v Schott Industrial Glass Ltd* [1981] FSR 289; and *Columbia Picture Industries Inc & Ors v Robinson & Ors* [1987] Ch 38; [1986] 3 All ER 338.
203. [1976] 1 All ER 779.
204. [1981] 2 All ER 76.
205. [1982] 1 MLJ 217. *Apparatech (M) Sdn Bhd v Ng Hock Chong* & Anor [2006] 2 MLJ 61, para. 27.
206. *Anton Piller KG v Manufacturing Processes Ltd & Ors* [1976] 1 All ER 779, per Lord Denning MR, p. 783.
207. *See Arthur Anderson & Co v Interfood Sdn Bhd* [2005] 6 MLJ 239, per Richard Malanjum JCA, para. 21, 'An *Anton Piller* order is just another form of injunction albeit unique in its application. Hence, it is a discretionary relief. It assumed the name from the decision of the English Court of Appeal in *Anton Piller KG v Manufacturing Processes Ltd* [1976] 1 All ER 779. This doctrine entered into our legal corpus through para. 6 of the Schedule to the Courts of Judicature Act 1964 in the same way as Mareva injunction did.'
208. *See*, for example, *Pentamaster Instrumentation Sdn Bhd v QAV Technologies Sdn Bhd* [2017] 11 MLJ 233, para. 18(2) and *Sigma Glove Industries Sdn Bhd and Ors v Ong Chin Kok and Anor* [2018] 8 MLJ 481, p. 491.
209. *Sigma Glove Industries Sdn Bhd and Ors v Ong Chin Kok and Anor* [2018] 8 MLJ 481, p. 491.
210. [1976] 1 All ER 779, per Ormrod LJ, p. 784.

The three preconditions were adopted by the court in *Apparatech (M)*.[211] In *Arthur Anderson & Co v Interfood Sdn* Bhd, the Court of Appeal restated the above preconditions and held that:

> It is settled that the basic requirements to be satisfied by an applicant for an Anton Piller order at an *ex parte* stage are as follows:
>
> (a) to disclose an extremely strong *prima facie* case,
> (b) that a refusal to grant the order will have a very serious effect to the applicant,
> (c) that it must be established that the defendant has in its possession the relevant documents and/or materials being sought for and that there is a real possibility that the defendant may destroy such documents and/or materials,
> (d) that the applicant is required to make a full and frank disclosure, and
> (e) that the order should contain the necessary undertakings and safeguards to be complied with upon its execution.[212]

In *Apparatech*, the court held that 'The plaintiff must show, in order to obtain an Anton Piller order, that there is a "very strong *prima facie* case against the defendant." To do this, the plaintiff must show that there is a valid cause of action and that judgment would be granted in favour of the plaintiff.'[213] However, in *Sigma Glove Industries Sdn Bhd and Ors v Ong Chin Kok and Anor*, the court, remarking on the less stringent threshold in *Apparatech*, referred to the Court of Appeal case of *Arthur Anderson & Co v Interfood Sdn Bhd* and the Singapore Court of Appeal case of *Asian Corporate Services (SEA) Pte Ltd v Eastwest Management Ltd (Singapore Branch)*. The court, noting that both these cases had applied the 'extremely *strong prima* facie case' requirement,[214] applied the same test.[215]

Failure to satisfy any of the preconditions would result in the order being set aside. In *Apparatech*, even though the defendants had not specifically pleaded that the plaintiff had failed to provide evidence that there is a real possibility that relevant materials may be destroyed, the court addressed this precondition.

4.5.2. Identification of the Specific Confidential Information Sought to Be Seized Is Important

Further, the affidavit in support of an ex parte Anton Piller order application must comply with all the procedural requirements stated in Order 29 rule 1(2A)(a)-(g) of the Rules of Court 2012 referred to earlier. As discussed earlier, one reason for the court setting aside the ex parte Anton Piller order in *Apparatech* was that the order 'was too wide, imprecise, vague and oppressive in the extreme and the defendants were put in

211. *Apparatech (M) Sdn Bhd v Ng Hock Chong & Anor* [2006] 2 MLJ 61, para. 48.
212. [2005] 6 MLJ 239, per Richard Malanjum JCA, para. 31. *See also Fileforce Sdn Bhd v Lai May Ting and Ors*, Suit No. WA 22NCVC-176-04/2018, dated 21.8.2019, where these preconditions were adopted.
213. *Apparatech (M) Sdn Bhd v Ng Hock Chong & Anor* [2006] 2 MLJ 61, para. 88.
214. *Arthur Anderson & Co v Interfood Sdn Bhd* [2005] 6 MLJ 239 and *Asian Corporate Services (SEA) Pte Ltd v Eastwest Management Ltd (Singapore Branch)* [2006] 1 SLR 901. *Sigma Glove Industries Sdn Bhd and Ors v Ong Chin Kok and Anor* [2018] 8 MLJ 481, p. 491.
215. *Sigma Glove Industries Sdn Bhd and Ors v Ong Chin Kok and Anor* [2018] 8 MLJ 481, p. 494.

a dilemma as to what documents were covered under the Anton Piller order'.[216] In *Arthur Anderson*, the ex parte Anton Piller order was set aside for procedural non-compliance with the provisions of Order 29 in that, *inter alia*, 'there was no clear and concise statement of facts stated which gave rise to the claim and the omission in the application and the supporting affidavit of a statement or reason as to the nature of the urgency thereby justifying the application to be made *ex parte*'.[217]

In addition, in cases involving breach of confidence, identification of the specific confidential information sought to be seized is important, not only in the statement of claim but also in the affidavit in support of the application for an ex parte Anton Piller order. In *Apparatech*, the orders were so general and wide ranging that the court held the 'Defendants were put in a dilemma as to what documents that were covered under the Anton Piller order.'[218] In *Sigma Glove*, the court observed that 'The statement of claim and the plaintiffs' affidavit in support of the ex parte Anton Piller order application did not specify the contents of the confidential information.'[219]

4.6. *Commercial or Industrial Significance*

The Anton Piller order is a mandatory order of the court authorizing the plaintiff to enter the premises of the defendant in order to search for materials and documents kept in the said premises and to inspect them physically and even remove them for safekeeping. The order may be granted at any stage of an action, even before the issuance of the writ of summons, when there is real risk of destruction or concealment of evidence by the defendant. When granted on an ex parte basis, it provides an element of surprise, thus preventing any attempt at destruction or concealment of materials and documents which may be relevant in any pending or intended litigation. A defendant who refuses to comply with the order may be subject to committal proceedings for contempt of court. However, a defendant can apply to set aside the Anton Piller granted ex parte. As it is a very draconian order, the plaintiff has to make sure that he complies with all the substantive and procedural requirements for obtaining such an order. Failure to do so would result in the ex parte Anton Piller being set aside, and the plaintiff would have to honour its undertaking to pay damages.

216. *Apparatech (M) Sdn Bhd v Ng Hock Chong & Anor* [2006] 2 MLJ 61, para. 54.
217. *Arthur Anderson & Co v Interfood Sdn Bhd* [2005] 6 MLJ 239, paras 46-47.
218. *Apparatech (M) Sdn Bhd v Ng Hock Chong & Anor* [2006] 2 MLJ 61, para. 54.
219. *Sigma Glove Industries Sdn Bhd & Ors v Ong Chin Kok & Anor* [2018] 8 MLJ 481, p. 496.

TOPIC 5 DAMAGES

Sik Cheng Peng

1. Legal Issues

A plaintiff seeking damages shall bear the onus of proving the loss or damage suffered. Difficulties, however, lie in quantifying and assessing the damages that a plaintiff is claiming. The plaintiff is required to present evidence at the stage of assessment of damages to support the claim for the loss or damage suffered as a result of the breach of confidence committed by the defendant.

2. The Statutory Law

Chapter VII of the Evidence Act 1950 (Act 56) is relevant in relation to the onus of proving loss or damage suffered in an assessment of damages. Section 101 of the Act places the duty on the party seeking judgment on any legal right or liability, whereas section 102 makes it clear that if a plaintiff fails to discharge his burden of proof, no evidential burden will shift to the defendant. Furthermore, section 103 of the Act provides where a person wishes the court to believe in the existence of any particular fact, the burden of proof on that fact shall lie on that person.

3. The Case Law

As the law stands now, there are only three reported judgments which directly dealt with the burden of proving loss during an assessment of damages for breach of confidence. The High Court in *Ampledeal (M) Sdn Bhd & 3 Ors v Laponie (M) Sdn Bhd & 3 Ors*[220] heard the plaintiffs' claim for general damages on various grounds including misuse of confidential information by the defendants. It held that the duty is placed on the plaintiffs to prove their actual loss or damage and this was not discharged by the plaintiffs who did not support the amount claimed by evidence or supporting documents. In *ZY Phyto Tech Industries (M) Sdn Bhd & Anor v Nazri bin Zakaria & Ors,* the High Court expounded on the principle of burden of proof in assessment of damages, namely, the party entitled to damages is under the duty to prove the loss or damage suffered while the other party only bears the onus to present evidence to rebut.[221] In the third case, *Lim Tze Sian v Coverright Surface Malaysia Sdn Bhd,*[222] the Court of Appeal addressed in detail the principles applicable to an assessment of damages for breach of confidence.

220. [2015] MLJU 1933.
221. [2018] 11 MLJ 110, para. 7-10.
222. [2017] 1 MLJ 418; [2017] 5 CLJ 150.

4. The Leading Case

The case of *Lim Tze Sian v Coverright Surface Malaysia Sdn Bhd*[223] is chosen as the leading case as it is delivered by the Court of Appeal, a higher court as compared to the High Court in the other two cases related to assessment of damages. In addition, this is also, so far, the only reported case of Malaysia which delved into the rules on assessment of damages for breach of confidence.

4.1. Case Information

Lim Tze Sian v Coverright Surface Malaysia Sdn Bhd [2017] 1 MLJ 418; [2017] 5 CLJ 150. Civil Appeal No: B-03(IM) (NCVC)-102–11 of 2015, Court of Appeal (Putrajaya), 28 November 2016. Abang Iskandar, Idrus Harun and Mary Lim JJCA.

4.2. Summary

The case concerned assessment of damages for an interlocutory judgment entered in favour of the respondent's counterclaim against the appellant. The respondent's counterclaim was for the losses resulting from the appellant's wrongful act of misusing the respondent's confidential information. During assessment of damages, the senior assistant registrar (SAR) assessed MYR 1 million as the respondent's loss of profit. The appellant appealed to the High Court which dismissed the appeal. Thereafter, the appellant appealed against the High Court's decision to the Court of Appeal raising questions on the assessment of damages, particularly whether the respondent had proved the losses suffered for the damages it was claiming. The Court of Appeal ruled in favour of the appellant as the respondent had failed to establish properly the loss claimed.

4.3. Facts

The appellant served a notice on the respondent on 1 October 2010 of his intent to resign with effect from March 2011. The respondent by a letter dated 21 January 2011 terminated the appellant's employment. Later, the appellant commenced an action to recover his outstanding salary and allowance from the respondent. The respondent counterclaimed a sum of MYR 1 million being the loss resulting from the appellant's wrongful act of disclosing and misusing the respondent's business information, confidential and intellectual property information. Due to the appellant's repeated non-attendance, his action was struck out and a judgment in default was entered for the respondent's counterclaim. It was ordered that damages were to be assessed by the SAR.

The High Court ordered the appellant to provide the respondent the details of profits he made from using the respondent's information. When the appellant failed to do so, the respondent issued a notice for assessment of damages and applied to the SAR

223. *Ibid.*

for directions. During the case management before the SAR, the SAR instructed the parties to file an affidavit each and written submissions, which both parties did. The SAR did not allow the calling of witnesses to prove damage on the basis that the quantum was only for loss of profit. The SAR then assessed a sum of MYR 1 million being the respondent's loss of profit. The sum was determined by the SAR after considering the respondent's losses indicated in the exhibits. The SAR was of the view that the respondent was under not duty to prove liability since judgment was already entered against the appellant.

On appeal, the award was affirmed by the High Court judge who held that 'the appellant had failed to adduce and rebut the documentary evidence in relation to the respondent's losses'.[224] The High Court judge did not express any opinion on the question of whether the SAR erred in refusing the calling of witnesses except stating that the use of affidavits was agreed upon by the parties. The appellant appealed to the Court of Appeal and raised issues on the matter of proving losses for an award of damages. More specifically, the questions considered by the Court of Appeal in the appeal were: first, whether both the SAR and the High Court judge erred in refusing the calling of witnesses during the assessment of damages; and second, whether the respondent had properly proved the quantum claimed.

4.4. *The Reasoning of the Court*

4.4.1. *Method of Assessment*

On the first question of whether the SAR and the High Court judge erred in refusing the calling of witnesses, the Court of Appeal expressed that if it was agreed between the parties that the assessment is to be by means of affidavit evidence, it would be improper for the appellant to break the promise.[225] Accordingly, the appellant cannot now complain about the method. The court, however, cautioned that affidavit evidence may have hearsay which should always be dealt with cautiously. Hence, where affidavit evidence is relied on, it is always open to either party to apply to cross-examine the deponent to verify the truth of the contents.[226]

4.4.2. *The Duty to Prove Loss*

The Court of Appeal ruled in favour of the appellant on the second ground of appeal. While a court hearing an appeal may not have had the opportunity to see, hear, and assess the witnesses' evidence, it is however obliged to scrutinize the evidence in order to determine whether assessment was done properly. In a case where assessment was based on affidavit evidence, the examination must be conducted on the affidavits and

224. *Lim Tze Sian v Coverright Surface Malaysia Sdn Bhd* [2017] 1 MLJ 418; [2017] 5 CLJ 150, para. 5.
225. *Lim Tze Sian v Coverright Surface Malaysia Sdn Bhd* [2017] 1 MLJ 418; [2017] 5 CLJ 150, para. 16.
226. *Lim Tze Sian v Coverright Surface Malaysia Sdn Bhd* [2017] 1 MLJ 418; [2017] 5 CLJ 150, para. 17.

exhibits as well as the submissions made by the parties.[227] Unfortunately, that was not reflected in the decision of the High Court judge who merely expressed that the appellant had not rebutted the documentary evidence.

The Court of Appeal held that consideration should have been made as to whether the SAR was right in holding that since the question of liability was settled by the judgment, it was thus unnecessary for the respondent to adduce proof of loss.[228] The Court of Appeal expressed that while the appellant's liability to pay was not a question, his liability to pay is still subject to proof.[229] Damage, or its existence, must be established; and the amount of the damage must be shown, via oral or documentary evidence or both; none of these was done in the assessment by the SAR.[230] The court stressed that the burden of proving loss on the balance of probabilities was with the respondent, which was never discharged by the respondent in this case. Since the burden was not discharged by the respondent, there was no question of rebuttal by the appellant.[231]

4.4.3. *Insufficient Evidence of Loss*

It was also found that the SAR had not properly examined the exhibits. The reasons given by the SAR for her decision were 'too broad brushed and generalized, and not fact specific'.[232] The Court of Appeal examined the affidavits and exhibits, namely, the respondent's audited statements of accounts for 2011 and 2012, the respondent's collective yearly sales analysis for 2010-2012, the analysis of sales to certain companies for 2010-2012, and a proforma invoice from a company signed by Patrick Teoh, a former sales manager of the respondent who resigned around the time the appellant left the respondent. The respondents claimed that all the exhibits indicated a significant drop of revenue as well as a similar drop in its sales, resulting from the appellant's act of sabotaging the respondent's business. The respondent, relying on the proforma invoice, claimed that both Patrick Teoh and the appellant had disclosed the respondent's customer information to the company which Patrick Teoh joined after resigning from the respondent company. Upon examination of the affidavits and exhibits, the

227. *Lim Tze Sian v Coverright Surface Malaysia Sdn Bhd* [2017] 1 MLJ 418; [2017] 5 CLJ 150, para. 18.
228. *Lim Tze Sian v Coverright Surface Malaysia Sdn Bhd* [2017] 1 MLJ 418; [2017] 5 CLJ 150, para. 20.
229. *Lim Tze Sian v Coverright Surface Malaysia Sdn Bhd* [2017] 1 MLJ 418; [2017] 5 CLJ 150, para. 21.
230. *Lim Tze Sian v Coverright Surface Malaysia Sdn Bhd* [2017] 1 MLJ 418; [2017] 5 CLJ 150, paras 21-22.
231. *See Bonham-Carter v Hyde Park Hotel Ltd* [1948] 64 TLR 177 per Lord Goddard: 'Plaintiffs must understand that if they bring actions for damages it is for them to prove their damages. It is not enough to write down the particulars and so to speak throw them at the court, saying: "This is what I have lost. I ask you to give me damages." They have to prove it.'
232. *Lim Tze Sian v Coverright Surface Malaysia Sdn Bhd* [2017] 1 MLJ 418; [2017] 5 CLJ 150, para. 23.

Court of Appeal held that these affidavits and exhibits did not prove how the alleged loss was attributable to the appellant.[233]

4.4.4. *Remoteness*

The Court of Appeal first emphasized that to succeed in claiming damages, the test of remoteness must be satisfied. In other words, the respondent must show that it had suffered loss of profits resulting from the appellant's breach of the confidentiality and non-competition agreement. If the loss is too remote, no compensation may be allowed. It is crucial to prove that the losses suffered by the respondent were caused by the appellant's act. The judgment in default entered against the appellant only established the fact of breach of confidentiality and breach of contract, but the matter of loss and the amount of the loss remain to be proved.[234] Reference was made to an unreported decision in *Taiping Poly (M) Sdn Bhd v Wong Fook Toh & Ors*[235] in which the Federal Court opined that the duty is placed on the plaintiff to prove the loss actually suffered due to the defendant's act and that the plaintiff is entitled to such damages as naturally flowing from such act.[236]

Upon examination of the affidavits and exhibits, the Court of Appeal held that they did not demonstrate how the alleged loss was attributable to the appellant on several grounds. First, the audited statements of account were incomplete sets of accounts, and thus making it 'unsafe and unreliable'.[237] Second, there was no proof that the respondent had always and consistently achieved an increase in its revenue or profits and that the trend would have continued so but for the appellant's acts.[238] Instead, the evidence indicated that the respondent had already sustained a reduction in its revenue collection before the period complained of with a higher percentage loss. Third, revenue does not necessarily translate into profits since profits depend on many factors such as operating expenses, investments, and borrowings. The court stressed that a reduction in revenue is not equivalent to a reduction in profit. In fact, the court observed that the respondent experienced an increase in its operating profit, profits after taxation, as well as retained profits.[239] None of these was considered by the SAR. Accordingly, the respondent's claim of a loss of profits was unsustainable.

---

233. *Lim Tze Sian v Coverright Surface Malaysia Sdn Bhd* [2017] 1 MLJ 418; [2017] 5 CLJ 150, para. 28.
234. *Lim Tze Sian v Coverright Surface Malaysia Sdn Bhd* [2017] 1 MLJ 418; [2017] 5 CLJ 150, para. 31. The Court of Appeal quoted the following from *Tan Ah Chio & Ors v Lua Kim Soon & Ors* [2015] 1 MLJ 334, 'It is trite law that a party claiming damages must prove actual losses suffered and that the losses suffered were caused by the opposing party's breach.'
235. Civil Appeal No. 02-44 of 2009.
236. *Lim Tze Sian v Coverright Surface Malaysia Sdn Bhd* [2017] 1 MLJ 418; [2017] 5 CLJ 150, para. 33.
237. *Lim Tze Sian v Coverright Surface Malaysia Sdn Bhd* [2017] 1 MLJ 418; [2017] 5 CLJ 150, para. 37.
238. *Lim Tze Sian v Coverright Surface Malaysia Sdn Bhd* [2017] 1 MLJ 418; [2017] 5 CLJ 150, para. 38.
239. *Lim Tze Sian v Coverright Surface Malaysia Sdn Bhd* [2017] 1 MLJ 418; [2017] 5 CLJ 150, paras 39-40.

Even assuming that there was substantial drop in revenue, the Court of Appeal held that there was no evidence showing that such drop was, in any way, caused by the appellant. The appellant was not the only or main sales personnel responsible for the sales.[240] On the contrary, it was admitted by the respondent that its former sale manager, Patrick Teoh, was the one who signed the proforma invoice for one of the sales. There was no explanation from the respondent as to how the losses were attributable to the appellant.

The respondent claimed that it experienced a significant drop in sales within the first two years upon the appellant's resignation by referring to the sales figures presented. According to the respondent, the drop in sales was a direct outcome of the appellant's act of sabotaging its business. However, the Court of Appeal found that this claim was not sustainable as certainly the drop in sales was not necessarily attributable to the appellant's cessation of employment. In addition, the respondent claimed that its profit margin was 20% of the yearly sales, which amounted to about MYR 18.3 million in loss of profits, but had limited its claim to MYR 1 million without giving any explanation for the decision.[241] In view of the incomplete audited statements and the unreliable yearly sales analysis, loss of profits alleged by the respondent was not established.[242]

The Court of Appeal remarked that the matter of damages is never arbitrary, and it has to be proved according to firmly established principles of compensation and based on reliable evidence.[243] It proceeded to rule that the SAR had failed to examine the evidence to determine if the claim of damage was indeed established. Had there been a proper scrutiny of the documents conducted, it would be obvious that the respondent's claim was not supported by the documents at all.[244]

4.5. *Legal Analysis*

4.5.1. *The Objective of Damages*

A flawed evaluation of a claim for damages may result in a failure of justice and departs from the object of an award of damages, namely, to place a plaintiff in a position he would have been if there was no breach or tort. Compensatory damages aim to compensate the loss suffered by the plaintiff and thus its assessment is based on the loss. Lord Wilberforce elucidated the general principle on assessment of damages in *General Tire and Rubber Co v Firestone Tyre and Rubber Co Ltd* as 'the measure of the

240. *Lim Tze Sian v Coverright Surface Malaysia Sdn Bhd* [2017] 1 MLJ 418; [2017] 5 CLJ 150, para. 41.
241. *Lim Tze Sian v Coverright Surface Malaysia Sdn Bhd* [2017] 1 MLJ 418; [2017] 5 CLJ 150, para. 46.
242. *Lim Tze Sian v Coverright Surface Malaysia Sdn Bhd* [2017] 1 MLJ 418; [2017] 5 CLJ 150, para. 47.
243. *Ibid.*
244. *Ibid.*

damages is to be, so far as possible, that sum of money which will put the injured party in the same position as he would have been if he had not sustained the wrong'.[245]

In cases relating to trade secrets, damages are usually granted to address the pecuniary loss that a plaintiff has experienced resulting from the misuse. General damages may also be granted in cases of breach of confidence or misuse of trade secrets if a plaintiff has suffered non-pecuniary loss. Aggravated damages, on the other hand, are determined with reference to the defendant's motive as well as the plaintiff's good reputation. Compensatory damages differ starkly from exemplary damages; the rationale of the latter is to punish.[246] An award of exemplary damages is, however, governed by a principle of moderation and restraint.[247]

4.5.2. The Burden of Proof

The principles governing the assessment of damages in breach of confidence cases are the same as that in breach of contract cases.[248] As explained by the English High Court in *Marathon Asset Management LLP v Seddon & Ors*,[249] the plaintiff may seek damages for the financial loss resulting from misuse of the confidential information, or in the absence of which, a remedy ordering the defendant to pay a sum of money representing the profit made by the defendant from the wrongful act.[250] In either case, the plaintiff must prove his case, namely, the fact of damage and its amount.[251] In the event where evidence proving the quantum of damages is absent, nominal damages may be awarded,[252] which may be seen in *Marathon Asset Management LLP v Seddon & Ors.*[253] Nonetheless, where a plaintiff has established that some substantial loss has been incurred, the difficulty of assessment due to the nature of the damage is no reason for awarding no damages or only nominal damages.[254] In other words, while it may be difficult to ascertain precisely the loss or damage sustained and thus the amount of damages, the court will nevertheless attempt to assess damages without fear or favour.[255]

245. [1975] 2 All ER 173 at 177; [1975] 1 WLR 819 at 824. The English Court of Appeal in *Dowson & Mason Ltd v Potter and others* [1986] 1 All ER 418; [1986] 1 WLR 1419 was of the view that the approach adopted by the court in *Seager v Copydex Ltd (No. 2)* [1969] RPC 250; [1969] 2 All ER 713 in assessing damages by reference to the value of the information misused by the defendant is not universally and generally appropriate. The fundamental principle is that as expounded by Lord Wilberforce in *General Tire and Rubber Co.*
246. *A v Bottrill* [2003] 1 AC 449; [2003] 1 LRC711; [2003] 1 NZLR 721 (PC), para. 20.
247. *See Rookes v Barnard* [1964] AC 1129; [1964] 1 All ER 367; [1964] 2 WLR 269 (HL), pp. 1227-1228.
248. *Fish & Co Restaurants Pte Ltd v MFM Restaurants Pte Ltd & Anor* [2009] SGHC 270; [2010] 1 1104.
249. [2017] EWHC 300 (Comm).
250. *Ibid.*, paras 154-156. The remedies of licence fee damages and an account of profits are two different methods of measuring the profits made by the defendant.
251. McGregor, Harvey, *McGregor on Damages* (Sweet & Maxwell, 18th ed., 2009), para. 8-001.
252. [2017] EWHC 300 (Comm), para. 157.
253. [2017] EWHC 300 (Comm).
254. *Chaplin v Hicks* [1911] 2 KB 786 per Vaughan William J.
255. *Sanders v Parry* [1967] 1 WLR 753.

In deciding the amount of damages to be awarded, the assessment may be based on loss of profits experienced by the plaintiff. Pritchard J in *Aquaculture Corp v New Zealand Green Mussel Co Ltd (No. 2)*[256] reminded that a degree of caution shall be exercised in doing so and that the plaintiff bears the burden of proving its loss.[257] The learned judge was of the opinion that if there is an error in achieving what must at best be rough justice, the error should be in the direction of being too conservative.[258]

Clearly, the burden of proving the loss or damage in assessment of damages lies on the party who is entitled to damages. The other party bears no onus of proof except to adduce evidence to rebut the claimed damage.[259] In *ZY Phyto Tech Industries (M) Sdn Bhd & Anor v Nazri bin Zakaria & Ors*,[260] the defendants were ordered to pay damages for the wrongful use of the plaintiff's confidential information and trade secrets, which will be assessed by reference to an account of profits from the plaintiff. However, during the assessment, the plaintiff adduced merely projected losses based on historical trends and sales estimates without presenting a profit and loss account. It was held that the plaintiff had failed to discharge the burden of proving the loss or damage it suffered. The case of *Ampledeal (M) Sdn Bhd & 3 Ors v Laponie (M) Sdn Bhd & 3 Ors*[261] is another example of unsuccessful endeavours by plaintiffs to prove the loss. In this case, the plaintiffs failed to obtain damages for the loss they claimed amounting to MYR 15.9 million as it was unsupported by evidence or any supporting documents.

4.5.3. *Proof of Loss*

Assessing damages for loss of profits is fraught with great difficulties. The court may resort to any relevant information which could help shed light on the loss that a plaintiff has suffered resulting from the breach of confidence. The Singapore High Court in *Fish & Co Restaurants Pte Ltd v MFM Restaurants Pte Ltd & Anor*,[262] for instance, in assessing the loss of profit resulting from a breach of undertaking, took note of the fact that other factors could have contributed to the plaintiff's loss of profit such as direct competition, pricing, and cannibalization. In ascertaining the loss of profit, the court referred to the Catering Trade Index for Restaurants for the corresponding period by the Department of Statistics of Singapore as an indicator of the industry trend.

The Court of Appeal in the case of *Lim Tze Sian* above applied the Federal Court decision in *SPM Membrane Switch Sdn Bhd v Kerajaan Negeri Selangor*,[263] which involved a claim for loss of profits calculated on the basis of commissions due to the appellant. The Federal Court pointed out that a calculation based on 'commissions' is very different from a calculation based on 'profits'. Awarding damages based on

256. (1986) 10 IPR 341.
257. *Ibid.*, p. 331.
258. *Ibid.*
259. *ZY Phyto Tech Industries (M) Sdn Bhd & Anor v Nazri bin Zakaria & Ors* [2018] 11 MLJ 110, para. 7.
260. [2018] 11 MLJ 110.
261. [2015] MLJU 37.
262. [2009] SGHC 270; [2010] 1 1104.
263. [2016] 1 MLJ 464; [2016] 1 CLJ 177.

commission completely ignores the fact that if the contract were properly performed, the appellant would have incurred expenses and operating costs. To award damages in such manner would place the appellant in a position well beyond that which it would rightfully be in had the contract been properly performed.[264]

The role of the court in assessment of damages was explained by the Court of Appeal in *Lim Tze Sian* as follows:

> Assessment of damages is a critical stage in the evaluation of any claim before the court. Inasmuch as the primary question of liability warrants careful consideration of the law and proper application of that law to the facts, so is the assessment of damages. Such exercise can sometimes be tedious as a mountain of 'information' is thrown at the court as purported evidence and justification for the claim. That is quite wrong. Parties must carefully prove their claim, and the court must evaluate the contentions, consider if the evidence brought is indeed relevant, true, and supportive of the claim, no matter how difficult or cumbersome. It is not enough for a court, especially one sitting at first instance, to simply say that it is satisfied that the claim is proved or not proved. Reasons must be articulated to explain why various pieces of evidence were either considered or not considered; and why and how the submissions from both counsel on the same were treated.[265]

As stated by Ong Hock Thye FC, as he then was, in *Guan Soon Tin Mining Co v Wong Fook Kum,*[266] an appellate court may interfere with an award of damages by a trial judge if the trial judge had acted on a wrong principle of law or had misapprehended the facts or had made a wholly erroneous estimate of the damage suffered.[267]

4.6. *Commercial or Industrial Significance*

The objective of an award of damages for torts is to compensate the plaintiff who suffers loss resulting from the wrong performed by the defendant. In circumstances where a plaintiff claims damages for the injury caused by the defendant's misuse of confidential information, damages may be ordered for financial loss or even non-financial loss in some circumstances. In either case, the plaintiff bears the burden to show the loss. It is vital for a plaintiff to prove not only the loss but also that the loss is linked to the wrong committed by the defendant.

Besides, a plaintiff must establish that the quantum of damages claimed is justified and supported by relevant evidence or documents. This is so even where a judgment on the defendant's liability on misuse of trade secrets has been granted since the question of liability is a matter separate from the assessment of damages. Where a plaintiff is seeking damages for loss of profits with reference to projected profits, the basis of the projection or estimation shall be justifiable and reasonable. Loss of revenue is not equivalent to loss of profits and thus would be insufficient to prove the damage allegedly suffered by a plaintiff.

---

264. [2016] 1 MLJ 464; [2016] 1 CLJ 177, para. 119.
265. *Lim Tze Sian v Coverright Surface Malaysia Sdn Bhd* [2017] 1 MLJ 418; [2017] 5 CLJ 150, para. 49.
266. [1997] 5 MLJ 632, p. 653.
267. *Kurdamai Construction and Engineering Sdn Bhd v Innoseven Sdn Bhd & Ors* [2014] 4 MLJU 1157 CA in which the Court of Appeal quoted the cases of *Davies v Powell Duffryn Associated Colleries Ltd* [1942] AC 601 and *Dingle v Associated Newspapers Ltd and Ors* [1964] AC 371.

CHAPTER 9

India

Prashant Reddy T.

OVERVIEW AND SUMMARY

Trade secret litigation in India has been a regular feature despite the fact that India does not have a statutory trade secret law. There has been some discussion within the government about introducing a statutory trade secret law and a draft bill was made public but never introduced in Parliament.[1] Rather, most of this trade secret litigation takes place under either contract law or the equitable 'duty of confidence' which was borrowed from the UK. A notable feature of the Indian approach to trade secrets is that there is no requirement for the information to have special commercial value. As a result, even personal information can be protected as long as it has remained 'confidential'.

If there is a contractual relationship between two parties, the contractual clauses will dictate the scope of confidentiality. This is a relatively straightforward application of the law. If there is no contractual relationship, the parties can fall back on the equitable 'duty of confidence' to seek an injunction against the disclosure of confidential information. Under the equitable duty of confidence, as long as the information is conveyed to the counterparty under a duty of confidence, the latter is expected to honour the obligation to maintain the information as confidential even in the absence of a contract. The test is as follows:

(i) the information disclosed was of a confidential nature;
(ii) it was communicated in circumstances importing an obligation of confidence;
(iii) there was an unauthorised use of this information.

1. Mihir Naniwadekar, *The Innovation Bill, 2008 and Trade Secrets: Part I*, SpicyIP (26 October 2008) https://spicyip.com/2008/10/innovation-bill-2008-and-trade-secrets.html. A draft of the law can be accessed here https://www.prsindia.org/uploads/media/draftinnovationlaw.pdf.

The circumstances of the case therefore greatly influence the outcome in such cases. For example, if one party discloses its confidential information to another during the course of negotiations for the purpose of contracting the latter's manufacturing services and the latter uses such confidential information to its advantage without the authorisation of the former, a court could conclude that duty of equitable confidence was in fact breached and order an injunction restraining the use of the information. Damages or an account for profits may follow if the plaintiff can establish losses.

The profile of typical trade secret litigation in India can be divided into two categories.[2]

The first and most significant category of litigation is in the context of the employer-employee disputes wherein employers try to sue former employees after they leave employment. This litigation is borne out of employment contracts. A significant portion of this litigation is focused on customer lists that employees may have accessed before leaving employment, usually to join a competitor or to set up their own business. The issue of whether such customer lists can be considered confidential has seen a fair degree of litigation with Indian courts generally siding with former employees. As a result, client lists in most cases are not considered confidential since the identity of potential clients is usually well known across a particular trade. A second component of employment-related trade secret litigation is the use of 'know-how' learnt by former employees and subsequently used by them while working for competitors. Such litigation is often linked to contractual non-compete clauses which forbid employees from working for competitors. While non-compete clauses are conceptually an entirely different issue from trade secrets, employers often try to link both issues by seeking an injunction to restrain employees from working with potential competitors because of the likelihood that they may disclose trade secrets to the competitors.

It is not necessary that a former employee will necessarily use the trade secrets for the benefit of his new employer, and as a result it will be difficult for employers to get an injunction on anticipated disclosure of their trade secrets. It should however be noted that Indian courts have a mixed record on this issue. Section 27 of the Contracts Act, 1872 does prohibit any post-employment restrictions on the practice of trade or a profession. This provision has unfortunately been interpreted inconsistently by Indian courts as a result of which some employers have managed to get injunctions restraining their former employees from joining competitors merely on the grounds that they may breach their duty of confidentiality despite being unable to provide substantial evidence to support their claims. There are other judges who have refused to grant such injunctions because of the absence of proof of actual breach of a duty of confidentiality. At most, such judges may pass an injunction restraining the former employee from disclosing any trade secrets once they begin working for a competitor. These injunctions do not preclude the former employee from taking up the new job; rather, they only pre-emptively restrain the former employee from disclosing the data in question.

2. For a more detailed classification *see* Prashant Reddy T., *The 'Other IP Right': Is It Time to Codify the Indian Law on Protection of Confidential Information?*, 5(1) The Journal of the National Law University Delhi, 2018, 1-21.

There are however others judges who decline to grant such orders because of the impossibility of monitoring employees who are working in the privacy of their new workplaces for potential breach of such injunctions. This of course does not preclude legal action if specific evidence regarding the breach of confidence comes to light. Collection of evidence in such cases is however not very easy, and India does not have any specific law reversing the burden of proof in cases dealing with breach of confidence.

The second category of trade secret litigation in India deals with cases where two parties are negotiating to enter into a deal with each other, and in the process disclose confidential information to the other party before having entered into any contract. The information could be anything from a movie script to cutting-edge technology. Typically, one of the parties attempts to use the information disclosed to it during confidential negotiations without the permission of the counterparty. Since there is no contract between both parties, there is no contractual obligation to keep the information confidential. In such cases, Indian courts have used the doctrine of equitable 'duty of confidence' developed by English courts to restrain parties from disclosing information that has been shared with them under circumstances implying a 'duty of confidence'. Since this doctrine can be invoked even if there is no valid contract between both parties, India has not really felt the lack of a statutory trade secret law.

A notable trend across Indian trade secret litigation is that most cases conclude once the court decides on the grant or denial of interim injunctions. The few cases that go to trial had to grapple with the procedural issue of maintaining secrecy of the confidential information being disputed by the parties. Indian courts are required by law to conduct all civil and criminal proceedings, especially trials, in an open court that is accessible by any members of the public. The concepts of 'open courts' and 'open justice' are deeply ingrained in the Indian judicial system and are seen as critical to maintaining public confidence in the judicial system. These principles have existed in India since the time of British rule. The conduct of judicial proceedings in full public gaze has been seen as the best safeguard against abuse of power by judges or other powerful litigants.

Exceptions to this general rule have been carved out through legislation or judicial precedents in cases where the ends of justice may be defeated or in case where the privacy of the individuals in sensitive case may be violated. For example, in cases involving prosecutions for espionage or in cases involving questions of national security, the courts may hold their proceedings behind closed doors. With time, the exceptions grew wider to include cases of sexual assault and divorces where the legislature sought to protect the privacy of victims or litigants. Exceptions to the open court rule in trade secret cases have been recognised by the judiciary in the passing. However, it is only recently that Indian courts have created an elaborate procedural framework governing the manner in which the confidentiality of information may be protected during judicial proceedings in trade secret cases. Borrowing from English jurisprudence, Indian courts have recently developed the concept of 'confidentiality clubs' to deal with cases where confidential information forms part of the evidence. In order to prevent the parties from gaining knowledge of each other's 'confidential information', only specific lawyers and experts of either side are given access to the confidential information under the obligation that it can be used only for the judicial proceedings and not disclosed to their respective clients. Some courts like the Delhi High Court, which sees the largest volume of intellectual property (IP) litigation in India, have created standardised rules to govern the creation of confidentiality clubs in cases involving confidential information. Although other courts do not have similar procedural rules in place, Indian law is flexible enough to allow them to create such a procedural framework for individual cases. The drawback of creating such exceptions to the 'open court' is that the process is likely to be abused by litigants who do not want excessive public scrutiny of even those cases that do not involve commercially sensitive information.

Till date, there has not been a single reported trade secret case where the court has awarded 'damages'. Most of these cases tend to settle after a decision is rendered on the grant of an interim injunction. In the remaining cases, there has never been a case where damages have been awarded. This is more a comment on the slow-paced progress of the Indian judicial system, than on the reluctance or otherwise of Indian judges to grant damages in such cases. In other IP cases, notably trademark infringement cases, damages have been granted in ex parte cases, i.e., where the defendant has not made an appearance in court thereby saving the court the requirement of carrying out a contentious trial.

While there is no statutory trade secret law criminalising the misappropriation of trade secrets, there have been cases where complaints have been filed under the Indian Penal Code (IPC), which is the ordinary criminal law in India, alleging 'theft' of trade secrets under provisions that criminalise offences against property. These include specific provisions criminalising the theft of papers by a servant or clerk of the employer. Prima facie, it appears that these cases are usually filed by employers to harass former employees and there do not appear to be any reported judgments recording convictions. The only judgments available in this regard are in cases where the accused petitions High Courts to invoke their extraordinary powers to quash criminal complaints before lower courts prior to a trial. In some of these cases, High Courts in short judgments have stated that customer lists cannot be classified as 'trade secrets' or 'property'.[3] The precedents on this point do not sufficiently clarify the position of law in such cases, and as a result of which, it may still be possible to file criminal complaints with the police under the IPC in cases involving confidential information. Apart from the IPC, it may be possible to prosecute persons under the Information Technology Act, for accessing information on a computer system without due authorisation. Such cases appear to be rare in the Indian context.

While the courts have evolved an adequate legal framework to protect trade secrets despite the lack of action by the legislature, these cases are typically too complex for the under-resourced judicial system in India. While cases with simple facts

3. *American Express Bank Ltd. v Priya Puri* 2006 (110) FLR 1061 ('The details of customers are not trade secrets nor they are the property was held in 140 Wash.381, 249 P. 782, *City Ice and Cold Storage Co. v. Kinnee*. In this matter the Supreme Court of Washington had held that customers are not necessarily trade secrets, nor are they property'). *Hemal R Shah v State of Gujarat* Special Criminal Application No. 1171 of 2009 before the High Court of Gujarat (27 December 2010).

are likely to be heard speedily at the interim stage, it is unlikely that the more complicated cases will even reach the interim stage since they require full-fledged trials which take a long time to progress through the Indian judicial system.

TOPIC 1 THE REQUIREMENTS OF TRADE SECRETS

1. Legal Issues

Typically, if a trade secret is being protected under contract law, there has to be a specific clause in the contract pertaining to confidentiality. While oral contracts are recognised in India and can be enforced, they can prove to be difficult in a court of law. The extent and form of trade secrets in such cases will depend on the language of the confidentiality clause in the contract. It should however be presumed that the information in question should have been remained confidential and not already existing in the public domain. This can be a tricky question in the context of 'customer lists', which is an issue that often crops up in litigation between employers and former employees.

Even if there is no specific clause regarding confidentiality, courts can read in a 'duty of fidelity' into the contract, so as to impose a duty of confidentiality on former employees when it comes to information that they have picked up during the course of their employment.[4]

The third and perhaps most important limb of trade secret law in India is the 'duty of confidence' that evolved under the law of equity in the UK and which has been adopted by Indian courts over the last couple of decades.[5] The uniqueness of this doctrine is that it can be applied even without the existence of a contract between two parties. The typical fact scenarios where this doctrine applies are cases of negotiations where one party discusses confidential information with the other party in the hope of entering into a commercial agreement. Even if the negotiations fail and a contract is not signed, the counterparty is not at liberty to use the confidential information for its own commercial advantage, and if it does so, it can be sued for breaching its equitable duty of confidence. The three-step test to establish a breach of equitable duty of confidence, as laid down by English courts,[6] and adopted by Indian courts, is as follows:

(i) the information disclosed was of a confidential nature;
(ii) it was communicated in circumstances importing an obligation of confidence;
(iii) there was an unauthorised use of this information.

This doctrine can be extended to any information regardless of its 'commercial value', and in the UK it has been used to protect even personal information from being disclosed.[7] As a result, this doctrine can be used even in privacy cases.

4. Andrew Frazer, *The Employee's Contractual Duty of Fidelity*, 131(1) Law Quarterly Review 53 (2015).
5. One of the first English decisions in this regard was *Coco v Clark* [1968] FSR 415.
6. *Ibid.*
7. *Duchess of Argyll v Duke of Argyll* [1965] 1 All. E.R. 611 (the facts in this case involved the Duchess seeking an injunction restraining the Duke from disclosing to the press personal information that she had conveyed to him in confidence).

2. The Statutory Law

As of now there is no statutory law in India that protects trade secrets. There has been no dedicated legislative effort since 2008 to create a special trade secret law in India. Hence, contract law and the equitable duty of confidence are the only legal routes to protect trade secrets in India.

3. The Case Law

While there has been significant trade secret litigation in the last few years, almost no cases have gone all the way till the Supreme Court. Most of these cases usually get decided before trial courts or at most before Division Benches of the High Courts, in their appellate capacity. Therefore, it is necessary to determine the contours of trade secret law from the judgments of different High Courts. The judgments of these High Courts are binding only on the district courts below them and not on other High Courts. In terms of subject matter, these courts deal with subject matters ranging from movie scripts to technology to customer lists.

4. The Leading Cases

4.1. Case I

This case was the first Indian case to deal with the equitable duty of confidence as laid down by the English courts.

4.1.1. Case Information

John Richard Brady And Ors. v Chemical Process Equipments Pvt. Ltd.[8] decided by the Delhi High Court on 6 July 1987.

4.1.2. Summary

In this case before the Delhi High Court, there was no valid contract between the plaintiffs and defendants. Since the plaintiff argued that the information was shared with the defendant on the condition that its confidentiality would be maintained, the court granted an interim injunction pending trial because the balance of convenience was found to be in favour of the plaintiff. The case opened the door to protect trade secrets in India under the equitable duty of confidence.

4.1.3. Facts

The plaintiffs and defendants were in talks to manufacture a 'Fodder Production Unit' (FPU) that was developed by the plaintiff. The plaintiffs provided the defendants with access to their technical material, detailed know-how, drawings and specifications

8. AIR 1987 Delhi 372.

under the express condition that the latter would maintain confidentiality of the know-how, etc. The collaboration did not go through as planned due to inability of the defendants to manufacture certain components. In the following months, the plaintiffs discovered that the defendants had visited their facilities to gain know-how and information about the workings of their FPU technology, without the permission of the plaintiff's management. Later the defendants began selling FPUs that were similar to the ones developed by the plaintiff. On discovering these sales, the plaintiffs sued for copyright infringement and breach of the equitable duty of confidence that the defendants allegedly owed to the plaintiffs.

While the agreement between both parties did have a confidentiality clause, the defendants argued that the agreement was not a valid contract because it had not been validly concluded nor acted upon by either party.[9] The judgment does not expand on this issue in further detail, but it is likely that the parties did not exchange consideration, without which a contract is not considered to be valid under Indian law.[10] The absence of a valid contract or a confidentiality agreement made this a unique fact situation before an Indian court because most previous case law on this issue dealt with contractual confidentiality.

4.1.4. *Reasoning of the Court*

The court's reasoning on the existence and breach of duty of confidence was as follows:

> 22. This is just the situation in which the Courts must enforce the general rules of equity and restrain breach of confidence as recommended in the leading Saltman's case, Saltman Engineering Coy. Ld., Ferotec Ld. and Monarch Engineering Coy. (MITCHAM) Ld. v. Campbell Engineering Coy., Ld. (1948) 65 RPC 203, by Patrick Hearn in his book the Business of Industrial Licensing, by Roskill, J. in Cranleigh Precision Engineering Ltd. v. Bryant 1966 RPC81, by Lord Denning, M. R. in Scager v. Copydex Limited 1967 RPC 349 and also by S. Ranganathan J. of this Court in Konrad Wiedemann Gmbh & Co. v. Standard, Castings P. Ltd. and Ors.[11]
>
> 23. In Saltman's case a question arose whether or not there was a viable contract and if not whether breach of confidence could in law have occurred. It was found by the Court of Chancery that there was in fact no binding contract and thus no breach of confidence. The Court of Appeal held to the contrary. The observations of Lord Greene M. R. made in that case apply with full force, to the plea raised by the Defendants in the present case. It was observed at page 216: –
>
>> 'The suggestion that no contract was made is used for some purpose which, again, I am afraid that I do not understand. It is suggested that the absence of a contract at that time in some way, at some time, modified or discharged the obligation of the Defendants to treat the drawings as confidential matter. It seems to me that it would not matter the least bit whether there was a contract or whether there was not a contract. I find as a fact, without hesitation, that there was a contract, but, contract or no contract, the Defendants got those drawings into their hands knowing, or knowing shortly afterwards, that they

9. *Ibid.*, at para. 21.
10. Section 10 of the Contracts Act, 1872 requires contracts to be made for consideration.
11. AIR 1987 Delhi 372 at para. 22.

belonged to Saltman, that they were obviously confidential matter, and they knew that they had got them into their hands for a strictly limited purpose. How on that basis they could say that the fact that there was no contract released them from any obligation of confidence I do not know, nor can I see how the fact, if it had been the fact, that there was no contract in June 1945 could in any way have affected their position after 22nd November. I have already said what the position was, in my opinion and, indeed, in the opinion of the Defendants' own witnesses at that date. I have already said that nothing happened at or after that date which could justify the Defendants in thinking that they were relieved from their obligation of confidence.'[12]

25. With regard to confidential information, Roskill J. in Cranleigh Precision Engineering Ltd. v. Bryant and Anr., 1966, RPC 81 observed at page 96 'the possessor of such information must be placed under a special disability in the field of competition in order to ensure that he does not get an unfair start.' Lord Denning, M. R. clarified in Seager v. Copydex Limited 1967 RFC 349 at page 368 that 'the law on this subject does not depend on any implied contract. It depends on the broad principles of equity that he who has received information in confidence shall not take unfair advantage of it'.[13]

'Balance of convenience is clearly in favor of grant of injunction to the plaintiffs. Unless the Defendants are restrained by grant of temporary injunction during pendency of the suit, irreparable injury and loss which cannot be estimated in terms of money will be caused to the plaintiffs by the Defendants continuing to manufacture, sell or deal in their Machine which is a substantial reproduction in three dimensional form of the Drawings of the plaintiffs' FPU in which Brady has copyright. It will also be in the interest of justice to restrain the Defendants from abusing the know-how, specifications, Drawings and other technical information regarding the plaintiffs' FPU entrusted to them under express condition of strict confidentiality, which they have apparently used as a "spring-board" to jump into the business field to the detriment of the plaintiffs.'[14]

4.1.5. *Legal Analysis*

The judgment of the Delhi High Court is not very clear in its analysis of whether the information was in fact of a 'confidential nature'. Going by the plaintiff's submissions, as recorded in the judgment, it appears that information about the FPU was not confidential since not only had one of the plaintiffs filed a patent application for the technology but also it was selling the technology in the market.[15] If a patent application for the technology was in fact filed, the information related to the technology was most certainly public knowledge because patent applications in India are advertised prior to the grant in order to enable the filing of pre-grant oppositions. In such an event, the information could not have been presumed to be confidential. Similarly, if the technology was being sold in the open market, it is difficult to argue that the technology in question was in fact confidential. It is therefore very doubtful as to whether the disputed information was even confidential to begin with.

12. *Ibid.*, at para. 23.
13. *Ibid.*, at para. 25.
14. *Ibid.*, at para. 38.
15. *Ibid.*, at para. 21.

Perhaps the court did not go into these questions in much detail because it was hearing the dispute at the interim pretrial stage and did not want to conduct mini-trial on the facts. However, most of these cases dealing with 'breach of confidence' rarely proceed to trial in India and tend to conclude after the interim stage. It is however unlikely that the information will be deemed to be confidential unless it pertains to internal processes or data of a commercial entity which has not been exposed to the scrutiny of the outside world.

4.1.6. *Commercial or Industrial Significance*

This particular case has proven itself to be a useful precedent for those fact scenarios where there is no contract between two parties because of unsuccessful negotiations. It should however be noted that these fact scenarios, where parties are compelled to invoke the equitable duty of confidence, are relatively rare and most trade secret cases arise in employment where contracts contain a boilerplate confidentiality clause. It is in industries like the entertainment industry where the equitable duty of confidence has been invoked a bit more frequently by scriptwriters who have discussed storylines and plots with production houses without signing a non-disclosure agreement.[16] In the absence of a statutory trade secret law, the equitable duty of confidence remains important because it is the only remedy for parties seeking to sue those defendants with whom they have no contractual arrangements.

4.2. *Case II*

This case dealt with the issue of whether customer lists of a logistics company could qualify as trade secrets protectable under the law and whether a former employee with access to such customer lists could be restrained from using such lists in the course of business. This issue has arisen quite often in the Indian context, and save for one exception, most courts have declined to declare customer lists as confidential even though the list itself may not have been public knowledge. This judgment is the latest on a frequently litigated issue before Indian courts.

4.2.1. *Case Information*

Navigators Logistics Ltd. v Kashif Qureshi[17] decided by the Delhi High Court on 17 September 2018.

4.2.2. *Summary*

The court declined to grant an interim injunction. The logic employed by the court in this case was that the list of persons active in certain business is publicly known and

16. *Zee Telefilms Ltd. & Film v Sundial Communications Pvt. Ltd.* 2003 (27) PTC 457 Bom.; *Beyond Dreams Entertainment Pvt. Ltd. & Ors. v Zee Entertainment Enterprises Ltd. & Anr.* 2015 (62) PTC 241.
17. 254 (2018) DLT 307.

not a secret and hence confidentiality cannot be claimed with respect to such information.

4.2.3. *Facts*

The defendants who were former employees of the plaintiff, which was a company engaged in the field of logistics and freight forwarding services, were sued for copyright infringement and also breach of a contractual trade secret clause after they joined a competitor of the plaintiff. The defendants had access to extensive information of the plaintiff, especially customer lists, and the plaintiff was keen on restraining the defendant from using such information to benefit its competitor. The plaintiff had substantial evidence from deleted electronic communications, which were recovered from the defendants' electronic devices, indicating that the defendants were planning on using the plaintiff's information for the benefit of the plaintiff's competitors.

4.2.4. *Reasoning of the Court*

> Confidentiality and secrecy is claimed in the same works in which copyright is claimed viz. data, information and trade secrets residing in the electronic devices without again specifying the particulars thereof or secrecy thereof. Mere mention of research process, financial / administrative and / or organizational matter or transaction or affairs of the company or invention or discovery or patent protection does not satisfy the requirements of pleadings. The plaintiff as per its own admission is engaged in the business of providing logistics and freight forwarding services and is not engaged in any research work; it was incumbent for the plaintiff to, in the plaint, plead how the data etc. in which confidentiality is claimed is different from data of any other entity engaged in such business and what is secret about the same and what steps besides the clause aforesaid in the letters of appointment of defendants no.1 to 8 have been taken by the plaintiff to maintain secrecy/ confidentiality thereof. The plaint in this regard is vague and cannot be put to trial. The whole purpose of pleadings in a civil suit is to let the opponent know the case to be met and which crystallizes ultimately in issues on which the parties go to trial. If such rules of pleadings are not to be adhered to, it will result in a fishing and roving enquiry and enable a party to the suit to secure a victory by springing a surprise during the course of trial. Similarly, an injunction qua confidentiality as sought, even if granted would be vague and unenforceable as aforesaid. This Court cannot pass such unenforceable order, the meaning whereof is not clear. It cannot be known, neither to the Court nor to the defendant as to what the defendant is injuncted from doing.[18]
>
> On facts as pleaded in plaint it appeared that there can be no confidentiality about such a list. Just like customers/clients of an Advocate practicing in the field of acquisition of land and determination of compensation therefor can comprise only of those whose land has been acquired and whose particulars are contained in the acquisition notification and/or award pronounced by the Land Acquisition Collector, similarly the list of customers/clients of the plaintiff, carrying on business in the field of logistic and freight forwarding, can only comprise of businesses/ industry requiring carriage of goods and material and none else. Names and

18. *Ibid.*, at para. 39.

> contact addresses of such businesses are easily available in public domain. Any competitor of the plaintiff worth its salt would also know of such businesses/ industry and be free to market his services to them, even if presently employing the service of the plaintiff. I am thus unable to fathom the confidentiality therein and during the hearing also repeatedly enquired about the same and also enquired about the particulars of other works/databases and in which also copyright and confidentiality was claimed. No answer was forthcoming. Every customer list cannot qualify as confidential information or a trade secret unless the confidentiality around such a list is of economic value/business value/commercial value. A thought also crossed my mind, whether not any employee of the plaintiff, dealing with the customers/clients of the plaintiff on behalf of the plaintiff, would have knowledge of the said customers/clients and their contact address even in the absence of a list and how could such an employee, when joining the employment of a competitor, be prevented from marketing the services of the competitor to the employees/clients at the address on which he was earlier servicing them under employment of the former employer and whether not it would amount to restraint of trade.[19]
>
> 42. In fact today, trade/business directories are available of each trade/business and wherefrom names and addresses of all in a particular trade/business/industry can be known.[20]
>
> 48. The plaintiff, on a reading of the plaint, is thus found to have not made out a case for permanent injunction restraining the defendants from divulging any trade secrets, research process, financial, administrative and/or organizational matters or any transactions or affairs of the plaintiff to anyone else and/or for recovery of damages therefor for the reason of the plaintiff having not pleaded that the defendants were privy to any such trade secrets or other such matters.[21]

4.2.5. Analysis

The court's reasoning had two prongs. It began with examining whether the plaintiff had established a case for confidentiality of its information. The court concludes that the plaint was vague on details as to how the confidentiality of the information was being maintained and how such information was different from other information being maintained by other commercial entities in the same field of business. This conclusion of the court explains why it is important for the plaintiffs in such cases to explain the reason as to why the contested information qualifies for protection as a trade secret.

The second prong of the court's reasoning was focused on the specific question of whether customer lists could even qualify as 'confidential information'. The court came to the conclusion that such information would most likely not qualify as a confidential information in most cases, especially in the logistics businesses as was the plaintiff's area of business. The court's reasoning was that information like customer lists would be easily known to everybody in the business. In addition, the court also pointed out how such information is usually published in the form of business

19. *Ibid.*, at para. 41.
20. *Ibid.*, at para. 42.
21. *Ibid.*, at para. 48.

directories therefore robbing any potential customer lists of the element of confidentiality.

4.2.6. *Commercial/Industrial Significance*

The judgment is of significant commercial importance because it reiterates once again that Indian courts will be deeply reluctant to protect customer lists in most industries.[22] The reiteration of the law on this point was important in the Indian context because of the frequency with which employers raise this issue in litigation against former employees. This judgment however does not create an irrebuttable presumption against the protection of customer lists as trade secrets. It should be possible to protect such lists as confidential if the plaintiff can demonstrate the steps taken to maintain the confidentiality of such information. If the confidential customer list can be shown to be unique, it may still qualify for protection as a trade secret.

22. Another such case in the banking industry where the court denied an injunction is as follows: *American Express Bank Ltd. v Ms. Priya Puri* (2006) IIILLJ 540 Del on 24 May 2006. A rare case where the court did intervene to protect client lists in the context of a lawyer's office is the case of *Diljeet Titus v Alfred A. Adebare and Ors.* 2006 (32) PTC 609 Del.

TOPIC 2 THE VALIDITY AND SCOPE OF CONFIDENTIALITY AND/OR NON-COMPETITION CLAUSES

1. Legal Issues

Section 27 of the Indian Contract Act, 1872 does forbid non-compete clauses and renders any such clause in a contract void. Despite the clarity with which the provision has been drafted, there has been significant confusion in judgments of the Supreme Court on the interpretation of this provision. There have been instances where Indian courts have restrained former employees from joining their competitors on the grounds that they would be in violation of the non-compete clauses, as well as the possibility that the employees may disclose trade secrets to the competitors. This is technically an incorrect understanding of the law because mere anticipation of disclosure of trade secrets is not reason enough to restrain future employment, and more importantly, the legislative history of section 27 indicates that the provision was meant to favour employees and not employers. The dominant trend in judgments by Indian courts in such cases has been to allow employees to join competitors once their employment contract has been terminated.

2. The Statutory Law

The text of section 27 of the Contracts Act, 1872 is reproduced below:

> 27. Agreement in restraint of trade, void. – Every agreement by which any one is restrained from exercising a lawful profession, trade or business of any kind, is to that extent void. –Every agreement by which any one is restrained from exercising a lawful profession, trade or business of any kind, is to that extent void.
>
> Exception 1. – Saving of agreement not to carry on business of which goodwill is sold. – One who sells the goodwill of a business may agree with the buyer to refrain from carrying on a similar business, within specified local limits, so long as the buyer, or any person deriving title to the goodwill from him, carries on a like business therein, provided that such limits appear to the Court reasonable, regard being had to the nature of the business.

At the time this provision was enacted in 1872, English common law generally allowed for partial restraints of trade if employers could prove that such restraints on trade were 'reasonable'. With time, it was felt that the restraint of trade clauses in common law had been allowed to mutate to an extent that it was having a detrimental effect on competition and the ability of employees to find alternative sources of employment. It was in this backdrop that the drafters of the Indian Contract Act, 1872 are said to have drawn inspiration from section 833 of the draft Code for New York,[23] which was being drafted in 1862 and which draft never translated into law in New York.[24] Section 833 was reportedly drafted with the express intent to dilute the existing

23. The judgment does not say which Code it was, most likely a commercial code https://indiankanoon.org/doc/1186410/.
24. *Superintendence Company of India v Krishan Murgai* 1980 SCR (3) 1278 (Minority concurring judgment of Justice A. P. Sen).

common law position of allowing for general and partial restraints in contracts on trade and employment. By incorporating this provision into Indian law, it appears that the drafters of the Indian Contract Act, 1872 wanted a clean break from the then-existing position of law under English common law.[25] However, the interpretation of section 27 by Indian courts has not been consistent, although an increasing number of judges in the recent past have leaned towards negating all post-contractual restraints on trade, thereby making it difficult for employers to restrain employees from working with competitors or setting up their own enterprises.

3. The Case Law

The reasoning adopted by the Supreme Court in this judgment was not convincing, and it is not surprising that some of the subsequent judgments of Indian courts on this issue have avoided applying this precedent.

4. The Leading Cases

4.1. Case I

4.1.1. Case Information

Niranjan Shankar Golikari v The Century Spinning & Mfg. Co.[26] before the Supreme Court of India on 17 January 1967.

4.1.2. Summary

This case dealt with an employee who left employment to join a competitor. The former employer sued the employee on the basis of an employment contract which had clauses on both non-disclosure of confidential information and a non-compete clause. The case was litigated all the way till the Supreme Court which ultimately restrained the former employee from working for the competitor for a certain period of time.

4.1.3. Facts

The respondent-company was a manufacturer of tyre cord yarn. It had signed a contract with two European companies for the sharing of their confidential technical know-how, data and documents. One of the terms of the contract required the respondent-company to sign non-disclosure agreements with all of its employees to keep all the technical know-how, etc., secret without disclosing to any other person. The appellant was a former employee who had signed an employment contract with the respondent-company. This employment contract had clauses requiring the employee to protect secret information, as well as non-compete clauses both during the course of employment and after the cessation of employment. The appellant left the

25. *Ibid.*
26. 1967 AIR 1098.

employment of the respondent-company before the expiry of the term of the employment contract but after having received training from the respondent-company about its secret manufacturing processes and machinery. After leaving the employment of the respondent-company, the appellant joined a competitor of the respondent-company at a higher pay. The respondent-company then sued the appellant for damages for breach of contract and also, for an injunction restraining the appellant from working with a competitor of the respondent-company. The trial court and the High Court ruled in favour of the respondent-company after which the appellant approached the Supreme Court for relief.

4.1.4. *Reasoning of the Court*

> The result of the above discussion is that considerations against restrictive covenants are different in cases where the restriction is to apply during the period after the termination of the contract than those in cases where it is to operate during the period of the contract. Negative covenants operative during the period of the contract of employment when the employee is bound to serve his employer exclusively are generally not regarded as restraint of trade and therefore do not fall under section 27 of the Contract Act. A negative covenant that the employee would not engage himself in a trade or business or would not get himself employed by any other master for whom he would perform similar or substantially similar duties is not therefore a restraint of trade unless the contract as aforesaid is unconscionable or excessively harsh or unreasonable or one sided as in the case of W.H. Milsted and Son Ltd.(3). Both the Trial Court and the High Court have found, and in our view, rightly, that the negative covenant in the present case restricted as it is to the period of employment and to work similar or substantially similar to the one carried on by the appellant when he was in the employ of the respondent company was reasonable and necessary for the protection of the company's interests and not such as the court would refuse to enforce. There is therefore no validity in the contention that the negative covenant contained in clause 17 amounted to a restraint of trade and was therefore against public policy.[27]
>
> The next question is whether the injunction in the terms in which it is framed should have been granted. There is no doubt that the courts have a wide discretion to enforce by injunction a negative covenant. Both the courts below have concurrently found that the apprehension of the respondent company that information regarding the special processes and the special machinery imparted to and acquired by the appellant during the period of training and thereafter might be divulged was justified; that the information and knowledge disclosed to him during this period was different from the general knowledge and experience that he might have gained while in the service of the respondent company and that it was against his disclosing the former to the rival company which required protection. It was argued however that the terms of clause were too wide and that the court cannot sever the good from the bad and issue an injunction to the extent that was good. But the rule against severance applies to cases where the covenant is bad in law and it is in such cases that the court is precluded from severing the good from the bad. But there is nothing to prevent the court from granting a limited injunction to the extent that is necessary to protect the employer's interests where the negative stipulation is not void. There is also nothing to show that if the

27. Paragraph 17 of 1967 AIR 1098.

> negative covenant is enforced the appellant would be driven to idleness or would be compelled to go back to the respondent company. It may be that if he is not permitted to get himself employed in another similar employment he might perhaps get a lesser remuneration than the one agreed to by Rajasthan Rayon. But that is no consideration against enforcing the covenant. The evidence is clear that the appellant has torn the agreement to pieces only because he was offered a higher remuneration. Obviously, he cannot be heard to say that no injunction should be granted against him to enforce the negative covenant which is not opposed to public policy. The injunction issued against him is restricted as to time, the nature of employment and as to area and cannot therefore be said to be too wide or unreasonable or unnecessary for the protection of the interests of the respondent company.[28]

4.1.5. Legal Analysis

4.1.5.1. The Disclosure of Trade Secrets Is Not Inevitable

The court justified the enforcement of the non-compete clause, for the remainder period of the original contract, on the grounds that it was a reasonable restraint that was limited in time and scope. The court reasoned that since the non-restraint clause applied only during the period when the original employment contract was meant to subsist, the appellant would not be rendered completely idle since there were other non-competing jobs where the appellant could seek employment. The court was of the opinion that such a restraint on the appellant's ability to work for competitors was required and justified in order to protect the respondent-company's interests. While these 'interests' are not clearly articulated in the judgment, it appears that the court was referring to the trade secrets of the respondent-company. The court does not directly state this, but it does endorse the reasoning of the lower courts which used the 'trade secret' logic to restrain the appellant from working for a competitor. The pertinent extract from the judgment is as follows:

> Both the courts below have concurrently found that the apprehension of the respondent company that information regarding the special processes and the special machinery imparted to and acquired by the appellant during the period of training and thereafter might be divulged was justified ... .

This reasoning prima facie appears to be flawed because the disclosure of trade secrets is not inevitable just because the appellant was going to work for the competitor. It is perfectly possible that the appellant could work with a competitor without revealing trade secrets, and in any event if there was evidence that trade secrets were in fact disclosed, an independent action could be filed in that regard for damages and an injunction. Injunctions cannot be granted in anticipation of a breach of a right, except in certain cases where quia-timet injunctions may be granted. For example, anticipation that a patent may be infringed because a company has secured

28. Paragraph 18 of 1967 AIR 1098.

regulatory approvals for a generic version has led to the grant of quia-timet injunctions.[29]

4.1.5.2. Section 27 Contracts Act Represented a Clean Break from English Law

More importantly though, the Supreme Court appears to have interpreted section 27 incorrectly. It assumes that reasonable restraints on trade and profession are permissible in employment contracts and cites a litany of English precedents to discuss the nature of such reasonable restraints regarding time and geographical spread. However, as pointed out in a subsequent, minority but concurring opinion of a different bench of the Supreme Court in a different case called *Superintendence Company of India v Krishna Murgai,*[30] section 27 of the Contracts Act represented a clean break from English law when it was drafted in 1872. The *Murgai* court delved deep into the legislative history to make a strong case against any kind of restraints on practice of a trade, post-termination of a contract, regardless of whether the restraint was reasonable or not. The *Murgai* court adopted a literal interpretation of section 27 of the Contract Act to arrive at this conclusion that no restraints could be imposed on a former employee's right to practise a trade or a profession.

4.1.6. Commercial or Industrial Significance

The *Golikari* case is a significant judgment since it was the first interpretation of section 27 by the Supreme Court since its creation in 1950. While it does have a strong legacy in Indian jurisprudence, there have been significant deviations from its interpretation of section 27 despite the judgment being a binding precedent on lower courts. This trend of deviation started off with the *Murgai* judgment but has subsequently spread to the High Courts and trials courts. For the most part, Indian courts in the last few decades appear to be uncomfortable with restraining former employees from engaging in a lawful profession to earn a living. This has meant that the Indian workforce has enjoyed more job mobility as the Indian economy has liberalised and grown.

4.2. Case II

This particular case provides an interesting contrast to the *Niranjan Golikari* judgment despite the fact that the Calcutta High Court is bound by judgments of the Supreme Court. This is a relatively rare occurrence in a common law jurisdiction like India where the hierarchy of courts is taken quite seriously.

---

29. Aparajita Lath, *Analysing the Pitfalls of Indian Patent Injunctions Based on Fear of Infringement,* 19 Journal of Intellectual Property Rights 253 (2014).
30. 1980 AIR 1717.

4.2.1. *Case Information*

Electrosteel Castings Ltd v Saw Pipes Ltd & Ors[31] decided by the Calcutta High Court on 4 October 2004.

4.2.2. *Summary*

The facts of this case involved the former employees of the plaintiff working for a competitor of the plaintiff. Since the plaintiff was in the business of manufacturing a specialised product and had a near monopoly over the product in the market, it was worried about the defendants disclosing its trade secrets to a new competitor that was in the process of entering the market. Like most former employers, the plaintiff also sued its former employees for alleged violation of a non-compete clause. Interestingly, the Division Bench of the Calcutta High Court declined to restrain the defendants from working for the plaintiff's competitor.

4.2.3. *Facts*

The plaintiff company was a manufacturer of special ductile iron pipes, and it was practically the only manufacturer of these pipes in India. Six of the seven defendants were former employees of the plaintiff. The employment contract contained standard clauses on protection of trade secrets as well as a non-compete clause prohibiting employees from working with a competitor for a period of five years after leaving the employment of the plaintiff.

The plaintiff company was suing its former employees because after they left the plaintiff's employment, they began working for a competitor which was entering the business of manufacturing similar ductile iron pipes. The plaintiff alleged that by working for a competitor, its former employees were in alleged violation of a non-compete clause in the employment contract.

Reasoning of the court

> 43. At its inception, therefore, the five-year period to work for a single employer is a good clause. Nobody can say at the inception that the employee will not work all five years actually with the same employer.
>
> 44. Suppose the clause also contains another term, like in the Golikari case, that in case of leaving employment midway, the employee will still not work with a competitor for the rest of five years. Is that a good clause? How can that not be a good clause because the Supreme Court granted injunction in the Golikari case?
>
> 45. Our respectful answer to these questions is that the clause is bad and against the express words of Section 27 insofar as it prevents the employees from working with a competitor even after leaving the first employment. But this clause does not taint the whole clause, i.e., if the employee is working with an employer, he will work with that employer only. This is clarified by the words of Section 27 that the bad clause is only 'to that extent void'.

31. (2005) 1 CHN 612.

46. Notwithstanding the partial potential or prospective voidness of this clause of restraint, the Court still retains a power of granting an equitable injunction for the period of five years during which the employee had agreed to serve the employer. This power the Court retains whether there is a bad clause restraining the employee, even after cassation of the first employment, from joining a second employer or not. In the Burn Company case, which was not restrictive clause, but still the Court granted an order of injunction on this basis. The basis was that five years had been agreed to be served, five years had not been served. It was not equitable for Madonald to go away and serve another employer in the facts and circumstances of that case. It was on this basis that the Golikari injunction would be made operative for the unexpired term of five years although there was coupled with it a restrictive clause not to work for a second employer even after leaving the first employment, and though the restrictive clause was void. The voidness of the clause does not take away the Court's equitable power to sustain the second employment. What parties cannot achieve by agreement, the Court can do by an order of injunction.

47. We are aware that the Hon'ble Supreme Court of India did not exactly proceed on this basis; however we have read the Golikari judgment more than once and in our respectful view what we have said above is nowhere in conflict with what the Supreme Court has laid down in the Golikari case.

48. It is because the Court has to deal with propriety of passing an order of injunction during the unexpired term of the agreed period of employment, that questions and consideration of reasonableness and fairness come in. When the agreed term is not served out, the Court has to weigh the circumstances and answer to itself the question whether the employee should serve out that unexpired term. The Court cannot directly grant an injunction compelling the employee to complete the balance period of employment. The Specific Relief Act directly prevents it. But the Court can grant a restrictive order of injunction stopping the employee from working with forbidden employers during the unexpired term. That is a permissible equitable order. No doubt, the Court indirectly almost forces the employee thereby to work with the first employer, but the enforcement is not absolute. It has been held and we respectfully agree that if the case is so extreme that the employee has no option but to work with the first employer or else starve, then the Court will ordinarily not grant an injunction.

50. What do we find if we apply these principles to our case? We find that no fixed period of employment is specified at all. The contract of employment is terminable with a month's notice. If a month's notice is served, it can at best be said that during that month the employee should not work with a competitor. Once the period of notice runs out, there is no breach of contract even if a competitor is joined, because the restrictive covenant of five years even beyond the agreed period of employment is void by reason of Section 27 of the Contracts Act.

51. On this simple basis we are of the opinion that there is no case for injunction made out against the employees.

61. The appeal and the application are both dismissed. We would have vacated the infructuous order of injunction which prevents the employees from divulging their know-how since there is no practical way of enforcing it or proving that they are divulging their know-how, as they will all be working with the first respondent in its privacy, yet we do not vacate that order of injunction as there is no cross-appeal.

4.2.5. *Legal Analysis*

4.2.5.1. No Point Granting an Injunction Whose Compliance Could Not Be Monitored

One of the most interesting aspects of the judgment is the last cited paragraph above, where the Calcutta High Court dismisses out of hand the request for an injunction restraining the defendants from disclosing any trade secret, on the grounds that there was no point in granting an injunction whose compliance could not be monitored because the employees would be working in the privacy of their new employer's factory. This is a rather unique conclusion because most courts tend to grant such injunctions with little thought on how compliance with such orders would be monitored. In fact, the correct approach would be to collect evidence on a breach of the contractual clause on trade secret before suing for an injunction.

4.2.5.2. Golikari Needs Not Be Complied with in a Rigid Manner

This judgment is also interesting because the Calcutta High Court appears to disagree with the Supreme Court on its interpretation of section 27 of the Indian Contracts Act. The Calcutta High Court categorically opined that section 27 did not allow for any post-contractual restraints and found the post-contractual restraint of five years to be void due to section 27. Although this conclusion is different from the Supreme Court's conclusion in the *Golikari* case, the High Court justified the outcome in the *Golikari* case on the grounds that an injunction is an equitable remedy and a court can choose to restrain employees from post-contractual employment in cases where judges feel that such a remedy is just and appropriate. The court therefore moved the focus of the entire discussion from section 27 of the Contracts Act to the principles of equity. The rationale offered by the court may not be entirely accurate because injunctions can only be granted to protect rights under the law. There has to be some basis in the law to restrain post-contractual employment and if section 27 basically voids all post-contractual restraints, then there is no question of an injunction.

Nevertheless, this judgment is important because the Calcutta High Court openly disagrees with the reasoning of the *Golikari* judgment, and although its attempt at an alternative reasoning is less than satisfactory, it provides the legal ammunition required by employees looking to convince other judges that *Golikari* need not be complied with in a rigid manner.

4.2.6. *Commercial or Industrial Significance*

Since this judgment was delivered in an appeal by a Division Bench of the Calcutta High Court, which is one of the older High Courts in the country, it can be considered to be an important judgment. Although not cited significantly by other High Courts, this judgment opens the door for future judges to disagree with the rationale of the *Golikari* judgment and deny injunctions on the basis of non-compete clauses whose intent is to protect trade secrets. There are other High Court judgments which have displayed a similar reluctance to follow the *Golikari* judgment to enforce post-contractual restraints with the intention of protecting trade secrets. Judgments like these offer employees more job mobility. One way to look at this issue is that greater employee mobility engenders greater competition and innovation.[32] The net effects for the Indian economy may therefore be positive. For employers looking to protect their trade secrets with greater certainty, the solution to their problems may lie in structuring employment contracts to stagger benefits or bonuses through the term of the contract and beyond in order to provide greater incentives to employees to continue working for them. Such a strategy may work better than a strategy of legal threats.

32. Mark Lemley & James H.A. Pooley, *California Restrictive Employment Covenants after Edwards*, 23(3) California Labor & Employment Law Review (2009).

TOPIC 4 'CONFIDENTIALITY CLUB' TO PROTECT THE SECRECY OF TRADE SECRETS DURING TRIALS

1. Legal Issues

The issue of maintaining the secrecy or confidentiality of trade secrets during trials is a crucial issue in a country like India which considers 'open courts' as one of the sacrosanct features of the justice system. The phrase 'open courts' refers to the requirement of holding all legal proceeding in a courtroom accessible to members of the general public. Such public proceedings are meant to instil confidence in the judicial process and act as a check against arbitrary action by judges. For the most part, Indian courts have adhered to this principle of 'open courts' quite strictly.

However, the Supreme Court never laid down precise procedures to shield confidential information from public scrutiny. Over the last decade as trade secret litigation picked up in India, some High Courts have tailored detailed procedures to shield confidential information from public scrutiny by allowing only certain persons on either side to view the confidential information for the purposes of the litigation.

2. The Statutory Law

Section 153B of the Civil Procedure Code (CPC) mandatorily requires the place of trial to be deemed to be an open court which can be accessed by members of the public. The same provision allows the presiding judge to curb access to the trial to any person or the public if he so thinks fit. The provision does not lay down any criteria to guide the judge regarding the type of cases where the public may be excluded from the courtroom, but it is very likely that trade secret cases will qualify as one of the cases where the general public is not allowed into the courtroom.

Apart from the CPC, there are other laws which have specific provisions that allow for 'in-camera' trials. For example, the Family Courts Act, 1984 allows for in camera trials in order to protect the privacy of parties. While Parliament has not enacted a similar exception for trade secret cases, the Delhi High Court has announced codified rules of practices to create a procedural framework that maintains confidentiality of information in cases where trade secrets are being litigated.[33] These rules of practice by the Delhi High Court, which were borne out of precedents in a trade secret case, allow for the filing of confidential information in a sealed cover, whose contents can be viewed only by members of a 'confidentiality club'. As per these rules, the members of the 'confidentiality club' shall comprise of three advocates, who are not in-house lawyers for either party, along with two external experts from each party.

Only the members of the confidentiality club are allowed to access the confidential documents of the opposite side or be present during hearings where the confidential information is being discussed before the court. These members of the confidentiality club are also under an obligation not to disclose the contents of the documents that they have seen to anyone else, although the rules in question do not mention the

33. Delhi High Court (Original Side) Rules, 2018 available at http://delhihighcourt.nic.in/writereaddata/upload/Notification/NotificationFile_8BP1BKKNT2G.PDF.

penalty for the unauthorised disclosure of such information.[34] It may be possible to hold members of the confidentiality club liable under contempt law for any violations of the confidentiality rules. It must however be noted that the Delhi High Court has deviated from these rules on more than one instance on the grounds that it would be unfair, and perhaps in violation of professional ethics rules, for lawyers to litigate on behalf of their clients without disclosing to them the information received from the opposite side. This was in response to an interpretation by the plaintiffs which argued that only external lawyers and external experts could view such confidential documents.[35]

Relevant extracts of the draft protocol[36] available in Annexure F to the Delhi High Court (Original Side) Rules, 2018 are reproduced below:

> CHAPTER VII RULE 17 PROTOCOL OF CONFIDENTIALITY CLUB: Procedure to be followed in dealing with confidential documents/ information
>
> Upon hearing of an application, the Court may allow constitution of a Confidentiality Club in the following manner: –
>
> a) All documents/ information considered as confidential ('Confidential Documents/ Information') by the Court shall be permitted to be filed in a sealed cover to be kept in the safe custody of Registrar General.
> b) Each party shall nominate not more than three Advocates, who are not and have not been in-house lawyers of either party, and not more than two external experts, who shall constitute the Confidentiality Club. Members of the Confidentiality Club alone shall be entitled to inspect the Confidential Documents/ Information.
> c) Members of the Confidentiality Club shall be allowed to inspect the Confidential Documents/ Information before the Registrar General, without making copies thereof. After the inspection, the Confidential Documents/ Information shall be resealed and kept in the custody of the Registrar General.
> d) Members of the Confidentiality Club shall not make copies of, or disclose, or publish the contents of, the Confidential Documents/ Information to anyone else in any manner or by any means, or in any other legal proceedings and shall be bound by the orders of the Court in this behalf.
> e) During recordal of evidence with respect to the Confidential Documents/ Information, only members of the Confidentiality Club shall be allowed to remain present.
> f) During proceedings of the Court, when the Confidential Documents/ Information are being looked at or their contents discussed, only members of the Confidentiality Club shall be permitted to be present.
> g) The Court may in its discretion and in an appropriate case, permit copies of the Confidential Documents to be given to the opposite party after redacting confidential information therefrom, if such redaction be possible and not otherwise.
> h) Any evidence by way of affidavit or witness statement containing confidential information derived from the Confidential Documents/ Information shall be

34. *Ibid.*, at Annexure F, Chapter VII Rule 17 – Protocol of Confidentiality Club.
35. *Interdigital Technology Corporation & Ors. v Xiamoi Corporation & Ors.* CS(COMM) No. 296 of 2020 decided on 16 December 2020.
36. The rules propose a draft protocol to institute confidentiality clubs. It is not binding on judges, and it is possible for judges to modify the protocol as per the facts of the case.

kept in a sealed cover with the Registrar General and would be accessible only to the members of the Confidentiality Club. However, a party filing such evidence by way of affidavit shall, if so directed by the Court, give to the opposite party a copy of such affidavit after redacting therefrom the confidential information, if such redaction is possible and not otherwise.

i) The Confidential Documents/ Information shall not be available for inspection after disposal of the matter, except to the Party producing the same.

j) In cases where the Confidentiality Club is constituted or documents are directed to be kept confidential, the Court may consider extending the time for filing of pleadings. However, the same shall be within the overall limits prescribed by the applicable provisions.

3. The Case Law

In one of the landmark cases, the Supreme Court explained the importance of 'open courts' in the following words:

> It is well-settled that in general, all cases brought before the Courts, whether civil, criminal, or others, must be heard in open Court. Public trial in open court is undoubtedly essential for the healthy, objective and fair administration of justice. Trial held subject to the public scrutiny and gaze naturally acts as a check against judicial caprice or vagaries, and serves as a powerful instrument for creating confidence of the public in the fairness, objectivity, and impartiality of the administration of justice. Public confidence in the administration of justice is of such great significance that there can be no two opinions on the broad proposition that in discharging their functions as judicial Tribunals, courts must generally hear causes in open and must permit the public admission to the court-room. As Bentham has observed: In the darkness of secrecy sinister interest, and evil in every shape, have full swing. Only in proportion as publicity has place can any of the checks applicable to judicial injustice operate. Where there is no publicity there is no justice. Publicity is the very soul of justice. It is the keenest spur to exertion, and surest of all guards against improbity. It keeps the Judge himself while trying under trial (in the sense that) the security of securities is publicity.[37]

In the same judgment, the Supreme Court also carved out an exception to this general rule of 'open courts' in cases where disclosure of information may adversely affect the subject matter of the litigation. One of the illustrative examples provided by the Supreme Court in its judgment were cases involving 'secret processes' where publicity may end up frustrating the relief sought by plaintiffs. The court stated the following in pertinent part:

> Similarly, in regard to litigation as to a secret process, where the effect of publicity would be to destroy the subject-matter, trial in camera would be justified, because in such a case, justice could not be done at all if it had to be done in public. In other words, unless it be strictly necessary for the attainment of justice, there can be no power in the court to hear in camera either a matrimonial cause or any other where there is a contest between parties. He who maintains that by no other means than by such a hearing can justice be done may apply. for an unusual procedure. But he must make out his case strictly, and bring it up to the standard which the

37. *Naresh Shridhar Mirajkar and Ors v State of Maharashtra and Anr* 1966 SCR (3) 744.

> underlying principle requires. He may be able to show that the evidence can be effectively brought before the court in no other fashion. In either case, he must satisfy the court that by nothing short of the exclusion of the public can justice be done.[38]

4. The Leading Cases

4.1. Case I

In this judgment, the Delhi High Court borrowed a framework formulated by English courts, to protect the confidential information being provided by the defendants to the plaintiffs in order for the plaintiffs to prove that their trade secrets were used without the authorisation of the plaintiffs.

4.1.1. Case Information

Mvf 3 Aps & Ors v Mr. M. Sivasamy and Ors[39] decided by the Delhi High Court on 31 August 2012.

4.1.2. Summary

This case before the Delhi High Court was one part of a transnational litigation spanning several countries between two European entities over secret recipes for an insecticide used to prepare nets that kept out mosquitoes. One of the key issues that arose before the Indian courts pertained to 'discovery' of documents and information from the defendants that were necessary for the plaintiffs to establish that their trade secrets had been used without the authorisation of the plaintiff. In the normal course, parties may seek 'discovery' of documents from each other in order to marshal the facts necessary to prove/defend their cases. In the case of trade secret litigation, one of the complications is maintaining the confidentiality of information exchanged during the 'discovery' process.

4.1.3. Facts

The plaintiffs were the leading manufacturers of insecticide-coated mosquito nets with sales across the world. The main defendants were the former employees of the plaintiff who had allegedly left with valuable trade secrets to set up competing concerns. These defendants had allegedly contracted with Indian companies for manufacturing the products that were the subject matter of the plaintiff's claim, which is why the plaintiffs had approached the Delhi High Court for relief against the defendants. The plaintiffs sought 'discovery' of the documents pertaining to the subject matter of the suit, including documents pertaining to the manufacture and sale of the defendants' competing products. The obvious problem that arose in this context was the protection of the defendants' trade secrets from being misused by the plaintiff, in the event that

38. *Ibid.*
39. MANU/DE/5492/2012.

the defendants' trade secrets were distinct and different from the plaintiff's trade secrets. The court was therefore faced with the dilemma of creating a procedural framework to protect all the trade secrets from being misused by either party.

4.1.4. Reasoning of the Court

The following order of the court makes multiple references to 'UK confidential documents' because the parties before the Indian court had initiated similar litigation before the English courts and had secured a detailed confidentiality order from the English courts. Since the questions of law and fact were similar before the Indian and English courts, the former referred to the orders of the latter classifying certain documents as confidential:

> 29. The above facts have been extracted by this Court from the three applications filed by the plaintiffs against the concerned defendants after passing the interim orders. No doubt, referring these statements made by the plaintiffs in the said applications does not mean that the plaintiffs do not have to prove the same at the time of hearing of the pending applications, but prima-facie, there is sufficient material placed on record and it has become necessary in order to determine the real issue involved in the matter, that the prayer made in the application be allowed in view of the guidelines issued by the Division Bench in the order dated 2nd August 2012.[40]
>
> 30. Under these circumstances, the present application is allowed. In order to devise a procedure to ensure the confidentiality of the information, documents, database etc. the following directions are passed ordering production of the same:
>
> (a) the plaintiffs' UK solicitors from the law firm of FIELD FISHER WATERHOUSE LLP will submit the 'UK confidential documents' as defined in paragraph 10(d) of the present application to the Registrar General of this Court in sealed covers/boxes within 8 weeks of this order subject to any constraints imposed upon them by the UK order dated July 02 2009;
> (b) the Registrar General will take the UK confidential documents in sealed covers/boxes on record;
> (c) The undertakings voluntarily submitted by the Members of the confidentiality club identified in Annexure IV to the application and those subsequently admitted to it in respect of the UK confidential documents ('the Members') will be applicable to the 'Indian Confidential Documents' as defined in Paragraph 10 (a), (b),(c), of the present application;
> (d) whenever these relate to or require any confidential documents to be relied on or quoted from or arguments addressed thereon will be conducted in camera or in Judge's chambers, with only the Members permitted to be present. If necessary, court may take the assistance by appointing an expert/advocate on the subject in order to arrive at a decision;
> (e) the Registrar General shall keep the documents in sealed covers under lock and key and allow access to the confidential documents only to the Members on the following terms: That the undertakings voluntarily signed and provided by the Members shall also be applicable to the Indian Confidential Documents which shall also comply the conditions governing the usage and reference to the UK

40. *Ibid.*, at para. 29.

Confidential Documents, which will be recognized and apply equally to the Indian Confidentiality Documents.

(f) That the sealed cover documents would be opened by the Court for its own perusal and reference and reseal these.

(g) That the Registrar General of this Court be empowered to de-seal the documents for inspection by Members in his presence, on formal request being made by either party to the Registrar General with simultaneous intimation to the opposite counsel who has the option to remain present for such inspection. The documents shall be resealed thereafter by the Registrar General.

This order of the court referred to an earlier order of an appellate court in the same litigation, wherein access to the confidential documents was limited to a 'confidentiality club' whose membership was limited to a selected number of lawyers and experts from either side, all of whom were required to sign a confidentiality agreement.[41] Only the members of this 'confidentiality club' were given access to the documents in the format and procedure as described above; i.e., the documents could be accessed only in certain locations and arguments involving the documents would be conducted in closed chambers not open to the general public.

4.1.5. Legal Analysis

This particular judgment of the court is significant because it creates a legal framework for maintaining confidentiality of trade secrets shared by the defendants with the plaintiff during the course of 'discovery' proceedings and subsequently at the stage of oral arguments. These 'discovery' proceedings under the CPC basically allow one party to seek documents/information from the other party in order to establish the facts at dispute during litigation. In the case at hand, since the plaintiffs required documentation from the defendant describing the secret recipe used by the latter, they requested for discovery of documents from the defendants. The concern for the parties in such cases, apart from maintaining confidentiality of the documents from the general public, is the disclosure of their trade secrets to their competitors.

The Delhi High Court attempts to address both these concerns. In order to protect the confidentiality of the documents vis-à-vis the rest of the world, the confidential documents were required to be stored in sealed boxes under lock and key within the court premises and accessed only under the supervision of the court staff. Any court proceedings involving these confidential documents would not be open to the members of the general public. With regard to the second concern, i.e., protecting the confidentiality of the documents vis-à-vis the competitors, the court restricted access to the documents only to members of the 'confidentiality club' which consisted of the lawyers of both parties and their independent scientific experts. All members of the confidentiality club were themselves subject to a confidentiality agreement, thereby restricting their ability to share the information with anybody else.

41. *M. Sivasamy v Vestergaard Frandsen A/S & Ors.* 2009(113) DRJ 820.

4.1.6. *Commercial or Industrial Significance*

While the orders in this case to protect the confidentiality of the information from disclosure do provide a procedural framework for judges dealing with trade secrets, it should be noted that trade secret cases in India almost never reach the stage of trial. Most of these cases end after a decision is rendered on interim injunctions. In fact, there does not appear to be a single reported judgment involving trade secrets that was delivered post-trial in India. Even in the case under discussion, there has not been a judgment on final merits. Only a series of interim orders was passed by the court. In this backdrop, the orders of the Delhi High Court in this case have only limited significance for future trade secret cases in India.

However, the fact that this order served as a template for the Delhi High Court to create a set of court rules in such matters makes the order a significant legal precedent. These new court rules on confidentiality clubs, etc., will hopefully bring about more procedural consistency in future cases, but their effectiveness in a complex trial setting is yet to be judged. The challenge for parties in such a setting is to be able to put up an effective legal defence despite not being able to share the confidential material widely among their legal or scientific teams.

4.2. *Case II*

4.2.1. *Case Information*

Transformative Learning Solutions Pvt. Ltd. v Pawajot Kaur Baweja & Ors CS (COMM) 817/2018 decided by the Delhi High Court on 17 July 2019.

4.2.2. *Summary*

The plaintiff had sued its former employees for breach of confidence, copyright infringement, etc., after they left its employment to set up their own business. The plaintiff sought an injunction against the defendants, restraining them from using the customer lists of the plaintiffs, which they considered confidential and copyright protected. During the course of the proceedings, the plaintiff asked the court to create a 'confidentiality club' as laid down in the Delhi High Court Rules in order to protect the confidentiality of the information that would be disclosed to the court during the course of the proceedings. The court declined to grant such an order because it felt that the defendants had to have access to these customer lists in order to defend itself. A review petition was filed by the plaintiff, which was dismissed by the Delhi High Court.

4.2.3. *Facts*

The plaintiff ran a company that offered educational courses on Ayurveda. The defendants were former employees of the plaintiff until they left to set up their own company and presumably offer similar educational courses. The plaintiff then sued the defendants for allegedly breaching their employment contracts and specifically sought an injunction restraining the defendants from using the confidential customer database of the plaintiff. The plaintiff requested the court to create a confidentiality club which could examine the customer lists of both parties in order to determine whether there was breach of confidence. The plaintiff wanted the confidentiality club to be designed in a manner to exclude disclosure of any information to the defendants, although their lawyers could view the information on the conditions that they did not disclose the same to the plaintiff. The court refused to grant such an order.

4.2.4. *Reasoning of the Court*

> 13. The senior counsel for the plaintiffs has else today also referred to Annexure-F to the Delhi High Court (Original Side) Rules, 2018 prescribing the 'Protocol of Confidentiality Club' and on the basis of Clause (b) thereof contended that the defendants cannot be members of the Confidentiality Club. It is argued that only the advocates and external experts can be members of the Confidentiality Club.
> 14. I have enquired from the senior counsel for the plaintiffs, whether not without even knowing what the confidential information is, from use whereof the defendants are sought to be restrained, the injunction cannot be enforced, inasmuch as a person can be restrained from doing a thing what he knows he has been so restrained from doing and not from doing what he does not know he is restrained from doing.
>
> 17. ... The counsel for defendant no.2 has also drawn attention to Rule 17 of Chapter-VII of the Delhi High Court (Original Side) Rules aforesaid, to contend that the same provides for constitution of the Confidentiality Club, 'as may be deemed appropriate in the facts of the case' and Annexure-F is only 'illustrative', as also stated in Rule 17. He thus contends that considering the nature of the dispute in the present suit, the contention, that the defendants cannot be members of the Confidentiality Club, ought not be accepted.
>
> 18. The counsel for defendant no.1 and 3 has also drawn attention to the orders dated 25th April 2018 and 11th May 2018 in this suit and has contended that the ex parte ad-interim injunction, on 11th May 2018 was with reference to the confidential information stated to be contained in the Pen Drive but which confidential information has not been disclosed to the defendants and the order is liable to be vacated. It is also argued that the reluctance of the plaintiffs to disclose their customer list, is an admission, of the defendants having no knowledge thereof. It is argued that the plaintiffs are indulging in a fishing and roving enquiry.
>
> 21. A civil lis,[42] governed by the CPC, requires each party thereto to have notice of the case of other, which is required to be met and the CPC does not permit any surprises. The trial and adjudication of a civil lis is regulated by pleadings and evidence, documentaries or otherwise, beyond pleadings is not permitted. The documents of each other are required to be admitted and/or denied and issues on which adjudication is required to be done, struck. No evidence, even if led, beyond pleadings is permitted to be led. Thus, the proceedings require complete disclosure.
>
> 22. Of late however, in respect of a certain class of suits, it was felt that documents filed should not be permitted to go in public domain, as happens on filing in the Court. Provision has thus been made for keeping such documents in a sealed cover, for eyes only of a limited number of persons who also agree / undertake not

42. Lis in Latin means litigation. Indian judges for some reason have a fondness for Latin.

> to divulge contents thereof to others. In some cases, as in cases of patent infringement or infringement of copyright in source code of a computer software, the need for a party to a lis to see the document may not arise as the opinion with respect thereto is to be given by the expert only.
>
> 23. However in the present suit to restrain defendants from using confidential information of plaintiffs and for ancillary reliefs, the defendants are permitted to defend the suit inter alia on the grounds, that the plaintiffs have no copyright in the customers list and even if the plaintiffs have a copyright, the defendants have not infringed the same. I may mention that the suit has been filed as a commercial suit and not as an ordinary suit. This suit, under Section 2(c) of the Commercial Courts Act, 2015, can qualify as a commercial suit only if arising out of intellectual property rights relating to trade marks, copyright, patent, design etc. and not if arising out of property rights or a tort. In such a suit, to ask the defendants to contest the suit without knowing the customers list in which copyright is claimed and without knowing what they are sought to be restrained from doing, would not only be unfair to the defendants but also would be contrary to procedure prescribed by law. The Advocates of defendants and experts, even if any possible in such scenario, cannot be expected to make pleadings, to meet the case of plaintiffs. The non-disclosure to the defendant sought by the plaintiffs, in my opinion deprives the defendant of opportunity of being heard and the right to defend the suit.

4.2.5. Legal Analysis

This case lays bare one of the critical questions of procedural justice and that is whether a party can be fully expected to defend themselves without access to all the documents that are otherwise accessible only to its lawyers? How can such a party advise its lawyer on the best defence? The case is a reminder that even though the Delhi High Court put in place rules governing 'confidentiality club', a court is not bound to allow for the creation of such a confidentiality club on the asking of the plaintiff. The decision to constitute such a club depends on the facts of the case and whether or not the defendant can defend itself in the facts of the case without access to the confidential documents. If the court is of the opinion that the defendant cannot provide his lawyers with adequate instructions, without access to the confidential documents, it may deny the creation of a confidentiality club excluding the defendants themselves. In such a case, although the information may still remain confidential vis-à-vis third parties, the defendants themselves may be given access to the information in question.

4.2.6. Commercial or Industrial Significance

This particular case raises the stakes for plaintiffs in cases involving trade secrets because if a judge declines to create a confidentiality club by excluding the defendants, the plaintiff will have to risk disclosing his confidential information to potential competitors without knowing how much information the defendant has had access to prior to the lawsuit. The fear of such an outcome can prevent lawsuits over trade secrets or at the very least lead to the withdrawal of lawsuits after the denial of a request to exclude the defendants from the confidentiality club. Such orders demonstrate the difficulty in balancing the ends of justice with the peculiarities of trade secret cases.

TOPIC 6 THE CRIMINAL PUNISHMENT FOR TRADE SECRET INFRINGEMENT

1. Legal Issues

While India does not have a specific trade secret law that criminalises the unauthorised use of trade secrets, there is no shortage of cases wherein employers have attempted to use conventional criminal law to prosecute former employees for taking away customer lists or other alleged trade secrets. A variety of existing provisions in the IPC dealing with crimes against property are invoked in such cases where trade secrets are involved.

2. The Statutory Law

IPC, section 405. Criminal breach of trust – Whoever, being in any manner entrusted with property, or with any dominion over property, dishonestly misappropriates or converts to his own use that property, or dishonestly uses or disposes of that property in violation of any direction of law prescribing the mode in which such trust is to be discharged, or of any legal contract, express or implied, which he has made touching the discharge of such trust, or wilfully suffers any other person so to do, commits 'criminal breach of trust'.

IPC, section 408. Criminal breach of trust by clerk or servant – Whoever, being clerk or servant or employed as a clerk or servant, and being in any manner entrusted in such capacity with property, or with any dominion over property, commits criminal breach of trust in respect of that property shall be punished with imprisonment of either description for a term which may extend to seven years, and shall also be liable to fine.

IPC, section 418. Cheating with knowledge that wrongful loss may ensue to person whose interest offender is bound to protect – Whoever cheats with the knowledge that he is likely thereby to cause wrongful loss to a person whose interest in the transaction to which the cheating relates, he was bound, either by law, or by a legal contract, to protect, shall be punished with imprisonment of either description for a term which may extend to three years, or with fine, or with both.

IPC, section 420. Cheating and dishonestly inducing delivery of property – Whoever cheats and thereby dishonestly induces the person deceived to deliver any property to any person, or to make, alter or destroy the whole or any part of a valuable security, or anything which is signed or sealed, and which is capable of being converted into a valuable security, shall be punished with imprisonment of either description for a term which may extend to seven years, and shall also be liable to fine.

Information Technology Act, section 72A. Punishment for disclosure of information in breach of lawful contract – Save as otherwise provided in this Act or any other law for the time being in force, any person including an intermediary who, while providing services under the terms of lawful contract, has secured access to any material containing personal information about another person, with the intent to cause or knowing that he is likely to cause wrongful loss or wrongful gain discloses, without the consent of the person concerned, or in breach of a lawful contract, such material to any other person, shall be punished with imprisonment for a term which may extend to three years, or with fine which may extend to INR 5,00,000, or with both.

3. The Case Law

Statistics regarding the successful prosecution of cases before district courts are unavailable. However, going by reported judgments from the High Courts, it appears that some of these cases are quashed even prior to any trial taking place. Yet, employers continue to file such cases because it provides for a means to get the police involved in their efforts to pressurise the former employee from not joining competitors. Depending on the provision that is being invoked, the police do have the powers to arrest without requiring a prior warrant from a court. The arrested persons have to be produced before a magistrate within 24 hours, and it is up to the magistrate to either grant bail or remand the accused to further custody.

The threat of such an arrest can have a disproportionate impact on any negotiations with the former employee. Criminal law thus has great nuisance value in such cases. Some High Courts have hinted that trade secrets are not property, therefore reducing the possibility of using conventional criminal law in their jurisdictions to prosecute cases involving unauthorised usage of trade secrets.[43] But this is not yet a nationwide trend.

4. The Leading Case(s)

4.1. Case Information

Pramod Son of Laxmikant Sisamkar ... v Garware Plastics and Polyester decided by the Bombay High Court on 29 August 1986 [1986 (3) Bom CR 411].

4.2. Summary

The petitioners who were engineers had left their employers to join another company. The former employers filed a criminal complaint against the petitioners under section 408 and section 420 of the IPC on the grounds that they had taken away proprietary documents and 'know-how' of their former employers for the benefit of their new employers. While the Judicial Magistrate did initiate criminal proceedings, the High Court quashed the complaint.

43. *American Express Bank Ltd. v Priya Puri* 2006 (110) FLR 1061 ('The details of customers are not trade secrets nor they are the property was held in 140 Wash.381, 249 P. 782, *City Ice and Cold Storage Co. v. Kinnee.* In this matter the Supreme Court of Washington had held that customers are not necessarily trade secrets, nor are they property'). *Hemal R Shah v State of Gujarat* Special Criminal Application No. 1171 of 2009 before the High Court of Gujarat (27 December 2010).

4.3. *Facts*

The two petitioners were qualified in instrumentation engineering. They had an employment contract with the respondent-company. They however left their employment with the respondent-company to join another company, presumably a competitor. Their former employer then accused them of taking away proprietary documents as well as using the special know-how they had gained through special training at their former employer's expense, for the benefit of their new employer. The former employer thus filed a criminal complaint with a Judicial Magistrate alleging that these activities of their former employees resulted in a criminal breach of trust under section 408 and cheating and dishonestly inducing delivery of property under section 420 of the IPC.

Under the Code of Criminal Procedure, 1973, the Judicial Magistrate can take cognisance of the complaint if it makes out a prima facie case of an offence. Once cognisance is taken, the matter can be referred to the police for further investigation and depending on the investigation, the accused may be either charged and tried or discharged if there is not adequate evidence. The accused may approach the High Court with relevant jurisdiction to quash the criminal complaint on the grounds that the basic ingredients of the crime have not been made out and that the Judicial Magistrate was wrong to take cognisance of the case. The former employees approached the Bombay High Court to quash the criminal complaints against them.

4.4. *Reasoning of the Court*

> 4. … In the instant cases, I may state that it is not necessary for me to consider the question whether the technical know-how gained by the petitioners by the special training during their service in the company is a 'property' or not within the meaning of section 405 IPC, because according to me the instant writ petitions should succeed upon the other requirements of sections 408 and 420 of I.P. Code which, as I would show lack in these complaints.
>
> '9. It is thus clear that neither in the complaints nor in the verification statement, any specific documents are mentioned which were in possession of the petitioners at the time they left the service. There is not even a general statement which documents of the company used to be in their possession during their services which they would be required to hand over at the time of leaving their service. In my view if there were any documents in possession of the petitioners which they did not return, it would be a fact which the company would certainly know and would have referred to, if true, in its complaints or at any rate in the verification statement of the Manager of respondent No.1 would have named them specifically instead of making a bald and vague statement in that regard. I may observe that the complaints in the instant cases are filed not by any layman but are filed by a reputed company normally assisted by legal Counsel. In the absence of the specific statement in regard to the documents in possession of the petitioners which they did not return, it is not possible to believe prima facie that there were certain documents in possession of the petitioners which they did not hand over at the time they left their service.
>
> 10. As regards the second aspect relating to the technical know-how, which, according to respondent No.1, the petitioners have gained during their special training in their service in the company, in my view, no offence can be said to be

> committed by the petitioners by merely carrying the said technical know-how in their hands. It is only when that technical know-how is used by them in contravention of the aforesaid provisions of their Agreement of Service that it can be said that any offence as alleged against them under sections 408 and 420 I.P.C. is prima facie committed by them.
>
> 11. ... It is also not disputed on behalf of respondent No.1-Company that the factory of the said company is not fully established but is in the process of being erected. It cannot, therefore, be said that the petitioners have any occasion to use, much less have used their technical know-how in the new company because the factory itself is not fully established and the production itself has not yet started in the new company. Unless the factory starts functioning it cannot be said that the petitioner has used their technical know-how in the said company.
>
> 11-A In my view these complaints are thus really premature. It cannot be said on the basis of the above facts that the petitioners have used the technical know-how of respondent No.1-Company which is a requirement for an offence under section 405 I.P.C. relating to criminal breach of trust. It cannot also be said till the technical know-how is used by them that they cheated the company by fraudulently or dishonestly gaining the technical know-how of respondent No.1-Company for being used in other company.

4.5. *Legal Analysis*

In this judgment, the court entirely sidesteps the argument that 'technical know-how' may not even qualify as 'property' and hence not liable to be covered under either section 408 or 420, both of which deal with crimes against property. This case represents a missed opportunity for the court to engage with the issue of whether 'technical know-how' or 'trade secrets' are 'property' for the purposes of criminal law. If 'technical know-how' or 'trade secrets' cannot be classified as 'property', it goes without saying that such cases cannot be filed against former employees. While it may be difficult for a court to declare that trade secrets will never qualify as 'property', since such a determination will be left to a case-by-case basis, the court could have quite easily declared that 'technical know-how' in the form of 'skills' does not qualify as 'property'. In some later cases, other High Courts have declared that 'customer lists', which is one of the most litigated issues in Indian trade secret cases, do not qualify as 'property'.[44]

4.6. *Commercial or Industrial Significance*

The commercial significance of this judgment is that it keeps open the door to using criminal prosecutions in trade secret cases, provided the trade secrets in question can be classified as 'property' as understood in the IPC. For example, documents or machines may be easy to classify as property. Technical skills or know-how will most likely be difficult if not impossible to classify as property under the IPC. The theoretical possibility of filing criminal cases can serve as a deterrent. But in reality, it should be noted that these cases are almost never successfully prosecuted.

44. *Hemal v State* SCR.A/117120/2009 decided by the Gujarat High Court on 27 December 2010.

PART IV Some References from the Occident

CHAPTER 10
Trade Secrets Protection in the European Union

Luc Desaunettes-Barbero

1. OVERVIEW

1.1. Historical and Institutional Background

Prior to the Trade Secrets Directive (TSD),[1] the legal protection of trade secrets inside the European Union (EU) was a patchwork.[2] Not only the Member States of the EU formally relied on different legal instruments but also the nature of protection itself diverged between the different legal orders.[3] Concerned that this disparity might negatively impact cross-border innovation within the European internal market and the competitiveness of European firms,[4] in 2016 the European legislator decided to

1. Directive on the protection of undisclosed know-how and business information (trade secrets) against their unlawful acquisition, use and disclosure, 2016/943, OJ L 157, 15.6.2016, pp. 1-18, 2016.
2. *See* the preparatory work undertaken by the European legislator prior to the adoption of the TSD, EU Commission, *Impact Assessment accompanying the proposal for a Directive of the European Parliament and of the Council on the protection of undisclosed know-how and business information (trade secrets) against their unlawful acquisition, use and disclosure*, 28.11.2013, SWD (2013) 471 final, 19-33 and Annex 9 (Impact Assessment) and HOGAN LOVELLS, *Report on Trade Secrets for the European Commission*, 2012, Markt/2010/20/D, accessible under https://op.europa.eu/en/publication-detail/-/publication/068c999d-06d2-4c8e-a681-a4ee2eb0e116. On the reasons for the adoption of the Directive *see also*: APLIN, 'A Critical Evaluation of the Proposed EU Trade Secrets Directive', 4 *Intellectual Property Quarterly*, 2014, 257, 258-260.
3. In Germany, trade secrets protection was primarily regulated in sections 17-19 of the former Act against Unfair Competition; it was regulated within Code on Industrial Property in Italy (former sections 98-99), and it was mainly the result of case law in France. *See* the conclusion of the EU Commission, *supra* note 2.
4. *See* Recitals 8 and 9 TSD: 'The internal market is affected in so far as such differences lower the incentives for businesses to undertake innovation-related cross-border economic activity, including research cooperation or production cooperation with partners, outsourcing or investment in

proceed with a harmonisation of the law by adopting a Directive aiming at ensuring 'that there is a sufficient and consistent level of civil redress in the internal market in the event of unlawful acquisition, use or disclosure of a trade secret'.[5]

To regulate a given area, however, the European legislator needs to rely on a competency recognised by the EU Member States,[6] and when making use of these competencies, it remains further bound by the subsidiarity and proportionality principles.[7] These principles explain the scope of harmonisation and the choice of legal instruments.

With regard to trade secrets, the EU legislator finds its competency and legal base in Article 114 of the Treaty on the Functioning of the European Union (TFEU), which, broadly speaking, allows the European Parliament and the Council to adopt the measures necessary for the functioning of the internal market.[8] Despite the generous scope of this base, the European legislator first estimated that it could only intervene to harmonise the civil dimension of trade secrets protection, with the result of leaving the possibility of criminalisation up to the Member States.[9] Furthermore, it also decided not to intervene in the contractual issues concerning employer/employee relationships, especially regarding the validity and scope of confidentiality or non-competition clauses.[10]

In terms of the instrument, the EU legislator took the decision to rely on a 'directive': a non-self-executing legislative act only binding on the Member States with regard to the result to be achieved, and which requires transposition in the law of each EU Member State.[11] The advantage of such an act is to allow the integration of a new regulatory framework while at the same time respecting the legal tradition and dogmatic logic of each Member State. The shortcoming is that, already at the transposition stage, potential divergences might arise, the legality of which depends on the freedom left by the Directive to the Member States.

---

other Member States, which depends on the use of information that enjoys protection as trade secrets. [...] In addition, there is a higher risk for businesses in Member States with comparatively lower levels of protection, due to the fact that trade secrets may be stolen or otherwise unlawfully acquired more easily.'

5. Recital 10 TSD.
6. Conferral principle: *see* Articles 4(1) and 5 of the Treaty on the European Union (TEU).
7. The subsidiarity principle requires the EU to act only when a given objective cannot be attained if handled at the level of the Member States. The proportionality principle limits the exercise of the EU legislative competency to what is necessary. *See* Article 5(3) and (4) TEU and Protocol No. 2 on the application of the principles of subsidiarity and proportionality, OJ C 202, 7.6.2016, pp. 206-209.
8. *See* Article 114(1) TFEU: 'Save where otherwise provided in the Treaties, the following provisions shall apply for the achievement of the objectives set out in Article 26. The European Parliament and the Council shall, acting in accordance with the ordinary legislative procedure and after consulting the Economic and Social Committee, adopt the measures for the approximation of the provisions laid down by law, regulation or administrative action in Member States which have as their object the establishment and functioning of the internal market.'
9. For more details, *see* section 7.
10. *See* recital 13 TSD. The impact of this choice will be analysed in detail in section 2.
11. Regarding the justification of this choice in comparison to a Regulation, which would have been self-executing and would hence have applied without requiring any transposition, *see* EU Commission, *supra* note 2, 66.

In this regard, two features of the TSD can already be noted. First, it is quite an extensive act – it is one of the most detailed pieces of legislation devoted to the civil protection of trade secrets. This level of detail consequently leaves narrow margins of manoeuvre to the Member States. Second, even if the TSD is said to be of minimum harmonisation, in the sense that Member States can foresee a stronger form of protection than what was foreseen in the Directive, this freedom is, however, strongly restricted by Article 1(1). This article indeed forces Member States to comply with several of the Directive's enumerated provisions, which have precisely the function of limiting the intensity of trade secret protection.[12]

Procedurally, the Directive entered into force in June 2016 and the Member States had two years – until 6 June 2018 – to transpose it.[13] It is still a recent piece of legislation upon which no decision from the Court of Justice of the European Union (CJEU) or of higher-ranking courts has been rendered.

1.2. Structure, Influence and Overall Balance

The TSD proposes a harmonisation of the civil provisions and remedies against misappropriation of trade secrets and has four chapters: the first defining the subject matter and scope of trade secrets protection; the second dealing with the means of acquisition, use and disclosure of trade secrets; the third covering the remedies and the securing of the procedures' confidentiality; and the fourth covering sanctions, reporting and final provisions directed at the Member States.

Overall, the system is strongly inspired by United States (US) law, in particular the Uniform Trade Secret Act (UTSA) and the Restatements. This influence of the US is easily explainable. The European legislator relied, as a starting point, on the only common denominator of all Member States, i.e., their acceptance of the trade secrets definition provided in Article 39(2) of the Agreement on Trade-Related Aspects of Intellectual Property Rights (TRIPS). Since the definition was itself taken from US law, the EU legislator's attraction towards the US legal framework was almost automatic.

This influence results in a system of protection built on a broad and fuzzy definition of trade secrets and on the recognition of far-reaching prerogatives for the holders of trade secrets. This potentially broad and intense protection is counterbalanced at the enforcement stage, where judges are accorded a strong power of appreciation. Hence, the established system has the advantage of flexibility, which should, at least in theory, avoid the dysfunctional effects resulting from an overprotection of trade secrets. However, it presents at the same time the flaw of lacking clear guidance concerning the way judges should make use of the offered flexibilities.

---

12. Article 1(1) TSD provides that 'Member States may, in compliance with the provisions of the TFEU, provide for more far-reaching protection against the unlawful acquisition, use or disclosure of trade secrets than that required by this Directive, provided that compliance with Articles 3, 5, 6, Article 7(1), Article 8, the second subparagraph of Article 9(1), Article 9(3) and (4), Article 10(2), Articles 11, 13 and Article 15(3) is ensured.'
13. As is usually the case, some States took more time to transpose it. For instance, even Germany's transposition was not completed until 18 April 2019.

1.3. A Broad and Fuzzy Definition

The definition of trade secrets provided in Article 2(1) TSD requires three conditions: the information at stake needs to be secret (i.e., not generally known); it needs to present a commercial value; and it must have been subject to reasonable steps of protection. It will be explained later that the contours of these conditions are blurred and their interrelations and respective added value uncertain. Overall, the definition portrays a potentially extensive subject matter.

1.4. A Strong Legal Protection

The far-reaching scope of the subject matter is complemented by an extensive protection organised around two mirror provisions – Articles 3 and 4 TSD – describing respectively *lawful* and *unlawful* acquisition, use and disclosure of trade secrets.

In this regard, the TSD explicitly recognises two lawful types of acquisition: 'independent discovery' (Article 3(1)(a)) and 'reverse-engineering' practices (Article 3(1)(b)). The clarification of the lawfulness of these two types of acquisition shows the intensity of the protection recognised: indeed, a different solution in these situations would almost amount to the recognition for the holders of trade secrets of a protection equivalent to the granting of a classical *erga omnes* intellectual property right over the information protected.

Article 3(1) TSD further extends the scope of the lawful means of acquisition through a general clause according to which a lawful acquisition might also occur by 'any other practice which, under the circumstances, is in conformity with honest commercial practices'. This clause, which could be seen as opening the scope of the lawful means, is immediately counterbalanced by a similar general clause, this time on the side of the unlawful means of acquisition, foreseeing as unlawful 'any other conduct which, under the circumstances, is considered contrary to honest commercial practice' (Article 4(2)(b)).

When it comes to the conducts explicitly recognised as unlawful, the Directive is very detailed. Article 4(2)(a) TSD considers first as unlawful any means of acquiring a trade secret from a given holder in the absence of its consent. Furthermore, the Directive not only considers unlawful acquisition as a trade secret violation but also encompasses behaviours concerning the use or disclosure of the information carried out either in the aftermath of an unlawful acquisition or in breach of a contractual agreement that limits the use or the disclosure of a given trade secret (Article 4(3) TSD). It should also be noted that the establishment of an unlawful acquisition, use or disclosure does not require the violator to present specific subjective qualities (for instance, of being a competitor or of acting with a commercial purpose). In other words, the TSD adopts a strict liability regime, meaning that the accountability of the violator is not a condition for the characterisation of the violation.

Lastly, third parties – i.e., individuals not having unlawfully acquired the information themselves or being in breach of a contract agreement – might also be found responsible for a trade secret violation according to Article 4(4) TSD. This extension of the personal scope of protection is particularly noteworthy when combined with Article 4(5) TSD that specifies that any act of commercialisation of a good, the characteristics of which significantly benefit from a trade secrets violation (infringing good),[14] is also constitutive of a trade secret violation. The inclusion of any behaviour concerning the commercialisation of an infringing good within the TSD's scope of protection is an interesting instrument that allows the effectivity of the European protection also against extraneous violations. Indeed, if an act of misappropriation in the sense of the TSD occurred in a third country – and therefore outside the territorial scope of the Directive – the trade secret holder will, however, enjoy a legal claim as soon as commercial actions occurred on the European internal market.

The establishment of these types of violation nonetheless requires the demonstration that the violator 'knew or ought, under the circumstances, to have known' that the trade secret was misappropriated.

1.5. Exceptions for Journalists and Whistle-Blowers

The absence of limitations concerning the addressees of the prohibitions during the legislative process generated a fear among journalists and civil society that undertakings could use the provision entailed in the TSD as a way to restrict the exercise of freedom of expression. These concerns were increased by the fact that during the time the European Parliament discussed the Directive, the disclosure of a tax avoidance scheme put in place in Luxembourg resulted in journalists and whistle-blowers responsible for these revelations being prosecuted.

To defuse these concerns, the Directive was amended with Article 5 entitled 'exceptions', according to which: 'an application for the measures, procedures and remedies provided for in this Directive is dismissed where the alleged acquisition, use or disclosure of the trade secret was carried out in any of the following cases: (a) for exercising the right to freedom of expression and information as set out in the Charter, including respect for the freedom and pluralism of the media; (b) for revealing misconduct, wrongdoing or illegal activity, provided that the respondent acted for the purpose of protecting the general public interest'.

1.6. Enforcement: The Requirement of an In-Depth Proportionality Analysis

When it comes to the enforcement of its material rules, the TSD stipulates in Articles 12-15 an arsenal comparable to what is classically recognised for intellectual property rights under the Enforcement Directive in Europe.[15] Article 12 TSD foresees the possibility for judges to grant injunctions and corrective measures including *inter alia* the cessation or the prohibition of the use or disclosure of the trade secret (Article 12(1)(a)), the prohibition of the production of infringing goods (Article 12(1)(b)), or

14. According to Article 2(4) TSD, infringing goods are 'goods, the design, characteristics, functioning, production process or marketing of which significantly benefits from trade secrets unlawfully acquired, used or disclosed'.
15. EU, Directive on the enforcement of intellectual property rights, 2004/48/EC, 29.04.2004.

the recall of these goods from the markets and their destruction (Article 12(2)(a),(c)). Article 14 TSD is then devoted to damages, the calculation of which follows the same triple damages calculation existing for intellectual property.[16]

Despite the alignment with the arsenal foreseen in the Enforcement Directive, the European legislator nevertheless decided not to refer to this legislation. The reason for this choice was the legislator's desire to see the judge taking on a different role when it comes to trade secrets. The Enforcement Directive is indeed often criticised as lacking flexibility and as being one-sided in favouring the rights owners.[17] Considering the breadth (and fuzzy nature) of both the subject matter and of the scope of trade secrets protection, such a one-sided and rigid enforcement could only have led to dysfunctional effects. This explains why the legislator imposed on judges a duty to carry out the in-depth proportionality test described in Article 13(1) TSD: '1. Member States shall ensure that, in considering an application for the adoption of the injunctions and corrective measures provided for in Article 12 and assessing their proportionality, the competent judicial authorities shall be required to take into account the specific circumstances of the case, including, where appropriate: (a) the value or other specific features of the trade secret; (b) the measures taken to protect the trade secret; (c) the conduct of the infringer in acquiring, using or disclosing the trade secret; (d) the impact of the unlawful use or disclosure of the trade secret; (e) the legitimate interests of the parties and the impact which the granting or rejection of the measures could have on the parties; (f) the legitimate interests of third parties; (g) the public interest; and (h) the safeguard of fundamental rights.'

The intensity of this proportionality analysis, which requires the judge to consider the interests of the trade secret holder, the violator and third parties, is an important novum for European law on immaterial goods. As a matter of fact, this in-depth proportionality assessment for trade secrets comes from the US, as Article 13(1) TSD is in fact almost a copy of §44(2) US Restatement (Third) of Unfair Competition.

2. THE REQUIREMENTS OF TRADE SECRETS

According to Article 2(1) TSD:

> 'trade secret' means information which meets all of the following requirements:
>
> (a) it is secret in the sense that it is not, as a body or in the precise configuration and assembly of its components, generally known among or readily accessible to persons within the circles that normally deal with the kind of information in question;
> (b) it has commercial value because it is secret;
> (c) it has been subject to reasonable steps under the circumstances, by the person lawfully in control of the information, to keep it secret.

16. *See* Article 13 Enforcement Directive, 2004/48/EC, *supra*.
17. *See* in this regard: Hilty, 'The Role of Enforcement in Delineating the Scope of IP Rights', *Max Planck Institute for Innovation & Competition Research Paper*, 2015, No. 15-03, 10f.

2.1. A Questionable Alignment with Article 39(2) TRIPS

The decision to rely on the TRIPS standard was expressly acknowledged by the European Commission (EC).[18] In its preparatory works, the EC explicitly refers to the TRIPS definition as a common benchmark for the definition of trade secrets within different EU Member States.[19]

If this choice was undoubtedly pragmatic, it also reflected the lack of clear understanding regarding the purpose of such a definition by the EU legislator. Recital 14 states that '[i]t is important to establish a homogenous definition of a trade secret without restricting the subject matter to be protected against misappropriation', which from a theoretical perspective is antinomic: the definition of an object aims precisely at setting out its limits. Therefore, if the definition does not aim at restricting the information to qualify as a trade secret, it serves no function. In reality, the European legislator refused to engage in discussions regarding the determination of what should be the proper scope of the subject matter of trade secrets and resorted to the broad TRIPS standard instead.

The recourse to the TRIPS definition is, from a substantive perspective, even more questionable. This definition is the result of compromise within an international negotiation, which often used 'constructive ambiguity' as a way to obtain an agreement between differing parties.[20] Furthermore, the basis for these negations was the definition provided in §1.4. UTSA. Yet, this definition was itself not the outcome of clear reflection concerning the *telos* of trade secrets, but merely an attempt to crystallise, in the form of requirements, several broad factors used by the US case law to identify protectable trade secrets.[21] This results in a fuzzy definition, and the proper meaning and scope of each of its requirements will need to be further specified in the future by case law.

2.2. Analysis of the Requirements

The first requirement of a trade secret is poorly defined, as it only provides that the information should not be generally known among or readily accessible to the persons normally dealing with the kind of information at stake. The wording of this requirement makes clear that no absolute secrecy is required. However, once this ceiling is set, no clear guidance is given concerning what should constitute the floor. It is, for instance, uncertain whether the court should recognise protection for a piece of

18. For a general discussion on the definition, *see also*: SILVA, 'What Exactly Is a Trade Secret under the Proposed Directive?', 9(11) *Journal of Intellectual Property Law & Practice*, 2014, 926 and f.
19. EU Commission, *supra* note 2, p. 21.
20. DE CARVALHO, *The TRIPS Regime of Antitrust and Undisclosed Information*, Kluwer Law International, Alphen aan den Rijn, 2008, p. 219, §39.2.23.
21. The first attempt to synthesise these factors came to the conclusion that 'an exact definition of a trade secret is not possible', *see* American Law Institute, *Restatement of Torts (first)*, 1939, §757, comment b), p. 6. This explained why the authors of these treaties choose to list six factors generally considered by courts. These factors that should have remained a bundle of indices were then crystallised in the form of requirements with the UTSA. Regarding this link *see* SANDEEN, 'The Evolution of Trade Secret Law and Why Courts Commit Error When They Do Not Follow the Uniform Trade Secrets Act', 33(3) *Hamline Law Review*, 2010, 493, 522.

information widely shared under a confidentiality agreement within a relevant group. The uncertainty concerning the way this threshold should be interpreted was already perceivable at the transposition stage. Hence, the French Parliament initially contemplated establishing a shallow threshold that would enable protection as soon as the information is not accessible to 'one' person usually processing this type of information,[22] before abandoning this formulation during the legislative process. The new Article L. 151-1. French Commercial Code hence refers to 'persons familiar with such information because of their sector of activity'. The final formulation, more in line with the Directive's prescriptions, however, as a result conveys the uncertainty concerning the threshold's interpretation to case law.

Similarly, the second requirement that the information should have economic value to enjoy protection did not specify the threshold for this value. In this regard, recital 14 TSD proposes some criteria of evaluation for economic value: 'such know-how or information should have a commercial value, whether actual or potential. Such know-how or information should be considered to have a commercial value, for example, where its unlawful acquisition, use or disclosure is likely to harm the interests of the person lawfully controlling it, in that it undermines that person's scientific and technical potential, business or financial interests, strategic positions or ability to compete'. However, criteria for carrying out a value evaluation are worthless without a definition of the threshold to be reached. It should also be noted that this second condition appears to establish a causality between the secrecy and economic value: the information is said to have 'commercial value because it is secret'. This link raises doubts concerning the independence of the two conditions and the added value of the economic value requirement. Should the information be considered as having value as soon as it reaches the secrecy requirement of the first condition? This was at least the reading of the German legislator at the transposition stage, which indeed decided to regroup the two conditions into one: 'For the purposes of this Act, a trade secret is information that a) is not generally known or readily available, either as a whole or in the precise arrangement and composition of its components, to persons in the circles that usually handle this type of information, and is *therefore* of economic value' (emphasis added).[23]

Equivalent criticisms also apply to the third requirement concerning the need for reasonable steps of protection to have been taken in order to keep the information secret. Regarding the intensity of these steps, Article 2(1) TSD simply explains that they need to be 'reasonable under the circumstance', without explaining what should be regarded as 'reasonable' and under which 'circumstances'.

As for secrecy, a stringent interpretation of the requirement, imposing upon the holder the establishment of a perfectly hermetic fortress, should be discarded. The premise of any trade secret case is a misappropriation claim, which necessarily entails

22. French Assemblée nationale, *Proposition de loi n°675 portant transposition de la directive du Parlement européen et du Conseil sur la protection des savoir-faire et des informations commerciales non divulgués contre l'obtention, l'utilisation et la divulgation illicites*, 28.03.2018, Article 1. *See also* the development by Silva, *supra* note 18, 928-929.
23. *See* section 2 No. 1(a) German Law on the Protection of Trade Secrets.

a situation in which the trade secret leaks out beyond its original owner's control. If the information could no longer be regarded as a trade secret in such a constellation, the whole legal arsenal would then be meaningless. Once this hypothesis is set aside, the absence of precision regarding the way in which courts should apply this requirement is further intensified by the breadth of conceivable measures, which range from material securities to actions aiming at increasing the awareness of those accessing the information to the recourse to contractual types of restraints.

Beyond this wide range of possibilities, the lack of explanation on the function that this separate requirement should fulfil further increases the uncertainty. The degree of secrecy and the economic value are intrinsic characteristics that directly impact the economic significance of a trade secret as an economic asset. In comparison, the efforts of protection constitute exogenous factors: their intensity does not influence the objective economic significance of the information. From this perspective, the steps of protection appear as contextual elements that, nevertheless, impact the protectability of given information. Theoretically, two possible functions seem conceivable. First, taking these measures could flag the interest of their holders in maintaining the information's secrecy. However, in such case, the threshold should be considered as very low since any notice would be sufficient to achieve this goal. Second, and more probably, the reasonable efforts could have an evidential function for the fulfilment of the other two requirements. The efforts could be seen as an indirect evidence that the information is not generally known and that it presents an economic value. However, in this case, the verification of this requirement becomes superfluous as soon as the other two conditions are established.

To summarise, the definition provided by Article 2(1) TSD appears as extremely fuzzy, leaving to courts the task of setting out the subject matter's limits without offering the necessary guidance. It will be necessary for the CJEU to establish how these requirements should be interpreted[24] and as a result to clarify the actual breadth of a trade secret's subject matter under EU law.

3. THE VALIDITY AND SCOPE OF CONFIDENTIALITY AND/OR NON-COMPETITION CLAUSES

The question of the validity of confidentiality and non-competition clauses was not harmonised within the EU. Their harmonisation remained explicitly outside the scope of the TSD. According to Article 1(3):

> Nothing in this Directive shall be understood to offer any ground for restricting the mobility of employees. In particular, in relation to the exercise of such mobility, this Directive shall not offer any ground for: [...] (c) imposing any additional restrictions on employees in their employment contracts other than restrictions imposed in accordance with Union or national law.

24. The EU legal order entails a so-called preliminary ruling mechanism, giving national courts the right (or imposing the duty) to refer an interpretation question of European law to the CJEU. This mechanism will play a fundamental role in establishing a corpus of cases for the interpretation of the TSD's provisions.

During the drafting of the Directive, a potential harmonisation of the conditions related to the validity and scope of these clauses was considered but eventually rejected.[25] The European legislator considered that making these clauses uniform at the European level would first turn out to be economically inefficient because it would be incapable of attaining the level of granularity permitted by *inter partes* agreements, and second, it would not increase the effectiveness of trade secrets protection since such clauses are a general matter of contract law.[26]

These arguments are highly questionable and in reality conceal a certain political reluctance of the European legislator to intervene in areas of law – notably when it comes to labour relationships – where Member States are very protective of their prerogatives.[27] Contrary to what seemed to be the EU legislator's assumption, a harmonisation of the conditions related to the legality of such clauses would indeed not have required a prescriptive uniformisation of their conditions. The imposition only of certain workable limitations on the market players' contractual freedom would have been entirely conceivable.

Furthermore, if the harmonisation of these clauses would by itself not have increased the intensity of trade secret protection, it would however have brought legal certainty to two structuring elements of the legal framework established by the Directive: (i) the requirement for the information to be the object of reasonable steps of protection; and (ii) the condition for a violation being a result of unlawful use or disclosure. The question of the validity of these clauses in fact plays an important role when it comes to the verification of the measures required to be taken in accordance with Article 2(1)(c) TSD. Contractual measures are one of the most relevant mechanisms that a trade secret holder might rely upon, especially with respect to employees dealing with the information at stake. More importantly, the validity of these clauses will also be decisive for assessing a violation.[28] Indeed, the TSD not only prevents the unlawful acquisition of trade secrets but also considers as a violation 'the use or disclosure of a trade secret [...] whenever carried out, without the consent of the trade secret holder, by a person who is found to meet any of the following conditions: [...] (b) being in breach of a confidentiality agreement or any other duty not to disclose the trade secret; (c) being in breach of a contractual or any other duty to limit the use of the trade secret'. The establishment of an unlawful use or disclosure as a result of contractual violation will hence necessitate the establishment of the validity of the violated clause. The absence of harmonisation of the standards on validity with respect to these clauses will therefore lead to differences in the intensity of protection from one

25. *See* in this regard EU Commission, *supra* note 2, pp. 244-245.
26. *Ibid.*
27. Comp. also: KNAAK, KUR, HILTY, 'Comments of the Max Planck Institute for Innovation and Competition of 3 June 2014 on the Proposal of the European Commission for a Directive on the Protection of Undisclosed Know-How and Business Information (Trade Secrets) Against Their Unlawful Acquisition, Use and Disclosure of 28 November 2013, COM (2013) 813 Final', 45(8) *International Review of Intellectual Property and Competition Law*, 2014, 953, 955, §8.
28. Also raising this issue, *see*: APLIN, *supra* note 2, 257, 270.

Member State to another and will oblige a new employer of a foreign worker to verify the law applicable in another Member State.[29]

4. THE BURDEN OF PROOF FOR TRADE SECRETS AND INFRINGEMENT AND ITS REVERSAL

The question of the repartition of the burden of proof among the parties is not expressly regulated within the Directive. It will therefore follow the principle of civil procedural law existing in each Member State. Two questions might arise with regard to the repartition of the burden of proof.

The first question is related to the lawfulness of a mean of acquisition not expressly listed as 'lawful' or 'unlawful' by the Directive. As explained above, Articles 3 and 4 TSD are two mirroring general clauses. This structure renders difficult the establishment of principle/exception ordering between the two provisions. In those countries which maintain this mirroring structure at the transposition stage,[30] a debate could therefore emerge regarding the determination of who should have the burden to demonstrate whether or not the behaviour at stake should be considered as lawful or not.[31]

Another equivalent question could also emerge concerning the exception under Article 5 TSD, which foresees *inter alia* that 'an application for the measures, procedures and remedies provided for in this Directive is dismissed where the alleged acquisition, use or disclosure of the trade secret was carried [...] for exercising the right to freedom of expression and information as set out in the Charter, including respect for the freedom and pluralism of the media'. There again, the text of the Directive does not clarify expressly who bears the burden to prove that the conditions of the exception are fulfilled. It could be argued that it is for the person benefiting from a provision to demonstrate that its conditions are fulfilled. However, Article 5 TSD would present no normative value since a party can always leverage a fundamental right justification. Another possible reading could be that Article 5 induced a reversal of the proof burden according to which it is the trade secret holders to demonstrate that the violator's behaviour does not fulfil the condition to be regarded as falling under the freedom of expression exception.

29. For detailed reports on the legal regimes in Germany, the Netherlands, France, Italy and Spain, *see* HEATH, KAMPERMAN SANDERS, *Employees, Trade Secrets and Restrictive Covenants*, Wolters Kluwer, Alphen aan den Rijn, 2017, pp. 61-199.
30. Germany made the choice to transpose the general clauses of Articles 3 and 4 TSD only at the level of unlawful acts. *See* German Law on the Protection of Trade Secrets, section 4(1) No. 2: 'A trade secret may not be obtained by any other conduct which, under the circumstances, is not in accordance with the principle of good faith having regard to honest market practice.' On the other hand, section 3 dealing with lawful behaviours does not entail any opening clause.
31. This question is also relevant in civil law countries, where the parties only have to present facts to the court, which is supposed to know the law ('*curia novit legem*'). Indeed, even in these countries, the burden to demonstrate 'usages' or a 'practice' is to be borne by the party who asserts it.

5. THE ORDER FOR PROTECTING THE SECRECY OF TRADE SECRETS DURING TRIAL

The TSD offers detailed measures when it comes to the protection of trade secrets during trial. An ineffective protection during the process was explicitly recognised as a potential downfall for any trade secret protection. Even recital 24 of the TSD recalls that: 'the prospect of losing the confidentiality of a trade secret in the course of legal proceedings often deters legitimate trade secret holders from instituting legal proceedings to defend their trade secrets, thus jeopardising the effectiveness of the measures, procedures and remedies provided for'. Two types of measures should be differentiated in this regard: (i) those aiming at securing and preserving the confidentiality of the proceedings and (ii) those opening the possibility of ordering provisional and precautionary measures before a definitive decision on the merits of the case.

5.1. Preservation of Confidentiality of Trade Secrets in the Course of Legal Proceedings

Regarding the preservation of the confidentiality of trade secrets during legal proceedings, Article 9 TSD foresees that:

> 1. [...] the parties, their lawyers or other representatives, court officials, witnesses, experts and any other person participating in legal proceedings relating to the unlawful acquisition, use or disclosure of a trade secret, or who has access to documents which form part of those legal proceedings, are not permitted to use or disclose any trade secret or alleged trade secret which the competent judicial authorities have, in response to a duly reasoned application by an interested party, identified as confidential and of which they have become aware as a result of such participation or access. [...]
>
>   The obligation referred to in the first subparagraph shall remain in force after the legal proceedings have ended. [...]
> 2. [...] the competent judicial authorities may, on a duly reasoned application by a party, take specific measures necessary to preserve the confidentiality of any trade secret or alleged trade secret used or referred to in the course of legal proceedings relating to the unlawful acquisition, use or disclosure of a trade secret. [...]
>
>   The measures referred to in the first subparagraph shall at least include the possibility:
>   (a) of restricting access to any document containing trade secrets or alleged trade secrets submitted by the parties or third parties, in whole or in part, to a limited number of persons;
>   (b) of restricting access to hearings, when trade secrets or alleged trade secrets may be disclosed, and the corresponding record or transcript of those hearings to a limited number of persons;
>   (c) of making available to any person other than those comprised in the limited number of persons referred to in points (a) and (b) a non-confidential version of any judicial decision, in which the passages containing trade secrets have been removed or redacted.
>
>   The number of persons referred to in points (a) and (b) of the second subparagraph shall be no greater than necessary in order to ensure compliance with the right of the parties to the legal proceedings to an effective remedy and to a fair trial, and shall include, at least, one natural person from each party

> and the respective lawyers or other representatives of those parties to the legal proceedings. [...]

Because of its level of detail, this provision does require an elaborated comment. The provision entails first a general duty not to use or to disclose any trade secrets released during the procedure, and second the possibility for the judges to restrict the access to documents or hearings in which trade secrets might be disclosed and to limit the number of persons having access to its final (and uncensored) decision.

Generally, all these procedural instruments try to find a balance between the necessity for efficient remedies and the rights to a fair trial and defence, both considered as fundamental rights under the EU Charter.[32] The search for the proper equilibrium between these opposite goals leads the EU legislator to foresee that the number of persons having full access to the documents and hearings should 'include, at least, one natural person from each party and the respective lawyers or other representatives of those parties to the legal proceedings'. The quality of this natural person is not explicitly specified in the Directive, but recital 25 leaves little doubt that the EU legislator has in mind that it should be the claimant and the defendant themselves.

This natural person presents two main differences compared to the legal representative, which might lead its presence obligation to become the Achilles heel for the efficiency of Article 9 TSD. First, these natural persons will not face professional sanctions if they disrespect a confidentiality obligation. Second, as opposed to the legal representatives, the activity of whom will in principle not benefit from accessing the secret at stake, the natural persons in question might have a direct commercial interest in gaining knowledge of it. Thereof, the presence of this actor to which the secret will necessarily be disclosed might already be sufficient to discourage him from the outset from engaging in a legal action.

5.2. Provisional and Precautionary Measures

When it comes to trade secret cases, the capacity to react quickly is essential. Trade secrets once they become easily accessible as a result of violation will no longer meet the subject matter requirement. To avoid irreparable harm by the time of the final decision, Article 10 TSD foresees the possibility for the judge to grant provisional and precautionary measures:

> 1. [...] the competent judicial authorities may, at the request of the trade secret holder, order any of the following provisional and precautionary measures against the alleged infringer:
>   (a) the cessation of or, as the case may be, the prohibition of the use or disclosure of the trade secret on a provisional basis;
>   (b) the prohibition of the production, offering, placing on the market or use of infringing goods, or the importation, export or storage of infringing goods for those purposes;

32. *See* Articles 47 and 48 EU Charter of Fundamental Rights.

(c) the seizure or delivery up of the suspected infringing goods, including imported goods, so as to prevent their entry into, or circulation on, the market.

2. [...] the judicial authorities may, as an alternative to the measures referred to in paragraph 1, make the continuation of the alleged unlawful use of a trade secret subject to the lodging of guarantees intended to ensure the compensation of the trade secret holder. Disclosure of a trade secret in return for the lodging of guarantees shall not be allowed.

6. THE DAMAGES

In cases where a loss was already suffered, damages might then be granted as per Article 14 TSD. Accordingly:

1. Member States shall ensure that the competent judicial authorities, upon the request of the injured party, order an infringer who knew or ought to have known that he, she or it was engaging in unlawful acquisition, use or disclosure of a trade secret, to pay the trade secret holder damages appropriate to the actual prejudice suffered as a result of the unlawful acquisition, use or disclosure of the trade secret. [...]
2. When setting the damages referred to in paragraph 1, the competent judicial authorities shall take into account all appropriate factors, such as the negative economic consequences, including lost profits, which the injured party has suffered, any unfair profits made by the infringer and, in appropriate cases, elements other than economic factors, such as the moral prejudice caused to the trade secret holder by the unlawful acquisition, use or disclosure of the trade secret.

   Alternatively, the competent judicial authorities may, in appropriate cases, set the damages as a lump sum on the basis of elements such as, at a minimum, the amount of royalties or fees which would have been due had the infringer requested authorisation to use the trade secret in question.

6.1. Need for Demonstration of the Violator's Accountability

According to Article 14(1) TSD, the ordering of damages is only possible against: 'an infringer who *knew or ought to have known* that he, she or it was engaging in unlawful acquisition, use or disclosure of a trade secret' (emphasis added). For the award of damages, the establishment of the accountability of the violator needs first to be established. This condition is important since the determination of the violator's accountability is not required as a matter of principle, both when it comes to the establishment of a trade secret violation[33] and for the ordering of corrective measures. The standard of accountability remains however low, since, according to Article 14(1), a simple negligence is sufficient.

33. The proof of accountability is already imposed as a condition for the characterisation of third-party violation: 'The acquisition, use or disclosure of a trade secret shall also be considered unlawful whenever a person, at the time of the acquisition, use or disclosure, knew or ought, under the circumstances, to have known that the trade secret had been obtained directly or indirectly from another person who was using or disclosing the trade secret unlawfully within the meaning of paragraph 3' (Article 4(4) TSD).

6.2. Calculation Method

The calculation method to establish the damages that should be awarded to compensate the actual harm suffered due to the violation is the same prevailing in classical intellectual property rights. Article 14(2) TSD allows courts to resort to a threefold calculation. Accordingly, the competent judicial authority can not only take into account the loss suffered by the trade secret holder as a result of the violation but also base its decision upon the unjust enrichment of the violator or even rely on an appreciation of the amount of royalties that the trade secret holder would have asked for from the infringer had the latter entered into a licence relationship. This calculation hence differs from the classical damages valuation applied under the civilian tradition of tort law, according to which damages should only aim at covering the loss suffered. The triple damages calculation indeed adds an element of deterrence: without going as far as punitive damages, the purpose is not only to repair the damage caused but also to suppress the economic attractiveness of a violation.

On the other hand, the TSD does not introduce punitive damages as a part of the legal arsenal, and recital 30 clarifies that: 'the aim of that alternative method [based on the royalties] is not to introduce an obligation to provide for punitive damages, but to ensure compensation based on an objective criterion while taking account of the expenses incurred by the trade secret holder, such as the costs of identification and research'. Punitive damages are not widespread, especially in civil law countries. Prior to the introduction of the TSD, the Commission noted in this regard that this tool was only available in Ireland and in the United Kingdom.[34]

7. THE CRIMINAL PUNISHMENT FOR TRADE SECRET INFRINGEMENT

Criminal punishment of trade secrets violation was considered as a policy option during the drafting of the Directive.[35] The European legislator ultimately decided not to foresee a criminal law protection of trade secrets for substantive and political reasons.

With regards to the substantive reasons, the EU legislator actually recognised that an encompassment of criminal law would entail a more coherent approach for the protection. However, it would, on the other hand, go 'beyond the existing situation regarding infringements to intellectual property rights'[36] under EU law. A criminal law protection of these rights was indeed considered at the European level in the context of the Anti-Counterfeiting Trade Agreement, but was finally abandoned after the rejection of this agreement by the European Parliament.[37] The second argument advanced against it was that the deterrence induced by criminal sanctions could also present some detrimental side effects from an innovation policy perspective: accordingly 'while the greater deterrence of misappropriators should provide additional incentives

34. EU Commission, *supra* note 2, p. 202.
35. *Ibid.*, p. 44, policy option 5.
36. *Ibid.*, p. 66.
37. EU Parliament, *legislative resolution on the draft Council decision on the conclusion of the Anti-Counterfeiting Trade Agreement*, 4.07.2012, P7_TA(2012)0287.

to innovate, these might be somewhat mitigated by overly conservative behaviour of some businesses fearing criminal consequences'.[38]

The political reasoning finds its roots in the specificities of the EU legal order explained in section 1. It would have been much more challenging for the EU legislator to obtain the acceptance of the Member States for such a criminal law protection. The EC makes no secret of this fact: it actually recognised explicitly that foreseeing criminal sanctions 'would result in higher legislative costs [...] as it would require the negotiation of two different legal instruments at the EU level and it would also require changes in national criminal law which is at the heart of national sovereignty'.[39]

It is undoubtedly this political argument that ultimately brought the EC to refrain from engaging in a process of harmonisation of the criminal law. Although the Directive does not itself criminalise these acts, it allows national lawmakers to engage in such a criminalisation. Indeed, according to Article 1(1), Member States may 'provide for more far-reaching protection against the unlawful acquisition, use or disclosure of trade secrets than that required by this Directive'. Some countries, such as Germany,[40] foresee a far-reaching criminal protection, whereas in others, like France,[41] criminal protection is almost anecdotal.

8. CONCLUSION

In comparison to the patchwork of legislations existing before, the enactment of the TSD can be praised as offering a higher degree of legal certainty for players active in several EU Members States. However, the scope of harmonisation remains limited due to political and institutional considerations, shelving the questions of the criminalisation of certain behaviours and of the validity of confidentiality and non-competition clauses.

Today, the EU and US share similar systems of trade secrets protection, consequently increasing their respective global influence. However, the alignment of these two legal orders should not lead to the conclusion that the solution they propose is necessarily of quality or effectiveness, and that it is the only conceivable regulatory path. This chapter demonstrates that the TSD exhibits a high degree of flexibility; it also, and foremost, presents a very fuzzy situation regarding both its conditions and the overall regulation *telos* that should guide courts in their interpretation. This should resonate as a warning for every lawmaker. The fact that the EU and US legal orders now exhibit similar systems of protection is not the result of a scientific process based upon a careful identification of the justifications and offering a strong and encompassing conceptual framework. The two legal frameworks are the outcome of incremental

38. EU Commission, *supra* note 2, p. 58.
39. *Ibid.*, p. 62.
40. *See* §23 German Law on the Protection of Trade Secrets.
41. In France, this protection is governed by an old norm. Article L-621-1 Code of Intellectual Property, which dates back to the nineteenth century, provides protection only to manufacturing secrets. For more details of this norm, *see* DESAUNETTES, *Employees, Trade Secrets and Restrictive Covenants in France*, in: HEATH, KAMPERMAN SANDERS (eds), Employees, Trade Secrets and Restrictive Covenants, Alphen aan den Rijn (Netherlands), 2017, 138-139.

developments that took place within US case law, and of political and practical considerations that led the European legislator, in its harmonisation attempt, to use this model of protection.

To conclude, if the EU example can be of any help for countries wishing to reform their trade secrets regimes, it is perhaps a warning against following the same sort of alignment with the US system. Other regulatory paths are possible. All regulatory work should, however, start with a clarification of the justifications for a legal protection of these immaterial assets.

Index

A

Acquisition, 10–13, 15, 24, 42, 61, 63, 73–74, 76, 79, 80, 89, 221, 234, 235, 280, 281, 321, 405, 434–437, 440, 442–444, 446, 448
Apportionment, 108–110, 112–113

B

Breach of confidence, 272–282, 288–290, 299–300, 325–326, 332, 344
Business information (commercial information, trade information), 8, 9, 27, 64, 72, 81, 85, 94, 104, 116, 117, 120, 122, 135, 160, 184, 226, 227, 232, 235, 237, 238, 240, 243, 244, 250, 257, 266, 318, 371, 387

C

Calculation of damages
  infringer's profit, 78, 109–111, 159, 262
  reasonable royalty, 55, 78, 108, 111, 167, 168
  royalty rate, 59–61, 78
Choice of law, 3, 16, 37
Civil remedy, 39
Classification theory, 40
Code/law
  Act on General Rules for Application of Laws (Tsûsokuhô), 34, 35, 37–42
  Agreement on Trade-Related Aspects of Intellectual Property Rights (TRIPS Agreement), 7–10, 178, 225, 226, 340, 435
  Anti-Unfair-Competition Law (AUCL), 115–118, 120, 126, 127, 129, 134, 135, 137–139, 143, 144, 150, 154, 155, 156, 160, 161
  Civil and Commercial Code, 225, 226, 246, 248, 251, 262, 265, 266
  Civil Code, 2, 7, 8, 54, 57, 77, 78, 90, 95, 96, 111, 117, 154, 171, 178, 188, 209
  Civil Procedure Law (CPL), 116, 146, 151, 152
  Civil Provisional Remedies Act, 47, 48
  Code of Civil Procedure (CCP), 15, 34, 35, 36, 39, 40, 43, 48, 75, 174–176, 197, 199, 200, 212
  Code of Criminal Procedure, 43, 428
  contract law, 26–27, 116, 130, 135, 250, 262, 395, 400, 401, 442
  Contracts Act 1950, 332, 349, 352–353, 371, 375, 377
  Contracts Act, 1872, 396, 408–409
  Defend Trade Secrets Act, 103, 271
  Fair Trade Act, 171, 178
  General Rules for Application of Laws (Hôrei), 34, 35, 37, 40

Industrial Technology Leak Prevention and Protection Support Act (ITPA), 72, 79
Intellectual Property Case Adjudication Act (IPCAA), 143, 171, 172, 174–176, 194, 197, 199–203, 208
labor contract law, 116, 130
labor law, 7, 26–27, 116, 130, 186
Labor Standards Act, 173, 186–188, 192–193
non-disclosure agreement (NDA), 227, 276, 377, 404, 409
Penal Code, 15, 79, 225, 226, 228, 398
Private International Law (PIL), 34, 37, 40, 42
tort law, 8, 44, 54, 71, 76, 78, 262, 447
Trade Secrets Act (TSA), 171–172, 184, 185, 192–193, 240, 241, 243, 262, 263
Unfair Competition Prevention Act (UCPA), 7, 27, 71, 79–80, 95–96

Compensatory measure, 27, 29–31, 33
Competitive advantage, 87, 88, 122, 125, 126, 148, 150, 153–155, 165, 221, 375, 376
Competitive business activities, 29, 30, 32
Competitive relationship, 30, 32, 56, 57, 86
Confidential information, 241–242, 272, 298–299, 306–307, 333, 351, 384–385
Confidentiality, 26–33, 74, 89–96, 129–136, 172–173, 186–193, 198, 203–206, 208, 246–253, 275–281, 283, 302–309, 315–316, 332–334, 349–358, 364, 408–425, 441–445
Confidentiality club, 397, 398, 417–425

Court
Appeal Court (Court of Appeal), 92, 99, 110, 229, 238–245, 265, 267, 323–325
Calcutta High Court, 412, 413, 415
Central Intellectual Property and International Trade Court (CIPIT Court), 226, 230–233, 238, 255–259, 261
Court of Appeals for Specialized Cases, IP&IT Division, 226, 233
Delhi High Court, 398, 401, 403, 404, 417, 418, 420, 422–425
Federal Court, 334, 335, 339, 349, 357, 360–366, 371, 378, 390, 393
IP High Court, 10, 16–19, 27, 30–33, 38, 46, 55–61
Seoul High Court, 92, 99, 110
Supreme Court, 68–69, 82–83, 100–103, 183–184, 197–198, 233–238, 247–253, 263–268
Supreme People's Court (SPC), 115, 160, 214
Taiwan IP and Commercial Court, 171–173, 175, 176, 179, 181–185, 188–191, 194, 195, 197, 198, 200, 201, 205, 206, 210, 214–216, 218–220

Criminal penalty (sanction, liability), 7, 13, 15, 28, 29, 44, 51, 63, 64, 72, 107, 176, 228–230

Customer
database, 311, 313–316, 344, 423
information, 19–21, 23–25, 55, 64, 103, 132, 163, 236, 294, 299, 307, 311, 314, 389
list, 9, 14, 18, 72, 104, 122, 132–134, 163, 179, 180, 184, 227, 263, 264, 299, 342, 348, 351, 354, 396, 398, 400, 401, 404–407, 423, 424, 426, 429

D

Damages
aggravated damages, 319, 323, 326, 328, 329, 339, 392
assessment of damages, 386-388, 391-394
compensatory damages, 153-155, 292, 315, 319, 322-325, 327, 329, 339, 391, 392
exemplary damages, 265, 268, 287, 292, 319-326, 328, 329, 339, 392
monetary awards, 78, 271, 285, 324, 326, 370, 375
nominal damages, 317, 319, 322, 327-329, 392
punitive damages, 2, 72, 108, 115, 117, 153-157, 160, 175, 176, 209, 210, 213-214, 229, 231, 262-264, 266-268, 319, 447
reasonable expenses, 125, 140, 155-157
sales profits, 154-156, 167, 168
statutory damages, 116, 117, 154-156, 159, 160
treble damages, 2, 78, 108,
Department of Intellectual Property (DIP), 238
Disclosure, 10-12, 380-381, 411-412
Discovery, 1, 50, 73, 76, 159, 198, 200, 203, 225, 228, 405, 420, 422, 436
Duty
duty of confidence, 90, 289, 297, 298, 310, 315, 316, 322, 343, 345, 362, 370, 395, 397, 400-402, 404
duty of fidelity, 276, 289, 294, 295, 297-300, 340-347, 370, 372, 400
fiduciary duties, 289, 291, 316, 320, 324, 326, 333, 364, 370, 372, 374-376
implied duty, 91, 295, 297-300, 304, 306, 316, 342, 343, 346, 354
implied obligation, 87, 276, 299, 331

E

Economic and Trade Agreement between the USA and China, 161
Economic espionage, 1, 117, 137, 161-163, 168, 176, 217-224
Electronic intrusion, 117, 144, 162
Employee, 95-96, 134-135, 223-224, 333, 347
Employment, 32, 134, 235, 347
Enforceability, 94, 173, 246-248, 250-252, 283, 302, 305-306, 362
Equitable obligation, 277-279, 285, 289, 331
Equitable remedy, 287, 290, 292, 326, 327, 331, 376, 415

F

Foreign trade secret infringement, 79
Fraud, 8, 10, 15, 62, 73, 144, 162, 176, 180, 227, 232, 338, 339, 429
Freedom
freedom of business, 27-29, 32, 33
freedom of profession, 96
freedom to work, 132, 134-135

G

General skills and knowledge, 95-96
Good faith, 16, 28, 80, 86, 92, 93, 143, 225, 228, 232, 252, 261, 277, 306, 333, 341-343, 345, 351, 353
Gross negligence, 11-13, 17, 38, 39, 53, 73, 74, 89, 112, 173

I

Important market players
Nippon Steel (NS), 59-61

POSCO, 59–61
Taiwan Semiconductor Manufacturing Company (TSMC), 173, 189–193, 219
United Microelectronics Corporation (UMC), 219–224
Samsung, 190

Imprisonment, 1, 15, 44, 62, 63, 117, 141, 162–164, 167, 171–173, 176, 205, 217, 218, 228, 229, 286, 426
In-camera procedure, 15, 48
Independent economic value, 72, 81, 85–87, 91
Infringement, 34–42, 62–70, 97–105, 134, 137–144, 150, 159, 161–168, 173, 174, 194–201, 209–216, 227–228, 334, 359–368, 426–429, 443, 447–448
Injunctive relief
- Anton Piller order, 290, 336, 378–385
- interim injunction, 38, 230, 254, 255, 260, 273, 335, 337–338, 350, 369, 370, 372–374, 376, 377, 397, 398, 401, 404, 423, 424
- interlocutory injunction, 77, 290, 291, 294–297, 321, 323, 324, 337–338, 369–377
- Mareva injunction, 290, 335–337, 381
- permanent injunction, 77, 97, 98, 100–104, 125, 151, 152, 211, 230, 254, 255, 406
- preliminary injunction, 90, 145–152, 175, 188, 230, 254, 261
- springboard injunction, 290, 291, 374–377

International jurisdiction, 3, 16, 34–42

J

Judicial interpretation, 115, 116, 120, 121, 125, 126, 131, 142

L

Lead time, 98–102, 104, 155, 165, 215
Legitimate interest, 24, 36, 41, 135, 192, 193, 281, 302, 303, 305, 306, 317, 367, 438
Loss
- actual loss, 2, 110, 117, 153–155, 159, 209, 210, 213, 214, 216, 262, 264–268, 317, 319, 320, 327, 328, 335, 338, 386
- substantial loss, 118, 392

M

Managed as a secret, 19–20, 72, 81–88
METI Commentaries, 9, 62
METI Guidelines, 17, 18, 21–23, 25
Ministry of Economy, Trade and Industry (METI), 17, 18, 21–23, 25
Mobility, 1–3, 7, 28, 70, 186, 192, 217, 223–224, 276, 412, 416, 441

N

Negative fact
- non-public domain, 17, 21, 24–25
- not generally known, 21, 24, 91, 120–122, 126, 133, 141–142, 340, 344, 436, 440, 441
- not publicly known, 8–10, 17, 21, 27, 49, 66, 81, 226, 243
- not readily available to the public, 10
- unknown to the public, 120, 122, 125, 126, 150, 236

Non-competition (compete), 3, 27, 30, 131, 237, 246–253, 258, 302–309, 333–339, 349–358, 390, 408–416, 434, 441–443, 448

O

Open court, 202, 397, 398, 417, 419

P

Pervasive view, 9, 50, 54
Pledge, 18, 30–32, 82, 109, 110
Preliminary showing, 143, 174, 175, 194, 199–201
Preservation
  behavior, 145–152
  evidence, 145, 146
  property, 145, 146
Presumption, 14, 52, 54, 61, 78, 106–108, 110, 111, 137, 230, 281, 284, 315, 407
Price list, 157, 311–316, 344, 379, 382
Prima facie evidence, 43, 127, 290, 310, 370
Principle of autonomy, 129
Proof
  burden of proof, 137–144, 174, 196–197, 201, 284, 310–318, 334–336, 359–368, 392–393, 443
  distribution of burden of proof, 137
  reversal of burden of proof, 310–318, 334–336, 359–368, 443
  shifting burden of proof, 111, 137–144
Proportionality, 190, 305, 308, 325, 434, 437–438
Prosecution only upon complaint, 44, Protective order
  confidentiality preservation order, 172–173, 202–206, 208
  investigation confidentiality protective order, 172–173, 202, 204–208, 218,
Provisional disposition, 43, 45–49
Provisional measure, 145, 147, 152, 254–256, 261
Public domain, 127, 179, 184, 241, 272–275, 288, 297, 315, 358, 371, 374, 376, 400, 406, 424
Public interest, 2, 15, 19, 131, 146, 151, 152, 175, 193, 228, 271, 272, 281–282, 284, 305, 307, 309, 356, 367, 373, 437, 438
Public order, 9, 41, 95, 131, 188, 202, 246–251, 267
Purpose of wrongful gain, 11, 27, 62–70

R

Ratio of the contribution (contribution rate), 58, 109–113, 159
Reasonable efforts, 81–88, 122, 441
Reasonable explanations, 137, 138, 143, 144, 311, 318
Recognizability, 9, 19, 21–23, 25
Relative secrecy, 272–274
Restraint of trade, 283, 302, 303, 305, 317, 332–334, 341, 347, 349, 350, 352–357, 362, 366, 371, 375, 377, 406, 408, 410
Restrictive covenants, 94, 288, 290, 302–309, 317, 349, 352, 361–363, 410, 414
Reverse engineering, 10, 24, 73, 87, 99, 100, 104, 116, 228, 436

S

Secrecy management, 17–25, 28, 81–88
Severity of the infringement, 162
Specific defense, 143, 174, 194–201
Suspension of infringement, 47

T

Technical information, 11, 24, 59, 60, 64, 72, 82, 91, 92, 109, 110, 115, 116, 123–125, 134, 135, 139–141, 147, 166, 274, 403
Technical know-how, 287, 409, 428, 429
Theft, 10, 11, 15, 71, 73, 79, 89, 144, 162, 176, 213, 214, 217–224, 227, 229, 232, 248, 398
Threshold of conviction, 161
Trade secret
  controller, 227, 230–232, 236–238
  misappropriation, 306–307

owner, 2, 27, 28, 52, 63, 84, 88, 98, 99, 101, 146, 152, 174, 175, 180, 183, 193, 204, 205, 209, 226–228, 231, 232, 234, 235, 237, 238, 246, 253, 260
specific trade secret, 209, 288, 298, 306, 426
Trade secret protection period, 99–104
Trade Secrets Directive (TSD), 433, 435, 436–438, 440–448

U

Unauthorized use, 3, 10–13, 43, 57, 72, 79, 226, 227, 280, 281, 287, 289–290, 300, 332, 340, 344, 345–348, 359, 360, 369
Unfair competition, 2, 7, 10–15, 17, 19, 27, 29, 37–43, 49, 52–55, 106, 107, 135, 171, 225
Unification theory, 40, 41
Usefulness (commercial value), 8–9, 21, 24
Utility, 8, 9, 24, 210–213, 215

W

Whistle blowers, 437
Wrongful act (unlawful act), 34–37, 39, 40, 76, 77, 254, 262, 266, 292, 326, 336, 374, 375, 377, 387, 392